College English & Communication

7TH edition

Sue C. Camp, Ed.D.
Broyhill School of Management
Gardner-Webb University
Boiling Springs, North Carolina

Marilyn L. Satterwhite
Business Division
Danville Area Community College
Danville, Illinois

 **Glencoe McGraw-Hill**

New York, New York
Columbus, Ohio
Woodland Hills, California
Peoria, Illinois

DEDICATION

With thanks for their encouragement and support, we would like to dedicate the seventh edition of *College English and Communication* to our families: Gladys, Charles Sr., Charles Jr. and Amber, and Charles III for Sue Camp; William, Marcy, and David for Marilyn Satterwhite.

Illustration Credits:

2, 9 Mark Burnett; 12 Patrick Ramsey/The Image Bank; 20, 26 Michael Newman/PhotoEdit; 32 Mark Burnett; 42 Alan Schein/The Stock Market; 46 SuperStock; 51 Benelux Press/Masterfile; 59 Uniphoto; 62 Flip Chalfant/The Image Bank; 182 Lou Jones/The Image Bank; 260, 264, 273, 282, 286, 298 KS Studios/Rick Weber; 304 Aaron Haupt; 344, 369 Doug Martin; 376 Aaron Haupt; 381 Doug Martin; 389 Ron Chapple/FPG; 393 Doug Martin; 403 Kevin Smyth/The Stock Market; 415 Mark Burnett/Glencoe File Photo; 417 Jose Palaez/The Stock Market; 426 Aaron Haupt; 431 Mugshots/The Stock Market; 439 Doug Martin; 440 B. Busco/The Image Bank; 446 Uniphoto; 456, 458 Doug Martin; 465 Jose Luis Pelaez/The Stock Market; 494, 552 Doug Martin; 558 Jon Feingersh/The Stock Market; 563, 570 Doug Martin; 579 Mark Burnett/Glencoe File Photo; 616 Doug Martin; 644 Doug Martin.

Cover illustration by Nikolai Punin/SIS.

Illustration on page 53 by permission of The National Association of Life Underwriters, Washington, D.C.

Library of Congress Cataloging-in-Publication Data

Camp, Sue C., (date)
   College English and Communication. —7th ed./Sue C. Camp,
Marilyn Satterwhite.
   p. cm.
   Rev. ed. of College English and communication/Kenneth Zimmer,
Sue C. Camp
    Includes index.
    ISBN 0-02-802168-1
1. English language—Business English. 2. English language—
Grammar. 3. English language—Rhetoric. 4. Business
communication. 5. Business Writing. I. Satterwhite, Marilyn L.
II. Zimmer, Kenneth, (date) College English and communication.
III. Title.
PE1479.B87C36 1997
808' .06665—dc21   97-29555 CIP

Glencoe/McGraw-Hill

*A Division of The **McGraw·Hill** Companies*

College English and Communication, Seventh Edition

Send all inquiries to:
Glencoe/McGraw-Hill
8787 Orion Place
Columbus, OH 43240

ISBN 0-02-802168-1

4 5 6 7 8 9   027   05 04 03 02 01 00

Brief Contents

CHAPTER 1 Understanding Communication 2

CHAPTER 2 Communicating Around the Globe 32

CHAPTER 3 Expanding Language Skills 62

CHAPTER 4 Applying the Mechanics of Style 182

CHAPTER 5 Reading Effectively 260

CHAPTER 6 Improving Listening Skills 282

CHAPTER 7 Sharpening Writing Skills 304

CHAPTER 8 Developing Speaking Skills 376

CHAPTER 9 Communicating Electronically 426

CHAPTER 10 Planning and Formatting Business Correspondence 456

CHAPTER 11 Writing Business Correspondence 494

CHAPTER 12 Improving Customer Service Communication 552

CHAPTER 13 Writing Reports and Special Communications 570

CHAPTER 14 Finding, Accepting, and Leaving Employment 616

ANSWERS TO CHECKUPS 652

REFERENCES 662

INDEX 663

Contents

Preface   ix

CHAPTER 1   Understanding Communication   2

Chapter Opening Case   3
Section 1.1   Effective Communication in Everyday Living   4
Section 1.2   The Communication Skills: Listening, Speaking, Reading, and Writing   17
Section 1.3   Applying Your Communication Skills in Business   24
Critical Thinking Case: The Cost of Poor Communication Skills   30

CHAPTER 2   Communicating Around the Globe   32

Chapter Opening Case   33
Section 2.1   Electronic Communication   34
Section 2.2   Domestic and International Communication   41
Section 2.3   Ethics and Professional Courtesy in Business Communication   50
Section 2.4   Nondiscriminatory Language   56
Critical Thinking Case: Communicating With Tact and Courtesy   61

CHAPTER 3   Expanding Language Skills   62

Chapter Opening Case   63
Section 3.1   Language Structure   64
Section 3.2   Nouns: Plural Forms   81
Section 3.3   Nouns and Pronouns: Possessive Forms   91
Section 3.4   Pronouns: Nominative and Objective Forms   99
Section 3.5   Verbs   109
Section 3.6   Predicate Agreement   128
Section 3.7   Adjectives   142

Section 3.8   Adverbs   152

Section 3.9   Prepositions   161

Section 3.10 Conjunctions   171

Critical Thinking Case: Dealing With a Supervisor's Errors   181

CHAPTER 4   Applying the Mechanics of Style   182

Chapter Opening Case   183

Section 4.1   Sentence Enders   184

Section 4.2   Commas   192

Section 4.3   Semicolons, Colons, and Dashes   211

Section 4.4   Quotation Marks, Parentheses, and Apostrophes   220

Section 4.5   Capitalization   230

Section 4.6   Abbreviations   240

Section 4.7   Numbers   249

Critical Thinking Cases: Checking for Errors in Written Copy;
The Importance of Keeping Confidences   259

CHAPTER 5   Reading Effectively   260

Chapter Opening Case   261

Section 5.1   Basics of Reading   262

Section 5.2   Improving Vocabulary Power   267

Section 5.3   Strategies for Comprehending and Retaining Content   272

Section 5.4   Effective Note Taking While Reading   276

Critical Thinking Cases: Dealing With a Challenging Reading Assignment;
Keeping Up With Your Professional Reading; Handling an Important
Reading Assignment   280

CHAPTER 6   Improving Listening Skills   282

Chapter Opening Case   283

Section 6.1   Basics of Listening   284

Section 6.2 Listening in Casual Conversations and Small-Group and Conference Settings   296

Critical Thinking Cases: Asking Someone to Speak More Clearly; How Not to Take Notes   303

CHAPTER 7 **Sharpening Writing Skills**   304

Chapter Opening Case   305
Section 7.1 Using Words Effectively   306
Section 7.2 Mastering Spelling Techniques   321
Section 7.3 Structuring Phrases and Clauses   330
Section 7.4 Writing Effective Sentences   338
Section 7.5 Building Effective Paragraphs   350
Section 7.6 Revising, Editing, and Proofreading   358
Critical Thinking Cases: Revising for Tact; Proving Yourself in Writing   375

CHAPTER 8 **Developing Speaking Skills**   376

Chapter Opening Case   377
Section 8.1 Basics of Oral Communication   378
Section 8.2 Nonverbal Communication and Speech Qualities   387
Section 8.3 Conducting Meetings and Communicating in Groups   399
Section 8.4 Formal and Informal Presentations   410
Critical Thinking Cases: Tacky Telephone Technique; Getting Ready for a Presentation   425

CHAPTER 9 **Communicating Electronically**   426

Chapter Opening Case   427
Section 9.1 Using Information Processing   428
Section 9.2 Using Telecommunications   434
Section 9.3 Considerations for Communicating Electronically   449
Critical Thinking Case: Selecting the Appropriate Technology   455

CHAPTER 10 Planning and Formatting Business Correspondence **456**

Chapter Opening Case	457
Section 10.1 Planning Messages	458
Section 10.2 Planning Memos	463
Section 10.3 Memo Types and Parts	471
Section 10.4 Letter Parts and Formats	477
Section 10.5 Stationery and Envelopes	487
Critical Thinking Case: Assuring Correspondence is Correct	493

CHAPTER 11 Writing Business Correspondence **494**

Chapter Opening Case	495
Section 11.1 Informing	496
Section 11.2 Requesting	499
Section 11.3 Responding to Requests	508
Section 11.4 Persuading	524
Section 11.5 Public Relations Letters	531
Section 11.6 Social-Business Communications	537
Section 11.7 Form Paragraphs, Form Letters, and Templates	545
Critical Thinking Case: A Public Relations Problem	551

CHAPTER 12 Improving Customer Service Communication **552**

Chapter Opening Case	553
Section 12.1 The Importance of Good Customer Service	554
Section 12.2 Maintaining Good Customer Service	556
Section 12.3 Improving Contact With Customers	561
Section 12.4 Responding to Customer Service Needs	566
Critical Thinking Case: Customer Dissatisfaction	569

CHAPTER 13 Writing Reports and Special Communications 570

Chapter Opening Case 571
Section 13.1 Gathering Information for Reports 572
Section 13.2 Technology and Reports 576
Section 13.3 Reviewing Articles and Documenting Sources 580
Section 13.4 Writing Informal Reports 586
Section 13.5 Writing Formal Reports 594
Section 13.6 Keeping Meeting Records 607
Section 13.7 Preparing News Releases 611
Critical Thinking Case: Doing Your Homework 615

CHAPTER 14 Finding, Accepting, and Leaving Employment 616

Chapter Opening Case 617
Section 14.1 Communicating in the Job Search 618
Section 14.2 The Effective Employment Interview 637
Section 14.3 Communicating and Your Career 647
Critical Thinking Case: Making a Mess of Marketing Yourself 651

ANSWERS TO CHECKUPS 652

REFERENCES 662

INDEX 663

Preface

Flexibility—the ability to be adaptable—certainly applies to business communicators. Due to the global nature of business and the impact of technology, you will be confronted with change throughout your career. To be a successful business communicator, you will need a solid foundation in grammar and mechanics and in reading, listening, speaking, and writing. In addition, you will need to understand how factors such as cultural diversity, ethics, nonverbal communication, and technology impact business communication.

College English and Communication, Seventh Edition, is designed to help you meet the challenges of business communication. In response to feedback from users of previous editions, the seventh edition retains the comprehensive, detailed presentation of previous editions and adds up-to-date coverage of key topics such as cultural diversity, ethics, electronic communication, and the Internet. In addition, the seventh edition offers expanded coverage of reading, listening, speaking, writing, reports, and employment communication.

College English and Communication, Seventh Edition, presents a dynamic combination of new and expanded coverage.

NEW COVERAGE

- Electronic communication—New Chapter 2 introduces some of the technologies used to communicate globally while Chapter 9 discusses in detail the implications for communicating electronically. Technology margin features throughout the text highlight technology-related concerns for communication. Additionally, discussion of the use and impact of particular technologies is integrated into appropriate chapters.

- Global communication—New Chapter 2 focuses on the considerations for communicating on a global basis, including factors dealing with cultural diversity, ethics, international communication, and nondiscriminatory language. In addition, World View margin features throughout the text offer insights into international communication.

- Customer service communication—New Chapter 12 discusses the importance of customer service in business communication, distinguishes between internal and external customers, and offers timely guidelines for dealing with the public.

- Internet and World Wide Web—Chapter 2 introduces the use of the Internet and the World Wide Web, and Chapter 9 expands on the applications of these on-line resources for business communicators. In addition, Chapter 13 discusses how to use the Internet and other on-line sources to research reports.

EXPANDED COVERAGE

- Chapter 3, the grammar chapter, offers expanded and reorganized coverage of the parts of speech as well as sentence structure and types of sentences.

- Chapter 5, a new chapter on reading skills, pulls together information on reading, vocabulary power, strategies for retaining and comprehending content, and note taking.

- Chapter 6, a new chapter on listening skills, offers expanded coverage of nonverbal communication and provides tips for improving listening skills.

- Chapter 7 combines the coverage of writing skills into one comprehensive chapter. Topics discussed in Chapter 7 include word choice; spelling; structuring phrases and clauses; writing sentences; building paragraphs; and revising, editing, and proofreading.

- Chapter 8, the speaking skills chapter, offers more coverage of communicating in groups and an expanded discussion of formal presentations, with tips for creating electronic visual aids.

- Chapter 10, the formatting chapter, combines the coverage of formatting memos and letters in one chapter for easy reference.

- Chapter 13, the chapter on reports and special communications, provides expanded coverage of conducting research and includes tips for searching the Internet and citing electronic sources.

- Chapter 14 provides up-to-date, expanded coverage of employment communication, including guidelines for three types of résumés and for creating an electronically friendly résumé.

FEATURES

College English and Communication, Seventh Edition, uses a variety of text and margin features to present concepts of interest and importance for business communicators. Text features in the student edition include:

- An opening case study at the beginning of each chapter introduces the chapter and presents a realistic business situation. You are invited to analyze the situation in the case as you study the chapter.

- Memory Hooks throughout the text present tips and acronyms for remembering important concepts.

- Four-color photographs and artwork provide visual reinforcement of communication principles and serve as starting points for discussion.

- Section Reviews in all chapters test your understanding of the section content and your ability to apply what you have learned to specific situations. These activities include Practical Applications, Editing Practices, and Critical Thinking Skills activities.

- Checkup exercises in Chapters 3, 4, 5, 6, and 7 quiz you on concepts just studied. Answer keys for the Checkups appear in the back of the text.

- A critical thinking case or cases at the end of each chapter give you the opportunity to apply what you have learned about chapter concepts to a real-world job situation.

Margin Features in the *Student Edition* Include:

Key Points, new to the seventh edition, highlight important concepts. Use these Key Points to help you summarize and review chapter content.

OOPS! features, new to the seventh edition, present humorous and challenging misuses of language and detail awkward or embarrassing workplace situations.

Technology features, new to the seventh edition, highlight the implications of using technology for communication and offer tips on how to apply a technology application to a specific task.

World Views offer insights into aspects of international communication. Issues such as cultural and language differences are discussed.

Margin Features in the *Instructor's Annotated Edition* Include:

School-to-Work/SCANS features identify workplace competencies addressed in each section and in each Section Review.

Go To features cross-reference related concepts in other chapters and provide correlations to related material in the *Student Activity Workbook, Transparencies,* and the *Computer Test Bank.*

Global Notes offer suggestions for increasing students' awareness of some of the international issues important in today's business communication.

- Teaching suggestions and notes at the point of instruction offer tips for introducing, reinforcing, and reviewing concepts. These suggestions are in addition to the teaching suggestions that appear in the front of the *Instructor's Annotated Edition.*

- Answer keys for Checkups and Section Reviews appear in the margins where space permits. Longer answer keys appear in the front of the *Instructor's Annotated Edition.* Answer keys for Checkups appear in the back of the student text.

COMPONENTS OF THE PROGRAM

The seventh edition of *College English and Communication* is a complete, well-rounded program that includes the following components:

- *Student Activity Workbook* with ample application and critical thinking activities. The activities for each chapter are organized by section and take a building-block approach. Each succeeding chapter builds on previous chapters. You will be asked to apply concepts that you learned in the current and previous chapters. The workbook activities are integrated, often calling on you to apply more than one skill to complete an activity.

- *Glencoe Interactive Grammar Student Software,* available on CD-ROM, contains a comprehensive set of grammar and mechanics exercises. The graphical interface allows you to draw lines, underline text, circle words, and insert punctuation to complete exercises. You may check your own work and receive immediate feedback on your answers. The program provides learning hints that explain grammar rules and definitions associated with each lesson. You can print your responses to exercises as well as answers to any incorrect items.

- *Instructor's Annotated Edition of the Student Activity Workbook* contains a page-for-page answer key for all activities, with the answer keys shown full size.

- *Transparencies* include a set of 100 two- and four-color transparencies that instructors can use for visual reinforcement and explanation of concepts from *College English and Communication, Seventh Edition.*

- *Computer Test Bank* provides comprehensive chapter tests for all 14 chapters of *College English and Communication, Seventh Edition,* with questions organized by section. Instructors have the option of using the prepared questions or adding their own questions. Question types include true/false, multiple choice, matching, completion, short answer, and essay.

- *Instructor's PowerPoint Presentation* Software presents PowerPoint slides that illustrate communication principles and guidelines related to reading, listening, speaking, and writing skills. Instructors may manipulate the slides as needed to tailor the presentation to the needs of the class.

Acknowledgments

We would like to thank Karen Schneiter of the Job Training Center in Rochester, Minnesota, for her consulting work in conjunction with Chapter 9.

We would like to thank the following educators for their invaluable comments and feedback on this revision. In particular, we would like to thank Marcy Satterwhite of Lake Land College, Mattoon, Illinois, for her input in developing the manuscript.

Janet S. Arena, Stone Academy, Hamden, Connecticut
Diana Beebe, InterVoice, Dallas, Texas
Connie Jo Clark, Lane Community College, Eugene, Oregon
Debbie Clark, Augusta Technical Institute, Augusta, Georgia
Evelyn V. Delaney, Daytona Beach Community College, Daytona Beach, Florida
Robin Delaney, Hickey School, St. Louis, Missouri
Phyllis Donovan, Bryant & Stratton, Buffalo, New York
Cheryl L. Draughter, Louisiana Technical College, New Orleans, Louisiana
Mildred S. Franceschi, Valencia Community College, Orlando, Florida
Joy L. Hanel, South Central Technical College, North Mankato, Minnesota
Gloria Huffman-Gregory, Trenholm State Technical College,
    Montgomery, Alabama
Donna Jarrett, Bradford School, Columbus, Ohio
Jane LaRose, Louisiana Technical College, Metairie, Louisiana
William M. Lewis, Western Business College, Portland, Oregon
Georgia E. Mackh, Cabrillo College, Aptos, California
Todd A. Maginnis, Churchman Business School, Easton, Pennsylvania
Dixie B. McIntosh, King's College, Charlotte, North Carolina
Virginia Melvin, State Technical Institute at Memphis, Memphis, Tennessee
Candyce H. Miller, Ricks College, Rexburg, Idaho
Nancy B. Moody, Sinclair Community College, Dayton, Ohio
Tiffinee Morgan, West Kentucky Technical School, Paducah, Kentucky
Paul W. Murphey, Southwest Wisconsin Technical College, Fennimore, Wisconsin
Linda S. Petraglia, The Stuart School, Wall, New Jersey
Eileen Rehm, Utica School of Commerce, Utica, New York
Amy L. Sanders, Bradford School, Pittsburgh, Pennsylvania
Imogene B. Shultz, Minneapolis Business College, Roseville, Minnesota
Shirley Sloan, Jefferson Community College, Watertown, New York
Clotilde Szajda, Dover Business College, Parsippany, New Jersey
Sherry W. Wise, South Georgia Technical Institute, Americus, Georgia

1.1   **Effective Communication in Everyday Living**

1.2   **The Communication Skills: Listening, Speaking, Reading, and Writing**

1.3   **Applying Your Communication Skills in Business**

Michelle works as a part-time assistant in the Archives Department at the Hometown Public Library while attending college. Her principal duties are to help patrons research their genealogy and use microfilm readers as well as to conduct research for mail-in research requests from across the country.

Michelle's supervisor, Roberta, is the director of the Reference Department, which is located in a separate part of the building along with her office. Michelle does not see her supervisor much, and they communicate mostly by notes and telephone messages.

On the occasions when they meet face-to-face, Roberta rarely initiates a greeting and often does not respond to Michelle's greetings. When they meet to discuss a problem, Roberta often interrupts Michelle as she speaks, waving her finger at Michelle in a scolding way.

When Roberta sends Michelle notes of instruction, she often misspells words and leaves words out, so it is difficult to understand the notes. In addition, Roberta often contradicts written instructions she had given earlier. For example, Roberta gave Michelle mailing instructions for sending replies to genealogy requests indicating that replies of more than five pages should be mailed in a 9 by 12 envelope instead of the standard No. 10 business envelope. Some weeks later, Roberta began sending back 9 by 12 envelopes Michelle had addressed for six- and seven-page replies. When Michelle asked Roberta about this, Roberta sent a note saying up to seven pages could be mailed in a No. l0 envelope.

Michelle was frustrated with the miscommunication that occurred between her and Roberta. Her frustration reached a breaking point when Roberta reprimanded Michelle for how she had distributed announcements for a computer training course Roberta was conducting for other library employees. Michelle had put the announcements in each person's mailbox in the break room instead of mailing them since Roberta was always reminding her to be cost-conscious. When Roberta saw the announcements in the mailboxes, she became very angry and told Michelle she should have mailed them to employees' homes.

As you read Chapter 1, identify some of the communication problems that Michelle and Roberta have, and think about how the problems could be eliminated or minimized.

Effective Communication in Everyday Living

OBJECTIVES:

After completing Section 1.1, you should be able to:

1. Identify the three types of communication and the four purposes of communication.
2. List and define the six components of communication.
3. Describe the factors that influence communication.
4. Discuss ways interpersonal skills affect communication.

Communication is simply mutual understanding.

—Stephen R. Covey, author and management consultant

Communication, very simply defined, is the exchange of information. Communication is a vital part of our everyday lives, beginning at birth. Very early in life, we learn to communicate our needs. A baby, for example, learns that crying makes a parent or caregiver respond quickly with attention, a dry diaper, food, or all three. As a child develops, communication becomes more complex. Speaking, listening, reading, writing, and even observing become part of the communication process.

Today, in addition to traditional methods of communication such as letters and telephone conversations, communicating by electronic media is becoming increasingly common. Electronic media such as voice mail, pagers, and videoconferencing allow people in different locations to exchange messages quickly and conveniently. This increased use of electronic media is changing communication practices, especially with regard to ethics and confidentiality. Chapter 2 introduces several forms of electronic media, and Chapter 9 offers guidelines for selecting the best technology for communicating electronically.

KEY POINT

The three main categories of communication are:
1. Oral.
2. Written.
3. Nonverbal.

TYPES OF COMMUNICATION

Communication can be divided into three main categories: oral, written, and nonverbal.

Oral Communication

Oral communication uses spoken words to exchange ideas and information. Examples of oral communication include one-on-one conversations, meetings, voice-mail messages, and teleconferencing. Spoken messages can be sent instantaneously and usually result in some immediate feedback. The disadvantage to oral communication is that there is often little opportunity to reflect on what is said.

Written Communication

Written communication can include letters, faxes, memorandums, electronic mail, reports, news releases, tables, diagrams, charts, and graphs. Written communication provides proof that the information was exchanged. The disadvantage to written communication is that immediate feedback may not always be possible.

Nonverbal Communication

Nonverbal communication is communication without words. Nonverbal communication is an important form of communication. Think about it. Without saying a single word, you can express your feelings with body language—gestures, facial expressions, and body movements or positions. For example, in the case study at the beginning of the chapter, Roberta's lack of acknowledgment of Michelle's greeting sent an unfriendly message.

Many times the nonverbal message is stronger and therefore more believable than the verbal message. The nonverbal message also may reinforce or contradict the verbal message.

Good communicators combine oral and nonverbal communication techniques to make their communication more effective. This important combination—or, even more so, lack—of skills, is easy to spot. Have you ever listened to a speaker who was an authority on a subject, but whom you considered boring because the speaker lacked any kind of nonverbal expression? Even if the subject interested you, you probably found it hard to keep your mind on the speech. Nonverbal communication can add emphasis and depth to spoken words and can even tell you whether or not to believe a speaker. Nonverbal communication plays an important role in the clear, effective exchange of messages.

KEY POINT

Listeners tend to believe nonverbal messages. "Actions speak louder than words."

PURPOSES OF COMMUNICATION

The first step in planning any message is to determine the purpose of your communication.

Recall for a moment what you said to various family members, friends, and school or business associates today. Every question you asked and every statement you made—from "How do you feel today?" to "I just found a ten-dollar bill!"—falls into at least one of the following four main purposes of communication:

- *To inquire.* "When did you learn to use this digital camera?"
- *To inform.* "This digital camera is six months old."

KEY POINT

The four main purposes of communication are:
1. To inquire.
2. To inform.
3. To persuade.
4. To develop goodwill.

- *To persuade.* "You really will save time and money if you use a digital camera."
- *To develop goodwill.* "Thank you for helping me select a digital camera."

You will learn how to plan business messages and determine the purposes of such messages in Chapters 10 and 11.

COMPONENTS OF COMMUNICATION

What can a speaker—even a great speaker—communicate if there is no one to listen? Keep in mind that communication can take place only if you have *both* a sender and a receiver. Each time you have a conversation with someone or exchange written messages, you should be aware of each component of the communication model as illustrated in Figure 1.1 below. The six basic components of communication are as follows:

1. *Message sender.* The sender composes the intended message. The sender could be a writer, a speaker, or a person who sends a nonverbal message through gestures and body language.

2. *Actual message.* The actual message may be written, oral, or nonverbal, or it may combine two or more types of communication. It may or may not be the message the sender intended.

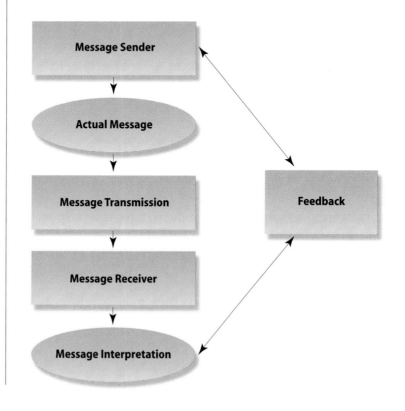

Figure 1.1
The Communication Model

Every exchange of messages, whether oral, written, or nonverbal, involves six basic components: (1) message sender, (2) actual message, (3) message transmission, (4) message receiver, (5) message interpretation, and (6) feedback.

3. *Message transmission.* The message can be sent or delivered in a variety of ways. *Written messages* can be sent in the form of letters, memorandums, and reports. Written messages could also be sent electronically using fax machines or electronic mail. *Oral messages* can be delivered through face-to-face conversations, meetings, presentations, and through telephone conversations and voice mail. *Nonverbal messages* include gestures, body language, and facial expressions.

4. *Message receiver.* The receiver takes in, or receives, the message. The receiver's knowledge, interest, and emotional state will affect how the message is received.

5. *Message interpretation.* The receiver interprets the message. The interpretation may be different from the intended message or the actual message.

6. *Feedback.* The sender and the receiver respond to each other in writing, orally, nonverbally, or in a combination of these ways. Feedback may include a written response, verbal questions, and nonverbal gestures such as body language and facial expressions.

FACTORS THAT INFLUENCE COMMUNICATION

Although the sender of a message knows the goals he or she wants to achieve, the sender must keep in mind four key factors that will influence the communication either favorably or unfavorably. To be an effective communicator, the sender should account for how the following four factors affect the communication process:

1. The background of the receiver.
2. The appearance of the sender or of the sender's communication.

KEY POINT

Four key factors influence a communication either favorably or unfavorably:
1. The background of the receiver.
2. The appearance of the sender or of the sender's message.
3. Barriers that might negatively affect the intended message.
4. The language and communication skills of the sender and the receiver.

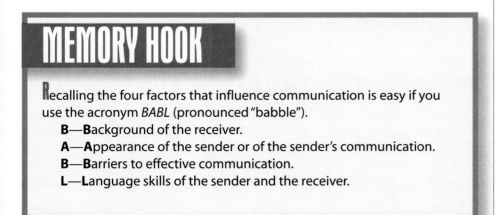

MEMORY HOOK

Recalling the four factors that influence communication is easy if you use the acronym *BABL* (pronounced "babble").

    B—**B**ackground of the receiver.
    A—**A**ppearance of the sender or of the sender's communication.
    B—**B**arriers to effective communication.
    L—**L**anguage skills of the sender and the receiver.

3. Barriers that might negatively affect the intended message.

4. The language and communication skills of the sender and the receiver.

Background of the Receiver

The following four background elements can play an important role in determining the receiver's possible reaction and response to the message.

1. The *knowledge* both the sender and the receiver already have about the facts, ideas, and language used in the message.

2. The *personality* of the receiver—-particularly the emotions, attitudes, and prejudices that are likely to influence the way the message is interpreted.

3. The receiver's *experiences* that are relevant to the message content.

4. The receiver's *interest and motivation* regarding the subject of the message.

To understand how these four factors can influence a receiver, imagine that you have just received a flyer from an office supply company explaining their latest sale. If you have not previously purchased supplies from this company, your *knowledge* of their quality and service is probably limited. Naturally, your reaction would be different from that of a person who is knowledgeable about the office supply company. If your *personality* is quite conservative, you have probably decided to make only a small purchase. However, if your *experience* with this company has been good, your *interest and motivation* probably grew the minute you saw the cost savings available from this type of sale.

The communicator who weighs all of these factors and anticipates the receiver's needs before preparing the message stands a greater chance that his or her message will be accepted by the receiver than the person who ignores these factors.

KEY POINT

A receiver's interest and motivation are often influenced by experience.

Appearance of the Sender or of the Sender's Communication

What do these three situations have in common: (1) a sloppy-looking speaker or salesperson, (2) a receptionist or telemarketer who does not speak distinctly, and (3) a letter filled with errors? They all transmit their messages in an unfavorable way. Every communication you transmit can be your goodwill ambassador and can help achieve a positive reaction if you remember that appearances do make a difference.

Figure 1.2

Physical appearance contributes positively or negatively to the impression a person makes. Which person's appearance makes the better impression? Why?

Barriers to Effective Communication

Barriers are factors that interfere with communication and might negatively affect the intended message. Barriers may include physical distractions, emotional distractions, and cultural and language differences.

Under what circumstances is the message received? For example, is the room noisy? too warm or too cold? poorly lighted? Is the receiver more concerned with some personal problem? Such distractions interfere with and draw the receiver's attention away from the message and create barriers to effective communication. Sometimes the resulting lack of concentration can lead to incomplete communication by message senders and erroneous conclusions by message receivers.

Physical distractions are usually easier to prevent in a speaking or listening situation because the surroundings can often be controlled or changed. In a writing or reading situation, however, the writer has little influence over the reader's surroundings. However, every writer can and should prevent the distraction of a sloppy-looking message or one that contains errors.

Emotional distractions on the part of the receiver can prevent him or her from concentrating on and giving full attention to the communication. Emotional distractions may include thinking about a personal matter or allowing an emotion such as anger to influence how you interpret a message.

Barriers such as language differences, inattention, and misunderstandings caused by different interpretations of a word or an expression can have a negative influence on the communication process. Cultural

KEY POINT

Three types of barriers to communication are physical distractions, emotional distractions, and language differences.

Misunderstandings can arise when someone uses the wrong word. Consider this statement made by an employee in a French hotel:

"Please leave your values at the front desk."

diversity can also be a barrier to effective communication. For example, executives in the United States and Japan might have different ideas about what constitutes politeness in a letter. Chapter 2 discusses cultural diversity in more detail.

Language and Communication Skills of the Sender and the Receiver

Every business person is involved in some form of communication and must be able to use language effectively to send and receive messages. Words are the major tools of language, and they must be chosen carefully to express the intended meaning. How well the sender of the message uses these tools and how well the receiver interprets their use are major factors in the effectiveness of the message.

In today's intercultural society, it is important for you to be sensitive to cultural diversity when using any form of communication. An awareness of, and respect for, cultural differences will help you to avoid stereotyping someone based on their background. You do not want to offend anyone.

Selecting the correct words to use is particularly important in cases in which there might be a language barrier—for example, if the receiver's first language is not English. Use of slang and jargon in communicating with people who do not understand the slang and jargon could also cause a barrier to communication.

As a message sender, you must communicate facts, ideas, opinions, and instructions in a coherent manner with a minimum of effort and with clarity, confidence, and knowledge. To do this, you must have a broad vocabulary with the ability to spell, pronounce, and select the correct words. You must be able to speak and write clearly, concisely, and without error. As a message receiver, you must also be able to read and listen with understanding. Both the sender and the receiver share the responsibility for effective communication. In the case study at the beginning of the chapter, what were Roberta's responsibilities as a message sender? What were Michelle's responsibilities as a message receiver?

In speaking situations, word choice, grammar, pronunciation, and listening are also factors in effective communication. A receiver may be distracted by incorrect grammar, incorrect pronunciation, or misused words and may not receive the intended message.

In writing situations something as simple as using the wrong word, making a spelling or grammatical error, using an incorrect format, or misusing a punctuation mark may change the intended meaning of the message. Even if the receiver understands the message, his or her opinion of the sender's intelligence and credibility may be negatively influenced by the error. For example, a receiver may not do business with a company because of a poorly written sales letter. The receiver may feel

World View

When communicating with someone whose first language isn't English, avoid using figures of speech such as "Don't bite off more than you can chew." Such expressions can be confusing because they don't mean what they literally say.

Omitting a punctuation mark can completely change the meaning of a sentence. Read these two sentences, and notice the difference in meaning.

The teacher said the student was very cooperative.

The teacher, said the student, was very cooperative.

In each sentence, who was cooperative?

that a company careless about its letters may also be careless about filling orders promptly and accurately.

Each of these tools of language is discussed more fully in later sections of this book. Keep in mind, however, that these tools apply not only to writing but also to reading, listening, and speaking. If the communication process is to be successful, the message sender must be an effective writer or speaker, and the receiver must be an effective reader or listener. As the receiver, you owe the sender the courtesy of paying attention to the message, even though you may be preoccupied with another matter.

RESPONSIBILITIES OF THE SENDER AND THE RECEIVER

As you can see from Figure 1.1 on page 6, both the sender and the receiver have responsibilities for ensuring that effective communication occurs. Let's take a look at the responsibilities of the sender and the receiver.

Evaluate Each Communication Situation

Effective communication requires the sender to understand his or her own intrapersonal communication. *Intrapersonal communication* refers to the way each person views and interprets information based on his or her previous life experiences. Intrapersonal communication (communication in your mind) must take place before you can communicate with another person. *Interpersonal communication* is communication that occurs between two people.

KEY POINT

Communication takes place when the intended message, the actual message, and the interpreted message are the same.

Avoid Miscommunication. Ideally, the intended message, the actual message, and the interpreted message will be the same. Miscommunication occurs when one or more of the three message components are different for either the sender or the receiver. For example, consider the following situation.

Even though Chris Miller, a college freshman, was upset with her semester grades, she knew she had to write home. Chris (*message sender*) sent a letter (*message transmission*) in which she stated her grades (*intended message*) to her parents: "I got only one D this semester (*actual message*)." When her parents (*message receivers*) read her letter, they interpreted it this way: "Chris got only one D this semester. That is much better than the three Ds she got last semester! (*interpreted message*)"

Miscommunication occurred because Chris's *actual message* did not accurately convey the facts. Chris received only one D this semester, but she also received two Fs. Because her parents want her to do well, they interpreted her message in a positive way.

Maintain Goodwill. Effective communication takes place when the message is received and understood. Keep in mind, however, that effective communication always maintains *goodwill* (favorable relations) between the sender and the receiver. You can tell a person no and make an enemy for life; but if you use a customer service approach and incorporate human relations skills into your communication, you are more likely to have an effective communication. Chapter 12 discusses customer service communication in more detail.

Remember that communication is effective when it:

- Enables the receiver to interpret the message exactly as the sender intended.
- Results in the desired response from the receiver.
- Develops goodwill between the sender and the receiver.

Give and Receive Feedback. Miscommunication and communication breakdowns can often be avoided by using the feedback technique. *Feedback* involves getting an oral, written, or nonverbal response from the receiver. In the process of transmitting a face-to-face message, the sender can use clues from the receiver to determine if the receiver is interpreting the message correctly. For example, a puzzled look on the receiver's face can signal that the message is confusing.

Asking questions is one way to get feedback. The sender can ask the receiver questions to determine whether the message is being received accurately. In turn, the receiver can ask the sender questions to clarify any content that is unclear. What feedback could Michelle have given Roberta in order to avoid some of the miscommunication that occurred in the case study at the beginning of this chapter?

Figure 1.3

Feedback from a listener may include facial expressions, posture, and eye contact. What might the listener's feedback indicate to the speaker? What could the speaker do to get oral feedback from the listener?

Feedback cannot be achieved so easily with written communication because the sender and receiver are separated and receiver response is usually not immediate. The wrong response, questions from the receiver, or no response may indicate a temporary breakdown in communication.

Understand Personal Needs

One significant factor in successful interpersonal skills is understanding the needs of the receiver of a message. Abraham Maslow, a famous psychologist, divided human needs into five levels.

1. *Physical needs.* Physical needs are essential to life and include food, clothing, and shelter. Until these basic needs are satisfied, receivers have difficulty thinking of anything else.

2. *Security needs.* Security needs include the desire to be safe from physical harm and mental abuse.

3. *Social needs.* Social needs, which are evident in everyone's desire to be part of a group, can be met through family, social contacts, work relationships, or other group situations.

4. *Esteem needs.* Esteem needs are satisfied through a feeling of self-importance, self-respect, prestige, power, or recognition. Winning a contest, being selected as chairperson of an event or organization, and receiving a scholarship are some situations that satisfy esteem needs.

5. *Self-actualizing needs.* These needs are met through a sense of achievement, competence, and creativity, and by helping others meet their own needs. People who reach the top in their fields often want to use their abilities and resources to benefit others. They may also want to help others attain similar success.

Figure 1.4 on page 14 illustrates Maslow's hierarchy of needs, with the lowest-level needs at the bottom and the highest-level needs at the top.

Assess the Needs of the Receiver

In order to communicate effectively, the sender must carefully examine each situation and assess the needs of the receiver. Needs motivate people to act or react in certain ways. Some theorists believe that a satisfied need is not a motivator. If you just ate two cheeseburgers, an order of fries, and a large milk shake, food would not be a motivator for you. However, if you had just been on a restricted diet, food could definitely be a motivator.

World View

Although English is becoming a global language, many know English as a second language and may have difficulty understanding it. People who are more proficient in their native language than in English will mentally interpret the English into their native language in order to understand what is said.

KEY POINT

Maslow organizes human needs into five levels:
1. Physical
2. Security
3. Social
4. Esteem
5. Self-actualizing

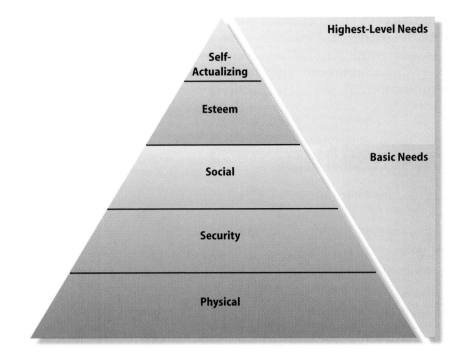

Figure 1.4 Maslow's Hierarchy of Needs

The basic needs are at the bottom, and the highest-level needs are at the top.

In many cases, the first three needs (physical, security, and social) are satisfied. However, the last two needs (esteem and self-actualizing) always have room for more satisfiers. By helping the receiver satisfy these two needs, the sender can improve communication. *Empathy,* imagining yourself in another person's situation, is a good way to determine the best motivator to get the desired action from the receiver.

Keep in mind that the receiver may be motivated by more than one need. For example, a person may accept a position as officer of an organization to satisfy both social and esteem needs.

To communicate effectively, you need to demonstrate human relations skills when interacting with others. Use the human relations techniques described in the following paragraphs as a guide.

Apply Interpersonal Skills

The average person speaks about 18,000 words each day. Most of those words are spent communicating on a one-to-one basis or in situations involving only a few people. It makes sense, therefore, that everyone should develop effective interpersonal skills.

Human relations skills, also known as interpersonal skills, involve the ability to understand and deal with people in such a way that a favorable relationship and goodwill are maintained.

Use the You-Attitude. Using the *you-attitude* when writing and speaking helps build goodwill and helps maintain an environment of friendliness. The you-attitude means putting your reader or listener first

KEY POINT

Using the you-attitude in speaking and writing helps to build and maintain goodwill.

and being considerate of the other person. An example of the you-attitude is "For your convenience we are extending our hours until 7 p.m."

The *I-attitude* is the opposite of the you-attitude; it is putting your own interests, well-being, and comfort ahead of anyone else's. An example of the I-attitude is "I have decided to extend our hours until 7 p.m."

Demonstrate a Positive Attitude. A good communicator demonstrates a positive attitude by building good working relationships with peers, superiors, subordinates, and customers and clients. Showing enthusiasm about your job and your organization, cooperating with others, and controlling your emotions are ways to demonstrate a positive attitude.

Be a Good Listener. A good communicator is also a good listener. It is important to listen carefully and to let the speaker know you are interested. Ask questions when you are unsure of the content of the message, and take notes when appropriate.

Maintain Confidentiality. A good communicator understands the importance of confidentiality. This means releasing information to authorized personnel only and releasing information at the appropriate time—not early and not late. Also, do not spread rumors—even if you believe they are true.

Be Considerate. Treat others as you would like to be treated. A good communicator is courteous, honest, and patient in dealing with other people and respects the opinions of others. This means using tact and diplomacy in some instances. It also means using words and terms that your receiver understands. Another way to show courtesy is to be prompt in answering correspondence and in returning telephone calls.

Recent studies indicate that workers need to possess good communication skills in order to be competitive in the changing workplace and in the global economy. Practicing the human relations techniques described in this section will help you improve your communication skills.

SECTION 1.1   REVIEW

Practical Application

1. Define *communication,* and list its four main purposes.
2. Explain the differences among oral, written, and nonverbal communication, and tell why each type of communication is essential to effective communication.

3. Name the four key factors that influence communication, and describe each one briefly.
4. List several basic human relations techniques that, if applied, could improve communication.
5. Define feedback and give some examples of oral, written, and nonverbal feedback.

Editing Practice

Spelling Alert! Write or type each of the following sentences on a separate sheet, correcting the spelling errors. A sentence may have more than one misspelled word.
1. A catalog will be cent under seperate cover since its so bulky.
2. Mrs. Ramirez ordered a blew chair because it matched her curtins.
3. What time are your planing to leave for Chicago?
4. He finaly finished the report yesteday.
5. Although John shiped the package last Tuesday, we did not recieve it until today.

Critical Thinking Skills

A. **Analyze:** Today, immediately after a conversation with a fellow student or employee, analyze what was said by jotting down answers to the following questions.
1. What was the sender's intended message?
2. What was the sender's actual message?
3. What was the receiver's interpretation of the message?
4. Were all three messages the same? If not, what factors may have caused a breakdown in communication?

B. **Classify:** Tell which human need or needs each of the following represents.
1. A heavy front door with a deadbolt lock and a motion detector light.
2. A jacket with your name and your organization's name embroidered on it.
3. The latest CD released by a popular recording artist.
4. Low-fat food and exercise.
5. Election as chairperson of an advisory council.
6. A successful recording artist giving an unknown singer a chance.
7. A carbon monoxide detector.
8. A request for you to design and paint a mural in the public library.
9. Owning an expensive car.
10. Basic clothing.

The Communication Skills: Listening, Speaking, Reading, and Writing

OBJECTIVES:
After completing Section 1.2, you should be able to:

1. Explain how the four communication skills are interconnected and how they reinforce one another.
2. Show how the four communication skills relate to your social, educational, and professional lives.
3. Give examples to illustrate the importance of listening, speaking, reading, and writing skills in your life.

For many of us, communication is first and foremost seeking to be understood, to communicate our ideas and opinions to others in an effective way. If we listen at all, it's usually with intent to reply. Seek First to Understand, Then to Be Understood.

—Stephen R. Covey, author and management consultant

Look around you. There are many good communicators. Some of the people you identify as good communicators may be friends, family members, teachers, or supervisors. Others may be national figures, such as radio and television personalities and political figures. What makes these people effective communicators? What can you do to become a more effective communicator?

In Section 1.1 you learned that communication is a two-way process that requires a sender and a receiver. You cannot communicate in a vacuum. You cannot communicate by speaking if there is no one to listen. You cannot communicate by writing if no one will read your words. Each side—sender and receiver—must do its part.

As you have probably noticed, communicators are paired: speaker-listener and writer-reader. *Oral communication* requires a speaker and a listener. Oral communication is most effective when the sender has good speaking skills and the receiver has good listening skills. Similarly, *written communication* requires a writer and a reader. Written communication is most effective when the sender has good writing skills and the receiver has good reading skills. In the situation described in the case study at the beginning of the chapter, how would you rate the effectiveness of Roberta's oral and written communication with Michelle?

If only half of the pair operates effectively, something is lost in the communication process. Suppose, for example, that someone writes a clear, step-by-step description of a certain business procedure. No matter how clear that message, some information will be lost if the reader does not focus full attention on the message or does not understand some of the words or references. The reader will not understand what the writer is trying to say. Communication, then, is a partnership in which each side has responsibility.

KEY POINT

Communication is a two-way process that requires a sender and a receiver.

COMBINING THE COMMUNICATION SKILLS IN YOUR SOCIAL, EDUCATIONAL, AND PROFESSIONAL LIVES

An essential ingredient of successful family, social, and business relationships is effective communication. A communication breakdown can lead to misunderstandings and serious problems in our personal and business lives. Good communication skills can affect most aspects of our relationships with others in a positive way.

Learning to be a successful, effective communicator is somewhat like learning to be a good basketball player or a good chess player. Once you have learned the basic skills, you become better and better as you practice the skills and gain confidence.

Listening, speaking, reading, and writing are important and useful skills in and of themselves. When used together, they reinforce each other, producing a higher, more efficient level of communication. Each of the four skills can be strengthened by being combined with the others. Take listening, for example.

Listening Skills

Listening is one of the primary means of receiving information. The problem with listening, though, is that if you miss something or forget part of what you heard, you cannot replay the message (unless, of course, you have recorded it). When you know something about the subject, however, when you have "read up on it" or "done your homework," you will find it easier to grasp the information presented orally. Reading, then, can reinforce listening; it helps you gain more from what you hear.

Common barriers or distractions to good listening fall into three categories—educational, environmental, and emotional-physical. *Educational* distractions include a lack of knowledge of the subject matter and vocabulary. *Environmental* distractions include external factors such as the temperature in the room, the noise level, and so on. *Emotional-physical* distractions include internal factors such as your state of mind or your health. For example, having a headache or being extremely worried about something can adversely affect your ability to listen.

Speaking, too, can reinforce your listening skills. As mentioned before, good listeners ask questions to clarify points and obtain additional information. Speaking can also be used as a memory aid. Repeating a person's name right after you hear it, for example, will help you remember the name.

Writing reinforces listening skills on an ongoing basis. You jot down the name and address of a restaurant someone recommends, or you take a telephone message for a coworker. You take notes when your supervisor explains how a job should be done. You can then refer to your notes when you need them. Listening skills are important in all aspects of your life.

MEMORY HOOK

Use these five strategies to enhance and reinforce your listening skills:

- *Read* to gain background information.
- *Repeat* a person's name when you are introduced to someone.
- *Ask* questions to clarify information.
- *Take* good notes.
- *Use* a tape recorder when permitted to record a lecture or meeting.

Your Social Life. In your social life good listeners—those who understand what the speaker is saying and why—are much in demand. We often choose a good listener as a good friend: someone to turn to when we want to talk about our problems or fears or to share our triumphs or joys. Good listeners often reap the benefit of the experience of others and enjoy the satisfaction of close, personal relationships.

Your Educational Life. Good listening skills help you absorb an instructor's lectures, explanations, and directions for assignments. The process of taking notes on the oral information enhances listening. Your notes provide a record of the information you received and enable you to review the information at a later time.

Your Professional Life. To see how listening is assisted by the other communication skills in your professional life, consider how Barbara Wright uses these skills in her job as an administrative assistant in a medical center. Listening is an important part of Barbara's job. She attends staff meetings where she listens to caseworkers and medical staff discussing current problems and cases. To help her remember what was discussed and what she is supposed to do, Barbara takes notes. After a meeting, she enters her notes on a computer, creating a permanent record and handy reference. In the meetings Barbara often hears references to medical procedures, drugs, and articles in medical journals. She finds that her background reading helps her to understand discussions at meetings.

Barbara also uses her speaking skills in her job. She asks questions and answers requests for information at the staff meetings, and she spends some time each day on the telephone, answering questions and providing information to coworkers and clients. Barbara has discovered that reading, writing, and speaking have helped her become a more effective listener.

Kristen was daydreaming about her weekend and not paying attention when the instructor announced that class would not meet tomorrow. Kristen was the only student who showed up the next day.

Speaking Skills

The communication skill you will probably use the most is speaking. Speaking can be an excellent way to transmit information. Speaking also comes into play as part of being a good listener. You provide feedback by letting the speaker know you understand, by offering advice, and by asking for more details.

Your Social Life. You use your speaking skills to share your thoughts, wants, accomplishments, and feelings with others. You also ask questions to gain information and show interest. Speaking can be face-to-face or over the telephone.

Your Educational Life. Asking questions, summarizing information, and expressing ideas are an important part of the learning process. Your spoken feedback tells your instructor what information you understand and what information needs clarification. Your speaking skills will help you master the course material.

Your Professional Life. Communicating by speaking is an important skill in the work world. Let's look at how Andrea Rosado uses speaking on her job as a paralegal. Andrea spends a good portion of her day speaking with attorneys, other paralegals, and clients. She makes telephone inquiries regarding legal cases she's working on, and she engages in discussions with attorneys and colleagues.

Reading, writing, and listening skills support Andrea's speaking skills. Andrea knows that reading is an essential part of her job. She must analyze the facts of a case and conduct research to identify laws, judicial decisions, and legal articles that may have a bearing on the

World View

To communicate effectively in a global environment, you need to consider various factors that make communication challenging. Some factors to consider include language differences, customs, and differences in viewpoints based on cultural and religious beliefs.

Figure 1.5

Good speaking skills can enhance your professional life. What speaking situations might you be involved in on the job?

case. Andrea uses her writing skills to prepare legal briefs and legal correspondence. Listening is also an important skill for Andrea. As a paralegal, she must listen to clients to obtain information and she must listen to instructions from her supervising attorney.

Reading Skills

Reading is one of the principal means of obtaining information. The information may be in printed form such as a book or magazine or in electronic form on a computer screen. Reading is an efficient way to learn because it allows you to control the flow of information. You can reread a passage you have not fully understood, and you can take notes, which will help you when reviewing the material. Reading allows you to skip over material you don't need.

Your Social Life.   Reading newspapers, magazines, and books helps you broaden your knowledge and understanding of the world and become a more interesting person. Reading gives you more information and ideas to share with others.

Your Educational Life.   In any kind of educational setting, reading is one of the principal means of gaining course-related information.

Reading skills are important for students at every level. Take Jim Hamid for example. Jim works for a travel agency during the day and attends a community college at night. Jim found the reading assignments for some of his courses difficult at first. However, things improved when he started taking notes on his reading. Taking notes helped Jim organize and remember the information. These notes made studying for exams easier, since Jim could review his notes rather than the entire text.

Jim discovered that he gets more out of a class when he has read the assignment ahead of time. The lectures help him review basic material and clarify difficult points. Jim has also found that he likes participating in discussions when he is prepared for class. Talking about the material in class reinforces Jim's reading and helps him master the material.

Your Professional Life.   Reading will be part of any job starting with the employment forms you must read when you are hired. Memos, letters, reports, computer manuals, schedules, procedures manuals, and policy manuals are a few of the documents that will require reading skills.

Writing Skills

Writing skills are important for creating and communicating information. Writing has many advantages, but its major advantage is that it provides a physical record of a communication that can be used as proof if necessary.

Your Social Life.   Writing is probably the communication skill that is least used in our personal lives today. Many of us tend to make a telephone call rather than write a personal letter to a friend who lives some distance away. However, receiving a letter from someone we care about can be a great pleasure—and the letter can be kept and reread many times. We also need writing skills to send a note of appreciation, for example, or to express condolence to a friend or family member.

In addition, we all have to use our writing skills when we take care of personal-business correspondence, such as letters of request, complaints, and notifications of a change of address. Committing your personal business to writing puts it on record. You have a dated copy of the request, complaint, or notification, and so does the recipient.

Your Educational Life.   Excellent writing skills can help you earn higher grades on research papers and tests. Writing about a subject helps you learn because you must think about the material and organize the information you have before you can start writing.

Your Professional Life.   On the job, you use your writing skills to compose electronic-mail messages, memos, letters, and reports. In many jobs writing is a supporting skill, but in some jobs such as that of newspaper reporter or author, writing is the primary skill. Writing, via some form of electronic communication, will become an increasingly important part of our lives in the future.

KEY POINT

Excellent communication skills are one of the most frequently listed requirements in want ads and in surveys of employers.

The Value of Good Communication Skills

As you can see, the four communication skills—listening, speaking, reading, and writing—apply to your social life, your educational life, and your professional life in much the same way. Good communication skills are a great asset in the learning process in any situation. Education does not usually end with high school, college, or professional training. You may, for example, attend job-related workshops on computer software, organizational skills, working in teams, or management. With the rapid rate of technological advancements, you can expect to have several different jobs during your working life. There will be new skills to learn and new technology to master. Your communication skills are tools that will help you to adapt to a variety of work situations.

The four communication skills are interconnected, and using all of them will strengthen your ability to communicate. Let's see how Renee Wong uses all four communication skills in her job. Renee works as a reporter on the *Centennial Times*. She has always liked to write and now has a chance to write full-time. Renee, though, has found that listening, speaking, and reading skills are crucial in writing newspaper articles.

For example, Renee had to read the minutes of last year's town meetings to get the history of the new recycling program. She found that she needed more information about recycling plans in other communities and the technology involved. Renee spent the morning in the public library, reading and taking notes. Next, she wanted to find out what various town officials and citizens thought about the new program. Was the proposed program worth the expense? Would it really help cut down the amount of garbage? Would the plastic bottles be processed and reused as promised? Renee drew up a list of questions before conducting her first interview. When Renee asked the questions, she listened carefully to the answers and took notes.

Finally, Renee had the material for her story, and she was able to plan what she was going to say and then to sit down at the computer and write.

When analyzing Renee's job, you see how the four communication skills are interconnected. Though you may use one skill more often than the others, those other skills do play a vital supporting role. Each of the communication skills—listening, speaking, reading, and writing—is strengthened and reinforced by the other skills.

SECTION 1.2   REVIEW

Practical Application

1. Describe how communication is a two-way process, and explain why communication skills are paired.
2. One of the communication skills is featured in each of the following examples. Explain how one or more of the other skills might be used in each situation to reinforce the main skill.
   a. Listening to a neighbor's complaints about a barking dog.
   b. Speaking to a group about the pros and cons of four popular word processing programs.
   c. Writing a report about public opinion on local property tax rates.
   d. Listening to an advisor in the school placement office explain what materials you will need to take when you go for a job interview.
   e. Reading several consumer and photography magazines in the library that evaluate videocassette recorders (VCRs). (You want to buy a VCR.)

Editing Practice

Proofreading. Proper proofreading involves checking the spelling of each word and the meaning of the word within the sentence.

Proofread the following paragraph. On a sheet of paper, make a list of all the errors. Then rewrite or type the corrected paragraph.

In accordance with our telephone conservation, we are senting you corected specifacations. Note that instalation of a two-way comunication systems is now required. Also, the thermastat is to be re-located to the upstair hall. Please send us your revise bid, propperly typed on your company stationary, no latter then Oct. 1.

Critical Thinking Skills

Analyze: Write a brief essay on the place of letter writing in either your social life or your business life. Give your opinion, supported by examples, on the following:
1. People write fewer letters nowadays.
2. Letter writing is a lost art.
3. Writing letters is a wonderful way to communicate with the people you care about.

SECTION 1.3

OBJECTIVES:
After completing Section 1.3, you should be able to:

1. Describe upward, lateral, and downward communication.
2. Define and give examples of internal communication, external communication, and tone.
3. Explain and give examples of the six Cs of business communication.

Applying Your Communication Skills in Business

If you can't write your idea on the back of my calling card, you don't have a clear idea.

—David Belasco, producer of Broadway musicals

THE IMPORTANCE OF GOOD COMMUNICATION IN BUSINESS

No matter what your job is, your working day is basically a constant flow of information. As an employee, you will communicate with customers or clients, coworkers, and managers in a variety of settings. You will communicate one-on-one and as part of a team. You will communicate not only by giving information but also by listening to or reading information provided by others. Doing so keeps you informed and enables you to tap into an endless supply of ideas and solutions.

Imagine that you are an employee who has made suggestions for improvement in the department or company. How would you feel if your supervisor listened to your ideas and actually put some of them into effect? You would probably feel great. You might respond by working even harder than you were working before. You would have experienced effective communication.

Flow of Communication

Communication not only links members of a certain department but also serves as a vital link between people in different departments. In a company each department functions as a spoke in a wheel; all the spokes are needed for the wheel to function properly. If several spokes are missing, broken, or not aligned properly, the wheel becomes wobbly and eventually will break.

Upward communication is communicating with people who rank above you. *Lateral* or *horizontal communication* is communicating with people who are at the same rank or level as you. *Downward communication* is communicating with people who rank below you. The direction your communication is flowing will influence how you communicate—the words you use and the method you choose.

Not only does good communication make a company operate efficiently, but also it creates a sense of unity—a team spirit—and a striving for common goals among employees.

Figure 1.6 below illustrates the flow of communication within an organization and shows the directions in which communication can travel. The arrows at both ends of a line show that communication flows both ways.

KEY POINT

Communication within an organization may be upward, lateral, or downward.

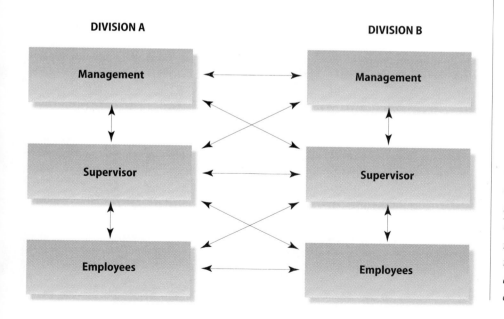

Figure 1.6 Flow of Communication Within an Organization

Communication within an organization flows in three directions—upwardly, laterally, and downwardly—to accomplish company objectives.

TYPES OF BUSINESS COMMUNICATION

Communication that takes place in a company or an organization falls into two categories: internal communication and external communication. The tone used in internal communication usually differs from that used in external communication. *Tone,* as it applies to business communication, usually refers to the general manner of expression or effect of a written document, conversation, discussion, or speech.

Internal Communication

Internal communication is the transmittal of information between and among persons within a business or organization. Within a company, internal communication is used to accomplish company goals and objectives. Managers must, for example, let employees know when and why a specific job must be done. On the other hand, nonmanagement personnel use communication for understanding and clarifying how a specific job must be done. Nonmanagement personnel communicate to convince management that their knowledge and personal attributes qualify them for pay increases or promotions. Other examples of internal communication include suggestions for improving products and services, and guidelines for completing a process.

Internal communication may be carried out with people in the same department, in other departments, and at other company locations.

Figure 1.7

Communicating in teams is an important aspect of internal communication. What qualities should team members demonstrate in order to communicate effectively as part of a team?

Also, employees may communicate individually or as members of a team. Internal communication may include face-to-face conversations, telephone calls, electronic-mail messages, and brainstorming ideas at a meeting.

In internal communication, a person's tone may be friendly and informal. As an employee, you must assess a situation and use the most appropriate tone. For instance, when telling a colleague about an idea you have to make your department more productive, you would use different words, different phrasing, and a different tone than if you were making the same suggestion to the manager of your department.

External Communication

External communication is the transfer of information to and from people outside the company. The goal of most of a company's external communication is to persuade the recipients to respond favorably to company needs. A sales letter, for example, tries to get a potential customer to buy a product or a service. A job listing tries to attract qualified personnel to fill a certain position.

In external communication, a person's tone more often is polite and formal. Using the right tone in external communication is more difficult, or more challenging, than using the right tone in internal communication because you are representing your company as well as yourself. Often, customers and clients will transfer their opinions of you and your communication skills to the company itself. They will base opinions not only on what you say or write but also on your appearance and manner. In other words, the whole package counts.

Although your physical appearance may not be so important as the content of what you say or write, your appearance creates a first impression. Keep in mind that the first impression you create will often influence how closely your customer or client will pay attention to what you have to say. As a result, your appearance (or the appearance of your communication) can work either for you or against you.

THE SIX Cs OF BUSINESS COMMUNICATION

Effective business communication meets the test of the six Cs—it is clear, complete, concise, consistent, correct, and courteous. The six Cs apply to any communication situation, whether you are speaking or writing, and whether you are communicating with someone inside or someone outside your organization. Using the six Cs will make your communication coherent and easy to follow.

World View

When writing to someone who may not be proficient in English, consider having the document translated. Have one translator convert the document into the receiver's native language, and have another translator convert the document back into English. Compare the two versions for accuracy.

—Sherron B. Kenton and Deborah Valentine, *Crosstalk: Communicating in a Multicultural Workplace*

KEY POINT

Effective business communication is (1) clear, (2) complete, (3) concise, (4) consistent, (5) correct, and (6) courteous.

Clear

It isn't enough to communicate so you can be understood; you must communicate so clearly that you cannot be misunderstood. Being specific rather than vague is a way to meet this test. If you call the floral shop and order a plant as a birthday gift for a coworker, will you be upset when you receive a bill for $68? Giving a price range of $15 to $20 when ordering the plant would eliminate this miscommunication.

Complete

Complete communication includes enough details so that the recipient will not need to ask for more information. Imagine receiving a notice from your doctor for a return visit on Tuesday at 3 p.m. at her office. Which Tuesday would you go? To be complete, a communication should answer the following questions: Who? What? Where? When? Why? and How? or How much?

Concise

Unnecessary words hamper communication because the extra words used to express the idea or thought clutter the message. The following sentence is wordy: "I am writing this letter to inform you that your airline tickets will be mailed ten days before your scheduled departure." Look how much more effective a more concise version is: "We will mail your airline tickets to you ten days before your scheduled departure." You've eliminated seven words, and none of the meaning is lost from the original message.

Consistent

All communication should be consistent in fact, treatment, and sequence. Consistency in *fact* refers to agreement with a source document or an established fact. For example, an open house scheduled for April 31 should be questioned since April has only 30 days. Consistency in *treatment* means treating similar items the same way. An example of consistent treatment would be using the courtesy title (*Mr.*, *Mrs.*, *Miss*, or *Ms.*) with the names of all recipients of a letter or indenting all paragraphs in a letter. Consistency in *sequence* refers to the arrangement of listings such as alphabetical, chronological, or numerical. Imagine a telephone book that is not arranged in alphabetical order. If a workshop is scheduled for three days, the dates should be given in chronological order (the order in which they occur), for example, May 3, May 6, and May 10.

MEMORY HOOK

The six Cs of effective communication are easy to remember because each one starts with the letter C.

Clear
Complete
Concise
Consistent
Correct
Courteous

To recall the six Cs, remember this sentence: Clara gave *clear, complete,* and *consise* directions on how to greet customers in a *consistent, correct,* and *courteous* way.

Correct

All the information in a message should be accurate—the content, the spelling, the capitalization, grammar, and punctuation.

Courteous

Your communication should use the you-attitude instead of the I-attitude. This means keeping the reader or listener in mind when you write or say something. Use positive words instead of negative words, and use tactful language. Use formats (lists, short paragraphs, tables) that are easy to read and comprehend.

SECTION 1.3   REVIEW

Practical Application

1. Define and give examples of internal communication, external communication, and tone.
2. Explain and give examples of the six Cs of business communication.

Editing Practice

Which of the six Cs of communication is violated in each of the following sentences?

1. We would like to take this opportunity to welcome all retirees.
2. We demand that you make a payment now.
3. The pictures will be sent seperately.
4. The sales manager told the associate that he would not attend the meeting.
5. The new Wal-Mart store will have the ribbon-cutting ceremony on Wednesday, August 28.
6. The prices will be $2, $6, and $4.

Critical Thinking Skills

Analyze: For each item, write a paragraph about what combination of communication skills you would use and why.

1. Applying for a job advertised in the want ad column in the newspaper that gives a box number for reply.
2. Receiving a message on your telephone answering machine to call an employer to set up an appointment for a job interview.
3. Preparing a research paper on a topic about which you have limited knowledge.
4. Conducting a workshop on refinishing furniture (assume you are not an expert).

CRITICAL THINKING CASE

The Cost of Poor Communication Skills. Mark Winters started a new position about six weeks ago as marketing associate for the Great Western Telecommunication Corporation. The corporation recently expanded and is now marketing upgrades and additional features for its existing telephone service. Technology features such as caller ID, voice mail, and videophone service are now available from Great Western.

On his first two weeks on the job, Mark went through extensive training to gain knowledge about the new features. Following the training, Mark's responsibilities included calling current customers who had returned interest survey cards and setting up appointments with them. He was expected to demonstrate the Great Western technology that would upgrade a customer's telephone service. Mark's goal was to schedule a minimum of 20 presentations each week and to sell the features to at least 60 percent of the potential customers.

After eight presentations, Mark had no sales. He had a wealth of complex information and terms at his fingertips and knew the features inside and out. Other marketing associates were selling the products, so Mark did not understand why he could not close a sale. After all, he used the same presentation each time and had it down cold. The presentations seemed to go well, but customers were always hesitant to commit themselves to the new technology features. They either told Mark no or said they wanted to "think it over."

Mark approached another associate, Lynn Moore, with whom he had developed rapport. Lynn started at the same time Mark did and had 12 sales to her credit. Mark asked Lynn to observe his next presentation and offer some suggestions. She readily agreed.

Lynn noticed that Mark talked too fast in his presentation. She also noticed that Mark was not making good eye contact with his prospects so he did not notice their puzzled looks and attempts to ask questions during his presentation.

In talking about caller ID—a device that displays the telephone number of the caller—Mark mentioned that the feature "did not work in all areas." What he meant was that caller ID did not identify calls received from areas that did not have the service yet. What the prospects heard was that since the unit did not work in all areas, it might not work where they lived, and therefore was useless to them. Mark understood the technical aspects of how voice mail worked, and he shared all the details with his prospects. Mary Cunningham, one of his prospects, said, "I don't think I could learn to use voice mail. It's too complicated."

After Mark and Lynn returned from the presentation where no sale occurred, Lynn said, "Mark, you really know the product inside and out, but I have several communication strategies that will help you to present what you know in a better way."

After reading Chapter 1, what do you think Lynn will suggest to Mark? Put yourself in the role of Lynn. Provide Mark with some specific, positive feedback that will help him improve the quality of his presentations and increase the possibility for potential sales.

CHAPTER 2

Communicating Around the Globe

SECTIONS

2.1 Electronic Communication

2.2 Domestic and International Communication

2.3 Ethics and Professional Courtesy in Business Communication

2.4 Nondiscriminatory Language

A Japanese automotive company was building a manufacturing plant in the Midwest. A major Japanese supplier of this company also decided to build a small manufacturing facility in a neighboring town. The supplier's company was run using a team approach, common in Japanese companies.

Ann Adams, a recently hired management trainee, was one of the few American employees in management at the supplier's company. Ann was unaware of the differences between Japanese and American culture, particularly concerning the concept of teamwork in Japanese businesses. She used business and social practices commonly used by American companies in the area.

One of Ann's assignments was to research different communication systems to be used at the plant. She contacted local telephone providers for information on costs and services available. Ann also did some research on her own using the Internet. After analyzing the different systems, Ann wrote a report comparing the systems and recommending the one to adopt.

Ann's managers were upset with her for making recommendations without first consulting them. In Japanese businesses, almost all decisions are made by a team. The managers were used to being part of the decision-making process.

Ann was unfamiliar with the management style for a Japanese company, and her Japanese managers did not understand that her American management style was quite different from theirs.

As you read Chapter 2, identify some of the problems Ann had in communicating with her managers from another culture, and describe how the problems could be eliminated or minimized.

Electronic Communication

OBJECTIVES:

After completing Section 2.1, you should be able to:

1. Describe four factors that affect productivity in the electronic office.
2. Give examples of electronic communication available by telephone and computer.
3. List several advantages to using electronic communication.

Now that computing is astoundingly inexpensive and computers inhabit every part of our lives, we stand at the brink of another revolution.

—Bill Gates, chief executive officer of Microsoft Corporation

In the above quotation, Bill Gates, head of one of the largest computer software companies in the world, is referring to a revolution in communication. Someday soon all computers will be connected in a global communication network. We will be able to communicate with others worldwide. Being linked in a computer network will allow us to access information from a multitude of sources. The Internet, a worldwide computer network, is only the start of this communication revolution. In addition to the Internet, other forms of electronic communication, including pagers, cellular phones, and electronic mail, offer expanded possibilities for communicating with others.

An increasingly important aspect of communicating on the job involves using technology to communicate with coworkers, customers, and suppliers. You probably will use technology to communicate with business people in domestic and even international locations. Whatever job you hold—that of accountant or computer programmer, paralegal or sales representative, teacher or technician—you will need to know how to use technology to be an effective communicator.

THE IMPACT OF TECHNOLOGY

Technology has definitely had an impact on business communication. Twenty years ago, the standard equipment used to transact business was the typewriter, the telephone, the copying machine, and the calculator. Now, companies and organizations are equipped with computerized information processing systems, including personal computers, computer networks, and electronic-mail systems. Employees working away from their offices use laptop computers, digital pagers, facsimile machines, and cellular phones. All of these devices help business people receive and transmit information faster and more efficiently.

Let's look at how technology has influenced the way businesses communicate, especially with regard to productivity.

KEY POINT

Technology allows business messages to be created and transmitted faster and more efficiently than in the past.

PRODUCTIVITY IN THE ELECTRONIC OFFICE

In order to provide quality products and services in a timely manner and to compete in the global marketplace, businesses use technology to enhance productivity. Technology affects productivity in terms of time, convenience, quality, and environment.

Time

Technology enables business communicators to perform tasks quickly and efficiently. For example, voice mail allows business people to send and retrieve telephone messages at a time convenient for them. Documents can be sent via computer networks and read on the computer screen instead of being sent by traditional mail. By rekeying the address only, identical original letters can be sent to many recipients.

Convenience

Technology offers the convenience of a variety of options for communicating information. Correspondence can be distributed by means of electronic mail, a modem, or a facsimile machine. Telephone callers can reach someone using voice mail or a cellular phone. Correcting errors in keyboarded documents can be done instantly by backspacing to eliminate incorrect keystrokes and then typing the desired keystrokes. Some software automatically corrects spelling and capitalization errors when the proper settings are selected. For example, if you type *teh* instead of *the*, the software automatically corrects the transposition when you touch the space bar. If you forget to capitalize a day of the week, the word is automatically capitalized when you touch the space bar.

Quality

Technology has improved the quality of communication. Voice mail enables both the caller and the recipient to leave more detailed and accurate messages. Because of the ease of correcting errors using electronic tools such as spelling checkers, grammar checkers, and thesauruses, documents produced in the electronic office are of high quality. Desktop publishing, scanners, and laser printers enable everyone to produce professional-looking documents. Today's software has hundreds of fonts and many sizes from which to choose as well as a variety of ways to emphasize text. Techniques for adding emphasis include using italics, bold, strikeout, tab settings, and so on.

KEY POINT

Technology allows businesses to:
1. Communicate information in less time.
2. Use convenient means of communicating.
3. Produce quality communications.
4. Automate routine tasks.

World View

With technology such as electronic mail and cellular phones, people around the world can communicate information more quickly than by using traditional mail or telephone services.

OOPS!

Players say the flow of exhibition games have been interrupted by too many fouls being called.
—*USA Today*

Environment

Technology has improved the office environment by streamlining many routine tasks. Voice mail has all but eliminated the need to take written telephone messages. Electronic forms of communication such as electronic mail have reduced the need for large numbers of paper copies to be made. People can access information on their computers and read the information on the computer screen instead of reading a printout.

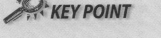
TECHNOLOGY AND ITS APPLICATIONS

Let's look at how some specific telephone and computer technologies are used to increase productivity in the electronic office.

Voice Mail

Voice-mail systems provide a fast, convenient way of managing telephone messages. With voice mail, a person can record greetings for incoming calls, listen to messages, and forward messages by using the telephone. A caller can leave a detailed message, including the reason for the call and information for reaching the caller. Instead of responding to a written telephone message, the sender listens to a caller's message at a convenient time and responds accordingly. Voice mail helps to solve the telephone-tag problem (repeated failure to make contact by phone even though both parties are trying). More importantly, you can use voice mail at any time of the day or any day of the week by dialing the voice-mail number directly.

Cellular Phones and Pagers

Cellular phones are portable phones that you can carry at all times in order to make and receive calls from almost any location, including while traveling in a vehicle, walking through the mall, or shopping at the grocery store.

Pagers, sometimes known as beepers, notify you by a tone or visual display that someone is trying to reach you. Both cellular phones and pagers are lightweight and small enough to carry in a pocket or a purse. With a cellular phone or pager you can contact people regardless of their location. When critical decisions or emergencies arise in business, it is advantageous to be able to reach a coworker who is away from the office.

Facsimile Machines and Scanners

Facsimile (fax) machines transmit exact copies of handwritten and typed documents as well as graphs, illustrations, and photographs. Both the sender and the receiver must have a fax machine. The fax machine scans the document and transmits it via telephone lines to the receiver's fax machine. Using a fax machine enables you to send a hard copy of the document within a matter of minutes.

Computerized Information Systems

Computerized information systems enable business personnel to handle a variety of tasks. One innovation that saves time and increases accessibility is the *computer workstation.* The computer workstation may be a microcomputer or personal computer operating independently or a computer terminal linked or networked to the company's main computer. Using the computer simplifies tasks such as creating spreadsheets, databases, and documents.

Personal Computers

A *personal computer (PC)* is a stand-alone computer with a *CPU* (central processing unit) and the necessary peripherals, such as a monitor, keyboard, mouse, and printer. An appropriate operating system and software must be installed to enable the computer to perform desired tasks.

The most frequently used type of software is *word processing software,* which provides a convenient way to produce error-free communications and eliminates the need for traditional time-consuming correction materials and retyping.

Spreadsheet software looks like an accountant's worksheet on screen and has rows and columns where numbers are entered. The user inserts formulas, and the software does the calculations.

Database software allows you to store information such as a mailing list with names, addresses, and telephone numbers. Information about each person can be sorted in several different ways, such as by ZIP Code, by state, or alphabetically by last name.

Desktop publishing software is page-layout software. The user places text and graphics on a page and can produce camera-ready copy on a laser printer. *Camera-ready copy* is any material that can be used for printing on a printing press or photocopying. Many organizations and individuals use desktop publishing software to prepare flyers, advertisements, newsletters, and booklets.

OOPS!

Juan's department had just begun using voice mail, and he was not in the habit of checking his messages. His supervisor left Juan a voice-mail message saying the total-quality management team meeting for the next day had been rescheduled from 2:30 p.m. to 1:30 p.m. Juan didn't check his voice-mail messages the next morning. He arrived an hour late for the meeting.

Electronic Mail

Electronic mail, or *e-mail,* is a keyboarded message transmitted instantly from your computer to the computer of your recipient via the Internet or other computer networks. Electronic mail can be sent to almost any place in the world, provided the sender and the recipient have access to a computer network. This technology benefits businesses because messages can be sent immediately, which virtually eliminates the lag time experienced with traditional mail delivery systems.

The Internet and the World Wide Web

The Internet is a system of computer networks that links computers from around the world in a large network. Internet users can send electronic-mail messages and gain access to databases almost any place in the world as Ann Adams did in the chapter opening case.

The World Wide Web is a segment of the Internet that presents information in multimedia form, including text, graphics, audio, and video. Information on the World Wide Web, or Web, is linked by means of connections that are made between data at different Web sites.

Laser Printers

A *laser printer* is a high-resolution printer that produces documents with the appearance of a professionally printed document. Businesses use laser printers to produce camera-ready copy. The professional look of laser-printed documents enhances the image and credibility of the company.

Modems

A *modem* is a device connected to, or included inside, a computer. It is used to exchange programs and data with other computers and to access on-line information services via telephone lines. A modem makes it possible to have instant access to all types of information.

Laptop Computers

A *laptop computer* is a portable computer that is lightweight and battery-powered. You can use a laptop computer to work on documents and even access information from or send information to an office computer in almost any location. With a laptop computer, business people can be productive during traditional downtime periods such as waiting for flights at airports and during flights.

World View

The Internet was developed in the United States in 1969. In 1973, England and Norway became the first countries with international connections to the Internet. As of 1995, over half of the Internet's registered users are located outside of North America.
—Michael Neubarth in *Internet World*

Technology offers a variety of options for communicating spoken and written messages. As a business communicator, you need to be sensitive to the needs and preferences of those receiving your communications. This sensitivity extends to considering which technology to use to convey a message. Chapter 9 discusses considerations for communicating electronically in more detail.

Keep in mind that although technology has dramatically changed the ways messages are created, transmitted, and received, the standards for business communication remain the same. Effective communication must still demonstrate the six Cs of business communication—clear, complete, concise, consistent, correct, and courteous.

World View

According to a recent *Frequent Flyer* poll of business travelers, 67 percent of the respondents generally take a laptop computer with them while traveling and 60 percent take a cellular phone.

SECTION 2.1   REVIEW

Practical Application

1. Describe how electronic communication affects office productivity in terms of time, convenience, quality, and environment.
2. Give three examples each of telephone and computer technologies used in today's offices.
3. For each of the following tasks, identify the means of communication that would be most appropriate. You may list more than one choice for each item, and you may list choices multiple times.

   electronic mail   laptop computer
   cellular phone   voice mail
   Internet

   a. Provide a coworker with specifications for a product update.
   b. Notify a traveling salesperson about a change in her schedule.
   c. Research databases for information on international communication.
   d. Contact a customer with price information.

Editing Practice

A. **Using Tact!** Each of the following items lacks sensitivity to the reader. Rewrite each one to correct the problem.
   1. We can't ship the shirt you ordered (catalog No. 456-861) until you tell us what color you want. Don't delay your order further. Send us the color today!

2. In our recent sales campaign, we sold 6,000 CD players. Your complaint is the only one we received. Even though 5,999 people were completely satisfied, we are shipping you a new CD player today.

3. The terms of our contract were clearly stated. We offered a discount if we received payment within 10 days. You took a total of 30 days to pay. Therefore, send us the $50 balance.

B. **Spelling Alert!** On a sheet of paper, rewrite each of the following sentences, correcting any spelling errors. If a sentence is correct, write *OK*.

1. Maria Gonzalas ocasionally asks for volunteers to go to the local high school and talk about their jobs.

2. Early next week, all supervisers must submit their buget requests for next year.

3. The Human Resource Manager was obviusly disatisfied with the quality of the job candidates.

4. When Paula proofred the manuscript, she noticed that three illustrations had been ommitted.

5. Suzy said that aproximately 100 employees had signed up for the wellness program.

6. The attornies for the defence and the prosecution agreed to settle out of court.

7. We will procede as soon as all the forms are signed.

8. The applicant said he was fluent in three langauges.

9. The annual report was sent to the stockholders on Tuesday, February 11.

10. Proofreading letters carefully before sending them to clients will help avoid possible embarassment.

Critical Thinking Skills

Evaluate: Interview someone in business, asking questions such as the following. Then evaluate the importance you think communication has in that business.

1. What percentage of your job is spent communicating?

2. What kinds of communication problems do you encounter on the job?

3. Do you think that the ability to communicate effectively will play an important part in the advancement of your career? Explain why or why not.

4. What has your company done in the past to improve the communication skills of its employees?

5. What suggestions do you have to improve the communications within your company?

Domestic and International Communication

You can make your world so much larger simply by acknowledging everyone else's.

—Jeanne Marie Laskas in Washington *Post Magazine*

OBJECTIVES:
After completing Section 2.2, you should be able to:

1. Define *culture*.
2. Give examples of some ethnic groups in the United States.
3. Explain what a multinational company is.
4. Give several examples of cultural differences between the United States and other countries.
5. Describe the differences and similarities between domestic and international communication.

With technological advances, our world is expanding each day. People can travel to almost any part of the world in a matter of hours; communications can travel to almost any part of the world in a matter of minutes or even seconds. As we communicate on an increasingly global basis, it is important to understand the people we communicate with and their cultural backgrounds.

Cross-cultural communication is communicating with people in the United States and other countries who are from a culture different from your own. In communication, it is important to understand and respect cultural differences and to be adaptable. Many of the same principles of cross-cultural communication need to be observed in both domestic and international communication.

DOMESTIC COMMUNICATION

The population of the United States is made up of people from many different races, religions, and cultures. *Culture* refers to the customs, beliefs, lifestyles, and practices of a group of people.

Throughout the United States different cultural and religious groups speak their traditional language and follow traditional customs and religious practices. Examples of such groups include:

- Chinese communities in Chinatowns in New York City, San Francisco, and other large cities.
- Hasidic Jewish neighborhoods in New York City and other large cities.
- Vietnamese communities in Minnesota, Wisconsin, and Texas.
- Amish settlements in the Midwest.
- West Indian communities in New York City.
- Polish neighborhoods in Chicago.
- Native American communities in the Southwest and the Northwest.
- Hispanic neighborhoods in Miami and in cities in southern California and southern Texas.

KEY POINT

The United States is made up of people from many cultures.

When working with people from different cultural, religious, and ethnic groups, keep in mind these guidelines.

- Research the customs of the communities in which you do business.
- Keep track of significant religious holidays that affect the company's employees and clients.
- Do not make comments or jokes based on cultural or religious practices.
- Do not imitate cultural language expressions or accents in an attempt to be friendly.

We need to be aware of, and respect, cultural preferences and beliefs if different from our own. Ann Adam's behavior in the chapter opening case revealed her lack of understanding of her company's management practices. This resulted in her managers being upset with her although she was following standard American business customs.

Being unaware of significant religious holidays can also create problems. For example, if a business conference is scheduled at the same time as the Jewish High Holy Days of Rosh Hashanan or Yom Kippur, Jewish members would find it difficult to attend.

Another example of lack of cultural knowledge is to not know the business protocol in a country where you and your company do business. This lack of knowledge can easily result in behaving in an impolite or disrespectful fashion. In Japan, for example, business cards are considered very important and are treated with care. It is considered very disrespectful to write on a person's business card.

Figure 2.1

Cultural communities in the United States offer residents and visitors contact with the customs and language of a particular culture. What are some characteristics of such communities?

Regional Differences

People in different geographic regions of the country use different words to express the same ideas. For example, a carbonated drink may be called a pop, soda, soda pop, or soft drink depending on whom you talk to and in what region of the country you live. The same is true of coffee, which may be called java, espresso, joe, cup of mud, or coffee.

Time Zones

From Nome, Alaska, in the west to Bangor, Maine, in the east, the continental United States spans seven time zones. This time difference is another factor that must be taken into consideration with some forms of domestic communication. When it is 9 a.m. in Maine, it is 6 a.m. in California and 4 a.m. in Hawaii. Most of the United States switches from standard to daylight savings time together; however, daylight savings time is observed all year in some areas (for example, in most of Indiana). Other areas of the country do not observe daylight savings time during any portion of the year (for example, most of Arizona).

Holidays

Most Americans celebrate the same federal holidays, but people in many groups and religions celebrate additional holidays. Even in some states the federal holiday celebrations may be observed on different days. For example, most states observe a federal holiday for Washington's birthday, which is February 22, on the third Monday in February. Because Illinois claims Lincoln as a native son, Illinois celebrates Lincoln's birthday instead of Washington's birthday. The holiday is celebrated on February 12, which is Lincoln's birth date, unless February 12 falls on a weekend; then the holiday is celebrated on the Monday or Friday closest to February 12.

You need to be aware of these cultural, regional, time zone, and holiday differences when sending business communications. Some of the same considerations regarding domestic communication also apply to international communication.

INTERNATIONAL COMMUNICATION

Many United States companies today have operations and offices in other countries. Likewise, many foreign companies have operations and offices in the United States. In other words, multinational companies are commonplace. A *multinational* company is a company that does business in or has operations in more than one country. If you are

KEY POINT

Differences in time zones across the United States affect working hours for businesses.

Tyrone Williams, who lives in Illinois, had a question about software he had received from Duckworth Digital Computing, a small, home-based company in California. Since it was 5 p.m., he thought it was too late to call—the business would be closed. The next day Tyrone called Duckworth Computing promptly at 8 a.m. and woke Mr. Duckworth.

an employee of a multinational company and you are based in the United States, you need to be aware of cultural and other differences when communicating with your company's offices in other countries.

For example, if you are an employee of a company with headquarters in Chicago and with plants in the Midwest, in the South, and in India, you need to be aware of time differences among the locations.

Language

Although English is recognized worldwide as the language of business, English is a second language for people in most other countries. Slang, clichés, and jargon make English one of the most complex languages in the world. When communicating with people in other countries, follow these guidelines.

- **Keep figures of speech and clichés to a minimum.** For example, instead of *right as rain*, use *right*. Instead of *to add insult to injury*, write *in addition* or *moreover*.
- **Avoid using cute, fancy, or trendy terms for standard English words.** For example, instead of *legal eagle,* say *lawyer.* Instead of *policy wonk,* use *policy expert.*
- **Use specific terms.** Instead of *just a little way down the road,* use *15 miles.* Instead of *unsanitary conditions,* say *unsafe drinking water.*
- **Be aware of the multiple definitions of words.** Some words carry more than one meaning and may be confusing to someone whose first language isn't English. For example, the word *bug,* may refer to an insect, the flu, or a computer-software virus. The work *break* in the sentence *There was a break in the negotiations* can refer to an opening (opportunity for agreement) or a halt (the stopping of talks). Make sure the context makes the meaning clear. This problem is especially troublesome in speech because words that are spelled differently may be pronounced similarly: for example, *sum* and *some.*
- **Avoid any form of slang or jargon.** American slang, such as *bad* meaning *good, cool* meaning *in style,* and *wicked* meaning *good, great,* or *in style,* would be confusing to a person whose first language isn't English.
- **Avoid using abbreviations or acronyms.** An *abbreviation* is a shortened form of a word or phrase. *Atty* is an abbreviation for the word attorney; *St.* is an abbreviation for Saint. An *acronym* is a word formed from the first letter or letters of each word in the phrase, such as *PIN* for *personal identification number* or *radar* for *radio detecting and ranging*. Acronyms may be unfamiliar, and abbreviations can stand for more than a single term. For example, does the abbreviation *IRA* mean *Irish Republican Army*

World View

Only 7 percent of the world's people speak English as a primary language, but 9 out of 10 Americans cannot speak, read, or understand any language but English.
—Gallup polls and UNESCO studies

OOPS!

Microsoft Corporation committed an oops in a Spanish-language version of its Microsoft Word software program. The thesaurus for the program suggested that *man-eater, cannibal,* and *barbarian* could substitute for the Spanish term for *black people.* The program also equated Indians with man-eating savages. Microsoft promised to correct the software.
—*The Wall Street Journal*

or does it mean *individual retirement account*? Does *CIA* mean *Central Intelligence Agency* or *cash in advance*?

- **Use visual aids.** Wherever possible use visual aids to clarify your message. A map, a sketch, or a picture usually enhances verbal or written communication.

If your message must be translated, be aware that many English words do not have an exact translation. Many companies have learned the hard way that some translations cause problems. In his book *The Tongue-Tied American* (Continuum Publishing Corporation, New York, 1980, pp. 6, 7, and 32), Paul Simon gives these examples of problem translations.

- Chevrolet would have a hard time selling its Nova model in Latin American countries. In Spanish, the phrase *no-va* literally means "It does not go."
- General Motors' slogan "Body by Fisher" translates to "Corpse by Fisher" in Flemish.
- The slogan "Come alive with Pepsi" translates to "Pepsi brings your ancestors back from the grave" in Chinese and translates to "Come alive out of the grave" in German.
- Parker pen put on a sales campaign in South America. A less-than-accurate Spanish translation promised buyers that the new ink in the pen would prevent unwanted pregnancies.
- Schweppes Tonic Water advertisements in Italy translated as "bathroom water."
- Cue toothpaste, a Colgate-Palmolive product, was advertised in France with no translation errors but *Cue* happens to be the name of a widely circulated pornographic book.

Because of these kinds of translation problems, companies sometimes change product names or slogans before marketing products in other countries.

Cultures

Many international cultures have a high regard for formality and social rules. In the United States most people are very time-conscious and punctuality is important. In many other cultures, it is not considered rude to be quite late for an appointment or to keep a person waiting for a long time.

Customs in various countries regarding clothing styles, greetings, and eye contact are also different. Some examples include the following:

- **Clothing styles.** Women in some cultures do not appear in public with their faces uncovered, while other cultures accept skimpy or topless swimwear in public.

KEY POINT

An English word or phrase often loses something in translation.

World View

When doing business with people in other countries, be aware of differences in etiquette and nonverbal communication. For example, most Europeans shake hands before and after social and business occasions. Japanese, on the other hand, usually bow instead of shaking hands.

Figure 2.2

Although the American custom of handshaking has been adopted by many cultures, it is polite to follow the greeting customs of a particular culture. Why is showing respect for other cultures important?

Marilyn and Bill had recently arrived in Belgium for a four-month stay to help with the start-up of a new plant. The first Saturday, they were invited to a company party at 6 p.m. at a local restaurant. They arrived about ten minutes before six and were surprised to find they were the first guests. They became worried when no one else had arrived by 6:20 p.m. Finally, at 6:35 p.m. the first guests arrived, and by 7:05 p.m. most guests were present and the group sat down to eat. In Belgium, arriving late is the custom, but Marilyn and Bill were embarrassed by not knowing this custom.

- **Greeting others.** In some cultures men kiss each other on the cheek or bow from the waist when they meet rather than shake hands as men and women do in the United States.

- **Eye contact.** In some cultures it is considered extremely rude to have direct eye contact with people to whom you are talking. By contrast, in the United States direct eye contact is expected. Lack of eye contact is interpreted as disinterestedness, unfriendliness, or perhaps even dishonesty.

It is important to learn about other cultures and countries so you are aware of cultural differences and can be patient and flexible in communicating with others. Just as many different cultures exist in the United States, other countries are also multicultural and include different ethnic groups. For example, in Belgium the population is divided into two major cultural groups—the Flemings and the Walloons. The Flemings live in North Belgium and speak Dutch, while the Walloons live in South Belgium and speak French. The differences in language and in other aspects of their culture have caused some friction between the two groups, even though the country is small and operates under one government. Good business communication can be hindered unintentionally by lack of knowledge about other countries and cultures.

There is an old saying, "When in Rome do as the Romans do," which is very appropriate to international communication. When you travel to another country, you have a responsibility to learn about the local customs and business practices to avoid offending anyone and to promote positive communication and business practices. Consult books on customs and business practices in other cultures to increase your cultural awareness. (See the list of references in the Appendix for suggestions.) When a person from another country or another culture communicates with you, you should recognize the cultural differences and not let those differences interfere with your communication.

Time Zones

The difference in time zones, as illustrated in Figure 2.3, must be considered in some forms of international business communication. When it is 9 a.m. in Chicago, it is 5 p.m. in Finland. If you are working in Chicago and wish to call a business in Finland, you will need to call before 9 a.m. in Chicago.

Vicky Stewart, an American executive, was walking down Michigan Avenue in Chicago with a Japanese trade representative on a cold, windy day. She said, "There sure is a nip in the air today." Vicky wasn't aware that *Nip* is a derogatory slang term for *Japanese*.

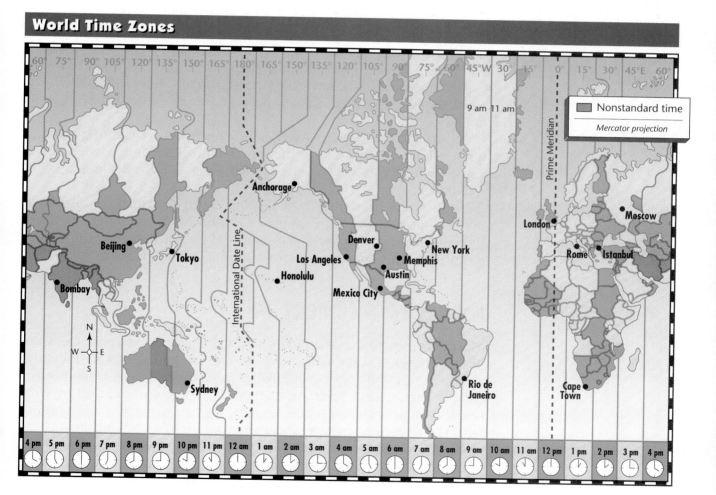

Figure 2.3 Map of International Time Zones

The earth's surface is divided into 24 time zones.

Holidays

Other countries celebrate different holidays from the ones celebrated in the United States, and businesses are closed on different days. For example, Independence Day (Fourth of July) and Thanksgiving are American holidays; those two holidays are normal working days in other countries. Likewise, other countries have their own national holidays. Even though the United States celebrates St. Patrick's Day informally, in Ireland it is a legal holiday. May Day on May 1 is a legal holiday in Great Britain. A holiday similar to our Independence Day is celebrated on different dates in these other countries:

Greece (Independence Day)	March 25
Italy (Liberation Day)	April 25
Japan (Constitution Day)	May 3
India (Independence Day)	August 15
France (Bastille Day)	July 14
Mexico (Independence Day)	September 16

The Christmas holiday is celebrated in different ways and on different dates in other countries. In the Netherlands, Belgium, and Luxembourg, St. Nicholas gives children presents on the eve of December 6. Children leave a snack (carrots) in their wooden shoes for St. Nicholas' white horse. December 25 in these countries is strictly a religious holiday.

In recent years African Americans have begun celebrating the cultural holiday Kwanzaa. It begins on December 26 and lasts for seven days. Each day is dedicated to celebrating a different principle of African culture.

The Islamic holy month of fasting, called Ramadan, is celebrated during September by Muslims in the United States and other countries. It is celebrated during the ninth month of the Muslim year. During the month Muslims may not eat or drink from dawn to sunset.

Measurements and Currency

Most of the world uses the metric system (a decimal system of measures based on meters, kilograms, liters, kilometers, and so on) for measurement. The United States uses English customary units of measurement (that is, feet, pounds, gallons, and miles). When communicating with someone who uses the metric system, don't assume they are familiar with the English system of measurement.

Most countries have their own currency. For example, Germany has the mark; Sweden, the krona; Mexico, the peso; and France, the franc. The exchange rate, the ratio at which the principal unit of two currencies can be traded, fluctuates daily.

In domestic and particularly in international communication you need to be aware of differences in language, time zones, holidays, and currency. Even more important to positive international communication is the need to be sensitive to people from other cultures, whether they live within the United States or in other countries.

SECTION 2.2   REVIEW

Practical Application

1. Define *culture.*
2. List examples of some cultural and religious groups in the United States.
3. Describe what a multinational company is.
4. Give examples of cultural differences between the United States and other countries.

Editing Practice

Proper proofreading involves checking the spelling of each word and the meaning of the word within the sentence. Proofread the following paragraph. On a sheet of paper, make a list of all the errors. Then rewrite or type the paragraph so that it is free of errors.

Inter culturel expereinces are important to help us understand people form all parts of the world. We tend to assume that everyone has the same beleifs, customs, and practises that we do. Being aware of these diferences will help us to be more tolerent and understanding of people from other cultures and contries.

Critical Thinking Skills

Analyze. Marcy White needs to telephone a customer in Paris to explain that merchandise that the customer has ordered cannot be shipped for another six weeks. Marcy knows that the customer speaks English. However, she cannot be sure that the customer will be the person who answers the phone. Marcy has never made an overseas phone call before. What does she need to know before she places the call?

Ethics and Professional Courtesy in Business Communication

OBJECTIVES:

After completing Section 2.3, you should be able to:

1. Define *ethics*.
2. Explain the purpose of a code of ethics.
3. Define *professional courtesy*.
4. Introduce two people to each other.

An act has no ethical quality unless it is chosen out of several choices.

—William James

The issue of ethics doesn't surface unless there are choices to be made. For example, if you find a billfold without identification on the floor in a store, you have several choices. Those choices would include (1) walking away and leaving the billfold on the floor, (2) turning the billfold in to the customer service desk, (3) sticking the billfold in your pocket and leaving the store with it, (4) taking out and keeping any money that was in the billfold and leaving the billfold on the floor, or (5) taking out and keeping any money that was in it and then turning the billfold in to the customer service desk. The ethical person will choose option one or two; the unethical person will make another choice.

ETHICS

KEY POINT

Ethics are the moral principles of right and wrong by which a person is guided.

We often hear about business practices being legal and being ethical. What is the difference? Laws determine whether or not something is legal. *Ethics* are the moral principles of right and wrong by which a person is guided. The goal of every business communicator is to conduct all business in a legal and ethical manner. It is possible for an activity to be legal but unethical. For instance, suppose you purchase a camera from a store with a 30-day return policy with the intention of using it for your vacation and then returning the camera for a full refund. Your behavior would be legal but unethical.

Treating Others With Honesty and Fairness

One way of incorporating ethics into business communication is to be honest and fair and to treat other persons as you would like to be treated. A new sales associate with no previous retail experience was advised by the hardware manager that a certain brand of mediocre-quality tools paid a higher commission rate than the top-quality tools. (A *commission* is a fee paid to the sales associate as a result of the sale.) The manager suggested making the following response to prospective customers who asked about the quality of the mediocre brand: "It is a very popular item." This statement implies that the tools are a good quality. While it is not a lie, the statement is misleading—and unethical.

Stating Facts Instead of Opinions

Business communication should be ethical and communicate information that is true. Another way of incorporating ethics into business communication is to use objective language and verifiable information. For example, suppose you are asked for a recommendation about a former employee's dependability for a job. Instead of saying "Sally will not be dependable," say "Our attendance records show that Sally missed work 11 times in the last three months." Stating a verifiable fact instead of your opinion lets the receiver form his or her own opinion of Sally. Many human resource departments have strict guidelines in place that specify how to respond to these queries.

Another example of providing honest, verifiable information occurs when a company requests a criminal background check on a prospective employee from a credit, health, and criminal reporting agency. If the reporting agency faxes the company a copy of a court record showing a misdemeanor conviction, the court record gives verifiable fact rather than opinion.

Description on the business card of a Chinese restaurant: "Mandarin, Szechuan, and Human Cuisine."

Figure 2.4

If you are faced with an ethical dilemma, it helps to discuss the matter with a valued friend or associate. How might you ask someone for such advice?

Ethical Communication

Ethical business communication should not withhold information that could cause the communication to be misinterpreted. For example, according to the news media, the United States tobacco industry allegedly withheld or misrepresented facts about the dangers of tobacco in reports to the public. Deliberately withholding information about the dangers of tobacco and misleading the public would be an example of unethical communication.

Another example of unethical communication would be an auto manufacturer's alleged failure to communicate to the public about defective parts on certain models of vehicles that are dangerous or life-threatening to the customers. Testing agencies who distort or skew the results of their vehicle safety tests are also unethical when they represent their skewed findings as fact.

A more subtle example of unethical communication occurs in the following situation. An environmental group releases data indicating the city water is unsafe to drink at the same time that the water company releases data indicating the city water is safe to drink. The water company tests samples of water at the water company and in homes throughout the city. The environmental group tests water at points along feeder waterways, just downstream from a golf course that uses fertilizer and other chemicals to enhance the appearance of the grass on the golf course. Both groups are accurately reporting the results of their tests. However, drinking water should be tested after it has been processed, treated, and released by the water company to homes and businesses. Clearly, since the two groups are using different sources for their data, the test results are different. Which group is releasing ethical communication?

Here are some other examples of the type of unethical communication you might encounter on the job: (1) Your supervisor asks you to "adjust" some figures in a report to make the results look better; (2) you work in the lab of a company that makes no-fat cookies, but you know they contain some fat; (3) your city promotes recycling to appeal to environmentalists, but you know that the "recycled" materials really go to the landfill with the rest of the garbage.

Maintaining Confidentiality

Confidential information is private or secret and should be released only to people with a proven need to know. Confidentiality is another important aspect of ethics. Right-to-privacy laws have been passed to legislate confidentiality in certain instances. For example, medical records, attorneys' client files, certain education and court records, banking and financial records, and so on are considered confidential information. Businesses and industries that develop new products and technologies, such as the electronics and pharmaceutical industries, have confidential information that should not fall into the hands of competitors.

KEY POINT

Confidential information is private and must not be shared without authorization.

It would be unethical communication to release confidential information to anyone who was not authorized to have access to it.

Code of Ethics

Being ethical means being honest, fair, and objective in all forms of communication. The true test of being ethical is to work toward the good of all rather than towards the good of a specialized group at the expense of some other group.

Some organizations and companies develop a written code of ethics so employees and customers or clients have a written record of the philosophy of the group. Figure 2.5 illustrates one such example of a code of ethics. A *code of ethics* states the goals of the group in terms of how the business operates and how it treats customers and competitors.

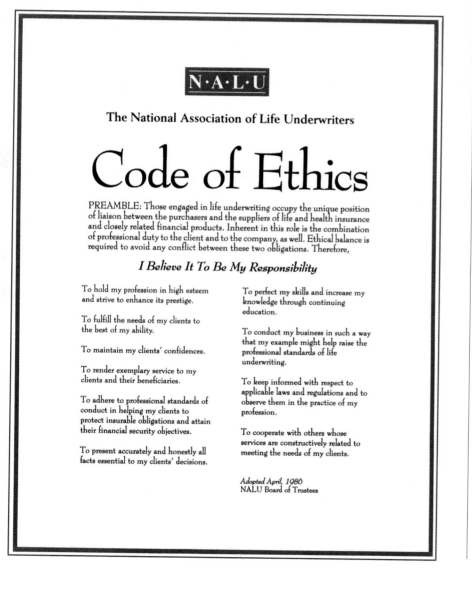

Figure 2.5
A Code of Ethics.

This illustration shows one organization's code of ethics. What are the advantages to a group or company of publishing a code of ethics?

PROFESSIONAL COURTESY

Professional courtesy, also known as business etiquette, is simply using good manners and appropriate behavior in business and business communication.

Making Introductions

One example of professional courtesy is *making introductions* when people do not know each other. In introducing people, the person you show greatest respect to is mentioned first. For example, "Alicia Lopez [your supervisor], I'd like you to meet Jerry O'Bryan [new employee]. Jerry is the new assistant in the Marketing Department."

Promptly introduce people to each other who have not met rather than leave them to introduce themselves. After you have been introduced to someone, make eye contact, smile, and acknowledge the introduction with a statement such as "I'm happy to meet you, Jerry" or "I'm pleased to meet you, Jerry." In the United States a firm handshake initiated by either person, regardless of gender, is appropriate. In other cultures there are different methods of responding to an introduction. For example, in the Japanese culture a bow from the waist is the accepted method for responding to an introduction. The lower the bow, the more respect for the individual.

Acknowledging Invitations and Thoughtful Actions

Another form of business etiquette involves acknowledging invitations for various events. If the invitation includes an *RSVP* notation, which is an abbreviation of a French phrase meaning *Please reply,* a reply by phone or in writing is required. A written invitation usually requires a written response unless a phone number is given. The host needs your reply in order to plan enough food, seats, handouts, individualized materials (such as name tags or name cards), table tents, and so on for the event. It is simply professional courtesy to let the sender know whether or not you will be attending. Occasionally, the notation *RSVP Regrets Only* appears on an invitation. That means you are expected to attend unless you reply that you are unable to attend.

Special favors done for you, such as a job recommendation, and thoughtful actions, such as sending flowers or a gift, should be acknowledged in writing with a thank-you note.

Observing Smoking Policies

Many states have laws governing smoking in public buildings and offices. It is common courtesy to limit smoking to designated smoking areas out of respect for people with allergies and respiratory health concerns.

SECTION 2.3   REVIEW

Practical Application

1. Define *ethics*.
2. Describe the purpose of a code of ethics.
3. Explain *professional courtesy*.
4. Introduce Harry Braun, company president, to Terri Prasad, the new marketing manager.

Editing Practice

Spelling Alert! Write or type each of the following sentences, correcting the spelling errors. A sentence may have more than one misspelled word.

1. Mr. Downing felt his bussiness math was the most valuable skill he had learned in school.
2. Accruels and defferals are difficult aspects of the accounting procedure.
3. Mrs. Soong does reel estate apraisals in addition to teaching at the college.
4. The whether was so cold that most of the plants died.
5. The hotel manager made an extra effort to accomodate the huricane victims.

Critical Thinking Skills

Evaluate: Joe Sandusky works as a graphic designer for a company that has a "no moonlighting" policy. (*Moonlighting* means holding a second job in addition to a regular job.) Although Joe knows of other places that allow employees to take on a limited amount of freelance work with a supervisor's permission, his employer never allows such outside work.

Joe has just had a car accident and needs $2,200 to pay for the repairs. Until he can come up with the cash, he will not be able to get his car back. His brother-in-law knows of a firm that is looking for someone to do graphic design work three hours a night for the next six weeks. The money that Joe would make doing this job would more than pay for the car repairs.

Make a list of the pros and cons of Joe's taking the freelance work. Also make a list of the pros and cons of Joe's turning down the work. Which decision do you feel Joe should make and why?

Nondiscriminatory Language

OBJECTIVES:

After completing Section 2.4, you should be able to:

1. Define *discrimination* and *discriminatory language.*
2. Describe gender-specific words and give some examples.
3. Change gender-specific words to generic, neutral words.
4. Change discriminatory language to neutral language.

Minds are like parachutes. They only function when they are open.

—Sir James Dewar

When you are communicating, it is important to avoid discrimination in what you say and do. *Discrimination* is the act of treating or judging someone on a basis other than that of individual merit. In speech and in writing, you should avoid using discriminatory language so as not to offend anyone. *Discriminatory language* refers to the biased statements and terms that are unfairly used to set an individual or group apart from others.

AVOIDING DISCRIMINATION IN COMMUNICATION

Develop the habit of using gender-neutral words and nondiscriminatory words to avoid offending any person or group.

Use Gender-Neutral Words

Gender-specific words indicate male or female. Such *gender-bias words* show favoritism toward or imply a greater importance of one gender over another. Gender-specific words do not accurately reflect today's world because men and women are considered equal in many respects. Gender-specific words and expressions are not appropriate in today's business communication. Instead, use gender-neutral words that don't emphasize male or female.

Gender-Specific	Gender-Neutral
businessman	business person, business worker
chairman	chairperson
fireman	fire fighter
foreman	supervisor
housewife	homemaker
mailman	mail carrier
newsman	newscaster, reporter
salesman	sales associate, salesperson
spokesman	spokesperson
stewardess	flight attendant
weatherman	weather reporter

KEY POINT

Gender-neutral words do not indicate male or female and do not show favoritism toward or imply a greater importance of one gender over another.

Avoid expressions such as "He's the best man for the job," which implies that men are more capable than women. Instead, say "He's the best person for the job." Similarly, avoid a phrase such as "executives and their wives," which implies that all executives are male. A more neutral statement would be "executives and their spouses."

Use Nondiscriminatory Words

In today's world, it is important to avoid offending or discriminating against anyone who may have different characteristics, beliefs, values, and attitudes from your own.

Use unbiased and nondiscriminatory language when communicating—especially when referring to a person's physical or mental condition, race, religion, age, and so on. This is a sensitive world; it is important to be aware of these differences and not offend anyone—even unintentionally. Always use bias-free language. Some words have negative connotations or meanings. For example, *handicapped* is more negative than *physically challenged*. Here are some guidelines for using nondiscriminatory language.

1. Describe people in terms of their skills and abilities, not in terms of their gender, race, cultural background, appearance, religion, age, or physical challenges.

   NOT: My assistant has great computer skills and is easy on the eyes too.
   BETTER: My assistant has great computer skills.

   NOT: A well-informed Asian doctor conducted the 10 a.m. tour.
   BETTER: A well-informed doctor conducted the 10 a.m. tour.

2. Don't make assumptions about people based on their gender, race, cultural background, looks, religion, age, or physical challenges.

   NOT: Eliot did well at the Harlem sales office because he is black.
   BETTER: Eliot did well at the Harlem sales office.

   NOT: Elderly clients are grumpy and hard to deal with.
   BETTER: When clients are grumpy or hard to deal with, we need to calmly and patiently explain the procedures.

3. Use preferred terms for different groups.

   African American, blacks (These terms are equally and widely acceptable. Be aware of groups such as West Indians and Black Muslims.)

   Asian (Do not use *Oriental*. Also, be specific if possible: for example, *Japanese, Chinese, Indian*.)

   English (Not all the British are English. Some are Welsh, Scottish, or Irish.)

   Hispanic (This term is generally acceptable. However, there are so many individual groups that it is best to be specific if possible: *Mexican-American, Puerto Rican, Brazilian, Central American*.)

   Jew (Do not use *Hebrew*, which refers to a language, or *Israelite*, which is a biblical term. Also, not all Israelis are Jews.)

   Muslim (Avoid using *Muhammadan*. However, *Moslem* is acceptable. Remember that not all Muslims are Arabs.)

KEY POINT

Nondiscriminatory language refers to a person's skills and abilities and does not make distinctions based on gender, race, culture, religion, age, or physical ability.

Native American (This term is generally acceptable. *American Indian*, but not *Indian*, which is used for natives of India, may also be acceptable. It is best to be as specific as possible: for example, *the Sioux, the Iroquois*.)

4. Use preferred terms to describe specific conditions.

NOT:	BETTER:
barren	childless
blind	*OK* or visually challenged
crazy	mentally ill
deaf and dumb	hearing- and speech-impaired
fat	overweight
handicapped, disabled, crippled	physically challenged
idiocy, moronism, cretinism	mental retardation

AVOIDING STEREOTYPING AND PREJUDICE

Stereotyping means generalizing in a positive or negative way about an entire group of people on the basis of a few examples or incidents or on the basis of preformed ideas. Our experiences or our attitudes may cause us to be prejudiced against the entire group of people. A *prejudice* is a negative attitude about an individual, a group, or a race, or about their supposed characteristics. Prejudices are conclusions that are drawn without sufficient facts. Some examples of stereotypes are:

Individual or Group	Stereotype
overweight people	lazy; overeat
people with poor grammar	lower class; uneducated; dumb
homeless people	lazy; bums
Asians	very intelligent; value education
young black people	good athletes
Italian men	good lovers
French men	very romantic
women	more creative than men; emotional
fraternity and sorority members	party animals
men with long hair	lower class; hippies
tall, slender women	would make good models
Hispanic people	migrants; speak very rapidly
people who talk slowly	dumb
people who speak with a southern accent	slow
people who speak with a New York accent	rude and curt
doctors or dentists	wealthy
attorneys	untrustworthy; mercenary

KEY POINT

Stereotyping means generalizing in a positive or negative way about an entire group of people on the basis of a few examples or incidents.

Your view or interpretation of events and people is based on your personal experiences and on information you have heard or read. If you have had a negative experience with your first contact with someone from a group, you tend to assume all people in this group are the same. For example, if your first experience with a cat was a bad one where you were hissed at, scratched, and bitten, you would probably hate cats from that point on. Whereas if your first experience with a cat had been with a soft, cute, cuddly, purring kitten, you would probably like cats.

DISCRIMINATORY ACTIONS

You can offend another person with your actions as well as words. When you are speaking to a person in a wheelchair, there is no reason to speak in a loud voice. A person in a wheelchair is physically challenged, not hearing-impaired. People who are blind are frequently spoken to in a loud voice. Remember, they are vision-impaired, not hearing-impaired. Likewise, people who wear a hearing aid frequently find that others speak to them as though they were hearing-impaired. The hearing aid usually corrects the hearing problem. Moreover, if the volume of speaking is much above normal, the voice of the speaker is distorted, and the volume on the hearing aid will need to be adjusted. People who don't speak English aren't deaf; they just don't understand. Don't shout; speaking louder won't help them understand, but speaking a little more clearly and slowly may help.

As you communicate in school and at work, strive to use language that is inclusive and not biased. Doing so will help you to avoid misunderstandings and to treat others equally and fairly.

World View

Sensitivity to other cultures is important to a company's image. MCI, a global communication company, did extensive testing of its latest logo. The new logo was tested in 40 languages—including Chinese, Japanese, Russian, and Arabic—to make sure there were no hidden meanings or offensive references.
—*USA Today*

A physically challenged person on TV made the comment that he resented people saying he was "tied to" his wheelchair. He made the point that his wheelchair enables him to get most places the rest of us do.

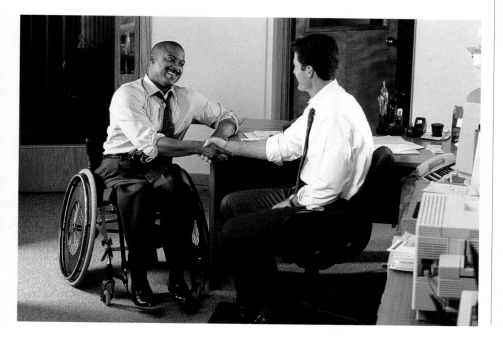

Figure 2.6

Nondiscriminatory behavior involves focusing on what you have in common with someone, rather than differences. How might you accomplish this?

SECTION 2.4   REVIEW

Practical Application

1. Define *discrimination* and *discriminatory language*.
2. Describe gender-bias and gender-specific words.
3. List at least four gender-bias or gender-specific words, and give a generic, neutral word for each one.
4. List at least four examples of discriminatory language, and give a neutral, nondiscriminatory substitute for each one.

Editing Practice

Using Nonbiased and Nondiscriminatory Language. Write each of the following sentences, correcting the biased and discriminatory language. A sentence may have more than one error.

1. The old mailman was very dependable.
2. My girl Friday is a cute brunette and has excellent telephone skills.
3. Her Catholic parents always stressed the importance of honesty.
4. The Hispanic, blind teacher made three important points at the meeting.
5. Danny Jones, the black quadriplegic, sang the national anthem at the ceremony.
6. Murry is definitely the best man for the job.
7. The salesman gave us a free gift for completing the credit application.
8. His Vietnamese mother was a strict disciplinarian.

Critical Thinking Skills

Analyze: Mary, whose ancestry is Polish, works at a medium-sized accounting firm. She likes the job and believes there is potential for career advancement. During the scheduled breaks several of the employees seem to have a never-ending supply of jokes about people of Polish ancestry that they tell so everyone can hear. Although the jokes are not directed at Mary, she is offended by them and feels humiliated. Mary is very close to her grandmother, who was born in Poland and moved to this country as a young woman. What should Mary do?

Communicating With Tact and Courtesy. Pete works for Soft-Tech, a California software company that is actively involved in international business. Clients from other countries frequently visit the office, and many of Pete's coworkers have traveled abroad on business. Indeed, Pete hopes that, in time, he too will get a chance to travel. Last week he attended a company seminar titled "The Clumsy American." The aim of the seminar was to make employees aware of appropriate—and inappropriate—behavior in dealing with people from other countries.

The seminar leader started the seminar with some actual examples of serious communication problems and errors that had occurred in the company and had prompted management to offer the seminar. Some of the examples used were as follows:

1. An employee from the California plant, where everyone wore casual clothes, dressed in blue jeans, boots, and a flowered shirt for a meeting with officers of a major bank customer in Chicago.

2. Plant employees tried to return calls to European customers after 10 a.m. California time.

3. California plant employees frequently tried to return calls to a major New York customer after 3 p.m. California time.

4. A conference call was scheduled with an Illinois bank on Lincoln's birthday.

5. A conference call was scheduled on May 1 with a vendor in England.

6. An employee who speaks only English tried to call an English-speaking employee of a French customer but had to go through a switchboard operator in France who spoke only French.

7. A lunch meeting with Jewish customers from Israel was scheduled during Yom Kippur.

8. At a meeting with some prospective clients who were Native American, the software company engineers talked down to the tribal representatives as if they were ignorant children. The tribe was run as a multimillion-dollar corporation, and the representatives were the chief executive officer (CEO) and the chief financial officer (CFO).

Why do you think the seminar was called "The Clumsy American"? In each of the examples that the seminar leader gave, suggest more appropriate ways to handle each situation.

Expanding Language Skills

3.1   **Language Structure**

3.2   **Nouns: Plural Forms**

3.3   **Nouns and Pronouns: Possessive Forms**

3.4   **Pronouns: Nominative and Objective Forms**

3.5   **Verbs**

3.6   **Predicate Agreement**

3.7   **Adjectives**

3.8   **Adverbs**

3.9   **Prepositions**

3.10   **Conjunctions**

Ashley had been working as administrative assistant to Mr. Moxley, the head of the shipping department, for about two years. When the administrative assistant to the company president retired, Ashley applied for the position. Ashley was disappointed when she did not get the promotion and asked Mr. Moxley if he knew the reason.

Mr. Moxley was quite candid. He reminded Ashley that all of her performance evaluations had indicated that she was weak in grammatical skills and that the reports and letters she produced always had to be corrected for grammatical errors. Mr. Moxley explained, "The company president has to have someone that he can depend on to make sure that his communications are correct."

When Ashley reminded Mr. Moxley that she had taken courses in grammar, Mr. Moxley replied, "Yes, I'm sure you have, but sometimes we need to refresh skills that are important in our job. The most convenient way is to review grammar concepts in a reference manual or a communications textbook. Another way to refresh grammar skills is to enroll in a course at a community college or private business school."

Ashley decided that she would not be passed over for the next available promotion. She searched her closets and found her communications text. She began to review the text immediately and placed the text beside her dictionary in the office as a ready reference—where the book should have been all along. After confirming that her company had a tuition reimbursement policy, Ashley enrolled in a grammar course at the local community college.

With the help of her grammar course, Ashley's grammar skills improved. As a result, her next performance evaluation was positive. Moreover, in the evaluation report Mr. Moxley wrote about Ashley's efforts to refresh her grammar skills to improve her job performance.

Ashley's efforts paid off. She got the next available promotion, which included a salary increase.

As you read Chapter 3, identify areas of grammar usage in which you could make improvement. Like Ashley, plan what you will do to strengthen your language skills.

LANGUAGE STRUCTURE

OBJECTIVES

After completing Section 3.1, you should be able to:

1. Identify the eight parts of speech.
2. Distinguish between a subject and a predicate.
3. Compare and contrast phrases, clauses, and sentences.
4. Recognize and write grammatically correct sentences.

I am the Roman king, and am above grammar.

— Sigismund, Holy Roman emperor

As you saw in the case study at the beginning of the chapter, Ashley found out that, unlike the emperor whose quotation introduces this section, she was not above grammar. Just the opposite. Ashley's inability to use correct grammar had a direct effect on how she performed her job and on whether or not she could advance to another job.

By reviewing grammar in her refresher course, Ashley found that terms such as *infinitive* and *predicate,* once difficult to understand, became simple to understand with a little practice. Ashley discovered that understanding basic grammar terms and knowing how to use grammar correctly help her speak and write more effectively.

As you study this chapter, view your instructor as the coach and yourself as a team player—not as a spectator. Just as in athletic competition, you will review the rules and practice applying them so that you can successfully compete when communicating in your chosen occupation.

THE PARTS OF SPEECH

All the many thousands of words in our language can be grouped into eight categories: nouns, pronouns, verbs, adjectives, adverbs, prepositions, conjunctions, and interjections. These categories are called the *parts of speech.* As you will see, each category, or part of speech, has certain characteristics. One of these characteristics is how the words from the category function in a sentence. Let's begin with nouns.

Nouns

The word *noun* is derived from a word meaning "name": A *noun* is the *name* of a person, place, thing, idea, concept, or quality. Nouns may be proper or common. A *proper noun* names a specific person, place, or thing. A *common noun* names a general person, place, or thing. The following list gives examples of proper and common nouns.

	Proper	**Common**
Persons:	Ms. Reynolds	associates
	Casey, David	students
	Natalie	patient
	Professor Johnson	client
	Dr. Partin	doctor

KEY POINT

The eight parts of speech categorize how words are used in sentences.

KEY POINT

Nouns name persons, places, things, ideas, concepts, or qualities.

	Proper	Common
Places:	New Orleans	universities
	Appalachian Mountains	restaurant
	East Coast	businesses
	Korea	home
	Middle East	stadium
Things:	United Nations	airplanes
	Golden Gate Bridge	videocassettes
	Xerox Corporation	computers
Ideas, concepts, or qualities:		democracy
		courage
		freedom
		patience

In a sentence, nouns function as subjects, direct objects, indirect objects, objects of a preposition, appositives, and complements. These functions will be discussed in later sections in Chapter 3.

Pronouns

Pronouns are words that *replace* nouns; for example, *I, you, he, she, it, we, they, me, him, her, us, them, my, mine, your, yours, his, hers, its, our, ours, their,* and *theirs.* Because they serve as substitutes, pronouns add variety to our speech and our writing and provide us with shortcuts.

KEY POINT

Pronouns are substitutes for nouns.

> *She* asked Antonio to order new stationery. (Another way of saying *"Anne asked Antonio to order new stationery."*)

> *She* gave *them* the keys to *their* offices. (Another way of saying *"The administrative assistant gave Alice and Ben the keys to Alice's and Ben's offices."*)

Since pronouns replace nouns, they also function as subjects, direct objects, indirect objects, objects of prepositions, appositives, and complements.

✔ CHECKUP 1

Identify the nouns and pronouns in the following sentences. On a separate sheet of paper, write the nouns and pronouns in each sentence. Label each noun *N* and each pronoun *P*. (Watch for nouns that have two or more words, such as *bulletin board*.)

1. Can we order a ticket for a play in New York City?
2. I am sure Yvette Wilson will make our reservations if we ask her.
3. They bought the software in Denver last month.
4. You and I will meet next Tuesday to discuss the proposed expansion.
5. She plans to visit Nashville and Memphis to tour the sights.

6. David and Tamara tell me the Midwest is their favorite part of the country.

Verbs

Verbs are words that express action, a state of being, or a condition. Verbs that express an obvious action are called *action verbs* because they give sentences life; they make sentences "move."

> Our company *imports* Swiss chocolate and *uses* it in various desserts. (*Imports* and *uses* are action verbs.)

> Ms. Kagami *bought* one Swiss chocolatier's inventory and *shipped* it to our Pennsylvania plant. (*Bought* and *shipped* are action verbs.)

> In fact, DeSuite Company *has been buying* chocolate from Switzerland since 1956. (*Has been buying* is an action verb that consists of more than one word.)

Some verbs do not indicate an obvious action but express a condition or a state of being. These verbs are called *linking verbs*. Linking verbs include forms of the verb *to be,* such as *am, is, are, was, were, be, been.* Linking verbs also include the sense verbs *look, feel, sound, taste,* and *smell,* as well as the verbs *appear* and *become.*

> Of course, I *am* delighted about Felipe's promotion, but his parents *are* thrilled. (*Am* and *are* are verbs that show state of being.)

> Henry's mother *feels* stronger as a result of her surgery. (*Feels* is a linking verb that shows a condition.)

> Mario *will be* an assistant manager in April. By that time Kathy *will have been* a manager for 12 years. (*Will be* and *will have been* are verbs. Note that each consists of more than one word.)

In a sentence, verbs function as predicates. You will learn about predicates later in this section.

✔ CHECKUP 2

On a separate sheet of paper, write the verbs in the following sentences.

1. Jill seems happy about her new responsibilities.
2. Denise was planning to call each new customer.
3. Martha hired two new sales representatives after she promoted William.
4. Mr. Linwood has been in Houston since February 10.

Using a separate sheet of paper, supply a verb for each blank in the following sentences, and indicate whether the verb is an action verb or a linking verb.

5. Shane _____ his associate degree in nursing in May and _____ his new job two months later.

6. He _____ proud of his degree and his new job.

7. Shane _____ his certification exam in early June.

8. He _____ to begin work on his bachelor's degree in nursing within two years.

Adjectives

Adjectives describe nouns and pronouns by limiting, or making more specific, the noun or pronoun. Another word for limiting is *modifying*.

Adjectives may show what kind of, which one, or how many.

What kind of: *hectic* schedule, *interesting* article, *expensive* equipment

Which one: her *former* supervisor, *that* report, *those* folders

How many: *one* employee, *several* clients, *few* tickets

The words *a, an,* and *the* are special types of adjectives called *articles:* *a* printout, *an* employee, *the* magazine. *A* and *an* are indefinite articles because they do not identify a specific item. *The* is a definite article because it identifies a specific item.

When adjectives describe nouns, as they do in the preceding examples, the adjective usually precedes the noun. When an adjective describes a pronoun, the adjective generally follows a linking verb such as *am, is, are, was, were, be, seem, appear, become,* and *been,* or a sense verb such as *feel, look, sound, taste,* or *smell.*

She was *impatient* with the slow growth of her investment. (The adjective *impatient* describes the pronoun *she.*)

They were *nervous* before their presentation. (*Nervous* modifies or describes the pronoun *they.*)

She feels *ill.* (*Ill* describes the pronoun *she.*)

Adjectives that follow linking verbs and sense verbs can also describe nouns.

Cathy feels *ill.*

Bob seems *happy.*

The group was *nervous* before its presentation.

KEY POINT

Adjectives modify nouns and pronouns.

Adverbs

Adverbs are also modifiers; like adjectives, adverbs *describe* or limit. Adverbs describe or modify adjectives, verbs, or other adverbs. They specify *how, when, where, why, in what manner,* and *to what extent.*

Anita was *unusually* quiet during the meeting yesterday. (The adverb *unusually* modifies the adjective *quiet.*)

KEY POINT

Adverbs describe adjectives, verbs, or other adverbs.

Joseph *nearly* fell on his face as he tripped over the telephone cord. (The adverb *nearly* modifies the verb *fell*.)

He ran *extremely well* in the Boston Marathon. (The adverb *extremely* modifies the adverb *well*; the adverb *well* modifies the verb *ran*.)

Note that many adverbs end in *ly* and are therefore very easy to identify:

bad*ly*	immediate*ly*	sudden*ly*
complete*ly*	successful*ly*	sure*ly*

We form these adverbs by adding *ly* to the adjectives *bad, complete, immediate, successful, sudden,* and *sure*.

Although most words that end in *ly* are adverbs, not all adverbs end in *ly*. Here are some adverbs that do not end in *ly*:

almost	much	quite	there
always	never	soon	very
here	not	then	well

✓ CHECKUP 3

Using a separate sheet of paper, identify the words in parentheses as either adjectives or adverbs.

1. They were (excited) about graduation.
2. The (beautiful) weather (here) attracts (many) tourists each summer.
3. Albert will forward the letter (immediately) to your (new) address.
4. Several (experienced) mechanics are (eagerly) waiting to begin work.
5. A (professional) presentation (always) has (attractive) visual aids.
6. The (last) person whom we interviewed was (more) qualified than we had expected.

Prepositions

Prepositions are connecting words that show the relationship between a noun or pronoun and other words in a sentence. Prepositions are always used in phrases, as shown in the following list.

Preposition	Prepositional Phrase
by	by the bus terminal, by tomorrow noon
for	for us, for Doris
from	from Maurice, from Mr. Ling
in	in the evening, in August
of	of the organization, of my friend
to	to the park, to my brother

In addition to the prepositions in the preceding table, there are many other commonly used prepositions, including these:

at	from	onto	through
after	into	over	with
before	on	out	

Prepositional phrases are very commonly used in sentences. A prepositional phrase contains an *object,* which is a person or thing that receives the action of the verb:

The pilot left here *after the meeting* and went directly *to the airport.*

At the airport she boarded the plane *with her crew.*

The horse leaped *over the fence, across the ditch,* and *over the hedges.*

Conjunctions

Conjunctions are words that *join* words, phrases, or clauses. Note how the conjunctions *and, but, or,* and *nor* are used in these sentences.

Clara *and* Jill attended the convention in Kansas City. (*And* joins two words—the nouns *Clara* and *Jill.*)

Their lawyers did not go to the meeting *but* to the gym. (*But* joins two prepositional phrases.)

Shannon will visit the construction site, *or* she will go to the main office. (*Or* joins two independent clauses.)

The defendant would not respond to their accusations, *nor* did she offer to answer any of their questions. (Nor joins two independent clauses.)

KEY POINT

Conjunctions join words, phrases, or clauses.

CHECKUP 4

On a separate sheet of paper, identify each word in parentheses as either a preposition *P* or a conjunction *C.*

1. (With) Ms. Greenberg's approval, the seminar will begin (on) Wednesday (or) Thursday.

2. The memo (to) Mr. Hansen gave the reason (for) the reprimand.

3. Matt did not order two (of) these trucks, (nor) has he ordered any other vehicles (through) our dealership (during) August.

4. Larry (and) Kim went (to) the electronics show (in) Detroit (with) their manager, Ms. Sullivan.

5. Tina likes the service station (on) the corner, (but) Fred prefers the one (on) Third Street.

Interjections

Interjections are words used alone that show very strong feeling. Interjections are often followed by exclamation marks, as shown in the following examples.

Congratulations! All your hard work has finally paid off handsomely. (Note that the interjection *Congratulations* is treated as an independent sentence.)

No! I never dreamed we would get their account.

THE SENTENCE

The parts of speech are used to form sentences, the basic units we use in reading, writing, and speaking. Our ability to use and to understand sentences effectively, therefore, determines our ability to communicate.

A *sentence* is a group of words that expresses a complete thought and contains a subject and a predicate. (An interjection such as "Yes!" "No!" or "Congratulations!" may be used as an elliptical expression that stands for a sentence. An *elliptical expression* can represent a complete statement or command and may be an answer to a question.) The subject and the predicate are the key elements needed to build a sentence. Let's look at subjects first.

Subjects

The *subject* of a sentence names (1) the person or persons speaking, (2) the person or persons spoken to, or (3) the person(s) or thing(s) spoken about. A subject is usually a noun or pronoun. Here are a few examples.

1. Who is speaking:

   I voted for Steve in the last election. (*I* is the complete subject of the sentence, the person who is speaking.)

   We bought new office furniture today. (*We* is the complete subject of the sentence, the persons who are speaking.)

2. Who is spoken to:

   You have been invited to speak at the banquet, Beth. (The subject *You* identifies the person spoken to, *Beth.*)

   You nominated me for president. (The subject *You* identifies the person spoken to.)

   Open a checking account. (Here the subject is still *you,* but this sentence is an *imperative sentence*—an order. In such sentences, the speaker usually directly addresses the person spoken to; therefore, it is clearly understood that the subject is *you.*)

3. Who or what is spoken about:

Ron purchased the house in November. (Who is spoken about? Answer: *Ron,* the subject of the sentence.)

Lisa is the manager of the Marketing Department. (Who is spoken about? Answer: *Lisa,* the subject of the sentence.)

She is the manager of the Marketing Department. (Who is spoken about? Answer: *She,* the subject of the sentence.)

In the last two examples, the person spoken about is referred to by name, *Lisa,* and then by the pronoun *She.*

Now that we have seen examples of *who* is spoken about, let's see examples of *what* is spoken about:

This insurance policy covers loss by fire and theft. (What is spoken about? Answer: *This insurance policy.*)

It covers loss by fire and theft. (What is spoken about? Answer: *It,* a pronoun that substitutes for the complete subject *This insurance policy. It* is the subject of the sentence.)

That disk belongs to Nicole. *Those disks* belong to Clarence. (*That disk* and *Those disks* are the complete subjects. *That disk* is the thing spoken about; *Those disks* are the things spoken about.)

She will attend the staff meeting. *They* will attend the staff meeting. (*She* and *They* are the subjects. *She* and *They* are the persons spoken about.)

Greg was quiet upset at the news.

✔ CHECKUP 5

On a separate sheet of paper, write the subjects of the following sentences. Determine whether each subject is (1) the person or persons speaking, (2) the person or persons spoken to, or (3) the person(s) or thing(s) spoken about.

1. Martin Ortega will be given the award.
2. Juanita Manahan will be the top sales agent for the month.
3. I feel that the price for the land is too expensive.
4. The reports will be finished by November 15.
5. Emilio and Dana will share the commission on the sale.

Simple Subjects. The *simple subject* is the main word or words in the complete subject—the core of the subject.

The *owner* of these condominiums is Amy Morina. (The complete subject is *The owner of these condominiums.* The main word, or simple subject, in this complete subject is *owner.*)

Five former *lawyers* in the Hills, Hills & Blackwell law firm have filed a complaint. (The complete subject of this sentence is *Five former lawyers in the Hills, Hills & Blackwell law firm.* Within this complete subject, the simple subject is *lawyers.*)

Because the subject of the first example is *owner,* not *condominiums,* the correct verb must be *is.* Because the subject of the second example is *lawyers,* not *firm,* the correct verb must be *are.* As you will learn in Section 3.6, knowing how to find the simple subject will help you make sure that subjects and verbs agree.

Compound Subjects. A *compound subject* is two or more subjects joined by a conjunction such as *and, but, or,* or *nor.*

> The *mechanics* and *technicians* at our local plant have requested additional safety procedures. (The complete subject is *The mechanics and technicians at our local plant.* There are two main words in this complete subject—*mechanics* and *technicians*— which are joined by the conjunction *and.* The compound subject is *mechanics and technicians.*)

> A *cruise* to Alaska or a one-week *vacation* on Maui is going to be the first prize. (The complete subject is *A cruise to Alaska or a one-week vacation on Maui.* The two main words in this complete subject are *cruise* and *vacation,* which are joined by the conjunction *or.* The compound subject is *cruise or vacation.*)

Every time you identify the subject correctly, you simplify your work in identifying the predicate. Reason: The predicate tells what the subject does, what is done to the subject, or the state of being of the subject.

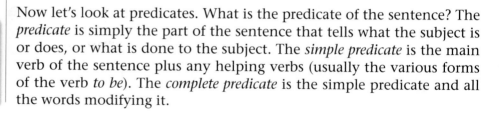
✔ CHECKUP 6

On a separate sheet of paper, write the simple subject or the compound subject for each sentence.

1. All employees submitted suggestions for solving the problem.
2. One seminar participant asked about tuition reinbursement programs for employees.
3. Has Harrison or Margaret made our flight reservations?
4. Four comprehensive folders on the Nelson case are filed in the cabinet beside my desk.
5. Two hair salons and a book store have shown interest in renting your building.

Predicates

Now let's look at predicates. What is the predicate of the sentence? The *predicate* is simply the part of the sentence that tells what the subject is or does, or what is done to the subject. The *simple predicate* is the main verb of the sentence plus any helping verbs (usually the various forms of the verb *to be*). The *complete predicate* is the simple predicate and all the words modifying it.

Ms. Schaefer *will organize the teams for the project.* (The simple predicate is *will organize,* which is what Ms. Schaefer will do. The complete predicate is *will organize the teams for the project.*)

Lisa and Max *are the managers of these departments.* (The simple predicate is *are,* which tells what Lisa and Max are. The complete predicate is *are the managers of these departments.*)

✔ CHECKUP 7

On a separate sheet of paper, write the complete predicate for each of the following sentences.

1. Tom and Gail are the newest members of our department.
2. Julia has enrolled in the computer applications course.
3. All applicants should have at least three years' experience.
4. My performance review is scheduled for March 15.
5. Our customers have responded favorably to the new ad campaign.

Normal Order: Subject, Then Predicate

The normal order of a sentence is subject first, then predicate.

Three members of management were at last night's meeting concerning health benefits. (The complete subject is *Three members of management.* The complete subject precedes the complete predicate, which is *were at last night's meeting concerning health benefits.* Therefore, this sentence is in *normal* order.)

At last night's meeting concerning health benefits were *three members of management.* (The words are the same, but the order is different. Now the predicate precedes the subject. This sentence, therefore, is not in normal order. It is in inverted order.)

Most questions are phrased in inverted order rather than normal order.

Has Bill estimated the cost of constructing the warehouse? (Why is this question in inverted order? The subject is *Bill,* and part of the verb—the word *Has*—precedes the subject. Normal order would be *Bill has estimated the cost of constructing the warehouse.*)

Now let's see why it is important to be able to distinguish between normal order and inverted order. What, if anything, is wrong with this sentence?

Where's the photographs that Andrea left for us?

Many people almost automatically start sentences with *Where's, There's,* and *Here's,* even when these words are incorrect. Normal order quickly points out the error.

The photographs that Andrea left for us *is* where? (Simply put, "The photographs . . . is where?" *Photographs is,* is incorrect; we must say "Photographs are." Thus, the correct form for the question is *Where are the photographs that Andrea left for us?*)

It is important to spot inverted order not only in questions but also in statements. Look at this sentence:

On the desk in my office is the photographs that Andrea left for us. (In normal order, this sentence reads "The photographs that Andrea left for us *is* on the desk in my office." The subject *photographs* is plural and does not agree in number with the verb *is,* which is singular. This error is masked by the inverted order. The original sentence should read *On the desk in my office are the photographs that Andrea left for us.*)

You will learn more about subject-verb agreement in Section 3.6.

Types of Sentences

You use sentences to make statements, ask questions, state a command or request, and express strong feeling. There are four types of sentences to serve these purposes.

Type of Sentence	Definition	Example
Declarative	Makes a statement.	You are tall.
Interrogative	Asks a question.	How old are you?
Imperative	States a command or request.	Proofread the letter.
Exclamatory	Expresses strong feeling.	I can't believe it!

✔ CHECKUP 8

On a separate sheet of paper, identify each of the following sentences as declarative (*D*), interrogative (*INT*), imperative (*IMP*), or exclamatory (*E*).

1. Who attended the conference?
2. Please give me the latest sales figures by tomorrow.
3. Both Stefanie and Boyd are candidates for the job.
4. Congratulations on winning the account!
5. Connie answered my question.

Clauses and Phrases

Words that are grouped together are classified as a *clause* if the group of words includes both a subject and a predicate. A group of related words that does *not* have both a subject and a predicate is called a *phrase*.

Clauses. If a clause (a group of words containing both a subject and a predicate) expresses a complete thought and can stand alone as a complete sentence, it is an *independent* clause. If the clause cannot stand alone, then it is called a *dependent* clause.

Review the following sentences. Note that each has a subject and a predicate and that each can stand alone. Each, therefore, is an independent clause.

Nathan Gilbert is a well-known expert in psychology. (The subject is *Nathan Gilbert,* and the complete predicate is the rest of the sentence. Because this group of words *can* stand alone, this is an independent clause.)

A video superstore is being built in the new mall. (Here, the complete subject is *A video superstore.* The complete predicate is the rest of the sentence. Because this group of words can stand alone, this is an independent clause.)

Now read the clauses that follow. Each has a subject and predicate but cannot stand alone. Therefore, these are dependent clauses.

If Jan Oberlin accepts the nomination. (The subject of this clause is *Jan Oberlin,* and the complete predicate is *accepts the nomination.* But does this group of words make sense by itself? No. This is a *dependent* clause. More information is required if this group of words is to make sense.)

When Rosemarie Terrazo returns from vacation (The subject of this clause is *Rosemarie Terrazo,* and the complete predicate is *returns from vacation.* However, the words do not make sense by themselves. This group of words is a *dependent* clause. As you read this dependent clause, ask yourself this: "What will happen *when Rosemarie Terrazo returns from vacation?*" Do you see that more information is required?)

Dependent clauses cannot stand alone as sentences; therefore, they must be joined to independent clauses for their meaning to be complete.

If Jan Oberlin accepts the nomination, she must resign her present position. (*She must resign her present position* is an independent clause. Thus the dependent clause *If Jan Oberlin accepts the nomination* is correctly joined to an independent clause.)

When Rosemarie Terrazo returns from vacation, she will review all of our progress. (Again, the dependent clause, *When Rosemarie Terrazo returns from vacation,* is joined to the independent clause, *she will review all of our progress.*)

KEY POINT

A *clause* is a group of related words that has a subject and a predicate. A *phrase* is a group of related words that does not have a subject or a predicate.

KEY POINT

An *independent clause* expresses a complete thought and can stand alone as a sentence. A *dependent clause* does not express a complete thought and cannot stand alone.

CHECKUP 9

Using a separate sheet of paper, determine which of the following groups of words are complete sentences and which are dependent clauses that are incorrectly treated as sentences. For each dependent clause, suggest an independent clause that would complete it.

1. Because Glenda Harris, the head nurse, will not return until next week, our weekly staff meeting will be rescheduled.

2. When Alexander meets with the hospital nursing staff.

3. Glenda and Jeff Feld will arrange a work schedule for each nurse.

4. Before the nurses meet to evaluate their patients.

5. If Glenda is unable to employ another nursing assistant by April 1.

Phrases. A *phrase* is a group of words that has neither a subject nor a predicate. As you study the following three kinds of phrases, note that none has a subject or a predicate.

Prepositional Phrases. A *prepositional phrase* consists of a preposition, an object, and any modifier of the object. Phrases such as *for the associates, in the office, among the interns, at the meeting, with Andrew Brewster, between you and me,* and *from Dr. Jenner* are prepositional phrases. The nouns and pronouns at the ends of prepositional phrases are not subjects; they are objects of the prepositions.

As you read the following examples, note how prepositional phrases can be used (1) as adjectives, (2) as adverbs, and (3) as nouns.

1. As adjectives:

   The woman *with the clipboard* is Betty Chung. (Which woman? The prepositional phrase *with the clipboard* describes the noun *woman*. Therefore, because it describes a noun, this prepositional phrase serves as an adjective.)

2. As adverbs:

   Dustin sent the report *to the committee chair*. (Sent it where? The prepositional phrase *to the committee chair* answers the question Where? This prepositional phrase serves as an adverb.)

3. As nouns:

   After 5 o'clock is the best time to meet.

Infinitive Phrases. An *infinitive* is the *to* form of a verb: *to read, to study, to analyze, to review, to compute, to question, to be, to have, to do,* and so on. An infinitive phrase includes the infinitive and any other words that are related to it. Infinitive phrases may be used (1) as nouns, (2) as adjectives, and, less frequently, (3) as adverbs.

1. As nouns:

   To develop new products is the objective of this department. (The complete infinitive phrase is *To develop new products;* the phrase is the subject of the verb *is*.)

2. As adjectives:

   Rachael Kirkland is the person *to ask about employment opportunities*. (*Here the infinitive phrase to ask about employment opportunities* modifies the noun *person* and therefore serves as an adjective.)

3. As adverbs:

   Pat bent down *to tie her shoe*. (Bent down for what reason? Here the infinitive phrase answers the question Why? The infinitive phrase *to tie her shoe* therefore serves as an adverb.)

Seen in a newspaper weather report: "The Mid-Atlantic region will be mostly funny."

MEMORY HOOK

Because infinitives begin with the word *to*, they may sometimes be confused with prepositional phrases beginning with the word *to*.

Infinitive	Prepositional Phrase
to write	to the committee
to see	to Professor Myers
to agree	to me

To avoid any possible confusion, remember that an infinitive is the *to* form of a *verb*. Simply test by using the infinitive as a verb: *I write, you see, they agree.* Using this procedure with prepositional phrases will yield gibberish. Try it!

Verb Phrases. In a verb phrase, two or more verbs work together as one verb. In such cases, the *main verb* is always the last verb in the phrase; the other verbs are *helping (or* auxiliary*) verbs.* Some common helping verbs include *is, are, was, were, can, could, has, had, have, should, will,* and *would.*

The architect *will complete* our house plans by May 1. (*Will complete* is a verb phrase. The main verb is *complete; will* is a helping verb.)

By May 1 our house plans *will have been completed.* (The main verb is *completed,* the last word in the verb phrase. *Will have been* is a helping verb.)

Verb phrases are often interrupted by adverbs, as shown in the following examples. Do not be misled by such interruptions.

The architect will *soon* be showing our house plans to the builder. (The verb phrase *will be showing* is interrupted by the adverb *soon.*)

The apartment residents have *already* been told about possible power outages tomorrow. (The verb phrase *have been told* is interrupted by the adverb *already.*)

✓ CHECKUP 10

Are the words in parentheses prepositional phrases (*PP*), infinitive phrases (*IP*), or verb phrases (*VP*)? On a separate sheet of paper, write *PP, IP,* or *VP* for each group of words.

1. Haley's poem (will be submitted) (to the contest committee) (by next Tuesday).   VP   PP   PP

2. (To attend the computer classes), customers (have been asked) (to register) (in advance).   IP   VP   IP   VP

3. Mr. Soo wants (to taste the recipe) when he goes (to the award presentation) (with Wendy Brennan).
4. (To become a chef) (at Antonio's), you (must have had) at least five years' experience (at a three-star restaurant).
5. Several violin classes (have been scheduled) (for elementary school children).

Sentence Fragments

Remember the definition for a sentence: *A sentence is a group of words that expresses a complete thought and contains a subject and predicate.* Note especially the word *complete.* Writing incomplete thoughts—called *fragments*—is a common but glaring error. You can distinguish between a complete sentence and a fragment by applying the "no sense, no sentence" rule. Look at the following examples:

Shannon Rogers wants to attend the seminar because the topic is the Internet. (This is a complete thought. This group of words makes sense. This is a sentence.)

When we receive Mr. Staley's approval, we will make a reservation for Ms. Rogers. (This thought is complete. This group of words makes sense, so it is a sentence.)

If, however, you try to split off part of the sentence (see the following examples), you create a fragment.

Shannon Rogers wants to attend the seminar. Because the topic is the Internet. (The first group of words is a sentence. The words *Because the topic is the Internet* do not make sense by themselves. The word *because* leads us to expect more. What happened *because the topic is the Internet?*)

When we receive Mr. Staley's approval. We will make a reservation for Ms. Rogers. (The words *When we receive Mr. Staley's approval* do not make sense by themselves; the word *when* leads us to expect more. It is not a sentence. What will happen *when we receive Mr. Staley's approval?* The second group of words is a sentence.)

In the preceding examples, the words *because* and *when* lead us to expect more. Each begins a clause that cannot stand alone. Note that the following words, like *because* and *when,* often introduce dependent clauses (clauses that cannot stand alone).

after	before	provided that	when
although	even if	since	whenever
as	for	so that	where
as if	how	than	wherever
as soon as	if	that	whether
as though	in case that	unless	while
because	in order that	until	why

Are the following groups of words sentences, or are they fragments? On a separate sheet of paper, identify each as a sentence or a fragment; then rewrite each fragment to make it a complete sentence.

1. Because two signatures are required for checks over $500.
2. If Mr. Cane decides to sign the contract.
3. Ralph or Julian will be chosen as our new paralegal.
4. The manager mandated the policy about five years ago.
5. Although her passport was valid at that time.

SECTION 3.1   REVIEW

Practical Application

A. On a separate sheet of paper, identify each word in parentheses as a noun, pronoun, verb, adjective, adverb, preposition, conjunction, or interjection. For each phrase in parentheses, identify the phrase by writing *VP* (*verb phrase*), *IP* (*infinitive phrase*), or *PP* (*prepositional phrase*).

1. (Steven) submitted his report on time, (but) his formatting was done (very) poorly.
2. (In 1999), (New York) (or) Orlando will be the site of (our) (national) convention.
3. (To distinguish between two candidates) is a (perplexing) task, but (we) will make the decision (in) November.
4. I (personally) (agree) that Miami would be the best (location) (for our January national meeting).
5. The (candidates) (should have known) the (issues) before (they) (entered) the campaign.
6. (Trainees) should be encouraged (to ask questions).
7. (Improvements) are always welcome (in this company).
8. A special award (will be given) (to associates) if they achieve perfect attendance.
9. Alice Freeman (and) Lana Patrick have (already) received bonuses for their (recycling) recommendation.
10. (Hooray!) (We) just (won) the department sales award (for) our entire region.

B. Identify the following clauses as dependent (*D*) or independent (*I*). On a separate sheet of paper, label each clause *D* or *I*.
1. When an increasing number of firms are striving for global competitiveness.
2. Before we see a significant upturn in the economy.
3. One of the most important signs that we have seen in terms of consumer buying power.
4. Discount retailers are winning the battle.
5. While more aggressive managers are searching for multitalented employees.
6. The manufacturing sector has been hardest hit.
7. To the degree to which trainees will take direction.
8. If they really want Carlotta Di Bello to approve the merger.
9. As soon as the results of the taste test have been tabulated.
10. In about a week we should know which brand was the top choice.

C. Read each of the following sentences carefully. Then, on a separate sheet of paper, (1) write the complete subject of each independent clause and (2) underline the simple or compound subject of that clause.
1. Eve and Eric Norton plan to use their basement as a dance studio.
2. As soon as the basement is renovated, their three assistants will begin teaching lessons there.
3. Students and their parents will tour the new studio during a reception on August 25.
4. Although renovating the basement is quite expensive, First Branch Bank has agreed to lend the couple most of the needed money.
5. While the basement is being renovated, Eric Norton will be getting estimates on paving the gravel parking lot that leads to the basement.
6. Prior to the opening of the dance studio, the Nortons and their assistants will install a new sound system.
7. In late July or early August, Mr. and Mrs. Norton will sell their old studio.
8. Their real estate agent has found a buyer for the old studio.
9. Located at the top of the hill are the only other houses on Amos Drive.
10. On the south border of the property are a pool and a lake.

D. On a separate sheet of paper, write *S* for *sentence* and *F* for *fragment*. For each fragment, add the words needed to change the fragment to a complete sentence.
1. What is your address?
2. As soon as we receive the loan application.
3. The two associates on the third shift who can do that work.
4. The supervisors and the associates agree with Dave's recommendation.

5. Can you remember how to use the presentation software?
6. Where are the designs for the new marketing campaign?
7. Even though these policies were in effect January through March.
8. At the fall festival in October, each hospital department will have a display demonstrating its specialty.
9. Filed away in storage are our outdated client files.
10. Until Mr. Kellogg endorses the new procedures that your committee suggested last February.

Editing Practice

Spelling and Grammar Alert! Can you find any spelling or grammatical errors in the following excerpt from an informal note written by an employee? Correctly write each sentence that has an error.

Here's the sales figures from January, Febuary, March, and April. If there is any posible explanation for the sales decline in March. I would appreciate having that information before our next staff meeting. We frequently have a decline in sales in Febuary but not in March. There is an upward trend, however, in April.

NOUNS: PLURAL FORMS

New words make their way into the world. But improper grammar and incorrect usage are examples of intellectual sloppiness and must be fought. Language must be precise or it is not language.

— Harold Schonberg

OBJECTIVES:
After completing Section 3.2, you should be able to:

1. Apply the basic rules for forming the plurals of most nouns.
2. Discuss solutions for forming difficult plurals.
3. Explain when to use a dictionary to determine how to form the plurals of nouns.
4. Describe plurals that often cause grammatical errors

When we say "several of our *customers,*" or "one *customer's* opinion," or "all *customers'* orders," we do not ordinarily think of the difference in the spelling of *customers, customer's,* and *customers'.* Because the pronunciation of all three forms is the same, in speaking we do not make errors when faced with a choice among these three words.

In writing, however, these three choices are not interchangeable. Each has its own distinct meaning and use. You must know, therefore, whether *customers* or *customer's* or *customers'* is correct in a particular sentence. In Sections 3.2 and 3.3 you will master the use of plurals and possessives. With this knowledge you can solve some common spelling problems. This section emphasizes forming plural nouns correctly.

THE BASIC RULES

Although you probably know the basic rules for forming plurals, review them to make sure that you *always* apply the rules correctly.

Plurals of Common Nouns

Most common nouns form their plurals by adding s to the singular form:

attorney	attorneys	diskette	diskettes
avenue	avenues	employee	employees
computer	computers	program	programs

However, nouns that end in *s, sh, ch, x,* and *z* form their plurals by adding *es* to the singular form:

class	classes
dash	dashes
wrench	wrenches
tax	taxes
buzz	buzzes

KEY POINT

Add *s* to form the plurals of most common and proper nouns. Add *es* to form the plurals of common and proper nouns ending in *s, sh, ch, x,* and *z*.

Plurals of Proper Nouns

Most proper nouns, or *names*, form their plurals by adding *s* to the singular form.

Brombecki	the Brombeckis
Ryman	the Rymans
Thornberg	the Thornbergs

Proper nouns that end in *s, sh, ch, x,* and *z* form their plurals by adding *es*—just as common nouns ending in these letters form their plurals.

Moss	the Mosses
Andrews	the Andrewses
Walsh	the Walshes
Holditch	the Holditches
Nix	the Nixes
Herz	the Herzes

Plurals of Compound Nouns

KEY POINT

Form the plural of a compound noun by making the main word in the compound plural.

A *compound noun* is a noun that consists of two or more words. Compound nouns may be written with a hyphen, with a space between the words, or as solid words. In any case, always make the main word (the most important word) in the compound plural.

attorney general	attorneys general
bulletin board	bulletin boards

chief of staff	chiefs of staff
editor in chief	editors in chief
general manager	general managers
major general	major generals
mother-in-law	mothers-in-law
notary public	notaries public
timetable	timetables

OOPS!

Dayton Industries hired two attornies to handle the real-estate purchase.

Plurals of Nouns Ending in *Y*

Singular nouns ending in *y* may form their plurals in one of two ways:

1. If the *y* is preceded by a vowel (*a, e, i, o, u*), add *s* to form the plural.

attorney	attorneys
convoy	convoys
turkey	turkeys
valley	valleys

2. If the *y* is preceded by a consonant, change the *y* to *i* and add *es*.

company	companies
faculty	faculties
territory	territories

Note that this rule does *not* apply to proper names ending in *y*. For proper names ending in *y*, add *s* to form the plural.

Langley	the Langleys
McCarthy	the McCarthys
Sally	two Sallys

✔ CHECKUP 1

On a separate sheet of paper, correct any errors in using plurals in the following sentences. Write *OK* if a sentence is correct.

1. All lens, including telephoto and wide-angle lens, will be on sale at discounts of up to 30 percent. [lenses / lenses]
2. Industry in these two countys is thriving because taxes are low. [counties]
3. The assistant district attornies who were assigned to this case are Jasper Garner and Celia Melendez. [attorney]
4. Kane, Inc., has subsidiaries in Charlotte and in Seattle. *OK*
5. Ellen Avery and her sister June want to buy this property, but the Averies have set a ceiling of $500,000 for both the building and the land. [Averys]
6. The last two attorneys general were responsive to the public. *OK*
7. One of the newly appointed editor in chiefs is Harriet C. Walberg. [editors]

8. The terms of Mr. Halper's will were that his three ~~daughter~~ *daughters*-in-~~laws~~ *law* must continue to operate his business.
9. Two ~~Barries~~ *Barrys*—Hillsburg and Parker—work in the communications center.
10. Stationery and miscellaneous ~~supplys~~ *supplies* are being stored in the hall cabinet.

SPECIAL PLURALS

Certain plurals cause problems for writers because these forms follow no regular rules. For example, how would you form the plural of the abbreviations *Mr.* and *Mrs.*? When you have reviewed these special forms, you will have no difficulty forming these plurals.

Plurals of Titles With Names

When forming the plural of a title *and* the name used with it, make *either* the title *or* the name plural—*not both*. (For example, *both Ms. Harrises* or *both Mses. Harris* not *both Mses. Harrises*.) Both plural forms are correct and mean the same thing. In ordinary usage, the trend is to make the last name plural rather than the title. Pluralizing the title is usually reserved for formal usage.

To help you form the plurals of courtesy titles correctly, review the plural forms of *Mr., Mrs., Ms., Miss*, and *Dr.*

KEY POINT

To form the plural of a title used with a name, make either the title or the name plural.

Singular	Plural
Mr.	Messrs.
Mrs.	Mmes.
Ms.	Mses.
Miss	Misses
Dr.	Drs.

Note the following:

1. *Messrs.* is derived from *Messieurs*, the French word for "Misters."
2. Likewise, *Mmes.* is derived from *Mesdames*, the French word for "My ladies," and is used as the plural of *Mrs.*
3. *Ms.* is considered nonsexist because it does not identify a woman's marital status, just as *Mr.* does not point out a man's marital status. The plural form of *Ms.* is *Mses.*

Now let's look at some examples of forming plurals of names with titles.

Singular	Plural Title	Plural Name
Mr. King	the Messrs. King	the Mr. Kings
Mrs. Amar	the Mmes. Amar	the Mrs. Amars
Ms. Desoto	the Mses. Desoto	the Ms. Desotos
Miss Harris	the Misses Harris	the Miss Harrises

If you are referring to two people who have the same courtesy title, use the plural form of the title, as in *Messrs. Long and King.*

Plurals With Apostrophes

In certain situations the apostrophe is used to form plurals. Specifically, use an apostrophe plus *s* to form plurals of lowercase letters and of lowercase abbreviations:

The *m*'s and *n*'s on this printer are unclear.

Our receiving department handles all *c.o.d.'s* for the plant.

To form plurals of capital letters and abbreviations ending with capital letters, add the lowercase *s* alone (*HMOs, VIPs, Ph.D.s, M.D.s, CEOs, V.P.s*). Add an apostrophe and lowercase *s* if adding the *s* alone causes confusion. For example, use *A's* instead of *As*, *I's* instead of *Is*, and *U's* instead of *Us* to avoid confusion.

An apostrophe is *not* required to form plurals in phrases such as *ups and downs, temperature in the 90s, dos and don'ts,* and *in the 1980s.*

Plurals With Special Changes

Anyone who speaks English has certainly noticed (and perhaps had difficulty with) irregularly formed plurals. Some common ones follow:

Singular	Plural
child	children
goose	geese
leaf	leaves
mouse	mice
ox	oxen
woman	women

CHECKUP 2

On a separate sheet of paper, correct any errors in using plurals.

1. Max asked us to send the registered letters to the Misses ~~Browns~~ Brown.

2. Our company stock is now selling at $10 a share, but it may soon reach the high ~~20's~~ 20s.

3. Because of her illness, she received two I's for her incomplete courses.
4. Yes, the Messrs. Randall are buying the office services company. *ok*
5. The ~~Jordan's~~ are staying with the president during the convention. *Jordans*
6. Both Jenny and Ned have worked in our Phoenix office since the 1980s. *ok*
7. Three of the ~~mans~~ *men* in the department requested the change.
8. Two men and two women partners were added to the firm: Mr. Crantz and Fenner and ~~Ms.~~ *Ms.* Hillsdale and Kramer. *Messrs.*

DICTIONARY "MUSTS"

Despite the many thousands of words that form their plurals according to basic, simple rules, some words follow no basic pattern or rule. To form plurals of such words, you must consult a dictionary. For example, plurals of words ending in *o*, *f*, and *fe* vary greatly. Study the following plurals carefully.

Plurals of Nouns Ending in *O*

Singular nouns ending in *o* preceded by a vowel form the plural by adding *s*. Some nouns ending in *o* preceded by a consonant form the plural by adding *s*; others, by adding *es*. Note the following examples.

Final *o* preceded by a vowel, add *s* for the plural:

folio	folios	studio	studios
ratio	ratios	video	videos

Final *o* preceded by a consonant, add *s* for the plural:

memento	mementos	tuxedo	tuxedos
photo	photos	zero	zeros

Final *o* preceded by a consonant, add *es* for the plural:

cargo	cargoes	motto	mottoes
echo	echoes	potato	potatoes
hero	heroes	veto	vetoes

Note that nouns that relate to music and that end in *o* form their plurals by adding *s: piano, pianos; alto, altos; oratorio, oratorios; solo, solos;* and so on.

POOPS!

We used two battery-operated ratios during the power outage.

Plurals of Nouns Ending in *F* or *Fe*

Form the plurals of nouns ending in *f* or *fe* in one of two ways: (1) by changing the *f* or *fe* to *v* and then adding *es*, or (2) by simply adding *s*.

Change *f* or *fe* to *v*, then add *es*:

half	halves	self	selves
knife	knives	shelf	shelves
life	lives	wife	wives

Simply add *s*:

belief	beliefs	proof	proofs
chief	chiefs	roof	roofs
plaintiff	plaintiffs	safe	safes

CHECKUP 3

On a sheet of paper, write the correct plural forms of the following nouns.

1. solo*s* video*s*
2. belief*s* loa*ves*
3. portfolio*s* ditto*s*
4. lea*f* thief*s*
5. tomato*s* mosquito*es*
6. watch*es* brush*es*
7. radio*s* concerto*s*
8. bailiff*s* handkerchief*s*
9. trio*s* volcano*es*
10. knife, gulf*s* *knives*

Plurals of Foreign Nouns

The plurals of foreign nouns form another category of dictionary "musts." As you can see in the following list, these plurals of words with foreign origin are not formed according to basic English rules.

Singular	Plural	Singular	Plural
addendum	addenda	basis	bases
agenda	agendas	crisis	crises
alumna	alumnae	diagnosis	diagnoses
alumnus	alumni	hypothesis	hypotheses
analysis	analyses	maître d'	maître d's
axis	axes	stimulus	stimuli
bacterium	bacteria	synthesis	syntheses

In addition, some words of foreign origin have *two* plural forms—the word's "original" foreign plural form (similar to the ones in the preceeding list) and an English plural form (a plural formed by treating the singular as if it were an English word).

KEY POINT

Plurals of foreign nouns that end in *um* are formed by dropping the *um* and adding an *a*.

KEY POINT

Foreign nouns that end in *is* in the singular are changed to *es* to form the plural.

Singular	Foreign Plural	English Plural
appendix	appendices	appendixes*
criterion	criteria*	criterions
curriculum	curricula	curriculums*
datum	data*	datums
formula	formulae	formulas*
index	indices	indexes
medium	media (media)	mediums (spiritualists)
memorandum	memoranda	memorandums*
nucleus	nuclei*	nucleuses
stadium	stadia	stadiums*
syllabus	syllabi*	syllabuses
vertebra	vertebrae*	vertebras

NOTE: * indicates the plural form that is preferred in English usage.

Troublesome Forms

The following nouns are *always singular* even though they end in *s*. Use a singular verb to agree with them.

aerobics	economics (science)	molasses	statistics (science)
aeronautics	genetics	news	
civics	mathematics	physics	

The following nouns are *always plural*. Use a plural verb to agree with them.

antics	pants	series	tidings
auspices	proceeds	slacks	tongs
belongings	riches	statistics (facts)	tweezers
jeans	scissors	thanks	winnings

The following nouns have only one form, which may be used either as a singular or a plural, depending on the intended meaning.

aircraft	deer	odds	sheep
Chinese	French	politics	shrimp
corps	moose	salmon	wheat

When modified by another number, the following nouns usually have the same form to denote either a singular or a plural number.

three *thousand* forms   four *score* years
five *hundred* applicants   two *dozen* seniors

✔ CHECKUP 4

On a sheet of paper, write the correction for any error with plurals in the following sentences. Write *OK* if a sentence is correct.

1. The scientists used the same three chemical ~~analysis~~ to reach their conclusions.   *analyses*

2. Jan bought four blouses and two pairs of pant~~s~~ **s**
3. The lab technician isolated three ~~bacterium~~ *Bacteria*
4. The proceeds from our raffle were given to the homeless shelter. *OK*
5. Hundreds of our recent alumni are coming to the reception to honor the university president at his retirement. *OK*
6. We received almost five ~~thousands~~ hits on our Internet Web site last month. *Thousand*
7. The chef asked that I purchase two ~~dozens~~ shrimps. *dozen* *Shrimp*
8. Two Chinese were the first delegates to offer to compromise. *OK*

SECTION 3.2   REVIEW

Practical Application

A. Select the correct or preferred plural noun for each item, and write it on a separate sheet of paper.
  1. Gordon bought over a hundred pounds of (potatos/**potatoes**) to bake for the banquet.
  2. His two (vetos/**vetoes**) were for significant decisions.
  3. The five stranded (**deer**/deers) were airlifted back to dry land.
  4. Jesse wrote one (memoranda/**memorandum**) this morning.
  5. Two new (formula/**formulas**) were developed to treat the weed problem.

B. Indicate whether each of the following nouns is always singular or always plural. Write *AS* to specify *Always Singular* and *AP* to specify *Always Plural.*
  1. news *AS*
  2. scissors *AP*
  3. economics *AS*
  4. aerobics *AS*
  5. slacks *AP*

C. For each noun, write the correct singular or plural form for those incorrectly used. Assume that the verbs in each sentence are correct. Write *OK* if a sentence is correct.
  1. What are the basis for your agreement?
  2. Three passersby stopped to assist the stranded motorist.
  3. As you suggested, we have already notified the two Mrs. Harrises of the good news.
  4. The cost of the new facilitys will exceed $3 million.

5. A recent survey showed several hundreds new computer businesses.
6. If we want the job done correctly, we'll have to do it ourselfs.
7. We tried to call Mr. Kelly several times, but none of the Kellies answered the telephone.
8. The local chamber of commerce prints a list of area church's.
9. Who won—the yea's or the nay's?
10. Since 1990 the Marxes have been trying to buy the last residential lot on the lake.
11. Only 15 CPA's have applied for the position in Germany.
12. Brent traded his two used stereoes for a new CD player.
13. Mr. Adams said that the old benchs in the cafeteria will be replaced with comfortable chairs.
14. Send copies to Messrs. Sharp, Turner, and Vance.
15. Most of my relatives have their own businesses.

D. Rewrite correctly any sentences with errors. Write *OK* for any sentence that is correct. (Note: In Sections 3.2 through 3.10, the last Practical Application reviews some of the principles presented in earlier sections.)
1. Several woman applied for the transfer.
2. Mrs. Nagata suggested that we set the VCR on one of the shelf at the back of the room.
3. He completed the training course successfully.
4. The office thermostat is generally set in the low 70s during the winter months.
5. Myra's new glass's make her look very studious.
6. Bert and Leslie have already spoke with Mr. Wexler about the shipping delays from his company.
7. I have been meaning to speak to her about her unprofessionally appearance.
8. The market price of our stock has risen almost 12 percent in only two weeks.
9. I wish that I could afford to buy you that new CD player, but business is a little slow now.
10. We will offer expanded stock portfolioes for new investors.

Editing Practice

Spelling Alert! Supply the correct plurals in the following paragraph on a separate sheet. (Hint: A *maid* of honor is an unmarried attendant, and a *matron* of honor is a married attendant.)

Kathi and Kati Bolinski, twin daughters of Al and Rita Bolinski, were married in a double ceremony respectively to John Whitmire and Wade Randolph. The brides chose one ceremony instead of two c_____ because they have always had a close relationship. M_____ Natalie and Deidre Bolinski, the brides' sisters, served as m_____ of h_____.

The _____, parents of the brides, entertained at a reception after the wedding. P_____ of both grooms honored the two couples at a dinner-dance after the wedding rehearsal. The couples will reside in adjoining duplex a_____. The adjoining d_____ are on the corner of Washington and Lafayette S_____.

Nouns and Pronouns: Possessive Forms

Write with nouns and verbs, not with adjectives and adverbs. The adjective hasn't been built that can pull a weak or inaccurate noun out of a tight place.

—E. B. White, in *The Elements of Style*

Nouns use the *possessive form* to show ownership. Errors in the use of the possessive forms of nouns and pronouns are common—and very noticeable—in writing, if not always in speaking. There are, however, some easy ways to master the correct usage of possessive nouns and pronouns. Study this section to learn about them.

POSSESSIVE FORMS OF NOUNS

To begin, remember this rule: An apostrophe is *always* used with a noun to show possession. The question is where to place the apostrophe. Let's review some of the specifics of using the apostrophe with nouns.

1. For a noun that does not end in *s*, add an apostrophe plus *s*. This rule applies to *all* nouns, whether they are singular or plural.

   The *man's* jacket and the *woman's* coat are in the locker room.

   The *men's* jackets and the *women's* coats are in the locker room.

2. For a *plural* noun that does end in *s*, add only the apostrophe.

   The *trainees'* day begins at 7:30 a.m.

   Six *months'* time has been allocated for training.

   The *Greens'* newest restaurant will be in South Dakota.

OBJECTIVES:

After completing Section 3.3, you should be able to:

1. Summarize the basic rules of forming the possessives of nouns.
2. Cite examples of correct possessive forms of compound nouns, of nouns showing joint ownership and those showing individual ownership, and of nouns used before gerunds.
3. Explain what to do when a noun that would ordinarily be in the possessive case is followed by an appositive.
4. Discuss the major confusion in using possessive forms of personal pronouns.

MEMORY HOOK

Remember that the possessive word comes *before* the object of possession.

the *manager's* reports (the reports of the manager, the reports belonging to the manager)

the *supervisor's* files (the files of the supervisor, the files belonging to the supervisor)

the *trainees'* day (the day of the trainees)

the *Greens'* newest restaurant (the newest restaurant of the Greens)

one *witness's* testimony (the testimony of one witness)

By separating the ownership words from the objects of ownership, you will be able to apply the rules of possession more easily.

3. For a singular noun ending in *s*, add an apostrophe plus *s* if the possessive form is pronounced with an added syllable.

One *witness's* testimony was especially effective.

My *boss's* recommendation was extremely helpful.

4. For a singular noun ending in *s*, add only the apostrophe if the possessive form is not pronounced with an additional syllable. This rule applies mostly to proper names that would sound awkward with the extra syllable.

Mike *Carothers'* promotion to vice president will be effective October 1. (The pronunciation of *Carothers's* would sound awkward.)

✔ CHECKUP 1

Correct any errors in the use of possessives in the following sentences. Write your corrections on a sheet of paper.

1. The new employees assignments are in their electronic mailboxes.
2. Our sales representatives' computers are leased.
3. One employee's suggestion asked that the company's vacation policy be changed.
4. Eagle Travel, Inc., makes all of our executive's flight reservations.
5. John Riley's stock portfolio has risen dramatically in the year.
6. The actress's own account of Hollywood's glamorous past will appear in Sunday's newspaper.

7. Ann's goal is to expand her father's software business.
8. Chris's latest research examines mens nutritional needs.

POSSESSIVE NOUNS IN SPECIAL CASES

Besides the basic rules of forming the possessives of nouns, there are a few special cases that need your attention. Study the following four discussions.

Compound Nouns

To form the possessive of a compound noun, make the *last word* in the compound possessive. If the last word ends in *s*, add an apostrophe; if the last word in the compound does *not* end in *s*, add an apostrophe plus *s*.

My *sister-in-law's* bid was accepted by the City Planning Department. (The bid belonging to my sister-in-law. *Law* does not end in *s*.)

Kelvin did not win first prize; *someone else's* entry won highest honors. (The entry belonging to someone else. *Else* does not end in *s*.)

Several *vice presidents'* assistants are being considered for the new position. (Assistants of several vice presidents. The last word, *presidents*, does end in *s*.)

Joint Ownership? Separate Ownership?

To show joint ownership (that is, two or more people owning the same thing), add the apostrophe (or the apostrophe plus *s*) to the last part of the compound.

Nancy and Larry's mother is the brains behind the family's graphic design business. (The mother of Nancy and Larry. Note the singular noun *mother* and the singular verb *is*.)

Abe and Frank's doughnut shop is located in Hickory Creek Shopping Plaza. (One shop belonging to both Abe and Frank.)

To indicate *separate ownership*, add the apostrophe (or the apostrophe plus *s*) to each part of the compound.

Erin's and George's mothers are the ones who started this service in 1993. (Here, we are talking about two different people—in other words, Erin's mother and George's mother.)

Lillian's and Dee's accounting firms are two blocks apart. (Lillian's firm and Dee's firm—two firms, each separately owned.)

Before a Gerund

A *gerund* is a verb form that ends in *ing* and is used as a noun. A noun or pronoun used before a gerund must be in the possessive.

KEY POINT

Joint ownership means that two or more owners possess a single thing together. *Separate ownership* means that each owner owns something individually.

Bill's proofreading was instrumental in *our* completing the project on time. *His* proofreading was instrumental in *our* completing the project on time. (Use the possessive *Bill's* or *His*, not *Bill* or *Him*, before the gerund *proofreading*. Use the possessive *our* before the gerund *completing*.)

Dave was unaware of *Martha's* leaving early. Dave was unaware of *her* leaving early. (The possessives *Martha's* and *her* are needed before the gerund *leaving*.)

As Appositives

An *appositive* is a word or a group of words that explains or gives additional information about the word or phrase that comes directly before it. When a noun that would ordinarily be in the possessive is followed by an appositive, the appositive must be in the possessive.

Mr. Ying's office is down the hall. (The office of Mr. Ying.)

Mr. Ying our *bookkeeper's* office is down the hall. (Note that *bookkeeper*, which is the appositive, is made possessive instead of the noun *Mr. Ying*.)

You can avoid this kind of awkward construction in most cases by rewriting the sentence.

The office of Mr. Ying, our bookkeeper, is down the hall.

✓ CHECKUP 2

On a sheet of paper, correct any errors in the use of possessives in the following sentences. Write *OK* if a sentence is correct.

1. Carmine and Rosa were engaged in June; Carmine and Rosa's wedding is now planned for October 8.
2. Deanna and Millie are sure that him helping us gave our company an edge on the competition.
3. Rachel certainly appreciated you sending us the order promptly.
4. I am sure that Donna's early response to the ad was a factor in her getting the job.
5. Shirley and Joe's oldest son graduates from community college in May.
6. Writing the letter was someone else's suggestion, not Rob's.
7. You know, of course, that the two supervisor's reports will be evaluated.
8. Marcus was glad to hear about us working together to complete the project.

POSSESSIVE FORMS OF PERSONAL PRONOUNS

You have seen that possessive forms of nouns *always* have apostrophes. Personal pronouns (*I, you, he, she, it, we, you, they*) become possessive either by adding just an *s* (as in *its*) or by changing their spelling. In the following list, notice that possessive forms of personal pronouns *never* have apostrophes.

KEY POINT

Do not use apostrophes with possessive forms of personal pronouns.

Personal Pronouns

Nominative Forms	Possessive Forms	
I	my	mine
you	your	yours
he	his	his
she	her	hers
it	its	its
we	our	ours
you	your	yours
they	their	theirs

Now study the following examples to see the correct uses of these pronoun forms.

Sarah asked *her* assistant to finish the interview.

The first vacancy is *ours*; the second one is *theirs*.

Please lend me *your* laptop computer; *mine* is at home.

Note that none of the above possessive pronouns has an apostrophe.

POSSESSIVE PRONOUNS IN SPECIAL CASES

The possessive forms discussed above are, unfortunately, easily confused with other similar words, which are compared below.

Its, It's

The possessive pronoun *its* (without the apostrophe) means "belonging to it" or "of it." *Its* is easily confused with the contraction *it's* (with the apostrophe), which means "it is." Use the contraction *it's* only when you mean "it is."

My new computer was expensive, but *its* speed is unbelievable. (Possessive pronoun *its*.)

Of course, *it's* thrilling to know that my students are getting good jobs. (*It is thrilling . . . .*)

Its estimated that 25,000 deaths and injuries would be prevented each year if all drivers and passengers always wore their seat belts.

Their, There, They're

Their, there, and *they're* are indeed pronounced alike. But *their* is the possessive of the pronoun *they,* meaning "belonging to them" while *there* (notice the word *here* within *there*) identifies a place. *They're* is a contraction; it means "they are."

> Holly and Fred said that *they're* eager to begin *their* vacation. (They are eager; vacation "belonging to them.")

> If we leave at 7 a.m., we should arrive *there* by noon. (*There* is an adverb that identifies a place; it answers the question Where? *There.*)

Theirs, There's

The pronoun *theirs* and the contraction *there's* are pronounced the same. However, *there's* means "there is" or "there has," and *theirs* means "belonging to them."

> The first ticket is reserved for Amelia; these three tickets are *theirs.* (Tickets "belonging to them.")

> *There's* the book we've been wanting! (*There is* the book . . . .)

Your, You're

The possessive pronoun *your* means "belonging to you," and the contraction *you're* means "you are."

> Leave *your* computer turned on if *you're* coming back soon. (Computer "belonging to you"; if *you are* coming back soon.)

Whose responsible for finding out who owns the property?

Our, Are

Actually, *our* and *are* should *not* sound alike when they are pronounced correctly. However, some people do pronounce *our* as if it were *are.* Thus errors in using *our* and *are* may be more common in speaking than in writing.

> *Our* tour director and *our* guide *are* planning a special dinner on *our* last night in Egypt.

Whose, Who's

Whose, the possessive form of the relative pronoun *who,* should not be confused with the contraction *who's,* which means "who is" or "who has."

> Do you know *whose* desk lamp this is? (Desk lamp "belonging to whom?")

> Do you know *who's* in charge of office furnishing? (*Who is* in charge . . . ?)

On a separate sheet of paper, correct any errors in the following sentences. Write *OK* if a sentence has no error.

1. The camper near the lake is ours; the camper near the trees is ~~there's.~~ *Theirs*

2. We will purchase the airline tickets when we know ~~whose~~ *who's* planning to travel to our plant in Mexico.

3. Norris will be ~~they're~~ *There* to introduce the speaker.

4. ~~Whose~~ *who's* on first shift tomorrow, Alan or Danny?

5. As Mr. Sinclaire emphasized, ~~theirs~~ *There's* one key to success: hard work.

6. Most of us prefer the red package because ~~its~~ *It's* so much brighter than the other choices.

7. Please call me when you're ready to discuss the proposed budget.

8. Although it is expensive and time-consuming, ~~its~~ *It's* certainly worthwhile to get a second opinion when surgery is recommended.

SECTION 3.3   REVIEW

Practical Application

A. On a separate sheet of paper, correct any errors in the following sentences. Write *OK* for any sentence that is correct.

1. Rex Clark's and Dina Poleto's boutique is one of the most successful in the resort area.
2. Let me know if your more interested in a home in the city or the suburbs.
3. Each paralegal's research was scrutinized.
4. Between you and me, the suggestion that I thought best was your's.
5. When James and I heard about the two weeks' delay in the electronics shipment, we checked for a quicker source.
6. Management agreed with him rejecting the defective computer chips.
7. Our computer desks are adjustable, and their easy to assemble.

8. The mens' department that sells expensive sports clothes is on the fifth floor.
9. Marty's and Andy's boss's are both graduates of Harvard.
10. Do you know whose in charge of the fund-raising event?

B. Correct any errors in the following sentences on a separate sheet of paper. Write *OK* if a sentence is correct.
1. Are you aware that they're both CEOs?
2. Please check in someone elses office for a blank diskette.
3. The results must be conclusive before tomorrows board meeting.
4. We reviewed all the analysis that were completed.
5. Everyone who saw Jill Carters résumé agreed that her credentials are certainly impressive.
6. Claudia requested about two dozens more parking passes for the Olympic trials.
7. To celebrate their continued superior sales, both Mr. Cleavers will receive a special ten-year award at the banquet.
8. There's few Andrew Lloyd Webbers writing musicals today.
9. Good childrens' roles in the theater are hard to find.
10. We are certain that the new musical will close in about six weeks time.
11. Karl, remember to dot your *i*'s and mind you're *p*'s and *q*'s.
12. Our seamstress's sewing machine does special design work using a computer.
13. Although Melani hasn't missed work, shes had a cold for the last two weeks.
14. Mickey's rewriting the lyrics helped us sell the song.
15. Him rewriting the lyrics took only three days.

Editing Practice

Call an Editor! Read the following excerpt. Then make any corrections necessary on a sheet of paper.

Cecil and I had spoke with Dr. Ray O'Mally about him conducting classes for our executives' on our new computer software. Dr. O'Mally and his wife are experts in information processing and have written several articles on this topic. Copys of there articles can be accessed on our computer network.

There's several dates in June available for the classes. Classes will be offered from 6:30 to 9:30 p.m. for five consecutive weeks on either Monday or Thursday nights. Both O'Mally's will be present for all sessions.

PRONOUNS: NOMINATIVE AND OBJECTIVE FORMS

A pronoun is a noun that lost its amateur status.

—Bill Watterson, cartoonist and creator of *Calvin and Hobbes*

W hen asked to identify the most important skills they seek in job applicants, most business executives put communication skills at the very top of the list. Indeed, when speaking or writing, workers are communicating their abilities to do their jobs well. To convince your colleagues of *your* ability to communicate well, you must be able to use the correct forms of nominative and objective pronouns and of pronouns ending in *self* in a number of different contexts.

OBJECTIVES:
After completing Section 3.4, you should be able to:

1. Describe the two uses of nominative pronouns.
2. List three ways in which objective pronouns are used.
3. Discuss special problems in selecting the correct case form of pronouns and tell how to solve these problems.
4. Explain the intensive use and the reflexive use of pronouns ending in *self*.

NOMINATIVE AND OBJECTIVE PRONOUN CASES

The term *case* refers to the form of a pronoun. There are three cases, or forms, of pronouns—possessive, nominative, and objective. The case of a pronoun shows how it relates to other words in a sentence.

In Section 3.3, you studied the possessive forms of pronouns. In this section, you will learn about the other two forms of pronouns—the *nominative* and the *objective* cases—and about pronouns ending with *self*. Study the forms of nominative and objective pronouns in the following tables.

Nominative Case		Objective Case	
Singular	**Plural**	**Singular**	**Plural**
I	we	me	us
you	you	you	you
he		him	
she	they	her	them
it		it	
who	who	whom	whom
whoever	whoever	whomever	whomever

Nominative-Case Pronouns

Learn these two rules for using nominative pronouns correctly.

Subject of a Verb. *Rule 1:* When a pronoun is the subject of a verb, the pronoun must be in the nominative case.

KEY POINT

Use nominative pronouns as subjects of verbs or as complements of being verbs.

To remember the exception rule about the infinitive *to be*, make this connection:

> *No* subject—*Nom*inative case

Let the *no* in the word *nominative* remind you to choose the nominative pronoun when there is *no* subject before the infinitive *to be*.

I have reviewed the income statement carefully. "(*I* [nominative case, singular] have reviewed," not "*me* [objective case, singular] have reviewed.")

She and Ricardo will speak at the luncheon. (*She*, [nominative case, singular] not *her* [objective case, singular].)

Who is the director of sales and marketing? (*Who* [relative pronoun in the nominative case] is the subject of the verb *is*.)

Complement of a *Being* Verb. *Rule 2:* The *being* verbs are the forms of the verb *to be*— *am, is, are, was,* and *were* and also *be, being,* and *been* used with helping verbs. A pronoun that completes the meaning of a being verb must be in the nominative case.

Perhaps it was (*they? them?*) who sent us these samples. (*Was* is a being verb, and the pronoun that follows it must complement the being verb. Therefore, the pronoun must be the nominative *they*.)

It must have been (*he? him?*) in the photo. (The nominative *he* is correct after the being verb must have been.)

Exception: One being verb has an exception—the infinitive *to be*. Do not use the nominative-case pronoun as the complement when *to be* is preceded immediately by a noun or a pronoun. Instead, use the objective case.

When she first answered the telephone, Olivia thought Jerry to be (*I? me?*). (Is there a noun or a pronoun immediately before the infinitive *to be*? Yes, *Jerry*. Therefore, do not use the nominative case—the answer is *me*. The exception rule applies.)

The patients appeared to be (*they? them?*). (Is there a noun or a pronoun immediately before the infinitive *to be*? No, there isn't. Therefore, choose the nominative form *they*. The exception rule does not apply.)

✓ CHECKUP 1

On a separate sheet of paper, correct any errors in the use of pronouns in the following sentences. Write *OK* if a sentence is correct.

1. Most of us agree that the candidate should be he.

2. Rescue squad members had suggested that the captain should be her.

3. When Ms. Bennet answered the telephone, she thought him to be I.

4. When a telephone caller asks for you by name, the correct response is "This is she" or "This is he."

5. If you were me, would you have objected to the testimony?

Objective-Case Pronouns

Use the objective-case pronoun forms *me, us, him, her, them,* and *whom* when the pronouns are *objects* of verbs (direct objects or indirect objects), of prepositions, or of infinitives. As you will learn in Section 3.5, an *object* is a person or thing that receives the action of a verb.

> The company tested *me* this morning. (*Me* is the direct object of the verb *tested*. It describes who is directly affected by the testing.)
>
> Gail had already given the photograph to *us*, so we made an extra print for *him*. (*Us* and *him* are objects of the prepositions *to* and *for*, respectively. *Us* and *him* are indirect objects—persons or things indirectly affected by the action.)
>
> To *whom* did Elaine send an Express Mail package today? (*Whom* is the object of the preposition *to*.)
>
> Mildred plans to call *them* this afternoon. (*Them* is the object of the infinitive *to call*.)
>
> Bob threw *him* the pillow. (*Him* is the indirect object of the verb *threw; pillow* is the direct object.)

Use the objective-case pronoun forms for *subjects* of infinitives:

> Lisbeth wants *us* to fly to Oregon in April or May. (*Us* is the subject of the infinitive *to fly*.)

Also, as you learned in the exception on page 100, use the objective-case pronoun following the infinitive *to be* whenever *to be* has a noun or a pronoun immediately before it.

> Greg mistook the candidates to be *us*. (The noun *candidates* precedes the infinitive *to be*; the objective *us* is correct.)

Special Problems of Pronoun Usage

In certain situations, selecting the correct case form of pronouns may be confusing. The following discussion will help you in such situations.

Who, Whom; Whoever, Whomever. You have already learned that the pronouns *who* and *whoever* are in the nominative case, and the pronouns *whom* and *whomever* are in the objective case. You also know that we use the nominative case (*who* and *whoever*) for subjects of verbs and for complements of being verbs. Use the objective case (*whom* and *whomever*) as you would use other objective forms—that is, for objects of verbs (direct objects and indirect objects) and for objects of

KEY POINT

Use objective pronouns as objects of verbs, prepositions, or infinitives; as subjects of infinitives; and as complements with the infinitive *to be*.

MEMORY HOOK

You know that *him* is in the objective case. Let the *m* in *him* remind you of the *m* in *whom* and in *whomever*, which are also in the objective case. You may even substitute *him* to test whether the objective case is correct.

> The doctor (*who? whom?*) Ed Billingsly recommended is Dr. Richard Bromberg. (Make this substitution: "Ed Billingsly recommended him." Because the objective case *him* is correct, the choice must be *whom*.)

> Patricia doesn't know (*who? whom?*) the director has selected. (Make this substitution: "the director has selected *him*." The correct choice, therefore, is *whom*.)

> We do not know (*who? whom?*) Dale Byrd is. (Make this substitution: "Dale Byrd is (*he*)." Because the nominative *he* can be substituted, the correct answer is *who*.)

prepositions. Still, many people have trouble with these pronouns—usually because of complications in context. Use the preceding Memory Hook to help you decide which pronoun case to use.

In Interrogative Sentences. Questions are generally worded in inverted order, that is, the subject comes after the verb. Therefore, in applying the Memory Hook test from this page to questions, change the sentence to normal order before substituting *he* or *him*.

> (*Who? Whom?*) is the doctor Ed Billingsly recommended? (Normal order: "The doctor Ed Billingsly recommended is *he*." A pronoun in the nominative case is correct because the pronoun follows a being verb. *Who*, then, is correct because it is in the nominative case and complements the being verb *is*.)

> (*Who? Whom?*) has the manager chosen? (Normal order: "The manager has chosen *him*." *Whom*, the objective case, is correct because *him* can be substituted and *him* is in the objective case.)

Of course, if the question is in normal order, simply substitute *he* or *him*.

In Clauses. When *who* or *whom* (or *whoever* or *whomever*) is used in a dependent clause within a sentence, you must (1) separate that clause from the rest of the sentence, (2) determine if the clause is in normal word order, and (3) proceed to substitute *he* or *him*.

1. Separate the clause, which *always* begins with the word *who, whom, whoever,* or *whomever*.

   We do not know (*who? whom?*) the caller could have been. (Separate the dependent clause from the rest of the sentence: "*who? whom?* the caller could have been.")

"To who it may concern ...."

Share this piece of information with (*whoever? whomever?*) you worked with on the Haggerty account. (Separate the clause: "*whoever? whomever?* you worked with on the Haggerty account.")

2. Change the inverted clause to normal order.

. . . (*who? whom?*) the caller could have been (Normal order: "the caller could have been *who? whom?*")

. . . (*whoever? whomever?*) you worked with on the Haggerty account (Normal order: "you worked with *whoever? whomever?* on the Haggerty account.")

3. Substitute *he* or *she* or *him* or *her* in each clause.

. . . the caller could have been *he* (Remember that a nominative form must be used to complete a being verb; thus *he* and *who* are correct.)

. . . you worked with *him* on the Haggerty account (*Him*, objective case, is correct, because *him* is the object of the preposition *with*. There-fore, *whomever* is correct.)

Note: Interrupters such as *I think, she says, you know,* and *we believe* should be omitted when selecting *who* or *whom* in clauses.

The supervisor (*who? whom?*) I believe we should hire is Celeste Harrill. (Separate the clause: "*who? whom?* I believe we should hire." Omit the interrupting words *I believe* and put the clause in normal order: "we should hire *her*." *Whom*, objective case, is correct because *her*, objective case, can be substituted.)

✔

On a separate sheet of paper, write the correct form of the pronoun in parentheses for each of the following sentences.

1. Peter Paterno, (who? whom?) we consider the best sales repre-sentative in our region, will lead the sales conference.

2. (Whoever? Whomever?) wrote the software manual did a terrific job.

3. We asked Jeanne, (who? whom?) has much experience in per-sonnel matters, for her recommendations.

4. Perhaps the person (who? whom?) you saw at the reception was Josh Williams.

5. McPherson is the designer (who? whom?) should be assigned to the project.

6. The lifeguard can reprimand (whoever? whomever?) does not observe the safety regulations.

On a separate sheet of paper, correct any errors in the following sen-tences. Write *OK* if the sentence is correct.

7. Do you know whom we should ask for a demonstration of the new color printer? who OK

8. No, I do not know whom ~~who~~ *ok* Vera asked for permission to borrow a company van.

9. Please give a carpet sample to whomever *whoever* asks for a one.

10. Please send a brochure to whomever you want. *ok whomever* *or*

Pronouns in Compound Subjects or Compound Objects. Compound subjects and compound objects are nouns and pronouns joined by *and* or *or*. When the pronoun is part of a subject, use the nominative case. When the pronoun is part of an object, use the objective case.

Nominative Case in Subjects	Objective Case in Objects
Ron and *I* want	for Ron and *me*
Mr. Rogers and *he* asked	asked Mr. Rogers and *him*
She and *I* will write	written by *her* and *me*
They and *we* agree	agree with *them* and *us*

Pronoun Phrases. When you are faced with a pronoun choice in phrases such as *we supervisors* and *us supervisors,* simply omit the noun following the pronoun and test the sentence with the pronoun choices.

(*We? Us?*) employees met with the insurance agent to discuss the supplementary policy. (Omit the word *employees*; then say "*We* met with . . ." and "*Us* met with . . ." Which pronoun would you choose? The nominative *we*, of course!)

Pronouns With *Than* or *As*. Another pronoun problem arises in sentences such as "Ted has more overtime hours than (*I? me?*)" and "The new policy affects Darlene as much as (*I? me?*)." When the word *than* or *as* is used in such comparisons, it generally represents an incomplete clause. By completing the clause, you will make your choice easy.

Ted has more overtime hours than I *have overtime hours*. (By completing the clause, you can see that *I* is the subject in the dependent clause. Subjects must be in the nominative case; me is in the objective case. Therefore, *I* is the correct choice.)

MEMORY HOOK

To simplify choosing the right pronoun in compounds, omit everything in the compound except the pronoun. Then say the sentence aloud, and the correct answer will be obvious.

Lynn Westin and (*I? me?*) leave for Mexico City on Monday. (When you omit the words *Lynn Westin and,* the answer becomes clear: "*I* leave . . ." not "*me* leave.")

Mitchell sent copies to Mr. Norton and (*I? me?*). (Omit the words *Mr. Norton and,* and the answer becomes obvious: "sent copies to . . . *me*.")

This new policy affects Darlene as much as *this new policy affects* me. (The missing words are *this new policy affects*, which were deliberately omitted in the original sentence because they are repetitive and because the sentence makes perfect sense without them. By completing the dependent clause, you will be able to make the correct pronoun choice.)

Pronouns as Appositives. As you learned in Section 3.2, an *appositive* is a word or a group of words used to explain or give more information about a preceding word or phrase. Note the appositives in italics in the following sentences.

Carole Wriston, the *principal owner of the condominium project,* elaborated on the storm damage in a television interview today. Her accountant, a *specialist in damage recovery,* commented on Ms. Wriston's statement afterward. (The appositives—the words in italics—help give additional information about *Carole Wriston* and *Her accountant,* the words that precede each of the appositives.)

A minor problem arises when choosing pronoun case in appositives such as these:

Two staunch supporters of the athletic program, Vance Olsen and (*she? her?*), explained their reasons for increasing the athletic budget.

We signed for the packages and gave them to the co-owners, Pam Marcelli and (*she? her?*).

In such instances, follow the instructions of the Memory Hook that follows.

MEMORY HOOK

To choose pronouns in the preceding examples, (1) omit the words that the appositive renames and then (2) omit the other words in the compound—that is, *use only the pronoun.*

1. Omit the words that the appositive renames:

   ...Vance Olsen and (*she? her?*) explained their reasons for increasing the athletic budget.

   We signed for the packages and gave them to ...Pam Marcelli and (*she? her?*).

2. Omit the other words in the compound appositive—that is, use only the pronoun:

   ...(*she? her?*) explained their reasons clearly. (Since you would not say "*her* explained," *she* is the correct pronoun.)

   We signed for the packages and gave them to ...(*she? her?*). (You would not say "delivered them to *she.*" The correct pronoun is *her.*)

On a separate sheet of paper, correct any errors in the use of pronouns. Write *OK* for any sentence that is correct.

1. Only Karen Rybnicek or him has the authority to grant a leave of absence.
2. Among the contributors to the blood bank were our two new interns—Pablo and she.
3. Alice assumed that none of we nurses wants to adopt the rotating shift scheduling plan.
4. The reprimands were sent to we three employees.
5. New procedures mandate that employees are to ask Dr. Graystone or I to approve travel reimbursements.
6. Most of the third shift associates voted for Gene and he.
7. Did you notice that most of the applicants were not as well prepared as her?
8. Two of our key personnel, Kevin and her, leave for the Germany tomorrow.
9. Between you and me, I know that Rochelle Rodriques will become divisional manager when Phillip Evans is transferred.
10. Jamira is certainly a more effective speaker than me.
11. Rosa asked we secretaries our opinions on the new voice-mail system.
12. As you can see, Corey keys much more quickly and accurately than she.

PRONOUNS ENDING IN *SELF*

The pronouns ending in *self* (*myself, yourself, himself, herself, itself, ourselves, yourselves,* and *themselves*) are called *intensive pronouns* and serve two functions: (1) to *emphasize* or *intensify* the use of a noun or another pronoun already expressed in the same sentence or (2) to *refer* to a noun or pronoun that has already been named in the same sentence (called *reflexive use*).

Intensive Use

Note how pronouns ending in *self* provide emphasis in these statements:

> Lucy *herself* announced the merger plans. (Much more emphatic than *Lucy announced the merger plans.*)

The manager asked Joseph *himself* to write the commercial script. (Much more emphatic than *The manager asked Joseph to write the commercial script.*)

Reflexive Use

Pronouns that end in *self* refer to a noun or a pronoun that has already been named elsewhere in the sentence.

The owners paid *themselves* a cash bonus. (*Themselves* clearly refers to *owners*.)

Joyce distributed all the copies but forgot to keep one for *herself*. (*Herself* clearly refers to *Joyce*.)

Common Errors

A pronoun that ends in *self* must have a *clear* antecedent within the sentence. An *antecedent* is a noun or a noun phrase that is referred to by the pronoun. Furthermore, the pronoun must be positioned correctly in the sentence. Note these examples of common errors:

Robert Montief and *myself* developed the strategy. (To whom does *myself* refer? It has no antecedent in this sentence. Instead, the sentence should be "Robert Montief and I developed . . . .")

When we asked the painter for his advice, he said that he prefers spray painting *himself*. (We know that the man does not want to spray paint *on* himself! Instead, the sentence should be ". . . he said that he *himself* prefers spray painting." The position of the pronoun ending in *self* must be correct.)

 **CHECKUP 4**

On a separate sheet of paper, correct any pronoun errors in the following sentences. Write *OK* if a sentence is correct.

1. Mr. Taylor specifically said that he wants to wax himself the car.

2. When they reviewed the magazine subscription list, they decided to cancel themselves most of them.

3. The president herself will talk to the staff about the new safety regulations.

4. The felon himself pleaded for mercy.

5. When Judith and myself volunteered to help, we did not realize how time-consuming the project would be.

6. As Scott and himself said, "Physical exercise stimulates the brain."

7. Bill and myself will start taking inventory Friday after work.

Practical Application

A. On a separate sheet of paper, correct any pronoun errors in the following sentences.
   1. The home office gave the award to the two top producers, he and she.
   2. She completed the contracts and delivered them to the Branleys and her.
   3. If our loan is approved, Danielle and myself will definitely buy the home health service company on Oak Street.
   4. Tim himself will be directing the advertising campaign.
   5. In threatening situations, the sheriff said that he preferred handcuffing himself first and asking questions later.
   6. Both of us thought the actor on the stage to be he.
   7. Whom in your opinion will be selected for advanced training?
   8. The Kelseys are the only ones whom I believe do not rent their mountain cabin.
   9. Us fire fighters were trapped temporarily on the second floor of the burning building.
   10. Are Gary and her going to the company dinner tonight?
   11. Steven cannot handle the pressure as well as she.
   12. Mrs. Mellinger's new assistants, whomever they may be, must begin working at least one day each weekend.
   13. Jeff Todaro is more resourceful than her?
   14. Two of the lawyers, Sheila and him, asked to be excused from the case because they knew the defendant.
   15. The manager gave Tom and myself the week off.

B. On a separate sheet of paper, correct any errors in the following sentences. Write *OK* if a sentence is correct.
   1. Yesterday Ms. Singh asked Joan and I to watch the bicycle race from her office window.
   2. Ask Mr. Freeman if he knows whose in charge of the reception arrangements.
   3. Luke Stevens, whom I know is a registered nurse, can help you.
   4. He and me studied nursing together at the community college.
   5. The two Marylou's were our supervisors at Memorial Medical Center.
   6. One of Andreas first patients was a well-known news broadcaster.
   7. In fact, he gave her a couple of autographed photoes.
   8. With fewer companys paying for their employee's health insurance, a serious crisis in health care is imminent.
   9. I myself think its time we found a way to help the homeless.
   10. Theirs nothing you can do but work harder.

Editing Practice

Plurals, Possessives, and Pronoun Usage. On a separate sheet of paper, rewrite the following paragraphs correcting errors in plurals, possessives, and pronoun usage.

As I am sure you know, our competitors are eager to compete with us for the Wolfe account. John and myself have begun the proposal process by reviewing the video's of there most recent advertising campaign. Here's the three areas of emphasis for selling their playroom equipment: safety, exercise, and cost.

This six month's project should incorporate your most creative thoughts. The president has issued herself a special incentive. If we get the Wolfe account, us, the advertising campaign staff, will get an extra weeks' vacation with pay.

Kaitlyn and Scot Wolfe want to work with our company. However, the Wolfes' are looking for the best advertising campaign available. Obviously, they will be spending much money on the campaign selected. You and me must give this project our best effort.

VERBS

Language is a part of our organism and no less complicated than it.

—Ludwig Wittgenstein, Austrian philosopher

Among the most serious and the most common errors we make as we speak and write are verb tense errors. Yet forming most verbs correctly is very easy, because most verbs follow one simple pattern, as you will see in the first half of this section. The verbs that do not follow this regular pattern are the ones that cause problems; these irregular verbs are discussed in depth in the second part of this section.

IDENTIFYING VERBS

As you read in Section 3.1, a *verb* is a word that describes an action, a condition, or a state of being. The verb in a sentence is referred to as a predicate. The following examples illustrate action verbs and two types of linking verbs.

OBJECTIVES:

After completing Section 3.5, you should be able to:

1. List and provide examples of the four principal parts of a verb.
2. Explain what makes most English verbs regular rather than irregular verbs.
3. Define the term *verb tense* and identify the six most commonly used verb tenses.
4. Discuss the differences between being verbs and transitive and intransitive verbs.

KEY POINT

Verbs may describe an action, a condition, or a state of being.

Action

In the following sentences, the verbs *supported, arrived, will write, is preparing*, and *will be competing* all describe actions.

Mark *supported* the proposal.

The UPS package *arrived* promptly at 8:30 a.m.

They *will write* all of the people who complained about the service interruption.

Mr. Marlowe *is preparing* the money order now.

Mrs. Santos *will be competing* in the upcoming marathon.

Condition

The verbs *seems, felt, became, appears*, and *grew* in the following examples all describe conditions.

Beth *seems* excited about her new job.

Gilbert and Fred *felt* better after the fumes dissipated.

Most of the trainees *became* fidgety during the explanation of benefits.

Ms. Cameron *appears* to be an excellent counselor.

Mr. Madison *grew* hungry before his medical tests were completed.

Being

The verbs *is, are, am, will be*, and *was* do not describe actions or conditions in the following sentences, yet each is a verb. These verbs are "being" verbs.

Lindsay *is* happy with the telecommunications system.

Joy and Bob *are* home from their trip to England and Scotland.

I *am* eager to begin working in my new position.

Ms. Wexler *will be* a likely nominee for employee of the month.

Mr. Nance *was* exhausted after his business trip to China.

Practice identifying verbs correctly—that's the first step in using verbs correctly.

✓ CHECKUP 1

Identify the verbs in the following sentences.

1. The assistant manager (has accepted) Jane's resignation.
2. Ben (seemed) convinced of her innocence.
3. Juan (was) in Memphis when the merger (was announced).
4. Barbara (invited) Marcia Berg to speak at the conference.

5. Both real estate agents (want) the corner property for their clients.

6. Laura and Will (are at) the airport to meet his flight.

REGULAR VERBS

As we speak and write, the verbs we use indicate the time of the action, the condition, or the state of being. We select a verb form to indicate the time when the action occurred: present time ("I laugh," "I am laughing"); a past time ("I laughed," "I have laughed," "I had laughed," "I was laughing"); or a future time ("I will laugh," "I will be laughing"). This time element for a verb is called its *tense*. Fortunately, most verbs in English follow the same simple pattern to indicate time. These verbs are *regular* verbs.

Principal Parts of Regular Verbs

Knowing how to form the principal parts of verbs is necessary if you are to use verbs correctly in communications. All verb tenses are formed from the principal parts of a verb. These parts are (1) the present tense form, (2) the past tense form, (3) the past participle, and (4) the present participle.

KEY POINT

The principal parts of a verb are the present tense, the past tense, the past participle, and the present participle.

MEMORY HOOK

How can you distinguish between the past tense form *called* and the past participle *called*? Answer: You cannot, except by seeing the word *in context* (how it is used in the sentence). *Remember:* A past tense form *never* has a helper (a helping verb); a past participle *always* has a helping verb *(have, has, had, shall have,* or *will have).*

Luke *called* us at 10 p.m. (Here, *called* is a past tense form; it has no helping verb.)

Wendy came at 11 p.m. to tell us about the meeting, but Luke *had called* us at 10 p.m. (Here, *called* is a past participle. When *called* is used with the helping verb *had,* the combination forms a tense called the *past perfect.* Together *had called* is a verb phrase or simple predicate and *called* is its main verb.)

PRINCIPAL PARTS OF REGULAR VERBS

Present Tense	Past Tense	Past Participle	Present Participle
move	moved	moved	moving
prepare	prepared	prepared	preparing
hire	hired	hired	hiring
call	called	called	calling
enter	entered	entered	entering
listen	listened	listened	listening
study	studied	studied	studying

Look at the table "Principal Parts of Regular Verbs" above. As you read this table, say to yourself "I move," "I prepare," and so on. Then notice that the past tense is formed simply by adding *d* to verbs that end in *e*. For verbs that do not end in *e*, add *ed: called, entered, listened.* For some verbs ending in *y*, change the *y* to *i* before adding *ed*.

Further simplifying this pattern for regular verbs is the fact that the past participle is the same form as the past tense. And the present participle is formed by adding *ing* to the present tense form. Note that for verbs ending in *e*, you must drop the *e* before adding *ing: moving, preparing, hiring.* Except for a limited list, all the verbs in English follow this pattern.

✔ CHECKUP 2

On a separate sheet of paper, copy the following chart. Then fill in the missing parts correctly for each entry.

Present Tense	Past Tense	Past Participle	Present Participle
1. paint	painted	painted	*Painting*
2. carry	carried	*Carried*	carrying
3. type	typed	*typed*	typing
4. answer	*answered*	answered	answering
5. bake	baked	baked	*baking*
6. mark	marked	*marked*	marking
7. marry	married	married	*marrying*
8. trust	trusted	*trusted*	trusting
9. use	used	used	*using*
10. walk	*walked*	walked	walking

KEY POINT

The last verb in the verb phrase is always the main verb.

Verb Phrases

As you read in Section 3.1, a *verb phrase* consists of the main verb and any helping verbs used together to function *as one verb*. A verb phrase may also contain an interrupting adverb. The main verb in the phrase is *always* the last verb. The other verbs are the *helping*, or *auxiliary*, verbs. Read the following examples carefully.

    can *move*   did *prepare*   will *hire*

The main verbs in the preceding three examples are *move, prepare,* and *hire.* The verbs *can, did,* and *will* are helping verbs. Note that *move, prepare,* and *hire* are the present tense forms listed in the table on page 112.

    has been *moved*   have *prepared*   will soon be *hired*

The main verbs are *moved, prepared,* and *hired,* which are the past participles listed in the third column in the table on page 112. The verbs *has been, have,* and *will be* are helping verbs. The word *soon* is an interrupting adverb.

    are *moving*   is *preparing*   will be *hiring*

Again, the last word in each phrase is the main verb: *moving, preparing,* and *hiring.* These are the present participles listed in the table on page 112. The words *are, is,* and *will be* are helping verbs.

Now note how verb phrases generally are used in sentences. Remember that the verb phrase can be interrupted by another word, most often an adverb.

> Kim *will be moving* into his new home next Friday. (The verb phrase is *will be moving;* the main verb is the last verb, *moving.*)

> Julie *has* also *been preparing* her portfolio. (The verb phrase *has been preparing* is interrupted by the adverb *also.* The main verb is *preparing.*)

> Our new vice president *has* already *been hired.* (*Hired* is the main verb in the phrase *has been hired. Already* is an adverb.)

In questions, the verb phrase is often more difficult to identify, because, as you have learned, the sentence order is inverted. Finding the verb phrase in inverted sentences is easier if you change the sentence to normal order first.

> When *did* Ms. Hua *purchase* new cellular telephones? (The verb phrase is *did purchase.*)

> *Have* Scott and Rhonda already *been accessing* the Internet? (The verb phrase *have been accessing* is tricky to identify because of the inverted order and the interrupting adverb *already.*)

✔ CHECKUP 3

Identify the verb phrases in each of the following sentences. For each phrase, write the main verb on a separate sheet of paper.

  1. Does Anne want to speak to the judge?

  2. Ahmed and Jim have already received the report.

  3. Greg and Cheryl have been waiting two years for this business opportunity.

4. Does William really (need another) copy) of these specifications?
5. Jonathan (will be)inspecting) all the elevators tomorrow morning.
6. Benita (can complete) this audit by Friday.
7. The actors (will enter) the theater through the stage door.
8. Janet (will introduce) the speaker.
9. Ms. Van Gilder (has been drafting) her will.
10. Lisa (has been promoted) to head nurse.

Verb Tenses

As we saw earlier in this section, the tense of a verb is the form that tells when the action did or will occur.

Present Tense.   Remember that terms such as *to spend, to run, to sell, to listen,* and *to call,* are *infinitives*. Omit the word *to* from these forms to create the present tense forms:

I call	we call
you call	you call
he	
she } calls	they call
it	

As you see, there are only two present tense forms, *call* and *calls*. Use *call* with *I, you, we,* and *they*. Add *s—calls*—to create the present tense of the verb form used with *he, she,* and *it* and with singular nouns.

We *call* every morning. (*Call* with the pronoun *we*.)

She *calls* every morning. Brad *calls* every morning. (*Calls* with the pronoun *he* and the singular noun *Brad*.)

They *enjoy* traveling. (*Enjoy* with the pronoun *they*.)

She *enjoys* traveling. Janie *enjoys* traveling. (*Enjoys* with the pronoun *she* and the singular noun *Janie*.)

The present tense is used to show action that is happening now. It is also used to indicate that something is always true (as in, "the sun *rises* in the east").

Past Tense.   The past tense is formed by adding *ed* to the present tense form (or *d* if the present tense form already ends in *e*).

I called	we called
you called	you called
he	
she } called	they called
it	

As you see, there is only one past tense form for a verb. (The only exception is the verb *to be*, which will be discussed later.) The past tense is used to indicate action that has already been completed.

KEY POINT

Regular third person singular verbs always end in *s*.

Future Tense. To form the future tense of a verb, use *will* or *shall* plus the infinitive form without the word *to*. In ordinary situations, use *will* to form the future tense. In formal situations, use *shall* to form the future tense for the first person (*I, we*).

I shall call	we shall call
you will call	you will call
he	
she } will call	they will call
it	

The future tense indicates action that is to take place in the future.

Each of the three tenses (present, past, and future) has a correlated *perfect* tense. As you read the discussion on these three perfect tenses, you will realize that they are very commonly used in our everyday conversation and our everyday writing.

Present Perfect Tense. The *present perfect tense* is used to show that an action began in the past and that it may still be occurring. This tense is formed by using the helping verb *has* or *have* with a past participle.

KEY POINT

All perfect tenses are formed with a helping verb and the past participle.

> Ruth *has redecorated* the first floor of the house. (Present perfect tense for an action that was begun in the past.)

> Jimenez and Alexander *have debated* the issue for at least ten years. (Present perfect tense for an action that began in the past and may be still continuing in the present.)

Past Perfect Tense. The *past perfect tense* is used to show which of two *past* actions occurred first. To form the past perfect tense, use *had* plus the past participle of a verb.

> Olivia *had signed* the agreement before she *received* the advice from her attorney. (The verbs *had signed* and *received* show *two* past actions. The past perfect tense *had signed* tells us that that action is the *first* past one. After that action was completed, a second action occurred—Olivia *received* something. *Received* is in the past tense to show that this action occurred second.)

Future Perfect Tense. The *future perfect tense* shows that an action will be completed by some specific time in the future. The action may have already begun, or it may begin in the future. The important point is that it will *end* by a specific future time. To form the future perfect tense, use the verb *will have* or *shall have* plus the past participle of a verb.

> The landscape artist *will have completed* her sketches long before the architect finishes his. (*Will have completed* is a future perfect tense verb describing an action that will end by some specific time—*long before the architect finishes his*—in the future.)

The Progressive Tenses. Closely related to the six tenses just discussed (present, past, future, present perfect, past perfect, and future perfect) are the *progressive tenses,* which depict actions that are still in progress.

Present Progressive Tense. As its name indicates, the *present progressive tense* describes an action that is in progress *in the present*. To form this tense, use *am, is,* or *are* with a present participle.

I *am using* this software program to balance my checkbook. (*Am using* shows action in progress now.)

You *are reading* Eduardo's proposal. (*Are reading* shows action in progress now.)

He *is driving* his friend's car. (*Is driving* shows action in progress now.)

Past Progressive Tense. Describe an action that was in progress at a certain time *in the past* by using *was* or *were* with a present participle.

They *were assessing* the losses when the insurance agent arrived. (*Were assessing* shows action that was in progress in the past.)

Future Progressive Tense. Describe an action that *will be* in progress at a certain time *in the future* by using *will be* or *shall be* with a present participle.

Maria *will be applying* for a scholarship next Friday. (Is this action in progress now? No. In the past? Again, no. *Will be applying* shows an action that will be in progress in the future—specifically, *next Friday*.)

Conjugating Regular Verbs. The table below, "Conjugation of the Verb *Hope*," presents an overview of the rules we have been discussing. It is a *conjugation table* and indicates the three elements that determine verb forms: person (*I, you,* and so on), number (singular or plural), and tense. Every regular verb follows the same basic conjugation pattern shown here. When you are unsure about the correct form of a particular regular verb, check that verb against the table.

KEY POINT

To use the conjugation table, substitute singular nouns in place of the pronouns *he* or *she* and plural nouns in place of the pronoun *they*.

CONJUGATION OF THE VERB *HOPE*	
Singular	**Plural**
Present Tense	
I hope	we hope
you hope	you hope
he, she, *or* it hopes	they hope
Past Tense	
I hoped	we hoped
you hoped	you hoped
he, she, *or* it hoped	they hoped
Future Tense	
I shall hope	we shall hope
you will hope	you will hope
he, she, *or* it will hope	they will hope
Present Perfect Tense	
I have hoped	we have hoped
you have hoped	you have hoped
he, she, *or* it has hoped	they have hoped

Singular	Plural

Past Perfect Tense

I had hoped	we had hoped
you had hoped	you had hoped
he, she, *or* it had hoped	they had hoped

Future Perfect Tense

I shall have hoped	we shall have hoped
you will have hoped	you will have hoped
he, she, *or* it will have hoped	they will have hoped

Present Progressive Tense

I am hoping	we are hoping
you are hoping	you are hoping
he, she, *or* it is hoping	they are hoping

Past Progressive Tense

I was hoping	we were hoping
you were hoping	you were hoping
he, she, *or* it was hoping	they were hoping

Future Progressive Tense

I shall be hoping	we shall be hoping
you will be hoping	you will be hoping
he, she, *or* it will be hoping	they will be hoping

✔ CHECKUP 4

On a separate sheet of paper, use each of the following regular verbs in a sentence.

1. have questioned
2. wished
3. has refused
4. evaluates
5. had remembered
6. are speaking
7. will have corrected
8. will be

IRREGULAR VERBS

Most verbs follow the regular pattern shown on page 116 for forming the present tense, the past tense, the past participle, and the present participle. However, there are 50 or more commonly used *irregular* verbs that do *not* follow this pattern. The rest of this section discusses these irregular verbs.

Principal Parts of Irregular Verbs

Review the table "Principal Parts of Irregular Verbs" on pages 118–119 in detail. During your review, try fitting some of the irregular verbs into the regular pattern. For example, say "speak, speaked" instead of "speak, spoke" or say "leave, leaved" instead of "leave, left." Can you hear the errors? For many of us, there is no alternative: we must memorize most of these forms, especially those that are used frequently.

PRINCIPAL PARTS OF IRREGULAR VERBS			
Present Tense	**Past Tense**	**Past Participle**	**Present Participle**
am	was	been	being
bear	bore	borne	bearing
begin	began	begun	beginning
bid (to command)	bade	bidden	bidding
bid (to offer to pay)	bid	bid	bidding
bite	bit	bitten	biting
blow	blew	blown	blowing
break	broke	broken	breaking
bring	brought	brought	bringing
burst	burst	burst	bursting
catch	caught	caught	catching
choose	chose	chosen	choosing
come	came	come	coming
do	did	done	doing
draw	drew	drawn	drawing
drink	drank	drunk	drinking
drive	drove	driven	driving
eat	ate	eaten	eating
fall	fell	fallen	falling
fight	fought	fought	fighting
flee	fled	fled	fleeing
fly	flew	flown	flying
forget	forgot	forgotten	forgetting
freeze	froze	frozen	freezing
get	got	got *or* gotten	getting
give	gave	given	giving
go	went	gone	going
grow	grew	grown	growing
hang (to put to death)	hanged	hanged	hanging

Present Tense	Past Tense	Past Participle	Present Participle
hang (to suspend)	hung	hung	hanging
hide	hid	hidden	hiding
know	knew	known	knowing
lay	laid	laid	laying
leave	left	left	leaving
lend	lent	lent	lending
lie	lay	lain	lying
pay	paid	paid	paying
read	read	read	reading
ride	rode	ridden	riding
ring	rang	rung	ringing
rise	rose	risen	rising
run	ran	run	running
see	saw	seen	seeing
send	sent	sent	sending
set	set	set	setting
shake	shook	shaken	shaking
sing	sang	sung	singing
sit	sat	sat	sitting
speak	spoke	spoken	speaking
stand	stood	stood	standing
steal	stole	stolen	stealing
strike	struck	struck	striking
take	took	taken	taking
tear	tore	torn	tearing
tell	told	told	telling
throw	threw	thrown	throwing
wear	wore	worn	wearing
write	wrote	written	writing

✔ CHECKUP 5

Using a separate sheet of paper, correct any verb errors in the following sentences. Write *OK* for any sentence that is correct. Refer to the table on pages 118-119 for help. (*Hint:* Remember that a past tense form *never* has a helper and that a past participle or a present participle *always* has a helper!)

1. Michael, of course, spoken about his experiences many times.

2. LaKisha had began her research paper weeks before her instructor assigned it to her.

3. Eric has went to the post office to get his package.

4. He stood at the door and knocked.

5. Ask Deidra if she seen the accounts payable file.

6. The police captain knowed the facts before the trial.

7. Company expenses have decreased over the past six months.

Being Verbs

The being verbs are the forms of the verb *to be.* They show no action. Study the present tense and the past tense forms that follow.

Present Tense

I am	we are
you are	you are
he	
she } is	they are
it	

Past Tense

I was	we were
you were	you were
he	
she } was	they were
it	

As you see, there are three present tense forms: *am, is,* and *are.* There are two past tense forms, *was* and *were.*

Verb Phrases With Forms of *To Be.* As you saw earlier in this section, verb phrases are formed by using helping or auxiliary verbs with (1) the infinitive form be, (2) the past participle form *been,* or (3) the present participle form *being.*

1. The infinitive form *be* with a helping verb: *will be, shall be, may be, can be, would be, might be,* and so on.

2. The past participle *been* with a helping verb: *has been, have been, had been, will have been, shall have been, could have been, might have been,* and so on.

3. The present participle *being* with a helping verb: *am being, is being, are being, was being,* and *were being.*

You will do well to memorize these eight forms of *to be am, is, are, was, were,* helper plus *be,* helper plus *been,* and helper plus *being.*

Because being verbs are so often used as helping verbs, be careful to distinguish between being verbs that are helpers and being verbs that are main verbs in the phrase.

Janis *should have been* here by now. (The verb phrase is *should have been*, and the main verb is *been*. This verb phrase is a being verb.)

That contract *should have been signed.* (Now the verb phrase is *should have been signed. Should have been* is only a helping verb. The main verb is *signed.* Only the helping verb is a being verb.)

Ned Pierce *is* the vice president of telecommunications. He *was* formerly the director of technical services. (Both *is* and *was* are being verbs. There are no helping verbs.)

World View

Canada is, by law, a bilingual country, with English and French the two official languages. About one-fourth of Canadians consider French their first language.

✔ CHECKUP 6

On a separate sheet of paper, write the verbs and verb phrases in the following sentences. Identify each being verb that is a main verb by writing *B* next to the verb.

1. Renaldo, the safety engineer for our plant, is at a conference.
2. Our company is proud of its community volunteer participation.
3. Incidentally, the jury has been deliberating for over a week.
4. Bob Hilton was employed as a consultant.
5. Both Ms. Delgado and Mrs. Pratt have been members of the advisory board for five years.
6. Most citizens, however, have been sympathizing with the defendant.

***Were* Instead of *Was*.** Good writing requires that we sometimes use *were* instead of *was* after *if, as if, as though,* and *wish*. Whenever such statements describe (1) something that is highly doubtful or impossible or (2) something contrary to fact or simply not true, use *were* instead of *was*. If, on the other hand, the statement *is true* or *could be true* (as often happens after *if*), then do *not* substitute *were* for *was*.

We wish it *were* possible for us to predict future stock prices, but SEC regulations prohibit us from making such claims. (It is not possible. Therefore, "We wish it *were*" is correct.)

If I *were* you, I would purchase this stock while it is still selling at 22. (Of course, I am *not* you—thus *were* is correct.)

Bill acts as if he *were* the only candidate for the position. (Bill is not the only candidate for the position, so this statement is contrary to fact and takes the verb *were*.)

If Michelle *was* here earlier, she probably left a message with her assistant. (Michelle could indeed have already been here; thus this statement could be true. Do *not* substitute *were* for *was*.)

On a separate sheet of paper, correct any verb errors in the following sentences. If a sentence has no error, write *OK*.

1. If Leslie were at work this morning, I certainly did not see her.
2. If I were President of the United States, I would make some drastic changes.
3. At times Richard acts as if he is the only detective in the state!
4. She has said that if she was younger, she would study real estate law.
5. Paul sometimes acts as if he was at a party instead of at work.

Lie, Lay; Sit, Set; Rise, Raise

Like the being verbs, *lie* and *lay, sit* and *set*, and *rise* and *raise* deserve very special attention. To be able to use these verbs correctly, you must first understand the distinction between transitive and intransitive verbs.

Transitive Verbs. A *transitive verb* is a verb that has an object or a receiver of the verb's action. To find that object, say the verb and ask "What?" or "Whom?" The answer to that question is the direct object. If a direct object follows a verb, that verb is transitive. Follow these examples:

1. Jillian accepted Jared's gift.
   a. Say the verb: *accepted.*
   b. Ask "What?" or "Whom?" Accepted *what?* Answer: Accepted *gift.* The object of the verb *accepted* is *gift.*
   c. Use the answer to determine whether the verb is transitive. Yes, accepted is transitive because it has an object, *gift.*
2. Ms. Nelson invited Susan to the business luncheon.
   a. Say the verb: *invited.*
   b. Ask "What?" or "Whom?" Invited *whom?* Answer: Invited *Susan.* The object of the verb *invited* is Susan.
   c. Transitive? Yes, *invited* is a transitive verb because it has an object, *Susan.*

   A *direct object* is a person or thing that directly receives the action of the verb. An *indirect object* is a person or thing that indirectly receives the action of the verb. The indirect object tells "to whom" or "for whom" something is done. Note that an indirect object does not appear

KEY POINT

Transitive verbs have direct objects that answer the question "What?" and indirect objects that answer the question "To whom?" or "For whom?"

without a direct object. Also, the indirect object will always appear *before* the direct object and is usually a person or persons rather than a thing. Look at these examples:

1. The flight attendant served the passengers a snack.
   a. Say the verb: *served.*
   b. Ask "What?" or "Whom?" Served *what?* Answer: Served *snack.* The object of the verb *served* is *snack.*
   c. Transitive? Yes, *served* is a transitive verb because it has an object, *snacks.*
   d. If *snack* is the direct object, what is passengers? *Passengers* appears before the direct object, it refers to persons, and it answers the question "To whom?" *Passengers* is the indirect object.

2. Adam gave the trainee the office key.
   a. Say the verb: *gave.*
   b. Ask "What?" or "Whom?" Gave *what?* Answer: Gave *key.* The object of the verb *gave* is *key.*
   c. Transitive? Yes, *gave* is a transitive verb because it has an object, *key.*
   d. If *key* is the direct object, what is *trainee? Trainee* appears before the direct object, qualifies as a person, and answers the question "To whom?" *Trainee* is the indirect object.

Sometimes the subject rather than the object of the sentence serves as the receiver of the verb's action. You can identify transitive verbs that are used this way because they include a being verb helper and a past participle.

The award *should have been given* to Tommy. (Do you have a being verb helper? Do you have a past participle? "Yes" to both questions. Therefore, this verb is transitive. What receives the action? Answer: *award.*)

The concert *was canceled,* according to Miriam. (Again, we have a being verb helper, *was,* and a past participle, *canceled.* Thus we know that the subject, *concert,* receives the action of the verb. *What* was canceled? Answer: *concert. Was canceled* is a transitive verb.)

Scott has been nominated to the Executive Committee. (What is the verb in this sentence? Is it transitive? If so, explain why.)

Intransitive Verbs. Verbs that do not have objects are *intransitive verbs.* Being verbs never have objects. Therefore, being verbs are never transitive; they are always intransitive.

Sam Cohen *visits* very often. (Visits *what?* Visits *whom?* No answer. *Visits* is an intransitive verb.)

Wanda Gordon *will leave* at 7 p.m., according to her itinerary. (The verb *will leave* has no object; it is an intransitive verb.)

KEY POINT

Intransitive verbs do not have objects.

Using a separate sheet of paper, identify the verbs and verb phrases in the following sentences. Then label each verb or verb phrase using *B* for *Being*, *T* for *Transitive*, or *I* for *Intransitive*.

T   1. Has Adriene <u>told</u> Marvin about the proposed personnel changes?

I   2. Both of them <u>have</u> apparently <u>left</u> already.

B   3. As always, Jon <u>has been</u> very helpful on our fund-raising venture.

T   4. A new security guard <u>had been appointed</u> as of last Thursday.

B   5. Rob <u>will be</u> in the office by noon.

T   6. Our next broadcast <u>will be televised</u> on June 15.

Using a separate sheet of paper, identify the direct objects (*DO*) and the indirect objects (*IO*) in the following sentences.

    7. Francine sent him an apology by e-mail. *(IO, DO)*

    8. The control tower gave the pilot the latest weather report. *(IO, DO)*

    9. Ken sold books and magazines to help finance his education. *(DO, DO)*

   10. The manager presented Fred and Marta perfect attendance awards. *(IO, IO, DO)*

Now review carefully the principal parts of the following irregular verbs.

Present Tense	Past Tense	Past Participle	Present Participle	Infinitive
lie	lay	lain	lying	to lie
lay	laid	laid	laying	to lay
sit	sat	sat	sitting	to sit
set	set	set	setting	to set
rise	rose	risen	rising	to rise
raise	raised	raised	raising	to raise

MEMORY HOOK

Now that you have learned to distinguish between transitive and intransitive verbs, you will have an easier time using *lie* and *lay, sit* and *set*, and *rise* and *raise*. The letter *i* is the key. Use the *i* in *intransitive* to remember that the *i* verbs—*lie, sit,* and *rise*—are intransitive and, therefore, do not have objects.

    *i*ntransitive   l*i*e   s*i*t   r*i*se

The other three verbs—*lay, set,* and *raise*— are all transitive.

You will probably notice that one common trap is to confuse *lay* in its present tense form with *lay* as the past tense form of *lie*. How can you tell which is which? You can tell by remembering what you have learned about transitive verbs.

Last Friday, Jenny (*lay? laid?*) the mail on the receptionist's desk.

After jogging, I usually (*lie? lay?*) down for about twenty minutes.

Yesterday I (*lie? lay?*) down for only five minutes or so.

Let's analyze these sentences. Does the verb in the first sentence above have an object? Yes, *mail*. Therefore, a transitive verb is needed. As you just learned, *laid* is the past tense form of the transitive verb *to lay*, so *laid* is correct.

In the second sentence, is there an object? No. (*Down* is not an object; it is an adverb.) Here you need a form of the verb *to lie*, so the answer is *lie*—I *lie* down.

In the third sentence, the word *yesterday* shows that the past tense is needed. Does the verb have a direct object? Answer: No. Thus the correct answer is *lay*, the past tense form of *lie*, an intransitive verb.

As you see, some thinking and analysis are needed when choosing among the forms of *lie* and *lay*, so do not choose hastily.

Now let's apply the same principles to the transitive verbs *set* and *raise* and to the intransitive verbs *sit* and *rise*.

Wallace and Jim (*sit? set?*) the flowers on the window sill before they left for lunch. (Is an object needed here? Yes. Which is the transitive verb? Answer: *set*. Set what? Set the *flowers*.)

As soon as the temperature (rises, raises), the air conditioner will automatically go on. (What is needed, a transitive verb or an intransitive verb? Answer: intransitive, because the verb has no object in this sentence. Which, then, is the intransitive verb? The *i* verb, *rises*.)

OOPS!

I lay the manual on the counter by the computer.

✔ CHECKUP 9

Practice your ability to use the verbs *lie, lay, sit, set, rise,* and *raise.* Write the correct verb for each sentence on a separate sheet of paper.

1. Ask the courier to (sit, set) the package on the desk.

2. Because Mandy felt ill, she (lay, laid) down after lunch.

3. The files that you were looking for had been (lain, laid) carelessly on a table in the reception area.

4. Please (rise, raise) to indicate an affirmative vote.

5. Mr. Rao will (rise, raise) the roof when he hears about this quality control problem.

6. When she works on special design proposals, Angela usually (sits, sets) at the computer in my office.

7. According to my new contract, my salary has been (risen, raised) by about 8 percent.
8. When you correct the draft for this special report, you should (sit, set) both margins for 2 inches.

SECTION 3.5   REVIEW

Practical Application

A. Using a separate sheet of paper, identify the verb phrases in the following sentences. For the main verb in each phrase, tell where it would belong on a chart of principal parts—under *Present, Past Participle,* or *Present Participle.*
1. The deed should be signed by noon today.
2. Betsy is being transferred to Denver in January.
3. Have they already hired a replacement for Sherry?
4. Denise is requesting an assistant during the peak season.
5. Joy and Heather arranged the documents.
6. Kendra has visited our Boston office three times.
7. On July 1, Sue will be recognized for 20 years of service.
8. Peggy easily finished the assignment by Friday.
9. The travel agent is now preparing a revised itinerary for Dr. Gregg.
10. We are ordering new equipment for our staff.

B. Practice your ability to form the principal parts of regular verbs by completing the following table. Use a separate sheet of paper.

Present Tense	Past Tense	Past Participle (Uses a helper)	Present Participle (Uses a helper)
1. explain	explained	explained	
2. approve		approved	approving
3. select	selected		selecting
4. address	addressed		addressing
5. stack		stacked	stacking
6. insure	insured	insured	insuring
7. bill		billed	billing
8. park	parked	parked	
9. argue	argued	argued	
10. require		required	requiring

C. Using a separate sheet of paper, identify the verb or the verb phrase in each of the following sentences. Label each choice *transitive* (*T*), *intransitive* (*I*), or *being* (*B*).
   1. They need more time to complete the order because of machinery failures.
   2. Additionally, nearly all airports have been requiring identification that includes a photograph.
   3. As a result of the delays, tempers are rising.
   4. How secure are our airports?
   5. A consulting firm is carefully studying this issue.
   6. Our crews have been very busy as a result of the storm.
   7. Weather related delays are happening more during the winter months.
   8. Work-related accidents have been decreasing.
   9. We should be finishing our feasibility study in about a month.
   10. Our article will be published in *Leisure Living* magazine.

D. On a separate sheet of paper, correct any verb errors in the following sentences. Write *OK* for any sentence that has no error.
   1. Josh has ~~risen~~ that same objection at every meeting. *raised*
   2. If I ~~was~~ Kathleen, I ~~would~~ ask for a promotion. *or were*
   3. The engineers promised us that the pipeline will have been ~~lain~~ no later than June 1. *laid*
   4. Lee has already ~~wrote~~ *written* to the administration about her concerns.
   5. The book that I misplaced was ~~laying~~ on my desk. *lying*
   6. When Mrs. Fontana arrived, we ~~raised~~ to greet her. *rose*
   7. At yesterday's meeting, Herb laid out a comprehensive emergency evacuation plan. *OK*
   8. Has Dana ever ~~flew~~ to Mexico before? *flown*
   9. Please lay those brochures on the shelf in your office. *OK*
   10. Sharon has lent us $200 to buy books for the literacy project. *OK*

E. Write five sentences that each contain a direct and an indirect object.

Editing Practice

Find the Errors. Check the following paragraph for errors in verb usage. Write the correct forms of verbs on a separate sheet of paper.

At tomorrow's meeting, we will be discussed the proposed manufacturing of several of our products by another firm. Many new issues will be risen that will be sensitive to some committee members. Please sit your personal feelings aside and look for the best outcome for the company. Incidentally, several members from management will be setting in on our meeting to get suggestions for dealing with the multitude of unanswered questions. An agenda for the meeting should be lain on your desk by 3:30 p.m. today.

The Right Word. Select the correct word for each of the following sentences, and write the words on a separate sheet of paper.

1. Earl suggested that we conduct a local (pole, poll) of fast-food restaurant customers.
2. The three-year guarantee is the (principle, principal) reason that we are buying our computers from you.
3. Dynamite Software has (its, it's) distribution center in Jackson, Mississippi.
4. Jim and Anni Ruth are now planning (they're, their, there) trip to Israel.
5. The campaign cost cannot (exceed, accede) $20,000.

SECTION 3.6

PREDICATE AGREEMENT

OBJECTIVES:

After completing Section 3.6, you should be able to:

1. State the basic rule of predicate agreement.
2. Explain how to determine whether a collective noun is singular or plural.
3. Describe subjects other than collective nouns that may be either singular or plural.
4. Identify relative-pronoun clauses and their antecedents.

Be sure that your subject and predicate is [sic] in agreement.

—C.B. Camp

Popular songs, television shows, and movies do little to avoid subject-verb agreement errors such as "he don't" and "I been." As a result, listeners and viewers hear such errors over and over so often that they may start to believe that "he don't" and "I been" are grammatically correct.

Well, they are *not!* Pay special attention to the subject-verb agreement rules to make sure that you *do* avoid such errors in your speaking and writing.

PREDICATE AGREEMENT WITH SIMPLE SUBJECTS

In Section 3.1 of this chapter, you learned about predicates and simple subjects. Now let's review the way that these elements are related.

Basic Agreement Rule

A predicate must agree with its simple subject in number and in person. This statement is the basic rule of agreement for all sentences. Remember, a complete predicate includes a complete verb, its complement, and any modifiers. Generally speaking, the complete predicate contains the complete verb and all the words that come after it. The verb within this complete predicate must agree with the subject of the sentence in both

KEY POINT

To agree in number, a singular noun takes a singular verb and a plural noun takes a plural verb.

number and person. In addition, if the predicate includes any pronouns that refer back to the subject, those pronouns must also agree with the subject in both number and person.

Agreement of Subject and Verb. Note how verbs agree in number with their subjects in the following sentences.

Walter Tate *wants* to approve the contract today. (The verb *wants* agrees with the subject, *Walter Tate*—both are singular.)

Walter Tate, our vice president, *wants* to approve the contract today. (Neither the subject nor the verb has changed. *Wants* agrees with *Walter Tate*.)

Two vice presidents *want* to approve the contract today. (Now the subject is the plural *vice presidents*. Therefore, the plural form *want*—not *wants*—is correct.)

Agreement of Pronoun With Subject. If the complete predicate includes a pronoun that refers to the subject, that pronoun also must agree with the subject in number.

Mr. Wayne wants to change *his* assignment in the company. (The singular pronoun *his* agrees with *Mr. Wayne*.

Mrs. Guzman is eager to receive *her* dividends. Mr. and Mrs. Guzman are eager to receive *their* dividends. (*Her* agrees with the singular *Mrs. Guzman*. In the second sentence, *their* agrees with the plural *Mr. and Mrs. Guzman*.)

 **CHECKUP 1**

Using a separate sheet of paper, choose the correct verbs and pronouns in the following sentences.

1. Lance Harrison (wants? want?) to close (his? her? its? their?) savings account.

MEMORY HOOK

Although plural *nouns* usually end in *s* or *es*, an *s* ending on a *verb* indicates that it is a singular verb. To help you recall this fact, remember that the word *singular* has an *s*; the word *plural* does not. And so it goes for verbs—singular verbs have an *s* on the end; plural verbs do not.

Singular Noun and Verb	Plural Noun and Verb
the *player wants*	the *players want*
one *salesclerk has*	all *salesclerks have*
Mrs. Salerno is	*Mr.* and *Mrs. Salerno are*

KEY POINT

To agree in person, a noun and a verb must both refer to (1) the person speaking (first person), (2) the person spoken to (second person), or (3) the person spoken about (third person).

2. The tour group (has? have?) changed (his? her? its? their?) destination since our Friday meeting with (his? her? its? their?) directors.

3. The Baxter Rehabilitation Center (is? are?) regarded as a leader in (his? her? its? their?) specialty.

4. The Casper Corporation (does? do?) not usually disclose (his? her? its? their?) financial statements.

5. Both accountants (is? are?) going to bring (his? her? its? their?) cash projection reports with (him? her? it? them?).

6. Betty Petrocinni, one of our senior associates, (is? are?) planning to liquidate (his? her? its? their?) company stock before (he? she? it? they?) purchases a retirement home in the mountains.

Simple-Subject Agreement Problems

The most common problems concerning agreement of subjects and verbs are reviewed in the following discussion. Study them carefully.

Inverted Sentences. Agreement problems most often arise when the subject is difficult to identify, as in sentences with inverted word order—where the verb comes before the subject.

Inverted Word Order

On your credenza (*is? are?*) the speakers. (At first glance, the subject and verb may appear to be "credenza is," but a closer look shows that the subject of this inverted sentence is *speakers*. The correct verb, therefore, is *are*.)

Other situations where sentences are in inverted order include questions and sentences beginning with *there*.

Questions

Are the speakers on the credenza? (Here the subject, *speakers*, comes after the verb, *are*, because the sentence asks a question.)

Sentences Beginning With *There*

There (*is? are?*) still several vacancies. (Until you identify the subject, *vacancies*, you cannot choose the correct verb, *are*.)

Do you know whether there (*is? are?*) additional elevators in the hotel? (The simple subject of the dependent clause "whether there (*is? are?*) additional elevators in the hotel?" is *elevators*. Therefore, *are* is the correct verb.)

Other examples of sentences begininng with *there* include those beginning with *there has been* and *there have been*.

Intervening Phrases and Clauses. Another construction that may confuse the writer or speaker is one in which words separate the subject from its verb. Again, the trick is to identify the simple subject.

The reason for the delays (*is? are?*) that wind damaged the amphitheater. (The subject is the singular noun *reason*. Therefore, the correct verb is *is*. Although the plural word *delays* immediately precedes the verb,

OOPS!

The mayor banded the use of pesticides in all city parks.

KEY POINT

In sentences starting with *there*, the true subject follows the being verb and determines the number of the verb.

delays is not the subject of the verb. *Delays* is part of the prepositional phrase *for the delays*.)

The business manager, who must sign all expense forms submitted by our executives, (*has? have?*) restricted the travel budgets for everyone. (The subject is *business manager*, not *executives*. Therefore, the correct verb is *has*.)

CHECKUP 2

On a sheet of paper, correct any agreement errors in the following sentences. Write *OK* if a sentence is correct. (Be sure to identify the subject for each sentence.)

1. Are you sure that there's no more than three restaurants within two miles of the proposed mall?

2. The entire pasture, except for the wooded areas, are to be seeded next month.

3. Our entire campus, which consists of over three thousand students, are inconvenienced when the water system is turned off for repairs.

4. Did you know that there's a few stubborn individuals who water their lawns when conservation is mandated?

5. When we checked the telephone directory, we found that there is only three area codes for that state.

6. There is, as you told me earlier, several explanations for increased traffic on the interstate highway.

Pronoun Agreement With Common-Gender Nouns. When the gender of a noun is clearly masculine (*man, father, brother, son*) or clearly feminine (*woman, mother, sister, daughter*), choosing between the pronouns *he* or *she*, *him* or *her*, and so on is no problem. Common-gender nouns are those that can be either masculine or feminine, such as *employee, student, teacher, officer, owner, secretary,* and so on. The traditional rule has been to use masculine pronouns to represent common-gender nouns. However, good communicators today avoid using masculine pronouns to refer to common-gender nouns. Instead, they use pronoun combinations such as *he or she, him or her,* and *his or her* to avoid suggesting either masculine or feminine gender.

KEY POINT

Use pronoun combinations such as *he* or *she* and *him* or *her* with common-gender nouns.

Every employee knows *his or her* role in the upcoming fire drill. (*His or her* agrees with the common-gender noun *employee*.)

An executive must be sure that *he or she* is familiar with the fire regulations. (*He or she* agrees with the common-gender noun *executive*.)

When such combinations are used too often, they make the message difficult to read. In such instances, consider using plurals to avoid the need for pronoun combinations.

Executives must be sure that *they* are familiar with the fire regulations. (*They* agrees with the plural *executives*.)

Indefinite-Word Subject. The indefinite pronouns *any one, anybody, anyone, anything, each, either, every, everybody, everyone, everything, neither, no one, nobody, nothing, somebody, someone,* and *something* are always singular. When they are used as subjects, and when they modify other subjects, their predicates must be singular. Use the following Memory Hook to help you remember the indefinite pronouns.

Each of the printers *has* a 10-foot cable that connects *it* to the computer. (The singulars *has* and *it* agree with the subject *each*.)

Each printer *has* a 10-foot cable that connects *it* to the computer. (Here *each* modifies the subject, *printer*. In all cases, *each* is singular.)

Anyone in your precinct who *wants* to volunteer *his or her* time should be sure *he or she registers*. (*Wants, his or her, he or she,* and *registers* are all singular and agree with the singular indefinite pronoun *anyone*.)

MEMORY HOOK

To remember the indefinite pronouns, memorize the phrase "**A**ll **e**mployees **n**eed **s**alaries." The indefinite pronouns are listed beneath the word in the phrase that shares the same first letter.

All	Employees	Need	Salaries
anybody	everybody	nobody	somebody
anyone	everyone	———	someone
anything	everything	nothing	something
any one	every one	no one	some one
———	either	neither	———
———	every	———	———
———	each	———	———

✔ CHECKUP 3

On a sheet of paper, correct the agreement errors in the following sentences. If a sentence is correct, write *OK*. For each sentence, identify the simple subject.

1. Anyone who wants to give blood in next week's drive should complete and return this form to his or her supervisor.

2. Every executive is permitted to use the exercise facilities, but he must present his identification at the desk when entering.

3. Nobody in these two divisions ~~have~~ **has** submitted his or her self-evaluation form.
4. Each of the administrative assistants ~~want~~ **wants** to get ~~their~~ **his or hers** own printer.
5. ~~Every~~ **his or her** manager in the region is sure to want ~~his~~ **his or her** staff members to participate in this management training opportunity.
6. **has** Neither of the medical centers we visited have enough parking for its patients.

PREDICATE AGREEMENT WITH SPECIAL SUBJECTS

Remember the basic agreement rule: *A predicate must agree with its simple subject in number and in person.* As you review some especially troublesome agreement problems, keep this rule in mind.

Collective-Noun Simple Subjects

A *collective noun* is one that refers to a group or a collection of persons or things; for example, *class, jury, audience, department, company, committee,* and *association*. Because a collective noun may be either singular or plural, its correct number may not be easily recognized. Use the following Memory Hook to help you.

MEMORY HOOK

When the class, jury, and so on acts *as one group,* treat the collective noun as *singular.* When the members of the collective noun act *as individuals,* treat the noun as *plural.*

In other words, remember:

One group is singular.

Individuals are plural.

In a major case, the jury (*does? do?*) not give (*its? their?*) verdict quickly. (Is the jury acting *as one group,* or is the jury acting *as individuals?* Answer: As one group. Therefore, treat *jury* as a singular noun: " . . . the jury *does* not give *its* verdict quickly.")

The jury (*is? are?*) arguing about the charges. (Is the jury acting *as one group,* or is the jury acting *as individuals?* In arguing, they would be acting *as individuals.* Treat *jury* as a plural noun: "The jury *are* arguing about the charges."

Foreign-Noun Subjects

Nouns of foreign origin do not form their plurals in the usual way. Review the list of foreign-origin nouns on pages 87 and 88. Always be careful to determine first whether the noun is singular or plural before deciding on the correct verb to agree with such nouns.

The basis for her statements (*was? were?*) unsound. (*Basis* is singular; therefore, the predicate must be singular. *Was* is correct.)

The bases for her statements (*was? were?*) unsound. (*Bases* is plural; therefore, *were* is correct.)

✔ CHECKUP 4

Make sure that the predicates agree with their subjects in the following sentences. On a separate sheet, write the correct verb, or write *OK* if a sentence is correct.

1. The unique criterion for the promotion decision among the assistant managers are [*is*] the ability to get along with others.
2. The media we prefer for our commercials is [*are*] television and radio.
3. If you want nutrition information, the analysis for each of our menu items are [*is*] printed in a pamphlet that is available on request.
4. The jury was [*were*] discussing the evidence among themselves.
5. The honors class are [*is*] leaving for a field trip on Saturday.
6. The audience were [*was*] told that there would be a delay.
7. Parentheses is [*are*] used to enclose bibliographic references.
8. The economic stimulus that is being used by the Federal Reserve have [*has been*] been criticized by some experts.

Part, Portion, or Amount Subjects

Other subjects that may be either singular or plural are those that refer to a part, a portion, or an amount of something. Thus *all, some, half, two-thirds* (or any fraction), and *none* may be either singular or plural depending on the nouns that they refer to. The noun may belong to an *of* phrase. To decide, find the answer to "Part of *what?*" "Portion of *what?*" "Amount of *what?*" In other words, use the complete subject (not the simple subject) for your answer.

Some of the condominium (*has? have?*) been remodeled. (Use *condominium has. Some* refers to the singular *condominium* in the prepositional phrase *of the condominium.*)

Use the following sentence to help you remember words that are used as indefinite-amount subjects:

People at **NASA** eat **M&M**s a **F**raction of the time.

None
Any
Some
All
More
Most
Fractions

Some of the condominiums *(has? have?)* been remodeled. (Use *condominiums have.*) Here *some* refers to more than one condominium and takes the plural verb *have.*

A Number, The Number

A number is always plural. *The number* is always singular. (Note that an adjective before *number* has no effect on the choice.)

A number of employees *have* requested a raise. (Use *have,* because *a number* is always plural.)

The number of employees *is* increasing. (*The number* is always singular, so *is* is correct.)

Use the acronym *APTS* as another way to remember that *a number* is always plural and *the number* is always singular.

A number
Plural
The number
Singular

On a sheet of paper, correct any agreement errors in the following sentences. Write *OK* for any sentence that is correct.

1. The number of available sources have risen to ten.
2. None of the condominiums was damaged by the hurricane.
3. Nearly two-thirds of the city was affected by the power shortage.
4. We know that a number of workers is concerned about the decrease in our life insurance coverage.
5. Some of the scientific equipment, Lara told me, was not adequately inspected before the expedition.
6. Some of the tools, as Caleb noted, has already begun to rust.

PREDICATE AGREEMENT WITH COMPOUND SUBJECTS

To complete your study of predicate agreement, you will now work on predicate agreement with compound subjects—that is, two or more subjects joined by *and, or,* or *nor*—and one other predicate agreement problem: agreement with the relative pronouns *who, that,* and *which.*

Subjects Joined by *And*

A compound subject joined by *and* is plural and must take a plural verb.

Ryan *and* Zach *have filed* their tax returns. (The compound subject *Ryan and Zach* is plural; the plural verb *have filed* is correct.)

A video company *and* a software distributor *have asked* for more information on the property. (The plural form *have asked* is correct because the compound subject is joined by *and*.)

Two exceptions to this rule are possible:

1. If the two nouns joined by *and* refer to *one* person, then that subject is really singular and takes a singular verb.

   My business partner *and* investment adviser *is* my brother, Tyler. (Although the compound subject is joined by *and*, only one person is serving as both *business partner* and *investment adviser*. The singular verb *is* is therefore correct.)

   Strawberries *and* cream *is* going to be served for dessert. (*One* dessert, *strawberries and cream,* is the intended meaning.)

   Note that if two different people or two different desserts were intended, the verbs would then be plural.

   My business partner *and* my investment adviser *are* not in agreement on this issue. (Two different people are intended.)

Sign seen in a chain of restaurants: "Be Cool in School! Good Grades Has Its Rewards."

Strawberries *and* ice cream *are* among the desserts included in the fixed-price lunch. (Here, two different items on the menu are referred to.)

2. If two or more subjects joined by *and* are modified by *each, every,* or *many a,* then the predicate is singular.

Each secretary and assistant *has* been asked to return the completed questionnaire to the personnel department by May 15. *Every* supervisor and manager *is* supposed to check the questionnaires. *Many a* factory, office, and store throughout the country *is* now following this procedure. (In each sentence, the predicate is singular because the subjects are modified by *each, every,* or *many a.* Members of the plural groups are being considered singly.)

✔ CHECKUP 6

On a sheet of paper, correct any agreement errors in the following sentences. Write *OK* for any sentence that has no error.

1. Many a lawyer and tax payer have complained about the complexity of income tax regulations.

2. Bacon and eggs are usually what I want for a midnight snack.

3. Pizza and dessert is at the top of most children's favorite-foods list.

4. Each returning patient and new patient are required to complete the medical history form.

5. Every partner and associate in the accounting firms we contacted are writing to their representatives to show support for the legislation.

6. The letter and the envelope is from two different qualities of stationery.

Subjects Joined by *Or* or *Nor*

For subjects joined by *or* or *nor,* simply match the predicate to the subject that follows *or* or *nor.*

The owner *or* her assistants (*is? are?*) going to discuss (*her? their?*) new spring clothing line at the sales meeting tomorrow. (Matching the predicate to the subject that follows *or,* the correct choices are *are* and *their.*)

The assistants *or* the owner (*is? are?*) going to discuss (*her? their?*) new winter clothing line at the sales meeting tomorrow. (Now the subject that follows *or* is the singular word *owner.* Therefore, the choices are *is* and *her.*)

Neither the owner *nor* her assistants (*knows? know?*) where the French designer went. (Which subject follows *nor?* Answer: the plural *assistants.* The choice, therefore, is *know.*)

Either the three Japanese couturiers *or* SmartShirt (*is? are?*) going to present (*its? their?*) collection this afternoon. (The subject that follows *or* is SmartShirt, singular; thus the choices are *is* and *its*.)

✔ **CHECKUP 7**

In the following sentences, select the words in parentheses that match the compound subject. Write your choices on a separate sheet of paper.

1. My brother-in-law or his colleagues (is? are?) interested in purchasing antiques for (his? their?) stores.
2. Either her associates or Laura herself (is? are?) going to lead the tour to France.
3. Either the salesclerks or Mrs. Paige (like? likes?) to present (their? her?) customers' jewelry in expensive gift wrap.
4. Neither Mrs. Paige nor the salesclerks (has? have?) volunteered to work Saturday evening to complete the inventory.
5. Consuelo Martinez or her buyers (has? have?) completed (her? their?) garment selection for the fall season.

PREDICATE AGREEMENT IN CLAUSES INTRODUCED BY RELATIVE PRONOUNS

The pronouns *who, that,* and *which* are called *relative pronouns* because they *relate* to other words (called *antecedents*). The antecedent of the relative pronoun is a noun or a pronoun that is usually immediately before the relative pronoun.

Grace Yancy is one *who* strives for perfection. (The relative pronoun is *who,* and its antecedent is *one.*)

Grace Yancy is one of those *who* strive for perfection. (The relative pronoun is *who,* and its antecedent is *those.*)

Grace Yancy is one of those people *who* strive for perfection all the time. (The relative pronoun is *who,* and its antecedent is the noun immediately before it, *people.*)

The calculator *that* is on the shelf works accurately. (If *that* is a relative pronoun, what is its antecedent? Answer: *calculator.*)

This special offer is good until Saturday, *which* is the last day of our sale. (The relative pronoun *which* refers to *Saturday,* its antecedent.)

Note that in each sentence the verb in the clause introduced by a relative pronoun agrees with the antecedent.

MEMORY HOOK

To choose quickly the correct verb in clauses introduced by a relative pronoun, omit the relative pronoun and use the antecedent as the subject of the clause. For example, omitting the relative pronouns from the immediately preceding sentences (page 138) would give:

one...strives
those...strive
people...strive
calculator...is
Saturday...is

Let's look at some other examples:

Tomas prefers one of those microwaves that (*has? have?*) rotating shelves inside (*its? their?*) ovens. (By omitting the relative pronoun *that*, you can determine the agreement: *microwaves...have...their*.)

Celeste Watson is one of those clerks who (*does? do?*) (*her? their?*) best selling under pressure. (Omit *who*, and you have *clerks...do...their*.)

Note: An exception is a clause preceded by *the only one*. Such clauses must take singular predicates.

Miriam is *the only one* of the members who *has cast her* vote for the expansion. (*Has* and *her* are correct.)

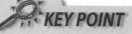

KEY POINT

Omit the relative pronouns *who, that,* and *which* to make finding the correct verb easy.

✓ CHECKUP 8

On a sheet of paper, correct any agreement errors in the following sentences. Write *OK* if a sentence has no error.

1. Zeb is one of those accountants who always double-check their figures.

2. Megan prefers one of those offices that has two windows in <u>it</u>.

3. Sabrina is the only one of the board members who wants to extend the city limits.

4. Yoshiko is one of those insurance sales representatives who personally collects from his clients on a monthly basis.

5. G. T. Hollender, Inc., is one of those dealerships which has shown an interest in leasing cars and vans.

6. We will soon close one of the several restaurants that is now operating at a loss.

Practical Application

A. On a sheet of paper, correct any errors in the following sentences. If a sentence is correct, write *OK*.

1. Each editor, proofreader, and designer were invited to an open house at the new publishing company.
2. As you probably already know, Mr. Mendoza is one of those architects who is always late in submitting plans to clients.
3. Neither the software nor the printer cable is with the computer.
4. In the Holiday Specialty Catalog is many different kinds of inexpensive but attractive items.
5. Don't Carlos know how to use his voice mail?
6. Because a number of people has complained about our statement format, we are now redesigning it to make it easier to understand.
7. Half of the area in the warehouses has been rented to the construction company.
8. Turkey and dressing is a traditional Thanksgiving menu item.
9. Every invoice and package that we ship customers are scrutinized by Wendy Cooper.
10. The manager or the stockbrokers was notified of the change in regulations.
11. To get a refund, each customer must show his or her receipt to the cashier.
12. There's the CDs that were damaged in shipping.
13. Some of the shipments to Europe has been delayed by the hurricane season.
14. The number of associates in the Chicago plant were higher than the number of associates in the Atlanta plant.
15. During the convention, members of the sailing association are staying at three hotels downtown.

B. On a sheet of paper, correct any grammatical errors in the following sentences. Write *OK* for any sentence that is correct.

1. Either Laura or Olivia should have corrected this data disk before they printed it.
2. Seth, my manager, whom did as much to win the award as me, gave me all the recognition.
3. Both brother-in-laws have donated time and materials to the building project.
4. After Amy and Kathy had spoke with Ms. Hamrick, we understood why Ms. Hamrick reassigned the project.
5. The jury was debating for two days about the guilt or innocence of the defendant.

6. Nearly three-fourths of the cars on the lot were damaged during the hailstorm.
7. Two forms of identification or a major credit card are required for cashing checks.
8. Have we received the Baxters contract?
9. Where's the monitor and the printer cable for this computer?
10. All the analysis that we received from our research and development department indicate that the new product is durable.
11. Please let me lay down before I fall down.
12. If him and I are selected, we will enjoy working on the Rodriguezes' beach house.

Editing Practice

Plurals and Possessives. On a sheet of paper, correct any errors in the following sentences. Write *OK* for any sentence that is correct.

1. Although all were subpoenaed, only two of the Davis's appeared at the trial.
2. Our organization sponsors the summer art programs for children from the local and adjoining communitys.
3. All these diskettes are ours; that box of diskettes is their's.
4. The Kellies may be attending the reception, but Mr. Kelly hasn't let us know definitely.
5. Although several of the window's were damaged, our insurance policy covers the cost of their replacement.
6. This copier quickly duplicates and collates, but our's works just as well, costs less, and staples.
7. David's article concerning the impact of electronic communications on the postal system appeared in yesterday's newspaper.
8. Her credential's are excellent for the position of grant writer for the university.
9. Among the cooking utensils that we import and sell are carving knifes, coffee makers, and woks.
10. I was not aware of Jordan having completed her associate of arts degree.

Using Your Computer. You typed the following copy quickly but didn't have time to proofread it. Do so now.

We appreciate your request for information about the Mountain Top Inn. To answer you questions about convention facilitys, we have enclosed our latest brochure.

As you will see in the brochure, the Mountain Top Inn can accomodate groups of from 50 to 300 people with equal ease—and with the same high-quality service that have made us famous for more than 40 years.

After you have read the brochure, please be sure to call Alicia Cortez, our convention manager, at (800) 555-1234. Ms. Cortez will be happy to answer any questions that you may has.

ADJECTIVES

OBJECTIVES:

After completing Section 3.7, you should be able to:

1. Define and state the importance of adjectives in effective speaking and writing.
2. Identify and describe the various types of adjectives.
3. Explain how to form the comparative and superlative forms of descriptive adjectives.
4. Describe situations in which compound adjectives are and are not hyphenated.

The adjective is the banana peel of the parts of speech.

—Clifton Fadiman, American writer and editor

Without adjectives, our speech and writing would be dull and lifeless. Used wisely, adjectives make nouns and pronouns interesting, vivid, and specific. This section will introduce you to the many kinds of adjectives and discuss the ways that we commonly misuse adjectives. A mastery of the use of adjectives will help make your speech and writing better tools for communication.

IDENTIFYING ADJECTIVES

Any word that modifies or describes a noun or a pronoun is an *adjective*. An adjective usually precedes the noun it modifies. It tells "what kind," "how many," "how much," "which one," and "in what order." Some of the most commonly used kinds of adjectives are described below.

Articles

The words *a, an,* and *the* are called *articles*. Note how these special adjectives are commonly used.

> *The* coach achieved *a* victory by encouraging *an* eager team to practice.
> We were sure that *a* new member would join *the* team today.

Descriptive Adjectives

The most commonly used adjectives are *descriptive adjectives*—the adjectives that describe or tell "what kind of."

> In a *strong, clear* voice, Andrea rejected the *irresponsible* policies that some *real estate* companies use to lure *unsuspecting* consumers into buying *overpriced* and sometimes *worthless* property. (*Strong, clear, irresponsible, real estate, unsuspecting, overpriced,* and *worthless* are descriptive adjectives.)

Possessive Adjectives

The possessive personal pronouns (*my, your, his, her, its, our,* and *their*) and possessive nouns (*Steve's, Hilary's, Betty's,* and so on) are adjectives that modify nouns.

> *Your* associate inspected *our* sketch and gave it to *Herb's* assistant.

KEY POINT

The article *an* is used before a word that begins with a vowel (except the long *u* sound) or an *h* that is not pronounced: an *editor,* an *hour,* but a *united nation. The* is called the definite article.

Limiting Adjectives

Adjectives that tell "how many," "how much," or "in what order" are called *limiting adjectives*.

The *top five* winners in the region will receive *more than ten* prizes each. (*Top* tells "in what order." *Five* tells "how many winners." *more than ten* tells "how many prizes.")

Each winner had sold *many* cars, trucks, and vans. (*Each* modifies *winner*; *many* modifies *cars, trucks, and vans*.)

Proper Adjectives

Proper nouns are very often used as proper adjectives.

Used as a Noun	Used as an Adjective
in *Detroit*	a *Detroit* restaurant
near *Portland*	two *Portland* citizens
to *Phoenix*	*Phoenix* businesses

Proper adjectives include words derived from proper nouns, such as *Mexican, British, Canadian,* and *Israeli*.

Compound Adjectives

Two or more words joined to modify one noun or pronoun form a *compound adjective*.

Alexander wanted a *long-term* agreement but signed a *one-year* contract instead. (*Long-term* modifies *agreement*, and *one-year* modifies *contract*.)

She is a well-known author of time-management books. (*Well-known* modifies *author*, and *time-management* modifies *books*.)

My sister works as a real estate agent. (*Real estate* modifies *agent*.)

KEY POINT

Avoid ill-matched or redundant adjective-noun combinations:
Active consideration
Grateful thanks
True facts
Unexpected surprise

Demonstrative Adjectives

The pronouns *this, that, these,* and *those* are demonstrative pronouns that can function as adjectives.

As Pronouns	As Adjectives	As Pronouns	As Adjectives
this is	*this* book	*these* are	*these* offices
that has been	*that* software	*those* might be	*those* computers

Note that *these* is the plural of *this*; both *these* and *this* indicate nearness to the speaker. *Those* is the plural of *that*, and *those* and *that* indicate distance from the speaker. Never use the pronoun *them* as a substitute for *these* or *those*!

KEY POINT

Demonstrative adjectives "point" to the noun or pronoun they modify.

Please return *those* disks to Mr. O'Leary. (Not *them* disks.)

These kinds of illnesses arise often during the winter season. ("*These* kinds", not "*them* kinds" or "these *kind*.")

✔ CHECKUP 1

On a separate sheet of paper, identify the adjectives in the following sentences and label each *possessive* (P), *limiting* (L), *proper* (PR), *compound* (C), *descriptive* (D), or *demonstrative* (DM). Disregard the articles *a, an,* and *the.* (*Note:* Some adjectives may fit in more than one category.)

1. Jack's brother announced that two well-known musicians will be featured at the spring concert.
2. In three months his younger sister will graduate from college and work for this company out of the Kansas City office.
3. In Bill's opinion, we should choose a six-month assignment in beautiful Hawaii.
4. One of Carla's crucial accounts is a new client who represents a West Coast insurance company.
5. These bonds are tax-free investments, according to their new prospectus.
6. The third T-shirt outlet we opened has contributed a substantial profit to our struggling company.
7. A special class is being organized for new employees to learn these important procedures.
8. The Dallas attorney who represents that enterprise asked our employees for their opinions on Goldberg's character.

COMPARISON OF ADJECTIVES

Descriptive adjectives can be compared. For example, *strong* and *clear* can be compared to show degrees of strength and clarity: *strong, stronger,* and *strongest; clear, clearer,* and *clearest.* These three forms of comparison are called the *positive,* the *comparative,* and the *superlative* degrees.

1. The positive degree expresses the quality of *one* person or thing.

   a *strong* foundation

   a *clear* day

2. The comparative degree allows us to compare that quality in *two* persons or things.

   a *stronger* foundation

   a *clearer* day

KEY POINT

The comparative degree compares two persons or things. The superlative degree compares three or more persons or things.

3. The superlative degree enables us to compare that quality in *three or more* persons or things.

> the *strongest* foundation

> the *clearest* day

Now that we know how the three degrees are used, we need to know how they are formed.

Forming the Comparative and Superlative Degrees

The comparative degree is formed by adding *er* to the positive or by inserting the word *more* or *less* before the positive form. The superlative is formed by adding *est* to the positive or by inserting the word *most* or *least* before the positive form.

Positive	Comparative	Superlative
quick	quicker	quickest
funny	funnier	funniest
poor	poorer	poorest
decisive	more decisive	most decisive
	less decisive	least decisive

In addition, some very commonly used adjectives form their comparative and superlative degrees by changing the form to another word completely. Memorize these for quick reference.

Positive	Comparative	Superlative
bad	worse	worst
good	better	best
little	less	least
many	more	most
much	more	most

The comedian was the most funniest person we had ever heard.

Selecting the Correct Forms

Adjectives of only *one* syllable are compared by adding *er* or *est* to the positive degree. Adjectives of *three* or more syllables add *more* or *less* or *most* or *least*. Adjectives of *two* syllables vary: some add *er* or *est*; others add *more* or *less* or *most* or *least*. Sometimes, an error may be obvious to you: *more useful*, not *usefuler; most useful*, not *usefulest.* If you are unsure, consult a dictionary.

Avoiding Comparison Errors

The following discussion highlights two of the most common comparison errors in using adjectives: making double comparisons and comparing absolute adjectives.

Making Double Comparisons. Do not mix the different ways in which adjectives can be compared—use only one comparative form at a time.

better, not *more better*
greatest, not *most greatest*

Comparing Absolute Adjectives. Adjectives whose qualities cannot be compared are called *absolute adjectives.* For example, a glass of water cannot be *fuller* or *fullest. Full* is already tops!

Here are some other adjectives that cannot be compared:

accurate	empty	round	unanimous
complete	immaculate	square	unique
correct	perfect	supreme	true
dead	perpendicular	ultimate	straight

Although they cannot be compared, the qualities of these adjectives can be approached, as indicated by the following:

more nearly accurate
less nearly complete
most nearly correct
least nearly perfect

You may hear (especially in advertisements) of products that are *most unique*, but *unique* really says it all. Remember that absolute adjectives cannot logically be compared.

✔ CHECKUP 2

On a sheet of paper, correct any errors in the use of adjectives in the following sentences. If a sentence is correct, write *OK*.

1. The soft drink dispenser is fuller than the water dispenser.
2. These apartments are ~~more~~ better than the apartments on Main Street because they are ~~more~~ quiet and ~~more~~ bigger
3. Mr. Hartzog is definitely a better instructor than Mr. Lloyd. Indeed, he is probably the best instructor in the school.
4. Brett thought that we had enough tea, but the pitcher was ~~very~~ empty.
5. Which ~~clothes~~ dryer uses ~~the most energy~~, Model GX34 or Model GX84?
6. Li Ping is ~~more happier~~ now that she is working with the homeless.
7. Which of the two homeless shelters is ~~largest~~, Memorial Center or Mercy Center?
8. The medical center staff agrees that Ashley's fund-raising campaign is ~~very~~ unique.

More Than Any Other, More Than Anyone Else

In comparisons with *more than*, be sure to include the word *other* or *else* if the person or thing is being compared with *other* members of the same group.

> Lisa is *more* ambitious *than anyone else* in the Marketing Division. (With the word *else*, the sentence clearly says that Lisa *is* a member of the Marketing Division. Without the word *else*, the sentence would indicate that Lisa is *not* part of the Marketing Division but is being compared with people who are in this division.)

> Travis is *more* creative *than any other* designer in marketing. (Travis *is* a designer in marketing. Without the word *other*, this sentence would indicate that Travis is *not* a designer in marketing.)

Repeated Modifier

In the following examples, repeating the modifier *a* (or *an*), *the*, or *my* indicates that *two* different people are intended.

> The analyst and *the* programmer (*was? were?*) formerly with Bates Computers. (Repeating *the* shows that *two* people—an analyst and a programmer—are referred to. *Were* is the correct verb.)

> The analyst and programmer (*was? were?*) formerly with the municipal government. (One person who is both an analyst and a programmer is referred to. *Was* is correct.)

For Added Polish

The following short discussions will help you make correct choices when referring to two or more than two persons or things.

Each Other, One Another. Use *each other* when referring to two in number; use *one another* when referring to three or more.

> Laura and Anita work very effectively with *each other*. (Two people.)

> Several administrative assistants talked with *one another* about the proposed civic club. (Three or more administrative assistants.)

Either, Neither; Any, Any One, No One, Not Any, None. Use *either* or *neither* when referring to one of *two* persons or things. When referring to *three or more,* use *any, any one, no one, not any,* or *none*.

> *Either* of the sales associates can locate the product on the shelf. (There are only two sales associates. Therefore, *either* is correct.)

> *Any one* of the small airlines will arrange a charter flight to Tortola for you. (There are more than three small airlines; *any one* is correct.)

KEY POINT

Use a dictionary or a writer's handbook to help you decide whether to hyphenate a compound adjective.

COMPOUND ADJECTIVES

Hyphenate most compound adjectives that appear before a noun:

air-conditioned buses
first-quality merchandise
fund-raising projects
no-fault insurance
a *one-year* contract
tax-free bonds
three-mile hike
up-to-date report

When they appear after the noun, compound adjectives such as *air-conditioned* and *tax-free* retain the hyphen. Most other compounds do not. Some compound adjectives that almost always take hyphens before or after nouns include the following:

adjective + noun + *ed*	open-ended; single-spaced
adjective + participle	high-ranking; soft spoken
noun + adjective	toll-free; year-round
noun + participle	computer-aided; decision-making

Before the Noun	After the Noun
air-conditioned buses	buses that are *air-conditioned*
tax-free bonds	bonds that are *tax-free*
a *well-known* artist	an artist who is *well known*

Longtime use has made the following compounds so familiar that they are no longer written with hyphens:

high school teachers	*real estate* services
a *life insurance* policy	*social security* benefits

When the adverb *well* is used with a participle as a compound adjective, it is usually hyphenated before and after the noun.

The well-known speaker gave us some well-timed advice. (*Well-known* and *well-timed* are compound adjectives.)

Confusion may result when *well* and a participle appear after the noun and the participle is part of the verb.

The speaker is well *known*. (In this sentence, well is an adverb and *known* is part of the verb. The two words do not form a compound adjective.)

✓ CHECKUP 3

Apply the rules just presented by correcting the following sentences on a separate piece of paper. Write *OK* for any sentence that is correct.

1. Mr. Haggerty's court appointed attorney was named this morning.
2. My accountant and my investment adviser are well known in this region.

3. Ask Justin or Sasha—any one of them should know the answer.

4. When Don and Tom get to know each other better, they will work with one another very, very well.

5. The Litton fax machine is more durable than any fax machine available today.

6. My secretary, Kerry Ranlo, types faster than anyone in the legal department.

7. Wilson Werner is a five time winner in the amateur golf tournament.

8. Shankar's proposal is better than any proposal that we have evaluated so far.

9. Adrian planned a 15 minute break after each two hour demonstration.

10. Analysis has indicated that word of mouth recruiting by our students and graduates is our most effective way to attract competent students.

"Child teaching expert to speak."
—*Birmingham Post Herald*

PREDICATE ADJECTIVE OR PREDICATE NOMINATIVE?

Can you tell the difference? Earlier in this section, we discussed *being* verbs—verbs that express a state of being rather than action. Being verbs include all forms of the verb *to be* (such as *am, was, will be, should have been*) and verbs like *feel, seem,* and *appear*. A *predicate adjective* follows a being verb and modifies or describes the subject of the sentence.

His voice seems forceful. (*Forceful* follows a being verb and modifies the subject *voice.*)

The nurse has been helpful. (*Helpful* follows a being verb and modifies the subject *nurse.*)

Predicate nominatives also follow a being verb, but they rename—not modify—the subject. Note the following examples.

Max was the most successful graduate. (*Graduate* follows a being verb and renames the subject *Max.*)

Dina will be my first choice. (*Choice* follows a being verb and renames the subject *Dina.*)

Pronouns can also be predicate nominatives. Note the following example.

The candidate is he. (*He* follows a being verb and renames the subject *candidate.*)

CHECKUP 4

On a separate sheet, identify the words in parentheses as either predicate adjectives (*PA*) or predicate nominatives (*PN*).

1. Spring semester seems (short).
2. Phyllis is the (newscaster) on Saturday nights.
3. Ms. McKibben is (capable) and (well-suited) for the position.
4. Juan is (president) of the local Rotary Club.
5. My preference for the trip is (Cancun).

SECTION 3.7   REVIEW

Practical Application

A. On a separate sheet of paper, correct any errors involving adjectives. Write *OK* if the sentence is correct.
  1. Because they cooperated with one another so well, Nikki and Anthony were able to file their response weeks before the July 10 deadline.
  2. Tourists may purchase last minute gifts at the duty-free shops at the airport.
  3. For security and privacy reasons, door-to-door soliciting is prohibited in all campus offices and in the student residence halls.
  4. The price is substantially higher, but this VCR is no more better than that one.
  5. Every board member is limited to a five-minute statement of his or her position on the planned merger of city and county police services.
  6. Most of them desks are too high for computer use.
  7. Unless otherwise specified, each machine is equipped with a 120-volt, 10-ampere motor.
  8. Pete and Vera evaluated both color printers carefully, and they recommended the one that was least expensive.
  9. Yes, these types of damages are covered by your insurance policy.
  10. Cooperation is often unusual when sales commissions are at stake, but our five real estate agents work closely with one another.
  11. The dermatologist's examination room has no windows, but it is well-ventilated and well-lighted.
  12. In less than three years, our new CEO (chief executive officer) has increased our exports more than any CEO of this company.

B. On a sheet of paper, correct any grammatical errors in the following sentences. Write *OK* for any sentence that is correct.

1. Harriet said that the Gillis's have plans to attend the training seminar.
2. Next week we will begin lying our plans for the Memorial Day sale.
3. Two photographers, Manuel Espinosa and her, have been asked to submit proposed magazine covers for January.
4. There has been several up-and-coming companys that will succeed.
5. Because of her pace-setting sales volume, Loretta receives a higher commission than anyone in our region.
6. The Cassidy Book Store recorded revenues of $3 million last year—their best year ever.
7. Whom has Isabel chosen to decorate the reception area, Hernando or him?
8. Has Darby or Kay flew to Honduras before?
9. Although I am uncertain, the person who called this morning could indeed have been her.
10. Vito been working in California ever since he was graduated from Central Community College.
11. If the Messrs. Faridays are available, please confirm that all three of them can attend Fridays meeting.
12. One managers' recommendation was to lease all of the companies vehicles instead of buying them.
13. Please find out who's recommendation this is.
14. Scot and me both enjoy working out at the gym downtown.
15. After meeting with Mr. Ortaki and she, please prepare a summary of your discussion and any conclusions the three of you reach.

Editing Practice

Plurals and Possessives. Correct on a separate sheet of paper any errors in the use of plurals and possessives. Write OK for any sentence that has no error.

1. Because Greta and Linda DePriest are well-known consultants in the advertising field, the DePriest's are certainly worth the high fee they charge.
2. Mrs. Shellsburg does not think its wise to spend so much money renovating an old home; she prefers buying a new one.
3. My sister-in-law's suggestion was, "Renovate the old home."
4. Beth's and Keely's yogurt shop will open on July 4 at the Westfield Mall.
5. Damon and I enjoyed Wanda working with us on the new decor.
6. Carol answering the telephone has saved us time and let us work more efficiently.

7. If the Hilton's accept our offer to purchase their land, our farm will become the largest dairy farm in the state.
8. As soon as you receive there airline tickets, please mail them to each of the tourists.
9. Our ministers' brother is a well-respected citizen in this community.
10. The two mechanic's finally finished overhauling the fleet of rental cars.

Using Your Computer. Proofread the following excerpt from a printout. Using a separate sheet of paper, rewrite the excerpt, correcting the errors.

A three day delay will cause us to get behind in our production schedule. Let me assure you that we will do our best to give you an on time delivery if at all possible.

Homonyms, Anyone? Correct any errors in the use of homonyms—words that look or sound alike but have different meanings—in the following excerpt. Spelling checkers will not identify these words as errors because the words are correctly spelled but misused.

Let's take a brake before we get to tired. When we get tired, we may lose hour patients and not make the rite decision. We no that we should consider the situation carefully.

OBJECTIVES:
After completing Section 3.8, you should be able to:

1. Discuss the ways in which adverbs are like adjectives and how these two parts of speech differ.
2. Explain how to identify the comparative and superlative forms of one-syllable adverbs and of adverbs ending in *ly*.
3. Name at least six conjunctive adverbs and six subordinating conjunctions and tell how each type is used.
4. Discuss several of the pitfalls of adverb use and ways to avoid them.
5. Explain how recognizing linking verbs can help eliminate adjective and adverb confusion.

ADVERBS

I love our American language as if it were my own child. I watch it grow, adding words from the streets and the sciences. I wince with pain when I see or hear a good old word being broken on the wheel of ill usages. It's as if my own child were having a finger snapped.

—Earl Ubell

Like adjectives, adverbs modify or describe. You will see several similarities between adverbs and adjectives as you read this section, including some common confusions in their use.

IDENTIFYING ADVERBS

An *adverb* is a word that modifies an adjective, a verb, or another adverb. Adverbs answer questions such as "Why?" "When?" "Where?" "How?" "How much?" and "To what extent?" Many adverbs are formed simply by adding *ly* to an adjective. (Adverbs that end in *y* change their *y* to *i* before adding *ly*.)

Adjective	Adverb
adequate	adequately
clear	clearly
happy	happily
immediate	immediately
perfect	perfectly

As you learned in Section 3.1, most words that end in *ly* are adverbs, but not all adverbs end in *ly*, as the following list shows:

also	never	soon
always	now	then
hard	often	there
here	quite	too
much	right	very

Note how adverbs are used in the following sentences.

Alex Murray will meet us *here*. (Meet where? Answer: *here*. The adverb *here* modifies the verb *meet*.)

That is a *very* good spreadsheet program. (*How* good? *Very* good. The adverb *very* modifies the adjective *good*.)

She worked *quite* well under the pressure of the tight deadlines. (*How* well? *Quite* well. The adverb *quite* modifies another adverb, *well*.)

Some words can be used either as adjectives or as adverbs, depending on their position in the sentence.

He swallowed *hard* and then started to speak. (Here *hard* is an adverb that modifies the verb *swallow*.)

Devin complained that painting the lawn furniture was *hard* work. (Here *hard* is an adjective that modifies the noun *work*.)

COMPARISON OF ADVERBS

Adverbs can be compared in much the same way as adjectives. To indicate the comparative and superlative forms of a one-syllable adverb, add *er* or *est* to the positive form:

fast, faster, fastest
late, later, latest
soon, sooner, soonest

For adverbs ending in *ly*, use *more* or *most* (or *less* or *least*):

quickly, more quickly, most quickly
quickly, less quickly, least quickly
confidently, more confidently, most confidently
skillfully, less skillfully, least skillfully

The judge ordered the defendant to sit down angrily.

World View

The English phrase "Out of sight, out of mind," when translated by a computer into Russian and then back into English, became "invisible maniac." As a test, a writer entered his own Russian version of the same English phrase into a similar computer. The computer translation was "blind and mad."

Certain adverbs form their comparative and superlative degrees by completely changing their forms:

well, better, best
badly, worse, worst
much, more, most

CONJUNCTIVE ADVERBS

Conjunctive adverbs, as their name tells, are adverbs that serve as conjunctions—words that *join*. These adverbs are also known as *transitional words*.

accordingly	likewise	still	whereas
consequently	moreover	then	yet
furthermore	nevertheless	therefore	
however	otherwise	thus	

These adverbs join two *independent* clauses, as shown in the following sentences:

Insurance premiums are a big expense; *moreover,* the premiums will go up again at the end of the year.

Our expenses through July 15 are about 10 percent over budget; *however,* we expect the expenses to decrease as our quality increases.

Note, again, that each sentence consists of two *independent* clauses joined by a conjunctive adverb.

ADVERBIAL CLAUSES

Subordinating conjunctions introduce *dependent* clauses that serve as adverbs modifying an adjective, verb, or adverb in the main clause. Here are some commonly used subordinating conjunctions:

after	before	unless
although	for	until
as	if	when
because	since	while

Note the following examples of adverbial clauses introduced by subordinating conjunctions:

Stacy Bancroft will become the executive vice president when Alex Fuentes retires. (The adverbial clause *when Alex Fuentes retires* modifies the verb *will become* in the main clause.)

Our new laptop computer will be successful *if we market it properly.* (The adverbial clause *if we market it properly* modifies the adjective *successful.*)

☑ **~~Checkpoint~~ 1**

Identify the italicized words in the following sentences by labeling each *simple adverb* (SA), *conjunctive adverb* (CA), or *subordinating conjunction* (SC).

1. *Since* Yoshi opened his computer repair service, he has been *extremely* busy.

2. Meg and Dimitri have requested an appointment *when* Mrs. Wolfe returns from Miami.

3. The deadline for completion of the computer files conversion is next Tuesday; our vice president, *therefore*, has approved our working overtime.

4. *If* you would like more information about our prototype for an electric car, please call our toll-free number.

5. The new copier works *quickly* and *quietly*; it does not, *moreover*, have paper jams as often as our last copier did.

6. Judy has been *unduly* busy *since* her assistant had to be out of work for knee surgery.

7. *Because* Cody was behind in his work, he stayed *here late* two nights this week.

8. Matt *specifically* stated that he wanted a media room; *accordingly*, his architect designed a *very* modern room wired for electronic devices.

PITFALLS OF ADVERB USE

In speaking and writing, be sure to avoid these pitfalls of adverb use.

Position of the Adverb

Place an adverb as close as possible to the word that it modifies. Sometimes the meaning of a sentence can be changed by the position of the adverb.

Only Miss Bianco has a solid oak credenza in her office. (No one else has one.)

Ms. Bianco has *only* a solid oak credenza in her office. (She has nothing else in her office, only a solid oak credenza.)

Ms. Bianco has a solid oak credenza *only* in her office. (She has one nowhere else but in her office.)

Double Negative

Adverbs that have negative meanings (*scarcely, hardly, only, never,* and *but*) should not be used with other negatives.

Clayton *has scarcely* any money left in his bank account. (Not: "Clayton *hasn't scarcely* . . . .")

With five copiers working, Peggy *could hardly* hear Patrick. (Not: Peggy "*couldn't hardly* . . . .")

Claire *couldn't help recommending* a possible solution. (Not: Clair "*couldn't help but recommend* . . . .")

Never or Not?

Never and *not* are both adverbs, and both have negative meanings. *Not* expresses simple negation, but *never* means "not *ever*" (note the word *ever*). Use *never* only when an appropriately long time is intended.

Ms. Holcomb has *not* sent me an e-mail this week. (*Never* would be incorrect because the meaning "*not ever* . . . this week" would be wrong.)

Phyllis has *never* been married. (Even though *not* could be substituted for *never*, *never* is a better choice because it indicates a longer period of time.)

Where for That

The subordinating conjunction *that* (not the conjunctive adverb *where*) should be used in expressions such as the following:

I read in the newspaper *that* the Acme Record Company is releasing his latest CD. (Not: "I read in the newspaper *where* . . . .")

We heard on television *that* the governor has endorsed Cecilia Kish for attorney general. (Not: "We heard on television *where*. . . ." But: "We toured the house where *the famous musician once lived.*")

Badly or Worst Way for Very Much

Too often, we hear people say *badly* or *in the worst way* when they really mean *very much*.

Evelyn said that she wanted a minivan *very much*. (Not: "wanted a minivan *badly*" or "wanted a mini van *in the worst way*.")

ADJECTIVE AND ADVERB CONFUSIONS

Several adjective-adverb pairs cause special problems for writers and speakers. In the following pairs, the adjective is listed first.

Bad, Badly

Bad is an adjective; *badly* is an adverb.

Darren performs *badly* under pressure. (Performs how? *Badly*. The adverb *badly* modifies the action verb *performs*.)

The problem in selecting between *bad* and *badly* arises following nonaction verbs:

Olivia felt (*bad? badly?*) when she learned of the storm damage. (Here, *felt* is a linking verb, not an action verb. The answer here will modify not the verb *felt* but the noun *Olivia*. Thus an adjective is required because an adverb cannot modify a noun: Olivia felt *bad* . . . .)

The being verbs—*am, is, are, was, were, be, been*, and *being*—are all nonaction, or linking, verbs. In addition to these, sense verbs such as *feel, appear, seem, look, sound, taste*, and *smell* can be used as nonaction verbs. Remember that adjectives, not adverbs, must follow linking verbs.

Mr. Trammel was (*happy? happily?*) when he heard about the picnic. (The being verb *was* links the subject *Mr. Trammel* to the adjective *happy*. The verb *was* shows no action.)

Mr. Trammel appeared (*happy? happily?*) when he heard about the picnic. (Like *was*, the linking verb *appeared* shows no action; thus the adjective *happy* is correct.)

The motorists were (*patient? patiently?*). (Because the verb *were* indicates no action, the adjective *patient* is correct.)

The motorists seemed (*patient? patiently?*). (Like the nonaction verb *were*, *seemed* links the noun *motorists* to the adjective *patient*; thus *patient* modifies *motorists*.)

Keep in mind that some of these verbs can also be used as action verbs. Analyze each sentence carefully.

Dr. Spragins felt carefully for a possible fracture. (Here, *felt* is an action verb; thus the adverb *carefully* modifies the verb *felt*.)

Real, Really; Sure, Surely

Real and *sure* are adjectives. Use the *ly* endings to remind you that *really* and *surely* are adverbs. In the following examples, note that you can substitute the adverb *very* or *certainly* whenever *really* or *surely* is correct.

Leah and Al were (*real? really?*) dedicated to helping children who were visually impaired. ("*Very* dedicated" makes sense. The adverb *really* is correct.)

Lucinda (*sure? surely?*) was smart to learn about mortgages before applying for one to finance here new home. (*Certainly was* makes sense. The adverb *surely* is correct.)

OOPS!

"Menu item: Dinner Special—Turkey $2.35; Chicken or Beef $2.25; Children $2.00"
—Richard Lederer, *Anguished English*

Good, Well

Good is an adjective, and *well* is an adverb. The adjective *good* can modify nouns and pronouns; the adverb *well* can modify adjectives and verbs.

> Dr. Colby always prepares *good* lectures. (The adjective *good* modifies the noun *lectures*.)

> Dr. Colby always prepares lectures *well*. (The adverb *well* modifies the verb *prepares*. Prepares lectures how? Prepares *well*.)

> *Exception: Well* can also be an adjective, *but only when referring to personal health.*

> Because Amanda did not feel *well*, she left the office early. (Here, *well* is an adjective referring to a person's health.)

Remember the term *well-being*, and you'll be sure to recall that *well* is an adjective only when it refers to health.

If you do not feel good, you should see a doctor.

Some, Somewhat

Some is an adjective; *somewhat* is an adverb. To use *somewhat* correctly, test to be sure that you can substitute the phrase *a little bit.*

> As we anticipated, Mr. Ellis was (*some? somewhat?*) surprised at the increase in sales. (Does *a little bit surprised* make sense? Yes—thus *somewhat* is correct.)

> As you requested, we have prepared (*some? somewhat?*) ideas for the advertising campaign. (Does *a little bit ideas* make sense? No—thus the adjective *some* is correct.)

Most, Almost

Most is an adjective, the superlative of *much* or *many*, as in *much, more, most. Almost* is an adverb meaning "not quite" or "very nearly."

> (*Most? Almost?*) assistant managers aspire to become managers. (Because *very nearly assistant managers* makes no sense, *almost* cannot be correct. "*Most* assistant managers" is correct.)

> Rafael brought (*most? almost?*) enough hard hats for everyone at the building site. (*Very nearly enough hard hats does* make sense. *Almost* is correct.)

✓ CHECKUP 2

On a sheet of paper, correct any adverb errors in the following sentences. Write *OK* if a sentence is correct.

1. Rafe appeared ~~angrily~~ angry at the idea of selling his mountain cabin.

2. Because of potential legal action, we were somewhat hesitant to OK discuss this sensitive issue with the employees involved.

3. After the laptop computer goes on sale, it will be a ~~real~~ *really* good deal.
4. Rhett was ~~some~~ *somewhat* amused by the true story that Sam related.
5. Most of us in the textile manufacturing business found the reports ~~real~~ disappointing.
6. *OK* After almost three months, the parcel delivery service is doing ~~really~~ very well.
7. *OK* Because he was rushed, Henry painted the door facings badly.
8. She was, of course, ~~sure~~ *surely* justified in her request for a security guard in the parking lot.
9. Needless to say, she and I felt ~~badly~~ *Bad* when we heard that Moira Foster was being transferred out of state.
10. Because you don't feel ~~good~~ *well*, James, we suggest that you work on your computer at home this week.

SECTION 3.8   REVIEW

Practical Application

A. On a sheet of paper, correct any adverb errors in the following sentences. Write *OK* if a sentence is correct.
  1. Because Joan has been late so ~~frequent~~ *frequently*, Mr. Smythe has put a reprimand in her personnel folder.
  2. Reynaldo ~~never told~~ *has did not* me that he left early this morning.
  3. We immediately noticed that Louis had slipped on the ice and that he needed help in the worst way.
  4. All of us were glad when we read in ~~the~~ *that* newspaper where the proposed bridge would be built next year.
  5. Although the grilled hamburgers do smell ~~deliciously~~, I really am not very hungry right now.
  6. *only* Nicole and I ~~only~~ know about the surprise birthday party; no one else knows about it yet.
  7. Management feels that discounting our retail prices should ~~surely~~ work very well during the holiday shopping season.
  8. Of course, we felt very ~~badly~~ when we heard of your transfer.
  9. Follow these suggestions, Sita, to make sure that you prepare your speech ~~good~~. *well*
  10. The exhibit sketch that Heidi and Mildred submitted ~~hasn't~~ *has* scarcely one new idea that will attract new customers.
  11. "Our company," Robert said, "has a real good chance of winning the softball game tonight."

12. Elisabeth appeared very poised as she approached the podium to speak. *OK*

13. Our temporary staffing needs will increase ~~some~~ *somewhat* during the summer months owing to employees' scheduling of their vacations.

14. Because our condominium is on the beach, we can clear/hear the waves hitting the shore.

15. Yes, I do believe that his studying at the community college will work out very ~~good~~ *well*.

B. On a separate sheet of paper, correct any errors in the following sentences. Write *OK* if a sentence is correct.

1. According to Morris's manager, Morris works ~~mostas~~ *almost* meticulously as Dennis.

2. Last year, Erin had three computer operators in her department; since the budget cutbacks, however, she hasn't but two computer operators. *has*

3. Here ~~is~~ *are* all the tools and supplies that you requested.

4. Of course, Warren and ~~myself~~ *I* will be glad to help you interview the prospective secretary.

5. As you can well imagine, the Jacksons were ~~really~~ *real* pleased to learn that their home loan has been approved.

6. Sophie went home from work because she wasn't feeling very ~~good~~ *well*.

7. Neither the two supervisors nor the two assistant supervisors ~~has~~ *had* volunteered to help with the blood drive.

8. Because Marisol been devoting most of her time to the upcoming annual sales meeting, she has hired part-time help to do some of her day-to-day tasks.

9. Tasha will help you process all ~~them~~ *those* orders tomorrow.

10. Maria sure does a ~~superb~~ *great* job of directing incoming telephone calls.

11. Are ~~these~~ *those* kinds of pen and pencil sets available through the catalog ordering department?

12. There's about three or four ways to set up this trust fund.

13. The babies in the new diaper advertisement must look healthy and happy.

14. Of course, only the Walshes have requested specific seats at the ceremony.

Editing Practice

Using Your Computer. Correct the errors as you type the following paragraphs.

Lindsay called the manager's office yesterday to request additional funds for her research project. She reported that she hasn't scarcely any money remaining in her budget.

She had read in the company magazine where more funds may be available by May. Lindsay definitely needs the funds now and is some frustrated because of the lack of response to her request for more funds.

PREPOSITIONS

Words are one of our chief means of adjusting to all situations of life. The better control we have over words, the more successful our adjustment is likely to be.

—Bergen Evans

OBJECTIVES:
After completing Section 3.9, you should be able to:

1. State the function of prepositions.
2. Explain why certain prepositions are used with certain words even though no rule is involved and suggest the best ways to learn these combinations.
3. Identify several pitfalls in the use of prepositions and cite the rules for avoiding those pitfalls.

Such prepositions as *for, in, of, on,* and *to* are used so often that we generally pay no attention to them. In order to avoid some common preposition errors, however, you must pay attention to the rules presented in this section.

IDENTIFYING PREPOSITIONS

A *preposition* is a connecting word. It connects a noun or a pronoun to the rest of the sentence. The preposition combined with that noun or pronoun makes up a *prepositional phrase.* Examine the following commonly used prepositions and some sample prepositional phrases. (*Note: But* is a preposition only when it means "except." In other cases, *but* is a conjunction.)

Prepositions			Prepositional Phrases
about	but (except)	off	*above* the sink
above	by	on	*after* our meeting
after	except	over	*before* your first lesson
among	for	to	*from* Gary and Mona
at	from	under	*into* the fray
before	in	until	*like* that newspaper
below	into	up	*off* the shelf
beside	like	upon	*to* the new restaurant
between	of	with	*with* my partner

The noun or pronoun that follows the preposition in a phrase is the *object* of the preposition. The phrase may include modifiers—for example, *new* in *to the new equipment* modifies *equipment,* which is the object of the preposition *to.* Also, a phrase may have compound objects, as in *from Jack and Ruth.*

Because prepositional phrases often interrupt the subject and the verb in a sentence, your ability to make subjects and verbs agree will sometimes depend on your ability to identify prepositional phrases. Examine the following examples.

The programmers *in this department* are reviewing the computer security rules carefully. (The prepositional phrase *in this department* separates the subject *programmers* from the verb *are*. A careless speaker, therefore, may incorrectly say "department *is*," which is wrong.)

One official *on both boards* has agreed to serve as mediator. (The prepositional phrase *on both boards* separates the subject *official* from the verb *has agreed*.)

✔ CHECKUP 1

Using a separate sheet of paper, identify the prepositions and the prepositional phrases in the following sentences.

1. Most of the reimbursement requests that Chantal laid on my desk have been approved and sent to the Accounts Payable Department.
2. Only one of the partners indicated that she was unhappy with the billing procedures.
3. Hayley went into the conference room, I think, with her assistant.
4. The final decision on the site of the midtown helicopter landing pad will be made by the planning board.
5. Because Mr. Yebio was in a hurry, Denny drove him to the airport.
6. You will need the theater tickets that were put in my desk drawer.
7. Between you and me, I do not believe that investing in that stock was a smart idea.
8. The main reason for the delay is that Jill is still on the telephone.

WORDS REQUIRING SPECIFIC PREPOSITIONS

Through years of use, certain expressions are now considered "correct," even though there may be no rule or logical reason to make them correct. Such usage, called *idiomatic usage,* governs many expressions in our language. The use of certain prepositions with certain words is idiomatic. Long-accepted use has made it correct to use these prepositions. Examples are given in the table "Idiomatic Expressions With Prepositions."

Idiomatic Expressions With Prepositions	
abhorrence *of*	abound *in* or *with*
abhorrent *to*	accompanied *by* a person
abide *by* a decision	accompanied *with* an item
abide *with* a person	acquit *of*

adapted *for* (made over for)
adapted *from* a work
adapted *to* (adjusted to)
affinity *between*
agree *to* a proposal
agree *with* someone
agreeable to (*with* is permissible)
angry *at* or *about* a thing or condition
angry *with* a person
attend *to* (listen)
attend *upon* (wait on)
beneficial *to*
bestow *upon*
buy *from*
compare *to* the mirror image (assert a likeness)
compare *with* the reverse side (analyze for similarities or differences)
compliance *with*
comply *with*
confer *on* or *upon* (give to)
confer *with* (talk to)
confide *in* (place confidence in)
confide *to* (entrust to)
conform *to*
 in conformity *to* or *with*
consist *in* (exist in)
consist *of* (be made up of)
convenient *for* (suitable for, easy for)
convenient *to* (near)
conversant *with*
correspond *to* or *with* (match; agree with)
correspond *with* (exchange letters)
credit *for*

deal *in* goods or services
deal *with* someone
depend or dependent *on* (but *independent of*)
different *from* (not *than* or *to*)
disappointed *in* or *with*
discrepancy *between* two things
discrepancy *in* one thing
dispense *with*
employ *for* a purpose
employed *at* a stipulated salary
employed *in, on,* or *upon* a work or business
enter *at* a given point
enter *in* a record
enter *into* (become a party to)
enter *into* or *upon* (start)
exception *to* a statement
familiarize *with*
foreign *to* (preferred to *from*)
identical *with*
independent *of* (not *from*)
inferior or superior *to*
need *of* or *for*
part *from* (take leave of)
part *with* (relinquish)
plan or planning *to* (not *on*)
profit *by*
in regard *to*
with regard *to*
as regards
retroactive *to* (not *from*)
speak *to* (tell something to a person)
speak *with* (discuss with)
wait *for* a person, a train, an event
wait *on* a customer, a guest

The idiomatic expressions that are used (and misused) most often are given special attention below. Be sure to learn to use these expressions correctly.

Agree With, Agree To

Use *agree with* when the object of the preposition is a person or an idea; use *agree to* when the object is not a person or an idea.

Does Esteban *agree with* Mr. Marlowe on the need to increase our stock price? (Because the object of the preposition is a person, the preposition *with* is correct.)

Yes, Esteban *agrees to* the proposal to increase our stock price. (Here, the object of the preposition is *proposal*; because the object is not a person or an idea, *agrees to* is correct.)

Angry With, Angry At

Use *angry with* when the object of the preposition is a person; use *angry at* or *about* when the object is not a person.

Josh appeared to be *angry with* Carole because of the delay in shipment. (*With* is correct because its object is a person, *Carole*.)

Josh appeared to be *angry at* the delay in shipment. (Now the object of the preposition is not a person; thus *angry at* or *about* is correct.)

Part From, Part With

Part from means "to take leave of"; *part with* means "to relinquish" or "to give up."

Part from is generally used when the object of the preposition is a person. *Part with* is generally used when the object is not a person.

As soon as we *part from* Mark Wesson at the luncheon meeting, we will return to the office. (*Part from* a person.)

Although we certainly appreciate the features of the new printers, we hate to *part with* our familiar old printers that were reliable and durable. (*Part with*, meaning "to relinquish" or "to give up.")

Discrepancy In, Discrepancy Between, Discrepancy Among

Use *discrepancy in* when the object of the preposition is singular. Use *discrepancy between* when the object specifically denotes *two* in number. Use *discrepancy among* when the object denotes three or more persons or things.

I checked the patient's chart carefully and found no *discrepancy in* it. (Note that *one* chart is mentioned.)

Compare these two diagrams carefully; then let me know if you find any *discrepancy between* the two. (Note that *two* graphs are mentioned.)

There were many *discrepancies among* the testimonies presented in the case.

In Regard To, With Regard To, As Regards

The three terms *in regard to, with regard to,* and *as regards* are equally correct, but be sure to remember that only the word *regard* (not *regards*) can be used in the phrases *in regard to* and *with regard to*.

Gary has already consulted Mr. Collette (*in? with? as?*) regard to the menu changes. (Either *in* or *with* is correct.)

(*In? With? As?*) regards the menu changes, please consult Mr. Collette. (Only *as* is correct—*as regards.*)

Note: In many cases, you can simplify and improve your sentence by substituting the word *about* for *in regard to, with regard to,* or *as regards.*

Gary has already consulted Mr. Collette *about* the menu changes.

Different From, Identical With, Plan To, Retroactive To

Memorize the correct prepositions that go with these phrases so that you will use them properly.

different *from* (not *than*)
identical *with* (not *to*)
plan *to* (not *on*)
retroactive *to* (not *from*)

✓ CHECKUP 2

On a separate sheet of paper, correct any preposition errors in the following sentences. Write *OK* for any sentence that has no error.

1. We wrote to him in regard to the warranty on his lawn mower.
2. Barbara and Bill said that the most difficult aspect of transferring to our Kentucky branch was parting from all their good friends. *ok*
3. Lindsey enthusiastically told us how the new manager is different than the previous one. *from*
4. Malcolm was angry at the newspaper carrier because the carrier tossed the newspaper into a mud puddle. *with*
5. Nathan plans on opening his graduation gifts at dinner. *to open*
6. The judge was amazed to find several discrepancies in the testimony. *ok*
7. Joe and I proofread both copies of the flight schedule; fortunately, we found no discrepancy in the two of them. *between*
8. According to both attorneys, the contract will surely be retroactive from October 1. *to*
9. This television is identical to the one that was damaged in shipping. *with*
10. Yes, Karen and I do agree with Ben concerning the need to upgrade our graphics software. *ok*

PITFALLS OF USING PREPOSITIONS

Deciding when to use *between* and when to use *among* is one preposition choice that traps many writers and speakers. Other pitfalls concern (1) adding unnecessary prepositions and (2) omitting prepositions that *are* necessary. Study the following to avoid the most common preposition pitfalls.

Between, Among

Use *between* when referring to *two* persons, places, or things, and use *among* when referring to three or more.

> The votes for the new city council president were divided *between* Paul and Ray. (Between two people.)

> The responses to our new product were divided *among* our three freelance consultants. (Among three consultants.)

Between may also be used to express a relationship of one thing to each of several other things on a one-to-one-basis.

> A separate agreement was signed *between* the parent company and each of the franchises.

Beside, Besides

Beside means "by the side of"; *besides* means "in addition to."

> Yes, the man seated *beside* Ms. Harris is Darryl Anderson, our guest speaker. ("By the side of" Ms. Harris.)

> Do you know who is scheduled to speak *besides* Mr. Anderson? ("In addition to" Mr. Anderson.)

Inside, Outside

Do not use the preposition *of* after *inside* or *outside*. When referring to time, use *within*, not *inside of.*

> The cloak room door is the first door *inside* the main entrance. (Not *inside of.*)

> We expect to have our budgets completed *within* the week. (Not *inside of.*)

All, Both

Use *of* after *all* or *both* only when *all* or *both* refers to a pronoun. Omit *of* if either word refers to a noun.

> All the singer's fans blocked the entrance to the theater. (*Of* is not needed.)

> All *of* them eventually dispersed without incident. (*Of* is required here.)

At, To; In, Into

At and *in* denote position; *to* and *into* signify motion.

> Edna arrived *at* the board meeting and immediately went *to* the podium. (*At* for position; *to* for motion.)

> They went *into* the hotel and set up the display *in* the main ballroom. (*Into* for motion; *in* for position.)

> *Note:* When either *at* or *in* refers to a place, use *in* for larger places and *at* for smaller places.

> Amanda lives *in* Cleveland County and teaches *at* the local community college. (Here *in Cleveland County* indicates the larger place; *at the local community college* indicates the smaller place.)

Behind, Not In Back Of

Use *behind*, not *in back of*. *In front of,* however, is correct.

> Until the presentation begins, place the promotional display *behind*, not *in front of,* the curtain.

From, Off

From is generally used with persons; *off* is used with things. (*Off* is used with persons only when something on the person is physically being lifted away.) Never use *of* or *from* after *off*.

> Get some extra fax paper *from* Celia. (Not *off Celia*.)

> After ten minutes, take the ice pack *off* your arm. (Something is physically being lifted away.)

> Let's take these photographs *off* the book shelf. (Not *off of* the book shelf.)

Where, Not Where . . . At or Where . . . To

Adding *at* or *to* to *where* is a glaring error in usage.

> We do not know *where* Dr. Carter is. (Not *is at*.)

> *Where* did Howard go? (Not *go to*.)

Help, Not Help From

Do not use the word *from* after the verb *help*.

> The lecture was so stimulating that we could not *help* asking Dr. Baglione some questions. (Not *help from asking*.)

Opposite, Not *Opposite To*

Do not use the word *to* after *opposite*.

> The post office is directly *opposite* the museum. (Not *opposite to*.)

Like, Not *Like For*

Omit the word *for* after *like*.

> Mr. Chowdhury told Ms. Stevens that he would *like* her to visit his waterfront property. (Not *like for*.)

✓ **CHECKUP 3**

On a separate sheet of paper, correct any preposition errors in the following sentences. Write *OK* for any sentence that has no error.

1. The project planning component was divided ~~between~~ *among* Rosa, Tim, and Omar.
2. When the rain started, we quickly ran ~~in~~ *into* a nearby restaurant.
3. Is the woman standing beside~~s~~ Vance the visiting physician that you spoke of?
4. Does the supervisor know where all ~~of~~ her employees are ~~at~~?
5. We know that the choir cannot help ~~from~~ singing when they are on the bus.
6. Do you know where the plumber and electrician have gone ~~to~~?
7. Let's leave all ~~of~~ these cables and tools in the truck.
8. Both ~~of~~ the squad members received awards for their roles in rescuing the children from the rising flood waters.
9. Bob's father would like ~~for~~ him to earn a scholarship.
10. We are sure that the ice cream store is opposite the cellular telephone office. *OK*
11. Perhaps you should go ~~in~~ *into* the new hospital to inspect its surgical facilities.
12. According to the e-mail this morning, we may donate blood tomorrow ~~inside~~ *within* of working hours.
13. Our new office is opposite ~~to~~ the city park.
14. The nurse will take the bandage ~~from~~ *off* your arm.
15. Place the hard drive in back *off* of the computer monitor.

SECTION 3.9 REVIEW

Practical Application

A. On a separate sheet of paper, correct any preposition errors in the following sentences. Write *OK* for any sentence that has no error.

1. When potential clients have been identified, the list is divided *among* ~~between~~ the three recently hired stockbrokers.
2. With regards to the retirement of the company president, I have been asked to hold a press conference tomorrow morning at 10:30.
3. The revised estimate is no different from the previous one.
4. Do you know yet what Ann plans to do in regards to the long-distance telephone service?
5. Abby found Harry's key ring inside of the paper tray on the copier.
6. Of course, we would like for Mrs. Stronberg to be our speaker at the retirement banquet.
7. You should ask Gracie where Lucy went to.
8. Emily and Lana will take all of these printouts off of the conference room table.
9. Pete's comments were almost identical to the comments we received from our consultant.
10. Most of us could not help from wondering why the product was selling so well.
11. As a matter of fact, Lyle was angry at the president until he realized that the transfer included a big promotion and relocation package.
12. Denise carefully checked the equipment bid to make sure that there was no discrepancy in it.
13. John's office is on the fifth floor and is opposite to Gerald's office.
14. Baxter dislikes parting from the antiques he has collected.
15. Who besides Abdul will be promoted in July?

B. On a separate sheet of paper, correct any grammatical errors in the following sentences. Write *OK* for any sentence that is correct.

1. You should order more of them T-shirts, because they're selling as soon as we put them on the shelf.
2. Does the hotel conform with the local building codes?
3. The chef who created these two delicacies are not giving anyone his recipe.
4. A number of complaints about this new model has been received by our product manager.
5. Yes, Luis usually works longer hours than me.
6. Do you know whose planning the video conference on our new products?

7. Bert Mason, who you met at the meeting last Wednesday, has just received his associate of arts degree in information systems.
8. Each of our various departments have their own employee lounge area.
9. Perhaps the reason Vanna doesn't feel good is that she frequently skips meals.
10. Don't Woody want to take our clients to play golf Friday afternoon?
11. Don't Sheila and Veralee want you and I to help them develop their film?
12. Among the swimming pools that we manage are the indoor pool at the Syms Hotel.
13. Every executive in the country will surely improve their time management skills by reading Larry Denver's informative new book.
14. Have you already invited the Delgado's to visit with us when they tour the United States?
15. Who, in your opinion, is the best chef in our hotel chain, Ron or he?

Editing Practice

Using Business Vocabulary. From the list below, select the word that best completes each sentence. On a separate piece of paper, write the corresponding letter of the correct word for each sentence.

a. comptroller
b. cumulative
c. enumerate
d. exorbitant
e. inexhaustible
f. unscrupulous

1. To make the transparencies easier to read, _____ the items listed on each one.
2. The first column lists July sales; each succeeding column lists the sales for the next month and the _____ sales for the fiscal year.
3. Mr. Dexter, the _____ of our company, assists with all our financial affairs.
4. The newspaper featured a story on _____ hardware stores that sold generators at _____ prices during the recent hurricane.
5. Our supply of raw materials is virtually _____, but transporting them to our factory is very expensive.

Writing Sentences. Each of the following terms is a must for your vocabulary and your spelling lists. Do you know the meaning of each term? Use each term correctly in a sentence. Write or type your sentences on a separate sheet of paper.

1. accommodate
2. cancellation
3. chief executive officer
4. comparable
5. essential
6. outrageous
7. potential
8. recommendation
9. strategic planning
10. survey

Conjunctions

With but *and* or, *the compound sentence becomes more thoughtful. The mind is at work, turning its thought first one way then another, meeting the reader's objections by stating them.*

—Sheridan Baker, *The Practical Stylist*

OBJECTIVES:

After completing Section 3.10, you should be able to:

1. Describe the three types of conjunctions and give examples of the use of each type.
2. Identify the pitfalls in the use of conjunctions and explain how to avoid those pitfalls.
3. Discuss ways of ensuring parallel structure with coordinating and correlative conjunctions.

A s you will recall from Section 3.1, a *conjunction* is a word that is used to *join* words, phrases, or clauses within a sentence.

The delivery *and* the installation are included in the quoted price. (In this sentence, the conjunction *and* joins the words *delivery* and *installation*.)

You may get a report from my office or from the laboratory. (The conjunction *or* joins two prepositional phrases, *from my office* and *from the laboratory*.)

Lee wants to buy a scanner for her computer, *but* she is waiting for the price to go down. (The conjunction *but* joins the two independent clauses.)

Writing varied sentences and punctuating them correctly become much simpler once you have mastered the uses of conjunctions. This section presents three different kinds of conjunctions, discusses the most common pitfalls in using conjunctions, and then considers parallel structure—an important topic that is closely related to conjunction use.

TYPES OF CONJUNCTIONS

There are three types of conjunctions: *coordinating, correlative,* and *subordinating conjunctions.* As you will see, coordinating and correlative conjunctions connect two or more items of equal grammatical rank.

Subordinating conjunctions, however, connect a subordinate clause to a main clause.

Coordinating Conjunctions

The four coordinating conjunctions—*and, but, or,* and *nor*—are very commonly used. Note that they connect only like elements of grammar: two or more words, two or more phrases, or two or more clauses.

> Tea *and* coffee are included with your meal. (The conjunction *and* connects two words, *tea* and *coffee*.)
>
> Tea, coffee, *and* dessert are included with your meal. (Here the conjunction *and* joins *three* words.)
>
> Lucille has been with clients *or* with her staff since early morning. (The conjunction *or* joins two prepositional phrases, *with clients* and *with her staff*.)
>
> Mr. Wilder planned to spend three days at the resort, *but* he couldn't get a hotel room. (The conjunction *but* connects two independent, or main, clauses.)

Correlative Conjunctions

Correlative conjunctions are pairs of conjunctions that are regularly used together to connect like elements. (Note, again, that both coordinating and correlative conjunctions connect *like* elements only.) The most commonly used correlative conjunctions are these:

> both . . . and
> either . . . or
> neither . . . nor
> not only . . . but also
> whether . . . or

Like coordinating conjunctions, correlatives connect words, phrases, or clauses—like elements of grammar.

> *Not only* Alex *but also* Karen will fly to Arizona next Monday. (Here the correlatives *not only . . . but also* connect two words, *Alex and Karen*.)
>
> Casey has been working on our annual report *not only* during the week *but also* during the weekends. (Two phrases, *during the week* and *during the weekends,* are joined.)
>
> *Not only* does Jeremiah intend to finish his dissertation, *but* he *also* plans to publish it. (Here two clauses are connected.)

Subordinating Conjunctions

Subordinating conjunctions join clauses of *un*equal rank. A subordinating conjunction introduces a subordinate (or dependent) clause and connects it to a main (or independent) clause.

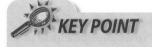

KEY POINT

Coordinating conjunctions and correlative conjunctions join like elements of grammar.

Although we located the main circuit breaker, we were unable to restore power to the third floor. (*Although* is a subordinating conjunction, and it introduces the subordinate clause *although we located the main circuit breaker.* Further, *although* connects this subordinate clause to the main clause.)

Ask Ms. Sanderson for an application form *if* you plan to apply for a job. (The subordinating conjunction *if* introduces the subordinate clause *if you plan to apply for a job* and connects this clause to the main clause.)

Study the following list of commonly used subordinating conjunctions so that you will be able to identify subordinate clauses.

after	before	provided that	when
although	even if	since	whenever
as	for	so that	where
as if	how	than	wherever
as soon as	if	that	whether
as though	in case that	unless	while
because	in order that	until	why

CHECKUP 1

On a separate sheet of paper, write the conjunctions used in the following sentences. Label each conjunction *coordinating* (CO), *correlative* (CR), or *subordinating* (S).

S 1. Jack will discuss his successes as soon as he returns from his mission to Africa.

S 2. While Ms. Poleta was on vacation, her request was reviewed by the personnel committee.

CR 3. Have you submitted both the application form and your rèsumè?

CO 4. Our consultant and the customer service manager carefully reviewed the complaints received during the last year.

S 5. If you prefer getting your mail at work, please give me that address.

S 6. Unless you find your wallet immediately, you must call and cancel the credit cards that were in your wallet.

CR 7. Richard, do you know whether Calvin or Gregg has called his insurance agent yet?

S 8. Yes, I'm sure that Calvin called her this morning.

CR 9. Please ask either Will or Sally to examine the evidence at the scene of the crime.

CO 10. You may subscribe to the magazine, or you may buy it at the newsstand.

PITFALLS OF USING CONJUNCTIONS

The following discussion focuses on two major conjunction pitfalls: (1) choosing a conjunction that does not accurately convey the meaning intended and (2) choosing a preposition when a conjunction is needed.

But or And?

The conjunction *but* provides a contrast while *and* simply joins two elements. Use *but* when a contrast is intended.

> The difference in price between the two models is minimal, *but* only one model is energy-efficient. (*But* for contrast.)

> The two models are similar in price and both are on sale. (*And* to join two items.)

Who, Which, or That?

Use *who* to refer to persons and *which* to refer to objects. Never say or write *and who* or *and which*.

> Send a copy of the memo to Dom Jarrett, *who* is the maintenance engineer. (*Who* refers to a person.)

> Thad asked us to present our concerns to the board, *which* is responsible for all major decisions. (*Which* refers to an object.)

That may be used to refer to persons, objects, or animals.

> The speaker *that* you heard is Howard Deville, a well-known economist. (*That* refers to a person. Note that *whom* could also have been used.)

> One idea *that* you will deem exciting is restoring the antique carrousel. (Here, *that* refers to an object.)

> The registered dog *that* Carrie sold was a dalmatian. (*That* refers to an animal.)

Since or Because, Not Being That

There is no such conjunction as *being that.* Use *since* or *because* instead.

> *Because* I had the flu, I decided to work at home yesterday and today. (*Because,* not *Being that.*)

The Reason Is That; Pretend That

Do not say or write "the reason is *because*" and "pretend *like.*" Instead, say "the reason is *that*" and "pretend *that.*"

> The reason for the delay in the flight arrival time is *that* violent storms prohibited the plane from taking off at the scheduled time. (Not *reason . . . is because.*)

Management will not, of course, pretend *that* the incident did not happen. (Not *pretend like*.)

Unless, Not *Without* or *Except*

Without and *except* are prepositions, and a preposition always introduces a prepositional phrase. Yet many writers and speakers incorrectly use these prepositions as substitutes for the subordinating conjunction *unless*. (*Remember:* A prepositional phrase consists of a preposition plus its noun or pronoun object and any modifiers.)

You cannot return the merchandise *without* Mrs. Hager's approval. (This sentence is correct. *Without Mrs. Hager's approval* is a prepositional phrase: *approval* is the object of the preposition *without*, and *Mrs. Hager's* is a modifier.)

You cannot return this merchandise *unless* Mrs. Hager approves it. (Again, this sentence is correct. The subordinating conjunction *unless* introduces a clause. An error occurs, however, when people incorrectly say or write *without Ms. Hager approves it*. The preposition *without* cannot introduce a clause.)

As, As If, As Though, Not *Like*

Remember that *like* is a preposition ("a car *like* mine") or a verb ("I *like* this model"). It is *not* a conjunction. Therefore, do not use *like* when *as, as if,* or *as though* is intended.

Kerrie acted *as if* she wanted to go home. (*As if,* not *like*.)

✓ **CHECKUP 2**

On a separate sheet of paper, correct any conjunction errors in the following sentences. Write *OK* for any sentence that is correct.

1. Edward was instructed not to pay the invoice unless he receives both shipments from the vendor.
2. You should, of course, act like you are interested in the meeting.
3. Ray, please do not use the expensive stationery except the mail is going outside the organization.
4. She told Bill not to sit around like he has no work to do.
5. Please make sure that Ms. Borelli doesn't leave without she approves the proposed expenditures.
6. Lanny said, "It seems like computers are everywhere."
7. Do not mail the check without you check to see if we have enough funds to cover it.
8. Beth's car is not the latest model on the market, and she is really enjoying driving it.

9. One reason for the decrease in computer prices is because ~~because~~ technology is continuing to advance. *that*

10. Caleb suggested several musicians which would be appropriate to play for the reception. *who*

Tammy speaks quietly and with confidence.

PARALLEL STRUCTURE

Observing the rules of parallel structure will provide balance to your writing. Look at the following examples:

Don's new assistant works quietly and accurately. (The conjunction *and* joins two parallel elements—two adverbs, *quietly* and *accurately*.)

Don's new assistant works quietly and with accuracy. (The same ideas are expressed here, but they are not expressed in parallel form. Now we have an adverb, *quietly*, joined to a prepositional phrase, *with accuracy*. These two grammatical elements are not alike; they are not parallel.)

Study the remainder of this section to ensure that you master parallel structure with coordinating and correlative conjunctions.

With Coordinating Conjunctions

KEY POINT

To balance sentences, present parallel ideas in parallel form.

Coordinating conjunctions connect *like* elements: an adjective with an adjective, a prepositional phrase with a prepositional phrase, and so on. Therefore, make sure that the elements before and after a coordinating conjunction match.

Our fire alarm system is checked carefully and (*regularly? with regularity?*). (An adverb, *carefully*, appears before the coordinating conjunction *and*; therefore, the adverb *regularly* should follow *and*. Together, *carefully* and *regularly* achieve parallel structure.)

Running the first mile is relatively easy, but (*finishing? to finish?*) the marathon is quite challenging. (Which choice matches *running?* Answer: *finishing*. Both *running* and *finishing* are gerunds.)

✓ CHECKUP 3

On a separate sheet of paper, balance the following sentences to make them parallel. Write *OK* if the sentence is already balanced.

1. "Both nurses," the patient commented, "~~and~~ seem to be professional and personable."

2. You may send us your travel plans by telephone, by fax, or ~~you can send them by~~ e-mail.

3. Cathy enjoys reading, exercising, and to travel*ing*

4. Fred, the cafeteria manager, said that the squash could be eaten steamed, fried, or ~~is edib~~le raw.

5. Our response should be courteous, quick, and with accuracy. ᴏᴠ⁓

6. The dietician told the patient that avoiding certain foods is necessary, but to exercise is ~~also~~ essential to his overall health program.

With Correlative Conjunctions

As you already know, correlative conjunctions are used in pairs. To achieve parallelism with correlative conjunctions, simply make sure that the element that follows the first conjunction is the same part of speech as the element that follows the second conjunction.

Priscilla wants *either* Ben *or* me to select the wall covering for the reception area. (The elements that follow *either . . . or* are the noun *Ben* and a pronoun *me*. Nouns and pronouns are considered like elements because pronouns are substitutes for nouns. Thus the phrase *either Ben or me* is parallel.)

The color green is predominant *not only* in the reception area's furnishings *but also* in its wallpaper. (Notice the parallelism of two prepositional phrases, one after each of the correlatives.)

Not only did the volunteers do all the painting, *but* they *also* hung the wallpaper. (*Not only* is followed by an independent clause, and *but also* is followed by an independent clause and may be interrupted by *they*. The sentence is parallel. Do not be misled by the inverted order of the first clause.)

Misplaced Conjunctions

Be sure that the placement of the correlative conjunction is correct. A misplaced conjunction can change the meaning of a sentence.

She likes *either* to eat pizza *or* to eat spaghetti. (Correct.)

She likes to eat *either* pizza *or* spaghetti. (Correct.)

She likes to eat *either* pizza or *to eat spaghetti.* (Wrong!)

✔ CHECKUP 4

On a separate sheet of paper, balance the elements joined by correlative conjunctions so that they are parallel.

1. Among the activities I like best are reading mystery novels and to "surf" the Internet.

2. In an effort to save fuel, we are trying to either form car pools or to use public transportation.

3. Coupons are usually either mailed to our best customers or to our prospective customers.

4. Our public relations brochure is both well written and has colorful illustrations.
5. For 50 years the antique shop has been owned either by Mr. Roselli or his father.
6. Selma neither went to the hospital nor to the clinic.

SECTION 3.1 REVIEW

Practical Application

A. On a separate sheet of paper, correct any conjunction errors in the following sentences. Write *OK* for any sentence that has no error.
1. Company policy states that checks for over $500 are not written without the vice-president's signature.
2. Company policy states that checks for over $500 are not written unless a manager signs them.
3. Joyce neither feels that overtime work nor temporary help is the solution to getting the job done.
4. During the trip, Lee spent money like it grew on trees.
5. The reason she is buying all those clothes is because she just got her first "real" job after completing her degree.
6. After about a month, they not only agreed to drop the law suit but also to accept a refund for the damaged merchandise.
7. The woman which you met in my office is one of the top five candidates for the job.
8. Please do not process this voucher without Mr. Williams signs it first.
9. Please do not process this voucher except Mr. Williams signs it first.
10. Your responsibilities will include calling prospective clients and to summarize their responses.
11. Being that our visiting Japanese customers like American food, we plan to have an American barbecue with the usual trimmings.
12. The real estate option runs out tomorrow, and we will be able to exercise the option before that deadline.
13. The job involves typing, operating prevalent software packages, and to file insurance claims electronically.
14. When you are questioning the suspect, it is a good idea to pretend like you know more than you actually do about the incident.

B. On a separate sheet of paper, correct any errors in the following sentences. Write *OK* for any sentence that has no error.
1. Did you read in our company newsletter where we may form a company computer club?
2. Cathy left a voice-mail message with Dr. Mendoza's service this morning, but Dr. Mendoza never called back.
3. Millicent neither completed the application correctly nor mailed it to the home office.
4. Many artists submitted their work to the show, but Paul's sculpture was the most unique.
5. In the company newsletter that was mailed yesterday is the announcements in regard to the yard sale to benefit children's charities.
6. If your looking for value, quality, speed, and compatibility, we believe that the Hi-Tech Computer is your best selection.
7. A large number of voters, according to Howard, was voting against the candidate.
8. Mr. Cassio believes that the Madison's are ready to buy a cellular phone.
9. Julio found one of those color printers that sells for under $500.
10. Last week Mr. Myers invited Della and I to tour his plant.
11. The vacant house on Oak Street is neither for sale or for rent.
12. No, Stephen, we have no stationery and not any fax paper.
13. Yes, there's been several problems with the dye on our last shipment of shirts.
14. Have you received any more information in regards to the changes in our medical and dental coverage?

Editing Practice

Using Your Computer. Type and print a corrected copy of the following paragraphs.

Beginning June 1, account executives must sign each new-account form, except that the office manager signs the form, before sending it to the operations manager. In signing the form, the account executive confirms that the client's name and address (as well as the details of the transaction, of course) is correct in every detail.

Remember that an error in a new-account form can delay the processing of the order. An error can also cause mistakes in billing transactions and in mailing statements.

Lets strive to get it right the first time! Thank you for you're assistance with the new-account form procedures.

Plurals and Possessives. On a separate sheet of paper, correct any errors in the following sentences. Write *OK* for any sentence that has no error.

1. Please check the ratioes that are listed in the first table in the report.
2. Julie and Lenny's new apartment is about three miles from the airport.
3. Tonights' performers, the five Messrs. Jackson, will surely entertain the audience.
4. My calculations do agree with your's.
5. No, I was not aware of Margaret leaving early, but apparently the boss gave her permission to do so.
6. The Ross's, who have been in Mexico for three weeks, were unable to attend the event.
7. One of the foremost childrens' clothing stores is Kids' Duds, a nationwide chain who's headquarters is in South Carolina.
8. According to the newspaper, his three brothers are all majors general in the Air Force.
9. Most of the designs that we reviewed showed creativity and flair; however, we all agreed that her's was the best.
10. When typing on-the-hour time, omit the zeroes; for example, type *2 a.m.*

Editing Practice

Proofreading. On a separate piece of paper, correct the errors in the following memo.

MEMO TO: All Employees

FROM: Richard Donne, Human Resources Manager

DATE: March 15, 19–-

SUBJECT: New Vacation Policy

I am pleased to announce a improvement to hour vacation policy.

The new policy enables not only full-time but part-time employees to receive more vacation time with less years of service than the previous policy. This new policy will be retroactive from January 1.

Please keep the enclosed copy of the new vacation policy for future reference. If you has any questions, please contact the Human Resources department.

Dealing With a Supervisor's Errors. Andrew Olson has been working for Ramseur Pharmaceuticals for almost two weeks now. He is administrative assistant to Helen Drexler, director of sales for Ramseur Pharmaceuticals. Just before lunch, Ms. Drexler gave Andrew a handwritten letter and asked him to type and send the letter to 25 of the company's best customers. Andrew read the letter and found two grammatical errors in it.

During lunch, Andrew seriously pondered what action he should take. As a new employee, he wanted to be sure that he approached the situation tactfully and that he did not offend Ms. Drexler. He remembered the bad experience he and his friend, Misha, had had during their first week at Ramseur.

The bad experience had happened about a week ago during lunch break when Andrew spotted a grammatical error in a bulletin board notice that was posted in the company cafeteria. He and Misha Benét, another new employee, were laughing at the error when Lenny Rivers stopped and asked, "What's so funny?"

Andrew replied, "Look at this gross error." He quoted from the posted bulletin board notice: "Everyone, including new employees, are invited to sign up for the one-day trip to New York City." Lenny looked puzzled; the sentence sounded correct to him. As Andrew and Misha chuckled, Andrew reread the notice emphasizing the error: "Everyone *is*, not *are*, invited."

Lenny, looking somewhat offended, replied, "I must have written this notice in a rush." He quickly removed it from the bulletin board and hastened to his office muttering as he went, "Just wait until those new folks make an error."

Knowing how he had unintentionally offended Lenny, Andrew wanted to make sure that he handled Ms. Drexler's errors appropriately.

1. Should Andrew type the letter as is and hope that when Ms. Drexler reviews it, she will discover her mistakes?

2. If Andrew typed the letter with the errors and Ms. Drexler didn't find the errors, what would he have to do?

3. How else could Andrew handle this situation?

4. What should Misha and Andrew have done when they found the grammatical error in the bulletin board notice?

4

Applying the Mechanics of Style

SECTIONS

4.1 Sentence Enders

4.2 Commas

4.3 Semicolons, Colons, and Dashes

4.4 Quotation Marks, Parentheses, and Apostrophes

4.5 Capitalization

4.6 Abbreviations

4.7 Numbers

Renata, born in Mexico, was the head teller of a large branch bank in a Texas city. Her native language was Spanish, but she spoke English quite well, even though she had lived in the United States less than two years. Renata studied English at a community college and learned to write English correctly. Her problem areas were capitalization and punctuation. She knew that if she were promoted to assistant branch manager, she would have to write many more memos, letters, and reports and would need to be a polished writer.

Renata checked with several schools in the area, but none of them had a course that would help her specifically with punctuation and capitalization. Renata talked with Consuelo, an associate of hers, about her writing concerns. Consuelo understood completely, because she had had a similar problem after learning to speak and write English. She recommended that Renata speak with Allison in the human resources department about her desire to improve her writing skills.

Allison was impressed with Renata's current English skills but even more impressed that she had diagnosed her own difficulty and that she wanted to overcome it. Allison ordered several books that Renata could work through on her own and also arranged for a retired high school English teacher to work with her one night a week.

As a result of her efforts, Renata made rapid progress. She had diagnosed her own difficulty and had sought assistance in overcoming it. What role will improving her skills play in Renata's chances for promotion?

As you read Chapter 4, follow Renata's example and identify areas of punctuation, capitalization, and numbers use in which you need to improve. What strategies will you use to help you improve your skills?

Sentence Enders

After completing Section 4.1, you should be able to:

1. Use periods correctly to end sentences.
2. Identify when, and when not, to use periods.
3. Correct errors in the use of periods.
4. Use question marks correctly after direct questions and in series of questions.
5. Use exclamation points correctly.

One who uses many periods is a philosopher; many interrogations, a student; many exclamations, a fanatic.

—J. L. Basford

Punctuation marks do for writing what pauses, changes in pitch, and gesturing do for speaking: They provide the necessary road signs to help readers and listeners understand our messages correctly. As you saw in the case study at the beginning of the chapter, Renata realized that her proficiency in using capitalization and punctuation directly affected her chances for promotion. The three punctuation marks discussed in this section—periods, question marks, and exclamation points—are used to end sentences. In addition, these marks have some other uses, which are also discussed in this section.

PERIODS

It's important to learn when to use periods and when not to use periods, as well as how to avoid some common pitfalls in using them.

When to Use Periods

KEY POINT

Use periods at the ends of statements, commands, requests phrased as questions, and indirect questions.

Use periods (1) to end declarative or imperative sentences, (2) to end requests that are phrased as questions simply for the sake of courtesy, and (3) to end indirect questions.

After Declarative and Imperative Sentences. Declarative sentences make statements, and imperative sentences order someone to act.

> All vacation requests must be submitted by Friday. (Declarative sentence.)

> Please submit your vacation requests by Friday. (Imperative sentence.)

After Requests Phrased as Questions. In an effort to soften commands and orders, speakers and writers often phrase such orders as questions. Because such statements are not really questions, use periods to end these sentences.

> Will you please reserve the room for our meeting. (Not a question—no answer is required.)

> May we have the entire order shipped by the fastest method. (A polite way of saying "Send the order as fast as possible." Not really a question.)

> Will you be able to install the computers next Monday? (This question requires a yes-or-no answer and, therefore, requires a question mark rather than a period.)

After Indirect Questions. An *indirect question* is a question restated as a declarative sentence.

> Rachel asked me if I had contacted Ms. Montez about the budget report. (The question is related as a declarative sentence, so it requires a period.)

> Stan, have you contacted Ms. Montez about the budget report? (Stated as a question, the sentence requires a question mark.)

CHECKUP 1

Which of the following sentences should end with periods and which should end with question marks? On a separate sheet of paper, write *P* for *period* and *Q* for *Question Mark*.

1. Christopher, may I ride home with you this afternoon
2. Kathi asked if she should work overtime
3. Will you please submit your goals for next year to Karen by Monday
4. May we schedule your dental appointment for Monday morning at 8:30
5. Phyllis asked Mr. Devoe if he plans to call his travel agent
6. Did Ms. Wellington respond to the questionnaire
7. May I please have your recommendations by return fax
8. Submit your suggestions to your supervisor before December 31

When Not to Use Periods

Do *not* use periods in the following instances.

After Sentences Ending in Abbreviations. Do *not* use two periods for sentences that end with abbreviations that require periods. If a sentence-ending abbreviation requires a period, let that period serve both functions.

> As previously announced, the bus tour will depart promptly at 7 a.m. (Not *7 a.m..*)

After Headings or After Roman Numerals With Names or Titles. A heading that is set on a separate line (for examples, see the headings in this textbook) should not be followed by a period. Also, roman numerals used with names or titles should not be followed by periods.

> Charles Camp III has been appointed director of marketing. (Not *Charles Camp III. has been . . . .*)

After Numbers or Letters in Parentheses. Do not use periods after numbers or letters enclosed in parentheses that precede enumerated items in a sentence.

Our employees have access to (1) America Online, (2) CompuServe, and (3) Internet of Shelby.

When numbers or letters are not in parentheses and are displayed on separate lines, use a period after each.

Our employees have access to:
1. America Online.
2. CompuServe.
3. Internet of Shelby.

Note: In the above example, each item in the list grammatically completes the introductory statement. Each item is the object of the preposition *to* in the introductory statement. Therefore, each item ends with a period. If the items did not grammatically complete the introductory statement, no periods would be needed.

If the introductory statement for a numbered list is grammatically complete, do not use periods after the items in the list.

Our employees have access to all the following:
1. America Online
2. CompuServe
3. Internet of Shelby

In addition, if each item in a list is a complete sentence or a long phrase, use a period.

After Even Amounts of Dollars. Except in tables (when it is important to align numbers), do not use periods or unnecessary zeros in even-dollar amounts.

Thank you for sending your *$100* payment so promptly. (Not *$100. payment* and not *$100.00 payment.*)

KEY POINT

Do not use periods after numbers or letters in parentheses or after even-dollar amounts.

✔ CHECKUP 2

On a separate sheet of paper, correct any period errors in the following sentences. Write *OK* for any sentence that is correct.

1. The enclosed materials include (1) a hotel reservation form, (2) a flight request form, and (3) a brochure describing tourist attractions.

2. Your corrected invoice for $114.00 is enclosed.

3. The new policy affects the following employees:
   a. Seasonal associates
   b. Part-time staff
   c. Temporary support personnel

4. Until July 15, you can join the new health club for $500. a year.

5. The best video slide demonstration was given by Dave Chadwick of Videocom, Inc..

6. The tour guide listed his complete name, Thurston P. Howell III., on the ship's passenger list.

Period Pitfalls

Using a period at the end of an *incomplete* thought, or fragment, is a *period fault*. Using a comma when a period is needed is a *comma splice*. Avoid these errors in your writing.

The Period Fault. An *incomplete* thought, or fragment, is not a sentence and therefore cannot stand alone. It should not end with a period. Generally, joining the incomplete thought to a main clause will solve the problem.

> Terri is taking a computer applications course. Because she believes it will help her get a promotion. (The second group of words cannot stand alone. This dependent clause should be joined to the preceding independent clause as shown in the following example.)

> Terri is taking a computer applications course because she believes it will help her get a promotion. (Now the dependent clause does not stand alone but is joined correctly to an independent clause.)

The Comma Splice. A comma by itself should *not* be used to join two independent clauses. A period is needed.

> Your seeds and bulbs are enclosed, a planting guide for your location will be mailed within ten days. (Put a period after *enclosed* to separate these two independent clauses.)

> Anthony is recruiting students to tour Israel, he said that the reservation deadline is July 1. (Again, these two independent clauses should be separated by a period.)

 CHECKUP 3

Are there any period faults or comma splices in the following sentences? Make any necessary corrections on a separate sheet of paper. Write *OK* for any sentence that is correct.

1. Since she came to work here a year ago. Andrea has had two salary increases.

2. Dr. Johnson is being honored at a luncheon Friday, she is retiring at the end of the year.

3. The cashier stamped the checks for deposit, he immediately placed them in the safe.

4. Even though Jan exercises daily at the spa for about an hour. She jogs two miles each evening.

5. Lenny was on vacation last week, but he called the office each day to check on his clients.

6. The flight was delayed for almost three hours. When a severe thunderstorm developed near the airport.

7. As we discussed at a recent committee meeting. We must continually update our technology.

8. Requests for specific software should be made by Monday morning, we get a discount on software ordered when we order our computers.

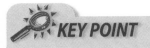
QUESTION MARKS

Use question marks after direct questions and in a series of questions.

After Direct Questions

Direct questions always end with question marks.

> Have you prepared your résumé?
>
> Mr. Montieth, have you received your bank statement yet?
>
> Should we mark these packages "Fragile"?
>
> Greta asked, "What time is your training session?"

Sentences that begin as statements but end as questions are considered questions. Use question marks at the end of such sentences.

> Kim mailed the contracts by Express Mail, didn't she? (The question at the end of the statement—*didn't she?*—requires you to put a question mark at the end of the sentence.)
>
> Lillian is planning to go to the health club today, isn't she? (Again, the question following the statement makes this an interrogative sentence. Use a question mark at the end of the sentence.)

In a Series of Questions

When a sentence contains a series of questions, the series may be joined by commas and a conjunction (like other series) and end with one question mark. Alternatively, each question may be separated from the main sentence and may have its own question mark. Note the following examples.

> Have you distributed copies of the accident report to the employee, her supervisor, and the human resources department? (The items in the series are joined by commas and the conjunction *and*. The sentence ends with a question mark.)
>
> Have you distributed copies of the accident report to the employee? her supervisor? the human resources department? (Each item in the series is separated from the main sentence, and each ends with its own question mark. Note that a lowercase letter begins each item to show that it is grammatically connected to the main sentence.)
>
> Will branch offices be located in Kansas City, in Phoenix, and in San Diego?

Question Mark Pitfall

So many questions include the word *why, ask,* or *how* that some writers automatically use a question mark at the end of any sentence with one of these words. However, many sentences with *why, ask,* or *how* are simply *indirect* questions—that is, declarative sentences.

> Mr. Porter asked why the fax machine had not been repaired. (This statement is an indirect question. Use a period.)
>
> Kate asked how we intended to increase production. (A statement, not a question.)

 **CHECKUP 4**

Are periods and question marks used correctly in the following sentences? On a separate sheet of paper, make any necessary corrections. Write *OK* for any sentence that is correct.

1. Doesn't Rachel know that the company softball game has been canceled because of heavy rain.
2. The manager asked how to use visual aids to improve his presentation?
3. Has the attorney already notified the client? the judge? the district attorney?
4. Ask the concierge when we should leave for the airport?
5. When will Shakeel complete his management training program?
6. Caleb knows how to use the presentation graphics software, doesn't he.
7. Ron asked Will if he had sold his car?
8. The toner cartridges for the laser printer are in the supply cabinet, aren't they.

EXCLAMATION POINTS

During the typical day, we see many, many exclamation points as we read signs and advertisements: "Special Sale!" "Limited-Time Offer!" "Hurry! Place Your Order Today!" The exclamation point is used to show strong emotion or feeling. An exclamation point can be used after a single word or at the end of a sentence. In business writing, exclamation points are limited to special uses.

> Congratulations! You have been named employee of the year.
>
> We were awarded the construction contract. What great news!
>
> James, your plan increased sales by 35 percent!

🔍 **KEY POINT**

Use exclamation points to show strong emotion or feeling.

Sometimes the exclamation point may replace a question mark when a question is really just a strong statement.

What happened to the fax machine! (This sentence is worded like a question but really is an exclamation.)

Do *not* overuse the exclamation point! Some inexperienced writers incorrectly use two or three exclamation points at the end of a sentence for extra emphasis. One exclamation point is enough.

SECTION 4.1   REVIEW

Practical Application

A. On a separate sheet of paper, correct any errors in the use of periods, question marks, or exclamation points in the following sentences. Write *OK* for any sentence that is correct.

1. Valerie asked Ken if he had notified his supervisor that he will be away for additional training the month of July?
2. Our summer intern is scheduled to report to work June 1, isn't she.
3. The sales representative quoted a price of $23,298.00, but the invoice price was $32,298.00. Ask the sales representative if this discrepancy is a typographical error?
4. The contract will be void unless it is returned by October 1, you should sign it and return it to me by messenger.
5. This 11 p.m. flight is the most economical. Although it is not as convenient as the flight at 6 p.m..
6. When you talk with the computer company, be sure that their price covers (1.) complete hardware and software installation, (2.) telephone support for trouble-shooting, and (3.) software training for five employees.
7. Do you know if Pete has passed his nursing examination yet.
8. Our financial planner recommends that we increase our:
   a. Life insurance for both adults
   b. Investments for the children's education
   c. Professional liability coverage
9. Lester wants to know if the copier has enlargement and reduction capabilities?
10. Should we open a video store in the Hickory Creek Mall? the West Gate Mall? the West Hills Outlet Mall?

B. On a sheet of paper, correct any errors in the following sentences. Write *OK* for any sentence that has no error.

1. Mrs. Garner, our purchasing agent, asked if the fax paper could be delivered today?
2. There's only five employees with over 30 years of service.
3. Because he is moving, Harry offered to sell his lawn mower for $100.00.
4. Dave Garcia sent my second set of car keys to Jeff and I by overnight parcel service.
5. We finished early, because finding the information was more easy than we thought it would be.
6. Veronica is certain that she will be able to attend the 7:30 dinner meeting, her plane lands at 5:30 p.m.
7. According to our procedures, each patients' chart is carefully checked before medication is given to him or her.
8. When Harold retired, his clients were equally distributed between Alan, Todd, and me.
9. Sometimes Ellen acts like she were the owner of the bank instead of a branch manager.
10. Please do not release the confidential personnel folders except I sign the release forms.
11. We stopped manufacturing the product. Because sales dropped drastically.
12. Keely estimates that this year's sales will be higher than any year in the company's history.
13. Usually, Betsy don't like to work on Saturday nights.
14. Do all design changes have to be approved by the architect? the builder? the homeowner?
15. Only one of the board members were in favor of renovating our existing office building.

Editing Practice

Are We in Agreement? On a separate sheet of paper, correct any agreement errors in the following sentences. Write *OK* if a sentence is correct.

1. Our real estate agent said that some of the retail office space have been sold to a developer from Arizona.
2. Madeline, here is the brochure and the article that you wanted to read.
3. The personnel files of persons hired before January 1, 1990, has been put on microfilm.
4. The number of loan applicants have increased since the new cars came on the market.
5. Every broker will be able to get their continuing education at the summer business conference.
6. Josh said that either rain or melting snow have caused the flash flooding in the valley.

7. A healthy diet and a regular exercise program is essential to maintaining physical fitness.
8. As you suggested, every hotel guest should have the opportunity to complete an evaluation of services that they received at the resort.
9. On the desk in Ms. Yamota's office is the reports on downtown traffic problems.
10. One of our recent reports contains an analysis of tourist visits to Myrtle Beach, South Carolina.

Spelling Alert! Using a separate sheet of paper, correct any misspelled words in the following excerpt.

As a valued customer of Swanson's Restaurant, you are invited to take advantage of the atached coupon that allows you to bring a guest for lunch at a reduce price. Your meal will be at the regular price; your guest's meal will be at half price. Lunch is served from 11 a.m. to 2 p.m. daily. This coupon offer is good on any Monday, Tuseday, or Wednesday during Septeber.

Thank you for your continued patronage.

SECTION 4.2   Commas

Commas are not a recent creation. Their use was described in the eighth century by an English monk named Alcuin who set down certain laws of grammar: "Let them (writers) distinguish the proper sense by colons and commas . . . and let them see the points, each one in its due place . . . ."

— John Tierney, *The New York Times*

OBJECTIVES:

After completing Section 4.2, you should be able to:

1. Use commas correctly in compound sentences and in a series.
2. Use commas correctly after introductory words, phrases, and clauses and before certain kinds of subordinate clauses.
3. Use commas correctly to set off interrupting elements, appositives, and related constructions.
4. Use commas correctly with consecutive adjectives and repeated expressions, for omissions, in direct address, and in numbers.
5. Correct errors in comma usage.

Effective speakers use pauses that enable their listeners to grasp and connect thoughts and to separate expressions that are not essential to the clarity of the message. Similarly, effective writers use commas to connect thoughts and to separate elements within sentences. You will find that using commas correctly will be an important asset to you in your business and personal writing.

A thorough discussion of the many uses of the comma follows. Study these applications so that you will be able to use commas correctly in all forms of business writing.

IN COMPOUND SENTENCES

To use commas correctly in compound sentences, you need to be able to distinguish a compound sentence from a simple sentence with a compound predicate. To accomplish this, let's review simple and compound sentences.

A *simple sentence* contains a subject and a verb. The subject or the verb may be compound. A simple sentence with a compound predicate has only one subject and a compound verb. Do *not* use a comma to separate a compound predicate.

> Betty moved to Charlotte last week and started her new job with Breyer Real Estate today. (*Betty* is the only subject for the two verbs in the compound predicate—*moved* and *started*. No comma is needed.)

> The Reynolds & Sturgis Company originally planned to build a mall on the acreage but later decided to sell the land instead. (*Company* is the subject for the compound predicate verbs *planned* and *decided*. No comma is needed.)

A *compound sentence* has two or more independent clauses, each with a subject and a predicate. Note in the following sentences how commas are used with the coordinating conjunctions *and, but, or,* and *nor* to join two independent clauses.

> Betty moved to Charlotte last week, *and* she started her new job with Breyer Real Estate today. (The comma and the conjunction *and* join two independent clauses.)

> The Reynolds and Sturgis Company originally planned to build a mall on the acreage, *but* it later decided to sell the land instead. (The comma and the conjunction *but* join two independent clauses.)

> Erin will take a refresher course in spreadsheets this semester, *or* she will take a course in database management. (The comma and the conjunction *or* join two independent clauses.)

> Grant does not plan to apply for the position, *nor* does he plan to transfer to another office. (The comma and the conjunction *nor* join two independent clauses.)

KEY POINT

Each clause in a compound sentence can stand alone as a sentence.

KEY POINT

Use a comma before the conjunctions *and, but, or,* and *nor* when they join two independent clauses unless the independent clauses are very short.

MEMORY HOOK

To help distinguish between a simple sentence with a compound predicate and a compound sentence, use the following:

Simple sentence with compound predicate
subject + verb + verb

Tim finished the analysis on time but *forgot* to report his results.

Compound sentence
subject + verb + conjunction + subject + verb

Tim finished the analysis on time, *but he forgot* to report his results.

A discussion of exceptions to the use of commas in compound sentences follows.

No Comma Between Very Short Clauses

When the independent clauses are very short, the comma is usually omitted. Read the following examples aloud; as you do so, note that each sentence sounds "natural" without a pause before the conjunction.

> Greta washed the car and Tom waxed it. (The two independent clauses are short; the comma between *car* and *and* may be omitted.)

> Nancy went to lunch and Rachel joined her later. (Again, two short independent clauses do not require a comma.)

Semicolon to Avoid Possible Misreading

If either clause of a compound sentence already contains one or more commas, a misreading may result. To avoid misreadings, use a semicolon, not a comma, to separate the clauses.

> This next benefits meeting will cover changing dental plans, submitting claims for reinbursement, and establishing flexible working hours; and a company-sponsored child-care center will be the topic of next month's meeting. (The semicolon provides a stronger break and prevents misreading *a company-sponsored child-care center* as part of the preceding series.)

When the two independent clauses in a compound sentence are very long, the brief pause of a comma to separate them may not be strong enough. A semicolon may be required. (Better yet, rewrite very long clauses as separate sentences.)

> The findings of our research staff clearly point to the possible effectiveness of polyvinyl chloride (PVC) as a replacement for the more expensive materials we are now using; and we fully support the need to fund further research to explore the uses of PVC for our entire line of products.

✔ CHECKUP 1

On a separate sheet of paper, correct any comma errors in these sentences. Write *OK* for any sentence that is correct.

1. The trial began at 10:30 a.m., but ended before noon.
2. We should fix his air conditioner immediately, or we should get someone else to fix it.
3. Martha drove, and Millie slept.
4. Calvin interviewed Ruth, Steve, and William, and Jim interviewed Ester, Sheila, and Wayne.

5. Gladys does not plan to fly to New York nor does she plan to drive; she plans to take the train.

6. Brent will officially retire in December, but will work part-time next year.

7. Scott will be transferred to Chicago in July but his replacement has not been appointed.

8. I telephoned the customer this morning but was disappointed with his attitude.

IN A SERIES

A *series* consists of three or more items in a sequence. As you will see in the following examples, the items may be words, phrases, or clauses.

> Vera checked the patient's *blood pressure, temperature, and pulse.* (A series of words. Note that a comma is used before the conjunction.)

> Many of our employees do volunteer work in hospitals, at homeless shelters, and for various charitable organizations. (A series of three phrases: *in hospitals, at shelters, for various charitable organizations.*)

> Clarence will head our Kansas City office, Wilma will fill Clarence's former position at headquarters, and Reba will become Wilma's assistant. (A series of three independent clauses.)

When *Etc.* Ends a Series

Etc. means "and so forth." Never write *and etc.* because that would mean "*and and* so forth"!

When *etc.* ends a series, use a comma before and after it unless *etc.* ends the sentence.

> Summer interns at the newspaper interview community leaders, research background information, write feature articles, *etc.* (A comma before *etc.* No comma after *etc.* because *etc.* ends the sentence.)

> We will meet the clients, take them to dinner, show them around the city, *etc.,* according to Jon's instructions. (A comma before and after *etc.*)

Semicolons Instead of Commas in a Series

When the items in a series are long clauses or if the items already contain commas, use a semicolon to provide a stronger break between items.

> Mr. Wells has asked us to do the following: place the cartons on shipping pallets; move the pallets to the warehouse entrance for shipment; and obtain a signed receipt showing the time the pallets were picked up by the shipper. (A long pause in between the items is helpful to the reader.)

KEY POINT

Use a comma before the conjunction when listing three or more items in a series.

During his first three months with the company, Bob met with clients in St. Marys, Georgia; Rock Hill, South Carolina; Calhoun, Tennessee; and Lufkin, Texas. (Using semicolons to separate the parts of the series enables the reader to grasp the meaning immediately.)

When Not to Use Commas

Do not use commas in the following situations.

At the End of a Series. Do not use a comma after the last item in a series (that is, the item following the conjunction) unless the sentence structure requires a comma. Only the items preceding the conjunction are separated by commas.

Leslie, Michelle, and Tamara are responsible for the orientation sessions for new employees. (No comma after *Tamara,* the last item in the series.)

Leslie, Michelle, and Tamara, who are training specialists in our home office, will conduct the orientation sessions for new employees. (The comma after *Tamara* is required because of the interrupting clause beginning with *who.*)

With Repeated Conjunctions. When the conjunction is repeated between every two items in the series, no commas are needed.

You may send us the contract by Express Mail or private courier or fax. (Because the conjunction *or* is repeated between items in the series, no commas are needed.)

In Certain Company Names. Write a company's name exactly as it is printed on the company's letterhead. Some companies write their names *without* a comma before *and;* others, *with* a comma. Follow the company preference. In all cases, no comma is used before an ampersand (&).

Kline, Cole, and Riverez Company bought the property. (Follows the official company name precisely.)

Dewey, Cheatum & Howe is a reputable accounting firm. (Never use a comma before an ampersand: &.)

OOPS!

The coach called out the players names.

✔ CHECKUP 2

Correct any comma errors in the following sentences on a separate sheet of paper. Write *OK* for any sentence that is correct.

1. You can use your cellular phone in your car, on the train or on your sailboat.
2. Adam, Ben, and Erin, our summer interns, will temporarily replace our vacationing employees.
3. At midnight, the security guard turns off the lights, locks the door, turns on the alarm, and etc.

4. The firm of Beddow, Beddow, & Smith filed the lawsuit.

5. Shorts, tees, and tanks, etc. will be on sale after July 4.

6. Coleen will request the van, Andrea will make the hotel reservations and Carmen will buy the theater tickets.

7. You can travel by van, train, or airplane, or if you prefer, you may drive your car.

8. David, Mark and Sean brought their gear and are going trout fishing on Saturday.

FOLLOWING INTRODUCTORY WORDS, PHRASES, AND CLAUSES

Commas follow introductory words, phrases, and clauses to provide a needed pause and thereby prevent possible misreading or confusion.

KEY POINT

Use commas after introductory words, phrases, and clauses.

Introductory Words

Commas follow introductory words at the beginning of sentences or clauses. Some of the most commonly used introductory words are listed below:

consequently	moreover	obviously
finally	namely	originally
first	naturally	therefore
however	no	yes
meanwhile	now	

Naturally, we were eager to hear the results of his medical tests. (The introductory word *naturally* is at the beginning of the sentence. A comma follows the word.)

The medical tests showed that his surgery had been successful; *naturally,* we were thrilled that he would soon return to work. (Here, the word *naturally* introduces the second clause in the sentence. Again, it is followed by a comma.)

We received the results from the medical tests today; we were, *naturally,* extremely happy that his surgery was a success. (Note that a comma is used before and after *naturally.*)

Introductory Phrases

Commas are often needed after infinitive phrases, participial phrases, and prepositional phrases.

After Infinitive Phrases. An infinitive phrase that begins a sentence or a clause is followed by a comma unless the phrase is the subject of the sentence or clause.

To finish the feasibility study, Linda will have to work late every night this week. (The infinitive phrase *to finish the feasibility study* introduces the sentence. It modifies the subject *Linda*.)

To finish the feasibility study is Linda's priority for the week. (Here, the infinitive phrase is the subject of the sentence.)

After Participial Phrases. A participial phrase is always followed by a comma.

Waiting for the clients to arrive, Susan reviewed the proposal she planned to present to them. (Use a comma after the participial phrase.)

Delayed by heavy traffic, Kim needed an extra two hours to complete the trip. (Comma after a participial phrase.)

Do not confuse participial phrases with gerund phrases. A *gerund phrase* is a phrase that contains a gerund. When it appears at the beginning of a sentence, a gerund phrase is always a subject. A participial phrase is always an adjective.

Maintaining law and order is every police officer's responsibility. (*Maintaining* is a gerund. The gerund phrase *Maintaining law and order* is the subject of the sentence.)

Maintaining law and order, the police officer improved the living conditions in our neighborhood. (Here, *Maintaining* is a participle—an adjective that modifies the subject, *police officer*.)

After Prepositional Phrases. Use commas after long prepositional phrases and prepositional phrases that contain verb forms such as gerunds.

For more detailed installation instructions, please call our toll-free number. (Long prepositional phrase.)

After stopping the runaway car, Nancy received awards from the mayor and the governor. (Note the gerund *stopping* in the prepositional phrase.)

Do not use a comma if the prepositional phrase is short or if it flows directly into the main thought of the sentence.

By tomorrow the cement should be dried and the driveway ready to use. (The prepositional phrase *By tomorrow* is short and flows directly into the sentence.)

Introductory Clauses

A comma is needed after a dependent clause that precedes a main clause. Note how the comma provides a necessary pause in the following example.

When David returned from his vacation, he met with the engineers who had several recommendations for solving the problem. (Comma after a dependent clause that precedes the main clause.)

To apply this comma rule, you must be able to identify the words and phrases that commonly begin introductory clauses. You will remember the following list better if you try using each word or phrase to introduce a clause.

KEY POINT

A *gerund* is a verb form that ends in *ing* and is used as a noun.

KEY POINT

Use a comma to separate a dependent clause from the main clause that follows.

after	how	though
although	if	till
as	inasmuch as	unless
as if	in case	when
as soon as	in order that	whenever
as though	otherwise	where
because	provided	whereas
before	since	wherever
even if	so that	whether
for	then	while

✓ CHECKUP 3

Correct any comma errors on a separate sheet of paper. Write *OK* for any sentence that is correct.

1. Unless Larry approves our recommendation we will not be able to begin today as we had anticipated.

2. To board an airplane each passenger must present identification that has his or her picture.

3. Unless you apply before October 1 you will not be considered for early admission to such a prestigious university.

4. To succeed as a sales representative, requires persistence, determination, and drive.

5. Mrs. Sandford finally gave her consent to the restructuring plan; she approved moreover hiring an additional sales representative for each region.

6. Before John was promoted to manager he worked at least 60 hours per week.

7. Whenever you return from your vacation we will start working on the proposal for Hempstead Company.

8. Installing the new software, took Steve and Delores all morning.

9. Installing the new software, Steve and Delores worked diligently all morning.

10. Haley should be able to leave Seattle early Friday morning; therefore she should arrive home by 7 p.m.

WITH A DEPENDENT CLAUSE FOLLOWING A MAIN CLAUSE

We have already seen that a dependent clause preceding a main clause is always followed by a comma.

> *As we discussed at our Friday meeting,* we will evaluate the commission rates for all sales representatives. (Comma after a dependent clause preceding a main clause.)

KEY POINT

When the dependent clause follows the main clause, use a comma *only* if the dependent clause offers *nonessential* information.

After Ms. Dameron has made her decision regarding recruitment, she will meet with each supervisor. (Comma after a dependent clause preceding a main clause.)

However, when the dependent clause *follows* the main clause, use a comma only if the dependent clause offers *nonessential* information—information not needed to complete the meaning. As you read the following examples, note how the dependent clauses differ.

We will evaluate the commission rates for all sales representatives, *as we discussed at our Friday meeting.* (The words *as we discussed at our Friday meeting* are not critical to understanding the meaning of the sentence. They merely provide extra information. A comma separates nonessential words.)

Ms. Dameron will meet with each supervisor *after she has made her decision regarding recruitment.* (No comma here because the clause *after she has made her decision regarding recruitment* is important to the meaning of the sentence. It provides *essential* information, *not* additional information. It tells precisely *when* "Ms. Dameron will meet with each supervisor.")

When writing such sentences, you will, of course, know the meaning you intend and will have an easier job of deciding whether a comma is needed or not.

WITH INTERRUPTING, PARENTHETIC, AND EXPLANATORY ELEMENTS

Use commas to set off nonessential information such as interrupting, parenthetic, and explanatory elements.

Interrupting Elements

Interrupting elements do not provide essential information. Use commas to set off interrupters.

The increase in annual profits, *naturally,* has elated the stockholders. (Commas set off the interrupting word *naturally*.)

Each division's proposed budget, *consequently,* can be increased because of the significant jump in profits during the last fiscal year. (Again, commas set off the interrupter *consequently*.)

Parenthetic Elements

As we speak and write, we add words, phrases, and clauses within sentences to emphasize a contrast, express an opinion, soften a harsh statement, qualify or amend meaning, and so on. These parenthetic elements should be set off by commas.

KEY POINT

To determine if an element is interrupting, parenthetic, or explanatory, do this: Read the sentence without the element. If the meaning of the sentence isn't affected, use commas to set off the element.

Any policy changes, *in my opinion,* must be approved by the personnel committee. (The parenthetic expression *in my opinion* is not essential to the meaning of the sentence and is set off by commas.)

The text of the policy manual, *but not the appendices,* has been approved by the executive committee. (The parenthetic statement separated by commas emphasizes the contrast.)

Explanatory Elements

Additional information that is not essential to the meaning of the sentence is set off by commas. To determine if information is nonessential, read the sentence without the information. If the sentence makes sense, use commas to set off the additional information.

The systems analyst, *suspecting a virus in the computer network,* issued an advisory memo to all network users. (Read this sentence aloud. As you do so, note how you would pause at the beginning and at the end of the participial phrase *suspecting a virus in the computer network.* Use commas to set off such explanatory elements.)

Harold VanDyke, *who developed this procedure,* is a third-shift supervisor. (The clause *who developed this procedure* is set off by commas. Again, read this sentence aloud to note how you would pause before and after the explanatory element.)

Note, however, that clauses that *are* essential are not set off by commas.

Our company has five third-shift supervisors. The third-shift supervisor *who developed this procedure* is Harold VanDyke. (In this sentence, the clause *who developed this procedure* does not provide *extra* information; it specifies *one* of the "five third-shift supervisors." Note that in reading this sentence aloud, you would *not* pause before and after the clause.)

KEY POINT

Who and *whom* clauses that are preceded by a specific name are *not* essential and, therefore, require commas.

✓ CHECKUP 4

Are commas used correctly in the following sentences? Make any necessary corrections on a separate sheet of paper. Write *OK* for any sentence that is correct.

1. The only accountant on our staff, who is a CPA, is Mitchell Poteat.

2. Please order additional stationery, if the special discount is still in effect.

3. An effective alternative Elaine and I think will be to reschedule the meeting after the holiday season.

4. The team members, not the manager, must determine the course of action.

5. The technician, who is installing the computer in the lab, is Arnold Johnson.

6. Steven waiting for the fax from our Michigan office did not go out for lunch.

7. One possible solution as we discussed yesterday is to order immediately the supplies that we anticipate using next week.

8. Mr. Tobias, who designs our luggage, met with the international sales manager yesterday.

9. The income tax attorney, whom you should consult, is Leslie Maxwell.

10. The dividends received but not the stock owned is called earnings.

WITH APPOSITIVES AND RELATED CONSTRUCTIONS

The use of commas with appositives, degrees and titles, calendar dates, and state names is explained in the following discussion.

Appositives

As you learned in Section 3.3, an appositive is a word or a group of words that gives more information about a preceding word or phrase. When an appositive is not essential to the meaning of a sentence, it is set off by commas.

> The new paralegal, *Beth Warren,* is working on the Taylor case. (The appositive, *Beth Warren,* offers additional information and is set off by commas.)

> The controller of Ace Accounting, *an adjunct professor at the community college,* is an expert in financial management. (The appositive, *an adjunct professor at the community college,* offers additional information and is set off by commas.)

When the appositive is very closely connected with the noun that precedes it, no commas are used to set off the appositive. This occurs most often with one- or two-word appositives such as names, which are read as a unit.

> My daughter *Marcy* will graduate in June. (The appositive *Marcy* is read as part of the unit *My daughter Marcy,* so no commas are used.)

> The motivational speaker *Tom Dickens* will accompany her to the convention. (The appositive *Tom Dickens* is closely connected to the noun preceding it; therefore, no commas are needed.)

> The year *2000* will mark the 100th anniversary of our firm. (Here, *2000* is essential to the meaning of the sentence. It is not set off by commas.)

KEY POINT

Use commas before and after an appositive that is nonessential to the meaning of the sentence.

If you were sharing your view on a subject, which sentence would you write?
Some changes in my opinion are necessary.
Some changes, in my opinion, are necessary.

Degrees, Titles, and Other Similar Terms

Several commonly used abbreviations offer additional information about the names that precede them. For example, *M.D.* following a person's name tells that he or she is a doctor of medicine, and *Inc.* following a company name tells that the firm has been incorporated.

Abbreviations such as *M.D.*, *Ph.D.*, and *D.D.S.* are always set off by commas when they follow a person's name.

> Joel F. Spragins, M.D., is an avid sailor.
>
> Frieda F. Brown, Ph.D., has a private counseling practice.

The abbreviations *Inc.* and *Ltd.* may or may not be set off with commas, depending on the preference of the company. Always follow the style shown on a company's letterhead.

> The credit services division of Sanford & Son, Inc., has moved to Las Vegas, Nevada. (*Sanford & Son, Inc.,* is the official company name.)
>
> Ms. Ramsey does freelance photography for Time Inc. in New York City. (*Time Inc.* is the official company name.)

Like *Inc.* and *Ltd.*, the abbreviations *Jr.* and *Sr.* may or may not be set off with commas. Follow the preference of each individual when writing *Jr.* or *Sr.* or roman numerals after a person's name.

> David D. Williams Jr. has been appointed assistant principal. (Mr. Williams prefers no commas setting off *Jr.*)
>
> Seth Nelson, III, is the president of Nelson Travels, Inc. (Mr. Nelson prefers to use commas to set off *III* following his name.)

Note that when commas are used to set off such abbreviations as *M.D.*, *Inc.*, and *Jr.*, they are used in pairs. Do not use a single comma to set off such abbreviations unless the abbreviation appears at the end of a sentence. If the person's preference is not known, do not use commas to set off *Jr.*, *Sr.*, or roman numerals after the name.

KEY POINT

Use a pair of commas to set off degrees, titles, and abbreviations used with names.

Calendar Dates

In month-day-year dates, the year is set off with two commas. In month-year dates, the commas are omitted.

> On *September 20, 1998,* we purchased the restaurant on Chatsworth Street.
>
> In *September 1998* we purchased the restaurant on Chatsworth Street.

When the month and day are preceded by the day of the week, use commas to set off the month and day.

> We will meet on *Tuesday, April 7,* to discuss the merger.

World View

Writing dates using numerals can lead to confusion. In many countries, the day of the month is placed before the month. Thus *5/9/99* means "5 September 1999"—not "May 9, 1999."

State Names

A comma is used to separate the city from the state and the state from the rest of the sentence.

> Our next national meeting will be held in *Dallas, Texas,* next March.

✔ CHECKUP 5

Are there any comma errors in the following sentences? Make any necessary corrections on a separate sheet of paper. Write *OK* for any sentence that is correct. (*Note:* Abbreviations used with names reflect the preference of the person or company.)

1. On July 1, 2002 our contract should be renegotiated.
2. One of our divisions Lensco Pharmaceuticals has been a leader in disease prevention.
3. Maggie Ward flew to Nashville, Tennessee to meet with the songwriter.
4. Send the damaged merchandise to Preston Discount and Salvage, Inc. tomorrow morning.
5. His wife Doris enjoys flying and skydiving.
6. A secretary in the Accounting Department, Rita Leonard will be our entrant in the keyboarding contest.
7. Joshua Bernard, one of our new employees, lived in Madison Wisconsin for five years.
8. On Monday George S. Paxton, Jr. will be here as a consultant to the president.
9. During July 1997 two hurricanes damaged our restaurant on the coast.
10. Two new staff writers, Bill Kline and Rob Billings were recently hired by the *Shelby Gazette*.

WHICH AND *THAT* CLAUSES

Clauses that are not necessary to the meaning of a sentence should be introduced by *which* and set off by commas. Clauses that are necessary to the meaning of a sentence are introduced by *that*. They are not set off by commas.

> Only the part of the roof *that was damaged by the storm* will be replaced. (No commas separating a "that" clause.)

> The damaged roof, *which includes the patio roof,* will be replaced. (The "which" clause gives additional information and is correctly set off by commas.)

KEY POINT

Which clauses include non-essential infomation and should be set off with commas. *That* clauses are necessary to the sentence and are not set off with commas.

COMMA PITFALLS

Here are two more comma pitfalls that trap many writers: (1) using a comma to separate a subject from its predicate and (2) using a comma to separate a verb or an infinitive from its object or complement.

Comma Separating Subject From Predicate

Never separate a subject from its predicate by a comma.

All written *requests* from our clients, *must be initialed* by the office manager before being given to the broker. (Wrong. No comma should separate the subject, *requests,* from its verb, *must be initialed.*)

All written *requests* from our clients, according to company policy, *must be initialed* by the office manager before being given to the broker. (Correct. Now *two* commas separate a phrase that gives additional information.)

Comma Separating Verb From Object

Never separate a verb from its object or complement with a comma. Likewise, never separate an infinitive from its complement with a comma.

Since 1990 Elise *has been,* one of the hospital's most dedicated *volunteers.* (Wrong. A comma should never separate a verb from its complement.)

Most of the staff were surprised *to learn, that Hank is retiring next month.* (Wrong. A comma should never separate an infinitive from its complement.)

 **CHECKUP 6**

Using a separate sheet of paper, find and correct any errors in the following sentences. Write *OK* for any sentence that is correct.

1. The enclosed bank statement which also includes an order form for additional checks is also available through our electronic banking system.

2. Several nurses on the third shift, are being considered for second-shift positions.

3. The newspaper editor is writing an article for the annual holiday edition of the newspaper, which has become an advertising tradition in our small community.

4. Our Myrtle Beach outlet which is one of the largest sportswear outlets in the South is our company's most profitable outlet.

5. Environmentalists have urged consumers to recycle products, that can be recycled effectively.

6. All fishing gear, that is listed in our catalog, may also be purchased in our outlet store at the mall.

WITH CONSECUTIVE ADJECTIVES

When two or more adjectives separately modify a noun, use a comma to separate the adjectives. To test whether the two adjectives *separately* modify the noun, use the word *and* between the adjectives, as shown below.

> Cheryl addressed the audience in a *dynamic, entertaining* way. (Comma between the adjectives *dynamic* and *entertaining.* Note that the word *and* can be used between the modifiers: in a way that is dynamic *and* entertaining.)

> Brian and Sara are creative, knowledgeable computer analysts. (Commas between the adjectives that *separately* modify the compound noun *computer analysts: creative* and *knowledgeable.*)

Note that no comma follows the last adjective in a series—that is, no comma separates the last adjective from the noun.

> The new outpatient clinic is staffed by skilled, experienced personnel. (No comma is used to separate the last adjective, *experienced,* from the noun *personnel.*)

> Oscar Weinstein's unique negotiation style is his greatest attribute. (Using the word *and* between the modifiers *unique* and *negotiation* makes no sense. These adjectives do not separately modify the noun *style.*)

> We discussed conservative financial investments with our adviser. (You would *not* say "investments that are conservative and financial." Here, the adjective *financial* modifies *investments.* But the adjective *conservative* modifies the unit *financial investments.* In other words, "financial investments that are conservative.")

✔ CHECKUP 7

Using a separate sheet of paper, insert commas as needed between adjectives in the following sentences. Test by using the word *and* between adjectives. Write *OK* for any sentence that is correct.

1. The earliest possible date that we can meet is December 9.
2. Their portfolio contains solid high-yielding investments.
3. Scott & Westin manufactures lightweight thermal coats.
4. Ms. Atkins has developed a creative talented consulting team of highly experienced professionals.
5. Ben is considered a brilliant ambitious resourceful trainee.
6. Jennifer and Jerry showed the slides of their fascinating educational trip to Asia.

FOR OMISSIONS, WITH REPEATED EXPRESSIONS, AND IN DIRECT ADDRESS

The comma is also used to save time and words, to emphasize an important thought, and to set off names and terms in direct address. These uses are discussed in this section.

Omissions

Sometimes writers can use the comma to avoid repeating words that have already been stated in the sentence. The comma makes the reader pause long enough to mentally supply the omitted words.

> Effective March 1, Mr. Yancy *will be in charge of* the Miller account; Ms. Duncan, the Gordon & Gordon account; Ms. Tanner, the Maxwell Shop account; and Mr. Little, the Harris Chemicals account. (Rather than repeat the words *will be in charge of* three times, the writer uses commas after *Duncan, Tanner,* and *Little* to indicate the omission and cause the reader to pause long enough to supply these words.)

KEY POINT

Commas are usually substituted for repeated words when the clauses are separated by a semicolon.

Repeated Expressions

Repetition is one of the most effective ways to emphasize an important point. Repetitions must be planned if they are to be effective, and the repeated words must be separated by a comma.

> Company policy states, "*Never, never* smoke in the warehouse." (Note the comma that separates the repetition *Never, never.*)

Direct Address

In writing, when we address people directly, we set off their names (or similar terms) with commas.

> As you may know, *Mr. Elliott,* this software program offers you direct on-line support.

> Without your encouragement and support, *Dr. Rybnicek,* I would not have recuperated so quickly.

✓ CHECKUP 8

Do the following sentences correctly illustrate use of commas for omissions, for planned repetition, and for direct address? Make any needed corrections on a separate sheet of paper. Write *OK* for any sentence that is correct.

1. The Birmingham plant is scheduled for a safety inspection on June 1; the Charlotte plant July 1; and the Nashville plant August 1.

2. Skydiving is a risky risky sport!

3. Ms. Adams we enthusiastically support your fund-raising plan.

4. To pass the licensing exam, each trainee will have to study many many hours.

5. We are proud to announce that Johnson, Inc., has donated $5,000 to United Way; Billings Industries $10,000; and Hills Communications $20,000.

6. Wesley's testimony was the truth absolutely the truth.

IN NUMBERS AND BETWEEN UNRELATED NUMBERS

Use a comma to separate thousands, ten thousands, hundred thousands, millions, and so on, in numbers of four or more digits. This function of the comma prevents misreading of numbers. Note that there is a trend towards omitting the comma in four-digit numbers like *$4,000*. However, if the four-digit number is used in the same sentence as a number with five or more digits, use the comma for consistency.

> Our sales exceeded *$10,000,000* last year and are estimated to be *$12,000,000* this year.

> During the past year, TechMart sold *9236* Swift 486 computer systems.

> Our subscription list was *9,500* last year; this year it is *10,500*.

When unrelated numbers are written together, use a comma to separate them.

> By October 1, 150 employees had completed the additional training. (The comma slows down the reader and makes each number distinct.)

KEY POINT

Separate unrelated numbers with a comma.

MORE COMMA PITFALLS

Now that you know all the important uses of the comma with numbers, be sure to master these principles for *not* using a comma with numbers.

In Numbers

Never use commas in the following numbers, regardless of the number of digits: years, page numbers, house and telephone numbers, ZIP Code numbers, serial numbers, and decimals.

in 2000	201-555-8234	3271 Washington Street
page 1418	11.37580	Detroit, MI 48266-1234

In Weights, Capacities, and Measurements

Never use a comma to separate the parts of *one* weight, *one* capacity, or *one* measurement.

> The videotape runs for exactly 1 hour 18 minutes 20 seconds. (No commas to separate the parts of *one* time measurement.)

✔ CHECKUP 9

Did the writers of the following sentences fall into any of the comma pitfalls described above? Correct any errors on a separate sheet of paper. Write *OK* for any sentence that is correct.

1. By 1999 100 new franchises will have been opened in 50 states.
2. The agenda intentionally allows 1 hour, 45 minutes for the question-and-answer period.
3. Pages 1,311 through 1,345 of the transcript cover the defendant's testimony concerning the $35000 payment.
4. In 1995 the Reilly Trucking Company relocated to 3,181 Filmore Street.
5. As you will see on Invoice 24353, 10 of the 12 items were shipped.
6. My copy of my life insurance policy, Policy 80,876, is in my safe deposit box.
7. The bookshelves are precisely 8 feet, 6 inches high.
8. Hilda received a yearly bonus of $9600; Andrea's was $10,500.

SECTION 4.2   REVIEW

Practical Application

A. Correct the following sentences on a separate sheet of paper. Write *OK* for any sentence that is correct.
1. We were amused to see the printing errors, that appeared in our competitor's latest flier.
2. One of the most interesting commentaries on the president's speech, appears in our local newspaper.
3. Amber will send you our internal audit report, as soon as it is printed.

4. Her husband Steve is an insurance executive in Sioux Falls, South Dakota.
5. The large items will be shipped by truck, or by airfreight.
6. For an incredibly low package price, you can fly to Miami, take a cruise to the Bahamas, take exciting sightseeing tours and fly back to New York City.
7. The company's goal is to add to, not detract from the advantages it enjoys in the marketplace.
8. The announcement, that the Broad River recreational area will be refurbished, excited the community.
9. Selling VitaLife stock according to my investment advisor is a good idea.
10. The proposal was scheduled for presentation on September 1; last-minute revisions however will delay the presentation until September 8.
11. When the mayor arrives we will begin the parade.
12. To produce a professional-looking mock-up you may wish to include computer-generated charts and other graphics.
13. The cost estimate was $9800; actual expenses, however, totaled $12800.
14. Patricia Fong, Ph.D. is the director of the community counseling center.
15. The new telephone system, which Mr. Nieves ordered last week, was activated today.

B. On a separate sheet of paper, correct any errors in the following sentences. Write *OK* for any sentence that is correct.
1. The speaking time will be divided between four candidates: Bill, Judy, Lourdes, and Nathan.
2. Several applicants, as you know, was interviewed, but only one met all our qualifications.
3. Isn't it obvious that preparing their proposal took much time and effort.
4. In my opinion, you should sell the stock today before it goes down.
5. If I was in Miami, Florida, or in Phoenix, Arizona, I wouldn't be shoveling snow now.
6. The orchestra will play in Lincoln, Nebraska February 20.
7. The SuperVideo VCR is neither inexpensive, nor easy to operate.
8. Whenever you are sad, set down and count your blessings.
9. John D. Harris, Jr., is laying in the middle of the gymnasium floor demonstrating a new exercise.
10. The first applicants' résumé is the best I've seen.
11. Is Denise Swartz one of the attorneys who we met last year in Detroit?
12. There were two Darryl's on the company bowling team.
13. Either Kathy or Sally are planning to work late Friday night to finish the booklets.

14. On March 5, 1905, the cornerstone was lain for the building that is now on the historic register.
15. Shelly and him will have to decide how to divide the assignment.

Editing Practice

Test Your Skills. As part of applying for a job with a major corporation, you have been asked to take an editing test. Read the following excerpt from a letter addressed to shareholders. Make any necessary corrections on a separate sheet of paper.

Most of you have already seen the article in the January issue of *Consumer Facts* naming our software as the number one comunications software in the nation. Needless to say, I am exceptionally proud of this accomplishment; and I congratulate our research and development staff, our marketing department and our office staff for achieving this recognition.

How did we accomplish this goal. We had competent, energetic dedicated people whom worked as a team. All of us should share in this recognition. Your the reason for our success. Thank you.

Semicolons, Colons, and Dashes

The dash says aloud what the parenthesis whispers. The dash is the more useful—since whispering tends to annoy—and will remain useful only if not overused.

—Sheridan Baker, *The Practical Stylist*

OBJECTIVES:
After completing Section 4.3, you should be able to:

1. Use semicolons correctly to join independent clauses.
2. Use semicolons and colons correctly before enumerations and explanations.
3. Use colons correctly to introduce independent clauses and for emphasis.
4. Use dashes correctly in sentences.
5. Correct errors in the use of semicolons, colons, and dashes.

This section discusses three marks of punctuation that are used *within* sentences—semicolons, colons, and dashes. These punctuation marks enable the writer to guide the reader through the message. At the same time, they enable the writer to add variety and interest to the message. Each mark has its own specific function.

SEMICOLONS

Semicolons are intended to make the reader pause; by providing timing cues, they guide the reader in understanding the message clearly. Semicolons are used (1) in place of a coordinating conjunction to join independent clauses, (2) before an introductory word that begins the second clause in a sentence, and (3) before explanatory or enumerating words.

KEY POINT

Semicolons are used before the second clause in a compound sentence when the conjunction is omitted, before an introductory word that begins the second clause in a sentence, and before explanatory or enumerating words.

In Place of a Conjunction to Join Independent Clauses

As we have seen, in a compound sentence two or more independent clauses are usually connected by a comma or commas and one or more coordinating conjunctions.

> Lucia completed her degree in physical therapy in May, *and* she started working at Cleveland Memorial Hospital in June. (This sentence is a compound sentence; it has two independent clauses connected by a comma and the conjunction *and*.)

The conjunction and comma in a compound sentence such as the one above may be omitted, and a semicolon may be used to replace them.

> Lucia completed her degree in physical therapy in May; she started working at Cleveland Memorial Hospital in June. (Here, a semicolon joins the two independent clauses, replacing the comma and the conjunction.)

Before a Second Clause Starting With an Introductory Word

In some compound sentences, the second independent clause starts with an introductory word such as the following:

accordingly	consequently	moreover
again	furthermore	nevertheless
also	however	otherwise
besides	indeed	therefore

In such sentences, use a semicolon before the introductory word that introduces the second independent clause. The semicolon provides the necessary pause between the independent clauses, and the introductory word provides a connection between the two clauses.

> Many of our guests made reservations before the special offer was introduced; *nevertheless,* we will give them the discount. (The semicolon separates the two independent clauses, and the introductory word *nevertheless* signals the reader to contrast the two clauses.)

> This corporate bond offers a 7 percent after-tax return; *consequently,* we are increasing our total investment. (Again, the semicolon separates the two independent clauses and tells the reader to pause. The introductory word *consequently* establishes a specific relationship between the two clauses; it shows that the second statement is a result of the first statement.)

Note that the introductory word is not always the *first* word in the second clause.

> Many of our guests made reservations before the special offer was introduced; we are pleased, *nevertheless,* to give them the discount.

> This corporate bond offers a 7 percent after-tax return; we are, *consequently,* increasing our total investment.

Before Explanatory or Enumerating Words

Use a semicolon before such terms as *for example, for instance,* and *that is* when they introduce an independent clause, an enumeration, or an explanation that is incidental to the meaning of the rest of the sentence.

> Elena is seeking to advance her career; *for example,* she has completed two advanced accounting courses at the university. (*For example* introduces an independent clause.)

> Robin suggested several ways to advertise our company; *for instance,* (1) develop a home page on the Internet, (2) send promotional flyers to potential customers, and (3) sponsor a trade show. (*For instance* introduces an enumeration.)

> List units of measurement as abbreviations; *that is,* 12 ft, 8 in, and 5 yd. (*That is* introduces an explanation.)

CHECKUP 1

Make any necessary corrections in the following sentences on a separate sheet of paper. Write *OK* if the sentence is correct.

1. Kevin is a full-time student, however, he does work at least ten hours per week.
2. Riding in a hot air balloon provides a beautiful view, as the sun rises, the sky has many different hues.
3. Policy mandates two signatures for checks over $1000, consequently, both Phil and Amy must sign the reimbursement checks.
4. Invoices should be paid within the discount period, paying within the allotted time saved us $23,500 last year.
5. Dr. Brown's lecture on phobias was intriguing, indeed, 25 people registered for counseling to treat various phobias.
6. The airplane's arrival was about one hour late; the delay was caused by poor weather conditions.
7. Andy will be transferred to Portland in January, we plan, therefore, to fill his position in early February.
8. We canceled our order for more fax machines, besides, most of our computers now have fax capabilities.

COLONS

Colons make readers pause and take note of what follows.

Before Listed Items

When an expression such as *the following, as follows, this, these,* or *thus* is used to introduce a list of items, it is often followed by a colon. The

KEY POINT

Colons are used instead of semicolons before listed items when the explanation or enumeration is anticipated.

list may appear on the same line as the colon, or it may start on a new line.

> Our next staff meeting will cover these topics: (1) research tools for paralegals, (2) new billing procedures, and (3) expansion of our client base.

> At our next staff meeting, we will discuss these topics:
> 1. Research tools for paralegals
> 2. New billing procedures
> 3. Expansion of our client base

Sometimes the words *the following, as follows,* and so on, do not directly lead into the list; for example, an interrupting sentence appears between the lead-in sentence and the list. In such cases, use a period, not a colon.

> We have amended the course requirements. The new requirements are as follows. They may be completed in any order.
> 1. Submit Form 470A.
> 2. Meet with your supervisor.
> 3. Request an examination date.

> (A period, not a colon, is used after *as follows* because the actual list does not follow directly. A sentence separates the lead-in *as follows* and the actual list.)

If a list of items is preceded by an introductory clause that does not express a complete thought, do not use a colon to separate the clause from the list.

> Most of our computers contain internal modems, CD-ROM drives, and built-in Internet access. (No colon is needed before the list of items since the clause *Most of our computers contain* is not a complete thought.)

Instead of Semicolons

You already have learned that semicolons are used before such expressions as *for example* and *that is* when these expressions introduce independent clauses, enumerations, and explanations that are incidental to the rest of the sentence. However, when the explanation or enumeration is anticipated, a colon is used instead of a semicolon.

> We have changed our procedure for accepting new patients: namely, the patient must submit a complete medical history, and the patient must present proof of insurance.

To Emphasize

KEY POINT

Use a colon to emphasize important thoughts.

Writers use colons most often to emphasize important thoughts or words.

> Jeri identified the most important feature: convenience. (The colon places special emphasis on *convenience.*)

> Remember: Beginning Monday, all employees must use their photo identification badges to enter the building. (More emphatic than *Please try to remember that beginning Monday . . . .*)

Capitalizing After Colons

Capitalize the first word following a colon if (1) it begins a complete sentence requiring special emphasis or (2) it begins a sentence stating a formal rule.

The personnel changes will affect two departments: accounting and marketing. (Not a sentence; the first word is not capitalized.)

Deborah stated an important reason for accepting the bid: It will cut costs. (Complete sentence; the first word is capitalized because the sentence requires special emphasis.)

The first step is the most important: Create an outline for your report. (Complete sentence; the first word is capitalized because the sentence states a formal rule.)

✔ CHECKUP 2

On a separate sheet of paper, correct any errors in colon use in the following sentences. Write *OK* for any sentence that is correct.

1. Only two employees were recognized for distinguished service: My partner and Ted Reynolds.
2. As soon as you hear the tornado alarm, follow this action. Go to the basement.
3. To be selected for a baseball expansion team, a city must have adequate support in these areas; demographics, economics, and facilities.
4. The concierge related this change in convention registration procedures, Registration is in the convention hall lobby instead of the main lobby.
5. We finally discovered why the mail had not arrived; The address was printed incorrectly.
6. Della gave three reasons for hiring Al. Each reason was justified.

DASHES

Dashes share some of the features of semicolons and of colons: All three make the reader pause—but dashes do so more forcefully. Compare, for example, the differences in impact of the punctuation in each of the following examples. Notice how the dash provides greater impact than either the semicolon or the colon.

Your Internet advertising will bring you the greatest return if you post ads on UniversalNet; this Internet service is the one most used by consumers worldwide. (A good sentence, but not a forceful one.)

KEY POINT

The dash provides a pause, indicates that something important will follow, and draws special attention to what follows. The dash is stronger than the semicolon and the colon.

For the best return on your advertising dollar, do this: Buy ads on UniversalNet, the most widely used Internet provider in the world. (This is a better sentence, a more forceful one.)

Your Internet advertising will bring you the greatest return if you post ads on UniversalNet—the Internet service most used by consumers worldwide. (The dash snaps off the main thought and thereby adds power to the rest of the message. This is the most forceful of the three sentences.)

The semicolon provides the needed pause between clauses. The colon provides more than a pause: It promises that something important will follow. The dash goes even further by drawing special attention to what follows the dash. Therefore, the dash makes the third example the strongest of the three.

For Forceful Summarizing and Forceful Repetition

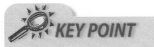

KEY POINT

Use dashes to indicate forceful summarizing, forceful repetition, and afterthoughts.

In your writing you may wish to summarize the main points of your message to make sure that your readers remember these key points. Repeating a key point is another technique that you can use to make a stronger impression on your readers. (The same is true when you are speaking.) When you are summarizing or repeating main points, use a dash to separate the summary or the repetition from the rest of the sentence.

Challenging games, helpful business programs, educational software—all are available at the CompuCenter nearest you. (The dash provides forceful summarizing.)

Remember to get all your computer supplies from CompuCenter—CompuCenter, where we keep you and your computer needs in mind. (Forceful repetition. Here, the writer deliberately repeats the most important part of the message—the store name.)

With Afterthoughts

To add variety to their writing, to arouse the reader's curiosity, to soften a statement that might otherwise offend, to provide special emphasis—for all these reasons, good writers *plan* their afterthoughts.

Our Memorial Day sale will surely save you money—and offer you some exciting *un*advertised specials! (To provide variety in writing style and to arouse the reader's curiosity.)

Of course, we wish that we could send you a free copy of our latest software as you requested—but company policy limits the free copies to educational institutions. (To soften a refusal.)

This discount coupon is sent only to our credit customers—no one else receives one! (To emphasize a statement.)

Using a separate sheet of paper, add dashes where needed. Write *OK* for any sentence that is correct.

1. Only three reservations remain for the Alaska cruise fax your reservation request to us today.

2. Our merger plans are almost complete but more about this at the meeting.

3. Our family will be unable to travel to Colorado—at least until after school is dismissed for the summer.

4. Tennis courts, golf courses, and swimming pools, these are but a few of the resort's recreational opportunities.

5. Get your photography supplies from the Shutter Shop, Shutter Shop, where we keep your camera needs in mind.

Punctuating Words Set Off by Dashes

Use dashes to set off words at the end of a sentence or within a sentence.

At the End of a Sentence. When you want to set off words at the end of a sentence, only one dash is needed. The dash is placed before the words to be set off; a period, question mark, or exclamation point then ends the sentence. No spaces are used between a dash and the word or words it is setting off.

> This computer package has several features not usually found at this low price—120 megabytes of memory, dual 3.5-inch disk drives, a CD-ROM, a 17-inch color monitor. (The dash precedes the words to be set off; a period ends this declarative sentence.)

Note that no punctuation is used before the dash unless an abbreviation or quotation precedes the dash. No punctuation ever follows the dash.

> We became partners with MegaSoft Inc.—Ms. Frasier approved the merger. (The period before the dash belongs with the abbreviation.)

Within a Sentence. To set off words within a sentence, two dashes are needed. Again, no punctuation is used before the first dash unless an abbreviation or quotation precedes the dash. The second dash may have a question mark or an exclamation point *before* it, but only if the words set off by the dashes require a question mark or an exclamation point.

> Our new vice president—have you met her?—will join us for lunch. (The dashes set off a question; thus a question mark precedes only the second dash. Note that the sentence ends with a period.)

> Nelson Carter won—for the third consecutive year!—the company golf trophy. (The words set off by dashes require an exclamation point. Note that the sentence ends with a period.)

Our bus was behind schedule because tariff was heavy.

Company recruiters—Bryan Gordon, Dawn Madison, and Phil Perkins are among them—have requested a merit-based compensation package. (No period before the second dash.)

Note in the above example that commas are used within dashes in the usual way. Note also that the first word after an opening dash is *not* capitalized even if the words between the dashes constitute a sentence.

✔ CHECKUP 4

On a separate sheet of paper, correct any punctuation errors in the following sentences. Write *OK* for any sentence that is correct.

1. Don ordered the snacks—bagels, pastries, and fruit—.
2. After she won the car—she won a brand new convertible!—she drove from coast to coast.
3. It will be Carrie and Steve—do you know either of them—? who will remove the virus from your computer.
4. Competence, personality, and hard work,—these traits form the foundation for promotions.
5. Your flight leaves Denver at 10:25 a.m.—but you should arrive no later than 9:25 p.m.
6. Please send the completed forms—is overnight delivery available—? by the quickest way.

SECTION 4.3   REVIEW

Practical Application

A. On a separate sheet of paper, correct any errors in the following sentences. Write *OK* for any sentence that is correct.
1. Dr. Wilson is a competent physician,—competent and very personable too.
2. Call us today to take advantage of: top quality, low prices, and free delivery.
3. The Grand Canyon—have you ever been there—? is one of the seven natural wonders of the world.
4. Our proposal was accepted August 25, however, it was later rejected.
5. Our proposal was accepted August 25, it was, however, later rejected.

6. Remember: absolutely no smoking is allowed in the explosives store room.
7. The first salary offer was reasonable—wasn't it $30,000—? but I negotiated a higher one.
8. Hampton Construction Company bid $255,000 on the project; Mauney, Inc., bid $252,000.
9. When the reporters bombarded me with questions, my response was always the same, no comment!
10. Investing has three possibilities (1) making money, (2) losing money, and (3) breaking even.
11. Paul's assistant is Darren Wilson, Anne's assistant is Darryl Wilson.
12. Clocks from Germany, cheese from Switzerland, coffee from Brazil,—these are products we usually import.
13. The following changes in the vacation policy will become effective December 1: As you read the changes, note that intended vacation days must still be specified at least 30 days ahead.
14. Our latest word processing software is temporarily unavailable— all other software can be shipped immediately.—but we can ship word processing software early Monday morning.
15. Three specialty stores—a pizza parlor, a video store, and an electronics showroom—have signed leases in the new mall.

B. On a separate sheet of paper, correct any errors in the following sentences. Write *OK* for any sentence that is correct.
1. The contract will be ready to sign, according to my attorney, within one weeks' time.
2. Please call Sam and me when your finished with that appointment.
3. Any customer who wants to enter the contest should give us their name, address, and telephone number.
4. Fred, as I am sure you know, is one of those journalists who verifies every detail.
5. All of our legal assistants' have the appropriate credentials.
6. As we reported to you, we gave all them people their luggage tags.
7. Beside her sports car, Aileen also has a boat and a camper.
8. As you noticed, Taylor couldn't hardly conceal her happiness.
9. Of course, Dave done seen his supervisor about next week's work schedule.
10. Why don't Max or Tim investigate Lenny's complaint personally?
11. We shipped their order today, it should arrive within three business days.
12. We do not accept cash payments after 11 p.m. Because it is not safe for us to do so.
13. Our profits were up considerably this year, in fact, they were up over 10 percent.
14. We will approve 20 people to work at home—they already have computers,—as soon as their modems are installed.
15. Alfred will sure walk better after he finishes his physical therapy.

Editing Practice

Using Business Vocabulary. On a separate sheet of paper, fill in each missing word with the correct word from the list below.

a. debit d. modem
b. exports e. virus
c. laptop

1. My computer wasn't operating properly, and the technician said that it had a ———.
2. Computers are usually connected to the information highway through a ———.
3. Donald takes his ——— computer with him when he travels out of town.
4. Imports refer to goods brought into the United States; ——— refer to goods shipped outside the United States.
5. A credit card charges purchases to your account; a ——— card takes money from your account.

Quotation Marks, Parentheses, and Apostrophes

OBJECTIVES:

After completing Section 4.4, you should be able to:

1. Use quotation marks correctly for direct quotations, definitions, special expressions, unfamiliar terms, titles of articles, and so on.
2. Use parentheses correctly to enclose words that give additional information and references.
3. Combine other punctuation marks correctly with quotation marks and with parentheses in sentences.
4. Use apostrophes correctly to form contractions.
5. Correct errors in the use of quotation marks, parentheses, and apostrophes.

Every quotation contributes something to the stability or enlargement of the language.

—Samuel Johnson, *Dictionary of the English Language*

Quotation marks serve primarily to tell the reader the exact words written or spoken by someone, but they also have other important uses. Parentheses share some (but not all) of the uses of commas and dashes. Apostrophes have one common use besides indicating ownership.

Knowing how to correctly use these three marks of punctuation will enhance your written communication skill.

QUOTATION MARKS

The common uses of quotation marks are described and illustrated in the following discussion.

For Direct Quotations

To indicate the *exact* words that someone has written or spoken, use quotation marks. In the following examples, note how commas, colons, and periods are used together with quotation marks.

KEY POINT

Quotation marks are used for direct quotations, definitions, special expressions, unfamiliar terms, and certain titles.

Ms. Ornette said, "Sam and I are taking a class in money management." (A comma precedes the direct quotation.)

"Sam and I are taking a class in money management," Ms. Ornette said. (A comma ends the quotation, separating it from the explanatory words that follow the quotation.)

"Sam and I," Ms. Ornette said, "are taking a class in money management." (Note how *two* commas are used to separate the interruption, *Ms. Ornette said.* The quotation marks still enclose the speaker's *exact* words.)

Ms. Ornette said: "Sam and I are taking a class in money management. We feel that we are not saving and investing enough of our salaries. In looking at our future, we saw that we will need to send two children to college and to finish paying for our home. Without planning and executing the plan, we will not be able to achieve our goals." (Use a colon before a long quotation, including a quotation of more than one sentence.)

"Sam and I are taking a class in money management," Ms. Ornette said. "We feel that we are. . . ." (Again, note that the interrupting expression is separated from the exact words of the speaker by a comma and a period.)

Remember that *indirect* quotations (restatements of a person's exact words) are not enclosed in quotation marks. Indirect quotations are often introduced by the word *that*.

She said that they were taking a course in money management. (This example is an *indirect* quotation.)

For Quotations Within Quotations

Use single quotation marks for words quoted within other quoted material.

KEY POINT

Single quotation marks are used for quoted words within other quoted material.

Mr. Santana asked, "Did she say '15 percent' or '50 percent'?" (Note the position of the question mark: It is *inside* the double quotation mark because the question mark belongs to the entire sentence but *outside* the single quotation mark.)

"In my opinion, this desktop publishing program is certainly not 'user-friendly,'" said Harvey. (A final comma is placed inside both the single and the double quotation marks.)

Harvey said, "In my opinion, this desktop publishing program is certainly not 'user-friendly.'" (A period that ends a quotation is also placed inside both the single and the double quotation marks.)

World View

In Great Britain the use of quotation marks is reversed. Single quotation marks (called *inverted commas*) enclose quotations, and double quotation marks enclose quotations within quotations: Mr. Santana asked, 'Did she say "fifteen people" or "fifty people"?'

For Definitions, Special Expressions, Unfamiliar Terms, Translations, and Slang

Use quotation marks to enclose definitions and special expressions following such phrases as *known as, marked,* and *signed.*

In computer terminology, *GUI* means "graphical user interface." (Quotation marks for definitions.)

Computer equipment known as "peripherals" includes printers, scanners, and modems. (Quotation marks for expressions following *called, known as,* and so on.)

Note: Words introduced by *so-called* do not require quotation marks since *so-called* itself provides them with sufficient emphasis.

Also use quotation marks for unfamiliar terms and for translations.

The illustration below shows a "light pen," which is used to read bar codes. (Quotation marks for unfamiliar terms.)

Par avion is simply the French term for "by airplane." (Quotation marks for translations.)

Slang may be deliberately used to add punch to a message, to attract attention, or to make a point. (Such uses should be limited.) Use quotation marks to enclose a slang expression, a funny comment, or a grammatical error. Note that instead of quotation marks, italics or underlining is now more commonly used with definitions and special expressions.

There is only one week left in the month, but Frank Stanley says the sales contest "ain't over yet!" (Quotation marks for intentional use of a grammatical error.)

The city editor said to "kill" that investigative report on contract fixing. (Quotation marks for a slang expression.)

World View

When communicating with someone whose native language isn't English, avoid using slang. Literal translations of slang expressions are likely to hinder rather than help the communication process.

✓ CHECKUP 1

Are quotation marks used correctly in the following sentences? Add quotation marks as needed and correct any errors on a separate sheet of paper.

1. "Write the client a letter tomorrow and enclose our investment proposal" said Shane.
2. "The new catalog said Pete will be distributed to customers by the first of the month."
3. We decided that the so-called "photo opportunity" wasn't worth our time.
4. The cartons containing the trophies were marked Fragile, of course.
5. Willis said, "Mark all the cartons Handle With Care."
6. The check was signed Stella Abernathy, but the teller said that the signature did not match the signature on file.

7. "Maria will attend only the morning session announced Mr. Norton because she must catch an early afternoon flight to Montreal."

8. Mr. Norton announced "Maria will attend only the morning session because she must catch an early afternoon flight to Montreal.

For Certain Titles

Use quotation marks for the titles of articles, poems, lectures, chapters of books, essays, and sermons and for mottoes and slogans.

> Arlen Honts wrote "E-Mail Etiquette," which appeared in the April issue of Technical Trends. (Quotation marks for article title.)

In the preceding example, note that while the article title is in quotation marks, the title of the magazine is underscored. In addition, book titles are underscored, as are the titles of newspapers, booklets, long poems, plays, operas, and movies.

> Tina's new book, Making Your First Million, was favorably reviewed in The Wall Street Journal. (Underscores for book title and for newspaper name.)

> This book, Securing Your Financial Future, contains a chapter entitled "Municipal Bonds Are Safe Investments," which I highly recommend. (Quotation marks for chapter title; underscore for book title.)

Note that underscoring in typewritten or handwritten copy is equivalent to *italics* in printed copy. Most word processing software and printers are capable of printing italics. Note, too, that while chapter titles are enclosed in quotation marks, other book parts are not. Words such as *preface, index, introduction,* and *appendix* are not enclosed in quotation marks. They are capitalized only when they refer to a specific part within the same book.

> Dr. Negbenebor, our economics professor, wrote the preface to the enclosed volume as well as Chapter 7, "Analyzing Trends."

> Refer to the Glossary for these definitions. (The sentence appears in the same book as the glossary.)

Technology

Use the italics feature of word processing software for titles of books, newspapers, booklets, long poems, plays, operas, and movies.

Punctuation at the End of Quotations

For a summary of how to use periods, commas, colons, semicolons, question marks, and exclamation points with quotation marks, study the following.

1. Periods and commas are *always* placed inside the closing quotation mark.

   "Prior to every scheduled meeting," said Ms. Botts, "the team leader will distribute an agenda to each of you."

KEY POINT

Periods and commas are *always inside* the closing quotation mark. Colons and semicolons are *always outside* the closing quotation mark. Question marks and exclamation points are *inside* or *outside* the closing quotation mark *depending on the context of the sentence.*

2. Colons and semicolons are always placed *outside* the closing quotation mark.

   Jim Hartman buys only stocks that are considered "blue chips": Kemper Metals, Inc.; Martin Industries; Webb Gas Company; and World Plastics.

   Mr. Carpenter thinks that all the estimates are "not in the ballpark"; for this reason, he has asked the companies to revise their estimates.

3. Question marks and exclamation points may be placed either inside or outside the closing quotation mark depending on whether or not the question mark or exclamation point is part of the quotation. Follow these rules to decide.

   a. If the quoted words are a question, then the question mark belongs with those quoted words. Place the question mark *inside* the closing quotation mark.

      Lance Carroll asked, "Do you think the sales forecast is realistic?" (Only the quoted words make up the question; thus the question mark belongs with the quoted words—*inside* the closing quotation mark.)

      Treat exclamations the same way as questions.

      Randy Hays said, "I can't believe that the computer network is down again!" (Only the words in quotations make up the exclamation; thus the exclamation point belongs with those words—*inside* the closing quotation mark.)

   b. If the quoted words do *not* make up a question (that is, if the quotation is part of a longer question,) then the question mark belongs to the entire sentence. Place the question mark *outside* the closing quotation mark.

      Do you agree with Russell Hardin that their reaction to the budget cuts was "mean-spirited"? (The entire sentence is a question; the quotation is only part of the question. The question mark belongs *outside* the closing quotation mark.)

      Treat exclamations the same way.

      Imagine calling these stocks "blue chips"! (The entire sentence is an exclamation; the quoted words are only part of the exclamation. The exclamation point belongs *outside* the closing quotation mark.)

MEMORY HOOK

To help remember how to use end punctuation with quotation marks, use this tip:

Periods and commas . . . . always inside
Colons and semicolons . . . . always outside
Exclamation points and question marks . . . where they belong

On a separate sheet of paper, correct any errors in the use of quotation marks. Write *OK* for any sentence that is correct.

1. The president included these people on his list of "key personnel:" Myrna Cloninger, Earl Godfrey, Darlene Gravett, Ruth Helton, Danny Shelton, and Duane Tarboro.

2. Impatiently waiting for his taxi to the airport, Demetri exclaimed, "Where is that taxi"!

3. Did you hear that one of the restaurant owners said she was "selling her business immediately"?

4. Ralph said that the budget requests were "ridiculously overstated;" moreover, he said that he wants each supervisor to revise and resubmit all requests.

5. Did Ms. McEntire specifically say "25 percent discount on all discontinued appliances?"

6. During her speech, she quoted a few lines from Robert Frost's well-known poem "The Road Not Taken".

7. Waste not, want not is an apt slogan for our cost-cutting campaign.

8. His new book, Interviews That Impress, has some excellent information that is not found in similar books.

PARENTHESES

Although commas, dashes, and parentheses share certain common uses, they should not be used interchangeably. Just as words that have similar meanings still have subtle distinctions, so, too, do commas, dashes, and parentheses have distinctions. The careful business writer is aware of these distinctions. Study the use of parentheses discussed here.

For Words That Give Additional Information

Commas, dashes, and parentheses may be used to set off words that give additional information. The words set off by commas may be omitted, but they generally add something to the main thought. The words set off by dashes are often given additional emphasis by the dashes. The words set off by parentheses, however, are clearly de-emphasized; they may be omitted.

**KEY POINT**

Parentheses are correctly used to enclose words that give additional information and to enclose references.

Kim Evans, after over 50 years of service, has finally retired. (The words set off by commas may be omitted, but they do add something to the main thought.)

Ms. Leonard selected four managers—including Jane Douglas in Human Resources—for the task force. (The words set off by dashes may be omitted; however, the writer deliberately uses dashes to draw attention to these words.)

In the past year, we lost only one account (Hannah Productions, which had small billings for the past five years). (The words in parentheses are extraneous; they contribute little to the main thought.)

For References

Parentheses are very useful for enclosing references and directions.

Refer to Appendix C (on page 572) for instructions on how to customize your keyboard.

Include your credit card information (account number and expiration date) on the payment form.

Punctuation With Words in Parentheses

Parentheses may be used to enclose some of the words within a sentence, or they may be used to enclose an entire sentence.

Parentheses Within a Sentence. No punctuation mark goes *before* the opening parenthesis within a sentence. Whatever punctuation would normally be used at this point is placed *after* the closing parenthesis.

When we meet next Friday (at the weekly budget session), we will discuss the new billing system. (The comma that is needed after the clause *When we meet next Friday* is placed *after* the *closing* parenthesis, not *before* the *opening* parenthesis.)

Mr. Walters suggested that we limit the number of overtime hours each week (to 5 hours for every employee), and a long discussion followed. (The comma needed to separate the two independent clauses is placed *after* the *closing* parenthesis, not *before* the *opening* parenthesis.)

Newton Tool Company estimated a unit cost of $2.62 (see the itemized statement enclosed); however, this cost applies only to manufacturing 100,000 units or more. (The semicolon is placed *after* the *closing* parenthesis.)

Note that these rules do not affect any punctuation needed *within* the parentheses. Study the following examples:

She will be based in one of the West Coast offices (either San Francisco, California, or Seattle, Washington), once she accepts the position.

I would like to revise the spreadsheet for the budget report (is it on this floppy diskette?) and ask Paul to comment on it.

If an independent clause in parentheses within a sentence is a question or exclamation, the question mark or exclamation mark is included within the parentheses. If the independent clause is a declaration, however, no period is used within the parentheses. Note, too, that when parentheses are included within a sentence, the first word in parentheses is not capitalized (unless, of course, the first word is a

Is her name Bev Saunders? (or is it Sanders).

proper noun) even if the words in parentheses are an independent clause.

> Hal Berger (he's the accounts receivable manager) is the person whom you should consult.

Parentheses for Complete Sentences. When the words enclosed in parentheses are entirely independent (that is, they are not part of another sentence), the first word in parentheses is capitalized and normal end punctuation is used before the closing parenthesis.

> As you can see, we have depreciated the equipment over a 5-year period. (Please see Appendix A, page 83.)

> Please be advised that payments received after the due date will not be credited to your account. (A late fee of $20 will be added to your next bill.)

✔ CHECKUP 3

Are parentheses used correctly in the following sentences? Correct any errors on a separate sheet of paper. Write *OK* if the sentence is correct.

1. Ms. Darnell insists that all these checks (every one of them!) be processed and deposited before 2 p.m.

2. If John and Sally buy a new car (We think they will do so.), we want them to get their loan from our bank.

3. Several telephone extension numbers were printed incorrectly in our new company directory (see errors marked) and these must be corrected without delay.

4. We will introduce the silver cleaning product at a special low price (say, $9.95); then, in three or four months, we can raise the price.

5. According to the revised company handbook (see the attached photocopy of page 34,) our vacation has been increased from two to three weeks.

6. Hayley International Travel, (formerly known as "Haley Travel Services,") is the best travel service in town.

7. Take advantage of this exciting offer to trade in your printer for a color printer for only $129.95. (This special offer ends March 15). Call us today!

8. Do you think Ellen will accept the transfer to the Denver office (after all, it is a lateral move?)

APOSTROPHES

As you learned in Section 3.3, the primary use of the apostrophe is to form possessives of nouns (*John's* office, several *technicians'* recommendations, and so on). A second common use of the apostrophe is to form

KEY POINT

Apostrophes are used to form possessives of nouns, to form contractions, and to show omissions in dates (*'98* for *1998*).

contractions—shortened forms of one or more words. (Note the difference between a contraction, such as *cont'd*, and an abbreviation, such as *cont.*—A contraction uses an apostrophe, and an abbreviation ends with a period.)

Contraction	Full Form
I'm	I am
you're, we're, they're	you are, we are, they are
she's, he's, it's	she is, she has; he is, he has; it is, it has
I've, you've, we've, they've	I have, you have, we have, they have
I'd, you'd, he'd, she'd, we'd, they'd	I had, I would; you had, you would; he had, he would; she had, she would; we had, we would; they had, they would
I'll, you'll, he'll, she'll, we'll, they'll	I will, you will, he will, she will, we will, they will
there's, where's	there is, there has; where is, where has
don't, doesn't,	do not, does not,
didn't, can't, couldn't, won't, wouldn't	did not, cannot, could not, will not, would not

Another use of the apostrophe is to show that the first two figures have been omitted from a year date; for example, '99 is a shortened form of *1999*.

SECTION 4.4   REVIEW

Practical Application

A. On a separate sheet of paper, correct any errors in the use of quotation marks, parentheses, or apostrophes in the following sentences. Write *OK* for any sentence that is correct.
   1. Since 1950 Maxwell Service Station has advertised its well-known motto: Service With a Smile.
   2. Mr. Jarvis said that "holiday bonuses will be distributed on December 15."
   3. We will place signs in the store windows (each sign will read "Closed for Inventory"!) and will advertise our after-inventory sale in the local papers.
   4. After viewing my advertising proposal, the client said, "Well done—looks great!"

5. Please take all these survey responses to Mr. Olson (is he still on the third floor) before you leave for lunch, Lamont.
6. Glenn Thomas asked for a list of movies that are rated "PG-13."
7. Mr. Wren's assistant couldnt reach him by cellular phone because the battery had run down.
8. When Diana completed her two-year degree, (she was graduated in '97) she began working for Ms. Werner.
9. As our attorney explained, *nolo contendere* is a legal term that means "no contest".
10. The new loan application (its already in use) can be completed on the computer instead of on paper.
11. Laura asked, "Which detectives are working during the holidays"?
12. "Perhaps" said Mr. Soutiere, we should evaluate your entire portfolio because your investment needs have changed."
13. Nearly 95 percent of our employees over 45 years old have signed up for the retirement seminar. (Our survey had shown that the majority of them were interested in preparing for this change in their lives).
14. "We asked some of our employees their views on the proposed changes in our shift schedules," said Ms. Jackson, "naturally, we felt that they should know that their suggestions are being considered."

B. On a separate sheet of paper, correct any errors in the following sentences. Write *OK* for any sentence that is correct.
1. "Without a doubt, we have produced the healthiest breakfast cereal on the market," said Lane Allen, "consequently, we must let the people around the world know the health benefits of our product."
2. The Index will lead you to pages in the book that deal with health issues for women (see page 1,142).
3. Esteban requisitioned enough printer ribbons, form-feed paper, floppy disks, and etc., for the entire office.
4. Nicole asked, "What is a non sequitur?" Sharon replied, "A non sequitur is a 'statement that does not follow."
5. "According to store policy," said Martha Drum, "A customer must show his or her driver's license to cash any check."
6. Bob Newberg is our new broker (he was recruited from a competitor.)
7. If you want more information on the family leave policy, call the human resources director, Angela Smith. (Her extension is 4378.)
8. A thorough explanation of the bank charges was included in the information booklet (see pages 12 through 14.).
9. After skimming the "preface," I decided to read the book.
10. Marcus' plan for restructuring the office is extraordinary, I think.

11. Remember this rule, No employee is permitted to enter the computer division without clearance from the president or the vice president.
12. Mr. Cooper said, "Because Casey been a nurse in our hospital for many years, we will certainly miss him when he moves to Asheville."
13. Jeff's article on investing tips, Planning Your Financial Future, will soon be reprinted in several magazines.
14. The investment seminar will cover (1.) buying and selling stocks, (2.) investing in government bonds, and (3.) selecting mutual funds.

Editing Practice

Making Sure Verbs Are in Agreement. On a separate sheet of paper, correct any verb errors in the following sentences. Write *OK* for any sentence that is correct.

1. Don't Mrs. Kilminster volunteer for the lunch buddy program at the elementary school?
2. More than a million dollars was paid in claims as a result of the tornado.
3. Sheila said that she been promoted twice since she came to work here.
4. Although a number of witnesses were questioned today, we have at least eight more to question tomorrow.
5. "The increasing number of tourists to this mountain area is encouraging," said the motel owner.
6. Kevin has already went to the hospital to visit with his aunt who had an appendectomy yesterday.

SECTION 4.5 Capitalization

OBJECTIVES:

After completing Section 4.5, you should be able to:

1. Use capitals correctly for the first words of sentences, direct quotations, and items in outlines and lists.

Don't use capital letters without good REASON.

—William Safire, in *Fumblerules*

The rules of capitalization help writers make words distinctive, emphasize words, and show that certain words are especially important. Some of the rules for capitalization are easy to remember because they are well known and long established. These rules are reviewed briefly in this section. Other capitalization rules may cause writers problems, however, and these pitfalls are also fully discussed here.

FIRST WORDS

Always capitalize the first word of the following:

1. A sentence or a group of words used as a sentence.

   The most recent information must be downloaded by tomorrow morning. (Complete sentence.)

   Yes, *tomorrow* morning. (Group of words used as a sentence.)

2. Each line of poetry (unless the original shows other capitalization).

   Let the downpour roil and toil!
   The worst it can do to me
   Is carry some garden soil
   A little nearer the sea.

   —Robert Frost, from "In Time of Cloudburst"

3. Each item in an outline or list.

   The results of the survey showed the following:
   1. Consumers dislike loud TV commercials.
   2. Viewers favor fewer commercial interruptions.
   3. Audiences respond to humorous commercials.

4. A sentence in a direct quotation.

   The 911 dispatcher emphasized the urgency of the situation: "Please rush to the fire at the oil refinery; there are still workers in the main building."

5. A complete sentence after a colon when that sentence is a formal rule or needs special emphasis.

   The store's rule is: Refund the customer's money if there is a receipt. (Rule.)

   Computer experts issue this reminder: Always check your disks for viruses. (For emphasis.)

6. The first word after a colon when the material that follows consists of two or more sentences.

   She described in detail the two main reasons for changing delivery services: First, lower rates will substantially decrease shipping costs. Second, expanded access to global markets will make it easier to reach overseas customers.

7. A salutation.

   Dear Dr. Ward:

8. A complimentary closing.

   Sincerely yours,

2. Use capitals correctly in headings and in titles of publications.
3. Correctly capitalize proper nouns, proper adjectives, titles, and names of commercial products.
4. Correct errors in capitalization.

 **KEY POINT**

Capitalize the first word of: a sentence, a group of words used as a sentence, each line of poetry, each item in an outline or list, a sentence in a direct quotation, a complete sentence after a colon, a salutation, and a complimentary closing.

MAIN WORDS IN TITLES

Always capitalize the main words of headings and titles of publications. Do not capitalize articles, conjunctions, and short prepositions (prepositions of three or fewer letters), unless they are the first word or the last word in the heading or title.

In this morning's edition of *USA Today,* under the headline "The Graying and Retiring of America's Seniors," Lavonda Silverstein commended the American Medical Association for its research on aging. (*The* is capitalized in the title of the article because it is the first word. The preposition *of* and the conjunction *and* are not capitalized in the article title.)

You should read "What Small Businesses Strive For," a well-written, perceptive article by Lucinda Borelli that appears in the current issue of *Today's Entrepreneur* magazine. (Here, *for* is capitalized because it is the last word in the title.)

Hyphenated titles follow the same rules:

In "Out-of-Work Blues," Denise Rosinni tells job seekers how to retain their self-esteem and their sense of humor.

Capitalize the first word that follows a colon or dash in a title.

Denzel Morris wrote the book *The Space Race: A Look Back.*

 **CHECKUP 1**

Make any needed corrections in the following sentences on a separate sheet of paper. Write *OK* for any sentence that is correct.

1. We are now reviewing our office furniture needs:
   1. one computer desk
   2. one printer table
   3. three leather desk chairs
2. Has the copier been repaired? no, it hasn't.
3. He is now writing "Tips For Business And Pleasure Traveling" for *International Business And Marketing* magazine.
4. At the close of the crash course to pass the state licensing exam, the instructor said, "continue studying two hours a day until you take the exam."
5. Monday's seminar includes the following: An introduction to exporting, the fundamentals of collecting for international sales, and testimonials by people involved in exporting.
6. I use the closing "sincerely" in all of my business correspondence.
7. This proposal is easier to follow than the one from Anderson & Son. significantly easier.
8. Remember: when using your personal car for business travel, write down your mileage so that you can be reimbursed.

9. Did you read the article "Labor-management Problems And How To Avoid Them"?

10. We are pleased to give you the good news: Sales and profits are up.

NAMES OF PERSONS

The problems surrounding the capitalization of names concern the use of prefixes such as the following:

D', Da, De, Di: *D'Amato, d'Amato; Da Puzzo, daPuzzo; DeLorenzo, De Lorenzo, deLorenzo; DiFabio, Di Fabio, diFabio.* Spell each name precisely as the person spells it.

L', La, Las, Le: *L'Engle, LaRosa, Las Varca, LeMaster.* Follow the capitalization, spelling, and spacing used by the person.

Mc, Mac: *McMillan, Macmillan, MacMillan.* The prefix *Mc* is followed by a capital letter and no spacing. The prefix *Mac* may or may not be followed by a capital.

O': *O'Brien, O'Toole, O'Malley.* The prefix *O'* is followed by a capital letter and no spacing.

Van, Von: *Van Fossen, van Fossen; van Hoffman; Von Huffman; von der Lieth, Von der Lieth, Von Der Lieth.* Follow the capitalization, spelling, and spacing used by each person.

In all cases, be sure to write each person's name precisely the way he or she writes it—this rule refers not only to capitalization but also to the spelling of and the spacing in names. Note, however, that even prefixes that begin with lowercase letters are capitalized when the surname is used without the first name.

Emile received a fax from Katherine la Salle today. (She writes her name *la*.)

He thinks La Salle's comments about the proposal are valid. (When her first name is not used, capitalize *la* to avoid misreading.)

NAMES OF PLACES

Capitalize names of geographical localities, streets, parks, rivers, buildings, and so on, such as *Europe, Westfield Road, Harris Park, Mississippi River, Metropolitan Medical Building.*

Capitalize the word *city* only when it is a part of the corporate name of a city: *Kansas City,* but the *city of Paris.*

Capitalize the word *state* only when it follows the name of a state: *Iowa State,* but the *state of Iowa.*

Capitalize the word *the* in names of places only when *the* is part of the official name: *The Hague,* but *the Maritime Provinces.*

KEY POINT

Capitalize the names of persons, places, things, and proper adjectives.

Capitalize *north, south, east,* and *west* whenever they refer to specific sections of the country and when they are part of proper names. They are not capitalized when they refer merely to direction.

> We established a shipping center in the East to expedite delivery in that region. (Specific part of the country.)

> Shannon's sales territory includes North Dakota. (*North* is part of a proper name.)

> Significant tornado destruction occurred 10 miles west of town. (Here, *west* simply indicates direction.)

NAMES OF THINGS

Capital letters identify official names of companies, departments, divisions, associations, committees, bureaus, buildings, schools, course titles, clubs, government bodies, historical events and documents, and so on.

> Matt and Patti are taking Microcomputer Applications at Central Piedmont Community College. (*Microcomputer Applications* is the official course title; *Central Piedmont Community College* is the official name of the school.)

> Matt and Patti are taking a microcomputer applications course at a nearby college. (No capitals.)

> Maria Dimitrios is a computer analyst for the Settlemeyer Manufacturing Company, which has offices here in the Metrolina Building. (Capitalize the official name of the company and the building.)

> She is a computer analyst for a manufacturing company which has its headquarters in this building. (No capitals.)

> The Direct Mail Department has leased an entire floor in the Handler Building. (Official department name; official building name.)

Capitalize the names of the days of the week, the months of the year, religious days and holidays, and the names of eras and periods: *Tuesday, Wednesday; March, June; Easter, Passover; the Roaring Twenties, the Middle Ages.* Do not capitalize the seasons of the year: *summer, fall, winter, spring.*

Mt. McKinley in Alaska is the tallest Mountain in North America.

PROPER ADJECTIVES

Capitalize proper adjectives, which are adjectives formed from proper nouns; for example, *American, Canadian, Puerto Rican,* and so on. (*Note:* Certain adjectives—*venetian* blind, *india* ink, *turkish* towel, and *roman* numerals, for example—are no longer capitalized, because through many years of use they have lost their identification as proper adjectives. Consult a dictionary when in doubt.)

Are capitals used correctly in the following sentences? Correct any errors on a separate sheet of paper. Write *OK* for any sentence that is correct.

1. The computers in schools association is exploring the possibility of moving its headquarters into the Hancock building.
2. The fireworks display sponsored by the city of Philadelphia on the fourth of july was spectacular, Hans von hoffman tells me. Also, von hoffman reports that the display was safe.
3. You should read the article on chinese exports in today's newspaper.
4. On the first monday in august, we will meet to plan our excursion to view the Autumn foliage.
5. Patricia DeMay supervises our mexican trade office.
6. The Rustic Furniture Company has a showroom in Sioux city, Iowa.
7. My associate von Aspern owns and manages the Sunrise Bed and Breakfast inn on lake Lure.
8. Eric's speech, "Creativity In Business: a Guide For Today's Entrepreneurs," offered many new marketing techniques.

CAPITALIZATION PITFALLS

The following discussion presents some useful solutions to some of the typical problems writers face in using capitals correctly.

Short Forms

Writers often substitute one word for the complete name of a person, place, or thing. Such substitutions are usually capitalized to give special distinction or emphasis, as when they indicate a specific person, place, or thing. Some short forms are capitalized if they are personal titles of high rank, organizational names, or governmental bodies.

The most recent biography of the General is entitled *Powell in the Pentagon.* (Here, *General* is a personal title of a specific person.)

She has written a biography about a general who was famous in the Gulf War. (Because *general* does not refer to a particular person, it is not capitalized.)

After the civil engineers completed their inspection of the Lincoln Tunnel, they issued a report stating that the tunnel needed routine repairs. (Lowercase the second *tunnel,* because it is a common noun.)

The words *company, department, association, school, college,* and so on, are not usually capitalized when they stand alone, even though they may substitute for the official name of a specific organization. The word *company* may be capitalized when it carries special emphasis, as in legal documents and minutes of meetings.

Her company developed the component with Glenn & Company.

Joseph visited the museum during a recent trip to Washington, D.C.

Two sales associates in our department were promoted.

The terms *government* and *federal government* are not capitalized. *Federal* is capitalized, however, when it is part of an official name, such as *Federal Communications Commission.*

Personal and Official Titles

Always capitalize a title written before a name.

Among the directors are Dr. Shirley Toney, former Senator Baker, and Professor Barbara Selph.

A title written after a name or without a name is capitalized when (1) it is the title of a high-ranking national or international official or (2) it is part of an address.

Kofi Annan, Secretary General of the United Nations, championed the development of a relief fund. (Always capitalize this internationally known title.)

In yesterday's editorial, she discussed the President's economic policies. (*President*—referring to the President of the United States—is always capitalized.)

Hosea Rodriques, president of Silicon Enterprises, Inc., plans to retire in December. (Do not capitalize *president* in such situations.)

Ms. Hillary Stevens, President
Stevens Electronics, Inc.
Post Office Box 975
Naperville, Illinois 60566
(Capitalize a title that is part of an address.)

When joined to titles, the prefix *ex-* and the suffix *-elect* are not capitalized. Also, *former* and *late* are not capitalized.

Among the dignitaries invited to the dinner was former Mayor Clay.

The late Senator Joe Joliet will be remembered for his strong stands on business ethics.

Governor-elect Wehunt said that she would balance the state budget within three years.

Next semester, ex-Senator Wheatley will teach a course in political science.

Commercial Products

Distinguish carefully between a proper noun that is part of the official name of a product and a common noun that names the *general* class of the product. For example, you would write *Arch Saver shoes,* not *Arch Saver Shoes,* because the official brand name is *Arch Saver.* Note the following:

Coke (Coca-Cola)	Scotch tape
Kleenex tissues	Xerox machine
Ping-Pong balls	Yellow Pages directory

 **CHECKUP 3**

Using a separate sheet of paper, correct any errors in the use of capitalization in the following sentences. Write *OK* for any sentence that is correct.

1. When your Manager speaks to the Rotary club thursday in our Private Dining Room, his remarks should address the business aspects of managing a Hospital.

2. Of course, you should send the quality control reports to the Quality Assurance Division in Lexington, Kentucky.

3. Ilene Cunningham, President of nashville Country Recordings, has announced that her company will construct its new facilities on Delmar Road.

4. These Tastee Cookies, made by a family-owned company, are low in sodium and high in fiber.

5. Which Advertising Agency currently has the Chef Camp Ribs account?

6. The staff members in the shipping and receiving department were instrumental in our firm's significant donation to the kennedy memorial hospital in Pocatello, Idaho.

7. Murphy Plastics is building an office and sound studio 12 miles West of Seattle, Washington.

8. Revirez Electronics will announce the appointment of a new President at a Monday morning press conference.

9. Throughout the country we lease over 12,000 General Motors Vans.

10. The federal Deposit Insurance Corporation is investigating the situation after receiving several complaints.

Practical Application

A. On a separate sheet of paper, correct any capitalization errors in the following sentences. Write *OK* for any sentence that is correct.

1. Our corporate offices are in Dallas, but our restaurants are located throughout the southwest, with most of them in the State of Arizona.
2. Cell-Tell Mobile Telephone Company has its satellite disk in the Southern part of the city of Charleston, South Carolina.
3. Your new sales territory will cover customers in the States of Alabama, Louisiana, and Mississippi.
4. Mr. Pomeranz wants to move from Utah to the east coast.
5. We are proud to announce that our Spring sales have exceeded our expectations.
6. During last year, our Company opened three outlet stores on the West Coast.
7. According to her press secretary, the Governor will be hospitalized for about five days.
8. Kent Mendoza, Vice President of Home Health Care, Inc., has an option to purchase the property.
9. Our communications director suggests that we use "sincerely" or "sincerely yours" to close most letters.
10. "Sailing In The Carribean: a Vacationer's Paradise" was the title of the article that inspired me to take the trip.
11. When we toured Washington, D.C., we visited the white house and the supreme court building.
12. Before Scott was named Manager of the Atlanta regional office, he spent several years supervising one of our District offices.

B. On a separate sheet of paper, correct any errors in the following sentences. Write *OK* for any sentence that is correct.

1. Is that doctor standing besides my sister the orthopedic surgeon?
2. Kelvin, do you know where Nancy and Artis went to?
3. No, Elvin, I do not know where they are at.
4. Do you have a modem like this one connected to your computer?
5. Ethel asked, "Why did you delete these files from the current directory, Mary"?
6. One of the insurance agents who you met at this afternoon's briefing is Tracy's brother.
7. Danielle Miller, former president of the University Cycling Association, has been named to the Governor's committee.
8. The only one of the staff members who was aware of the merger, was Odell Oliver.

9. Because Jaya has been on an overseas assignment her college intern has been writing articles for her.
10. Penny, the assistant, sometimes acts like she was the department head.
11. The updated 911 emergency system, according to the city manager, will be operational inside of five days.
12. The U.S. Small Business Administration is a federal government agency that helps businesses continue in operation.
13. Don't Arnold know that he should be on time for meetings?
14. When Donna recovered from her surgery, she could not help but tell the doctors and nurses how much she appreciated their assistance.
15. Where's the book and articles that I sent you from the conference?

Editing Practice

Using Your Computer. On a separate sheet of paper, edit the following sentences to correct any errors they may contain. Write *OK* for any sentence that is correct.

1. According to the newspaper, the refund for the unapproved rate increase in utilities is retroactive from last May.
2. Mr. Wilson confirmed that a federal government agency had been involved with regulating the companies involved with interstate commerce.
3. We heard on television where no one was injured when the airplane made an emergency landing.
4. As you can well imagine, Amber was real happy when she heard that she had passed her comprehensive examinations.
5. Being that you were 30 minutes late for the meeting, we cannot pay you for the entire two-hour meeting.
6. You should not schedule the meeting for early Wednesday morning without you make sure that Jerry Pomeranz will be back from his business trip.
7. This letter is in regards to the contract you mailed to me.
8. This stack of invoices will be divided between the three computer operators for processing.
9. There is a discrepancy among the dates on the contract and the dates in the file.
10. Gale is seated besides Laura.
11. We will get the latest sales figures off Susan.
12. Ms. Graves told Bart she would like for him to conduct the meeting.

Abbreviations

It may help to think of abbreviations as belonging to the same class of objects as instant coffee, powdered eggs, and TV dinners. They don't take up much space and they're great when you're in a hurry, but they never have the taste of the real thing.

—William A. Sabin, *The Gregg Reference Manual*

Abbreviations provide writers with shortcuts, and shortcuts are certainly appropriate *at times*. As a business writer, you must know when abbreviations are acceptable—and when they are *not*. In addition, you must know the correct forms of those abbreviations.

PERSONAL NAMES

Study the following rules for using abbreviations before and after personal names.

Before Personal Names

Many of the titles used before personal names, such as *Mr., Mrs.,* and *Dr.,* are abbreviations.

Singular	Plural
Mr.	Messrs. (from the French, messieurs)
Mrs.	Mmes. *or* Mesdames
Ms.	Mses. *or* Mss.
Miss	Misses
Dr.	Drs.

Other titles used before personal names are spelled out whether the full name or only the last name is given: *Governor* Wadsworth, *Superintendent* Davis, *Representative* Foster, the *Honorable* Betty W. Gilmore, the *Reverend* Jim Bracket, *General* Streeter, and so on.

After Personal Names

Academic Degrees and Similar Abbreviations. Abbreviations of academic degrees and religious orders and similar abbreviations generally have internal periods: *M.D., D.D.S., Ph.D., D.V.M., Ed.D., S.J., D.D.* Check your dictionary whenever you are not sure of the abbreviation.

KEY POINT

Use a comma before an abbreviation that follows a name.

Do *not* use *Mr., Ms., Mrs., Miss,* or *Dr.* before a person's name that is followed by an abbreviation of an academic degree or religious order.

Lucy S. Miller, M.D. *or* Dr. Lucy S. Miller (Not *Dr. Lucy S. Miller, M.D.*)

Patricia Hong, Ph.D. or Dr. Patricia Hong (Not *Dr. Patricia Hong, Ph.D.*)

Other titles before the person's name may sometimes be appropriate:

Reverend Matthew Billings, S.J.

Professor Hillary R. Rawlings, Litt.D.

Note that in a sentence, any such abbreviation following a name must be set off with *two* commas, unless the abbreviation ends the sentence.

Lucy S. Miller, M.D., is the subject of today's "Pediatric Medicine" column.

Jr. and Sr. Omit the comma before *Jr.* and *Sr.* when either follows a person's name unless the person specifically uses a comma, as some people still do.

Mr. David Garcia Jr.

Dr. B. Harrison Philpott, Sr. (Dr. Philpott *does* use a comma before *Sr.*)
Do not use *Jr.* and *Sr.* with a person's last name only.

Ms. Owens faxed the summary to Charles J. Smith Sr., and Mr. Smith responded immediately.

Initials

Initials are abbreviations of names; in some cases, the initials *are* names because they do not really stand for anything. Write an initial with a period and a space after it (always following, however, a person's individual preference).

Will E. A. speak at the conference next year?

If possible, talk with E. A. Neelon before noon.

Note: Reference initials written at the end of memos and letters are usually written with no periods and no spaces. See Sections 10.3 and 10.4 for examples.

✓ CHECKUP 1

Are abbreviations used correctly in the following sentences? Correct any errors on a separate sheet of paper. Write *OK* for any sentence that is correct.

1. Our building was inherited by the four Messrs. Donhurst.

2. Ms. Moncrief sent a fax to Robert T. Gordon Jr., and Mr. Gordon Jr. responded within an hour.

3. Sen. Abernathy announced his retirement, which would be effective at the end of the calendar year.

4. Dr. Jacquelyn R. Benton, M.D., will be associated with the pathologists who are already practicing at the hospital.
5. Ms. Evelyn S. Stanley, Ph.D., has resigned her university position to devote full time to her research projects.
6. While Mister Clary is on vacation, one of his many assistants will handle any urgent matters.

COMPANIES AND ORGANIZATIONS

Always write the name of a company or an organization precisely as its *official* name (on its letterhead stationery) is written:

Ramsey & Ramsey Inc.	Bug Busters Pest Control Company
Lane and Stillman, Inc.	Chandler Bros. Moving & Storage
Bits 'n' Bytes Software	J. B. Williams & Sons
J. L. Austin Construction Company	The Brown/Carscadden/Partin Group

Inc. and *Ltd.*

As with *Jr.* and *Sr.,* omit the comma before *Inc.* and *Ltd.* in company names. Again, however, always follow the *official* name.

Dynamic Inc. specialized in software development.

Sherry works for McNeil & Masters, Ltd., in Atlanta.

Note in the last example that *two* commas were used to set off *Ltd.* within the sentence.

All-Capital Abbreviations

Many names of organizations, associations, government agencies, and so on, are abbreviated in all-capital letters with no periods or spaces between the letters:

AAA	American Automobile Association
AFL-CIO	American Federation of Labor and Congress of Industrial Organizations
AT&T	American Telephone and Telegraph
FBI	Federal Bureau of Investigation
IRS	Internal Revenue Service
NYSE	New York Stock Exchange
UPS	United Parcel Service
USDA	United States Department of Agriculture

An *acronym* is a shortened form of a name. The acronym is formed from the initials letters of the words in the complete name. Pronounce an acronym as you would a word.

NASA   *National Aeronautics and Space Administration*
OPEC   *Organization of Petroleum Exporting Countries*
PIN   *Personal Identification Number*

The call letters of broadcasting stations are always written in all-capital letters without periods.

WBTV-FM   WSPA-TV   KCBT   NPR

United States should not be abbreviated as a noun. When *United States* is abbreviated as an adjective (before the name of a government agency, for example), periods are used.

the U.S. Department of Commerce   U.S. Air Force

BUSINESS ABBREVIATIONS

In addition to their use with personal names and in the names of companies and organizations, abbreviations are used in many other instances in business correspondence.

Address Abbreviations

Street Names. On envelopes, space restrictions sometimes make the use of *St.* and *Ave.* necessary. In letters, however (and on envelopes whenever possible), avoid abbreviating the words *Street, Avenue,* and so on. When abbreviations such as *NW, SW,* and *NE* appear after street names, use a comma to separate the street name from the abbreviation. (Note that the abbreviations *NW, SW,* and so on, should be spelled out in other cases.)

    221 East Third Street

    1828 West Dixon Boulevard

    186 Graham Avenue, NW

Post Office Box Numbers. The words *Post Office* may or may not be abbreviated with box numbers.

    Post Office Box 249 *or* P.O. Box 249

City Names. Except for the abbreviation *St.* in such city names as *St. Louis* and *St. Paul,* do not abbreviate city names.

State Names. With inside addresses or correspondence, use either (1) the two-letter abbreviations of state names or (2) the spelled-out name. The U.S. Postal Service prefers the two-letter state abbreviations on envelopes. In both cases, always use a ZIP Code (See the inside back cover for a list of two-letter postal abbreviations).

KEY POINT

In addresses, you may spell out or use abbreviations for the words *Street (St.), Avenue (Ave.), Boulevard (Blvd.),* and *Post Office (P.O.* or *PO).*

Mr. J. C. Pharr
Hayne Boulevard
New Orleans, LA 70124-1299

or New Orleans, Louisiana 70124-1299

When state names are used elsewhere (that is, not on envelopes or with inside addresses), spell them out or, if abbreviations are appropriate, use the traditional state abbreviations, such as *Conn.* or *Calif.*

Do not be surprised to see mail with computer-printed labels in all-capital letters with *no* punctuation and nearly every word abbreviated. Many companies that send large mailings use this style. The U.S. Postal Service prefers, but does not require, that this style be used for envelope addresses.

MR J C PHARR
ST LOUIS HOSP
2885 WOODLAWN ST
ST LOUIS MO 63121-1234

Units of Measure

General Use. In routine correspondence, units of measure are spelled out: *yards, pounds, kilograms, degrees, meters, gallons,* and so on. Use figures with units of measure.

Photographs submitted for the contest must be 4 inches by 6 inches.

Soft drinks are packaged in economical 2-liter bottles.

The sample that we tested contained about 3 grams of zinc.

Technical Use. In technical work and on invoices, units of length, weight, capacity, area, volume, temperature, and time are usually abbreviated. Among the commonly used terms are these:

cm	centimeter, centimeters	L	liter, liters
ft	foot, feet	lb	pound, pounds
g	gram, grams	m	meter, meters
gal	gallon, gallons	mm	millimeter, millimeters
in	inch, inches	oz	ounce, ounces
kg	kilogram, kilograms	pt	pint, pints
km	kilometer, kilometers	yd	yard, yards

Expressions of Time

Write *a.m.* and *p.m.* in lowercase letters with periods but with no spacing. Always use figures with these abbreviations, and do not use *o'clock* with *a.m.* or *p.m.* Remember: *a.m.* means "before noon" and *p.m.* means "after noon."

The van will leave our offices at 8:30 a.m. on Monday. (Not *8:30 o'clock a.m.*)

World View

Most countries outside the United States use the metric system of weights and measures. It is useful to know how to convert from one system to another. For example, a visitor from Japan who is planning to drive from Los Angeles to San Francisco may find it helpful to know the distance in kilometers as well as in miles.

Days and Months

The days of the week and the months of the year should be abbreviated only when space forces the writer to do so (as in tables and lists). In such cases, use the following abbreviations. Note that *May, June,* and *July* are not usually abbreviated.

Days of the Week	Months of the Year
Sun., Mon., Tues. (*or* Tue.), Wed., Thurs. (*or* Thu.), Fri., Sat.	Jan., Feb., Mar., Apr., May, June (*or* Jun.), July, (*or* Jul.), Aug., Sept., Oct., Nov., Dec.

No. for *Number*

The abbreviations *No. (for Number)* and *Nos. (for Numbers)* are used only before a figure: *License No. 83465-75J; Patent No. 293,667;* and so on. Note that *number* is spelled out when it is the first word in a sentence and that it may be omitted after such words as *Room, Invoice,* and *Check.*

> Have you found copies of the following purchase orders: Nos. 232-76, 232-78, and 232-81? When you do, bring them to Room 2127.

> Number 6232 is the only outstanding check, Ms. Kent.

> *Note:* The symbol # may be used on forms or in technical copy.

Miscellaneous Abbreviations

In addition to the abbreviations discussed so far, there are many more that are used in business, including these:

ASAP	as soon as possible
atty.	attorney
CAD	computer-assisted design
CEO	chief executive officer
ETA	estimated time of arrival
OTC	over the counter
PE	price-earnings (ratio)
RAM	random-access memory
reg.	registered
ROM	read-only memory
YTM	yield to maturity

Check a dictionary or another reference book for a complete list of terms and their acceptable abbreviations.

✓ CHECKUP 2

Are abbreviations used correctly in these sentences? Correct any errors on a separate sheet of paper. Write *OK* for any sentence that is correct.

1. Allison now lives in Forest City, N.C. where she works for WBBO radio.
2. Since the box weighs more than 50 lb, we cannot ship it by City Parcel Service.
3. The technician asked how much R.A.M. and R.O.M. we have on each of our computers.
4. The parcel delivery service guaranteed that the package would arrive before 10:30 AM.
5. Governor Maxwell has scheduled a news conference on Wed., Dec. 9, at 3:30 p.m.
6. The lab sample is about 2 inches long, which is equal to slightly more than 5 CM.
7. Jeff Yoder moved to Ft. Wayne, IND., after he retired from IBM.
8. After she speaks in Tex., Millie will travel to Calif. and to Ore.

SECTION 4.6   REVIEW

Practical Application

A. On a separate sheet of paper, correct any errors in abbreviation use in the following sentences. Write *OK* for any sentence that is correct.
   1. Has Mister Worthy filed a complaint with the US Department of Commerce?
   2. The U.S.D.A. offers a variety of services to American citizens.
   3. Station WRXY-FM, which broadcasts books to its listeners, has almost 50 percent of the morning commuter audience.
   4. One of our music professors, Dr. Stephen Plate, Ph.D., holds Copyright No. 899,987,789.
   5. An investigative reporter for W.X.R.T. interviewed our CEO about our policy on defective merchandise.

6. Last semester Prof. Kilpatrick taught economics at the Las Vegas campus of the Univ. of Nevada.
7. To increase your gas mileage, just add 2 oz of Formula X-213 to every 14 gal of gasoline.
8. No. 324-431 is the only file that was removed during the robbery.
9. Both the buyer and the seller agreed to meet on Mon. a.m.
10. Mr. Morrison is in Room 2914 of the Hillcrest Regional Medical Center.
11. Katrina S. Norton, M.D., works in the emergency room every Sat. night.
12. When do you think that Sen. Houston's assistant will be in the office?
13. We celebrated five years of successful business at this location on Jan. 15, 1997.
14. His two pieces of luggage weighed 65 lb. each.
15. Hayley now works for T.W.A. in LA, doesn't she?

B. On a separate sheet of paper, correct any errors in the following sentences. Write *OK* for any sentence that is correct.
   1. Our marketing function is handled through our N.Y. office.
   2. Soon-Jae writes our television commercials because he is such a creative, talented experienced writer and artist.
   3. Our raw materials will be depleted by Thursday or Friday, you should, therefore, fax an order to our supplier immediately.
   4. Our warehouse is located on Seventh Ave. near the baseball stadium.
   5. Do you plan to run for gov. in the November election?
   6. The hurricane has made a turn toward the U.S., a warning will be issued immediately.
   7. You should ask your attorneys advice before you sign any contracts.
   8. Traffic circles in England are called roundabouts.
   9. Either Roger or Manuel are going to coach the Graham Elementary School football team.
   10. Mr. Parker asked, "will you rent a car for me to drive while I am in San Francisco"?
   11. In the doctor's office <u>is</u> the file with Dana's test results from the specialist and the file with her medical history.
   12. Mr. Dunkirk announced that we raised more than $3,000 for U.N.I.C.E.F.
   13. After the press conference is over, try to interview Mr. Dixons assistant.
   14. Where should we send his mail to, Jane?
   15. The post office was already closed; thus, we decided to let the mail just lay on the desk until tomorrow morning.

Editing Practice

Plurals and Possessives. On a separate sheet of paper, rewrite any sentences that contain errors. Write *OK* for any sentence that is correct.

1. Ruth, we are depending on you designing the advertisement for us.
2. The nurse's lounge is on the third floor of the hospital's west wing.
3. In about six weeks time, you should have recovered from your surgery and be back at work.
4. Do you know whose being considered to head the special project?
5. My client keeping daily notes on his situation certainly helped clarify the case for the judge.
6. We learned that their are five flights to Denver that would arrive in time for the meeting.
7. Are you sure that Rachael's signing all checks is a good idea?
8. As you probably read in the insurance claim, the Baxters car and roof were damaged during the recent hailstorm.
9. Deana and Nancy's jobs are very different, even though they are both restaurant managers.
10. The football tickets are mine; the basketball tickets are theirs.

Spelling Alert! Using a separate sheet of paper, correct any spelling errors in the following sentences. Write *OK* if a sentence has no error.

1. After much research and consideration, we are reccommending that you not sell the acreage until after the first of the year.
2. When Albert completed his tax forms in the personel office, he listed four dependants.
3. Our research and developement staff conducted many scientific studies to document our claims that our pain reliever is effective in less than 20 minutes.
4. The consultant showed us how to write effective memorandoms and letters.
5. Will you please print the address lables for the company newsletter.
6. Most of our employees are sincerly interested in having an attic sale to provide scholarships for our employees' children.
7. Both defendants in the case stated that they had alibis during the time of the crime; charges were subsequently dropped.
8. The newspaper reports were clearly eroneous; there is no truth to the allegations.
9. We have an assistant manger on each shift to handle any problems that arise.
10. We ordered stationery, envelops, fax paper, and computer disks.

Numbers

When you can measure what you are speaking about, and express it in numbers, you know something about it.

—William Thomson, Lord Kelvin, British mathematician

Numbers are commonly used in business to express sums of money, quantities for orders, discounts, time, measurements, percentages, addresses, dates, sales statistics, versions of computer programs, and so on. Business writers know that the correct use of numbers is often critical to clear, accurate communication. Errors in number use can cause more than simple confusion; they can be expensive, time-consuming, and exceptionally disruptive.

Be sure to follow these principles of number usage, and make it a habit to proofread numbers carefully whenever you write business messages.

USING WORDS TO EXPRESS NUMBERS

Why is it important to know when to express numbers in figures and when to express them in words? One reason is that long-established use dictates certain rules. Another reason is that figures and words have different effects on different readers. The use of figures, for example, tends to emphasize a number, while the use of words tends to de-emphasize a number: *$100* is more emphatic than *a hundred dollars*. Thus we use figures when the number is a significant statistic or deserves special emphasis, while we use words for numbers in a formal message and for numbers that are not significant and need no special attention.

The business writer must know the general rules for expressing numbers in words and for expressing them in figures and must be able to manipulate the rules when it is necessary to achieve a greater degree of formality or to provide greater emphasis. First, we will discuss when the writer should use words to express numbers. Then, we will discuss when the writer should use figures to express numbers.

At the Beginning of a Sentence

At the beginning of a sentence use a spelled-out word, not a figure, to express a number. If writing the word seems awkward, then reword the sentence so that the number does not occur first.

> Seventy-seven percent of the customers we surveyed said that they were satisfied with our sales and delivery procedures. (Not *77 percent . . . .*)

OBJECTIVES:
After completing Section 4.7, you should be able to:

1. Determine when to express numbers in words and when to express them in figures in sentences.
2. Use ordinal numbers correctly in business communications.
3. Use correct punctuation and symbols with numbers.
4. Correct errors in the use of numbers.

KEY POINT

Use figures to emphasize a number; use words to de-emphasize a number.

KEY POINT

Spell out numbers that begin sentences.

Of the customers we surveyed, 77 percent said that they were satisfied with our sales and delivery procedures. (Better than *Seventy-seven percent . . . .*)

Numbers From *One* Through *Ten*

In business correspondence, the numbers from one through ten are generally spelled out.

> According to the personnel director, we hired eight new accountants in May.

> Ben's restaurant is located on Sixth Avenue. (Note that the ordinal numbers *first* through *tenth* are also spelled out.)

Fractions

Fractions are expressed in words in general business correspondence.

> About one-third of the people surveyed said that they were dissatisfied with our banking services.

> Only one-fourth of our commissioned brokers were at the regional meeting.

However, a mixed number (a whole number plus a fraction) is expressed in figures by using a decimal or a fraction.

> Our riding stable is located on 6.5 acres of land near the Blue Ridge Mountains. (The figure *6 ½ acres* is also acceptable.)

Indefinite Numbers

Spell out indefinite numbers and amounts, as shown in these phrases:

> a few million dollars
>
> hundreds of telephone calls
>
> several thousand people

Ages and Anniversaries

Ages are spelled out—unless they are significant statistics.

> Mr. Varma, our chemist, is forty-two years old today.

> Amy Bancroft, who is in her late sixties, is our top investigative reporter.

> Allison Buie, 27, has been appointed director of accounting. (A significant statistic.)

When ordinal numbers are used for ages and anniversaries, they are generally spelled out.

> her twenty-first birthday
>
> our thirty-first wedding anniversary

KEY POINT

Spell out the numbers from one through ten.

She celebrated her 10th anniversary with the company.

But when more than two words are needed to spell the number, or when special emphasis is desired, express the numbers in figures.

our city's 125th anniversary (Not *one hundred and twenty-fifth.*)

A 10th Anniversary Sale! (For emphasis.)

Centuries and Decades

Centuries are generally expressed in words.

the nineteen hundreds (But for emphasis, *the 1900s.*)

the twentieth century

nineteenth-century factories

Decades, however, may be expressed in several ways.

the nineteen-nineties *or* the 1990s *or* the nineties *or* the '90s

 **CHECKUP 1**

On a separate sheet of paper, correct any errors in number use in the following sentences. Rewrite the sentences if necessary. Write *OK* for any sentence that is correct.

1. 12 applicants have already called about renting the condominium.

2. The local newspaper estimated the crowd at a few 1,000.

3. We received hundreds of résumés in response to our classified advertisement.

4. The museum curator thought the painting might be the work of a 18th-century French artist.

5. The consultant's recommendations, which should be about 9 pages long, will be mailed to us tomorrow.

6. Lane & Company bought this building in the early 1970's, when it cost less than $200,000.

7. We have allocated about 1/10 of next year's budget to renovating our facilities.

8. 22 percent of our telephone customers were satisfied with their long-distance service.

9. Customers between the ages of 55 and 60 will get a 10 percent discount on their purchases; customers over 60 will get 15 percent.

10. One sales representative has ten and a half times more expenses than any other producer.

USING FIGURES TO EXPRESS NUMBERS

Polished communicators insist on expressing numbers correctly. The following simple rules will guide you in choosing between figures or words to express a number.

For Numbers Higher Than *Ten*

As you know, the numbers from one through ten are spelled out. Numbers higher than ten are expressed in figures.

> At last week's auction, 86 cars, vans, and trucks were sold.

> This 22-page manual lists and explains our rules and regulations.

However, express related numbers in the same way. If any of the numbers are above ten, express all the numbers in figures.

> At Friday's meeting, we will need 6 tables, 36 chairs, and 2 laptop computers. (Because one of the related numbers—the numbers in the series—is above ten, all are expressed in figures.)

Note: Figures are more emphatic than words because figures stand out clearly (especially when they are surrounded by words). Therefore, when greater emphasis is required for a number from one to ten, use a figure to express that number. For example:

> for 10 minutes (More emphatic than *for ten minutes.*)

> a 3-year loan (More emphatic than *a three-year loan.*)

For Sums of Money

Sums of money are written in figures.

> Marsha's travel expenses totaled $892.63.

> We gave her an advance of $800. (Not *$800.00.* The extra zeros are unnecessary.)

> We budgeted between $5,000 and $6,000.

> The unit cost is estimated to be 45 cents. (Not *$.45.* Use the symbol ¢ in tables and in technical copy only.)

Note, however, the following usage for related numbers in the same sentence.

> The unit cost will be $.65 for the small vase and $1.12 for the large vase.

Words *and* figures are often used to express amounts of a million or more.

> $7 million *or* 7 million dollars

> $15.5 million *or* 15.5 million dollars

To avoid misreading, be sure to repeat the word *million* in expressions such as this:

> between $3 million and $4 million (Not *between $3 and $4 million.*)

KEY POINT

Related numbers are numbers that refer to the same or similar things.

Also be sure to treat related numbers in the same way.

between $500,000 and $1,000,000 (Not *between $500,000 and $1 million.*)

Remember that indefinite amounts are spelled out:

Nathan's tax refund amounted to a few hundred dollars.

Bill and Sarah bought about a hundred dollars' worth of software at the clearance sale.

In Addresses

Use figures for house numbers except for *One*. For street numbers, spell out the ordinal numbers *first* through *tenth*. Use figures for all other street numbers.

The post office is located at One Prescott Street. (Spell out *One* when it is a house number.)

The video store that was at 246 East 14th Street is now located at 486 East 12th Street.

When the house number and the street number are not separated by *East, West*, or a similar word, use the ordinals *st, d,* and *th* with the street number.

3214 85th Street (The ordinal *85th* helps to prevent possible confusion.)

ZIP Code numbers are always given in figures.

New York, New York 10020 (Note that no comma precedes the ZIP Code number.)

New York, NY 10020-1221 (Nine-digit ZIP Code number.)

✔ CHECKUP 2

Correct the following sentences on a separate sheet of paper. Write *OK* for any sentence that is correct.

1. Depending on the weather, the construction project will take from 9 months to 1 year to complete.

2. Commercial paper is an unsecured note that has a maximum maturity of two hundred seventy days.

3. The new color printer cost $360.00, but we will get a 10 percent discount if we pay cash.

4. If you pay 50¢ per day for your coffee, your coffee costs you $2.50 per week.

5. At the coin operated laundry located at One Washington Lane, you can wash a load of clothes for $.75.

6. Our fleet of vehicles includes five vans, seven trucks, and 15 cars.

7. This particular van has twelve seats but very little luggage capacity.

8. The courier service guaranteed delivery by 10 a.m. today to Dr. Darlene Gravett, 203 13 Avenue.

9. Recent storm damage was estimated at 10 million dollars.

10. According to preliminary estimates, the potential market for this product is between $7 and $8 million.

With Units of Measure and Percentages

Use figures with units of measure and with percentages, as shown in the following examples:

Each bedroom measures 12 feet by 14 feet.

This computer screen measures 17 inches diagonally.

Each vial contains exactly 5 cubic centimeters of the serum.

You will receive a 20 percent discount if you pay cash.

Note: Use the symbol % only in tables and forms. In other cases, spell out *percent*.

With Decimals

Decimal numbers are always expressed in figures:

Mix this compound with water in a ratio of 4.5 parts compound to 1 part water. (A ratio may also be expressed as follows: *4.5:1 ratio of compound to water.*)

When no number appears before the decimal, add a zero to help the reader understand the number quickly.

A very slight decrease—0.5 percent—was reported for the month of April. (Without the zero, the reader might read *.5 percent* as *5 percent* instead *of five-tenths of a percent.*)

With *a.m.* and *p.m.*

As you already learned, always use figures with *a.m.* and *p.m.*

at 11 a.m.

between 10:15 a.m. and 11:15 p.m.

With *O'Clock*

With the word *o'clock,* either figures or words may be used. For greater emphasis and less formality, use figures. For more formality but less emphasis, use words.

OOPS!

Our open house will start at seven p.m.

You are cordially invited to join us at eight o'clock on Friday, the first of July, to celebrate the one hundredth anniversary of the founding of Campbell Enterprises. (*Eight o'clock* is more formal than *8 o'clock*.)

All authors are invited to a brunch and book-signing party to be held at the Kingston Inn on Friday, August 25, at 11 o'clock.

In Dates

Use figures to express the day of the month and the year in dates:

March 19, 1999 (Not *March 19th, 1999*.)

When the day is written before the month, use an ordinal figure or spell out the ordinal number.

the 4th of June *or* the fourth of June

the 21st of April *or* the twenty-first of April

Note: The ordinal figures are *1st, 2d, 3d, 4th,* and so on.

With Consecutive Numbers

Consecutive numbers should be separated by a comma when both numbers are in figures or when both are in words.

In 1997, 230 employees were hired for the Centerburg plant.

Of the original seven, two employees still remain in the Huntsville office.

But if one word is in figures and the other is in words, no comma is needed.

On May 12 two executives retired from Piedmont Industries Inc.

When one of the numbers is part of a compound adjective, write the first number in words and the second number in figures (unless the second number, when spelled out, would be a significantly shorter word). Do *not* separate the numbers with a comma.

two 9-page booklets (But *200 nine-page booklets.*)

fifty $10 bills (But *100 ten-dollar bills.*)

 CHECKUP 3

Correct any number errors in the following sentences on a separate sheet of paper. Write *OK* for any sentence that is correct.

1. To clean your tires, mix three and a half parts of Tirex to two parts water.

2. Your interest on your savings account is 2.8 percent.

3. A fireworks exhibition has been scheduled for the third of July at the mall.

4. According to the memo, the teleconference will begin at 4:30 p.m. and will end by 6:30 p.m.

5. Albert rented a storage room that is twelve feet by twenty feet.

6. Our contract was signed May 2nd, 1996.

7. The press conference is scheduled for three o'clock Tuesday afternoon.

8. By July 30 87 employees had registered for our stop smoking program.

SECTION 4.7   REVIEW

Practical Application

A. On a separate sheet of paper, correct any errors in number use in the following sentences. Write *OK* for any sentence that is correct.

1. Don said that our Web site has been accessed three thousand five hundred times since the first of the year.

2. Kevin and Allison Dalton have bought a small farm that has ten and a half acres.

3. Robert said that the difference between the estimated cost and the actual cost was minimal (only .6 percent).

4. Jonathan picked up 150 thirty-two-cent stamps at the post office today.

5. Almost 1/3 of our employees have indicated that they are willing to work on Saturdays.

6. Ms. Noblitt said, "We are proud to announce that all 5 of our divisions showed a profit for the 3rd consecutive year."

7. If you buy all four dish gardens, the cost will be $15.00 each.

8. Because your session is being televised, you must begin promptly at 11:05 a.m. and end precisely at 11:55 a.m.

9. The construction loan for Livingston Industries is two and a half percent higher than the prime rate.

10. Have you seen the new townhouses on 3rd Avenue?

11. Our goal is to increase our profits by 10.5% before the end of the year.

12. Your first day of vacation is the 9 of August, isn't it?

13. The unit cost for printing these brochures is $0.22 in quantities of 10,000 but only $0.19 for 25,000 or more.
14. Each lifelike reproduction stands 18 inches high and weighs about 10 pounds.
15. Murphy Teague, age 28, is a full partner with the accounting firm of Lawson, Davis, and Anders.

B. On a separate sheet of paper, correct any errors in the following sentences. Write *OK* for any sentence that is correct.
1. Entries for the first contest must be postmarked by June 15, for the second contest July 15.
2. Our accountants requested a three month extension in filing our tax returns.
3. Our biggest competitor, Hi-Tech Supply company, is spending a bundle on advertising and has captured at least 70 percent of the market.
4. When the tax season ends April 15 we will switch to our new computer system.
5. Based on our research, you Caleb must decide if we should open a branch in Salem.
6. Please call me immediately if your selling your camper and camping supplies.
7. JoAnne DeAngello is the only one of the sales representatives who like the new computerized order forms.
8. Patrick and Joe read the entire report last night but they were unable to get their revisions printed before our meeting this morning.
9. Enclosed are two copies of the contract; sign both copies and return them to me by February 12th.
10. Do you subscribe to "Business Week " magazine?
11. Between you and I, Mr. Lindsay, I doubt that we have seen the last of this matter.
12. At the luncheon on Friday, I met William A. Spielmann, the recently appointed President of Telmar Tools.
13. Because the cost of buying 20 new cars is out of the question until June 30. We decided that leasing them is our only option.
14. Scott suggested that we run three two page ads about a month apart.
15. The new policy for requesting medical leaves are not very clearly stated in the company newsletter.

Editing Practice

Using Your Computer. Proofread the following excerpt on your computer screen. Correct any errors.

Please send me five hundred copys of your booklet, *Using Credit Effectively,* which were advertised in the October issue of *Personal Finance Monthly.* I have enclosed a check for seventy-five dollars to cover the cost of these booklets.

Correcting a Letter. Proofread the following letter and correct any errors.

September 10 19—

Ms. Renee Watson
15 Oak Limb Drive
Altamonte Springs, FL 32714

dear Ms. Watson:

Welcome to the Sunset family! As the proud owner of a new Sunset sedan, you has our best wishes.

At Sunset, we take great pride in treating each car owner as an individual. To help us meet your needs please take a few minutes to complete the enclosed questionnaire and mail it too us. The information you provide will help us customize the maintenance schedule for your new sedan. All you will need to do is drive to your local service center we will handle the rest.

Our records show that you choose the 2-year or 20000-mile warranty. If you would like to extend your coverage, keep our 3-year and 5-year warrantys in mind.

If you have any questions, please call me at 1-800-555-6191.

Sincerely,

Michael Benton
Service Manager

Checking for Errors in Written Copy. Juanita Lourdes works as an administrative assistant at Centennial Travel Agency. One of her responsibilities is to revise, edit, and format a monthly newsletter that is sent to all business customers. Andrea Jeager, a travel agent, is reponsible for writing the draft of the newsletter and then submitting the draft to Juanita.

Because of a busy schedule, Andrea didn't take the time to carefully check the draft as she usually did before giving it to Juanita. Also, Andrea submitted the draft a week late, which left Juanita with just one day to complete the newsletter.

As Juanita reviewed Andrea's draft, she found differences in the way Andrea was punctuating sentences. Juanita also noticed that Andrea used both figures and words for the same types of numbers.

Juanita knows that she must complete the newsletter on time, but she is uncertain about how to go about this task. Should she format the newsletter first and then check the content for errors? What resources could Juanita use to help her check the use of punctuation and numbers?

The Importance of Keeping Confidences. As an assistant in the human resources department, you hear a lot of confidential information being discussed. The human resources manager recently resigned, and another employee is trying to find out who the next manager will be. You know who the replacement is.

The curious employee has tried such tactics as these to find out the information:

"You have a really important position. I'm sure you know who the new manager will be."

"The person who used to have your job would have told me what was going on."

"If you tell me who the replacement is, I won't tell anyone else. I promise."

Should you reveal the name of the new human resources manager? How could revealing this information affect your job?

SECTIONS

5.1 Basics of Reading

5.2 Improving Vocabulary Power

5.3 Strategies for Comprehending and Retaining Content

5.4 Effective Note Taking While Reading

Glen Maguire always wanted to work at Midwest Credit Services. The company was growing, the pay and benefits were excellent, and he had several friends who worked there and were very happy. Glen worked hard in school and took all of the microcomputer courses he could. He knew computer skills would be very important in securing a job with Midwest Credit Services.

Glen learned from his friends which word processing software package Midwest Credit Services used. In his microcomputer software class, Glen learned all the standard features taught as well as several advanced ones not covered in his class. Glen, however, did not like to read, and he was very critical of the software manuals, claiming they were too technical for anyone to understand. Glen's learning style was to learn from the teacher's explanations or from a lab assistant's demonstrations instead of reading the manual.

At last the day was approaching for Glen's graduation, and he eagerly applied for a position at Midwest Credit Services. The interview went well. He had all the computer skills listed in the position description, and he was offered a position. Glen accepted and started to work the next week. He loved the job, and everything was going smoothly.

One Monday morning about six months after Glen started his job, his supervisor, Nancy Sykes, came in and said, "Our technical support staff loaded new word processing software on your computer over the weekend. Here is the documentation manual; I'm sure you'll have no trouble making the switch." Glen asked about taking a class, but he was told that funding for training was not available. Nancy commented that if Glen knew one word processing program, he should be able to easily learn a new program.

Glen attempted to read through the manual, but he gave up in frustration. He now realized that reading skills were even more important on the job than they were in school.

As you read Chapter 5, note some strategies that Glen could use to improve his reading skills.

Basics of Reading

OBJECTIVES:

After completing Section 5.1, you should be able to:

1. Identify four types of reading and explain the differences among them.
2. Explain how to increase your reading speed.

People cannot become truly knowledgeable without being excellent readers.

—Bill Gates, founder and chief executive officer of Microsoft Corporation

As suggested by the quotation from Bill Gates at the beginning of this section, skillful reading is essential for success in college and in business. Students are tested on what they have read, and employees are often held accountable for actions based on their reading. In the medical field, important decisions about patient care are based on the ability of employees at all levels to read and correctly interpret medical information. In the business world, multimillion-dollar decisions are made based on employees' ability to read, interpret, and apply information.

KEY POINT

Reading skill is measured by how quickly you read and how thoroughly you comprehend the information.

ASSESSING READING SKILL

A person who can read quickly and efficiently may be able to handle more work than a slow reader. Because reading speed sometimes affects how much work an employee can do, it may affect the employee's value to the company. Reading speed, then, is one important measure of reading skill.

Speed, however, counts little if the reader does not understand what is being read. Reading well requires much more than moving your eyes rapidly over the words on a page. The reader must comprehend ideas and absorb information. Therefore, reading comprehension is a second important measure of reading skill.

Do you fully understand the material that you read? Does it take you much longer than other people to read material at school or at work? If your reading speed and comprehension need improvement, you can benefit from the following reading-improvement program.

IMPROVING YOUR READING SKILL

Many people have benefited from reading-improvement courses offered by schools, business organizations, and private institutes. The results are often well worth the time and money. You can also complete several tasks on your own to improve your reading skill.

Adjust Your Reading Rate to the Material and Your Purpose

You should adjust your reading speed to the kind of material you are reading and to your purpose for reading it.

Reading for Pleasure. When you are reading for entertainment—novels, magazines, newspapers, and so on—you do not need to absorb every detail or remember a long list of specific facts. You should be able to read this kind of material quite rapidly—at a rate of about 400 words per minute.

Reading for Specific Data. When you are looking for specific names, dates, or numbers or other specific items of information, you should be able to locate the items by scanning a page, without reading every word. An example would be looking up a word in the dictionary. Use the same scanning technique when you want to identify the most important ideas in reading material. Then, stop only to read significant phrases.

Reading for Retention or Analysis. Textbooks and other materials present content you need to master. You may need to memorize information or analyze the concepts so that you can interpret, explain, or apply the material to other situations. This kind of reading, therefore, requires concentration and a slower reading rate.

Checking and Copying. This kind of reading includes such activities as proofreading typewritten or printed copy, checking invoices, and verifying the accuracy of information on a computer screen that was typed from a printed or handwritten document. Checking one copy against another or one column of figures against another calls for great concentration because an error of one digit, one letter, or one syllable could change the entire meaning or accuracy of a document. As a result, such reading must be done carefully, with close attention paid to every detail.

CHECKUP 1

Write your answers to the following questions on a separate sheet of paper.

1. Identify two measures of reading skill.
2. List the four purposes for reading.
3. Which two purposes for reading require less reading time? Which two purposes for reading require more reading time?

Increase Reading Speed

You will always read magazines, newspapers, and novels faster than you read complicated material. However, you can improve your speed of both types of reading by following these suggestions.

The memo stated: "The files will be destroyed on July 25." July 15 is the date that should have been indicated. The person who requests the files on July 20 may find they have already been destroyed.

Add to Your Vocabulary. Enlarging your vocabulary will help you read faster and improve your comprehension. You will have fewer unfamiliar words to look up, and you will understand complex concepts more easily. One of the best ways to increase your vocabulary is to read a variety of materials, including newspapers, magazines, and professional journals.

Read in Thought Units. Since all words are not of equal importance, read in thought units rather than word by word. Thought units are groups of words that are related in some way, such as adjectives and the nouns they modify (my sister Marsha), or a verb and its modifier. You can develop your visual span of a thought unit by forcing your eyes to take in more words at each pause. With fewer pauses on each line of print, you will naturally read faster. For example, read the following lines.

1. unyqpr
2. traffic newspaper telephone fish
3. Read in thought units.

Although you had no difficulty reading each of these lines, you should have spent progressively less time on each line. In the first line, you had to read each letter individually; in the second, you read each word separately; but in the third, your eyes could take in and read the whole sentence with one glance.

You should be able to read a line in a newspaper column with only one or two eye pauses and to read a book-width line with only four or five eye pauses.

Figure 5.1

You can expand your vocabulary by reading a variety of materials. What are some examples of materials you might read to expand your vocabulary?

Keep Your Eyes Moving From Left to Right. Always force yourself to concentrate on what you are reading so that you do not have to go back to read a phrase a second time. Moving your eyes to reread something interrupts your progress and slows you down. To help keep your eyes moving from left to right, use your index finger to guide your eyes as you read a line of type.

Avoid Vocalization. Avoid spelling or pronouncing the words—even silently—as you read them. Such vocalization limits you to reading only as fast as you can read aloud.

Read Only Word Beginnings. Many words can be identified by reading only their beginnings. For example, you should be able to recognize the complete words from these first syllables: *remem—*, *sepa—*, *funda—*, *catal—*, and *educa—*. Then you should be able to tell from the rest of the sentence whether the exact ending of each word should be *remembering* or *remembrance; separate, separately,* or *separation;* and so on. For instance:

> Did he remem—*(remember)* to sepa—*(separate)* the old catal—*(catalogs)* from the new catal—*(catalogs)?*

By following the above suggestions, exercising your willpower, and continually practicing rapid reading, you are certain to increase your reading speed.

World View

In some Japanese writing as well as Arabic, the characters are read from right to left, not left to right.

SECTION 5.1   REVIEW

Practical Application

A. To test your reading speed, have someone time you with a stopwatch (or a watch with a second hand) as you read the following selection from *Peter Norton's Introduction to Computers* (Glencoe/McGraw-Hill, Westerville, Ohio, 1995, p. 93).

One of the great promises of the computer revolution was "the paperless office," an office that requires no printed forms or records because everything is stored electronically. Such an office is certainly possible: records can be kept in databases; correspondence can be sent by electronic mail or FAX modem and never printed.

Unfortunately, few offices even approach this ideal. In fact, many use more paper as a result of computerization. Part of the problem is that changing documents on the computer and printing revised copies is so easy that it's more efficient to proofread your work in hard copy (on paper) than to read it over and over on the screen. When creating text documents, for example, people tend to print every draft, so they often use much more paper than they would if they had to retype the whole document every time they made a change.

On the other hand, some developments in the computer industry have discouraged wasted paper. The steady growth of data communications has been a boon from environmentalists' point of view. The modem, for example, allows computer users to trade data over the telephone lines, instead of printing it out and sending it through the mail. Electronic mail has the potential to eliminate printed correspondence. In offices where electronic-mail systems have been adopted, an office memo need never appear on paper. The sender can simply type the message on a computer and enter the names or electronic addresses of the recipients, and the message arrives immediately. The popularity of WYSIWYG (What You See Is What You Get) monitors, which let you see on screen what a printed page will look like, also encourages users to print their documents less often.

(286 words)

How long did it take you to read the selection? Use the following chart to compute your reading speed. Because the selection is 286 words long, your speed is 286 words per minute (wpm) if you took 1 minute, 143 words a minute if you took 2 minutes, and so on.

15 seconds	1,144 wpm
30 seconds	572 wpm
1 minute	286 wpm
1 1/2 minutes	214 wpm
2 minutes	143 wpm
2 1/2 minutes	119 wpm
3 minutes	95 wpm
3 1/2 minutes	83 wpm
4 minutes	71 wpm

B. One excellent reading habit that will help you improve reading speed is to read only the beginnings of familiar words rather than the entire words. Test your ability to do this by reading as rapidly as possible the following paragraph, in which the endings of some familiar words have been omitted.

The right atti_____ makes all the diff_____ in the out_____ expres_____ of your pers_____. This inv_____ your atti_____ toward your work, tow_____ your emp_____, tow_____ life in gen_____. You reveal your atti_____ tow_____ people in the way you resp_____ to sugg_____. You can reject them in a self-right_____, almost indig_____ manner. Or you can adopt an indiff_____, "don't care" atti_____. These are both neg_____ resp_____. The pos_____ resp_____ is to accept sugg_____ and crit_____ thought_____ and graciously. Then you can act upon them acc_____ to your best judg_____, with resul_____ self-impr_____.

Editing Practice

Finding the Errors. Copying amounts of money, form numbers, dates, and other figures often results in errors because of reading mistakes. Even the most conscientious proofreader can miss an error. Compare the original list (A) with the copied list (B) to determine if any items have been copied incorrectly.

List A	List B
1. 789836B	789863B
2. 4328765	4328765
3. $2786.54	27866.54
4. 9833V39	9833V39
5. LT817745	LT187745
6. u897V229	U897v229
7. Wjkti	wkjti
8. June 23, 1997	June 23, 1979
9. 23 gross @$32	32 gross @23
10. S768R3456J789	S768R3546J789

Improving Vocabulary Power

SECTION 5.2

My father still reads the dictionary every day. He says your life depends on your power to master words.

— *Arthur Scargill, British politician*

OBJECTIVES:
After completing Section 5.2, you should be able to:

1. Identify strategies for increasing your vocabulary.
2. Use a dictionary to obtain information about the spelling, hyphenation, pronunciation, origin, and meaning of words.

Reading and vocabulary are closely related. Reading will increase your vocabulary, and increasing your vocabulary will make you a better reader.

WHAT TO STRIVE FOR

A good vocabulary is a vast and complex structure that must be built piece by piece. Your curiosity will give you the necessary energy to build your vocabulary, but you will also need to become word-conscious, to practice using new words, and to use a dictionary.

Become Word-Conscious

Curiosity is your natural ally in building an effective vocabulary, so use it to your advantage. Remember a word you see or hear for the first time (or write it down) until you can get to a dictionary. Find the meaning of the new word, and fit the meaning into context. Becoming word-conscious means satisfying your curiosity every time you encounter a new word.

Once you become word-conscious, you will be amazed to discover how many new and interesting words you come across each day. You will hear new words in class, on the job, on radio and television, and in the movies and the theater. You will see new words in newspapers, magazines, textbooks, novels, advertisements, and even on package labels.

Keeping a notebook of new words will speed your progress. Keep a record of words and their definitions, and review them from time to time. If you hear a new word, be sure to note its pronunciation. If you read a new word, be sure to note its spelling. New slang expressions are worth noting too. You should always label them as slang, however, and realize that they are inappropriate in most business situations.

Practice Using New Words

A new word really becomes a part of your vocabulary only when you use it in speaking and writing. As soon as you are certain that you understand the meaning and shades of meaning of a new word, use it in business and social conversation or correspondence. Each new word makes possible greater variety and precision in word usage. In turn, verbal variety and verbal precision increase your power to express and advance your views.

Use the Dictionary

Although you have thousands of words stored in your memory, you will encounter new words in your reading. Using a dictionary will not only help you locate the meaning and usage of an unfamiliar word for the particular item you are reading but also enrich your vocabulary for future occasions. As you expand your vocabulary and sharpen other verbal tools, you will become a more effective reader, speaker, and writer.

The dictionary is the most used and most useful reference for those in search of the meaning of a word. Learning to use the dictionary is part of learning to use the language. Every successful business professional and student should keep a dictionary within reach and be adept at using it.

The choice of a dictionary is important. A standard abridged (concise) dictionary serves the needs of most students and business professionals. (The dictionary used as the source for this discussion and throughout this text, except where noted, is *Merriam-Webster's Collegiate Dictionary, Tenth Edition,* Merriam-Webster, Inc., Springfield, Mass., 1996.) A pocket-sized dictionary should not be your standard dictionary reference because such dictionaries contain too few words and provide limited information about each word.

Word Information in the Dictionary

You will find information about a word's pronunciation, definition, origin, and synonyms helpful in learning the meaning and usage of words. Refer to the dictionary entry for the word *business* as it appears in Figure 5.2 for examples of these features.

Pronunciation and Division Into Syllables. Immediately after the regular spelling of a word, the dictionary shows the word's phonetic spelling. This feature indicates how the word should be broken into syllables, how each syllable should be pronounced, and which syllable or syllables should be stressed. If phonetic symbols are new to you, refer to the section of the dictionary that explains them. Many dictionaries have a convenient phonetic guide on every page or on every other page.

Look again at the sample dictionary entry in Figure 5.2. The dictionary shows that the pronunciation of *business* is *biz-nes.* The hyphen indicates a syllable break. *Merriam-Webster's Collegiate Dictionary* and some other dictionaries show major and minor stresses by placing a stress mark (a vertical mark) *before* the stressed syllable or syllables.

Word Origin. A word's origin, also called its *etymology* or *derivation,* is interesting and informative and often fixes the word's meaning in

KEY POINT

Dictionaries provide information about the spellings, definitions, pronunciations, and synonyms for specific words.

Technology

When traveling you may find a handheld electronic speller more convenient than a regular dictionary.

World View

Many foreign words have come into common use in English. Examples include *exposé; aloha; touché; répondez, s'il vous plaît (R.S.V.P.).* Consult a dictionary to familiarize yourself with the spellings and pronunciations of these words.

---

busi·ness \'biz-nəs, -nəz, *Southern also* 'bid-\ *n, often attrib* (14c) **1** *archaic* : purposeful activity : BUSYNESS **2 a :** ROLE, FUNCTION ⟨how the human mind went about its ~ of learning —H. A. Overstreet⟩ **b :** an immediate task or objective : MISSION ⟨what is your ~ here⟩ **c :** a particular field of endeavor ⟨the best in the ~⟩ **3 a :** a usu. commercial or mercantile activity engaged in as a means of livelihood : TRADE, LINE ⟨in the restaurant ~⟩ **b :** a commercial or sometimes an industrial enterprise; *also* : such enterprises ⟨the ~ district⟩ **c :** usu. economic dealings : PATRONAGE ⟨took their ~ elsewhere⟩ **4 :** AFFAIR, MATTER ⟨the whole ~ got out of hand⟩ ⟨~ as usual⟩ **5 :** CREATION, CONCOCTION **6 :** movement or action (as lighting a cigarette) by an actor intended esp. to establish atmosphere, reveal character, or explain a situation — called also *stage business* **7 a :** personal concern ⟨none of your ~⟩ **b :** RIGHT ⟨you have no ~ speaking to me that way⟩ **8 a :** serious activity requiring time and effort and usu. the avoidance of distractions ⟨got down to ~⟩ ⟨she means ~⟩ **b :** maximum effort **9 a :** a damaging assault **b :** REBUKE, TONGUE-LASHING **c :** DOUBLE CROSS **10 :** a bowel movement — used esp. of pets
syn BUSINESS, COMMERCE, TRADE, INDUSTRY, TRAFFIC mean activity concerned with the supplying and distribution of commodities. BUSINESS may be an inclusive term but specifically designates the activities of those engaged in the purchase or sale of commodities or in related financial transactions. COMMERCE and TRADE imply the exchange and transportation of commodities. INDUSTRY applies to the producing of commodities, esp. by manufacturing or processing, usu. on a large scale. TRAFFIC applies to the operation and functioning of public carriers of goods and persons. *syn* see in addition WORK

Figure 5.2

Dictionary Entry.

This dictionary entry provides extensive information about the word business.

By permission. From Merriam-Webster's Collegiate® Dictionary, Tenth Edition ©1996 by Merriam-Webster, Incorporated.

one's memory. The origin of the word *radar*, for example, is the phrase "*ra*dio *de*tecting *a*nd *r*anging." This information will help us remember the word's correct meaning and spelling. As you know, words that are formed, like *radar*, from the initial letters of a compound term are called "acronyms." When you know their etymologies, acronyms are easy to remember.

Definition. A good dictionary lists all of a word's definitions, usually in the order in which they developed. Often the dictionary gives examples of the word's use in more than one sense. For example, see Figure 5.2, in which the entry for *business* shows several examples of the word's use.

Inflectional Forms and Derivatives. The dictionary shows the irregular plural of nouns, the past tense and participial forms of irregular verbs, and the comparative and superlative forms of irregular adjectives and adverbs. After the definition of the noun *contract*, for example, are its derivative noun *contractibility* and its derivative adjective *contractible*. The entry for the irregular verb *fall* gives its past tense, *fell*; its past participle, *fallen*, and its present participle, *falling*.

Synonyms. For many entries the dictionary also lists synonyms—words that have almost the same meaning as the entry. Synonyms for the entry word are often shown in small capital letters. The entry for *invent* lists three synonyms, one of which is shown below. Note that although *invent* and *discover* have what the dictionary calls a "shared meaning element," each word has its own distinct shades of meaning.

Edward Mellanby did not *invent* vitamin D, but he did *discover* it.

The Wrights did not *discover* the airplane, but they did *invent* it.

Illustrations. A dictionary sometimes uses illustrations to make a word's meaning clear. Illustrations are especially helpful in understanding definitions of terms that denote complex physical forms and objects. The meanings of some of these terms are difficult to grasp from words alone but become clear at once after a look at an illustration. Can you visualize a *nautilus* without the aid of an illustration? a *filigree*? a *pagoda*? After looking at the illustrations in a good dictionary, you will have no difficulty understanding these terms.

The salesperson insured us that we were receiving the best deal.

World View

A knowledge of prefixes will help you understand the difference between words that sound similar but have different meanings, such as *export* and *import*. The root *port* comes from the Latin *portare*, meaning "to carry." The prefix *im-* means "in" or "into"; the prefix *ex-* means "from" or "out of." Thus imports are carried in, while exports are carried out.

✔ CHECKUP 1

Use a dictionary to answer the following questions. Write your answers on a separate sheet of paper.

1. List the most common definition for the word *occasion*.
2. Write two synonyms for the noun *quality*.
3. Divide the word *incorporated* into syllables.
4. List two inflectional forms for the word *accomplish*.

SECTION 5.2   REVIEW

Practical Application

A. Using a dictionary, find a synonym for the underlined word in each of the following phrases, and write your answers on a separate sheet of paper.
   1. A thorough report
   2. A complex problem
   3. A heavy burden
   4. A hard choice
   5. A good mechanic

B. For a speech you are preparing, you refer to the following people. Using a dictionary, find the pronunciation of each name. On a separate sheet of paper, provide some identifying information about the person.
   1. Carnegie
   2. Pepys
   3. Lehman
   4. Walesa
   5. Goethe

C. In the same speech, you refer to the following places. Using your dictionary, find the pronunciation of these places. On a separate sheet of paper, write where they are located.
   1. Beijing
   2. Glasgow
   3. Rhine
   4. Lake Leman
   5. Sault Sainte Marie

D. The following words should be part of your vocabulary. On a separate sheet of paper, write the most common definition for each word. Then correctly use each word in a sentence.
   1. excise
   2. lien
   3. merger
   4. teamwork
   5. ecology
   6. franchise
   7. mortgage
   8. investment
   9. accrual
   10. appreciation

E. In each of the following pairs, which is the preferred spelling?
   1. traveling, travelling
   2. salable, saleable
   3. center, centre
   4. envelope, envelop (noun)
   5. instalment, installment

6. judgement, judgment
7. sizeable, sizable
8. adviser, advisor

Editing Practice

Hidden Pairs. From each group of words below, two can be matched because they are similar in meaning. Find each pair of similar words, and write the letters that indicate the pairs.

Example: (a) practice (b) proscribe (c) placate (d) preempt (e) appease.
Answer: c, e

1. (a) wield (b) procure (c) dispense (d) obfuscate (e) obtain
2. (a) circumstance (b) sanitation (c) cenotaph (d) situation
   (e) accident
3. (a) dispense (b) depreciate (c) spend (d) disburse (e) disperse
4. (a) dispatch (b) keep (c) locate (d) retain (e) indicate
5. (a) unlawful (b) illegible (c) ineligible (d) unreadable
   (e) uncouth
6. (a) deny (b) alleviate (c) ease (d) impound (e) obfuscate
7. (a) wretched (b) depicted (c) obsolete (d) antiquated
   (e) meticulous
8. (a) new (b) innovative (c) despicable (d) deplorable
   (e) neutral

SECTION 5.3 — Strategies for Comprehending and Retaining Content

OBJECTIVES:

After completing Section 5.3, you should be able to:

1. Explain the purpose of scanning or previewing material before reading it.
2. Discuss the difference between reading and comprehending the material.
3. Describe strategies to use to improve retention.

The way a book is read—which is to say, the qualities a reader brings to a book—can have as much to do with its worth as anything the author puts into it.

—Norman Cousins

Many students have the idea that they will not have to read when they finish their education. With the amount of information doubling every few years, the ability to read will be even more important in the future than it is today. Employees at all levels will have to read to keep up with the changes in their jobs.

UNDERSTANDING WHAT YOU READ

Reading is more than the physical act of looking at words on a page or a computer screen. Have you ever read something only to find that when you're finished, you have no idea what you read? The words might as well have been in a foreign language that you do not understand. Just as you can hear something but not listen, you can read words but not understand or remember what you read.

Improve Reading Comprehension

The ability to read fast is important in our productivity-oriented business world. But even more important than reading speed are *comprehension* (understanding) and *retention* (remembering). Many of the suggestions made for increasing reading speed will also contribute to greater comprehension. However, here are some additional hints.

Scan or Preview Material. Before actually beginning to read, scan the material. If you are reading a book or a report, look over the table of contents. Also check to see if a glossary is included, or any other features that might help you understand the book. If you are reading a chapter in a book or a section in a report, read main headings and subheadings. Also look at illustrations and read captions and numbered passages. This preliminary overview will help you determine your purpose for reading and will also help you identify important points. After completing your reading of the whole piece, you will have read the most important points twice. Thus, your memory of these parts will be reinforced.

KEY POINT

Scan the table of contents, headings, and other features to get an overview of the material.

Figure 5.3

Scanning or previewing material is especially helpful when you are dealing with technical or detailed information. What types of materials might you scan or preview on the job?

Read the Material. As you read, you need to focus your full attention and concentrate on reading. Reading is the *receiving* of written communication. However, reading is not synonymous with *absorbing* the information contained in the written communication. Comprehending what you read is an active process. Your mind must work to understand the information you are reading.

As Glen discovered in the case study at the beginning of this chapter, written information is a main source for learning new concepts and gaining knowledge. As a reader you must uncover the information you need and relate it to knowledge you have already acquired. Look for the main ideas, and constantly relate what you already know to new material being presented.

Your environment and state of mind will enhance or detract from your comprehension. It is extremely difficult to watch an action-packed TV show and read technical material at the same time. Constant interruptions from other people or from the telephone cause you to lose your concentration. After an interruption, it takes a few minutes to refocus. If you are worried about something or thinking of another project, your concentration, and consequently your comprehension, will suffer. It is important to learn to focus your full attention on the material you are reading in order to comprehend and retain the information.

Take Notes. To help you remember what you have read, take notes that include the main ideas. How do you find these main ideas? Usually, writers deal with only one main idea per paragraph, and they often place that main idea in a topic sentence, often the first sentence in the paragraph. In addition to the main idea, you should also note the facts, examples, and supporting points that explain, support, or develop each main idea.

When you are reading for specific information such as a flight number, a part number, or an account number, it is important to make a written note of the information. The written specifics are a convenient way to refer to the data.

You should also make note of unfamiliar words you encounter while reading. Look up the meanings of these words, and add the words to your personal vocabulary. The more words you know, the easier it is to read and comprehend information.

Make an Outline. One way to organize your notes about what you have read is to make an outline. In an *outline,* you list the main ideas on separate lines, with supporting points listed underneath. Number the main ideas, beginning at the left margin, and indent supporting points, as in the following example.

   I. Computer storage devices
     A. Hard-disk drive
     B. Floppy disks

  II. Computer input/output devices
     A. Keyboard
     B. Mouse
     C. Monitor

MEMORY HOOK

To help you remember the five strategies for improving reading comprehension and retention, use this sentence:

Smart **r**eaders **t**ry to **m**aximize **r**etention.
Scan or preview material.
Read.
Take notes.
Make an outline.
Reread and review.

Technology

The outline feature in many word processing programs may align roman and arabic numbers at the left. You can change this set-up to align the numbers or letters on the period.

When you make an outline, use short phrases or sentences. Your outline should include just enough information to remind you of a concept, without including all the details.

Reread and Review. How often you reread or review material will depend on its difficulty and on how you plan to use the information it contains. Often, quick scanning or rereading of your notes will be adequate for review if the first reading was done carefully. However, if the material is technical and filled with new concepts and specific subject matter jargon, including new vocabulary, it may be necessary to read the text a second or third time to fully comprehend the material.

If you follow the suggestions made in this section and apply yourself seriously to a reading-improvement program, you will see results. Not only will you be able to understand more of what you read, but also you will retain more information about what you read.

KEY POINT

Use a highlighter pen to identify important material in your notes. Underline or mark with an asterisk information stressed by the instructor or the writer.

SECTION 5.3   REVIEW

Practical Application

1. Explain the benefits of scanning or previewing material before reading it.
2. Describe the difference between reading something and comprehending what you have read.
3. List five strategies for improving retention.

Critical Thinking Skills

Analyze: Read the following paragraph. Identify the main idea and two supporting points you would write if you were taking notes.

There are three important traits every employee should possess in order to be valuable to an employer. Customers and clients expect prompt, conscientious service, so being dependable is extremely important. Technology changes things so rapidly today that an employee must have the ability to learn quickly in order to keep current. Although technology skills are indispensable to employers if their organizations are to survive, the employee's ability to get along with other employees so he or she can be part of the team is also important.

OBJECTIVES:

After completing Section 5.4, you should be able to:

1. Understand the importance of note taking.
2. List two reasons for taking notes while reading.

Effective Note Taking While Reading

The shortest pencil is better than the longest memory.

—Unknown

ROUTINE NOTE TAKING FOR COMPREHENSION

The process of writing information increases your ability to comprehend and remember it. The purpose of taking notes while you read is to highlight the most important points in the material.

Find the Important Points

Important points in written material are often indicated by formatting techniques such as headings and bold or italic type.

How do you find the most important points? Important points in written material are often indicated through formatting techniques. Text material is usually broken down into sections by headings, and important words or phrases are in bold or italic type. Sometimes key points are formatted in a special way, such as in a box or with shading around or behind the text or by placing key points in the margins as this book does. Another method of emphasizing important points is to number them or put them in a bulleted list.

Preview the Material

Before taking notes, scan the material by reading the headings and the summary. This preliminary step will give you an overview of the material you are reading. If you are reading a textbook for a course, always read the exercise or assigned work before reading the chapter. This helps you focus on what you need to learn from your reading and identify information on which you need to take notes.

To preview material, follow these steps:

1. Read headings.
2. Read the first paragraph of the chapter, section, or article.
3. Read the first sentence of each of the remaining paragraphs.
4. Read the last paragraph of the chapter, section, or article.
5. Review any illustrations.

By previewing material you can anticipate what information will be presented.

Note Taking From a Single Source

Sometimes you need notes from a single source such as a textbook, a periodical, or computer documentation. If you have your own copy or a photocopy of the material, you could:

- Underline or highlight the important points.
- Make notes in the margins.

If you do not have a personal copy of the material, you will need to take notes from the source by following the note taking tips in the next section.

Tips for Taking Notes

Notes are a condensed version of the important points in an article or chapter. Follow these tips when taking notes:

- Use lined paper or note cards, and list each new idea on a new line.
- Use phrases, not complete sentences, to save time.
- Use abbreviations when possible.
- Never take verbatim notes (unless you need a direct quote), even if you know shorthand.
- Use pen rather than pencil (a pencil point gets dull and pencil lead can smear).
- Use underlining and asterisks to indicate important points.
- Number items, put information in bulleted lists, or use an outline to make it easier to review notes.

KEY POINT

Taking notes as you read is one way to increase your understanding of the material. This strategy is especially helpful when you must remember and apply what you have read.

- Leave space in the margins for additional notes later.
- Write on only one side of the paper or note card.

NOTE TAKING FOR RESEARCH

Most research begins with a review of the available sources on the subject. Available sources—sometimes referred to as *secondary sources*—can include books, periodicals, encyclopedias, government reports, and electronic media. Starting your research by researching existing materials saves time because you aren't reinventing the wheel—repeating research that has already been done.

Note Cards

Taking notes from printed materials is a good way to organize and summarize important points you wish to remember. If the material is not lengthy, photocopy it and highlight or underline with colored ink the important points. Marking the main points will speed up the note taking process.

Notes can be taken on 3 x 5 or 4 x 6 or 5 x 7 lined note cards, on lined paper, or on a computer. However, cards are preferred over sheets of paper because cards are sturdy, which makes them easier to handle. Make a separate note card for each fact to facilitate sorting and organizing your research.

After highlighting or underlining the main points in the material, write your notes on note cards. Several purposes are served by writing note cards:

Technology

Many word processing software programs have a note taking or outline feature that allows you to arrange and rearrange notes on the page. Some programs also allow you to expand notes into narrative copy without retyping the information from the notes.

1. Rereading the article and summarizing the information in your own words makes the information clearer in your mind, which results in an easier job of compiling the report.
2. It is easier to work from summary notes that contain relevant information than to read and scan the entire source again.
3. Notes can easily be rearranged to follow the outline or organization chosen for your report.

Tips for Note Cards

Follow these suggestions when writing note cards.

- Summarize the content in your words unless you need a direct quote. Put direct quotations in quotation marks so you'll know they are direct quotations.
- Write the name of the general subject matter at the top of each card to make it easier to sort cards later.

- Include source information on each note card (author's name, title of publication, date, page number, and any other pertinent information).

Taking notes is an effective way to focus on and remember the main points of material you read. By summarizing the main points in your own words, you increase your ability to apply the material to specific situations later on.

SECTION 5.4   REVIEW

Practical Application

1. Write a short paragraph explaining the importance of note taking for comprehension and research.
2. Give two reasons for taking notes while reading.

Editing Practice

Proofreading. On a sheet of paper, compare the items in List A and List B to determine if the items are identical. If the items are identical, write *yes*; if they are not identical, write *no*.

List A	List B
1. Smith	Smithe
2. 35124	35124
3. JR7486376	JR3486376
4. bloomencourt	bloomen court
5. 35 pkgs @$83	35 pkgs @$38
6. 331-36-4962	331-36-4926
7. IROC3976	IRCO3976
8. Sally Martin	Sally Marten
9. financial	financail
10. businessman	bussinessman

Dealing With a Challenging Reading Assignment. Rachel Graham is a paralegal with Byers & Stratus, Inc., a large law firm. She has been on the job for ten months and has finally reached a point where she is able to stay caught up with completing her tasks.

Just today, Rachel's supervisor, Louise Gutierrez, asked Rachel to research information for an upcoming court case. This case is an important one and will require at least 15 hours of research a week for the next two months. Because of a staff shortage, Rachel is being asked to take on this project in addition to maintaining her current duties.

Part of the challenge of this assignment will be to take detailed notes on the cases she researches. Although she successfully completed courses on conducting legal research and taking notes, Rachel is apprehensive about working on such a high-profile case, in addition to completing her regular tasks.

1. Given the time constraints of the project, what can Rachel do to make her reading more productive?

2. What strategies might she use to record and summarize the information?

Keeping Up With Your Professional Reading. Richard Perez has just graduated from college and started work in the sales department at Datamatic, Inc. He is telling another employee, Judy Okano, how glad he is to be finished with school.

"It's great," says Richard. "I don't have to study for tests any more, and I don't have all that reading to do all the time. I haven't read anything except *TV and Video* in six weeks."

"What about keeping up with changes in our field?" asks Judy. "You know that the competition is coming out with new products all the time, and state and federal regulations keep changing. How can you do a good job if you don't know what's going on?"

"Oh," Richard says. "I hear quite a bit from other people in the office. Besides, when would I have time to read? I work all day, and I have a long commute besides."

1. Why is it important to read about what's happening in your profession on a regular basis?

2. What kinds of materials should Richard be reading in order to stay up to date?

3. When might he be able to find time for professional reading?

Handling An Important Reading Assignment.   Alissa, a management trainee with Madison Shipping Company, is helping her supervisor research new federal regulations for exporting goods. As part of her research, Alissa must review several binders of material and prepare a summary of her findings.

Although she is a competent reader, Alissa is overwhelmed by the amount of material she has to read. To complicate matters, she has only a month to complete this assignment, which is in addition to her regular duties.

What can Alissa do to make best use of her reading time? What strategies could she use to increase comprehension and retention?

CHAPTER
6
Improving Listening Skills

Harry Jarvis, director of human resources at a large manufacturing firm, employs college students as interns during the summer. He tries to make the internship meaningful for the students and involves them in a wide range of experiences.

This summer, Mr. Jarvis hired Amy Ford and Bill Leonard to work in his department. The company is planning a stop-smoking campaign. Because his department will be instrumental in this effort, Mr. Jarvis decided to attend a six-hour conference designed to assist companies with their stop-smoking campaigns. Even though the conference costs $200 per participant, Mr. Jarvis asked Amy and Bill to attend with him.

Amy and Bill were not thrilled about attending the seminar. Neither of them had ever smoked, and attending the seminar meant leaving the plant at 5:30 on Saturday morning to travel for two hours to attend the conference.

About an hour after the first session began, Amy leaned over to Bill and said, "I'm bored, I don't feel well, and I'm cold. I'm going to get some coffee. Besides, we are at the back and Mr. Jarvis will never miss me." Amy had accidentally left the prescription medication for her sinus infection at home and was experiencing some discomfort.

After Amy left, Bill tried to listen, but the speaker spoke in a boring monotone and kept saying "uh" and "you know." From time to time, Bill found himself distracted by music from a dance recital being held in the ballroom next door.

Bill and Amy had selected seats at the back of the room. Even though Bill was straining to hear what was being said, he could actually hear less than half of the words. When Amy returned with her coffee, she asked if she had missed anything. Bill, not having paid attention, said no. Then he commented on the speaker's personal appearance: "I bet she could get a job haunting houses on Halloween."

"Her outfit looks like something from the sixties," Amy added.

Then Amy said, "I wonder what we did to deserve having to sit through this? We will never have to use this information; neither of us smoke. Besides, this nonsmoking campaign is a complex issue, and my head hurts so bad that I can't concentrate."

Bill responded, "Look on the bright side; the conference will be over in two more hours. I'm tired because I had guests last night, and I'm not interested in this stuff." His mind then turned to ideas for a quick dinner for his guests.

On the way home, Mr. Jarvis asked Amy and Bill to bring their notes to his office Tuesday morning at 10:30. "I'll be interested in seeing what you picked up that I missed," Mr. Jarvis explained. "We need to get started on this campaign right away," he further commented. Amy and Bill looked at each other; they had not taken any notes.

As you read Chapter 6, identify actions Bill and Amy could have taken in order to deal with barriers to listening and to increase their retention of the information they heard.

SECTIONS

6.1 **Basics of Listening**

6.2 **Listening in Casual Conversations and Small-Group and Conference Settings**

Basics of Listening

OBJECTIVES:

After completing Section 6.1, you should be able to:

1. Identify the four components in the listening model.
2. Explain how hearing differs from listening.
3. Describe the difference between active and passive listening.
4. Describe how to overcome listening barriers.
5. List strategies for improving listening skill.

We have been given two ears and but a single mouth in order that we may listen more and talk less.

—Zeno of Citium, Greek philosopher

You may be surprised to learn that you spend more of your time listening than you spend talking, reading, or writing. Surveys have shown that the majority of business people spend roughly 70 percent of their working day engaged in communication; about half of that time is spent listening. However, most people remember only about 25 percent of what they hear. They hear but do not really listen.

THE LISTENING MODEL

As shown in Figure 6.1, the listening model has four components:

1. *Hearing*—the physical ability to perceive sounds. For example, you may hear a nearby conversation or the hum of a computer without focusing on these sounds.
2. *Listening*—the act of filtering out distractions to allow you to comprehend the meaning of sounds. For example, when you ask someone a question you then listen for a response.
3. *Interpreting*—a mental function whereby you analyze the sounds that you comprehended. You relate what you have heard to information and experiences with which you are familiar.
4. *Retaining*—the act of remembering the interpreted sounds for later use.

As you can see from the listening model, you do not decide what sounds you will hear, but you can decide what sounds you will listen to and concentrate on.

KEY POINT

Every day, business people spend more time listening than they do speaking, reading, or writing.

LISTENING—A NEGLECTED SKILL

Listening is a little like breathing. You began listening many years ago without ever studying how to listen or being aware of the way you were listening. Listening is different from the other communication skills in that you were not taught to listen. When you were learning to talk, someone corrected you if you made mistakes or mispronounced words. Learning to read and write involved even more formal instruction and practice. Most people assume that listening is automatic, but it is really an acquired skill.

KEY POINT

Hearing is automatic, while listening is an acquired skill.

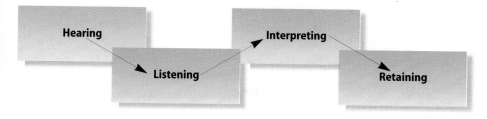

Figure 6.1 The Listening Model

The listening model involves hearing, listening, interpreting, and retaining.

The first step in becoming a better listener is to make listening less routine. You need to be aware of the kind of listening that is required in each situation and to learn how to make your listening more productive.

KINDS OF LISTENING

Basically, there are two kinds of listening: *passive* and *active*. The difference between these two kinds of listening is the level of the listener's involvement.

Passive Listening

Passive listeners concentrate at a low level and absorb just enough of the speaker's words to stay involved in the conversation or speech. They actually understand or remember little of what is said. Often, passive listeners let the speaker's inflection or tone of voice signal when they should react by nodding, smiling, or saying "I see." Such reactions can suggest that the speaker has the listeners' attention even though that may not be the case.

Passive listening is appropriate only when you are listening for pleasure and when it doesn't matter whether or not you retain what you hear. Imagine yourself in a comfortable chair reading a magazine and listening to some music or to a television show. In such situations, you are listening passively because you don't need to hear and absorb every note of the music or every word that is said. Often, you use the music or talk as background and listen attentively only when you hear something, such as a news bulletin, that catches your interest.

Active Listening

In the workplace or in school, passive listening is inappropriate. Instead, you must listen actively, with a higher level of concentration, because you are listening for information. You need to listen carefully to an instructor's explanation of an assignment or to your supervisor's directions about the procedure to follow in performing a particular task. Workplace conversations are filled with names, dates, places, prices, requests, and suggestions, and each is important.

KEY POINT

Passive listening is appropriate when it is not important to remember what you hear.

OOPS!

Phyllis was preoccupied with her mother's recent illness and was passively listening to her supervisor, Gail, ask her to make hotel reservations for a visiting consultant. Phyllis, not paying attention, wrote down the wrong date. As a result, Phyllis failed to reserve a hotel room for the consultant, and she had some explaining to do to Gail.

KEY POINT

Active listening is appropriate when you need to remember the information you hear.

Active listeners concentrate at a high level on what is being said, and they participate mentally. The salesclerk must hear the customer's requests and preferences; the bank teller must hear the correct amounts and denominations; the travel agent must hear the correct times, dates, and destinations; the medical assistant must hear the doctor's instructions for patient care. To be successful in any workplace environment, therefore, you will need to know how to listen actively.

Listening is the main way of finding out what is going on around you. Active listening provides you with vital information and signals. If you are prepared to listen, you are more likely to receive the information you need from friends, instructors, coworkers, and supervisors. Listening is one of the primary means of gathering the information that is necessary in your life and your work.

OVERCOMING LISTENING BARRIERS

Being a good listener can make the difference between being a mediocre employee and a good employee. Unfortunately, no one is born with good listening skills. Becoming a good listener requires conscious effort. It takes continued practice to overcome the following listening barriers.

1. Not concentrating on what is being said.
2. Becoming distracted by noise.
3. Talking instead of listening.
4. Having preconceived thoughts and opinions.
5. Not being interested in what is being said.

Figure 6.2

Active listening involves concentrating on the speaker's voice and blocking out distractions. What are some things you can do to minimize distractions?

Concentrate on the Speaker's Message

One of the keys to effective listening is realizing that it is your responsibility to stay focused. Often the listener blames his or her lack of concentration on the fact that the speaker is boring or that the listener has something else on his or her mind. Sometimes, instead of listening, a person makes the decision to "tune out" and asks a friend or coworker to explain the gist of the message later.

Most people—even good listeners—occasionally find that they have lost their focus when they should be listening. When this happens to you, simply refocus your attention by saying to yourself something like the following: "Mind come back to where your body is." Then, immediately refocus on the listening task.

Use Filters to Manage and Control Noise

Noise can affect your ability to listen. The two basic kinds of noise are external noise and internal noise. *External noise* includes sounds from conversations, radios, televisions, machinery, and so on. *Internal noise* includes distractions such as pain, fatigue, preoccupation with other thoughts, worry, or a personality conflict with the speaker.

Effective listeners must filter out both external and internal unwanted noise. They must be proactive in avoiding the noise they can control and managing the noise that they cannot control. For example, they can turn down the volume on a radio, but they can't turn down the noise of the machinery that they are operating. However, they can manage the machinery noise by wearing ear protection. Taking a pain reliever and getting enough sleep would be ways of controlling the internal noise of a headache and fatigue.

KEY POINT

To manage noise, a listener should identify what noise can be controlled and what noise cannot be controlled.

Resist Talking Instead of Listening

As a listener, you must keep this factor in mind: When you are talking, you cannot be listening effectively. It is impossible to be a sender and a receiver at the same time. You can become your own distraction.

As a listener you may be tempted to interrupt the speaker in order to make a point or to share information that you feel is important. However, a listener should resist the urge to interrupt. Wait until the speaker has finished making a point, then respond with an appropriate comment.

Avoid Bias and Stereotypes

As a good listener, you do not allow your ideas to interfere with listening to the ideas of another. First of all, although you may be aware that

KEY POINT

To avoid bias towards a speaker, always assume that you can learn something from him or her.

a speaker's ideas or opinions clash with your own, you cannot know for sure what someone is going to say until you actually hear it. Second, you may know the speaker's views but not the reasons for those views; passing judgment without hearing the speaker's arguments would be premature. Third, even if the speaker advocates ideas or supports a course of action that you oppose, you still should listen carefully. By listening you will learn about the opposing view and be able to argue against it more effectively. Listening could change your mind or could reconfirm your own theory.

Make sure that you are not against a speaker's view because you dislike some of the speaker's personal characteristics, mannerisms, or appearance. Such judgments are superficial and unfair.

Listen With a Positive Attitude

To be a good listener, you don't have to want to hear what the speaker has to say. However, to be an effective listener, you do have to keep an open mind and believe that the speaker might have something useful to offer.

Usually it is easy to see how adopting a positive listening attitude is in your best interest. For example, the main purpose of attending a lecture or a class discussion is to learn; therefore, if students want to learn, they will also want to listen. In the business world, the employee who wants to do a good job will listen carefully to the supervisor's explanations and directions. To be productive, supervisors also need to listen carefully to the workers' problems and needs. Good listeners learn to listen even when they don't *want* to listen.

TURNING GOOD LISTENING SKILLS INTO EFFECTIVE COMMUNICATION

Think back to the most recent occasion when someone told you how to do something new. Did you listen carefully and understand fully what you were supposed to do, or did you realize a few minutes later that you had actually missed or misunderstood certain steps in the directions? Suppose you had to ask for the directions to be repeated. Use the list of listening barriers on page 286 to determine what prevented you from hearing all the directions the first time.

CHECKUP 1

Answer *T* for *True* and *F* for *False* for the following questions. Write your answers on a separate piece of paper.

1. When you listen for pleasure, you should always listen actively.
2. When you listen for information, you should listen passively.
3. Internal noise is caused by the listener.
4. Business people spend more time each day speaking than they do listening, reading, or writing.
5. One way to manage external noise is to wear hearing protection.
6. To listen with a positive attitude, you must want to hear what the speaker has to say.

IMPROVING YOUR LISTENING SKILLS

When you read, you may sometimes let your attention wander from the writer's message because you know that you can return later to read the words you missed. Spoken words, however, do not wait for the listener. They disappear. In most listening situations you have only one chance to absorb and comprehend a speaker's words, so you cannot let your attention wander.

Imagine yourself in this situation. As your flight taxies down the runway, the flight attendant gives the routine speech about safety and emergency procedures. The flight attendant and the topic are boring; the plane's air conditioning has not yet reached a comfortable temperature, and the person seated next to you is listening, unfortunately, at the same level you are. After a smooth take-off, the pilot levels off at 33,000 feet. Suddenly, the plane loses cabin pressure and the oxygen masks drop before you and your seatmate. You immediately realize that you should have focused on the flight attendant's speech. You can't do an instant replay of the speech. You just have to improvise. After a few minutes, cabin pressure is reestablished, and the flight continues without incident. During the safety instruction speech, you and the other passengers should have been active—not passive—listeners.

One reason that listeners stop paying attention is that they can hear faster than the speaker can speak. The average person can say 125 to 150 words a minute, but a good listener can process 300 or more words a minute. Because of this ability to understand faster than people speak, listeners tend to relax and listen to only part of what is being said. Missing a sentence, however, or even a single word could change the speaker's message. If you don't want to run the risk of misunderstanding the message or missing an important part of it, you have to listen *actively* to everything that is said. However, it is humanly impossible to listen attentively all the time. At some point you will need to take a break—mentally and physically—from listening. You might think about how the topic of the conversation or speech relates to a situation in your life. After taking a short break, mentally bring yourself back to the active listening mode.

World View

Listening behavior varies from culture to culture. African listeners may look away from you instead of maintaining eye contact. Japanese listeners often close their eyes when they are concentrating.

KEY POINT

Because listeners can comprehend spoken words almost twice as fast as speakers can talk, they relax and listen to only part of what is said. This casual listening can lead to confusion or misunderstanding.

Evaluate Your Skills

Everyone has listening weaknesses. Before you can improve your listening skills, you need to understand where your skills fall short—in other words, to identify your weaknesses. Begin by answering the following questions.

LISTENING CHECKLIST

❑ Have you had your hearing tested recently?

❑ Do you try to filter out distracting sights and sounds when you are listening to someone?

❑ Do you avoid interrupting speakers before they finish expressing their thoughts?

❑ Do you avoid doing something else—such as reading—while trying to listen?

❑ Do you always look at the person who is talking to you?

❑ When people talk to you, do you try to concentrate on what they are saying?

❑ Do you listen for people's ideas and feelings as well as for factual information?

❑ Do you believe that you can learn something from others?

❑ If something is unclear, do you always ask the speaker to repeat or explain information?

❑ Do you ever refuse to listen because you do not agree with the speaker's ideas?

❑ Do you ever stop listening because you do not like a speaker's appearance or mannerisms?

❑ Do you ever think about what you will say next while another person is talking?

❑ Do you ever have to ask the speaker to repeat some important information because you cannot remember what was said?

❑ Do you ever let your mind wander because you believe that what the speaker is saying will not interest you?

❑ Do you sometimes stop listening because you feel that you need to spend too much time and effort to understand what the speaker is saying?

If you are an excellent listener, you should have answered yes to the first nine questions and no to the last six. However, even if you had a perfect score, the following suggestions may still help you improve your listening skills.

Prepare Yourself Physically and Mentally

Listening is a combination of physical and mental activities. Although the mental part of listening is more complex, you must also remember to deal with the physical part.

If you are experiencing any hearing difficulties, schedule a hearing examination with a medical professional. Identify any deficiencies and deal with them appropriately. Some people are born with hearing deficiencies; others encounter them as a result of accidents, illness, or exposure to loud noises such as the noise of machinery or equipment at work. Most companies that have excessive noise in the workplace require their employees to wear hearing protection to prevent damage to this vital sense. Unprotected exposure to loud sounds, whether work-related or leisure-related, will permanently damage your hearing. The public health service in your community may have information about local agencies that give free hearing tests.

The most important factor in effective listening is being mentally prepared. Mental preparation involves a receptive frame of mind and certain communication tools, such as an extensive vocabulary. Good listeners try to clear their minds of extraneous thoughts—meeting car payments, making a dental appointment, deciding where to eat lunch, making plans for the weekend—so that their minds are open to receive the speaker's message.

The general vocabulary you acquired in high school and college may not be adequate for effective listening in the workplace. Almost every field has its own special vocabulary, and the listener must master this vocabulary to understand the material under discussion. If you work in a computerized office, for example, you will probably need to be familiar with such terms as *default drive, local area network,* and *file server.* To master the special vocabulary of the field you work in, ask people in your company to recommend appropriate books. Then, as you read, write down any unfamiliar words and look them up in the dictionary. Follow the same procedure when you talk with and listen to coworkers and supervisors.

KEY POINT

Well-developed listening skills help the listener hear the information; a well-developed vocabulary helps the listener comprehend what he or she hears.

Set Listening Priorities

Because you are often bombarded with several messages at once, you have to set listening priorities. When more than one listening opportunity is available to you, you must determine which one deserves your

OOPS!

The witness described the suspect as "a white male between 35 and 40 years old with short, straight brown hair and a mustache wearing a baseball cap."

focus. For example, while your instructor is discussing electronic mail, the person behind you might be talking about weekend plans, and in the background you may be aware of an ambulance siren and a honking horn. If your priority is to listen for information on electronic mail, you must concentrate on the primary message (the lecture) and try to block out the conversation and noises, which are barriers.

Make Good Use of Free Time

As you read earlier, a listener can comprehend words at least twice as fast as most people can speak. To some listeners, this extra time is a problem because they allow their thoughts to wander from the subject. Active listeners, however, use this free time to concentrate on the speaker's words so that they can better understand what is being said. Specifically, good listeners use their free time to accomplish the tasks outlined in the following Memory Hook.

MEMORY HOOK

To make the best use of your free time while listening, you should:

Identify the speaker's ideas and the connections among the ideas.
Summarize the main points of the message.
Assess the correctness or validity of the message.
Formulate appropriate questions.
Associate the speaker's ideas with other known concepts.
Consider specific ways the information might be used.
Take notes to assist in better recall.

Use the phrase *IS A FACT* to remember these strategies.

Identify Ideas and Relationships. As you begin to grasp the speaker's ideas, look for relationships among them. For example, which idea is most important? Do the other ideas support the main one? What is the speaker leading up to? Can you anticipate what the speaker is going to say next? What cues are given by the speaker to show the relationships among the ideas?

Imagine you are listening to the following excerpt from a speech.

Two major costs in operating a modern business are absenteeism and tardiness. For instance, if a company with 1,000 employees averages 50 absences a month, and the average daily rate of pay is $100, the company loses $5,000 a month, or $60,000 a year. Such a loss takes a sizable amount of the company profits.

Notice that the first sentence (in italics) contains the main idea. The word *major* is a cue to the importance of that first sentence. In the next sentence, the speaker also uses the phrase *for instance* as a cue to indicate that what follows will support the main idea. Good speakers use verbal cues such as these to indicate important ideas.

Verbal Cues for General Listening	Verbal Cues for Class Lectures
first second third another consideration on the other hand the most important thing finally in summary	You'll see this information again. This concept is important. Remember how to apply this information.

Speakers also use many nonverbal cues, such as pauses and changes in volume or tone of voice. Speakers reinforce certain points by using body language such as gestures, nodding or shaking the head, or counting on their fingers. They also reinforce points by writing the points on flip charts or using visual aids such as handouts, overhead transparencies, or computer-generated presentations. All these cues help you identify the speaker's ideas and see the interrelationships among them.

Summarize Main Points. As you listen, you should summarize the speaker's words by paraphrasing them in your own words. By reducing the speaker's message to its most basic terms, you will be able to understand and remember the message better. The following example (from Lois Schneider Farese, Grady Kimbrell, and Carl A. Woloszyk, *Marketing Essentials*, 2d ed., Glencoe/ McGraw-Hill, New York, 1997, p.183) shows how you might paraphrase the speaker's points in your own words.

KEY POINT

Paraphrasing involves putting the speaker's ideas into the simplest, clearest, and most direct words possible without changing the intended meaning.

What the Speaker Is Saying	Your Summary of the Speaker's Points
Empathy is the essence of customer-oriented selling. Empathetic salespeople are able to see things from a customer's point of view and be sensitive to a customer's problems. For example, such a salesperson might say, "I can understand why you feel that way. If I were in your situation, I would feel the same." But the salesperson must be sincere in this. Customers are astute and can tell when salespeople don't mean what they say. When customers sense that you have their best interests at heart, they let down their defenses and begin really listening to you.	Salespeople should see the situation from the customer's point of view and be sympathetic but sincere in their comments.

World View

The same gesture may mean different things in different cultures. For example, in some cultures (as in India) people nod "yes" by moving their heads back and forth, much as Americans might indicate "no."

Assess the Message. As you summarize the speaker's message and see the organization and the relationship structure of the speaker's ideas, you probably will find yourself beginning to agree or disagree with the speaker. When this happens, try to trace your response to the speaker's reasons or arguments. Ask yourself if the arguments and ideas of the speaker really lead to his or her conclusions. Also determine if the speaker is trying to convince you with reason or to persuade you by pleading, coaxing, or insisting. Make sure that you are not in favor of the speaker's views simply because they are presented with humor, enthusiasm, or charm.

Formulate Questions. Formulating questions helps you stay focused on what the speaker is saying. You might ask questions to clarify a point that is unclear or to determine if you have interpreted the material correctly.

Associate Ideas With Familiar Concepts. As you listen to the speaker's ideas, relate this information to what you already know about the topic or related topics. Doing so allows you to more quickly grasp the information the speaker is presenting.

Consider Ways to Use the Information. One of the best ways to absorb what a speaker is saying is to determine how you can use the information. For example, if you are responsible for handling customer inquiries, you can directly benefit from listening to your supervisor's explanation of a new procedure for dealing with customers.

Take Notes. You are most likely to take notes in meetings or in a lecture or conference setting. As you will learn in Section 6.2, taking notes is an excellent way of recording spoken information for future reference. Notes, however, should be more than just aids to memory. They should also be tools that help the listener concentrate on the speaker's message.

As you think about what you have just read, keep in mind that effective listening is a skill, and like any other skill it requires practice. Therefore, you should take every opportunity at work and at school to practice the listening techniques discussed here.

✔ CHECKUP 2

Answer *T* for *True* and *F* for *False* for the following questions. Write your answers on a separate piece of paper.

1. A speaker can talk twice as fast as a listener can comprehend spoken words.
2. Having your hearing checked is one way to physically prepare yourself to listen.
3. The general vocabulary you developed in high school is adequate for effective listening on the job.

4. When you paraphrase a speaker's thoughts you put them in your own words.
5. Speakers may use body language to reinforce certain points.

SECTION 6.1   REVIEW

Practical Application

Write your answers to the following questions on a separate sheet of paper.
1. Describe the four facets of the listening model.
2. Explain the difference between hearing and listening.
3. What is the difference between an active listener and a passive listener?
4. Name five barriers to effective listening. List some strategies for overcoming these barriers.
5. What should you do if you realize that you are no longer focused on a lecture that you need to understand?
6. The listener has the responsibility for listening even when the speaker is boring. Do you agree? Why or why not?
7. Select at least three possible areas of employment. List five specialized vocabulary words from each area that you might hear used on the job.

Editing Practice

Speaking Contextually. Some of the following sentences contain words that are not used correctly. On a separate sheet of paper, correct each sentence that contains a word that does not fit the context, or write *OK* after each correct sentence.
1. The defendant is to be arranged in court next week.
2. Professor Mason accused the university of infringing on his patent rights.
3. Don said that discrimination of confidential information is prohibited.
4. Software knowledge has a direct affect on how effectively you use a computer.
5. The manager asked for the corporation of everyone in dealing with the problem.

Critical Thinking Skills

Evaluating. A good listener is able to distinguish between facts and opinions. On a separate sheet of paper, identify each of the following statements as a fact or an opinion.

1. The campus police shouldn't tow away as many cars as they do.
2. Your new suit gives you a very professional appearance.
3. The videotape on gun control was biased.
4. Phil told me that he had a flat tire this morning.
5. If you speed on the interstate highway, you may get a ticket.
6. Six hours of math is a requirement for graduation.
7. Grocery prices and gas prices are up 3 percent.
8. Not using your air conditioner will reduce your fuel bill.
9. Biology is a boring subject.
10. Alice's new computer has 1.6 megabytes of memory.

SECTION 6.2

OBJECTIVES:

After completing Section 6.2, you should be able to:

1. Identify techniques for listening in casual and small-group conversations.
2. Identify good listening techniques for conference situations.
3. List tips for effective note taking.

KEY POINT

Being attentive and showing interest are two attributes of good listeners.

Listening in Casual Conversations and Small-Group and Conference Settings

When people talk, listen completely. Most people never listen.

—Ernest Hemingway

Most employers will tell you that effective listening skill is important in their specific work environments. Employees with poor listening skills can be costly. Poor listening can cause mistakes, misunderstandings, lost sales, lost customers—and subsequently lost jobs on the part of employees who simply did not listen!

LISTENING IN CASUAL CONVERSATIONS

When you start naming your best friends, the names at the top of the list are those with whom you confide when you have concerns or share happiness when something great happens in your life. The primary reason that these people are at the top of your list is that they are good listeners. Good listening helps build friendships; it also helps build professional relationships. You can use the following techniques to help establish rapport in small-group conversations. The techniques, with the exception of the nonverbal techniques, are also useful for telephone conversations.

Listen Attentively

The ability to listen attentively is one of the most important skills connected with effective oral communication. Being attentive and showing interest in the other person are two attributes of the good listener that lead to more effective communication. For example, if a customer verbally complains to you about something over which you have no control, help soothe the customer by listening attentively. Often, you need not say anything, because what the customer most wants is for someone to listen.

World View

If needed, offer to provide sign language interpreters or language interpreters to improve the listening of those who have difficulty hearing or difficulty comprehending English.

Listen for Ideas and Feelings

A good listener listens for ideas and feelings as well as for factual information. A good listener also listens for the tone of the speaker's voice to pick up subtleties in meaning. Read the following statement out loud:

Thanks, Fred, for your help on the project.

If the sentence were expressed sincerely, it would indicate that Fred helped with the project. On the other hand, if the sentenced were expressed sarcastically, it would indicate that Fred had helped little, if any, with the project. Try reading the sentence aloud attempting to convey sincere appreciation and then sarcasm.

World View

Acceptable forms of communication differ from culture to culture. For example, in Japan, it is uncommon to maintain direct eye contact with a speaker.

Establish Eye Contact

A speaker likes to have the listener's complete attention. One way to communicate your interest in what the speaker is saying is to establish eye contact. However, do not stare at the speaker, which is rude. Instead, glance away periodically to rest your eyes.

Use Body Language to Show You Are Listening

As a listener, you can use body language to convey to a speaker or speakers your interest in what they are saying. Here are some nonverbal cues that let people know that you are listening to them.

KEY POINT

Use body language to convey your interest in what a speaker is saying.

1. Stand or sit facing the people in your group.
2. Give the speaker your undivided attention. In other words, don't continue reading a report or working on your computer

Figure 6.3

Listening is one means of feedback that you can give team members. What are some examples of nonverbal feedback that a listener might give a speaker?

during the conversation. Also, don't look at your watch frequently. Glancing at your watch signals that you do not have time to listen.

3. Use facial expressions to convey that you are listening intently to the conversation. Nodding affirmatively encourages a person to continue the conversation.

4. If it is appropriate, take notes about the conversation. For example, taking notes when a supervisor is giving instructions on a new procedure demonstrates that you realize the importance of the conversation. The notes will later help you perform the procedure correctly.

5. Be sure to follow the listening customs of different countries. For example, standing too close to somone is considered rude in the United States. Some cultures have strict rules regarding male and female interactions.

LISTENING IN CONFERENCE SITUATIONS

Many people think that the last lecture they will hear is in a college setting. Not true! To keep up with the changes occurring in their professions, employees at all levels are involved in frequent training or retraining. This updating can take place within the organization's walls, at conference centers, or by teleconference. Modern technology has made it possible for people at several locations to participate in a conference at the same time. For example, the speaker may be in Florida, and the listeners can be scattered throughout the United States or other parts of the world. Depending on the technology available at various locations, the conference may be one-way, with no interaction between the speaker and the listeners, or two-way, which allows for interaction between the speaker and the listeners.

In addition to conferences, employees must attend meetings held by their supervisors. In most cases, the employees are held responsible in some way for retaining the information disseminated. The following techniques for effective listening in a conference situation will also be helpful in improving listening skills in classroom lecture situations.

Determine Your Listening Objectives and Prepare Accordingly

Know why you are attending the session, and know what the expected outcomes are. Are you attending the session to learn new software your company is implementing by the first of the month? Are you expected to learn the software well enough to operate it and teach it to your coworkers?

Find out the subject matter to be covered, and learn something about it before you attend the session. If you know, for example, that you are going to attend a training session on a specific software application, you should read a manual or book about the subject before you attend the session. This preparation gives you a frame of reference that prepares you to absorb the information that you will hear. Keep in mind that homework doesn't end with college.

Overlook Personal Characteristics of the Speaker

Don't prejudge a speaker on the basis of personal characteristics such as mannerisms, voice, speech patterns, or appearance. Ignoring such features may be impossible, but good listeners must not confuse the speaker's message with the manner of speaking or the speaker's appearance.

Listeners can manage their adverse feelings for the speaker by putting themselves in the speaker's place. How might the listener react if he or she was doing the speaking?

Choose Comfortable Seating

Arrive early and, if possible, choose a seat at the front and center of the room. Select a location that limits distracting sights and sound. Choose a seat away from the windows if you think that sun glare would be a distraction. If you feel that the hallway will be noisy, choose a seat as far away from the door as possible. If you have either a visual or a hearing deficit, choose a seat that offers you the best opportunity to see and hear the speaker.

Technology

Videoconferences allow employees to communicate with counterparts in other countries without the need to travel, thus saving time.

KEY POINT

One way to determine your listening objectives is to find out what the expected outcomes are.

World View

Be patient with persons who speak with an accent that is different from your own. Focus on the words and not how they are spoken. Also be patient with persons who are trying with some difficulty to speak your native language.

Prepare for Comfort

Physical discomforts are big distractions. If you have a tendency to get chilled while sitting still in an air-conditioned room, you should take a sweater or suit jacket with you. A room that is too warm could also be a factor.

Ask Questions If Permitted

Most speakers will state their preference as to the appropriate time for questions. Some prefer to be interrupted with questions during the session. Other speakers prefer to answer questions at the end of the session. Asking questions at very large or formal conferences is often inappropriate.

Take Notes

Technology

In some meetings or conferences, you may be allowed to use a tape recorder to record the presentation.

KEY POINT

Note taking is no substitute for active listening.

As a listener, you should concentrate on taking notes on key ideas or concepts. You will be glad later that you did take notes. Information that was completely clear in the meeting or conference can become vague or unclear before you actually apply it. Some tips for taking notes appear on page 301. You will probably want to add your own tips to the list.

Avoid Substituting Note Taking for Active Listening. Occasionally, listeners will just "try to get it all down on paper," while promising themselves that they will review their notes later. When this happens, the listener transfers the information to paper without thinking about what was said. As a result, very little learning takes place because thinking is at the core of attentive listening and note taking.

If possible, compare your notes with those of another attendee. This comparison should help fill in gaps for both of you.

KEY POINT

To improve retention:
- Read your notes within 24 hours.
- Highlight only major points in your notes.

Read Your Notes Within 24 Hours. Read your notes as soon as possible after taking them but definitely within 24 hours. Reading your notes soon after taking them will enable you to include any necessary explanations or additions while the information is still fresh in your mind. A significant amount of forgetting takes place after 24 hours. Read your notes again within the next 48 hours and again as time permits until you have mastered the information.

Highlight Major Points. Use a highlighter pen or underscoring to emphasize major points in your notes. Some people have a tendency to color the entire page with a highlighter. This practice defeats the purpose of highlighting. Highlight only the major points.

Type and Print Notes as a Learning Strategy

If the material is unusually hard to master, you may choose to type and print your notes while the information is still fresh in your mind. Typing the information helps you learn it, and having the neat printout makes your notes easier to read, study, and share with others.

Tips on Taking Lecture or Meeting Notes

- Have two pens and a notebook or legal pad for taking notes.
- Write the date and the topic at the top of the page.
- Begin a new page for each meeting or session.
- Write additional notes directly on handouts.
- Leave a wide left margin in your notes in which you can write additional information later.
- Don't take down everything that the speaker says. If you do, you will miss some of the main points.
- Listen for cues that something is important. Some examples follow: "Here are three tasks that you should complete before the interview"; "This concept will be on your exam"; "Let me summarize the points that I have made today."
- Note the content of visual aids such as posters, slides, and transparencies.
- Record only the main points and important details; as time permits, go back and fill in details in the left margin.
- Use your own set of symbols to indicate information that needs special treatment. For example:
  - * Something that needs follow-up.
  - ! Important fact or critical information.
  - ? A point that is unclear.
  - \> Something that you want to ask the speaker about when questions are appropriate.
  - ■ Topic that needs further study or research.
- Ask questions if permitted.

As you can see, listening skill can be improved. The challenge is yours. You must be proactive, and you must practice the listening and note-taking tips presented.

Practical Application

A. Answer the following questions related to the case study at the beginning of this chapter.
   1. Why did Mr. Jarvis invite Amy and Bill to the conference?
   2. What evidence do you have that Amy and Bill were not listening with a positive attitude?
   3. Were Amy and Bill able to overlook the personal characteristics of the speaker? Why or why not?
   4. Was there any evidence that Bill may have a hearing deficit?
   5. What could Amy and Bill have done to physically and mentally prepare themselves to listen?
   6. List any external and internal noise that was a part of the situation.
   7. How could Amy and Bill have managed and controlled the internal and external noise?
   8. How would you rate Amy's and Bill's preparation for the conference?
   9. Should Mr. Jarvis have told Amy and Bill to take notes? Why or why not?

B. **Test Your Note-Taking Skill.** Listen to a specific news broadcast assigned by your instructor. Take notes and bring them to class. After getting to class, compare your notes with the notes of several classmates. Determine if there are any discrepancies between your notes and the notes taken by your classmates. What are some factors that may account for the discrepancies?

C. With a team of three or four classmates, write a description of a job situation that demonstrates some of the listening techniques presented in this chapter. Include examples of poor listening techniques. Analyze your case by listing the good and poor listening activities presented. Role-play the case for the class, or record it on videotape to show to the class. After you present the case to your class or show it on videotape, ask your classmates to identify good and poor listening techniques that they saw. Choose a leader from your team to moderate the discussion of your team's case.

Editing Practice

On a separate sheet of paper, correct any errors in the following sentences. Write *OK* if the sentence is correct.
   1. My desk is more clear than Alma's.
   2. The better restaurant in New York City is Maria's Italian Garden.
   3. My office is more larger than yours.
   4. This year's expenses are higher than last year's expenses.
   5. Of the three ideas, Benton's is the more practical.

Asking Someone to Speak More Clearly. Janet Alvarez was recently hired as a medical transcriptionist in the medical practice of Drs. Vance and Davis. Both doctors use dictating equipment for their correspondence and reports. Janet is having difficulty understanding the medical terms that Dr. Vance uses, but she hears Dr. Davis quite well.

At first, Janet thought that possibly she had a hearing problem. She asked the previous medical transcriptionist if she had had difficulty understanding Dr. Vance. When the previous medical transcriptionist acknowledged difficulty understanding Dr. Vance, Janet knew that she must talk with Dr. Vance and ask her to speak more distinctly.

How should Janet approach this problem with Dr. Vance? What might Janet say to Dr. Vance?

How Not to Take Notes. Marlene works as a financial assistant at Target Financial Services. She has been asked to participate on a committee that will examine the company's accounting procedures. Determined to make a good impression at the first meeting, Marlene concentrated on taking notes. She spent most of her time writing word-for-word what others were saying. Instead of looking at the person speaking, Marlene looked over her notes to see if she had any questions about the topic. Marlene was so busy taking notes that she didn't hear the team leader ask her for her opinion.

What strategies could Marlene use to improve her listening skills?

CHAPTER 7

Sharpening Writing Skills

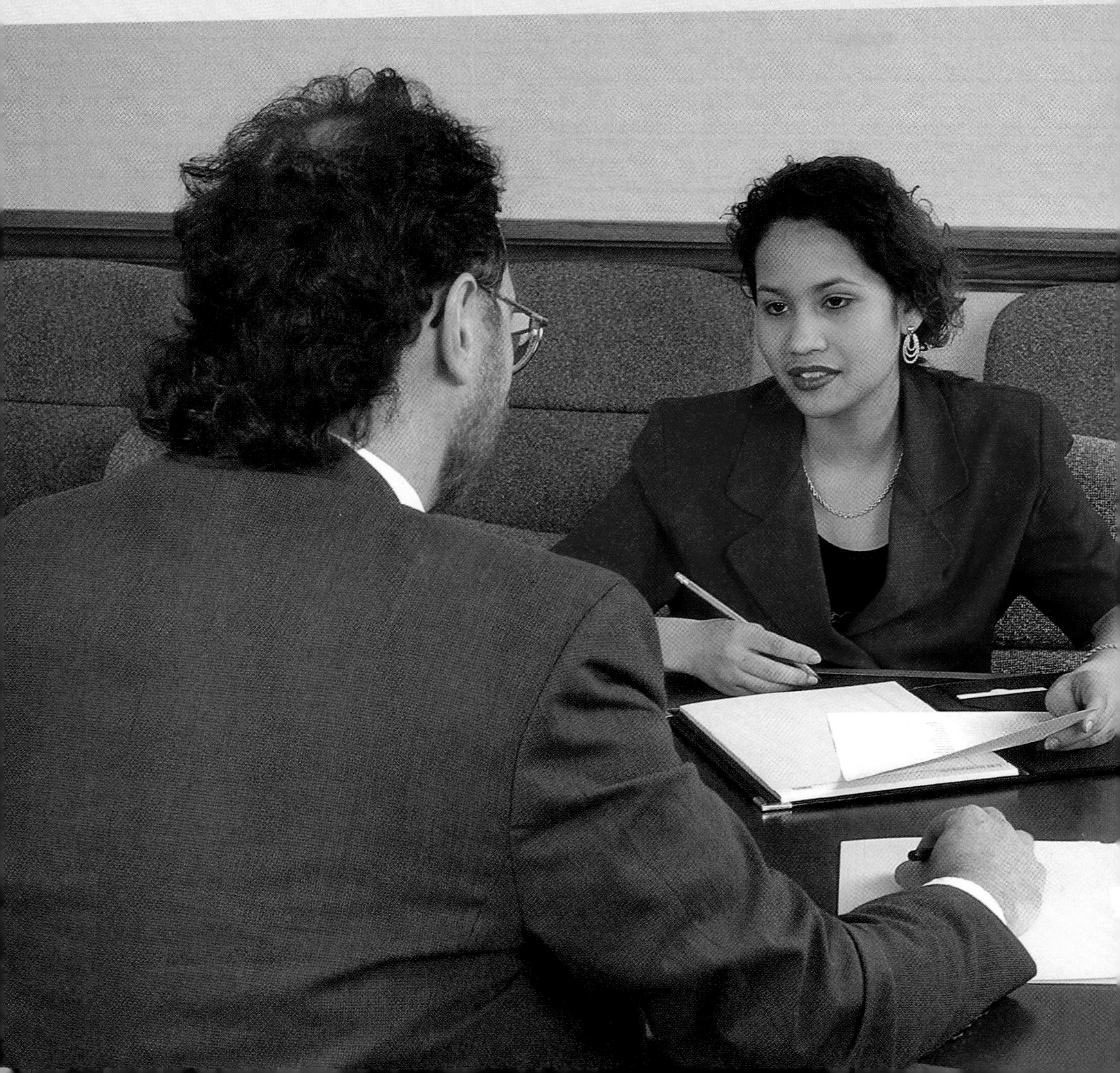

7.1   **Using Words Effectively**

7.2   **Mastering Spelling Techniques**

7.3   **Structuring Phrases and Clauses**

7.4   **Writing Effective Sentences**

7.5   **Building Effective Paragraphs**

7.6   **Revising, Editing, and Proofreading**

Joan will graduate from her community college in two weeks with an associate degree. Joan excelled in accounting courses, getting mostly As. In other courses, such as communications, Joan averaged a C.

On Monday, Ms. Arendas, Joan's accounting instructor, told Joan about an excellent accounting position that would become available at a nearby hospital in about two weeks. "Joan," she said, "If you are interested, I would advise you to apply for the position. I would be happy to recommend you."

Joan was delighted. "I am definitely interested," she eagerly replied to Ms. Arendas.

Ms. Arendas arranged the interview for Joan. "You will meet with Mr. Tallenega, the human resources manager. He said you will take a test after the interview and that you should plan to spend about two hours at the hospital."

Joan went for the interview, which she felt went quite well. Then, Mr. Tallenega took Joan to the hospital library to give her the test. Joan was surprised to see that the test was a writing test.

"Mr. Tallenega," Joan commented, "I applied for an accounting position, and this test is asking me to write a memo and to correct the grammar and punctuation in a letter."

"You have the right test, Joan. We know that you can do accounting, because you have excellent grades in all of your accounting courses. In this accounting position, you will have contact with hospital board members and local business executives. You will be asked to write reports regarding your accounting work and to present the reports to board members. We must have someone who can speak and write well," Mr. Tallenega said.

After completing the interview and the test, Joan drove back to the college to talk with Ms. Arendas. "Do most accounting jobs require writing skills?" she asked.

"Certainly many of them do. Both the Certified Professional Accountant (CPA) Exam and the Graduate Management Admissions Test (GMAT) have a writing component. The fact that these two tests stress writing is an indication of the importance that professionals place on writing."

"Ms. Arendas, it's just not fair. I really want this position. Do you think that I will get it?"

As you read Chapter 7, identify strategies that Joan could use to develop her writing skill.

Using Words Effectively

OBJECTIVES:

After completing Section 7.1, you should be able to:

1. Use a dictionary to obtain information about the spelling, definition, capitalization, and hyphenation of words.
2. Use a thesaurus to find words that will make your writing more precise.
3. Avoid using words that are incorrect, overused, out of date, or inappropriate for the audience.

Never use a foreign phrase, a scientific word, or jargon word if you can think of an everyday English equivalent.

—George Orwell, "Politics and the English Language"

Words are the elements we use to communicate messages in writing. When we write, we create pictures with words—just as artists create pictures with paints. To be effective in your written communication, you must learn to use words—the tools of language—effectively. Fortunately, help is available in two valuable reference books: the dictionary and the thesaurus. As you study this section, note how Joan could use a dictionary and a thesaurus to improve her writing skills.

THE DICTIONARY

The dictionary is the most useful word reference for business writers. You should always keep a dictionary nearby and know how to use it.

Word Information

As a writer, you will probably use the dictionary to find information on the spelling, definition, capitalization, and hyphenation of words, as well as synonyms and other information that will help you use words effectively. As an example of the detailed information provided by a dictionary entry, review the entries for the words *complement* and *compliment* in Figure 7.1 on page 307.

Spelling.   The dictionary entries in Figure 7.1 show in bold type how the words *complement* and *compliment* are spelled. Keep in mind that many words have more than one spelling. Spellings that are equally correct are joined by *or,* as in "adviser *or* advisor." When one spelling is less commonly used, the dictionary joins the spellings by *also,* as in "lovable *also* loveable."

Definition.   A good dictionary lists all of a word's definitions, usually in the order in which they developed historically. Often the dictionary gives examples of the word's use in more than one sense. For example, see Figure 7.1, where the entry for *complimentary* shows several examples of the word's use.

Capitalization.   The dictionary may show if a word is to be capitalized when it is not the first word of a sentence. For example, the word

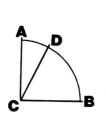

¹com·ple·ment \'käm-plə-mənt\ʼ n [ME, fr. L complementum, fr. complēre to fill up, complete, fr. com- + plēre to fill — more at FULL] (14c) **1 a** : something that fills up, completes, or makes perfect **b** : the quantity or number required to make a thing complete ⟨the usual ~ of eyes and ears —Francis Parkman⟩; *esp* : the whole force or personnel of a ship **c** : one of two mutually completing parts : COUNTERPART **2 a** : the angle or arc that when added to a given angle or arc equals a right angle in measure **b** : the set of all elements that do not belong to a given set and are contained in a particular mathematical set containing the given set **c** : a number that when added to another number of the same sign yields zero if the significant digit farthest to the left is discarded — used esp. in assembly language programming **3** : the musical interval required with a given interval to complete the octave **4** : an added word or expression by which a predication is made complete (as *president* in "they elected him president" and *beautiful* in "he thought her beautiful") **5** : the thermolabile group of proteins in normal blood serum and plasma that in combination with antibodies causes the destruction esp. of particulate antigens (as bacteria and foreign blood corpuscles)
²com·ple·ment \-ˌment\ *vi* (1602) *obs* : to exchange formal courtesies ~ *vt* **1** : to be complementary to **2** *obs* : COMPLIMENT
¹com·pli·ment \'käm-plə-mənt\ *n* [F, fr. It *complimento*, fr. Sp *cumplimiento*, fr. *cumplir* to be courteous — more at COMPLY] (1654) **1 a** : an expression of esteem, respect, affection, or admiration; *esp* : an admiring remark **b** : formal and respectful recognition : HONOR **2** *pl* : best wishes : REGARDS ⟨accept my ~s⟩ ⟨~s of the season⟩
²com·pli·ment \-ˌment\ *vt* (1735) **1** : to pay a compliment to **2** : to present with a token of esteem

complement 2a: *ACB* right angle, *ACD* complement of *DCB* (and vice versa), *AD* complement of *DB* (and vice versa)

Figure 7.1 Dictionary Entries for Complement and Compliment.

Dictionary entries show the spelling, pronunciation, synonyms, and meanings of a word.

Source: Merriam-Webster's Collegiate Dictionary, 10th ed., *Springfield, Mass. 1996, pp. 235–236.*

MEMORY HOOK

To use the dictionary effectively, follow these guidelines for verifying the spelling of a word:

- Place the letters in their correct order; for example, *neither*, not *niether*.
- Avoid inserting extra letters in a word, as in the incorrect *athaletic* (instead of *athletic*).
- Include all the letters that are in the word; for example, *mortgage*, not *morgage*, and *business*, not *busness*.
- Verify that the word is not some other word with a similar spelling. Read the definition. For example, would you give someone *complementary* tickets or *complimentary* tickets?
- Pay close attention to compound words to determine whether they are written as one word *(checkpoint)*, two words *(check mark)*, or a hyphenated word *(drip-dry)*.
- Include any accent marks that are part of a word. For example, *exposé* is a noun that means "the revelation of something discreditable"; but *expose* is a verb that means "to cause to be visible."

south used as a direction is usually not capitalized, but when it refers to a specific region, as in *the South*, it *is* capitalized.

Hyphenation. Dictionary entries use centered periods to indicate the correct places for hyphenating words:

com•mu•ni•cate
con•trol
ap•pre•ci•ate *but* ap•pre•cia•tive

Sometimes a word must be divided at the end of a line of writing. Unless the word is divided correctly, the reader may be confused. Here is an example of this kind of problem:

Please sign and return the enclosed statement promptly if you want a refund.

Pronunciation and Division Into Syllables. Immediately after the regular spelling of a word, the dictionary shows the word's phonetic spelling. This feature indicates how the word should be broken into syllables, how each syllable should be pronounced, and which syllable or syllables should be accented. If phonetic symbols are new to you, refer to the section of the dictionary that explains them.

Look again at the sample dictionary entries for *complement* and *compliment* in Figure 7.1 on page 307. The entries show the pronunciation of both words is 'kam-ple-ment. The hyphens indicate syllable breaks. The accent mark indicates the syllable that should be stressed when pronouncing the word.

Inflectional Forms and Derivatives. *Inflectional forms* are forms of a word that show tense, number, and other meanings. For example, *goes* is an inflectional form of *go*. A *derivative* is a word formed from another word. For example, *affirmation* is a derivative of *affirm*.

The dictionary shows the irregular plurals of nouns, the past tense and participial forms of irregular verbs, and the comparative and superlative forms of irregular adjectives and adverbs. After the definition of the noun *contract,* for example, are its derivative noun *contractibility* and its derivative adjective *contractible*. The entry for the irregular verb *fall* gives its past tense, *fell,* its past participle, *fallen,* and its present participle, *falling*.

Synonyms. For many entries the dictionary lists *synonyms*—words that have almost the same meaning as the entry. As an example, the entry for *complement* in Figure 7.1 on page 307, lists the synonym *counterpart;* the entry for *compliment* lists the synonyms *honor* and *regards*. Note that although synonyms have what the dictionary calls a "shared meaning element," each has its own distinct shades of meaning, as shown in the following examples of synonyms for *invent*.

Edward Mellanby did not *invent* vitamin D, but he did *discover* it.

The Wrights did not *discover* the airplane, but they did *invent* it.

KEY POINT

Many dictionaries have a convenient phonetic guide on every page or on every other page.

World View

Although British English and American English use many of the same words, these words can have quite different meanings. For example, an American might use the word *sharp* to describe someone who is quick and intelligent. However, in Britain, the word *sharp* would mean someone who is devious.

—Roger E. Axtell, *Do's and Taboos of Using English Around the World*

KEY POINT

Synonyms for an entry word are often shown in SMALL CAPITAL LETTERS.

Other Information

In addition to word information, a good abridged dictionary contains the following special sections that a writer may find helpful.

Signs and Symbols. This section consists of signs and symbols frequently used in such fields as astronomy, biology, business, chemistry, data processing, mathematics, medicine, physics, and weather. This section could be helpful in verifying the correct use of symbols in technical documents.

Biographical Names. The names of famous people, each with the proper spelling and pronunciation, are listed. Biographical data such as dates of birth and death, nationality, and occupation are also given. Use this material for checking the pronunciation of names or for identifying unfamiliar names encountered in reading or conversation.

Geographical Names. This section provides information about places—name, pronunciation, location, population, and so on. This section, therefore, can be helpful when you are checking the spelling of place names in correspondence.

Handbook of Style. Included in this very useful section are rules on punctuation, italicization, capitalization, and plurals; citation of sources; and forms of address.

KEY POINT

A good dictionary includes information on geographic names and names of famous people, as well as charts of measurements and a list of common abbreviations.

Technology

Many software programs contain an electronic dictionary and thesaurus to use in verifying the spelling of a word or selecting a synonym.

THE THESAURUS

If you know a word, the dictionary will give you its meaning. The thesaurus works the other way around: If you have a general idea of the meaning you want to convey, the thesaurus will give you a choice of specific words to express it. Look up the general idea, and then choose the word or expression that best fits your meaning.

Roget's International Thesaurus and *Merriam-Webster's Collegiate Thesaurus,* two popular references, are arranged differently. *Roget's* has two parts: the main section, which lists synonyms and associated words, and the index to the main section. To find a synonym for a word, for example the adjective *careful,* look up the word *careful* in the alphabetic index. There you will find entries followed by a key number, as in the following example:

KEY POINT

The thesaurus offers a selection of different words or expressions related to the same idea.

careful
adj.   attentive 530.15
          cautious 895.8
          conscientious 974.15
          economical 851.6
          heedful 533.10
          judicious 467.19
interj. caution 895.14

The key numbers refer to numbered paragraphs in the main section. Thus, if *cautious* is closest to the idea you wish to convey, turn to entry 895 in the main section (organized numerically) and find paragraph 8 for a listing of synonyms.

Merriam-Webster's Collegiate Thesaurus is organized like a dictionary, with one list of entries arranged in alphabetic order. To find synonyms for *careful,* just turn to the entry *careful.* Within this entry capital letters are used for the word *cautious,* an indication that more information can be found at that entry, which is also given in alphabetic order. *Bartlett's Roget's Thesaurus* has 350,000 references and includes contemporary words, phrases, foreign expressions, idioms, and many quotations.

To Find the Most Suitable Word

Imagine that you are a writer of advertising copy, working on an advertisement about new fall fashions. One aspect you wish to emphasize is the smartness of the clothes. Using your thesaurus, you can find that *smart* may be expressed by the words *chic, fashionable, dapper, well-groomed, dressed up,* and *dressy,* among a number of other words and expressions.

To Avoid Overusing a Word

Suppose you have written a letter in which you use the word *great* several times. Consulting the index of your thesaurus, you find a list of other adjectives, such as *grand, chief, important, large,* and *famous.* When you check these references, you discover additional words and expressions that are synonyms of *great.* You now have at your disposal a wide choice of words that you can use in place of *great.*

To Find the Most Specific Word

Sometimes you have a general word for an object or idea in mind, but you want to use a more specific word. For example, you may be discussing the possibility of taking a *trial* vote, but that is not the specific word you are seeking. You look up the word *vote* in the thesaurus. Among the many choices shown is the expression *straw vote,* which is precisely the expression you are seeking.

To Replace an Abstract Term

Imagine that you are writing a memorandum and that you wish to replace the word *precipitous* in the phrase *a precipitous decision.* Among the substitutes that you would find in your thesaurus are *hasty, abrupt, hurried,* and *sudden.*

ELECTRONIC DICTIONARY AND THESAURUS

Most word processing programs have an electronic dictionary and a thesaurus you can use to verify the spelling of a word or to find suitable synonyms. An electronic dictionary will highlight misspelled words, such as *apreciate* for *appreciate*. An electronic thesaurus will suggest possible synonyms for a word. If, for example, you have used the word *extravagant* three times in a report, you could check your thesaurus to find appropriate synonyms to substitute. Synonyms listed would include *abundant, excessive,* and *lavish.*

IMPROVING WORD CHOICE

The words that you use can earn the respect and admiration of those with whom you communicate, or they can mark you as unimaginative—and even uneducated. The words you use can even brand you as insensitive. To be an effective communicator, you must use the right word at the right time. Also you must use words correctly, you must avoid overusing words, and you must be able to predict how readers will interpret the words you use.

KEY POINT

Words not only communicate ideas but also stir emotions, either favorably or unfavorably.

THE CORRECT WORD

Careful writers know the difference between correct and nonstandard usage. Usages that are unacceptable in standard English must be avoided in business writing.

Some nonstandard usages result from errors; for example, the use of *irregardless,* which is not a word, for *regardless.* Some are correct words used incorrectly; for example, the use of *accept* for *except.* Some are glaring grammatical errors.

When you make these errors, readers may know your meaning, but they may not have a positive view of your competency and expertise.

Homonyms

Homonyms are words that look or sound alike but have different meanings. Choosing the incorrect word (although it may sound or even look correct) is one of the most frequently committed errors in word usage.

For example, the tenants of a large apartment building receive a letter urging "all the *residence* to protest the proposed rent increase." This important message might cause confusion because the writer cannot distinguish people, *residents,* from a place, *residence.* Another letter writer might place an order for a ream of *stationary,* much to the amusement of the *stationer* supplying the goods.

KEY POINT

Homonyms are words that look or sound alike but have different meanings.

OOPS!

A teacher received the following note from a student's father. "John was sick yesterday. Please execute him."

KEY POINT

Pseudohomonyms are words that sound somewhat alike but have different meanings, such as *advice* and *advise*. When pronounced correctly, these words do not sound alike.

The chart entitled "Easily Confused Words" on pages 312 and 313 lists some homonyms that every business writer should know and use correctly.

Pseudohomonyms

Pseudohomonyms are words that sound somewhat alike but have different meanings. When pronounced correctly, these words do not sound *exactly* alike. For example, the statement "Ortiz, Sanders, and Valentine placed orders for $800, $1,000, and $1,300, *respectfully,*" is incorrect. The writer has confused the word *respectfully* (meaning "courteously") with *respectively* (meaning "in the order given"). The pseudohomonyms that give the most trouble are listed in the following chart.

Easily Confused Words	
Homonyms	
ad, add	forth, fourth
aisle, isle	foul, fowl
allowed, aloud	gorilla, guerrilla
altar, alter	grate, great
ascent, assent	hear, here
assistance, assistants	hole, whole
attendance, attendants	idle, idol
aural, oral	instance, instants
bail, bale	intense, intents
base, bass	lean, lien
berth, birth	leased, least
born, borne	lessen, lesson
brake, break	lesser, lessor
canvas, canvass	loan, lone
capital, capitol	mail, male
cereal, serial	medal, meddle
cite, sight, site	miner, minor
coarse, course	overdo, overdue
complement, compliment	pain, pane
core, corps	passed, past
correspondence, correspondents	patience, patients
council, counsel	peace, piece
dependence, dependents	pedal, peddle
discreet, discrete	plain, plane
dew, do, due	presence, presents
dual, duel	principal, principle
foreword, forward	raise, raze

rap, wrap
residence, residents
right, write
sole, soul
some, sum
stake, steak
stationary, stationery
straight, strait
taught, taut

their, there, they're
threw, through
to, too, two
vain, vane, vein
waist, waste
wait, weight
waive, wave
weak, week
weather, whether

Pseudohomonyms

accede, exceed
accept, except
adapt, adopt
addition, edition
adverse, averse
advice, advise
affect, effect
allusion, illusion
anecdote, antidote
appraise, apprise
carton, cartoon
casual, causal
clothes, cloths
choose, chose
conscience, conscious
cooperation, corporation
corespondent, correspondent
dairy, diary
deceased, diseased
decent, descent, dissent
deference, difference
desert, dessert
detract, distract
device, devise
disburse, disperse

disprove, disapprove
elicit, illicit
eligible, illegible
emigrate, immigrate
eminent, imminent
expand, expend
facilitate, felicitate
fiscal, physical
formally, formerly
ingenious, ingenuous
later, latter
liable, libel
loose, lose, loss
moral, morale
our, are, hour
persecute, prosecute
personal, personnel
precede, proceed
quite, quit, quiet
reality, realty
recent, resent
respectfully, respectively
statue, statute
suit, suite
than, then

The biologist identified the mushrooms that were audible.

Spelling

If you were a business executive, would you hire an engineer whose résumé listed a degree in *compewter* science? Would you hire someone who had taken courses in *acounting*? Poor spelling would make you doubt that these people could do the jobs that they sought. Good spelling shows people the results of careful, hard work. Avoid being a poor speller by using a dictionary either in printed form or electronic form.

MEMORY HOOK

Look up and remember the difference between prefixes that have similar meanings. Such words can be confusing.

biweekly—occurring every two weeks
semiweekly—occurring twice a week
disinterested—impartial
uninterested—bored; unconcerned
interstate—between states
intrastate—within one state

You can improve your spelling by giving careful attention to the similarities and differences between homonyms or pseudohomonyms and to the suggestions in Section 7.2. The most important step to improved spelling, however, is developing the dictionary habit.

WORDS SUITED TO THE AUDIENCE

In a letter to a customer, a computer specialist would lose the attention of the audience if, in discussing how a computer could be useful to everyone, he or she used such technical terms as *backups, checkdisk,* and *batch file.* By using nontechnical terms, the writer could better hold the attention of the audience. Using a specialized vocabulary that is unfamiliar to an audience is as serious a mistake as speaking in language that is unknown to an audience. Communication takes place only when a writer chooses words geared to the interests and knowledge of that audience.

WORDS WITH VARYING CONNOTATIONS

KEY POINT

Denotation is the meaning of a word that is listed in a dictionary. *Connotation* is the meaning readers associate with the word.

The dictionary meaning of a word (*denotation*) is often different from its *connotation,* which is the meaning readers associate with the word based on their experiences and emotions. For example, a solitary person might be called a *wallflower,* a *recluse,* or a *rugged individualist.* The wrong choice of terms can distort the writer's meaning and perhaps even offend someone.

Look at the shades of meaning in the two words *cheap* and *inexpensive.* Only an unskilled writer or speaker would use the word *cheap* to mean *inexpensive*. Certainly, no salesperson would make that mistake. *Cheap* means "worthless or shoddy"; *inexpensive* refers only to cost, not to quality. Sometimes an *inexpensive* suit is a bargain; a *cheap* suit never is.

Whenever you are in doubt about a word's meaning, check the dictionary before using the word. If there is no time to look up the unknown word, then phrase your idea in a way that avoids the unknown term.

WORDS TO AVOID

Building a successful business or career requires building goodwill. Because words play a vital part in establishing goodwill, a skilled communicator chooses words or phrases that the reader and listener can both understand and appreciate. In general, this means choosing positive rather than negative terms, presenting information directly and without repetition, and using fresh and current expressions rather than outdated and overused ones.

If an English-speaking person knew enough Spanish, he or she would be bilateral.

Avoid Negative Words

Which of the following statements is more likely to build or retain customer goodwill?

> You neglected to specify the sizes and colors of the dress shirts you ordered. We cannot ship the order with such incomplete information.

> The four dozen dress shirts you ordered will be shipped as soon as you tell us what sizes and colors you prefer.

The second statement is the better selection, although both statements try to convey the same idea. The second statement is positively worded and avoids such unpleasant expressions as *you neglected* and *cannot ship the order with such incomplete information*. Negative words are almost sure to evoke a negative response. The customer reading these negative words may cancel the order or may choose a different supplier for future orders.

Words create negative responses when the reader feels blamed or accused. Most expert business writers consider *failed, careless, delay,* and *inexcusable* negative words, regardless of how the words are used, and recommend avoiding these words. Actually, such words are unpleasant primarily when they are accompanied by *you* (*you failed*) or *your* (*your delay*). *Your oversight, your error,* and *your claim* signal the reader to react negatively; but *our oversight* and *our error*—though not necessarily wise choices of words—carry an entirely different impression.

The following words sound negative when used with *you* or *your*. To maintain goodwill, avoid using these words.

blunder	damage	inability	regret
careless	defective	inadequate	trouble
claim	delay	inferior	unfavorable
complaint	error	mistake	unfortunate
criticism	failure	neglected	unsatisfactory

Eliminate Unnecessary Words

Words that are repetitious are a waste of the reader's time. Such words clutter the message and can distract, delay understanding, and reduce emotional impact. The italicized words in the following expressions are unnecessary and should be omitted.

adequate *enough*
as yet
at above
up above
both alike
new beginner
cooperate *together*
same identical
lose *out*
meet *up* with
modern methods *of today*
over *with*
customary practice

connect *up*
continue *on*
and etc.
as to whether
past experience
free gratis
inside *of*
my *personal* opinion
rarely (seldom) *ever*
repeat *back* or *again*
refer *back*
exact same
true facts

Avoid Out-of-Date Words

Words that are out of date suggest that the writer is behind the times. Imagine the reaction to a sign that says "Eschew Smoking"! In certain uses, the words below have a similar effect.

advise *or* state (for *say, tell*)
beg (as in *beg to advise*)
duly (as in *comments are duly noted*)
esteemed (as in *my esteemed colleague*)
herewith (except in legal work)
kindly (for *please*)
party (for *person*, except in legal work)
same (as in *we will send you same*)
trust (for *hope, know, believe*)
via (for *by*)

Avoid Overused Words

Replacing overused words with more exact and colorful terms can make your writing lively and interesting. The adjective *good* is overused and weak: a *good* maneuver, a *good* negotiator, a *good* speech, a *good* worker. Instead, for greater interest, say a *clever, smart,* or *skillful* maneuver; a *patient, forceful,* or *crafty* negotiator; an *eloquent, informative,* or *engrossing* speech; a *qualified,* an *intelligent,* or a *competent* applicant.

Adjectives such as *awful, bad, fine, great,* and *interesting* are also overused. The following sentences show how meaningless these words can be.

Avoid: The new guidelines on hiring workers will result in a *bad* situation.

Use: The new guidelines on hiring workers will result in a (*difficult, painful,* or *troublesome*) situation.

Avoid: Kari Michaels gave an *interesting* sales presentation.

Use: Kari Michaels gave an (*informative, enlightening,* or *educational*) sales presentation.

Avoid: We have an *awful* backlog of orders.

Use: We have (*an enormous, a gigantic,* or *an overwhelming*) backlog of orders.

Avoid Clichés

Clichés are overworked expressions such as *crystal clear, needs no introduction,* and *at a loss for words* that long ago lost their strength. Outdated expressions such as *attached hereto, attached herewith please find,* and *under separate cover* still find their way into business documents, creating the perception of a stale, backward organization.

The use of clichés exposes a lack of imagination—the tendency to repeat the familiar, even when the familiar is not worth repeating. Clichés waste time, obscure ideas, and bore readers and listeners. Your imagination is sure to provide better expressions once you resolve to avoid clichés.

Some commonly overused words and expressions, together with suggested substitutions for them, are listed in the following chart.

Cliché	Substitute
along the lines of	like
asset	advantage, gain, possession, resource
at all times	always
by the name of	named
deal	agreement, arrangement, transaction
each and every	each *or* every
face up to	face
factor	event, occurrence, part
field	branch, department, domain, point, question, range, realm, region, scene, scope, sphere, subject, theme
fix	adjust, arrange, attach, bind, confirm, define, establish, limit, mend, place, prepare, repair

World View

In international communication, avoid using American expressions that may be unfamiliar to your audience, such as "Let's talk turkey" and "Will this idea float?"

Cliché	Substitute
inasmuch as	since, as
input	comment, information, recommendation
in the near future	soon (or state the exact time)
line	business, goods, merchandise, stock
matter	point, question, situation, subject (or mention what is specifically referred to)
our Mr. Smith	our representative, Mr. Smith
proposition	affair, idea, offer, plan, proposal, recommendation, undertaking
reaction	attitude, impression, opinion
recent communication	letter of (give exact date)
say	articulate, assert, declare, exclaim, express, mention, relate, remark

USE CREATIVITY TO ACHIEVE VARIETY

Although there are reference books to help you achieve variety in expression, you cannot expect to find ready-made words and phrases to express every idea. Achieving variety in word usage requires creativity.

Select Suitable Synonyms

Choosing suitable synonyms is the most direct means of achieving variety in your vocabulary. Although synonyms have the same basic meaning, each synonym has a different shade of meaning. To select the synonym that best expresses a specific idea, you must go beyond the basic idea and learn the distinctions.

Sometimes a dictionary can help you create a phrase to achieve variety. Under the word *explore*, for example, the *Merriam-Webster's Collegiate Dictionary* lists no synonyms, but look at its definition: "to investigate, study, or analyze . . . look into . . . examine minutely . . . make or conduct a systematic search." Thus, instead of using *explore*, you can make a phrase to fit: "*study* the options," "*examine* the records *minutely*," "*systematically search* the files."

Use Appropriate Antonyms

An *antonym* is a word that means *exactly* the opposite of another word. For example, *light* is an antonym of *dark*. Antonyms may also be formed by the addition of such prefixes as *il, in, ir, non,* and *un* before a word. For instance, *legible* becomes *illegible; credible, incredible; abrasive, nonabrasive; acceptable, unacceptable;* and so on.

Skill in the use of antonyms opens broad possibilities to the writer. While *additional* reading sounds like an added burden, *unrequired* reading sounds as if it might even be fun. It is sad when the dead are *forgotten,* but sadder still when they are *unmourned.*

Choose Descriptive Words

Descriptive words make readers or listeners "see" what is being described. Notice how the first sentence uses abstract words and the second sentence uses specific words to call an image to mind.

Vague: Our new building is well located and the apartments are comfortable.

Descriptive: Our new high-rise building is located on a quiet, tree-lined street near the center of town. The apartments are spacious and equipped with all the latest modern conveniences.

Using descriptive words will improve your written messages, but developing this skill requires much work and practice. To develop this skill, visualize a complete picture of what you want to describe, then consult the thesaurus until you find the most specific descriptive terms that apply. First comes the idea, then the full picture, and finally the right words. Use this technique to compose messages that hold the attention of your readers.

KEY POINT

Use a thesaurus to search for specific terms to make your writing more descriptive.

SECTION 7.1   REVIEW

Practical Application

A. Using a thesaurus, list on a separate sheet of paper three words that can be used to replace the underlined word in each of the following phrases:
   1. A <u>dynamic</u> presentation
   2. A <u>beautiful</u> view
   3. A <u>good</u> person
   4. A <u>good</u> book
   5. A <u>good</u> employee

B. In each of the following sentences the writer confused two similar words. Using a separate sheet of paper, replace the incorrect word with the correct one. Define both the correct and the incorrect words.
   1. The spreadsheet should give the some of all our invoices.
   2. Wallace Carpenter asked that the breaks on his company car be inspected.
   3. Your property is being considered as a cite for the new manufacturing plant.

4. Jan and Hilton called to say that there flight will be late.

5. Joyce Brown submitted the logo for our new stationary.

C. In each of the following pairs, which is the preferred spelling? Use a dictionary to check your answers.

1. acknowledgment, acknowledgement
2. traveling, travelling
3. canceled, cancelled
4. envelope, envelop (noun)
5. installment, instalment
6. judgement, judgment
7. sizeable, sizable
8. advisor, adviser

D. Which words in the following sentences are used incorrectly? On a separate sheet of paper, write the incorrectly used word and next to it the word you would use in its place.

1. The nursing supervisor complemented both nurses on their quick action.
2. Reprimands will be issued to drivers who accede the posted speed limit in company cars.
3. The lawn chairs have canvass covers.
4. Ms. Westin is adverse to changing the work schedule.
5. Hurricane Bob's impact was not quiet as severe as anticipated.

Editing Practice

Hidden Pairs. From each group of words below, two of the words are synonyms. Find each pair. On a separate sheet of paper, write the letters that indicate the pairs.

Example: (a) practice (b) proscribe (c) placate (d) preempt
(e) appease   Answer: c and e

1. (a) compensation   (b) consideration   (c) pay
   (d) compensatory   (e) satisfaction
2. (a) hearing   (b) audit   (c) examine   (d) listening   (e) seeing
3. (a) suspense   (b) procure   (c) dispense   (d) distort   (e) obtain
4. (a) circumstance   (b) sanitation   (c) deduction   (d) situation
   (e) accident
5. (a) dispense   (b) depreciate   (c) spend   (d) disburse
   (e) disperse
6. (a) dispatch   (b) keep   (c) retain   (d) locate   (e) indicate
7. (a) unlawful   (b) illegible   (c) ineligible   (d) unreadable
   (e) uncouth
8. (a) ease   (b) alleviate   (c) deny   (d) impound   (e) obfuscate
9. (a) wretched   (b) depicted   (c) obsolete   (d) fastidious
   (e) meticulous
10. (a) neutral   (b) innovative   (c) despicable   (d) positive
    (e) new

Descriptive Words. Rewrite these sentences, substituting exact, descriptive words for the italicized words.

1. Laura has a *good* work record.
2. The fan had a *bad* motor.
3. Both the engineers and the technicians are *happy* with the design.
4. Our customer-service representatives receive *good* training.
5. Chemistry is a *hard* course.

Why Be Trite? Rewrite these sentences using lively and different words for the trite, italicized expressions.

1. Business-card-sized telephones may well be the ultimate portable phones; *be that as it may,* they initially will be very expensive.
2. Jaya is more interested in the *nuts and bolts* of the product than in the history of the product's development.
3. Our guide was a *tower of strength* during the unexpected snow storm.
4. Sarah advanced in the company by *the sweat of her brow.*
5. Despite high mileage and heavy use, the old trucks seems *none the worse for wear.*
6. *In this day and age,* everyone must be computer literate.

Mastering Spelling Techniques

SECTION 7.2

OBJECTIVES:
After completing Section 7.2, you should be able to:

1. Describe the rule of doubling a final consonant, giving examples to illustrate the rule.
2. Discuss at least three other spelling principles that almost always hold true.
3. Name two ways to ensure the correct spelling of words for which there are no rules.

A word is not a crystal, transparent, and unchanged; it is the skin of a living thought and may vary greatly in color and content according to the circumstances and time in which it is used.

—Oliver Wendell Holmes, Jr.

As Joan found out in the opening case study, many employees screen applicants by giving them grammar and spelling tests. Such assessment of an applicant's writing skill is important because misspelling a word in a document makes both the writer and the organization look unprofessional. To increase your chances for employment and advancement, make every effort to improve your spelling.

GUIDES TO CORRECT SPELLING

Although there are many variations in the spelling of English words, some spelling principles always hold true. Every writer must know and be able to apply these principles—the basic guides to correct spelling.

Final *Y*

Many common nouns end in *y: company, industry, entry, territory, warranty, supply, day, attorney, survey.* The spelling of plurals of these common nouns depends on whether the *y* is preceded by a consonant or a vowel.

- If *y* is preceded by a consonant, change *y* to *i* and add *es: company, companies; entry, entries; industry, industries; supply, supplies; territory, territories; warranty, warranties.*
- If *y* is preceded by a vowel, leave the *y* and just add *s: attorney, attorneys; day, days; survey, surveys.*

Ei and *Ie* Words

Among the most frequently misspelled words are these: *believe, belief, conceive, conceit, deceive, deceit, perceive, receive, receipt, relieve,* and *relief.* Use the following Memory Hook to help you remember when to use *ie* and *ei*.

KEY POINT

When *y* is preceded by a consonant, to make the plural change *y* to *i* and add *es*. When *y* is preceded by a vowel, add an *s*.

KEY POINT

Use the combination *li* and *ce* in *Alice* to remember that the correct spelling after *l* is *ie* (believe); after *c, ei* (receive).

MEMORY HOOK

To spell *ei* and *ie* words correctly, remember this saying:

Use *i* before *e*
Except after *c*
Or when sounded like *ay*
As in *neighbor* or *weigh*.

Exceptions: Words in which *ei* makes a long *e* sound (*either,* caffeine, and seize); the words foreign, height, and forfeit.

Endings *Ful, Ous, Ally, Ily*

To spell the endings *ful, ous, ally,* and *ily* correctly, remember the following:

- The suffix *ful* has only one *l: beautiful, careful, masterful, meaningful, skillful.*

- An adjective ending with the sound "us" is spelled *ous: humorous, miscellaneous, obvious, previous, various.*
- The ending *ally* has two *l*'s: *basically, finally, financially, incidentally, originally.*
- The ending *ily* has one *l: busily, gloomily, hastily, necessarily.*

Doubling a Final Consonant

Knowing when to double a final consonant before adding an ending to a word is a matter of distinguishing between vowel sounds.

Words of One Syllable. If you can hear the difference between long and short vowel sounds, you can tell whether or not to double the final consonant of a one-syllable word. If the vowel sound is long, do *not* double; if the vowel sound is short, double the final consonant. *Exception:* Do not double the final consonant of words ending in *w* (*saw*) or *x* (*fix*).

hope	hoping *(long vowel)*
mope	moping *(long)*
plane	planing *(long)*
scare	scaring *(long)*
stripe	striping *(long)*
tape	taping *(long)*
weed	weeding *(long)*
mix	mixing *(ends in x)*
hop	hopping *(short vowel)*
mop	mopping *(short)*
plan	planning *(short)*
scar	scarring *(short)*
strip	stripping *(short)*
tap	tapping *(short)*
wed	wedding *(short)*

Words of More Than One Syllable. The only rule needed is this one: Double the final consonant if the last syllable of the base word is accented, if the vowel sound in the last syllable is *short,* and if the suffix to be added begins with a vowel.

commit	committed, committing
equip	equipped, equipping
occur	occurred, occurrence, occurring
omit	omitted, omitting
prefer	preferred, preferring *(but* preference*)*
regret	regretted, regretting, regrettable
transmit	transmitted, transmitting

In each of the following base words, the accent is on the *first* syllable; therefore, in the preferred spelling, the final consonant is *not* doubled.

benefit	benefited, benefiting
cancel	canceled, canceling *(but* cancellation*)*
differ	differed, differing

KEY POINT

For one-syllable words, do not double the final consonant before adding an ending if the vowel sound is long. Double the final consonant if the vowel sound is short.

edit	edited, editing
equal	equaled, equaling
offer	offered, offering
travel	traveled, traveler, traveling

On a separate sheet of paper, correct any misspelled words in the following sentences. Write *OK* for any sentence that is correct.

1. Lamont used the videocassette when tapping the newscast.
2. We transmited the message by fax late yesterday afternoon.
3. Invitations should be mailed four weeks before the weding.
4. Tomeika offered to work late during the summer months.
5. The sales manager assigned the two new sales territorys to Paul Chen and Anita Foster.
6. Dr. Mallory, the surgeon, said that scaring would be minimal.
7. I beleive that we can save money and energy by adjusting the thermostat a few degrees.
8. The sale will feature miscellanious tools and kitchen items.
9. Judge Sanders felt that the testimony was not necessarilly accurate.
10. Nancy was moping because she was mopping the floor.

DICTIONARY ALERTS

Even the best spellers need to use a dictionary. However, no one has time to look up every word. Therefore, you should learn how to recognize spelling pitfalls—words that are most likely to be misspelled. These pitfalls alert careful spellers to consult the dictionary.

The most common spelling pitfalls are presented here. In addition, you may have your own personal spelling pitfalls. *Remember:* Use the dictionary whenever in doubt, but especially if the word in question contains one of these prefixes or suffixes.

Word Beginnings

These pairs of prefixes—*per, pur, ser, sur*—present a spelling difficulty because the words in each pair sound alike. Study the following words:

permanent	purchase
personal	purpose
persuade	pursuit

KEY POINT

Identify your personal spelling pitfalls, and use a dictionary to verify the spelling of these words.

serpent   surplus
serenity   surprise
service   surtax

Word Endings

The following groups of word endings are tricky because they have similar sounds or because they may be mispronounced. The spellings of these endings, however, differ. Do not try to guess at spellings of words with the following ending sounds.

"Unt," "Uns."   The endings *ant, ance, ent,* and *ence* are all usually sounded "unt" and "uns." Because there are so many words with these endings, they are spelling danger spots. They must be spelled by eye, not by ear. Some common words with these endings are in the following list.

accountant	compliance	dependent	existence
defendant	maintenance	incompetent	independence
descendant	perseverance	permanent	interference
tenant	remittance	silent	occurrence

"Uhble," "Uhbility."   The sound "uhble," which might be spelled *able* or *ible,* is another trap. The alert writer consults a dictionary in order to avoid misspelling words that end in *able, ible, ability,* or *ibility.* Some common "uhble" and "uhbility" words are the following:

changeable	collectible	availability	credibility
movable	deductible	capability	flexibility
payable	illegible	predictability	possibility
receivable	reversible	probability	visibility

✔ CHECKUP 2

On a separate sheet of paper, correct any misspelled words in the following sentences. Write *OK* for any sentence that is correct.

1. This versatile jogging suit is reversable.
2. The judge was concerned about the credibility of the defendent and the witness.
3. Contributions to charitable organizations are tax deductable.
4. Catherine pursuaded me to accept the remittence offered by the tenant.
5. Committee members were quite perplexed when they learned of the surplus of available funds.
6. Dr. Robichek's handwriting is almost illegable.

"Shun," "Shus." Words ending with the sound "shun" might be spelled *tion, sion, cian, tian, sian, cion,* or *xion.* The ending sound "shus" might be spelled *cious, tious,* or *xious.* Learn the spelling of the words listed here.

ambition	ignition	anxious	malicious
collision	profession	conscientious	pretentious
complexion	suspicion	conscious	superstitious
dietitian	technician	fictitious	suspicious

"Shul," "Shent." The ending that sounds like "shul" is sometimes spelled *cial* and sometimes *tial.* A "shent" ending might be spelled *cient* or *tient.* Study the following words and learn how they are spelled.

artificial	deficient
beneficial	efficient
essential	impatient
judicial	omniscient
partial	proficient
substantial	quotient

✔ CHECKUP 3

On a separate sheet of paper, correct any misspelled words in the following sentences.

1. The physician's assistant noticed the patient's pale complection.
2. Baxter Fieldsberg, our college summer intern, is both aggressive and ambicious.
3. Andrew was ankcious about the medical procedure, even though his physician explained that the test was painless and routine.
4. Carlotta is a capable and consciencious counselor.
5. New employees found the orientation meeting very benefitial.

"Ize," "Kul." The ending "ize" might be spelled *ize, ise,* or even *yze (analyze).* A "kul" ending could be spelled *cal* or *cle.* A careful writer, therefore, consults a dictionary for words with these endings. Study the following "ize" and "kul" words.

apologize	advertise	identical	obstacle
criticize	enterprise	mechanical	particle
realize	improvise	statistical	spectacle
temporize	merchandise	technical	vehicle

Ar, Ary, Er, Ery, Or, Ory. Words that end in *ar, ary, er, ery, or,* or *ory* should be recognized as spelling hazards; you should always verify each spelling. For example, *stationary* (motionless) and *stationery* (paper) end

World View

Be aware that the British rules for spelling differ somewhat from ours. For instance, in England, the word *labor* is written with *ou* instead of *o (labour)* and the word *recognize* is written with an *s* instead of a *z (recognise).*

with the same sound, but they are spelled differently. Memorize the spellings of the following words:

calendar	temporary	stationery	laboratory
grammar	advertiser	debtor	
customary	adviser	advisory	
stationary	customer	inventory	

"Seed." Although only a few words end with the sound "seed," they are often written incorrectly because the ending has three different spellings. As shown in the following table, only one word ends in *sede* and only three words end in *ceed*—all other "seed" words are spelled *cede*.

sede	ceed	cede	
supersede	exceed	accede	precede
	proceed	cede	recede
	(*but* procedure)	concede	secede
	succeed	intercede	

KEY POINT

Only one word ends in *sede* (*supersede*) and only three words end in *ceed* (*exceed, proceed,* and *succeed*). All other "seed" words end in *cede*.

CHECKUP 4

On a separate sheet of paper, correct any misspelled words in the following sentences.

1. Dust particals and moisture caused the computer keys to stick.
2. We will need to order additional stationary to maintain our inventery.
3. Abe, our Realtor, gave us calenders that advertise his company.
4. Reports with statisticle and technicle information are hard to write.
5. His performance exceded our expectations.

YOUR SPELLING VOCABULARY

Business writers cannot take the time to verify the spelling of every word. They must, therefore, take the time to learn the correct spellings of the words used most often in their written communications. Knowing how to spell troublesome words requires more than memorization. You must analyze each word and fix in your mind its peculiarities. Use strategies like the ones shown in the following Memory Hook.

MEMORY HOOK

Remember the spellings of troublesome words by using tips such as these:

accommodate (two *c*'s, two *m*'s)
aggressive (two *g*'s, two *s*'s)
convenient (*ven, ient*)
definite (*ni*)
develop (no final *e*)
embarrass (two *r*'s, two *s*'s)
forty, fortieth (the only *four* words without a *u*)

ninth (the only *nine* word without an *e*)
occasion (two *c*'s, one *s*)
privilege (*vile*)
recommend (one *c*, two *m*'s)
repetition (*pe*)
separate (*par*)
until (only one *l*)

SECTION 7.2   REVIEW

Practical Application

A. Without using a dictionary, write the correct forms of the words enclosed in parentheses on a separate sheet of paper.
1. His goal to graduate from college a semester early is an (attain) one.
2. Has the college established an (advise) board?
3. The merger proved (advantage) to both companies.
4. According to the warranty, the vendor is responsible for the (maintain) of the computers.
5. It was (presume) of the customer to go to the head of the line.
6. That idea was (scrap) by the engineering team.
7. Mr. Poletta made it (abundant) clear that he preferred to be transferred.
8. What are the (eligible) requirements for the scholarship?
9. Hillary is (commit) to providing quality patient care.
10. Dominique has the (flexible) to work both jobs.

B. On a separate sheet of paper, make any spelling corrections needed in these sentences. Write *OK* for any sentence that is correct.
1. By accepting 25 new members, Matt's fraternity will sermount its preset financial difficulties.
2. After confering for three hours, the technisions solved the problem.
3. Ricardo will be faxxing our response today.

4. Your reservations were cancelled when we did not receive your check by the deadline.
5. We heard the huming of the chain saw as Millie cut the fire wood.
6. The entire situation was embarassing for everyone concerned.
7. Dr. Kilpatrick, a local veterinarian, has several lovible puppies for sale.
8. Shawna prepared a list of the uncollectable accounts.
9. Unfortunately, crime has been increasing steadely.
10. Turnover, according to our statistics, is noticebly high.

C. On a separate sheet of paper, write correctly any words in the following letter that are misspelled.

Dear Mr. Hempstead:

Thank you for leting me speak with you and your very consciensious staff last Wednesday and demonstrate our new excercise equipment. I enjoyed meeting everyone at Action Graphics.

As I mentioned, you will recieve a 10-percent discount on a purchase worth $10,000 or more. Orders placed within two weeks of the demonstration will be delivered free of charge within ten business days. You will also get a 10-percent discount on any supplys ordered with the equipment.

Your health club members will enjoy useing equipment that has been reccommended by fitness experts around the world. Some members may like to view the enclosed video, which has testimonials by several entertainment and sports figures whose credability in the fitness arena is valued.

Should you need additional information, please call me at 1-800-555-6837. Please order within two weeks to take advantage of our special promotion. You will find that our equipment excedes your expectations.

Sincerly,

Editing Practice

Using Business Vocabulary. On a separate sheet of paper, write the letter and the correct word from the following list to complete each sentence. Each word is used only once.

a. delinquent
b. perplexed
c. personal
d. personnel
e. principal
f. principle
g. secede
h. supersede
i. retrieval
j. visualize

1. Several nations are planning to _____ from the international trade alliance because they feel it is too restrictive.

2. What is the total dollar amount on all _____ accounts that are at least 60 days past due?
3. Mr. Hemano was _____ by the detective's contradictory phone messages.
4. The police artist's sketch helped us _____ the assailant.
5. Software Sales and Service developed a sophisticated _____ system for all our stored files.
6. The new contract we signed with the real estate agent will _____ any previous agreements and will give him exclusive rights to market our home.
7. Dan asked for my _____ opinion on his establishing a line of credit with his house as collateral.
8. In planning for retirement, my _____ concern is maintaining an acceptable monthly income.
9. Our technical _____ have all received safety training.
10. Although we stand to gain little from the lawsuit, Mr. Delano feels winning is a matter of _____.

Structuring Phrases and Clauses

OBJECTIVES:

After completing Section 7.3, you should be able to:

1. Recognize and correct errors in thought units composed of words, phrases, and clauses.
2. Recognize and correct errors in pronoun references.
3. Correct *this* and *thus* faults.

The surest way to arouse and hold the attention of the reader is by being specific, definite, and concrete. The greatest writers—Homer, Dante, Shakespeare—are effective largely because they deal in particulars and report the details that matter. Their words call up pictures.

—William Strunk, Jr. and E. B. White, *The Elements of Style*

A combination of words that properly belong together is called a *thought unit*. One example of a thought unit is a noun or pronoun and its modifiers; another example is a verb and its complement. When the words of a thought unit are placed correctly, the reader can understand the meaning quickly and easily. When the writer incorrectly places the words of a thought unit, however, the reader may get a mistaken idea of the writer's meaning. Sometimes the mistaken idea is laughable, but in business such mistakes are more likely to cause problems or confusion, as in the following example.

Incorrect: Calling the meeting to order, the new autofocus camera drew the praise of the marketing director.

Introductory phrases and clauses logically lead the reader to the words that directly follow. However, in the preceding example a camera cannot really call a meeting to order. In order to avoid a confusing statement such as this one, the writer should group together words whose meanings belong together.

Correct: When the meeting was called to order, the new autofocus camera drew the praise of the marketing director.

WORDS IN THOUGHT UNITS

Sometimes a confusing, laughable, or simply false meaning is conveyed because a single word is not connected with its proper thought unit. The following advertisement is an example of a misplaced adjective.

Incorrect: Gigantic men's clothing sale begins today!

The modifier *gigantic* has been misplaced—it seems to indicate that *gigantic men's* is a thought unit. However, few men want to be described as *gigantic*. The correct thought unit is *gigantic sale*.

Correct: Gigantic sale of men's clothing begins today!

Misplaced adverbs can also cause confusion.

Incorrect: The idea for changing our sales emphasis came to me after I had opened the meeting suddenly.

What happened suddenly—the opening of the meeting or the idea for the sales emphasis?

Correct: The idea for changing our sales emphasis suddenly came to me after I had opened the meeting.

OOPS!

Lettuce will stay crisper if you put your head in a plastic bag before refrigerating it.

PHRASES IN THOUGHT UNITS

Incorrectly placed phrases, as well as incorrectly placed words, can completely change the meaning of a message. Careful writers edit their work meticulously to see that they have placed phrases correctly.

Incorrect: This hard drive can be installed by anyone who has studied the computer manual in ten minutes.

No computer manual could be studied in ten minutes, but someone who had studied the computer manual for a reasonable length of time could probably install a hard drive in ten minutes.

Correct: This hard drive can be installed in ten minutes by anyone who has studied the computer manual.

Now read the following classified advertisement and see the confusion that results from an incorrectly placed thought unit.

Incorrect: Two-story townhouse apartment for rent. Ideal for working couple with balcony.

How many working couples can there be who have a balcony but don't have an apartment?

Correct: Two-story townhouse apartment with balcony for rent. Ideal for working couple.

Two misplaced phrases can be even worse than one. Imagine receiving a direct-mail advertisement that contains the following sentence.

Incorrect: Our interactive, high-resolution games are guaranteed to give you hours of entertainment without qualification for your home computer.

The correct thought units are *games for your home computer* and *guaranteed without qualification*. The following revision would be more likely to encourage you to order a game or two.

Correct: Our interactive, high-resolution games for your home computer are guaranteed without qualification to give you hours of entertainment.

CLAUSES IN THOUGHT UNITS

KEY POINT

Clauses contain a subject and a predicate.

Misplacing a car is a bigger mistake than misplacing a bicycle. We shouldn't be surprised, then, to learn that a misplaced clause can have even more devastating consequences than a misplaced word or phrase. How would the public react if the president of your company made the following announcement?

Incorrect: Our goal in marketing is to encourage the public to try our products until our health foods become better known.

The sentence sounds as if once the products are better known, no one will want to buy them. Moving the *until* clause clears up the matter.

Correct: Until our health foods become better known, our goal in marketing is to encourage the public to try our products.

Because clauses pose a special hazard since they often are used to explain people's motives. Consider the following statement.

Unclear: The clerk hardly listened to the customer's complaint because she was concentrating so intensely on completing the form.

Was the clerk or the customer completing the form? While the original sentence is not wrong, the following sentence better describes the situation.

Clear: Because she was concentrating so intensely on completing the form, the clerk hardly listened to the customer's complaint.

AMBIGUOUS *WHICH* CLAUSES

KEY POINT

The noun or pronoun modified by the *which* clause usually appears immediately before *which*.

The word *which* is a relative pronoun that refers to another word in the sentence. If the *which* clause is misplaced, the word being referred to is unclear and confusion will result.

Unclear: Our gallery has a book on important nineteenth-century American paintings, which you can purchase for a special price of $19.95 plus postage.

Placing *which* immediately after *paintings* is confusing. Can the *paintings* be purchased for only $19.95? The writer of the sentence actually intended to say that the book could be purchased for $19.95.

Clear: Our gallery has a book, which you can purchase for a special price for $19.95 plus postage, on important nineteenth-century American paintings.

While clear and a definite improvement, the rewritten sentence would gain force and polish if the *which* clause were removed as in this revision:

For a special price of $19.95 plus postage, you can purchase our gallery's book on important nineteenth-century American paintings.

Although it is acceptable for *which* to refer to a general idea rather than to a single noun, the writer must take extra care to see that the reference is clear. In the following sentence, the pronoun reference is ambiguous.

Unclear: Further resistance to the board of directors will only jeopardize your job, which neither of us wants.

The problem is that the *which* clause may refer either to the general idea *will only jeopardize your job* or to the single noun *job*. *Which* seems at first to belong to the thought unit *your job*. If neither of the persons referred to wants the job, why should either one care whether the job is jeopardized? A revision would clear up the confusion.

Clear: Further resistance to the board of directors will only jeopardize your job, and we do not want that.

Here is an example of a *which* clause making clear reference to a general idea:

Ms. Bergen predicted that an out-of-court settlement would be reached, which is precisely what happened.

Used with care, *which* clauses achieve a degree of clarity that it would be difficult to equal in as few words. Note the following sentence.

Read clause 5, which contains the productivity standards under the new contract.

She died in the home in which she was born at the age of 88.

WHO DID *WHAT?*

In written business communications, the writer must make it absolutely clear *who* has done or will do a specific action. Sometimes, however, the writer confuses the thought by connecting the wrong person, place, or thing with an action. As a result, the intended meaning is not conveyed to the reader. Such a violation of the thought-unit principle can cause doubt or uncertainty as to *who* did *what*.

Faulty: If not satisfied, we will refund your money.

The thought unit is *If not satisfied, we.* The meaning here is that we (the manufacturer) are the ones who might not be satisfied. If a customer returned the goods and asked for a full refund, could the manufacturer refuse on the grounds that the manufacturer was well satisfied with the customer's money? The correct meaning is immediately apparent to the reader when the sentence is revised.

Correct: If you are not satisfied, we will refund your money.

Occasionally, if the who-did-what principle is violated, the sentence becomes ridiculous, for an object, not a person, seems to be performing an action.

Faulty: Receiving the customer's urgent request, the order was immediately processed by Maria.

The thought unit *Receiving the customer's urgent request, the order* suggests that the order was receiving the request. This kind of phrasing shows a serious lack of communication know-how. In a revision, Maria performs the action.

Correct: Receiving the customer's urgent request, Maria immediately processed the order.

Here is another illustration of this type of error:

Faulty: After climbing to the top of the tower, the whole city lay spread before us.

What does the thought unit *After climbing to the top of the tower, the whole city* mean? How could a city climb to the top of the tower? In a revision, the people would perform the action.

Correct: After climbing to the top of the tower, we saw the whole city spread before us.

A who-did-what violation, sometimes called a *dangling modifier,* does not necessarily occur at the beginning of a sentence. For example, note the error in the following sentence.

Faulty: Mr. Collins saw the prospective customer leaving the stockroom.

As written, the thought unit is *customer leaving the stockroom.* Where was Mr. Collins when he saw the customer, and why was the customer in the stockroom? Most likely it was Mr. Collins who was leaving the stockroom. In order to eliminate the confusion, the writer should revise the sentence.

Correct: Leaving the stockroom, Mr. Collins saw the prospective customer.

Now read the following sentence, which is another example of unclear word reference.

Faulty: Rolanda Wilson was promoted to branch manager, thus confirming everyone's opinion that she is the most qualified person for the position.

Thus, as used here, is ambiguous. The thought could have been expressed more clearly and more directly by eliminating *thus.*

Correct: Rolanda Wilson's promotion to branch manager confirms everyone's opinion that she is the most qualified person for the position.

Amanda said to call them for a copy of the health plan.

CONFUSING PRONOUN REFERENCES

Each pronoun borrows its meaning from a noun. When the writer fails to make clear which noun a pronoun refers to, the pronoun loses its meaning or assumes an incorrect and unintended meaning. One vague or mistaken pronoun reference can garble an entire message. The careful writer checks each pronoun used in order to make certain that its reference is clear.

Confusing *He* or *She*

When you use either the pronoun *he* or *she,* you must make certain that the antecedent—the noun to which the pronoun refers—is clear. If more than one man or more than one woman is mentioned in the sentence, place the pronoun as near as possible to the person to whom you refer. The following sentence leaves the reader wondering "Who returned from the meeting?"

> **Unclear:** Ms. Onuma asked Helen to write a report immediately after she returned from the regional sales meeting.

Does that *she* in this sentence refer to *Helen* or to *Ms. Onuma*? If the reference is to *Ms. Onuma,* then the sentence should be revised as follows.

> **Correct:** Immediately after she returned from the regional sales meeting, Ms. Onuma asked Helen to write a report.

If, on the other hand, Helen is the one who attended the meeting, then the sentence should read:

> **Correct:** Immediately after Helen returned from the regional sales meeting, Ms. Onuma asked her to write a report.

Confusing *It*

Using the pronoun *it* to refer to something that is not immediately clear is a common mistake.

> **Unclear:** I will place the football in the kicking tee, and when I nod my head, kick it.

Kick what? This *it* could result in a painful injury. The word *it* must be replaced by the noun to which it should refer.

> **Correct:** I will place the football in the kicking tee, and when I nod my head, kick the ball.

Other Confusing Pronoun References

Speakers who are uncertain of their sources frequently use the vague "they say" as a reference. Writing that uses the same vague reference is considered amateurish; in written communication, references must be definite and exact or else they are confusing.

Vague: They say that the joint venture between Eastern Rail/Road Transport, Inc., and the Baltic republics will be launched early next year.

Who is meant by *they* in the preceding sentence? To be more precise, a writer should replace the vague *They say* with a more exact reference.

Clear: *International Market News* reports that the joint venture between Eastern Rail/Road Transport, Inc., and the Baltic republics will be launched early next year.

Another type of reference that is puzzling and annoying to a reader is an unclear pronoun reference.

Faulty: Although I dictated all morning on Tuesday, the word processing operator input only two of them.

The thought unit *two of them* is vague. Two of what? stories? letters? reports? news releases? A clear and explicit thought could be communicated by revising the sentence.

Correct: Although I dictated all morning on Tuesday, the word processing operator input only two of the letters.

CORRECTING *THIS* FAULTS

A common writing fault is the use of *this* to refer to an entire preceding thought. This lack of precision sometimes forces a reader to read a sentence several times to understand the writer's meaning. Inexact use of *this* can detract from the point the writer is trying to make.

Faulty: Employees can't find parking spaces. This has existed since we hired 50 new employees.

To what does the *this* refer? *This* refers to the *shortage of parking spaces*. Stating the point specifically makes the meaning clear.

Correct: Employees can't find parking spaces. This shortage of parking spaces has existed since we hired 50 new employees.

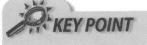

KEY POINT

To correct *this* and *thus* faults, ask yourself "*This* what?" or "*That* what?" Use your answers to these questions to complete the thought.

SECTION 7.3   REVIEW

Practical Application

A. On a separate sheet of paper, rewrite each sentence, making sure all thought units are clear.

   1. Zach put the video into the VCR, which everyone had been waiting to see.

2. The veterinarian was unable to complete the exam for the dog's owner because she was nervous.
3. Tim ate the donuts at the bakery with sticky fingers.
4. Walking on crutches, stairs were difficult to climb for Rick.
5. Having forgotten to save the document before turning off the computer, the letter had to be retyped by Juanita.
6. Sitting close to the hotel window, the snow-covered mountains are visible on a clear day.
7. The new computers, with little or no training, can be operated by skilled technicians.
8. Your rental agreement says that you may not have animals or children unless caged.
9. After much calculating, the checkbook finally balanced.
10. The mixer truck was wrecked by a substitute driver only half full of cement.
11. The excellent theater critic's review boosted ticket sales.
12. While working in our office, the printer noise was distracting to the visiting auditors.
13. Covered with proofreaders' marks, Ms. Raincloud sent the draft back for corrections.
14. After working a 12-hour shift, his head ached and his feet hurt.

B. On a separate sheet of paper, rewrite the following sentences to eliminate confusing pronoun references. Use the explanations in parentheses as a guide.
   1. Although we interviewed 30 applicants, we hired only 3 of them. (*Them* refers to nursing assistants.)
   2. The computer terminal is on my desk. Please don't move it for any reason. (*It* refers to the computer terminal.)
   3. Ms. Moreno was offered a five-year lease or a ten-year lease. She will probably sign it next week. (*It* refers to the longer lease.)
   4. Dave asked Lenny to review the proposal as soon as he received it. (Dave received the proposal.)
   5. Beth saw Cathy when she was in San Francisco last month. (Beth was in San Francisco.)
   6. Juan and Fredrico completed the product analysis, but he wrote the report. (Juan wrote the report.)
   7. Susan told Amanda that her explanation was not clear. (Susan's explanation was not clear.)
   8. They think that more research should be done before the medication is approved. (*They* refers to Dr. Sean Miller and Dr. Lucy Spragins.)

C. On a separate sheet of paper, rewrite each sentence, correcting the *this* or *thus* faults.
   1. The meeting adjourned without taking any action or making any decisions thus causing us to be dissatisfied.
   2. When we transferred the files, several folders were misplaced. This was not Dexter's fault.

3. When the power was unexpectedly interrupted, several computer files were damaged. This will cause us to work late.
4. The company's top designer was not able to work with us because she was on vacation when we launched the project. This has affected the quality of our project.
5. Steven ignored his father's good advice thus proving that he was stubborn.

Editing Practice

Pronoun Usage. On a separate sheet of paper, correct the pronoun errors in the following sentences. Write *OK* for any sentence that is correct.

1. What one of the account representatives will be transferred?
2. Whom is going to the sales conference in Montana next week?
3. The article was written by she last summer.
4. The fee will be divided between you and I.
5. Durability and appearance are it's strong points.
6. Its not clear which letter arrived first.
7. Gordon, Lori, and him volunteered to work overtime for two weeks.
8 They are planning to ride with us to the convention.
9. Who's performance should be evaluated?
10. Will you give your expense report to Andrea or I?

Writing Effective Sentences

OBJECTIVES:

After completing Section 7.4, you should be able to:

1. Compose sentences that use the you-attitude and positive words.
2. Use planned repetition for emphasis and avoid writing sentences with excessive repetition of sounds.
3. Use subordination and coordination properly, and correct *so* and *and so* faults.
4. Use the active and passive voices appropriately.

Long sentences in a short composition are like large rooms in a little house.

—William Shenstone, English poet

A well-written letter, memo, or report flows smoothly. The reader is more aware of the flow of ideas than of individual sentences, clauses, and phrases. Nothing should interrupt the reader's concentration—no awkward phrases, vague references, or unbalanced constructions.

Because a well-written document flows so easily, the reader may feel that the words flowed as easily from the writer's mind. In reality, however, the first draft was probably full of awkward phrases, vague references, choppy sentences, and unbalanced constructions. The writer took the time, however, to look for problems in the rough draft and then applied good writing techniques to eliminate the problems. As you study this section, identify strategies that Joan from the opening case study could use to write effective sentences.

KEY POINT

A good written communication flows smoothly, allowing the reader to absorb ideas without interpretation stemming from poor writing.

WORD USAGE

Writers combine words to make sentences and sentences to make paragraphs. You cannot write effective sentences without using the right words. Here are some suggestions for writing effective sentences.

1. Use the you-attitude and positive words.
2. Use planned repetition of words to emphasize important points.
3. Use pleasant-sounding words instead of harsh or awkward-sounding words.

Use the You-Attitude

Sentences that use the you-attitude emphasize the reader instead of the writer. By focusing on the reader, you are more likely to gain his or her acceptance or cooperation. Compare the following sentences.

I-Attitude: I would like to thank you for your interest in Micro Computer Solutions, Inc.

You-Attitude: Thank you for your interest in Micro Computer Solutions, Inc.

I-Attitude: We need to receive your reply to this offer no later than Thursday, April 5.

You-Attitude: Please send us your reply to this offer no later than Thursday, April 5.

KEY POINT

The you-attitude focuses on the reader. The I-attitude focuses on the writer.

One way to achieve the you-attitude in business writing is to use *you* with positive words. Such words create a receptive, pleasant impression in the mind of a reader. Compare the positive words and the negative words in the following chart.

KEY POINT

Positive words make a pleasant impression on the reader.

Positive Words

advancement	courage	happy	success
agreeable	eager	integrity	warmth
capable	easy	pleasure	welcome
cheerful	fun	profit	

Negative Words

anxious	complaint	failure	problem
apologize	damage	incapable	sad
blame	difficult	loss	sorry
cannot	dishonest	not	wrong

Note how using a negative word with *you* can result in a negative sentence. Such sentences should be reworded to make them more positive.

Negative: You were not late in making deliveries last month.

Positive: You made all your deliveries on schedule last month.

Use Planned Repetition of Words

Although careless repetition of words shows a lack of imagination, *planned* repetition can sometimes achieve striking emphasis of an important idea. Repeating the words *too* and *flexible* in the following examples helps to emphasize each point.

She arrived *too* late *too* often to keep her job.

Take advantage of our *flexible* hours to keep your schedule *flexible*.

Repetition is most often used in advertisements where the major goal is to make readers remember the name and purpose of the product. Sometimes the goal is accomplished by simple repetition of the name. Clever writers manage to vary the order of the repeated words to prevent monotony, as in the following sentence.

Flexicise Workouts will add muscles to your body, and Flexicise Workouts will add body to your muscles.

Use Pleasant-Sounding Words

Excessive repetition of certain vowel or consonant sounds can create tongue twisters that detract from the message. Even when reading silently, the reader cannot ignore a sentence like the following.

Selina sold seven synthetic slipcovers on Saturday.

Such repetitious sounds can cause problems other than tongue twisters. Although easy to say, the following sentence is hardly pleasant to hear.

Steer your weary, dreary body to O'Leary's Health Club.

Avoid using words with unpleasant sounds, and do not attempt to write business letters that sound musical or poetic. A business document should be courteous and concise. For the greatest effect, concentrate on that function.

✔ CHECKUP 1

Rewrite the following sentences to use either the you-attitude or pleasant-sounding words. Use a separate sheet of paper.

1. I have enclosed the samples requested in your April 5 letter.
2. The Thornton account takes up three thick files.

3. Include your payment with the completed order form.

4. Give me a response by Friday.

5. To avoid being a failure, you should try harder.

PROPER SUBORDINATION OF IDEAS

Proper subordination of ideas depends on the ability to determine the differences between an important idea and a lesser idea. The important thought is expressed as a main clause, and the lesser idea is properly written as a subordinate clause. This principle can be remembered as follows: Main idea—main clause; subordinate idea—subordinate clause. Subordinate clauses begin with subordinate conjunctions such as *because, since, when,* and *although.* Consider the following sentence.

KEY POINT

Express the most important thought as a main clause and the lesser thoughts as subordinate clauses.

Weak: Your proposal is interesting, although it does not meet our specifications.

Which statement is more important—*your proposal is interesting* or that *it does not meet our specifications*? That the proposal does not meet the specifications is the more important idea; therefore, it should be expressed as the main clause, as in the following example.

Better: Unfortunately, your proposal does not meet our specifications, although we did find it interesting.

Coordinate and Subordinate Ideas

When a sentence contains two ideas of equal importance, divide the sentence into two main clauses. Use a coordinating conjunction (*and, but, or, nor*) to join the ideas, as in the following sentences.

KEY POINT

When a sentence contains two ideas of equal importance, divide the sentence into two main clauses.

Wade will review the cost estimates, and Lynn will write the bid.

The work is difficult, but the rewards are great.

On the other hand, writing power is diminished when the writer fails to see that the thoughts belong not in two main clauses but in a main clause and a subordinate clause.

Weak: Other candidates were equally qualified, but the marketing director selected Laurel for the sales position.

This sentence places equal stress on what the writer considers to be two main ideas. The emphasis should properly be placed on the director's choosing Laurel even though others were qualified. For force, as well as for clarity, the sentence should be rewritten.

Better: Although other candidates were equally qualified, the marketing director selected Laurel for the sales position.

Eliminate Interrupting Expressions

Some writers unwittingly destroy the forcefulness of proper subordination by writing the lesser idea as an interrupting expression. For instance, read the following sentence.

Weak: You are, considering the risks involved in such an investment, very fortunate.

The main thought, *you are very fortunate,* is interrupted by the lesser idea, *considering the risks involved.* This interruption breaks the flow of the main thought and detracts from the force of the statement. Properly written, the sentence should read as follows.

Better: Considering the risks involved in such an investment, you are very fortunate.

Stronger: You are very fortunate, considering the risks involved in such an investment.

Correct *So* and *And So* Faults

Whenever you read a sentence that uses *so* and *and so* to introduce a clause, you can improve the sentence by substituting a more meaningful conjunction. Notice how weak the connection is between the two clauses in the following sentence.

Weak: Elena has been a dedicated literacy volunteer for ten years, so we gave her a special tribute at last night's fund-raising dinner.

The first clause gives the reason for the second clause. *Because* is a better choice for joining clauses that give causes and results. The following sentence is stronger, clearer, and more polished than the previous version.

Better: We gave Elena a special tribute at last night's fund-raising dinner because she has been a dedicated literacy volunteer for ten years.

And so is not a two-word conjunction. It is two separate conjunctions used to form a vague connection between two clauses. Consider the following sentence.

Weak: Mr. Velez is a talented graphic designer, and so we recommend that you hire him.

The first clause is the reason for the second. The relationship is easier to detect in the following revision.

Better: We recommend that you hire Mr. Velez because he is a talented graphic designer.

✓ CHECKUP 2

In the following sentences, make the corrections indicated in parentheses. Use a separate sheet of paper.

1. Some additional options were presented, but the manager decided to go with Susan's proposal. (Subordinate an idea.)

2. The report is due March 4, and Jeff has been working long hours on the calculations. (Subordinate an idea.)

3. We are, despite the costs involved, committed to expanding our markets overseas. (Eliminate an interrupting expression.)

4. Our accounting department is understaffed, and so we propose hiring three additional accountants. (Correct the *and so* fault.)

5. Save the files in a new directory on the computer. Print a copy of each file. (Coordinate ideas.)

ACTIVE VERSUS PASSIVE VOICE

Voice is that property of a transitive verb that shows whether the subject acts or is acted upon. In the active voice, the subject is the doer of an action; in the passive voice, the subject is acted upon. Any verb phrase composed of a past participle with a being verb helper is in the passive voice: *will be shipped, has been sent, was done, is frozen.*

Passive: A program upgrade *was sent* to us by the software company.

Active: The software company *sent* us a program upgrade.

The active voice expresses thoughts in a stronger, livelier way than does the passive voice. Compare these two sentences:

Passive: Your order *will be shipped* on Monday, July 8.

Active: We *will ship* your order on Monday, July 8.

Both sentences state the same information, but the active voice sentence is more direct. In the following pair of sentences, note that the sentence using the active voice makes a stronger point than the weak, passive voice does.

Passive: Last year our telephone systems *were sold* to three out of every four new businesses in the city.

Active: Last year, we *sold* our telephone systems to three out of every four new businesses in the city.

The passive voice has its uses in business writing, usually to soften the impact of negative news. In the following sentences, note how the sentence using the passive voice is the more diplomatic of the two.

Active: Because the college *did not send* us a copy of your transcript, we *cannot consider* your application to our program at this time.

Passive: Your application to our program *will be considered* when a copy of your transcript *is sent* to us by the college.

KEY POINT

In the active voice, the subject performs the action; in the passive voice, the subject receives the action.

KEY POINT

Use the active voice to express thoughts in a strong, direct way.

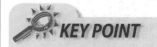

KEY POINT

In business writing, the passive voice is often used to soften the impact of negative news.

Figure 7.2

Using the active voice and the you-attitude are two strategies for writing effective messages. What are some other strategies a writer can use to compose a successful message?

KEY POINT

Treat like elements in a like manner.

PARALLEL STRUCTURE

Parallel structure is a must for similar parts of a sentence. A noun should be parallel with a noun, an adjective with an adjective, and a phrase with a phrase. For example, look at this sentence.

Unparallel: The new staff assistant is eager, diligent, and has much knowledge.

Lack of parallel structure causes the sentence to lose momentum. The writer erroneously coordinated two adjectives and a clause. In the following revision, note how the writer has coordinated the three adjectives, making the sentence grammatically parallel and effective.

Parallel: The new staff assistant is eager, diligent, and knowledgeable.

In the paragraphs that follow, you will study techniques for balancing comparisons, modifiers, verbs, prepositions, conjunctions, and clauses.

Balance Comparisons

Comparisons are balanced only if they are complete. They can be complete only if they include all the necessary words. The omission of one necessary word can throw a comparison out of balance, as in the following sentence.

Unbalanced: Recent studies show that women spend more money on eating in restaurants than men.

As written, the sentence could mean that women spend more money on eating in restaurants than they spend on men. The comparison lacks balance, as well as sense, because an essential word is omitted. One word, properly placed, can make the meaning of the sentence clear.

Balanced: Recent studies show that women spend more money on eating in restaurants than men *spend.*

Or the sentence could be rearranged.

Balanced: Recent studies show that women spend more money than men *do* on eating in restaurants.

Here is another unbalanced comparison.

Unbalanced: Ms. Ridgeway's role in the corporation is more than a financial analyst.

This sentence lacks sense because essential words have been omitted. The following revision improves the clarity.

Balanced: Ms. Ridgeway's role in the corporation is more than *that of* a financial analyst.

An unbalanced comparison like the one that follows provides a chance for skillful revision.

Unbalanced: Celia can program just as well, if not better, than George.

Disregarding the words set off by commas, the sentence reads as follows: *Celia can program just as well than George.* However, no one would say *as well than.* The first revision below is acceptable, but the second one is a much better sentence.

Balanced: Celia can program just as well *as,* if not better than, George.

Balanced: Celia can program just as well *as George,* if not better.

Balance Modifiers

Omission of single-word modifiers can destroy the balance of a sentence in several ways. Such an omission can produce, for example, an illogical message.

Incorrect: The company is hiring a receptionist and field engineer.

Failure to write *a* before *field engineer* makes *a receptionist and field engineer* refer to one person. It is unlikely that one person could serve in this dual capacity.

Correct: The company is hiring a receptionist and *a* field engineer.

Balance Verbs

Structural balance demands that whenever the parts of verbs in compound constructions are not exactly alike in form, no verb part should be omitted. The following sentence breaks this rule.

Incorrect: Rhonda always has, and always will, do a good job.

The word *do* cannot act as the main verb for the auxiliary verb *has. Has* requires the past participle *done.* Without the word *done,* the

When stopped, the feet are needed by the cyclist to balance the motorcycle.

KEY POINT

Omitting one modifier can change the meaning of a sentence.

In accordance with your instructions, I have renewed my license in the enclosed envelope.

sentence seems to read "Rhonda always has *do* and always will do a good job." The verbs required in this compound construction are not exactly alike in form; therefore, all verb parts should be included.

Correct: Rhonda always *has done* and always *will do* a good job.

The following sentence shows the same kind of error.

Incorrect: Your revised report was received today and copies sent to the members of the advisory committee for their comments.

The omission of the auxiliary verb after *copies* makes the sentence read "Your revised report was received today, and copies *was* sent to the members of the advisory committee for their comments." The plural noun *copies* requires a plural verb; therefore, the sentence should be revised.

Correct: Your revised report was received today, and copies *were* sent to the members of the advisory committee for their comments.

Balance Prepositions

The omission of a preposition can also throw a sentence off balance. Usage requires that some words be followed by specific prepositions. (See pages 162–163 for words that require specific prepositions.)

When two prepositional constructions have the same object, use the preposition that is correct for each construction.

Incorrect: Senior documentation writers must demonstrate expertise and knowledge of software programming.

In this sentence *expertise* and *knowledge* both are modified by the prepositional phrase *of software programming*. However, it is incorrect to say "expertise *of* software programming." The correct preposition to use with *expertise* is *in*. To be balanced the sentence should read as follows.

Correct: Senior documentation writers must demonstrate expertise *in* and knowledge of software programming.

Balance Conjunctions

In speech, subordinating conjunctions, particularly *that* and *when,* can often be omitted without causing any confusion. In writing, however, such omissions may destroy the balance of the thought units of a sentence and confuse the reader. Read the following example aloud.

Weak: Marc often talks about the time he had neither money nor position.

If this were an oral communication, the speaker could make the meaning clear by pausing slightly after the word *time*. The reader, however, might see the thought unit as *Marc often talks about the time he had,* with result that the words following *had* would not make sense. The reader would have to reread the sentence to understand the meaning. In business communication, you want the reader to understand the message the first time it is read. The sentence should be revised as follows.

Better: Marc often talks about the time *when* he had neither money nor position.

The following sentence may also be misread.

Weak: I searched and discovered the contract folder was missing.

The reader may see *I searched and discovered the contract folder* as one thought unit. The subordinating conjunction *that* adds clarity.

Better: I searched and discovered *that* the contract folder was missing.

Balance Clauses

Another mark of writing distinction is to avoid incomplete (elliptical) clauses whenever failure to write the complete clause would confuse the reader. In the sentence *You are a faster typist than I,* the meaning "than I am" is clear. But note the following sentence.

Unbalanced: Did Mr. Norville pay the bill or his accountant?

This sentence could be interpreted as follows: "Did Mr. Norville pay the bill, or did he pay his accountant? It could also be interpreted this way: "Did Mr. Norville pay his bill, or did his accountant pay the bill?" The following sentence clarifies the intended meaning.

Balanced: Did Mr. Norville pay the bill, or did his accountant pay it?

SECTION 7.4   REVIEW

Practical Application

A. The sentences below repeat similar sounds too often. On a separate sheet of paper, rewrite the sentences to make them less distracting to the reader.
   1. Mr. Randolph missed Miss Vester's call.
   2. The board became bored by noon.
   3. A pair of paralegals perused the contracts.
   4. My attorney summarized some of his comments.
   5. The cashier's check cleared up the confusion.

B. On a separate sheet of paper, rewrite each sentence to use positive words.
   1. Installation instructions for your new exercise equipment should not be difficult to understand.
   2. Bank tellers should not be dishonest.
   3. I failed to complete the project by today, but I will finish it by tomorrow.
   4. Your qualifications and lack of experience do not match our hiring needs at this time.
   5. Discuss any complaints during your European tour with our 24-hour customer representatives.

C. Rewrite these compound sentences, subordinating the less important ideas. Use a separate sheet of paper.
   1. Attendance at the concert was good, and all of the parking spaces were taken.
   2. You have successfully completed our management training program, and you will get a promotion.
   3. Our electrical service was interrupted last night by a storm, and I could not print my report.
   4. The stadium was enlarged, and the seating capacity is now 108,000.
   5. Your property is in an ideal location, and we are going to buy it.

D. On a separate sheet of paper, rewrite each sentence, correcting the *so* and *and so* faults.
   1. My flight to Juneau was canceled, so I spent an extra night in Seattle.
   2. Reanza has been promoted, so we wonder who will be named to fill her position.
   3. The shipment was damaged in transit, and so I refused to accept it.
   4. The contractor was concerned about the rising cost of raw materials, so she added 5 percent to her estimated price.
   5. He injured his back while operating the forklift, and so he applied for insurance benefits.

E. Rewrite each sentence to change the voice of the verb. Use a separate sheet of paper, and follow the directions in parentheses.
   1. Changes in the tax laws were outlined by Rita Polaski, and the consequences of the tax laws were explained by Pablo Candeleria. (Change to the active voice.)
   2. Potential environmental hazards that would be caused by pollution were discussed by the Sierra Club members. (Change to the active voice.)
   3. Juan was praised by Mrs. Bonner when his proposal was accepted by the mayor. (Change to the active voice.)
   4. We cannot approve your credit application because of your short employment history. (Change to the passive voice.)
   5. The new smoking policy was reviewed by the department managers. (Change to the active voice.)

F. Using a separate sheet of paper, rewrite each sentence to balance the elements.
1. Omar reminded me about the time he had neither money nor employment.
2. I have much respect and confidence in Mr. Jansen's ability.
3. Teale Investment Consultants advertised for a broker and account executive.
4. We need temporary personnel to type documents, to proofread correspondence, and answering the phone.
5. Dannielle's computer skills are as good, if not better than, those of other applicants.
6. Her business sense is as sharp, if not sharper than, theirs.
7. Did Alexis call the client or her secretary? (Who called the client?)
8. I have, and will continue to try, to contact his attorney.
9. Our research shows that women own more stock than men.
10. In Shannon's briefcase were a calculator, pen, legal pad, and umbrella.

Editing Practice

Choosing the Right Word. On a separate sheet of paper, write the word that correctly completes each sentence.
1. Megalli Orman, (formally, formerly) our president, chairs the board.
2. Most customers are completely satisfied with (their, there) catalog purchases.
3. Tim O'Leary is more qualified (than, then) William Evans.
4. Camden Company plans to (adapt, adopt) its first official ethics statement at the noon meeting.
5. Employees can (access, excess) the computer files by telephone if they have the right modem.
6. Calvin gave me some helpful (advice, advise) when I came to work here.
7. The printing company delivered our letterhead (stationary, stationery) yesterday.
8. Much deliberation (preceded, proceeded) the decision to borrow money to purchase the new manufacturing equipment.
9. For the second consecutive quarter, Samuel (lead, led) the trainees in establishing new accounts.
10. Sean's research (cited, sighted) several studies that support our position.

Building Effective Paragraphs

OBJECTIVES:

After completing Section 7.5 you should be able to:

1. Write paragraphs that have one main idea, sentences that relate to the main idea of the paragraph, and messages that have a definite purpose.
2. Write paragraphs that are of a reasonable length.
3. Use transitional words and phrases to connect sentences and paragraphs.
4. Use variety in sentence length and sentence structure to make written communication more interesting.

To write simply is as difficult as to be good.

—W. Somerset Maugham, English novelist

Writing effective paragraphs requires writing good sentences and connecting the sentences to get the message across to the reader. Each sentence should support the main idea of the paragraph. If sentence structure is faulty or if paragraph organization is poor, the whole communication will fail.

ONE PURPOSE, ONE IDEA, ONE THOUGHT

To be effective, a written message should have one purpose. Each paragraph in the message should have one main idea. Each sentence in a paragraph should have one main thought that supports the main idea of the paragraph.

Message	→	One purpose
Paragraph	→	One main idea
Sentence	→	One main thought

MESSAGE CONTROL

A written communication such as a letter or a memorandum should be limited to one main purpose. Two or more main purposes within a message can cause confusion or can make one idea seem more or less important than another. In the following examples, note how the first message covers more than one purpose, while the second message focuses on one purpose.

More Than One Purpose

Thank you for inquiring about our automobile loans. Enclosed is a loan application form for your review.

You may also be interested in our certificates of deposit. We offer variable interest rates for three-month, six-month, and nine-month certificates.

One Purpose

Thank you for inquiring about our automobile loans. Enclosed is a loan application form for your review.

We offer flexible payment schedules for all automobile loans so that you can select a monthly payment that fits your budget.

PARAGRAPH CONTROL

To achieve paragraph control, the writer should relate all sentences to the main idea of the paragraph and keep paragraphs a reasonable length. In addition, the writer should use transitions and make sound paragraphing decisions.

Paragraph Unity

The main idea of a paragraph is usually stated in a topic sentence. This topic sentence is often the first sentence in the paragraph. All other sentences in the paragraph should support the main idea, creating *paragraph unity*. For example, in the following paragraph, note how all the sentences relate to the main idea about techniques for improving your memory.

> There are several techniques for improving your memory. One technique is to use certain images to remember the names of people and things. For example, to remember the name of an important client, Ms. Flowers, you could remember her picking flowers. Another technique is to use a word or an acronym to remember a concept. For example, use the word *homes* to remember the names of the Great Lakes: *Huron, Ontario, Michigan, Erie,* and *Superior.* Still another memory technique is to associate a list of items with traveling a particular route. Each item becomes a part of your walk along this route. For instance, to remember the items on a grocery list, you might picture yourself putting a gallon of milk in the mailbox as you walk to your neighbor's house.

Before writing the first sentence of a paragraph, the writer should have the main idea of the paragraph clearly in mind. The writer must know where the paragraph is going before attempting to guide the reader there. The writer who does not know what conclusion the paragraph is to have should stop writing and start thinking.

KEY POINT

The topic sentence contains the main idea of the paragraph. All other sentences support the main idea.

KEY POINT

Achieving paragraph unity requires the writer to focus on one main idea.

Paragraph Length

In general, a paragraph should have no more than six to eight lines. If the development of the main idea requires more than six to eight lines, the writer should carry that thought over to another paragraph. Readers seem to need visual breaks (paragraphs) but not continuity breaks (interruptions in the message content). Visual breaks allow the reader to pause and think about the material presented.

Transitional Words and Phrases

Transitional words and phrases provide connections between sentences and between paragraphs. Skillful use of transitional words and

KEY POINT

Transitional words and phrases signal relationships between sentences and between paragraphs.

phrases can move the reader through the communication—from one idea to another—without a break in continuity that could detract from the message.

The following chart lists some common transitions you could use to show how items, ideas, or events are related to one another.

Transitional Words and Phrases		
Indicate Sequence		
after	during	later
as soon as	finally	meanwhile
at present	first (second, third,	next
at the same time	fourth)	soon
before	immediately	then
Show location		
above	below	outside
ahead	higher	
behind	inside	
Compare or Contrast		
also	however	on the other hand
although	instead	rather
both	likewise	similarly
but	neither	still
by contrast	nevertheless	yet
even though	on the contrary	
Add Information		
also	despite	moreover
and	equally important	next
another	further	one reason
as well	furthermore	
besides	in addition	
Provide an Example		
for example	namely	that is
for instance	specifically	
in particular	such as	
Add Emphasis		
after all	even more	in fact
again	for this purpose	more important
especially	indeed	
Indicate a Result or Conclusion		
as a result	consequently	therefore
because of	finally	thus

Note the transitions used in the following examples.

Sequence: *After* he receives the spreadsheets, Ned will compile the final report.

Location: *Below* is a list of specifications.

Emphasis: *More important,* this new insurance policy will be cost-effective for all employees.

Conclusion: *Therefore,* in recognition of Michelle Wellington's outstanding sales record, we are naming her Employee of the Year.

As you read the following message, note the length of the paragraph and the lack of transitions.

> We were surprised to hear that you did not enjoy your tour of Denali National Park in Alaska last month. We feel that our literature gave you an accurate impression of what to expect. Our literature states that "Explorer Nature Tours are not for the faint of heart. Our naturalist guides take you to some of the most remote and pristine areas on Earth where you will see scenic landscapes and encounter native wildlife." Our tour literature does not explicitly say that you will wake up to find a grizzly bear in your tent, as you did. We do indicate that such encounters are a remote possibility. Our experienced guides handled the situation quickly so that no harm resulted. We regret that you did not enjoy your tour. We must remind you that our policy, as stated in the tour literature, does not permit us to give you a complete refund. In your situation, we are willing to make an exception to our no-refund policy.

Let's look at how the preceding paragraph could be improved by making several shorter paragraphs and adding the transitions shown in italics.

> We were surprised to hear that you did not enjoy your Explorer Nature Tour of Denali National Park in Alaska last month. We feel that our literature gave you an accurate impression of what to expect. *For instance,* our literature states that "Explorer Nature Tours are not for the faint of heart. Our naturalist guides take you to some of the most remote and pristine areas on Earth where you will see scenic landscapes and encounter native wildlife."
>
> *Although* our tour literature does not explicitly say that you will wake up as you did, to find a grizzly bear in your tent, we do indicate that such encounters are a remote possibility.
>
> *Fortunately,* our experienced guides handled the situation quickly so that no harm resulted. *Nevertheless,* we regret that you did not enjoy your tour.
>
> We must remind you that our policy, as stated in the tour literature, does not permit us to give you a complete refund. *However,* in your situation, we are willing to make an exception to our no-refund policy.

Paragraphing Decisions

Paragraphing decisions can create an attractive, uncluttered format that makes business documents easier to read and understand. Ideally, content determines paragraph length. However, when it is practical, adjust paragraphs to fit the guidelines in the checklist on page 354. *Remember:* These are guidelines, *not* hard-and-fast rules.

KEY POINT

Careful paragraphing decisions can improve the appearance and readability of a document.

Paragraphing Guidelines

Follow these paragraphing suggestions to improve the appearance and readability of a document:

- Keep the first and last paragraphs short, usually two to five lines each.
- Keep middle paragraphs an average of four to eight lines in length, and make them longer than the first and last paragraphs.
- Combine several short paragraphs to avoid a choppy appearance.
- Avoid writing several long paragraphs.
- Avoid a top-heavy appearance (beginning paragraphs too long); avoid a bottom-heavy appearance (ending paragraphs too long).
- Use an odd number of paragraphs. Three paragraphs look better than two, and five paragraphs look better than four.

SENTENCE CONTROL

Maintaining sentence control is one way to improve the readability of a document. *Readability* refers to the ease with which something can be read. Sentence length and sentence structure are two factors that affect readability.

Variety in Sentence Length

Long sentences tend to be harder to understand than short ones. Yet, short sentences can seem choppy and boring. What is the solution to the sentence-length problem? Variety.

Most sentences should range in length from 10 to 20 words. This range is a guide. To provide variety, some sentences will have fewer than 10 words; others will have more than 20 words.

Extremely long sentences seem to bury the main thought. Beyond a certain length, sentences seem to grow weaker with each added word. This unnecessary length frustrates most readers. Overly long sentences may be grammatically correct, but often they are wordy. Compare the following examples.

Wordy: Thank you for informing us in your letter of May 30 that you still have not received the illustrated *Complete Guide to Organic Gardening* that we shipped to you by parcel post on or about last May 1, but there's no need for you to worry because we are going to send you another copy of this excellent handbook on the techniques of successful gardening without chemicals.

World View

When corresponding with someone who doesn't know English very well, avoid writing very long sentences and paragraphs.

KEY POINT

Most sentences should be from 10 to 20 words long.

The reader has to digest far too many words to learn that another copy of the book will be sent. The writer could have expressed the thought more clearly and concisely in separate, shorter sentences.

Better: Thank you for letting us know that your copy of the *Complete Guide to Organic Gardening* has not reached you. We are mailing you a new copy at once.

On the other hand, a succession of short sentences weakens writing, because the reader is jerked along from thought to thought.

Choppy: I received your proposal yesterday morning. Your approach to tracking inventory in our distribution center is interesting. We have a manufacturing committee meeting next Monday. I will present your proposal at that time.

Instead of writing a stop-and-go paragraph like the one above, the writer should smooth out the bumps, as in this revision.

Better: Your proposal arrived yesterday morning. In my opinion, your approach to tracking inventory in our distribution center is promising. I intend to present your proposal to the other members of the manufacturing committee when we meet next Monday.

In some situations, the planned use of short sentences can be very effective. Short sentences are useful to bring out a series of important facts, to emphasize a point, and to break up a series of longer sentences.

The Fast-Action camera is made especially for quick-moving action photography. Its autofocus feature prepares you for your next shot a fraction of a second after you press the shutter. You just point and shoot—there's no need to focus! Its easy-open back permits you to insert a new roll of film faster than you can in any other camera. You can reload in 15 seconds! Best of all, the Fast-Action camera is equipped with a built-in computerized flash that works on a rechargeable battery. The camera provides a flash only when it's needed! See your dealer for complete details.

Variety in Sentence Structure

A communication that lacks variety lacks interest. One sure way to produce a dull communication is to use only simple sentences. Equally dull is a communication with all compound sentences or one with all complex sentences. Your goal should be to vary the sentence structure of a message.

In the following example, note how too many compound sentences and too many *ands* make the paragraph dull.

Lengthy: Your new Metro Spirit coupe costs more, *and* it offers a variety of convenient standard features. The fuel-injected engine is durable, *and* you will enjoy its trouble-free operation. The engine uses less fuel while idling, *and* it uses less fuel on the road. Our coupes stand up to years of wear *and* have a high resale value. You chose the right car, *and* you will find this out in the coming years.

In the following revision, note how variety in sentence structure improves the paragraph.

Most drivers use the right foot to control the brake pedal, while using the same pedal to control the accelerator.

Better: Your new Metro Spirit coupe costs more, *but* it offers convenient standard features. *Because* the fuel-injected engine is durable, you will enjoy years of trouble-free operation. You will use less fuel *both* when idling and when moving. *Finally,* because Spirit coupes stand up to years of wear, they have high resale value. The years will prove that you chose the right car.

SECTION 7.5   REVIEW

Practical Application

A. Using a separate sheet of paper, edit the following paragraph. Make sure that each sentence has one main thought and that each sentence supports the main idea of the paragraph. If the paragraph contains more than one main idea, break it into two or more paragraphs. Omit sentences that do not support the main idea of the paragraph.

   The computer operator's body should be erect; he or she should sit well back in the chair and learn forward slightly from the waist. Feet should be placed firmly on the floor. Typing speed increases only through practice. The body should be about a handspan from the front of the keyboard. Sitting too close to the computer can cause bottom-row errors, just as sitting too far way can cause top-row errors. Most printers offer several font sizes. Likewise, sitting too far to the left or right causes errors in using the opposite hand.

B. The following paragraph contains short, monotonous, simple sentences. Rewrite the paragraph, varying the sentence structure. Some sentences will be combined. Use a separate sheet of paper.

   There will be a reception on Friday, December 28. It will honor LaShon Oduba. He has been the purchasing director for 25 years. He is retiring on December 30. The reception time is 5:30 p.m. to 7:30 p.m. It will be held in the corporate dining room. Everyone is invited.

C. Each of the following paragraphs contains one sentence that does not relate to the main idea of the paragraph. The sentence, however, does relate to the main idea of another paragraph. On a separate sheet of paper, rewrite the letter, putting the misplaced sentences in the *correct* paragraphs.

   Dear Mr. O'Malley:
   Thank you for requesting information about Ocean View Family Campground. Baby-sitting services are available ($4 per hour) through the local teen club.

Free activities include morning aerobic workouts, afternoon water games, and nightly movies. Shuttle bus service to the village, panoramic boat tours, and water skiing—all reasonably priced—are offered daily.

You may select various optional services, which are available at very low rates. Cable television, water connections, and electrical hookups are the most popular selections. Each Saturday night, the camp recreation director arranges such free entertainment as puppet shows, folk singing, and short plays.

The enclosed brochure lists our rates. Our grounds, arranged to provide privacy, can comfortably accommodate tents, camping vehicles, and mobile homes. Please telephone us soon to make sure that you get the reservations you want.

Sincerely yours,

D. On a separate sheet of paper, rewrite each sentence that has a grammatical error. Write *OK* for any sentence that is correct.
1. Both employees explained their absences to Kyle and I.
2. Hal Owens and me were invited to the ribbon-cutting at the new county office building.
3. When was the chain saws shipped?
4. Maria and myself will drive to Atlanta after work today.
5. After being hired, each new employee must have a physical.
6. The committee that coordinates volunteer services meet tomorrow morning at 10:30.

Editing Practice

Making Connections. Rewrite the following paragraphs on a separate sheet of paper. Add transitional words and phrases to connect the ideas.

Thank you for telling us about your experience with our products. We have strict quality control procedures. Some defective products may be getting by our inspectors.

Of course, comments like yours help us improve. We have already initiated actions that may be helpful. We respect your opinion. We plan to try your suggestions for a while and monitor the results. We may explore other options for quality control.

Your special order is ready and will be shipped some time later today. Thank you for your feedback. We sincerely appreciate your business.

Revising, Editing, and Proofreading

OBJECTIVES:

After completing Section 7.6, you should be able to:

1. Describe *revising, editing,* and *proofreading.*
2. Explain the importance of revising your written communications.
3. Use a revision checklist to improve the organization, wording, and tone of your written communication.
4. Apply the six Cs of editing to your written communication.
5. Explain why proofreading written work is essential.
6. Follow the five steps in proofreading.
7. Use proofreaders' marks and technology when revising, editing, and proofreading.

Revise, edit, and proofread because pobody is nerfect.

—S. C. Camp

After writing the initial draft of a document, writers go through these three steps—revising, editing, and proofreading. Some do all three tasks simultaneously, and some writers focus on one step at a time. Revising improves the content and organization of writing; editing refines the revised draft and adds polish; proofreading spots typographical and grammatical errors.

As you learn to revise, edit, and proofread, you will be more effective if you concentrate on each step individually.

USING PROOFREADERS' MARKS

When revising, editing, and proofreading documents, use proofreaders' marks as a quick, simple way to indicate changes or corrections in handwritten or typed copy.

The proofreaders' marks shown in Figure 7.3 on pages 359 and 360 are standard marks used to indicate corrections in handwritten or typed copy. Study the marks and become familiar with their use.

Some of the proofreaders' marks are particularly useful in reorganizing the content of a memo, letter, or report. You can easily see from Figure 7.4 on page 361 how to use these marks to indicate the relocation of small and large segments of text. Simply identify the material to be moved by marking the beginning and the end of the segment with a vertical line and labeling the block with a letter of the alphabet. You can also use this block identification to mark material that should be checked for accuracy before the final document is printed or typed. Place a question mark in the margin next to the block. Include marginal notes as needed for clarification.

Once you have marked changes and corrections on the hard copy, it is a simple process to make the changes on the computer. Remember to proofread the document after it has been printed to make sure all the indicated changes have been made correctly and no further errors have been made.

CAPITALIZATION	Capitalize a letter	texas	Texas
	Lowercase a letter	This	this
	Capitalize all letters	Cobol	COBOL
	Lowercase a word	PROGRAM	program
	Use initial capital only	PROGRAM	Program

CHANGES AND TRANSPOSITIONS	Change a word	price is only $10.98 $12.99	price is only $12.99
	Change a letter	deductable	deductible
	Stet (do not make the change)	price is only $10.98 are	price is only $10.98
	Spell out	2 cars on Washburn Rd.	two cars on Washburn Road
	Move as shown	on May 1 write him	write him on May 1
	Transpose letters or words	the time the of meeting	the time of the meeting

DELETIONS	Delete a letter and close up	strooke or strooke	stroke or stroke
	Delete a word	wrote two two checks	wrote two checks
	Delete punctuation	report was up to date	report was up to date
	Delete one space*	good day	good day
	Delete space	see ing	seeing

INSERTIONS	Insert a word or letter	in office buildng the	in the office building
	Insert a comma	may leave early. . . .	may leave early, . . .
	Insert a period	Dr Maria Rodriguez	Dr. Maria Rodriguez
	Insert an apostrophe	all the boys hats	all the boys' hats
	Insert quotation marks	Move on, she said.	"Move on," she said.
	Insert hyphens	up to date report	up-to-date report
	Insert a dash	They were surprised even shocked!	They were surprised —even shocked!
	Insert parentheses	pay fifty dollars $50	pay fifty dollars ($50)
	Insert one space	mayleave	may leave
	Insert two spaces*	1. The new machine	1. The new machine

(Continued on page 360.)

Figure 7.3 Proofreaders' Marks.

Proofreaders' marks provide a standard set of symbols for marking corrections.

FORMAT SYMBOLS: BOLDFACE AND UNDERSCORE	Print boldface	Bulletin
	Remove boldface	**Bulletin**
	Underscore	Title
	Remove underscore	Title

FORMAT SYMBOLS: CENTERING	Center line horizontally	] TITLE [

FORMAT SYMBOLS: PAGE AND PARAGRAPH	Begin a new page	*pg* . . order was delivered today by common carrier. We have all the . . .
	Begin a new paragraph	. . . order was delivered today by common carrier. We have all the . . .
	Do not begin new paragraph (run in)	. . . order was delivered today by common carrier. *No* We have all the materials . . .
	Indent five spaces	*5* We have the raw materials in our warehouse. Production will . . .

FORMAT SYMBOLS: SPACING	Single-space	SS [XXXXXXXXXX XXXXXXXXXX
	Double-space	dS [XXXXXXXXXX XXXXXXXXXX
	Triple—space	ts [XXXXXXXXXX XXXXXXXXXX

Figure 7.3 **Proofreaders' Marks. (continued)**

WHAT IS REVISING?

Revising is the process of "seeing again." In other words, when you revise, you have to stand back from your work and read it with fresh eyes in order to improve the writing. To do that, you need to allow some time to put your writing aside for a few hours or even for a day. Then you should be able to read what you have written more objectively—as your potential audience will read it.

KEY POINT

Revising improves the content and the organization of writing.

Revision	Edited Draft
Identify block	[A] and the catalog/will be mailed.
Insert identified block	Your order‸will be mailed.
Delete identified block	Your order [A] and the catalog/will be mailed
Move identified block*	Your order [A] and the catalog/will be *move* [A] shipped. The invoice‸will be mailed.
Query identified block*	Ed will retire at the age of/96/ ?[B] (Are the numbers transposed? Verify age.)
Query identified block*	Make my reservation for/June 31/ ?[C] (June has only 30 days. Verify date.)
Query conflicting blocks*	Call me Monday/morning at/8 [D] ?[E] /p.m./ (Morning or p.m.? Verify time.)

Figure 7.4 Proofreaders' Marks for Editing.

Using proofreaders' marks to indicate copy to be moved or verified is convenient when you are writing a document as part of a team. More than one person can work from the marked copy at the same time.

Checking Purpose, Audience, and Tone

Revising is not a hit-or-miss procedure. You need to ask yourself specific questions when revising any piece of writing. To begin the revision process, you should always ask questions about the purpose, audience, and tone of your message.

Is the Purpose of the Document Clear?   If your purpose, for example, is to persuade your reader to take a certain action, does that message come across clearly, without possibility of being misunderstood? If your purpose is to inform, have you included all pertinent information? If your purpose is to promote goodwill, have you used appropriate wording?

Is the Writing Tailored to the Audience?   To tailor the writing to the audience, consider your audience's familiarity with the subject. Suppose you must write a memo to new employees about company copying and mailing procedures. Did you consider that your audience—the new employees—know very little about the company, its policies, or other procedures? Did you use any terms, abbreviations, or references that might not be understood by the new employees?

Is the Tone Appropriate for the Audience?   *Tone* usually refers to the general effect a piece of writing creates. For example, the tone of your writing could be formal or informal, serious or humorous, positive or negative. Although seldom stated directly, the tone is inferred by the reader through the choice of words and other elements of style. For example, if you were writing a memorandum to a supervisor, you

KEY POINT

When you begin revising a document, check for clarity of purpose, suitability to the audience, and appropriateness of tone.

"Police union to seek blinking arbitration."

—*The News,* Groton, Connecticut

would avoid a negative, critical tone—even if you were reporting on some aspects of company procedures that needed improvement.

To keep the attention of your audience, you should establish a positive, upbeat tone that offers constructive suggestions for dealing with problems and challenges.

Reviewing the Organization

After answering the basic questions about purpose, audience, and tone, you should examine the organization of your message.

Is the Organization Logical? Begin the message with a strong opening paragraph or introduction that states the main idea or purpose of the message. The middle paragraphs should sufficiently support or explain your stated purpose, and the conclusion should summarize your ideas or arguments.

One way to make sure that your writing has a logical organization is to prepare an outline before you begin to write. Then follow that outline carefully as you write.

Do All Sentences Stick to the Point? As you review the organization of your message, pay particular attention to any sentences that seem to stray from the main idea of each paragraph. Such sentences usually contain unnecessary details or information that should be deleted because they detract from the message and create confusion. For example, if you were making the point in a report that good math skills are necessary for all entry-level jobs in your company, you would be wandering off the subject if you described your own math training.

Are Transitions Used to Connect Ideas? If your paragraphs are complete and if you have presented them in a clear, logical order, you should then make sure that you have included effective bridges or transitions between ideas, sentences, and paragraphs. Refer to the list of transitional words and phrases on page 352 for some common transitions to use.

Use Revision Checklist 1 on page 363 to improve the content, organization, and wording of your messages.

> **KEY POINT**
>
> Use transitions to help the reader move smoothly from one idea, sentence, or paragraph to another.

Reviewing the Language

Once you are confident that you have included all the necessary information, take a close look at the words that comprise the sentences and paragraphs.

Are Words Used Correctly? First, make sure that you have used each word correctly. If you are unsure of the meaning of a word, either look it up in a dictionary to make sure the word is appropriate or find an alternative word that expresses your exact meaning.

Purpose, Audience, and Tone

- ❐ Is the purpose clear?
- ❐ Is the wording suited to the audience?
- ❐ Is the tone appropriate?

Organization

- ❐ Is the content complete?
- ❐ Is the organization of the message logical?
- ❐ Does the message have a strong introduction, middle, and conclusion?
- ❐ Do all sentences relate to the main idea of each paragraph?
- ❐ Are appropriate transitions used to connect sentences and paragraphs?

Are the Words Vivid and Specific?　Now determine whether the words you have chosen will have the effect you intend. The purpose of all writing is to transfer your thoughts and ideas—as completely and as forcefully as possible—to someone else. Colorful, vivid, and specific words accomplish that purpose more easily than others. See page 319 for additional discussion of descriptive words.

When you revise, always examine your writing to make certain that the nouns, adjectives, and verbs are precise and sufficiently descriptive to convey your message. Use a thesaurus or a dictionary to find replacements for dull or overused words.

Are Any Words Overused or Unnecessary?　Check to see whether you have used the same words or expressions over and over. Readers sometimes become annoyed at such unnecessary repetition. For example, if you find that you have repeatedly used the word *told* throughout a report, consult a thesaurus for alternative words, such as *related, announced, declared, asserted, directed,* or *replied.* You will avoid repetition and at the same time describe more clearly the various ways people speak or make statements.

Is the Sentence Structure Varied?　Most people write exactly as they speak, and most people begin sentences with the subject. The monotony of this sentence structure is much more noticeable in a letter or report than it is in conversation. You can reduce reader boredom by adding some variety. For example, occasionally begin a sentence with an adverb or an adverb phrase, a participial phrase, or a prepositional phrase.

Subject: *Employees* often have to wait in line for 15 minutes in the cafeteria.

Adverb: *Often* employees have to wait in line for 15 minutes in the cafeteria.

KEY POINT

Use vivid, specific words to create concrete images in your readers' mind.

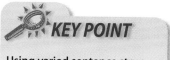

KEY POINT

Using varied sentence structure holds a reader's interest.

Prepositional Phrase: *In the cafeteria,* employees often have to wait in line for 15 minutes.

Is the Message Written in Active Voice?   Another important step is to see if verbs are in the active voice wherever possible. In the active voice, the subject is the doer of the action; in the passive voice, the subject is the receiver of the action. Your writing will be much livelier if you use the active voice. Compare the following sentences.

Active: The president of the company read the long-awaited announcement.

Passive: The long-awaited announcement was read by the president of the company.

Use Revision Checklist 2 to improve the language use in your messages.

Revision Checklist 2

Language Use

- ❏ Do the meanings of the words used fit the content of the message?
- ❏ Are there any dull or overused nouns, adjectives, or verbs that could be replaced with more colorful, specific words?
- ❏ Are there any repeated words or expressions that could be deleted?
- ❏ Should synonyms be used to make the message clearer and more forceful?
- ❏ Are the sentence beginnings varied?
- ❏ Are sentences written in the active voice whenever possible?

Revising With Grammar Checkers

A *grammar checker* such as Grammatik is software that evaluates grammar and suggests ways to improve the grammar and wording of a document. Grammar checkers identify certain weaknesses such as errors in subject-verb agreement, overuse of the passive voice, lack of variety in sentence structure, and wordiness.

Some grammar checkers estimate the reading level of a text segment. You can revise your document if the reading level is too high or too low. For example, if your company is inviting employees' children to attend a summer day camp, you could use a grammar checker to make sure the invitation is written so children can comprehend it.

Most grammar checkers highlight "potential" errors. You, as the writer, must decide if the highlighted text contains an actual error. You must also determine how to correct the error. You must ask yourself

Technology

For each error highlighted, the computer grammar checker displays the rule and explanation of the error, along with an example of how to correct that type of error.

these questions: Is what I typed correct? Should I make a change? What is the correct change? Although grammar checkers can be very helpful, they should not replace detailed revising and editing.

WHAT IS EDITING?

Editing is the process of checking a revised draft to make sure it meets the criteria of the six Cs of communication. That is, you make sure the document is clear, complete, concise, consistent, correct, and courteous. Editing not only helps improve the quality of your document but also helps improve your skill as a writer.

Editing skill is important for anyone involved with written communication. The purpose of editing is to make the document as effective as possible. You can improve a document by using the questions posed in the following Editing Checklist.

KEY POINT

Editing refines the wording of a revised draft.

Editing Checklist
☐ Is the message clear?
☐ Is the message complete?
☐ Is the wording concise?
☐ Is the wording consistent?
☐ Is the wording correct?
☐ Is the message courteous?

THE SIX Cs OF EDITING

Editing a document to follow the six Cs of communication ensures that your message is straightforward and uses the you-attitude.

Is It Clear?

Business communications are written to get action—not to entertain or increase the vocabulary of the reader. Good business writers use simple words and proper English and make every effort to avoid clichés. Documents should be coherent; that is, they should flow appropriately. Using transitional words and phrases contributes to clarity.

Is It Complete?

A complete message includes all necessary information. Because the writer is so familiar with the message, omitted details are not always

obvious to the writer. These missing details may, however, be obvious to the reader. Imagine receiving a brochure for a business seminar that gives only the hour, place, and topic of the seminar. The message is incomplete without the date. Further communication would be needed to clarify the information.

Is It Concise?

Unnecessary words, phrases, clauses, sentences, and paragraphs are a barrier to effective communication. Needless repetition of words decreases the effectiveness of your message because the reader must read a lot of words to get a little information. To make your writing concise, include only necessary words and avoid repeating the same words several times in a message.

Is It Consistent?

Business messages should be consistent in fact, treatment, and sequence. A message is consistent in fact if it does not contradict itself, an established fact, or a source document.

Treating similar items the same way results in consistency in treatment. Follow these guidelines:

- When listing both men's and women's names, use courtesy titles for all or none of the names: *Mr. Lawrence, Ms. Ruiz, Mrs. Thomas.*

- Use a consistent style in writing numbers and amounts. For example, *$1,000* and *$10,000, 36 customers* and *67 customers.*

- Use the same formatting, such as indenting paragraphs, throughout a document.

- Use special formatting techniques such as underlining and italics consistently for names of books and titles of articles.

- Use a consistent sequence (alphabetical, chronological, or numerical) to improve the flow of a message. For example, list names in alphabetical order to avoid conveying unintentional bias by listing one person's name before another's.

Is It Correct?

Accuracy in content, typing, and mechanics (capitalization, grammar, spelling, punctuation, and so on) makes the message more effective. Proofread the document to eliminate these kinds of errors.

Is It Courteous?

Courtesy means that the document is eye-pleasing, reader-centered, and positive. In addition to using the you-attitude and positive words, follow these suggestions for achieving courtesy:

- Select fonts that are easy to read. Cursive type fonts (*Cursive*) and solid-capital fonts (ALL CAPITALS) are more difficult to read than the more traditional fonts, such as Courier, with both upper and lowercase letters. Also, use a standard font size, such as 12 point. Very small fonts are difficult to read.

- Create an eye-pleasing communication by using several short paragraphs instead of one long paragraph.

- Position your document attractively on the page, including enough white space (blank space) to make the page appear uncluttered.

- Use a table format or a bulleted or numbered list for appropriate information to add visual variety and to make reading easier.

If you were Joan from the opening case study, describe how revising and editing could improve your writing.

In a newsletter, a vice president wrote the following: "I always want to be king to those living in areas that have experienced natural catastrophes."

WHAT IS PROOFREADING?

Proofreading is the process of examining a document to find errors that should be corrected. Sometimes proofreading is a verification process, such as checking a letter typed from a handwritten rough draft. There may be no document for comparison, however, when you are proofreading your own work. In either case, you should look carefully for errors in capitalization, content, format, grammar, word usage, number usage, punctuation, spelling, typing, and word division.

To be a good proofreader—to be able to identify errors—you must be familiar with all of these types of errors. If you are unsure of a spelling, a usage, and so on, rely on reference sources. You may, for example, see the word *reccomendation* and wonder whether it is spelled correctly. After checking a dictionary, you change the word to *recommendation*.

The proofreading process should begin in the early stages of document preparation and continue through each stage, including the final copy. In other words, check the document for errors before keyboarding

KEY POINT

Proofreading should be done throughout the writing process—at the draft stage, at the revision stage, and at the final printed document stage.

from notes, a handwritten draft, or a typed draft. Today, with the use of electronic communication such as electronic mail, some documents are not printed before transmission. However, for important documents, when errors could be extremely devastating, proofreading a printed document is a necessity.

Responsibility for Quality

Business writers are responsible for the quality of their communications no matter who prepares the final document.

Office personnel sometimes overlook the proofreading process because each person expects someone else to do it. The keyboarder may think that the document originator will proofread each communication. The writer may think that the keyboarder will find and correct all errors before submitting the document for final approval or signature. Ideally, proofreading is a team effort. Both the keyboarder and the writer should carefully proofread each document. The final responsibility, however, definitely rests with the writer.

Proofreading for Yourself and for Others

Proofreading is an essential step in the writing process, whether you are proofreading your own work or someone else's. As a student or as an office professional, you must get into the proofreading habit. Grades will suffer if errors are found on a research paper, and a potential salary increase or promotion may be lost if errors are found in a sales report you prepared. Habitual proofreading problems may even result in a loss of one's position.

In a business situation, you may have responsibilities for writing memos or reports. You would, therefore, need to proofread your own work. Often, a coworker, realizing the importance of an error-free document, will ask you to check his or her work for errors. Occasionally, you might ask others to proofread your work, but you do not want to convey to them that you lack proofreading skills. If you keyboard business letters, reports, or other correspondence, you must proofread as an important step in document preparation.

Proofreading your own writing is usually considered more difficult than proofreading the work of others for two reasons. First, you, as the writer, may tend to be overconfident, believing that you corrected all errors during the keyboarding process. Second, you may be overly familiar with the document, which may cause you to "read" what you *intended* to type instead of reading what you *actually* typed. Have you ever had this experience? A friend reads something you wrote and almost immediately finds an error that escaped your detection. This friend provided the benefit of a fresh set of eyes and therefore was neither overconfident of keyboarding accuracy nor overly familiar with the document.

KEY POINT

The final responsibility for the quality of the document rests with the writer.

KEY POINT

Ideally, proofreading should be a team effort of all those involved with the document preparation process.

I was absent from work yesterday because I had a head.

Proofreading and Technology

Technology offers some assistance in proofreading for spelling and keyboarding errors. Most word processing programs have spelling checkers that will locate words not recognized by their built-in dictionaries. However, spelling checkers will not locate a missing word or a misused word if it is correctly spelled. For example, the error in the following sentence would be undetected if you relied on a spelling checker alone.

Incorrect

We submitted the completed form *bye* March 2.

Hour company *if* the number *won* manufacturer of plastic containers in *their* country.

Correct

We submitted the completed form *by* March 2.

Our company *is* the number *one* manufacturer of plastic containers in *the* country.

Some spelling checkers will find repetition errors like this one:

He gave me *the the* calendar.

Technology streamlines the process of making identical changes, called *global changes,* throughout a document. Suppose, for example, you mentioned the name *Steven Smathers* five times in a document. After keyboarding, you learn that the correct spelling is *Stephen Smathers*. Using the global function, you would have to make the correction only once; the other four changes would be made automatically.

Proofreading on the computer screen is similar in many ways to proofreading a printed page. However, you must condition your eyes

Technology

Even though computers have made changing and correcting documents easier, automated equipment is only as good as the person operating it.

and mind to this different medium. Note the following techniques that are useful for finding errors on the computer screen.

Checklist for Proofreading on the Computer Screen
❏ Spell-check the document.
❏ Use a grammar checker to detect usage errors.
❏ Scroll through the document, proofreading line by line as each line appears at the bottom of the screen.
❏ Move the insertion point through the document checking each word as the insertion point encounters it.
❏ Use a piece of paper or your finger to guide your eyes as you proofread line by line down the screen.

Try each method and select the ones that work best for you. Some writers make the mistake of waiting until they print the document before proofreading it. You should do your first proofreading on the screen, make the necessary changes and corrections, and then print a copy. You should also proofread the printed copy to make sure that your changes were entered correctly. Experience will help you build confidence and skill in proofreading on the computer screen.

IMPORTANCE OF PROOFREADING

Uncorrected errors create a bad impression. They also can cost your company money and cause other problems. Consider these two examples.

Suppose, in a handwritten draft, you quote a price of $32,453 for a new minivan. When the final copy is keyboarded, the price is incorrectly listed as $23,453. If not detected, this simple transposition of numbers could cost your company $9,000. Correcting the error after the customer receives the incorrect quotation would cause ill will, the loss of a sale, and possibly legal action.

Suppose, on a travel itinerary, the airplane departure time is erroneously listed as 10:50 instead of the correct time of 10:05. This simple transposition could cause the recipient to miss the flight.

In both examples, efficient proofreading would result in the error being caught. For this reason, executives encourage the detection and correction of errors to prevent problems. Therefore, it is essential that you approach proofreading in a systematic way.

Steps in Proofreading

After using the electronic tools available to you, such as spelling checkers and grammar checkers, use the Proofreading Checklist as part of

The farmer bought 200 cows for his diary.

on-screen proofreading and later when proofreading printed documents. You need not use *all* these techniques in every document.

Proofreading Checklist

☐ Use a bright-colored pen when inserting proofreaders' marks. The bright colors make changes easier to spot.

☐ Quickly scan for such obvious problems as format errors. Are the date and other standard parts included in letters and memos? Do all headings in a report follow the same format?

☐ Check typeface styles and sizes. Is the same font style and size used for similar headings?

☐ Turn the document upside down to check for spacing and placement errors.

☐ Superimpose subsequent drafts over previous drafts and hold the superimposed drafts up to a light to detect possible errors.

☐ Read carefully for correct content, making sure that there are no factual errors and that no words, sentences, paragraphs, and other portions of text were omitted.

☐ Make sure that text that has been moved electronically does not appear in both the original position and the new location.

☐ Read for correct capitalization, grammar, word usage, number usage, punctuation, spelling, typing, and word division.

☐ Read the document backward, from right to left, to help detect spelling and punctuation errors by concentrating on each word separately.

☐ Give special attention to locations where errors frequently occur: (*a*) at the end of a page and the top of the next page, (*b*) in line endings and line beginnings, (*c*) in numerical and alphabetized lists, and (*d*) in cross-references to items ("for example, see the map on page 3") that appear on other pages of the text.

☐ As a separate step, check all numbers and technical terms for accuracy. Use a calculator to add columns of figures. This process verifies that the total is correct and that the figures contributing to the total are correct.

☐ Ask a coworker to proofread the document.

☐ Read the document aloud. Reading aloud increases concentration and thus helps you identify awkward sentences and other problems that might not be as obvious when you are reading silently.

☐ After making all changes and corrections, check the final copy to verify that changes were correctly made and that no new errors were introduced.

World View

Proofreading place names and personal names from other languages such as Spanish, Chinese, and Japanese is a particular challenge. Consult a dictionary for the language or a style guide for guidance in terms of spelling and use of accent marks.

Practical Application

A. For each underlined word or combination of words in the following sentences, find a more colorful synonym in a thesaurus. Then rewrite the sentences on a separate sheet of paper, replacing each underlined word with a synonym.
1. Slow drivers <u>annoy</u> my brother.
2. Nate's <u>accident</u> occurred when he <u>fell</u> on the ice.
3. Everyone saw the <u>fancy</u> box on Catherine's desk, but no one knew what was inside it.
4. Rafael <u>told us</u> a <u>funny</u> incident that happened yesterday.
5. Dana <u>quickly ate</u> the food on her plate.

B. On a separate sheet of paper, write *Yes* if the names are the same in both columns. Write *No* if they are different.

1. Antionné Jacqués   Antionné Jacques
2. I. Anthony Negbenebor, Ph.D.   I. Anthony Negbenebor, PH.d.
3. Sabine Reyes Ulibarri   Sabine Reyes Ulibarrí
4. Dr. Ricardo E. Rosa   Dr. Ricardo E. Rosa
5. Señora Angelica R. Guzman   Señora Angelia R. Guzman
6. Mario Albierto Iglesia   Mario Albierto Iglesia
7. Ejauhase Ushomo   Ejuwhase Ushomo
8. Mr. and Mrs. Mark Rice   Mr. and Mrs. Mark Rice
9. Mr. and Mrs. Kevin Dalton   Mr. and Mrs. Kevin Dalten
10. Dr. Santiago H. Espinosa   Dr. Santiago H. Espinosa

C. On a separate sheet of paper, write *Yes* if the items are the same in both columns. Write *No* if they are different.

1. 789836B   789863B
2. $3786.45   37866.45
3. 9833V39   9833V39
4. LT817745   LT187745
5. www.glotel.net/~adave/ html/loco.html   www.glotel.net/~adave/ html/loco.html
6. 9-011-234-1-86382   9-011-234-1-86382
7. July 21, 1997   July 12, 1997
8. 23 case @$32   32 cases @$23
9. S768R3456J789   S768R3546J789
10. 9-011-44-01-3827142   9-011-44-01-327142
11. $212,845,321.32   212,845,321.32
12. 905-682-1482   905-682-1482

13. June 27, 1999	June 27, 1999
14. 1995-1999	1985-1999
15. 125,673,281	125,683,281
16. 489 pages	498 pages
17. 28027-3925	28027-3925
18. 12:38.09 a.m.	12:38.09 p.m.
19. 214-778-8685	214-778-8685
20. 1,787 pounds	1,787 pounds

D. On a separate sheet of paper, edit each sentence to make any necessary corrections.
  1. Dr. Sam Martinez autographed copys of his latest book, *Healthy Eating for Busy Executives*.
  2. His letter was mis interpreted by the the newspaper editor.
  3. Phils Deli Shop opens dialy at 10:30 a.m. and closes at 8 in the evening.
  4. The camera were shipped February 10, and the film.
  5. Mrs. Anderson I apprecciate you willingness to participate our in fund-raising events.
  6. The shipment will arrive in 3 days.
  7. Many business expenses are tax deductable.
  8. Tom an Mariel are looking forward to Their Summer Vacation.
  9. Alexandra went to Mexico, and to south America.
  10. We need a new Zip CODE Directory.

E. On a separate sheet of paper, edit the following sentences to eliminate unnecessary words and to use clearer wording.
  1. We found the new computers to be adequate enough.
  2. Kindly return your completed form by August 4.
  3. All committee members need to cooperate together.
  4. Almost all of the gratis samples have been given away.
  5. Our past experience with this supplier has been positive.

F. On a separate sheet of paper, edit the following sentences to eliminate inconsistencies.
  1. Mark Rummel and Ms. Frances Weekley conducted the training session.
  2. Over 70 percent of our clients travel in April, June, and May.
  3. Of the 7 applicants, only three have programming experience.
  4. We ordered the books *Legal Procedures* and NOT LIABLE for the law library.
  5. Doctors Klein, Smyth, and Jergens are opening a new office.

G. On a separate sheet of paper, edit the following sentences to make them positive and to achieve the you-attitude.
   1. If you are unable to understand the operating instructions for your computer, please call our toll-free number for assistance.
   2. Your delay in completing the report put us behind schedule.
   3. We are sorry we cannot ship your complete order at this time.
   4. I need you to process the patients' insurance forms by this afternoon.

H. On a separate sheet of paper, rewrite the following paragraph, making any necessary changes and corrections. Assume that Monday is July 1.

   Nancy Threlkeld will assume the position of Director of Employee Activities on Monday, July 1. In this position, she will be in charge of and responsible for athletic teams, organizations, trips, and all other social events sponsored by our company. On Wednesday, July 3, she will attend a conference to learn about activities offered by other companies. She will have a meeting Tuesday, July 2, at 2:30 p.m., in the Recreation Hall, to get your suggestions for August and September activities.

Editing Practice

Choosing the Right Word. On a separate sheet of paper, make a list of words used incorrectly in the following paragraph. Beside each incorrect word, write the correct word that should have been used.

   In the passed ate weaks, my assistance have placed twenty adds in you're newspaper. As you may no, their was some confusion about the invoice. Your paper accidentally build us twice for the same advertisements. Will you please make an appropriate adjustment to our account. Advertising with you has been affective in increasing our sales, and we plan to buy more advertising space soon.

Revising for Tact. Martin Reeves works as the administrative assistant to Kelly Austin, the human resources director of a large manufacturing company. Kelly relies on Martin to edit and proofread all her correspondence.

Kelly has drafted a memo to be distributed to all employees and has asked Martin to finalize the memo.

Read the following paragraph from the memo, which is the first notice regarding the abuse of coffee breaks. If you were Martin, what changes would you make to improve the memo? Keep in mind that your revision should be tactful in order to foster cooperation.

Employees are spending too much time in the coffee room. They are spending their time drinking coffee, rather than doing their work. The coffee room was first opened five years ago. The room temperature is always uncomfortable. It might be stopped by the senior officers if people don't stop misusing the privilege of using it. I would be very sorry to see that happen.

Proving Yourself in Writing. Megan, an accountant with Dandridge Associates, has been with the company two years. During that time she has worked hard to prove herself. She completes her work on time and under budget, she looks for creative solutions, and she accepts additional responsibilities. Megan wishes to advance to a higher-level position within the company. As part of the advancement-seeking process, she has decided to write a memo to her supervisor. In the memo, Megan plans to analyze her strengths and weaknesses, her reasons for seeking promotion, and her qualifications for promotion.

Adopt the role of Megan. Write the body paragraphs of the memo that you would write to your supervisor. Keep the guidelines for writing effective sentences and paragraphs in mind as you compose your message.

As Margaret Reilly enters the reception area of the Carrigan Building, she is greeted by the warm smile and friendly voice of the receptionist asking, "May I help you?" She replies, "I'm Margaret Reilly. I have a ten o'clock appointment with Ms. Truillo, the director of marketing."

"Ms. Truillo's office is on the fifth floor, Suite 528. She is expecting you; I'll let Ms. Truillo know that you are on your way to her office," the receptionist responds. She then directs the caller to an elevator.

Margaret is favorably impressed with the Carrigan Company as a result of this first encounter with one of its employees at the company's headquarters. Margaret's initial contact with the Carrigan Company was a telephone call to discuss her company's services in developing presentations for clients. Now she will be meeting with the director of marketing, who has expressed an interest in having Margaret's company develop presentations for the Carrigan Company. If Margaret gets the account, one of her main responsibilities will be to design and present electronic presentations for Carrigan's sales and marketing campaigns. She would also develop presentations for Carrigan when area schools, colleges, and civic groups request a speaker from the company.

As Margaret steps from the elevator on the fifth floor into the marketing department of the Carrigan Company, she notices that the staff members are busily engaged in a variety of activities. A young man approaches her. "Good morning, Ms. Reilly; I'm Bradley Smith, Ms. Truillo's administrative assistant. Ms. Truillo will be with you as soon as she completes a conference call with three of our European sales representatives. Please make yourself comfortable. Would you like a cup of coffee or tea?"

"Thank you, no," Margaret answers as she glances around the busy office. She notices several associates quietly engaged in telephone conversations. In one corner, someone is explaining and demonstrating how to operate a new copying machine. Margaret notices that the copying machine demonstration is being interpreted into sign language for one of the office associates. In a glass-enclosed conference area, a small group is seated around a conference table, participating in a teleconference. Margaret's communication instructor was right—oral communication *does* play an important role in the daily activities of every office employee! Then, as Margaret is shown into Ms. Truillo's office, she realizes how fortunate she is to have had training in oral communication. She is about to make a presentation to an important potential client, and now is the opportunity for her to put her oral communications training into action.

As you read Chapter 8, identify some strategies that Margaret could use to make a successful oral presentation.

SECTIONS

8.1 Basics of Oral Communication

8.2 Nonverbal Communication and Speech Qualities

8.3 Conducting Meetings and Communicating in Groups

8.4 Formal and Informal Presentations

Basics of Oral Communication

OBJECTIVES:

After completing Section 8.1, you should be able to:

1. Explain the importance of oral communication in business.
2. Describe the various forms of oral communication.
3. List guidelines for effective one-on-one communication.
4. Discuss basic procedures for meeting the public.
5. Describe proper techniques for originating and receiving telephone calls.

One does not speak unless he can improve upon the silence.

—Chinese proverb

As you saw in the case at the beginning of the chapter, Margaret was convinced of the importance of oral communication in the business world. This conviction, however, grew after her visit to the Carrigan Company. From the receptionist who greeted her in the lobby to the director of marketing, information was continually being transmitted orally from one employee to another; from employees to customers and vendors; and from customers, vendors, and other outsiders to employees of the firm. The success of any business organization depends, to a very large degree, upon the success of its members in making themselves understood and in persuading others to accept their ideas.

THE IMPORTANCE OF ORAL COMMUNICATION IN BUSINESS

Although written communication is important in transacting business, oral communication is used more often and by more people. Some business positions require the use of oral communication almost exclusively, and the people who fill these jobs are hired on the strength of their ability to speak well. Sales associates, administrative assistants, customer-service representatives, paralegals, and medical assistants—all these people must be highly skilled in oral communication. These and other business professionals make extensive use of oral communication in carrying out their job responsibilities.

Your ability to speak clearly, correctly, and convincingly will play a vital role in helping you achieve success in the business world. On many occasions, you will do much of the talking. You will seek to solve problems; you will participate in and conduct meetings and small-group discussions; you will speak to supervisors and colleagues, to the public, and to business and professional groups. In your daily contacts with those inside and outside your organization, you will use oral communication to make requests, provide instructions, and give information.

KEY POINT

Oral communication is used more often than written communication and by more people.

KEY POINT

The effectiveness of your oral communication both inside and outside the organization will influence your chances for personal success.

THE ROLE OF ORAL COMMUNICATION IN BUSINESS

Business professionals use oral communication in a variety of ways and settings. Professionals depend upon oral communication when engaged in such activities as the following.

- *Explaining or reporting to supervisors, subordinates, and associates on the same level.* Report to a supervisor about the status of a project; direct a coworker to complete a task.
- *Giving information to customers and potential customers.* Answer face-to-face or telephone inquiries about items or services offered by your company; give presentations describing products and services provided.
- *Acquiring information necessary to conduct the everyday affairs of business.* Speak with vendors and suppliers to request information about products or order supplies; speak with outside consultants such as accountants, attorneys, and computer specialists.
- *Participating in meetings.* Meet with coworkers and supervisors to discuss current and future projects; meet with consultants or customers to discuss products and services.
- *Participating in informal discussion with fellow employees.* Ask coworkers to contribute for flowers for a hospitalized colleague; plan recreational functions for employees; attend an informal get-together for employees at someone's home.
- *Giving instruction to an individual or a group.* Train new employees; instruct customers in the use of newly purchased products; instruct patients in caring for themselves.
- *Interviewing employees and prospective employees.* Interview job applicants; participate in performance appraisals.
- *Participating in social-business conversations.* Engage in conversation with representatives from civic and professional organizations; congratulate associates and business acquaintances on their accomplishments.
- *Giving formal speeches before groups.* Give a speech before a civic group; talk to a class of college students about your work experience.

These are just a few examples of oral communication activities that take place every day in professional settings—activities that rely for their success almost wholly upon effective oral communication.

OOPS!

Job applicant at an interview: "I have an obsession for detail; I like to make sure I cross my *i*'s and dot my *t*'s."

FORMS OF ORAL COMMUNICATION

Oral communication occurs in many different forms, some used more frequently than others. Among the most commonly used methods of oral communication are the following:

- *Face-to-face conversations*—interviews, sales, social-business situations, informal discussions with coworkers.
- *Group discussions or meetings*—employee group discussions, team meetings, meetings of business and professional organizations.

- *Telephone conversations*—with a colleague, a supervisor, a customer, or a supplier.
- *Voice-mail messages*—recording a telephone message for someone to hear at a later time.
- *Formal speeches*—debates; panels; addresses to employees, the public, customers, or professional groups.
- *Instruction*—conducting training for new employees such as sales representatives and users of information processing systems.
- *Dictation and recording*—dictating letters and memos for transcription or recording meetings electronically.

Each of these forms of oral communication requires a slightly different technique. The difference may be (1) the amount and kind of preparation, (2) the manner in which the voice is projected, or (3) the style in which the speaker makes the presentation. For example, speaking over the telephone requires a knowledge of how far to hold the telephone mouthpiece from the lips and how much the speaker's voice should be projected. Leading a meeting requires a knowledge of parliamentary procedure. Teaching a class requires that the instructor know how to ask questions properly. Participating in a team meeting requires the ability to think quickly and to put thoughts into understandable language without hesitation.

EFFECTIVE BUSINESS RELATIONSHIPS THROUGH ORAL COMMUNICATION

Good oral communication establishes an environment that encourages a flow of information and ideas between management and employees. When employees can discuss their ideas and concerns freely and easily, morale is likely to be high—and when morale is high, work efficiency is greater. Personal conferences with employees, committee meetings, team meetings, and informational question-and-answer sessions are some of the situations in which oral communication contributes to improved relations between employees and between management and employees.

Oral communication contributes to effective public relations by ensuring that every spoken communication with a caller or visitor is a positive experience. Every employee who has contact with the public plays an important role in developing and promoting the company image. From the receptionist to the chief executive officer, those who speak for the company *are* the company to the people who do business with that organization.

The manner in which a customer is treated on the telephone or in person is just as important in developing goodwill as good written

Technology

Cellular phones, in-flight telephone services offered by airlines, and pagers make oral communication accessible in a wide variety of places.

KEY POINT

To improve public relations, make sure that oral communication with customers is a positive experience.

Figure 8.1

Effective oral communication is extremely important in promoting good public relations. How can an employee's oral communication influence the public's impression of an organization?

communication is—sometimes even more important. *All* employees—technicians, salespersons, administrative assistants, accountants, paralegals, medical assistants, receptionists—create a public image of the company they represent by the manner in which they speak to current and potential clients and customers. A curt or rude employee can cause a business to lose sales—and even to lose customers of long standing. In a telephone conversation or a face-to-face conversation, the employee must, through the words and tone used, make these customers feel that their interests are important and that the company wants them to be satisfied.

KEY POINT

Every contact with the public helps develop and promote the company image.

IMPROVING YOUR ORAL COMMUNICATION SKILLS

The case study at the beginning of this chapter illustrates how oral communication can influence a person's initial impression of a company. The receptionist's greeting certainly contributed to Margaret's positive impression of the company. Also, it is clear from the case study that a variety of speaking situations play an important role in the performance of many employees' daily tasks.

The manner in which you use your oral communication skills at work can either help or hinder you in performing your everyday activities and advancing to higher positions.

Guidelines for one-to-one
communication:
- Listen attentively.
- Use the person's name.
- Permit others to talk.
- Compliment when suitable.
- Keep conversations concise.
- Establish the best
  atmosphere.

COMMUNICATING ONE-TO-ONE

High on the list of communication activities for most business employees is communicating orally on a one-to-one basis. Business employees talk with colleagues in their own departments, with their supervisors, with top management, and with service personnel many times during the working day.

In addition, many employees talk either on the telephone or in person with individuals outside the company—customers, clients, patients, sales representatives, suppliers, visitors, and various people soliciting or giving information. Many business employees depend heavily on their oral communication skills to earn their living—sales representatives, personnel interviewers, and customer service representatives are just a few examples.

Use the following suggestions as guidelines for communicating effectively on a one-to-one basis, whether speaking to someone in person or over the telephone.

Listen Attentively

Listening attentively and showing interest in the other person are just two attributes of a good communicator. In a one-to-one or telephone conversation, you alternate between the roles of speaker and listener. As a speaker, part of your responsibility is to listen to what the other person says, to be courteous, and to get the necessary information. For example, a sales associate should listen to a customer's inquiry or complaint in order to know how to answer the customer. A medical assistant needs to ask questions and then listen to the patient's responses to find out about the patient's illness.

Use the Person's Name

KEY POINT

Using a person's name during
a conversation demonstrates
your interest in what is being
said.

Be certain that you clearly hear the name of the person whom you have met or talked with on the telephone for the first time. Repeat the name right after it is given to you: "I'm happy to meet you, Ms. Althanais." If you aren't absolutely sure of the person's name, ask that it be repeated; you can say, "I didn't hear your name clearly" or "How do you pronounce (or spell) your name?" Then, after hearing the name, pronounce it aloud in order to fix it in your mind. Whenever it is appropriate, use the name once or twice during the conversation: "Yes, I understand, Ms. Althanais." Finally, always be sure that you say the person's name in your good-bye: "Good-bye, Ms. Althanais; I enjoyed talking with you."

Permit Others to Talk

Don't do all of the talking. Give the other person a chance to talk, while you listen attentively. Watch for signs that the other person wants to say something or is becoming bored and not listening carefully. No matter how interesting you think the conversation is or how well informed or articulate you think you are, you must give your listener a chance to speak. Otherwise, you will not keep your listener's attention and respect. For example, you might ask questions to let the listener know you are interested in receiving feedback.

Compliment When Suitable

Compliments are always welcome, so compliment someone whenever the occasion is suitable. Paying a compliment is especially effective during tense situations. If a valued employee or a customer has a complaint that you cannot justify or remedy, you can put that person in a better frame of mind for a no answer by paying a compliment. For example, compliment the employee for work well done and compliment the customer for paying promptly. However, never pay a compliment unless you can do so honestly and convincingly. Insincerity is easily detected.

Keep Conversations Concise

Since time is valuable, you should keep your conversations to the point. If you are asked for opinions, give them clearly and concisely. Being concise, however, does not mean you must be brusque. Try to sense the amount of information the situation calls for and act accordingly. Most people do not want to hear unnecessary details or to listen to prolonged excuses for your inability to do something they have requested. Give enough information to satisfy the listener. If you are in doubt, the best policy is to keep your conversation short.

Establish the Best Atmosphere

One way to establish good relations with colleagues and customers is to create a relaxed, conversational atmosphere. You can accomplish this in one-to-one conversations by sitting or standing so that there are no physical barriers between you and the listener. When speaking on the telephone, focus on the conversation instead of doing other tasks, such as working at the computer. Giving the other person your undivided attention shows courtesy and respect.

COMMUNICATING BY TELEPHONE

Communicating by telephone requires techniques that are somewhat different from those used in one-to-one conversations. Since the speaker and the listener in a telephone conversation are unable to see

KEY POINT

In all conversations, be generous with praise when it is timely and when it is deserved.

each other, they must depend entirely upon their voices to communicate friendliness, interest, and a willingness to be helpful.

The telephone is one of the most important communication media in business. You must use it with great skill, whether you are speaking to callers from inside or outside the organization.

Although we are familiar with using the telephone, we may not be using it properly. Some of the following suggestions may seem obvious. Nevertheless, you should read them carefully and follow them whenever you use the telephone for either personal or business use.

- Talk directly into the mouthpiece.
- Talk slowly and naturally. Exaggerate your enunciation slightly. Do not shout.
- If you must transfer a caller to someone else in the company, say, "If you will please hold for a moment, I will transfer your call." Give the caller the name and phone number of the person to whom you are transferring the call, in case the transfer does not go through. Stay on the line to announce the transfer.
- If, while talking, you must put down the receiver, either put the caller on hold or place the receiver on a book or magazine rather than on a hard surface.
- Place the receiver gently in the cradle when you hang up.

Courtesy is the key to effective telephone communication. Greet all callers pleasantly. This pleasantness is achieved both by the words you use and by the tone of your voice. If you know who the caller is, use a greeting such as "Good morning, Mr. Random" or "Hello, Teresa." If you do not know who the caller is, identify yourself first: "Ms. Rossi speaking" or "Karen Jergens." When answering the telephone for a department, identify both the department and yourself: "Accounting Department, Ms. Jung."

Your voice should be friendly and your manner courteous, regardless of who is calling. This manner is especially important when you are talking to outside callers. Remember that the impression created by your voice should be that of a friendly smile. Show the caller that you want to be helpful: Always listen attentively and don't interrupt. Make an occasional comment such as "Yes" or "I understand" to let the caller know you are listening. Use the caller's name at least once before hanging up, and conclude the call with a remark like "Thank you for calling, Ms. Dawkins" or "We will look into the matter for you right away, Mr. Koch."

Originating Calls

To make the best use of your telephone time, follow these suggestions for originating calls:

KEY POINT

Smile as you speak on the telephone. The smile will relax your facial muscles and vocal cords, making your voice sound relaxed and pleasant.

1. Plan the conversation before you call. A little preparation will save both time and money. If your conversation will be an involved one, jot down notes in advance.
2. Identify yourself promptly and state the purpose of your call. For example, say, "This is Manuel Sully of Miracle Plastics. I would like to speak to the person in charge of new accounts."
3. Be prepared to leave a voice-mail message if the person you are calling does not answer.

Receiving Calls

To ensure efficient use of the telephone when you receive a call, follow these suggestions:

1. Answer promptly and identify yourself immediately. You should answer at the first ring, if possible, and not later than the second ring.
2. Respond to inquiries graciously; take notes; and verify important details such as account numbers, model numbers, dates, and names.
3. At the close of the conversation, take the required action. Be certain that you keep all the promises you make to the caller.
4. Allow the caller to hang up first.
5. If you are going to be away from your telephone, leave a voice-mail greeting that indicates the type of message callers should leave in your absence.
6. If you must put a caller on hold, inform the caller of this fact. Ask the caller if he or she would prefer to be placed on hold or would prefer for you to return the call later.

SECTION 8.1   REVIEW

Practical Application

A. For each of the following business positions, indicate the oral communication activities that you think would be typical in that position. Use a separate sheet of paper.
1. Administrative assistant
2. Paralegal
3. Medical assistant

    4. Accountant

    5. Sales representative

B. On a separate sheet of paper, under three headings—Home, School, Business—list as many oral communication activities as you can.

C. You are an administrative assistant for Ronald Quinn, the president of Quick-Read Books, a discount book publisher. Mr. Quinn has placed you in charge of making arrangements for a conference with Quick-Read's main suppliers to be held at your company's headquarters next month. One of your responsibilities is to contact the suppliers and arrange for their travel and hotel accommodations. On a separate sheet of paper, outline the notes you would make to prepare for making the calls. Include details such as the dates, times, and information on how to reach you.

D. Practice reading aloud the following instructions for talking on the telephone so that you do not sound as though you are reading the material or have memorized it. Then make a tape recording of your presentation to determine if you achieved your goal. Review the tape to see if you enunciated distinctly.

    Clear enunciation is extremely important if you wish to be understood by the listener. Each word and each syllable must be pronounced distinctly. Your voice should be well modulated, and you should move your lips, tongue, and jaw freely. Hold the mouthpiece about an inch from your mouth, speaking directly into the receiver. Keep your mouth free of gum, candy, and other objects that could affect your pronunciation or cause you to slur your words. You can usually tell if your words are being heard clearly by the number of times the listener asks you to repeat what you have said.

E. Without using any gestures or diagrams, give oral directions for the following situations:

    1. How to get from your classroom to the campus library.

    2. How to get to the administration building of your school from your classroom.

    3. How to fold a letter for insertion in a standard-sized envelope.

F. Orally describe an object without telling the class what the object is. If you have described the object clearly, the class should be able to identify it from your description.

Editing Practice

Spelling and Vocabulary. Some of the following sentences contain spelling errors; some test vocabulary; some are correct. Using a separate sheet of paper, correct each incorrect sentence. Write *OK* for any sentence that has no error.

1. How will the new policy effect office morale?
2. What plans does your company have for desposal of used paper?
3. Which proceedures apply to this job?
4. Let's plan a luncheon to celabrate Pat's promotion.
5. What was the occasion for the early closing of the store?
6. The new computer equiptment arrived this morning.
7. Have you recieved the specifications yet?
8. The new superviser was formally introduced to the employees today.
9. I adviced the new employee to take a public speaking course.
10. On which sight will the new factory be build?

Critical Thinking Skills

Justify. Be prepared to take the affirmative or negative side in a debate on this topic. *Resolved:* That entry-level business employees do not need effective oral communication skills as much as more experienced business employees.

Nonverbal Communication and Speech Qualities

It's a luxury to be understood.

—Ralph Waldo Emerson

In most business situations, oral communication is used at least as often as, if not more frequently than, written communication. Furthermore, obtaining a good position and succeeding in it depend very heavily upon persuasive oral skills. For these reasons, it is important that you pay attention to two major factors that determine a person's effectiveness in communicating orally—physical appearance and speech qualities.

APPEARANCE

Except for situations involving the telephone or voice mail, the speaker is visible to the listener and creates a visual impression that often influences the acceptability of his or her words to that listener. This first

SECTION 8.2

OBJECTIVES:
After completing Section 8.2, you should be able to:

1. Use body language effectively in oral communication.
2. Demonstrate good grooming and appropriate dress in various oral communication situations.
3. Use speech qualities effectively when speaking to others.
4. Distinguish between enunciation and pronunciation.
5. List four steps for improving enunciation and pronunciation.

impression is based primarily on the speaker's posture, gestures, eye contact with the listener, body and head movements, and overall personal appearance—dress, grooming, and so on.

In both casual and formal speaking situations, a speaker's physical appearance often sets the stage for the acceptance or nonacceptance of the speaker's words. A person who makes a good physical impression quickly gains the interest of listeners. Of course, a speaker must have something interesting and worthwhile to say—and must say it in an effective manner—to hold the attention of the listeners for any length of time. However, the first barrier to effective oral communication will be overcome if the speaker has good posture, is dressed appropriately, is well-groomed, and uses eye contact to make each listener feel that he or she is being spoken to directly.

Posture

Many people underestimate the importance of good posture to overall good physical appearance. Regardless of how tall you are, always stand up to your full height. You'll find that good posture will help you develop better breath control. Good posture will also make you appear more confident and give your listeners the impression that you know what you are talking about and that your message is important. Of course, no speaker should appear stiff or pompous; you don't want to look like a stick of wood. Instead, develop a natural posture, constantly reminding yourself to stand erect, with shoulders back and stomach in.

Gestures

While you are talking, do not distract your listeners by pulling at your clothing, putting your hands to your face or hair, or toying with an object such as a paper clip, a rubber band, or your eyeglasses. Listeners will become distracted by your physical maneuvers and will lose track of what you are saying.

If you are standing, place your arms and hands in a relaxed position at your sides (rather than behind your back of folded in front of you). From time to time, make natural gestures. If you are delivering a speech and there is a lectern in front of you, you may wish to place your hands on either side of it. However, remember *never* to lean on the lectern!

When you are talking from a sitting position, you will be heard better if you sit slightly forward in your chair. Rest your arms and hands in your lap, on the arms of the chair in which you are sitting, or partially on the edge of the table or desk in front of you. However, never rest your elbows on the desk or table. Lazy-looking speakers encourage apathy on the part of their listeners.

KEY POINT

A speaker's physical appearance affects the listener's acceptance or nonacceptance of the speaker's words.

KEY POINT

Good posture helps improve your voice quality and gives you the appearance of authority.

World View

Certain common American gestures are considered rude in other cultures. For example, the "OK" gesture made with the thumb and forefinger is considered obscene in some European countries.

Figure 8.2
A speaker's facial expression influences the listener's impression of the speaker. What can speakers do to become more aware of their facial expressions?

Facial Expressions

A speaker's facial expression influences the listeners' impressions. A relaxed, pleasant, interested expression will create a better atmosphere for communicating than a wrinkled brow and turned-down mouth. As you look in a mirror from time to time, see whether your facial expression captures your personality as others see it.

- Are your facial muscles relaxed?
- Is your smile natural, pleasant, and genuine?
- Does your facial expression convey interest and enthusiasm?

Practice developing animation and showing enthusiasm in your facial expression.

Eye Contact

One of the best ways to show interest is to look at your audience, whether that audience includes just one person or more than a hundred people. Everyone likes to feel directly addressed by the speaker. Therefore, your eyes should never leave your listeners for any extended period of time; it's hard for them to stay interested when you are looking constantly at your notes, at the ceiling, or out the window. When talking to one or two people, look them squarely in the face without staring at them, unless you are directing their attention to a visual aid. When speaking to a large audience, move your eyes over the entire audience; look into the faces of your listeners and not over the tops of their heads.

Body Movement

Body movement also contributes a great deal to the physical effect a speaker creates. The effective speaker never paces back and forth, because excessive movement will distract listeners. You may turn from side to side or move forward to add emphasis to a remark. Occasionally, you may even want to take a step toward your listeners to emphasize an important point or a step sideways to signal a transition in what you are discussing. If you are using a chart or other visual aid, move to the visual aid from time to time.

Nervousness

When you are talking to a group, pretend that you are carrying on a face-to-face conversation with just one person in the group. Remember that the audience is just as eager for you to perform well as you are to do so. Don't be upset if you are nervous—even experienced speakers are. Feeling nervous is a result of anxiety about doing a good job, and most authorities believe that a little stage fright provides needed tension.

Grooming and Dress

Personal appearance—grooming, cleanliness, and attire—is also an important factor in effective oral communication. How you look and dress expresses your personality just as much as your speech and conduct do. Good appearance gives you confidence. Appearing clean and neatly dressed; avoiding extremes in jewelry, hairstyles, and clothing styles; and selecting clothing and accessories that are tasteful and in harmony with one another are some of the factors of personal appearance that you should consider.

SPEECH QUALITIES

Although a speaker's physical appearance creates the first impression on listeners, the quality of speech may have an even greater influence on them. The quality of speech is determined by these voice attributes: volume, pitch, tone, rate, enunciation, and pronunciation.

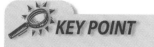
KEY POINT

When speaking, face your listeners as much as possible and stay in one place most of the time.

Force (Volume)

For oral communication to be effective, your voice must be clearly heard. Sufficient volume, achieved through good breath control, is important. If your voice is too soft and you have trouble being heard, practice breathing deeply and controlling your breath with your diaphragm and abdominal muscles, just as a singer does. The large abdominal cavity should be used to store a supply of air that can be released evenly to produce a clear, sustained tone. How much force you must use is determined by the acoustics in the room in which you are talking, the size of your audience, and whether or not you are using a microphone or other electronic device to amplify your voice.

KEY POINT

The force, or volume, needed is determined by the acoustics of the room, the size of your audience, and the availability of a microphone.

Pitch (Voice Level)

A speaker's voice will be more audible if it has a pleasing pitch. *Pitch* refers to the level of a sound on a musical scale. Practice can help correct the shrillness of a voice that is pitched too high or the excessive resonance of a voice that is pitched too low. Another pitch-related problem is the constant pitch that results in a monotone. An effective speaker varies the pitch of his or her voice to help communicate the message. The rising and falling of voice pitch is called *intonation*. Intonation can indicate that a statement is being made, that a question is being asked, or that a speaker is pausing.

A drop in pitch usually signals finality or determination and is, therefore, used at the end of a declarative sentence. For example, in reading the following sentence you should close with a drop in pitch.

I cannot *possibly* explain all the software applications, especially in ten minutes. (Emphasize the word *possibly*.)

A rise in pitch can signal a question or an expression of suspense, doubt, or hesitation. Read the following sentence, closing with a rise in pitch.

What *more* can I do? (Emphasize *more*.)

Gliding the pitch up and down or down and up usually expresses sarcasm or contempt, as in the slang expression "Oh, yeah?"

The most important aspect of pitch is variation. Variation of pitch not only helps hold listeners' attention but also helps listeners know the exact meaning intended by the speaker. A rise in pitch can stress important words. Using the same pitch for each element can stress comparisons; pitching the first element high and the second low, on the other hand, can denote contrasts.

Notice the different shades of meaning that emerge as you read the following sentences and emphasize the italicized words.

Tony gave her the special assignment. (Tony did, not someone else.)

Tony *gave* her the special assignment. (She did not earn it.)

KEY POINT

An effective speaker uses variation in pitch to hold the listeners' attention and to convey meaning.

Tony gave *her* the special assignment. (Only she was given the special assignment.)

Tony gave her the *special* assignment (The particular, or special, assignment.)

Tony gave her the special *assignment*. (He gave her the special assignment, not something else special.)

Tone

The tone of your voice often reveals your attitudes and feelings. A pleasant and cheerful tone is desirable because it will have a good effect on your listeners. On the telephone, the tone of your voice must substitute for your facial expression. In addition, you can use variation in tone, as well as in volume and pitch, to add interest to your speaking voice. The kind of tone you use should be appropriate for the words and ideas you are expressing.

Speaking Rate (Tempo)

The rate at which you speak should be varied to avoid extremes in either direction. Most people tend to speak too rapidly. Although you should not speak so rapidly that your words are not understood, neither should you speak so slowly that your listeners lose track of what you are saying. Regulate your rate of speaking so that you can say each word clearly. The listener should hear each word without difficulty.

A good speaking rate is 125 words a minute; oral reading rates tend to run slightly faster—about 150 words a minute. To determine what a rate of 125 words a minute sounds like, read aloud the paragraph below in a half minute. Reread the paragraph as many times as necessary until you achieve the desired rate. At the end of 15 seconds, you should be at the diagonal line. Use this line as a guide to increase or decrease your speaking rate.

> A good speaker talks slowly enough to be understood by the listeners and speaks in a pleasant voice, articulating and pronouncing each word correctly and distinctly. To develop a good / speaking voice, you must spend sufficient time practicing the elements of good speech. An effective speaker is a definite asset to a business and will usually find more opportunities for advancing in the job. (64 words)

Changing the rate contributes to variety, as well as to clarity. Important words and ideas should be spoken slowly; unimportant words or phrases, more rapidly.

Try to speak in thought units so that you can assist the listener in interpreting your words. If the sentence is short, the thought unit can be the entire sentence, as in "My job is very exciting." When there are several thought units within a sentence, pause slightly after each thought group.

> My job is very exciting; / but I must admit, / some days are almost too exciting.

Use pauses to stress major points. By pausing between major points or after important statements, you add variety and emphasis to the points you want your listeners to remember.

ENUNCIATION AND PRONUNCIATION

In business—and even in social situations—poor enunciation can lead to costly delays, unnecessary expense, and the loss of goodwill. That is why it is so important for all business employees, particularly those who have face-to-face or telephone contact with customers and vendors, to both enunciate and pronounce words clearly and correctly.

Although the terms *enunciation* and *pronunciation* are closely related, they do have slightly different meanings. Understanding the difference between the two terms and making a strong effort to eliminate the barriers to effective enunciation and pronunciation will help you improve your speech.

Enunciation

Enunciation refers to the distinctness or clarity with which you articulate or sound each part of a word. For instance, saying "offen" for *often* or "gonna" for *going to* are examples of careless enunciation. Careless enunciation often occurs in *ing* words, such as "willin" for *willing* and "asking" for *asking*. Also, when we speak rapidly, most of us have a tendency

Because of her manager's poor enunciation, Mona transcribed a statement from his dictation as "forty wall units for $14,000" instead of "fourteen wall units for $14,000." If her supervisor hadn't spotted the discrepancy in the letter, the mistake could have been costly.

 **KEY POINT**

Enunciation refers to the distinctness or clarity with which speakers sound each part of a word.

Figure 8.3

Proper enunciation is important in telephone conversations. What might be some consequences of poor enunciation?

to run our words together, dropping some of the sounds. Saying "dijago" for *did you go* and "meetcha" for *meet you* are examples. A person who slurs too many words is likely to be misunderstood or not heard at all, particularly over the telephone or on transcribing equipment. It is annoying for both the listener and the speaker if the listener must ask the speaker to repeat something several times. Such difficulties can often be avoided if we simply speak more slowly and more carefully.

Pronunciation

Pronunciation refers either to the sound that a speaker gives to the letters or letter combinations that make up a word or to the way in which the speaker accents the word. Note the following examples of mispronunciation and correct pronunciation.

Incorrect Pronunciation	Correct Pronunciation
pro•*noun*•ci•a•tion	pro•*nun*•ci•a•tion
li•*ba*•ry	li•*bra*•ry
com•par'•able	com'•par•able

Of course, there are regional differences in pronunciation; and, in addition, a number of words have more than one acceptable pronunciation. In the latter case, the dictionary lists the preferred pronunciation first.

Many difficulties in pronunciation arise because some letters or combinations of letters are pronounced one way in some words and another way in others. For example, the combination *ow* has an "oh" sound in *know* but an "ow" sound (as in *ouch*) in *now*. Other difficulties in pronunciation arise because a letter may be sounded in some words but silent in other words. For example, *k* is sounded in the word *kick*, but it is not sounded in such words as *know* and *knee*. Consult the dictionary whenever you are in doubt about the pronunciation of a word.

Pronunciation errors are most likely to occur with (1) unfamiliar words, (2) words of foreign origin, (3) names, and (4) multisyllable words. Such errors tend to distract the listener and may give the impression that the speaker is careless or uneducated. The business employee who is eager to succeed does not wish to be marked with either of these labels.

Improving Enunciation and Pronunciation

Follow this four-step plan to help you improve your enunciation and pronunciation:

1. Use the dictionary to determine the preferred pronunciation of words about which you are uncertain.
2. Speak slowly enough, and with sufficient care, so that each letter in a word is sounded as it is supposed to be sounded and so that words are not run together.

KEY POINT

Pronunciation refers either to the sound that a speaker gives to the letters or letter combinations that make up a word or to the way in which the speaker accents the word.

World View

International business people sometimes have difficulty in pronouncing English words. For example, the letter *g* may be pronounced hard (as in *go*) or soft (as in *gem*). A European visitor to the United States went to a fast food restaurant and ordered a *ham-bur-jer.*

—Roger E. Axtell, *Do's and Taboos of Using English Around the World*

3. Learn to use your jaw, your lips, and your tongue (the speech organs) properly.

4. Practice frequently the correct enunciation and pronunciation of words that are often mispronounced or poorly enunciated.

Relax Your Jaw. Most sounds require adequate jaw and mouth movement to achieve clear pronunciation. If such sounds are forced through a locked jaw, they are certain to be muffled and indistinguishable.

Keeping your jaws locked tight, try to pronounce these words—*neither, capable, try*. Can you understand what you are saying? You cannot, and you could not expect any listener to understand words that are pronounced in this manner.

To be an intelligible speaker, you must move your jaw freely between an open and a closed position. Say each of the vowels and notice the different positions of your jaw as you say *a, e, i, o, u*. Compare your jaw positions as you say first the sound "ow," as in *how*, and then the sound "oo," as in *room*. When you say "ow," your jaw is dropped. However, when you say "oo," you move your jaw slightly if at all.

Practicing the following phrases will exercise your jaw and help make it flexible.

going to go	down and out	up and around
around and away	sky high	down, up, and out
I've been	you've been	I've seen

Now practice saying these sentences to prove that your jaw is flexible enough so that each word is clearly enunciated and pronounced.

Shelly placed the parcel on the table today.

Many men and women strive to attain power, prestige, and financial security.

Please telephone (805) 555-8867 this morning.

Your flexible jaw will contribute to better speech through clearer enunciation.

Move Your Lips. As you were practicing the preceding words, phrases, and sentences, you probably noticed that in addition to the up-and-down movement of your jaw, your lips were assuming many different positions. Six consonant sounds are made by action of the lips. The lips are closed for the sounds "m," "b," and "p." The lower lip touches the edges of the upper front teeth for the sounds "v" and "f." The lips are rounded for the sound made by *w*, as in *woman*.

Poor enunciators do not move their lips very much; as a result, their speech is often unintelligible. The good speaker, on the other hand, uses a variety of lip positions. The "oo" sound in *who, lose, shoe*, and *do* requires rounded lips. The lips are widely stretched for the "e" sound in *me, we, key*, and *see*. In words like *few, boys, use*, and *how*, the speaker is required to use two different lip positions. The sound of "ow," as in *how* and *now*, requires that the jaw be dropped and the lips be rounded to form a circle.

KEY POINT

To improve enunciation and pronunciation:
- Relax your jaw.
- Move your lips.
- Develop a lively tongue.

While using proper lip positions, practice these words. First read across and then read down the columns.

wasting	mine	voice	very	wonder	pension
vocal	very	wary	file	victory	violent
winter	when	why	food	cost	careful
cool	mister	many	time	meaning	forceful

Now practice the following phrases, making certain that you avoid lazy lip movements.

office manager	readily available	answer the telephone
lose the money	when we go	empty the basket now
many men may	very fine work	what we wear

Make sure you move your lips sufficiently to enunciate clearly each word in the following sentences. Practice the sentences until every sound is clear.

Peter Piper picked a peck of pickled peppers.

She sells seashells by the seashore.

How now, brown cow?

The rain in Spain falls mainly on the plain.

The whistling west wind whipped the whispering trees.

Develop a Lively Tongue.　Repeat several times: *The tip of my tongue moves lively in my mouth.* Do you feel the lively movement of your tongue as you say these words? Try saying the same sentence with your tongue held loosely in your mouth, using a minimum of movement. Do you notice the lack of clarity? In order to enunciate precisely, to make your speech clear, you must move your tongue to several positions—the front of your mouth, the back of your mouth, the roof of your mouth, and even between the top and bottom rows of teeth for the "th" sound heard in *either, this,* and *that.*

Now that you know how a lively tongue feels, stand in front of a mirror as you practice the following words.

feel	forward	seal	sadly	saw	suit
main	many	some	sight	peace	mail
twine	train	later	legal	poster	port

Did you feel the lively movement of your tongue? Now practice these words, which require your tongue to be placed between your teeth.

think	thought	either	neither	loath	thorough
then	the	with	whether	through	wrath

Using the lively tongue that you have learned to develop, practice the following phrases and sentences until each sound is clearly enunciated.

Health, wealth, and happiness.

Actually colder than yesterday.

The attempted assault and battery.

Through thick and thin.

The thirty-three discounts are listed on page three.

Nothing gained, nothing lost, and nothing accomplished.

If you follow the suggestions in this section, you will find that your speaking will improve and that improved speech will quickly become easy and natural for you.

SECTION 8.2   REVIEW

Practical Application

A. Reread the case at the beginning of this chapter. Assume that you are a candidate for Margaret Reilly's job. List your strengths and weaknesses, including such factors as your personality, the first impression you make on others, your personal appearance, your facial expressions, and your mannerisms. Briefly comment on each of these factors. Would you be a likely candidate for this position? Why or why not? Would it be possible for you to overcome any deficiencies that you perceive that you have?

B. Read each of the following sentences aloud three times. Each time, emphasize a different word in the sentence, which will change the meaning of the sentence.
   1. Michael mailed the letter yesterday morning.
   2. I liked Los Angeles more than any other city I visited on my trip.
   3. Did you see Hosea at the banquet this week?
   4. If possible, please arrive earlier on Tuesday.
   5. Please forgive me for arriving so late.

C. Read the following sentences silently once or twice. Then, standing in front of the class, read them aloud from beginning to end. Try to keep your eyes on the audience as much as possible.
   1. Barry is never late for work, if he can avoid it.
   2. I doubt very much that I will be able to attend the booksellers convention next week.
   3. No, in my opinion, the new computer does not perform so efficiently as the old one.
   4. What difference does it make whether or not I attend your cousin's graduation next Tuesday?
   5. Do you really think that he will deliver the main speech at the awards banquet?

D. Read the following paragraphs silently twice. Then, standing in front of the class, read them aloud, keeping your eyes on the audience as much as possible.

1. When you are communicating face-to-face on a one-to-one basis, don't do all the talking. Give the other person a chance to talk while *you* listen attentively. Watch for signs that the other person wants to say something or is becoming bored and not listening carefully. No matter how interesting you think the conversation is or how well informed and articulate you think you are, you must give your listener a chance to speak. Otherwise, you will not keep his or her attention and respect.

2. Most people take telephone usage for granted—and this is one of the reasons so many office workers are ineffective telephone communicators. Too many employees assume that a business telephone conversation is the same as a personal telephone call. Actually, the telephone is one of the most important communication media in business, and you must use it with great skill, especially when you are talking with outside callers and with superiors in the office.

3. Nearly every speech of any length is brightened considerably by touches of humor and by human interest narratives. Of course, such stories should not dominate the speech. Observe the following rules: Use stories and jokes that add interest to the subject or illustrate a particular point. Before telling a joke to an audience, test it on friends to make sure it has a punch line. Make sure that stories and jokes do not offend or embarrass the audience. And time your stories to make sure that they are not too long.

Editing Practice

Synonyms or Antonyms? In each numbered list below, two words are synonyms or antonyms. For each item, identify the pair by letter and indicate whether the words are synonyms or antonyms. Use a dictionary if necessary.

1. (a) busy   (b) boisterous   (c) happy   (d) quiet   (e) clever
2. (a) phlegmatic   (b) stolid   (c) involuntary   (d) sordid   (e) respiratory
3. (a) faultless   (b) modest   (c) serious   (d) pretentious   (e) extraneous
4. (a) apathy   (b) hope   (c) enthusiasm   (d) vision   (e) thoughtfulness
5. (a) demise   (b) undershirt   (c) death   (d) contrive   (e) expire
6. (a) excellence   (b) disparity   (c) slander   (d) reference   (e) equality
7. (a) contract   (b) report   (c) letter   (d) model   (e) agreement
8. (a) sagacity   (b) hypocrisy   (c) opener   (d) glamour   (e) candor

9. (a) contingent   (b) erudite   (c) new   (d) erratic   (e) consistent
10. (a) affable   (b) garrulous   (c) gracious   (d) precious   (e) joyous

Editor's Alert. Thoroughly examine the following sentences for needed corrections. Make those corrections, rewriting any poorly worded sentences on a separate sheet of paper. Write *OK* for any sentence that has no error.

1. The messengers bicycles should not be parked in this area.
2. Ther're no reason for you to be sent on assignment to the Riviera.
3. Will you and him please go to Peoria instead.
4. Carl bought three airline tickets to Peoria at $150 each, for a total cost of $450.
5. Please continue on as though nothing were said.
6. Complete your questionaire, and hand in your asignment before you leave.
7. You should follow-up on your *Road and Driver* peice while you're in Peoria.
8. This company has always in the past—and always will—be noted for its fair treatment of all employees.
9. The new assignment schedule was only given to Morgan and I last week.
10. 10 writers begged to be sent to Peoria.

Critical Thinking Skills

Analysis. Select three prominent people (in politics, sports, or the arts) who frequently appear before the public in some type of speaking role. List the factors—pro and con—that affect their speaking effectiveness.

Conducting Meetings and Communicating in Groups

SECTION 8.3

Are meetings held because "Two heads are better than one"?

—Anonymous

OBJECTIVES:
After completing Section 8.3, you should be able to:

1. Discuss the steps to take to prepare for effective meetings.
2. Discuss the steps to take to lead effective meetings.
3. Describe the interaction method of conducting meetings.
4. Name the six basic rules for effective participation in meetings.

Meetings are among the most important ways to exchange ideas and report information within businesses. A meeting may involve a supervisor and an employee, several employees at various levels, and employees and vendors or customers. With an increase in global competition, many businesses are adopting a team

World View

Many United States companies have formed partnerships with international companies. In such companies that use a team approach, team members may consist of several people at different locations around the world.

approach to conducting business. Using the team approach helps involve employees at all levels in planning and decision making. Rather than working independently, employees work in groups in which they share ideas and responsibilities.

As a business communicator, you are likely to have frequent opportunities to participate in a variety of capacities in many types of meetings. You might be selected as a member of a *standing* (permanent) committee that meets regularly, such as a planning committee or a finance committee. You may also serve on an *ad hoc* (temporary) committee formed for a particular purpose, such as a grievance committee. You may even be selected as chairperson of one of these committees, with the responsibility for planning and conducting the meetings. After attending meetings during working hours, many business professionals often go to meetings and serve on other committees outside the company—for example, in professional, cultural, social, religious, political, and civic groups.

PLANNING MEETINGS

The success or failure of a group meeting is very often determined by preparation. Skillful planning can turn an ordinary meeting into an extremely profitable experience for each participant. Without careful advance work, the most promising meeting can result in a waste of time for everyone.

Prepare Thoroughly

A successful meeting or conference requires that the leader or leaders prepare in advance to make all the necessary arrangements and to contend with any problems that may arise. Preparations should include determining the starting time, the length, and the site of the meeting; the names of those who are to attend; and the objectives to be accomplished at the meeting.

Notification of a meeting is usually done by memorandum. The memo, accompanied by an agenda, should include the time, date, and location of the meeting. An *agenda* is a list of the topics to be discussed and the names of the people who are to lead the specific discussions. Some tips for agendas follow:

- Send the agenda as far in advance of the meeting as possible to allow the participants ample time to prepare for their roles. For a monthly meeting, send the agenda at least a week ahead of the meeting date. For a weekly meeting, send the agenda two or three days before the meeting.

- List topics in the order in which they will be discussed. Refer to Figure 8.4 on page 401 for a sample agenda.

Figure 8.4   Agenda.

An agenda lists the topics to be discussed at an upcoming meeting and includes the time, date, and location of the meeting.

DUNN AND BROOKS, INC.

AGENDA

Monthly Directors' Meeting
Thursday, May 25, 19—
9 a.m.-12 noon

Main Conference Room

1. Call to order

2. Approval of minutes of April meeting

3. Announcements

4. Old Business:
    a. Report on employee benefits committee
    b. Review of hiring procedures

5. New Business:
    a. Review of international sales
    b. Recommendations for new headquarters location
    c. Report on employee training programs

6. Adjournment

KEY POINT

Before the meeting takes place:
*   Prepare thoroughly.
*   Check the meeting site.
*   Arrive early.

*   Under "New Business," list the most important items first in the event that there is insufficient time to discuss them all.

*   Include a suggested time limit for the discussion to encourage completion of the agenda.

Check the Meeting Site

Arrangements for the meeting site must be planned so that the room, the furniture, and the equipment to be used are set up in time for the meeting. The following is a list of routine tasks associated with meeting preparations.

- Reserve a meeting room with enough tables and chairs. Arrange seating so that participants have eye contact with one another, such as around a conference table.
- Check the ventilation, room temperature, and lighting.
- Request any special equipment, such as a computer or an overhead projector, and make sure all equipment is working properly.
- Have an extra bulb for the projection equipment.
- Arrange for refreshments if appropriate.

In order to start the meeting promptly, check at least 45 minutes before the meeting to ensure that everything in the room is ready. By checking in advance, you can avoid delays by taking care of any problems before the meeting begins. Problems are more easily solved if they are discovered in a timely fashion.

Arrive Early

The leader of the meeting should arrive a few minutes early to check the facilities and to set an example for the participants. Arriving early also gives the leader a chance to greet the participants and offer them a copy of the agenda. Even though everyone should have an advance copy of the agenda, not everyone will remember to bring it to the meeting. Extra copies of reports or other papers to be discussed should also be available, even though copies may have been distributed in advance.

MANAGING MEETINGS

Being able to run a meeting smoothly is an important skill to acquire. You can follow the same guidelines for a small informal meeting as for a large conference.

Establish a Businesslike Atmosphere

The chairperson or facilitator sets the tone of the meeting. If the leader begins late or is slow to start the meeting, the participants are likely to lose whatever enthusiasm they may have had when they came to the meeting. Generally, it is best to start a meeting precisely at the scheduled time, even though there may be latecomers. Starting at the appointed time encourages participants to be punctual.

Guide the Discussion

The good leader talks as little as possible and draws out the opinions of the participants. Instead of doing most of the talking, a skillful leader

KEY POINT

During the meeting:
- Establish a businesslike atmosphere.
- Guide the discussion.
- Encourage participation.
- Discourage excessive talkers.
- Keep the discussion pertinent.
- Summarize periodically.
- Know when to conclude.

Figure 8.5

A key to a successful team meeting is to encourage all participants to contribute to the discussion. How can you encourage participation in a discussion?

brings out each participant's best ideas. The leader's function is not to show how much he or she knows but to steer the discussion in the proper direction. An experienced leader knows that the greater the participation—that is, the more minds constructively at work on a problem—the better the chances of accomplishing the meeting objectives.

Encourage Participation

Everyone invited to a meeting should be able to make some contribution to the discussion. Sometimes, ground rules are needed to encourage the members of the group to participate. The leader of the meeting should make it clear that individuals are not allowed to interrupt the person who is speaking. Speakers should know that they will be able to express their ideas without being criticized or attacked.

Some people are shy and will not say anything unless they are encouraged to speak. The leader should make a statement that offers encouragement; for example, "Andrea, you have had much experience in advertising. What do you think of William's layout for next week's ad?" or "Antonio, we would be interested in having the benefit of your experience in designing the home page for our Internet site."

A leader can encourage positive participation by complimenting a speaker who has made a worthwhile contribution; for example, "Thank you, Camilla, for that timesaving suggestion" or "That's an excellent idea, Ms. Ferragano. Can you tell us a little more about how that plan would function?"

Comments of this type are effective when they are obviously sincere. Negative comments, on the other hand, discourage participation and should, therefore, be kept to a minimum and be presented so tactfully that they do not discourage others from making suggestions. "If that idea could be implemented in a cost-effective way, our problem would be solved." The previous sentence tactfully says that the idea will not work because it costs too much.

Discourage Excessive Talkers

In any group there will always be one or two people who want to do all the talking. Unless these persons are listed on the agenda as principal contributors, they should not be permitted to monopolize the discussion. A leader should be firm in preventing a single person from taking over the meeting. "That's very interesting, Thad, but I think we ought to hear from Hannah" or "let's get back to you a little later, Helen; I think we would all be interested in hearing as many points as we can in our brief meeting."

Keep the Discussion Pertinent

Meetings sometimes tends to get off the track. All too often, a subject comes up that is of genuine personal interest to all those present at the meeting but has little or no bearing on the main topic. When side issues begin to waste valuable time, they must be cut off tactfully by the leader and the discussion must be brought back on track. "That certainly was an interesting experience, Lamont, but let's get back to our discussion on the employees' handbook. Yolanda, what changes do you think are necessary in the section on retirement?"

Usually you can keep the discussion on track without being rude to anyone, but bluntness is sometimes necessary as a last resort. "Kyle, time is getting away from us, and we want to avoid having to call another meeting to settle this problem. Do you have any specific solutions?"

Summarize Periodically

The group leader should always listen attentively but does not need to comment except, perhaps, to stimulate further discussion. "Excellent—that's an interesting point. I gather that you think this plan will be more effective than the one we have been following. Is that a correct assumption?" Above all, the leader should not tear down ideas or argue with participants; doing so will only discourage others in the group from expressing themselves. The leader of the meeting is only one member of the group; thus it is usually poor practice for the leader to judge every idea expressed instead of letting other members of the group participate.

From time to time, the chairperson should summarize the major points that have been presented. "We all seem to agree that we should not add more branch stores at the present time. Instead, you feel we

Jon motioned that the policy be approved.

should enlarge the existing branches and increase our advertising budget. Is that correct? Well, let's discuss which branches should be enlarged and how we should make use of an increased advertising budget. Brian, do you have any suggestions regarding which branch stores should be enlarged?"

Know When to Conclude

If the chairperson has prepared the agenda carefully and has conducted the meeting efficiently, the meeting should end close to the time scheduled for adjournment. If the discussion seems likely to extend beyond the closing time and it is important to continue, get the approval of the group; for example, "Ladies and gentlemen, it is five minutes of twelve, and it looks as though we won't get out of here by noon. Shall we continue the discussion, or would you rather schedule another meeting for this afternoon?"

After the meeting, the recorder should prepare the minutes and distribute them as soon as possible. Memorandums should be written to those who are assigned special responsibilities at the meeting.

CONDUCTING FORMAL MEETINGS

Many groups conduct their meetings on a formal basis, following parliamentary rules. If you are elected to office in such a group, you should read *Robert's Rules of Order,* the standard guide to parliamentary procedure.

Using the Interaction Method

The interaction method, which encourages participation by group members, is another way of conducting meetings. (Michael Doyle and David Strauss, *How to Make Meetings Work,* Berkley Books, 1993, pp. 85–87.) There are four key roles: the facilitator, the recorder, the group member, and the manager-chairperson. The interaction method has a built-in system of balances that keeps each of the key roles in check.

1. The job of the facilitator is to propose procedural guidelines and to make sure that everyone has a chance to participate.

2. The recorder stands in front of the group and writes down the main ideas of the speakers in their own words. The group members can watch the creation of this group memory and can make any needed corrections immediately.

3. The group members must make sure that the facilitator and the recorder perform their functions properly and that the ideas of the speakers are recorded accurately.

 **Technology**

Many companies use teleconferencing to minimize travel time and expense in conducting meetings. Teleconferencing enables group members at different locations to communicate using text, audio, and video.

4. The manager-chairperson is an active participant in the meeting but does not run it. In the end, however, the manager makes the decisions and can accept or reject the ideas of group members. The manager-chairperson has the role of group member during the meeting.

PARTICIPATING IN MEETINGS

Everyone invited to participate in a group discussion has an obligation to contribute his or her best thinking and suggestions. Here is an opportunity to exhibit your interest in, and knowledge about, the work you are doing. Too often, time and money are wasted because employees take meetings for granted and do not contribute their maximum effort to the discussion. They often come to a meeting unprepared, uninterested, and uninspired. The six basic rules for participating effectively in a meeting are:

1. Prepare for the meeting.
2. Express opinions tactfully.
3. Make positive contributions.
4. Be courteous.
5. Keep remarks concise and pertinent.
6. Take notes.

Prepare for the Meeting

The first rule for effective participation in a meeting is to come prepared. Learn all that you can about the topics to be discussed at the meeting. If there is an agenda, study each item carefully and learn more about topics that are unfamiliar to you. For example, if the subject of personnel evaluation is to be discussed, be sure that you know what the current company procedures are for evaluating personnel and the advantages and disadvantages of these procedures. You may refer to books or articles dealing with this topic or examine company forms that are currently in use. In addition, you might get the opinions of knowledgeable people who will not be present at the meeting. If there is to be a discussion of a revision of the evaluation form, study the form thoughtfully, try it out yourself, and ask various people who use the form to tell you what they like and do not like about it.

Being prepared also means coming to a meeting with a set of well-founded opinions. Opinions that are worth listening to in a business meeting are the ones backed up by facts. People are often opposed to a new idea merely because they don't know enough about it. Make certain that you can supply facts that will support your opinions and that will help convince others of the validity of your position.

KEY POINT

To prepare for a meeting, read about the topic and discuss the topic with knowledgeable people.

Express Opinions Tactfully

When someone asks you for your opinion or when you volunteer an opinion, be tactful in expressing yourself. Often, opposing points of view can cause strong disagreement. No matter how strongly you may feel, your chances of winning that person's support are better if you are tactful in presenting your views.

For example, don't say, "You're wrong, and here's why." Instead, you might say, "Your point of view certainly has merit, Henry, but I have doubts because . . ."

Never tell someone that he or she is wrong—*wrong* is a strong term, and your right to use it requires indisputable evidence. In selling your point of view, you will find the "Yes, but . . ." technique is more effective; in other words, acknowledge the other person's point of view and show your respect for it. Then present your own ideas. For example, "Yes, I agree that the solution seems simple and that your idea represents one way to approach the problem, but . . ."

In expressing yourself, separate facts from opinions. Label as facts only those statements for which you have solid evidence. Opinions should be signaled by such phrases as "It seems to me," "As I understand it," or "In my opinion."

Make Positive Contributions

Most meetings are held for the purpose of solving problems, and problems cannot be solved in a negative atmosphere. Participants must be willing to approach a problem with the attitude that the only way to solve it is to present as many ideas as possible. No one should immediately veto an idea; instead, each person should try to see the idea's merits and to enlarge upon the idea's possibilities, no matter how weak the idea may seem at first. To dismiss ideas before they are fully aired is not only rude but also extremely disheartening to those who are genuinely trying to reach intelligent decisions.

Be Courteous

The ideal meeting is one in which everyone participates freely. A speaker who monopolizes the discussion will discourage the participation of others. Even though you may be more knowledgeable about the topic than anyone else in the group, you should never display your knowledge in an offensive, overbearing manner.

More victories have been won in group discussion by modesty and tact than will ever be achieved by overaggressiveness. Don't jump in while others are speaking; wait your turn patiently. Show interest in what others are saying. You will win more support by listening and taking notes on remarks by others than by interrupting their remarks—regardless of how inane the remarks may seem to you. Acknowledge that others may have as much information or insight as you have or perhaps even more than you have.

Courteous group members do not (1) resort to sarcasm when they disagree with someone, (2) interrupt the person who is talking, (3) fidget, (4) gaze into space, or (5) carry on side conversations with other members of the group while someone else is speaking. If someone interrupts you while you are speaking, say something like "Please let me finish" and continue with the point you are making.

Keep Remarks Concise and Pertinent

Some participants in a meeting take a roundabout route to reach the point they want to make. They ramble endlessly. If you have something to say, get to your point quickly. Meetings become boring and unproductive mainly because participants insist on relating personal preferences, experiences, and opinions that have little or no bearing on the discussion at hand.

Take Notes

It is a good idea to develop the habit of taking notes at meetings, because the act of taking careful notes (1) keeps you alert, (2) tells speakers that you consider their remarks worth remembering, and (3) provides a valuable reference source both during and after the meeting. Take notes not only on what the speaker is saying but also on what *you* want to say when it is your turn to speak. Jot down your key remarks in advance so that your comments are well organized and complete.

World View

Cultures around the world have different cultural norms for pausing, interrupting, and overlapping in speech.

SECTION 8.3 REVIEW

Practical Application

A. Make a list of the steps you would take to prepare a meeting room for an all-day discussion.

B. Prepare the body of an interoffice memorandum to all supervisors, calling a meeting at which you and they will discuss the orientation program for all new employees. You want the supervisors to evaluate the present program, to talk with new employees hired since

January 1 of this year, and to do some research regarding orientation programs used in other local businesses. These aspects will be discussed at the meeting, and the supervisors will draw up a revised program that will be put into effect September 1. Supply any other information you feel would be helpful.

C. Evaluate your ability to conduct a meeting, using as guidelines your previous experience, if any, and the qualities you consider necessary in an effective leader of group discussions.

D. How does one establish a businesslike atmosphere at a meeting?

E. Prepare an agenda for an ad hoc committee on which you are to act as chairperson. Select a discussion topic of your own choice. Then develop a list of topics concerned with phases of this subject and assign them to individuals in your class. Use the sample agenda on page 401 as a guide.

F. At a meeting of the Employee Retirement Planning Committee, Marietta Hart was assigned the responsibility of gathering information about the facilities for the retirement banquet and dance. Write the body of a follow-up memorandum to Ms. Hart reminding her of the assignment. Supply all the details for the memorandum, including the date, time, location, and number of attendees for the banquet.

Editing Practice

Applied Psychology. The wording of the following letter excerpts does nothing to cement good human relations. Revise the sentences.
1. You made an error of $25 in totaling our last statement.
2. We fail to understand why you claim that the two lamp bases do not match.
3. We are unable to grant you credit because you are a poor payer.
4. You claim that your check was sent last week, but we have not yet received it.
5. You have put us through a great deal of trouble getting the merchandise to you on the date you requested.

Critical Thinking Skills

Evaluate. Read the following statements made by group discussion leaders. If the statement is not an appropriate one, what should have been said?
1. "I don't think that idea would work."
2. "We'd like to hear more about the plan."
3. "What has been your experience with this problem?"

Formal and Informal Presentations

1. Realize the role that presentations play in the job environment.
2. Prepare for a presentation.
3. Explain how to convey a professional image.
4. Relate suggestions for fielding questions.
5. List ways to manage stage fright.
6. Evaluate your own presentation.
7. Introduce a speaker.

To keep an audience's attention, make sure your speech is full of visual images. Examples are an excellent means of creating pictures.

—Phyllis Martin, in *A Word Watcher's Handbook*

Most professionals routinely make presentations as part of their job. They may be addressing a student group that is touring their facility, making a formal sales presentation to a prospective client, or explaining a proposed policy to the hospital board. Being able to develop and make formal and informal presentations is a competence that you should achieve. Practice is the best way to improve your presentation skills.

THE IMPORTANCE OF DEVELOPING PRESENTATION SKILLS

For many business professionals, the ability to speak effectively to groups is an important requirement of their positions.

A business executive may be expected to represent the company before professional organizations or cultural, civic, religious, or educational groups. These outside speaking duties are beyond those duties involved in speaking to members of one's own organization at employee meetings or at board meetings or at stockholders' meetings.

However, even those who are not top executives often are called upon to participate in activities involving speeches before either large or small groups—instructing subordinates, reporting to an executive committee, introducing a speaker, explaining a new company policy to a group of employees, or greeting a group of visitors.

A speech, like a letter, reflects an image of the organization that employs the speaker. An effective speech, like an effective letter, should convey a message clearly and convincingly and, at the same time, it should build goodwill. Since nearly everyone is called upon at one time or another to "say a few words" to an audience, every business employee should be prepared to represent his or her company in a way that will reflect favorably on the company.

KEY POINT

The ability to speak effectively to groups is an important requirement for many business professionals.

Preparing for a Presentation

Preparation is the key to a good presentation. You have an obligation to prepare and to deliver a presentation that will be worthwhile for your audience.

Analyzing Your Audience

One of the first steps in preparing for a presentation is to analyze your audience. You should learn everything you can about your audience, including their knowledge of, and interest in, the subject. Doing so helps you plan what to say. The following tips will help you analyze your audience.

1. Determine the occasion for your presentation. It is a staff meeting? birthday dinner? retirement banquet?

2. Tailor every presentation to the audience and to the occasion or theme of the meeting.

3. Respect your audience. This includes remaining within your allotted time. Using more time than allowed is discourteous. A good speaker knows the requirements of the program and adapts to them.

4. Put yourself in the shoes of the people who will be listening to your presentation and ask, "Would this speech be interesting to me?"

5. Find out such things as gender, job titles, education, interests, and general age range of the audience.

6. Find out how many people will attend so that you can prepare enough handouts.

7. Determine how much your audience knows about your topic. Your audience may know much about your topic or very little.

8. Choose the appropriate level of communication. Talking over the heads of your audience or talking down to them is considered rude. A good rule-of-thumb is to talk just a little below the level of the audience so that they can understand you easily.

World View

In cross-cultural communication, learn all you can about the beliefs and attitudes of the audience. For example, Asian audiences generally favor the needs of the group over the needs of the individual.

Developing Your Speech

The second step in preparing a presentation is developing your speech. Sometimes you are asked to speak about a specific topic; other times, you may choose your own topic. Whatever your topic, you should always have a strong introduction and conclusion. A brief but strong introduction grasps your audience's attention and gives a clear understanding of what you intend to talk about. You may choose to use a question, a startling fact, or a true story to introduce your topic.

The text, or "meat," of your presentation should have substance for your listeners. You should develop your points and support them. Be careful to avoid information overload. Most audiences will remember about five major points. You may want to use a handout to reinforce your major points.

Your concluding remarks should be well prepared, and you should end on a positive note. Remember that your audience, during these last critical minutes, is formulating a lasting impression of you and your presentation. A strong conclusion summarizes your major points and helps the audience remember what you said. Here are some tips to help you develop your speech.

KEY POINT

Use "nickel" words (short and easy-to-understand words) instead of "dollar" words (long words used in a futile attempt to impress listeners).

Content

1. Determine the purpose for your presentation, and make sure that it is clear in your mind.
2. Brainstorm ideas about the subject and outline your presentation, keeping the organization simple.
3. Write your ideas about the subject in words that your audience can understand.
4. Do whatever research is necessary. A good guideline is to know ten times more about your subject than you are able to say during the allotted time. This extra knowledge will help you field questions and feel self-confident.

Clarity

1. Be specific, avoid making too many broad generalizations, and stay on your subject.
2. Don't try to ad-lib or add material on the spot.
3. Use repetition as an effective way to emphasize main points.
4. Summarize after each main point.
5. Explain difficult points as you go along, and define unfamiliar terms the first time that you mention them.
6. Do not use abbreviations, acronyms, or technical terms that are unfamiliar to the audience.
7. Bring the presentation to a deliberate conclusion. Reemphasize the basic message, and summarize your main points.

Treatment

1. Try to give an overall impression of the subject rather than just facts and figures. The audience will get bored if all you do is give statistics.
2. Use illustrations and examples to help your audience relate to your content.
3. Use human interest stories and phrases that appeal to the senses and tend to create pictures in the minds of your audience.

Humor

1. Use humor only if you are comfortable with it. Omit telling jokes if you know that you always forget the punch line or that no one ever laughs at your jokes.

2. Remember that starting with a joke is risky. If the joke bombs, recovering is almost impossible.

3. Use humor only if it pertains to your topic.

4. Do not make fun of an individual or group of individuals. If you are questioning whether to use a specific joke, the rule of thumb is don't use it.

5. If there are humorous aspects to your subject, make reference to them. Humor can be a true story that has a humorous side. A speaker telling how to give CPR might say, "When you first see a person lying down, check to see if he or she is breathing. I almost gave CPR to a person who was simply sleeping."

World View

Be particularly careful in using humor in speaking to an international audience. A joke based on a current topic in the United States is likely to be unfamiliar to the audience.

MEMORY HOOK

When trying to decide whether or not a certain anecdote, joke, or story would be appropriate, use the following rule of thumb:

When in doubt, leave it out!

Getting Ready

After you have analyzed your audience and developed your presentation, you should prepare your notes and rehearse. Speakers, just like musical performers and actors, should practice before the actual presentation. Here are some tips to help you get ready for the presentation.

1. Develop speaking notes from the text of your presentation.

2. Write your notes on index cards, not full sheets of paper. Sheets of paper look unprofessional, and even the slightest movement of papers will cause noise, which will be amplified if you are using a microphone.

3. Use a larger size print on your note cards, which will allow you to see the text easily. The distance from the lectern to your eyes will probably be slightly greater than your normal reading distance.

4. Use a brightly colored highlighter pen to mark important points.

5. Don't put your notes on the podium ahead of time. The speaker before you may inadvertently remove them.

6. Indicate on your note cards the visual aid that should be used at that particular point in the presentation.

7. Practice until you feel confident and can coordinate your visual aids with your presentation.

8. Rehearse for timing. Plan what you can cut if it becomes necessary and what you can add if you finish ahead of schedule.

9. If possible, rehearse in the room in which you will be presenting with the equipment you will be using.

10. Practice with a microphone if you will be using one.

11. Videotape your presentation to detect and fine-tune details such as speaking too fast, speaking without expression, and using distracting mannerisms.

12. Remember that skipping meals before you speak can take the edge off of your energy level. Overeating can cause you to become sluggish.

13. Determine the best location for visual aids.

14. Make sure that the audience can hear you. Ask for a microphone if you know that you have difficulty projecting in a large room.

15. Examine podium lighting to make sure that you can read your notes.

16. Adjust the room temperature if possible. Set the temperature a few degrees below the comfortable level. The temperature will rise when people assemble in the room.

17. Make sure that all equipment is working properly.

18. Prepare a brief autobiographical sketch to send to the person introducing you. Take an extra copy with you to the presentation.

MEMORY HOOK

Number your note cards for a speech. If you drop them, they can easily be put back into the correct order.

KEY POINT

Visual aids should support and enhance your presentation and should reduce the amount of effort that your listeners need to understand what you are saying.

Creating Visual Aids

The next step in preparing for a presentation is creating your visual aids. Visual aids should support and enhance your presentation and should reduce the amount of effort that your listener needs to understand what you are saying. Remember that visual aids are *not* the presentation and that good visuals are *not* a substitute for good content. Visual aids can include slides, handouts, overhead transparencies, videos, demonstrations, actual samples, and computerized slides.

Presentation software such as PowerPoint will let you generate electronic slides that can be projected onto a screen or printed as transparencies for overhead projector use. See Figure 8.6 for a sample slide. Presentation software allows you to develop text and enhance it using color, a variety of typefaces and type sizes, and clip art.

Additionally, presentation software can be used to write, edit, and print the speaker's outline or notes, as well as to produce handouts that have a professional appearance.

One of the major advantages of using presentation software is that you can update your electronic slides within a few moments. This convenient updating is particularly helpful for sales representatives who use PowerPoint presentations when making sales calls. Many sales representatives use laptop computers to present product information to small groups. If they are speaking to a large group, they can connect their laptop computer to a larger television screen.

Your content will determine the best visual aid to help you get your points across. Remember, the quality of your visual aids strongly influences your audience's perception of you. The following checklist will help you prepare your visual aids.

- ❏ Use PowerPoint or some other presentation software to make your visuals look attractive and professional.
- ❏ Make sure all information on the graphics is correct and up to date.
- ❏ Make visuals large enough to be read from all parts of the room.

KEY POINT

Remember that visual aids are *not* the presentation and that good visuals are *not* a substitute for good content.

Figure 8.6   PowerPoint Slide.

Visual aids such as PowerPoint slides can be easily developed and adapted using computer software.

- Use an appropriate number of visuals in relation to the length of your presentation. Oversaturating your presentation with visuals loses an audience.
- Use color effectively to make your visuals more interesting and pleasing to the eye.
- Keep visual aids simple and uncluttered. Visuals that require lengthy explanations are ineffective.
- Limit each slide or transparency to three to four lines of text; six lines should be the maximum.
- Use block lettering, not fancy or script type. Limit type sizes to three per visual. Using more than three sizes complicates the visual.
- Use uppercase and lowercase letters. Solid capitals are hard to read.
- Use bullets to emphasize important points.
- Vary the visuals. Use a combination of pictures, graphs, and cartoons.
- Label and number visual aids, and note the label and the number in your note cards.
- Make the slides, overheads, and flip charts easy to transport.
- Test visual aids before the presentation.
- Use slides or transparencies instead of a blackboard or flip charts. You can face your audience and maintain eye contact while using these visual aids.
- Complete your remarks about a transparency or PowerPoint slide before showing the slide. Once the slide goes up, your audience will focus on it rather than on what you are saying.
- Don't stand between the audience and the visual aid.
- Use a pointer to direct attention to the visual aid.
- Use a good handout to give additional, in-depth information.
- Number or color-code handout pages to make it easier for audience members to locate a specific page when you refer to it during your presentation: "Find page 7" or "Turn to the blue page in your handouts."
- Leave generous margins on handouts so that your audience can take notes.
- Always include your name, postal address, e-mail address, and fax and telephone numbers on your handouts.

KEY POINT

For maximum effectiveness, visual aids should be:
- Correct
- Up to date
- Readable
- Uncluttered
- Visually interesting

Conveying a Professional Image

Now that you have finished your preparation, you should be concerned with conveying a professional image during your presentation. You should realize that audience members start forming their opinions of you as soon as they see you. Be sure that you are dressed appropriately, and demonstrate a professional image as you enter the room and walk to the podium. After you are introduced, walk to the podium with confidence and purpose.

The following tips should help you convey a professional image.

1. Be real, be sincere, be yourself. Being pompous or arrogant destroys audience rapport.

2. Remember that much of your message is communicated nonverbally through your posture, tone of voice, expressions, gestures, attire, and so on.

3. Be well-groomed. Make sure that your hair is neat and your clothes are fastened.

4. Decide what you will wear for your presentation in time to have your garments pressed or cleaned.

5. Select clothes and accessories that do not detract. You want your audience to notice that you look professional, not that you wore a loud tie or gaudy jewelry. Wear comfortable shoes that are appropriate for the occasion.

6. Use appropriate facial expressions.

7. Avoid mannerisms that take your listener's attention away from your content. Lean toward your audience, not away from it.

8. Use relaxed, natural movements and appropriate gestures. Moving around while you are speaking conveys confidence; exhibiting a stiff, statue-like posture conveys apprehension.

Figure 8.7

The hallmarks of an effective speaker are courtesy, sincerity, and confidence. How can you project these traits in giving a presentation?

9. Avoid rocking back and forth, standing on one foot, chewing gum, or jingling keys or coins.

10. Walk confidently to the podium, and stay poised throughout your presentation.

11. Use your best manners. If you are speaking at a dinner meeting, your audience will be observing your table manners.

Delivering Your Presentation

Now, you are ready to actually deliver your presentation. You should greet your audience and convey your pleasure at being asked to speak to them by smiling and using a friendly tone. In greeting your audience, you should observe the courtesies that are dictated by the formality of your speaking situation. For example, at a committee meeting, you might say, "Madam Chair and Committee Members." A simple "Good morning" would be appropriate in casual circumstances.

Probably, the most-mentioned expectation that an audience has for a speaker is that the speaker not read his or her presentation. A second expectation is that the speech be substantive. The third expectation is that the speaker should end on time. The smart speaker, when assigned 45 minutes, plans on 35 to 40 minutes. This leeway makes certain that the speech will not run overtime. If there are 5 to 10 minutes left, the time may be used to answer questions. Following are some suggestions for improving your delivery.

1. Deliver your presentation; don't read it. Memorizing or reading a presentation makes you seem insincere, apprehensive, and unprepared.

2. Use an outline on your note cards. Writing out every word on note cards will confuse you during the presentation.

3. Radiate energy, be enthusiastic, and be sincere.

4. Maintain eye contact. Focus on one person for several seconds, letting the person sense that you are talking to him or her. Then, focus on someone else in another segment of the room.

KEY POINT

Audiences expect the speaker to:
- Not read the presentation.
- Make substantive comments.
- End on time.

MEMORY HOOK

Put prompts or reminders to yourself on your note cards. For example, you could put a smiley face to remind you to have a pleasant expression. You could write SLOW UP! on several cards if you have a tendency to speak too fast. A clock drawing would remind you to check your time.

5. Speak at a slow, deliberate pace, and pause occasionally. Silence can be an effective way to get your audience's attention.

6. Concentrate on your words so that you do not slur your speech.

7. Properly pronounce words; use correct grammar; and choose appropriate vocabulary.

8. Stay focused and keep ideas moving.

9. Adjust your volume to enable everyone in the room to hear you.

10. Deliver your first words in a loud voice to gain your audience's attention.

11. Never turn your back on your audience.

12. Speak to your audience, not to your visual aid. Face your audience. Don't turn your back as you explain visuals.

13. Repeat important points. Audience members are more likely to remember details that they hear more than once.

14. Avoid fillers such as *uhs, ums,* and clichés such as "to make a long story short" or "That reminds me of a story . . ."

15. Monitor expressions and nonverbal cues to determine if your audience is confused, listening, disagreeing, or bored. Respond by adjusting your presentation accordingly.

16. Use appropriate gestures to emphasize major points.

17. Coordinate content and visual aids. Do not put up a visual aid until you are ready for it.

18. Anticipate potential noise such as people talking in the halls or sirens. When noise occurs, keep your composure and pause for the noise to end.

19. Stay within your assigned time limit.

20. Leave time for questions from your audience.

Fielding Questions

You should cultivate a positive attitude about questions from your audience. Good questions can help clarify important concepts, identify misunderstandings from audience members, and recognize specific areas that they want to know more about. Most presentation situations offer a question-and-answer period. When someone asks you a question, acknowledge the person and listen closely to the question. Following are some guidelines for fielding questions.

1. At the beginning of your presentation, tell your audience your preference for handling questions—at the end or as they occur throughout the presentation. An inexperienced speaker may prefer handling questions at the end.

2. If you like handling questions throughout the presentation, you may want to stop at convenient points and ask for questions.

 **KEY POINT**

Good questions can help clarify important concepts, identify misunderstandings from audience members, and recognize specific areas that they want to know more about.

3. Repeat the questions for the audience members who may not have heard them. Restating the question gives you time to formulate your response.

4. Ask for clarification if a question is unclear to you.

5. Give brief, direct answers to questions.

6. Try to anticipate possible questions by the audience, and think of answers in advance.

7. If you don't know the answer to a question, don't make up one. Ask the person to leave a business card with the question on the reverse side—tell him or her that you will send the answer soon.

8. Stay calm and polite if you receive antagonistic questions. Avoid displaying negative emotions.

9. Never permit an antagonistic audience member to speak from the microphone. Always maintain control of your temper and control of the presentation.

10. If the audience member continues to be confrontational, offer to talk with the person after the session ends.

Managing Stage Fright

What are the symptoms of stage fright, or speaker's anxiety? Some speakers report cold hands, sweaty palms, shaky knees, or a quivering voice. Others sense a pounding heart. Most experienced and inexperienced speakers have anxiety when addressing a group of people. Experienced speakers, however, value the benefits produced by speaker's anxiety and attempt to convert the anxiety into a positive energy that keeps them sharp and alert during their presentations.

If you experience stage fright, remember that nervousness is normal and that you are not alone in this emotion. Most people list the fear of speaking in public as their number one fear, above snakes and dying. Experienced speakers do not eliminate stage fright, but they learn how to live with it and how to manage it. Following are some suggestions for managing anxiety.

1. Prepare adequately. The key to conquering stage fright is preparation.

KEY POINT

Experienced speakers attempt to convert speaker's anxiety into a positive energy that keeps them sharp and alert during their presentations.

KEY POINT

Remember that speaker's anxiety is normal and that you are not alone in this emotion.

MEMORY HOOK

Good advice for managing stage fright used to appear on the lid of a popular brand of mayonnaise: "Keep cool, but don't freeze."

2. Master your content and visual aids to boost your self-confidence.

3. Because much of the anxiety comes as you begin your presentation, make sure that you are especially prepared with a very strong opening.

4. Go to the meeting room early, and talk with members of your audience. Introduce yourself to those whom you do not know, and have an informal conversation with those you already know.

5. While in the rest room or other private place, loosen up by bending from the waist and letting your hands and arms hang limp.

6. Just before you go to the podium, take three deep breaths to help you relax.

7. When you are speaking, focus on your topic and your audience.

8. Develop a positive attitude toward speaking. Speak every time you have the opportunity, whether at school, work, club meetings, or church or synagogue functions.

Evaluating Your Presentation

After each presentation, you should evaluate yourself. Also, ask a friend or coworker if he or she will constructively criticize your presentation and be receptive to any suggestions received. Try to complete the evaluation within two to three days after the presentation, while you still clearly remember the details. This self-evaluation process will help you become a better speaker. Here are some evaluation techniques.

1. Seek constructive criticism of your presentation from people you respect.

2. Maintain a good attitude about negative comments.

3. Profit by your mistakes, and convert them into a learning experience.

4. Note any segments getting several questions. Possibly your content was incomplete or unclear in this particular area.

5. List any changes you would make if you were presenting the same topic soon.

6. Compare yourself with others who spoke on the same program.

7. List your assets and liabilities that are related to speaking.

8. Accept as many opportunities to present as possible. Each speaking experience and subsequent evaluation will help you improve your presentation skills.

9. Keep a presentation file. The file will be helpful should you be asked to speak to the same group again or another group on the same or similar topic. Include your evaluation in this file.

INTRODUCING A SPEAKER

One of the most important speaking assignments is introducing a speaker. A good introduction sets the stage for the main address. If the introducer does an outstanding job, the main speaker's task is greatly simplified. In introducing a speaker, observe the following points.

1. Use an appropriate, brief introduction.
2. Set the stage for the speaker.
3. Keep your eyes on the audience.
4. End with the speaker's name.
5. Make closing remarks brief and appropriate.

Use an Appropriate, Brief Introduction

The audience has come to hear the speaker, not the person who is introducing the speaker. Therefore, keep the introduction short—not more than two or three minutes in length. Avoid giving specific information on the topic; the speaker will do that.

When you are introducing a speaker, avoid such trite expressions as "The speaker for this evening needs no introduction," "I give you Professor Terricita Gomez," or "Without further ado, I present Dr. Henry Co."

Set the Stage for the Speaker

Do some research on the speaker. Find out from the speaker's friends, associates, or assistant some personal traits or achievements that do not appear in the usual sources. A human interest story about the speaker's hobby, family, or generosity will warm the audience. Although you should have a complete résumé supplied to you itemizing the speaker's experience, education, and attainments, you do not need to use them all. An audience is quickly bored, and sometimes a speaker is embarrassed by a straight biographical introduction, no matter how impressive the speaker's background is. Give only the most significant dates, positions, and accomplishments. You need only to convince the audience that the speaker is qualified to speak on the topic assigned, is worth knowing, and has something important to say.

Keep Your Eyes on the Audience

Do not turn from the audience to face the speaker you are introducing—always keep your eyes on the audience. After you have made the introduction, wait until the speaker has reached the lectern before seating yourself.

End With the Speaker's Name

Many successful toastmasters recommend that you not mention the speaker's name until the very end of the introduction. During the introduction refer only to "our speaker." Then, at the end of the introduction, say something like, "It is my pleasure to present Dr. William B. Stowe."

Make Closing Remarks Brief and Appropriate

At the end of the speaker's remarks, someone on the platform or at the speaker's table should assume the responsibility for closing the meeting. If the speech was a particularly effective one, you may say with sincerity, "Thank you, Mr. Cronkite, for your most informative and insightful message. We are most appreciative. Members of the audience, the meeting is adjourned."

On the other hand, if the speech has been average or even disappointing, as indicated by the audience reaction, you may close by merely saying, "Thank you, Dr. Billingsly, for giving us your ideas on how to manage a multinational sales force. Members of the audience, thank you for coming to our meeting, and good night."

Under no circumstances should you prolong the closing remarks. If the speech was a good one, there is nothing more you can contribute to its effectiveness. If the speech was a poor one, the audience is probably tired and eager to leave.

SECTION 8.4 REVIEW

Practical Application

A. Identify a person whom you feel is an excellent speaker. List at least five reasons for your selection.

B. List three topics about which you feel qualified to speak. Using presentation software, or other available means, prepare two electronic slides or overhead transparency masters that could be used to illustrate each topic.

C. Prepare and present a three-minute informal presentation to your class on how to do something; for example, how to change a flat tire or how to balance a checkbook. You must use visual aids. As you present, try to make each person in your audience feel as though you are talking individually to that person.

D. Prepare and present a five-minute formal presentation to your class on a topic related to you intended career. Extensive study of your topic must be evident in your presentation. You must use visual aids. To give you experience in fielding questions, you must open the floor for questions at the end of your presentation.

E. You will introduce your instructor at a dinner for the May graduates of your school and their guests. Ask your instructor to supply needed biographical information. The topic for his or her presentation will be "Technology and Your Future." Be sure to use an appropriate attention-getting introduction that will encourage the audience to listen.

Editing Practice

Editing for Context. Rewrite any sentence containing words that do not fit the context. Write *OK* for any sentence that has no error.

1. The threat of a tax audit compiled us to consult with our tax attorney.
2. Did you receive all the items listed on the manifest?
3. His actions did not ward our taking any steps at this time.
4. Their quite concerned about environmental issues.
5. Sign the affidavit where indicated.
6. Please call the personal office to arrange a preliminary interview.
7. All the employees will benefit tremulously from the changes.
8. The error demented our confidence in his ability.
9. We attended to complete the project by Saturday.
10. To countenance serious problems, we must make drastic budget cuts.

Critical Thinking Skills

As a member of the activities committee at your company, you have been asked to make a presentation to all employees regarding company-wide activities for the upcoming year. Among the activities are a blood drive in February, a food drive for the local food bank in April, a company picnic in July, and an adopt-a-family program for the December holidays.

Develop an outline of the presentation you would give to encourage all employees to participate in these activities. Analyze the audience, and determine what visual aids would be appropriate. Also, prepare a list of questions you might be asked, and include possible answers you could give.

Tacky Telephone Technique. Critique the following telephone conversation between a customer and Donna, an accounting clerk in the credit department. Based on the following conversation, what should Donna do to improve her telephone technique?

Donna: Hello.
Customer: This is Martin Pattee. Who is this?
Donna: Who do you want?
Customer: I was trying to reach the credit department.
Donna: This is the credit department.
Customer: Is Laurel Ortega there?
Donna: Yes, she is.
Customer: May I speak with her, please?
Donna: What about?
Customer: I'm calling in regard to a billing error on my monthly statement.

Getting Ready for a Presentation. Ritsuko Kimura is a travel agent for World Wide Travel. She is about to make an important presentation to the company's management committee, and she wants it to be the best-organized and most convincing presentation she can give.

As part of her preparation, Ritsuko decides to copy her entire presentation on note cards in order to remember all the points she wants to make. To make her presentation as informative as possible, Ritsuko has included 12 key points that she wants to make. For each key point she has included at least two visual aids for reinforcement.

Ritsuko has asked you, a coworker, to listen to her rehearse her presentation, and you agree. Ritsuko begins her presentation with a joke for which she gives the wrong punch line. In making her points, Ritsuko frequently reads from her note cards and infrequently makes eye contact with you. Her visual aids include an average of seven to ten lines of type, and the charts and graphs are too small to be readable. In addition, Ritsuko delivers her presentation in a monotone, making it difficult to keep from becoming bored.

If you were Ritsuko's coworker, what constructive criticism would you offer to help her improve her presentation? Be specific in your suggestions.

SECTIONS

9.1 Using Information Processing

9.2 Using Telecommunications

9.3 Considerations for Communicating Electronically

Caroline Sturgis, administrative assistant to the human resources manager of a medical products company, often has to assist her supervisor in planning meetings for various levels of staff personnel. Just this morning Stephen West, her supervisor, announced that he needs her to set up a two-day conference of all department heads to do strategic planning for the next five years.

This meeting will be held about 1,500 miles away, in Chicago. Mr. West has asked Caroline to tell all department heads the dates and location of the conference. She is to find out who can attend. Caroline has decided to accomplish this task by using voice mail since all the participants are in the same facility.

Once Caroline receives the replies to her voice-mail messages, she can make appropriate hotel arrangements. She will let the hotel representative know how many meeting rooms are needed as well as the sizes and number of guest rooms. Mr. West has asked Caroline to book the airline flights for all the participants attending the conference. (Jill, a coworker, has just told Caroline about checking airline fares on the Internet to find the most current information available.) In particular, Mr. West would like Caroline to find out if any participants have special needs or preferences, for example, if the participant is a vegetarian, or uses a frequent flyer account, or prefers a nonsmoking room. Caroline has decided to create a form to gather all the information she will need.

Just two days after Caroline started planning for the conference, Mr. West asked her to include all district and regional sales managers in these plans. Originally, Caroline was going to send her survey form through the office mail, but now, needing information from people off-site, she has decided to fax the surveys instead.

By the end of the week, Mr. West has given Caroline a tentative agenda that needs to be coordinated with the presenters. Times, dates, equipment needs, and so on must be considered. With so much information yet to get, Caroline needs to make the best use of the technology available to her.

As you read Chapter 9, identify various forms of technology that Caroline could use to accomplish her tasks. In addition, assess the considerations Caroline must keep in mind as she decides which technology to use.

Using Information Processing

The computer revolution is the most advertised revolution in world history. Yet one of the funny things about it is that we probably still underestimate its impact.

—Herman Kahn, American futurist

OBJECTIVES:

After completing Section 9.1, you should be able to:

1. Describe information processing.
2. Identify the benefits of using word processing software.
3. Discuss what components are available in most integrated software packages.
4. Identify advantages of using an integrated software package.
5. Describe desktop publishing and the types of documents produced using this technology.
6. Explain what scanners do.

KEY POINT

Technology has revolutionized the workplace by allowing individuals to create and send messages faster and more efficiently.

During the last 20 years, technology has provided major developments for communication using stand-alone computers and specialized software for all types of information processing. In some businesses, these computers are operated independently. However, the trend is to merge them into a total system—an information processing system.

INFORMATION PROCESSING

Information processing is the manipulation of data by electronic means to collect, organize, record, process, distribute, and store information for decision-making purposes. It can relieve office personnel of routine, time-consuming, repetitive work.

For example, a *spreadsheet* program is a computerized version of an accountant's ledger. In its most simplistic form, a spreadsheet can calculate columns or rows of numbers and automatically recalculate the spreadsheet if any numbers are changed. A spreadsheet puts numerical data into a format that can be used for decision making, forecasting, and analysis. This type of software can also transform the information into a visual aid that clearly shows the relationships and trends expressed by the numerical data, as illustrated in Figure 9.1. In practical terms, spreadsheets allow businesses to keep and update accounting, inventory, and sales records; to project revenue and expenses for specific time periods based on assumptions; and to perform "what if" analyses to determine costs.

A database is another information processing tool that manipulates data efficiently and in a timely fashion. A *database* stores and organizes facts and figures in electronic files. Companies and organizations rely on databases for up-to-date lists to make timely and accurate reports and decisions. Information in a database is divided into fields; each field is used for a specific type of information. For example, in a database of employees' names, separate fields would be used for each employee's name, job title, telephone extension, and for the date the employee was hired, as illustrated in Figure 9.2.

There are two types of databases: internal and external. An *internal database* is used within a company, such as a database of financial

	A	B	C	D	E
1	Region	1st Quarter	2nd Quarter	3rd Quarter	4th Quarter
2	Northeast	11,926	9,625	10,015	15,217
3					
4	Midatlantic	14,607	11,413	12,699	16,700
5					
6	Southeast	10,180	11,817	12,798	14,654
7					
8	Midwest	12,015	10,860	11,399	15,675
9					
10	South Central	15,258	13,560	11,208	13,195
11					
12	Northwest	16,295	12,330	12,403	14,995
13					
14	West	15,884	13,639	12,925	15,839

Figure 9.1

Sample Spreadsheet Entries.

Spreadsheets are useful for organizing and analyzing numerical information.

information about a company. An *external database* is a collection of information available to various companies, organizations, and individuals, such as databases of government information. (External databases are discussed in Section 9.2 as part of on-line databases). An internal database may be used to create and update a membership list or a list of customer names and addresses, to generate mass mailings, to prepare a list of past-due accounts, to keep track of inventory, or to create an electronic catalog of products manufactured by the organization.

Much of the information processed and stored in a computer is either confidential or necessary for the continued success of company operations. For this reason, management should protect company records from accidental security breaks, from unintentional destruction, and from unauthorized access.

Employee Name	Job Title	Extension	Hire Date
Avila, Barbara	Personnel Director	2572	04/16/92
Burns, Timothy	Sales Manager	2257	10/27/94
DeAngelo, Susan	Administrative Assistant	2129	05/05/95
Fallon, John	Senior Accountant	2941	11/21/94
Fischer, Andrew	Computer Programmer	2827	01/15/96
Leon, Marlene	Sales Associate	2648	03/01/94
Marshall, Burt	Computer Technician	2815	06/10/97
Minette, Anthony	Marketing Manager	2278	09/07/95
Quintana, Ernesto	Accountant	2965	09/15/90
Russell, Jan	Sales Associate	2374	10/01/96
Shafir, Sharda	Marketing Manager	2239	05/09/95
Wilkins, Scott	Sales Associate	2761	06/22/95
Zawlinski, Rick	Vice President, Sales	2422	08/10/91

Figure 9.2

Sample Database Entries.

Businesses use databases to compile and sort information about employees, clients, customers, and patients.

WORD PROCESSING

The term *word processing* refers to the process of taking spoken, hand-written, and typed words and presenting them in final keyboarded form. Once the material is entered into the equipment and is properly formatted, it becomes a document.

Word processing equipment evolved from the automatic typewriters that appeared on the market in the 1960s. Since that time, there have been many improvements and developments by different vendors. One of the main benefits of word processing technology is that it has text-manipulation capabilities. In other words, text can be added, deleted, moved, corrected, and revised before the final document is printed. In addition, after a document has been printed, it can be stored electronically and retrieved at a later time for further revisions or copied to create new versions. The use of word processing equipment has saved companies countless hours formerly spent keyboarding correspondence and other documents on a typewriter.

Word processing is accomplished by dedicated word processors, microcomputers with word processing software, or a company's computer network. *Dedicated word processors* are designed and used primarily for word processing applications, although some of them also have calculating functions. *Microcomputers,* or personal computers (PCs), have word processing capabilities—usually through a software program (a set of instructions) written specifically for that purpose. Some companies access word processing programs stored on a company's computer network.

Several features of word processing software facilitate the easy and efficient production of documents. What are some of the benefits of using a word processing software package?

- You can emphasize portions of text by using boldface, under-lining, or italics. Also, font (type) styles and sizes can be changed.
- You can use the search-and-replace feature to insert and delete information as well as the cut-and-paste tool to move or copy information from one location in a document to another. These features eliminate the need to rekey a document.
- Document readability is improved. You gain confidence in your ability to produce an accurate document when you use a spell checker, a thesaurus, and a grammar or style checker.
- You can customize documents using special features such as mail merge, headers and footers, and footnotes and endnotes.
- Special templates provide preestablished margins, type sizes, and positioning of elements such as the date line.

Because revisions are easy to make, writers using word processing software are much more likely to revise a document. In addition to the ease of producing documents, users report significant time savings and increased confidence in the accuracy of their work.

KEY POINT

Word processing software allows the user to create, revise, and store a document electronically.

KEY POINT

Revisions can be accomplished with a minimum of effort when a word processing software package is used.

INTEGRATED SOFTWARE

Software packages, called *suites,* that contain spreadsheet, database, word processing, graphics or presentation, and sometimes communication software are very common today. Microsoft Office, Corel Word-Perfect Suite, Lotus SmartSuite, and Microsoft Works are examples of integrated software packages. The main advantage of integrated software is you can quickly switch from one application to another and you can easily insert files from one application to another because the software programs are compatible. Information entered in one application can be used in all other applications of the software. For example, a spreadsheet can be inserted into a word processing file and linked to it so that if you change a number in the spreadsheet, the software automatically updates the number in the word processing file.

The database software portion of an integrated software package organizes information into lists that may be retrieved and then formatted into a number of report formats. The information that is stored in a database may be sorted into a particular format or searched to identify only those data that meet certain conditions. For example, assume you work for the local chamber of commerce. The executive director of the chamber of commerce wants an alphabetical listing of the membership, with those organizations that have belonged for the longest period of time listed first. You would retrieve your database and then sort it on two fields; first you would sort based on the numbers of years of membership (descending) and then on the names of the members (alphabetical or ascending). Once your sort is complete and the data have been formatted into a list or other useful form, you might want to import the

Figure 9.3

Integrated software packages enable business people to prepare reports using several applications, such as word processing, databases, and spreadsheets.

list into a report that you are writing in word processing so the list becomes a part of the report.

The graphics or presentation software portion of an integrated software package is used to prepare visual aids. In many cases, a template for creating the visual aid is available; however, the user may also create his or her own format. Once the document has been entered, the visual aids can be made into transparencies or slides. A hard copy can also be made by simply printing out a copy of the visual.

The communication component of an integrated software package typically includes the software necessary to use electronic mail, or e-mail, and possibly a built-in fax feature. These communication technologies are discussed in detail in Section 9.2.

DESKTOP PUBLISHING

In recent years desktop publishing programs have gained in popularity. These specialized software programs enable the user to lay out pages that combine text generated by a word processing program, illustrations created on a graphics software program, and clip art. The document is manipulated through the use of photographs, charts, ruled boxes, graphics, typefaces, columns, and so on. With desktop publishing software, users function as writers, editors, and page-layout designers. This means that the software operator has control not only over what is written but also over how the document is presented on the page.

The advantage of using desktop publishing is twofold—a reduction in cost and a reduction in the time to prepare a professional-looking document. Brochures, booklets, catalogs, newsletters, annual reports, prospectuses, letterheads, business cards, and direct-mail advertisements require a professional typeset appearance. All these documents can be created using a desktop publishing program and a laser printer instead of using a commercial printer. One caution: If the operator is not skilled in design, the documents created and produced using the desktop publishing software may not be of the desired quality.

OPTICAL CHARACTER RECOGNITION (OCR) AND SCANNING

Text, data, and graphics can be scanned from hard copy to electronic format through the use of hand-held or desktop scanning equipment. *Scanners* take printed text and translate it into electronic files. Scanned text and images can be stored in many word processing or graphics formats so they can be easily revised. This convenience eliminates the time-consuming task of rekeying text or recreating data and graphics.

A specialized form of OCR equipment is used by the U. S. Postal Service to sort mail. The scanning equipment reads the ZIP Code on mail and sorts each piece by destination. Many word processing software packages can print the scannable bar code that represents the ZIP Code.

World View

Computer-generated visual aids are appropriate for all cultures. Such visuals look professional and indicate that the presenter is prepared.
—Sherron B. Kenton and Deborah Valentine, *Crosstalk: Communicating in a Multicultural Workplace*

KEY POINT

Desktop publishing programs enable the user to combine text and graphics in a document.

Technology

Desktop publishing programs often contain clip art—a gallery of pictures that can be added to a document.

Practical Application

1. Identify three benefits of using word processing software.
2. List the applications available in an integrated software suite.
3. Describe two advantages to using desktop publishing software.
4. Identify three examples of clip art you could use when preparing your company's monthly newsletter. Articles scheduled for the issue include "Exercise for a Healthy Life," "Upcoming Software Training," "New Savings Plan Offered to Employees," and "Time Management." If possible, provide printouts of the clip art you choose.

Critical Thinking Skills

Assume you are the administrative assistant to the executive director of the alumni association at Best West University. Read questions a, b, and c and the situations that follow. Give appropriate advice about what should be done in each situation, and then justify your recommendations.

a. What document(s) do you need to prepare?
b. What information should be included in each document?
c. What type of technology discussed in Section 9.1 would you use to accomplish the tasks?

1. In the fall Best West University begins its annual fund drive. Members of this graduating class will be setting up a phone bank and calling graduates to see if they will contribute. You are to prepare the materials that students will refer to while working the phone banks.
2. Once pledge cards are filled out during the telephone campaign, they are returned to you for tabulation and organization.
3. You need to coordinate a follow-up campaign for the graduates you were unable to reach during the telephone campaign.
4. Once the fund-raising campaign is complete, you will need to prepare a rough draft of a report with all the details of the campaign for your supervisor.
5. The final step is to report the results of the campaign to all alumni through the quarterly alumni magazine.

Using Telecommunications

OBJECTIVES:

After completing Section 9.2, you should be able to:

1. Define *telecommunications*.
2. Identify the differences between a traditional message and an electronic message.
3. Describe how voice mail works.
4. Discuss the advantages and disadvantages of voice mail.
5. Identify when to use a fax machine.
6. Discuss the impact of the Internet on business today.
7. Compare and contrast e-mail, electronic bulletin boards, and chat rooms.
8. Compose an e-mail message based on the guidelines presented.
9. Identify specific situations in which videoconferencing would be the most appropriate technology to use.

The newest computer can merely compound, at speed, the oldest problem in the relations between human beings, and in the end, the communicator will be confronted with the old problem of what to say and how to say it.

—Edward R. Murrow, broadcast news journalist

*T*elecommunications is the transmission of information by a combination of telephone lines, satellites, or networks. Because of the need for instant communication and as a result of rising postage costs, many companies are using telecommunications of various types to transmit information.

TELEPHONE COMMUNICATION

Besides the telephone, telephone communication includes voice mail, fax machines, videophones, pagers, and cellular phones.

Telephone

The telephone call is a simple, familiar form of telecommunications, and the telephone is the most widely used piece of equipment in business today. Today there are more than 285 million telephones in the world, and nearly half of them are in the United States. These statistics emphasize how much we depend on the telephone to give and receive information.

When would you choose to use the telephone to transmit a message? Typically, if you have a fairly simple or uncomplicated message and need an immediate response, the telephone is probably a good option. The telephone, however, does not provide you with written documentation of the message. If a written record is needed, put your message in writing or follow up the phone call with a written message. The type of message you are conveying will also determine whether you should use the phone, meet in person, or write. Before picking up the telephone to deliver a message, ask yourself the questions in the Memory Hook on page 435.

Telephone companies offer a variety of special services including telecommunications devices for the deaf (TDDs) and caller ID, which displays the caller's name and telephone number and the time and date the call was made. Speed dialing, call waiting, call forwarding, and conference calling are other services that are available in most areas.

KEY POINT

The telephone is ideal for delivering short, uncomplicated messages and messages that require an immediate response.

To decide if the telephone is appropriate for delivering a message, ask yourself these questions:

- Is my message simple enough that all details can be clearly conveyed over the telephone?
- Do I need written documentation of this message?
- Is the topic of my message one that is appropriate to transmit over the telephone?

Instantaneous feedback, personal contact with the receiver of the message, and virtually no time lag between the time a call is placed and the time it is received—all are advantages of using the telephone in your business or personal life. Probably the most widely recognized disadvantage of the telephone is "telephone tag." In telephone tag you are unable to reach the person you called on the first try, and both parties make repeated attempts to contact each other.

Voice Mail

Voice mail is a telephone feature that allows you to leave a spoken message for someone you are trying to reach but who is unavailable. Your spoken message is converted to a digital code that is stored on magnetic disks in a computer until it can be played back by the intended recipient. The voice-mail messages are stored in an electronic "mailbox." They may be retrieved at any time for playback, may be deleted or restored for future use, may be forwarded to another location, or may be sent to several people's mailboxes.

The advantages of using voice mail are:

- No phone calls are missed.
- Calls are handled quickly and efficiently because there is no telephone tag.
- A worker's productivity is increased because incoming calls do not require the receiver to stop what he or she is doing to take the message.
- Messages are accurate because another person does not have to write a message for the recipient.
- Time-zone barriers are eliminated because voice mail may be used at any time of the day or any day of the week if you call the voice-mail number directly.

World View

People around the world use different telephone greetings.
Japan: *Moshi moshi* (Hello)
Italy: *Pronto* (I'm ready.)
Russia: *Slushaiyu* (I'm listening.)
Spain: *Digame* (Speak to me.)

KEY POINT

A user can access voice mail at any time from any telephone by using a specified access code.

- Voice mail is a convenience for people who work out of the office and have only a limited time each day within which to make calls and leave messages.

As with most technologies, there are also some disadvantages to voice mail.

- Callers sometimes have to listen to long greetings before they can leave a message.
- Some people dislike the depersonalization of voice mail; they like the human touch and would much rather interact with people than machines.
- Voice mail may give the impression that the receiver's time is more important or valuable than the caller's time.

If you are using voice mail as a receiver, be sure to:

1. Record a personalized message that includes your name and organization. To show callers you're managing your voice mail efficiently, change the message daily to reflect the current date and what your availability will be for that day.
2. Include in your recorded greeting any special directions for leaving voice-mail messages.
3. Provide an emergency number or the name of someone who can give the caller immediate attention.

As a receiver, you can notify callers to expect that their voice-mail messages will be returned within a day if you are in and out of your office; two days if you are out of the office for a day; and a week if you are gone for more than three days.

As a caller using voice mail, you should always:

1. Start the message with your name, business affiliation, and telephone number.
2. State the purpose of your call and just enough details to allow the receiver to assess the urgency of the call.
3. Close your message by restating your name, organization, and telephone number; summarizing the main points of your call; and identifying a convenient time for the receiver to return your call.

When leaving a message on someone's voice mail, give all information in a professional manner. Avoid stammering, which shows lack of organization, or speaking so quickly that your message is unintelligible. When leaving your phone number or address make sure to pause so that the receiver can write down the information easily. If the voice mail picks up your call on the first ring or before the first ring, the person you are trying to reach may be on the phone; if the phone rings three to five times, the receiver is probably away from his or her desk or not taking calls.

Routine, simple messages are ideal for transmission through voice mail. These routine messages could include giving or requesting infor-

Voice-mail greeting:
Hello, this is Melanie Spiegel at *The Evening Herald.* If you would like to pace a classified ad . . . .

mation. For example, you might call a supplier to ask that all bills for goods purchased by your company be sent to Mr. Stan West in the accounting department by December 20. This routine message could easily be transmitted through voice mail. Another example of effective voice mail would be to notify staff members of an upcoming meeting and ask them to respond to you if they plan to attend.

Fax Machines

Voice is not the only way that data can be transmitted electronically. Today printed words and graphic images may also be sent electronically through a facsimile (fax) machine. A *fax machine* transmits copies of printed documents using telephone lines that connect the sender and the receiver. (It may help to think of a fax machine as a long-distance copier.) A one-page fax can be sent 24 hours a day to anywhere in the world in less than a minute. The recipient does not have to be present to receive the fax. Portable faxes are available; they give travelers the ability to transmit documents from different locations, including their vehicles. Costs for using a fax machine with the telephone lines are based on phone charges.

There is also communication software that includes integrated fax, e-mail, and graphics applications. With this software you are able to do *multitasking*—that is, to perform more than one task at the same time. With multitasking, the software enables you to complete one task and move on to another while the first task is being completed in the background. For example, you may transmit a fax in the background while simultaneously typing a letter.

Some businesses and individuals have a fax machine and a telephone hooked up to the same phone line. The same telephone number is used for both applications. With this type of setup, the phone line cannot be used simultaneously for faxes and phone calls.

Businesses are increasingly using fax machines for several reasons:

- Faxes save time—they take about the same length of time as a telephone call.

- Faxes can be received at any time of day, making it convenient to do business with organizations in other time zones.

- Faxes provide the hard copy that is sometimes required for documentation purposes.

Some disadvantages to using faxes include the following:

- Faxes lack confidentiality, unless the recipient is the only person who has access to the fax machine.

- Faxes may be delayed in reaching the addressee. For example, if the receiving fax machine is out of paper, it cannot print the message until paper is added. Thus the receiver may not get the fax when the sender intended.

Technology

Some computers are equipped with built-in fax capabilities. The fax is stored as an electronic file on the computer's hard drive.

Videophones

Videophones are also known as picture phones; they allow both parties to see each other as they are talking. For example, one person can point to information on a graph while discussing the material. Seeing such demonstrations as well as observing body language enhances communication. This service is available through many telephone service providers.

Pagers

Pagers, sometimes called beepers, are battery-powered devices that signal you when telephone messages are received. If you want to be accessible at all times without being tied to a specific location, you need a pager.

While pagers have been around for a while, they are still an evolving technology. There are several types of pagers available with a variety of features. The basic pager may sound a tone, vibrate, or use a blinking light to alert the user of the pager to an incoming message. An alphanumeric pager allows callers to leave short messages. Two-way pagers allow you not only to receive a message but also to respond directly from your pager unit.

Another type of pager offers voice capability; it is like a voice mail–pager combination. The pager connects the caller with your voice-mail box and then alerts you when the message is complete. You can store voice-mail messages and then play them back just as you would if you had dialed into your voice-mail system.

Darla was attending the funeral of a business colleague, and she forgot to turn off her beeper. She was embarrassed when the beeper went off during the service.

Cellular Phones

A *cellular phone,* or cell phone, is a wireless telephone that transmits voice and data messages in the form of radio signals. A cellular phone can be carried with you so you can be reached 24 hours a day whether you're at work, at the airport, at dinner, or shopping. Calls can be forwarded from your telephone to your cellular phone, or you may have an assigned phone number for the cellular phone.

It is irritating and distracting to be interrupted by the ringing of a cellular phone or the beeping of a pager. In public locations where conversation is expected, using a cellular phone or pager is not inappropriate. However, at formal meetings, in the classroom, social occasions, meals, and similar events, you should turn off your cellular phone or switch it to a silent-alert mode, if one is available.

Calls made or received on a cellular phone are paid for on a by-the-minute basis. Therefore, you should organize your thoughts carefully so you can present your message clearly and concisely and minimize costs. One of the advantages of using a cellular phone is the convenience of

Figure 9.4

Cellular phones offer the convenience of communicating from almost any location. In what business situations would access to such technology be important?

using it almost anywhere. However, be aware that using a cellular phone while you are driving can be a serious safety hazard.

TELECONFERENCING

Teleconferencing allows people in different locations and time zones to meet electronically. Teleconferences are sometimes referred to as *electronic meetings*. By holding teleconferences, executives can substantially reduce the high costs of traveling to face-to-face meetings: transportation, hotel accommodations, food, and travel time. Electronic meetings are usually very efficient because the participants must be well prepared (the cost of an electronic meeting directly depends on the amount of time you use the equipment).

Teleconferencing facilities are available in many large companies while small companies can rent teleconferencing services.

Audio Teleconferencing

An audio teleconference (formerly called a *conference call*) is the simplest, least expensive, and most commonly scheduled kind of teleconference.

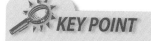

KEY POINT

Teleconferences enable business people at sites around the world to exchange information using equipment with audio and video transmission capabilities.

A telephone or speakerphone and the conference feature are all that is needed to connect all parties taking part in the conference. In most audio conferences, the people who participate know one another and feel comfortable conducting business in this forum. An audio conference works well for exchanging information, giving directives, resolving minor conflicts, conducting collaborative problem solving, and presenting simple proposals. However, audio conferences are not as effective as face-to-face meetings if your goal is to generate ideas through a brainstorming session that requires personal interaction.

Videoconferencing

Even though videoconferencing has been available since the 1970s, it did not become widely used until the 1990s when businesses were looking for ways to reduce travel costs.

The *videoconference* takes advantage of all media—audio, graphics, and video. A specially equipped room is necessary for a videoconference; this equipment consists of cameras, monitors, multiple microphones, and special transmission lines for transmitting audio and video information. A fiber-optic network, which can transmit digital signals, is provided by the telephone company. Many companies are now installing videoconferencing equipment on site so they don't have to rent rooms and equipment at an off-site location.

A major advantage of videoconferencing is that you are able to have face-to-face communication (including receiving feedback and seeing nonverbal communication cues) with the participants at other

Figure 9.5

Videoconferencing offers the advantage of face-to-face communication and immediate feedback. What are some other benefits of videoconferencing?

locations. Common uses of the videoconference include product presentations, new-product announcements, personnel training, and brainstorming sessions like the one shown in Figure 9.5.

There are several disadvantages that you should consider if you are working with videoconferencing. When a camera is introduced into any situation, the disruption may cause a loss of spontaneity, and participation may be inhibited. Also, some people simply do not relate well to a video screen and tend to focus on other things. This type of teleconferencing works well if your group is relatively small, with perhaps four to six people at each site.

Distance Learning

Some technology can be used to bring the class to the student rather than the student to the class site. *Distance learning,* sometimes called educational teleconferencing, uses closed-circuit television and feedback audio equipment to transmit classes to remote areas or to another location within a school or business. Students participating in distance learning can contact the classroom when they have questions.

A distance learning situation might be similar to the scenario that follows:

KEY POINT

Schools and businesses use distance learning to offer courses and training at distant sites.

> A well-known management consultant is giving a workshop on time-management skills in a city approximately 1,500 miles from your place of business. Since your organization cannot afford to send you to this meeting, your employer has decided to pay a fee so you can participate in the videoconference of the workshop. Because your business does not have videoconferencing equipment, you go to the local community college campus and attend the workshop in the videoconference classroom. Once there, you are seated in a room with monitors and microphones. You listen to and watch the presentation on the monitors. As the workshop draws to a close, the consultant asks if there are any questions. You are given a microphone and the camera is on you as you ask your question. The consultant then answers your question directly. Participants at other sites can see and hear what is happening.

COMMUNICATION NETWORKS

Two or more computers connected together to share information are a *network.* Connecting different pieces of electronic equipment in a network makes it possible to transfer information from one place to another more easily than ever before. Communication lines link computers to other computers, to word processors, to printers, and to databases. These communication networks can be set up within an organization for internal communications, or they can be used to communicate anywhere in the world with other organizations that have compatible equipment.

KEY POINT

Many businesses and organizations are linked within a site and with outside sites by means of communication networks.

Local Area and Wide Area Networks

One type of network is the local area network. A *local area network (LAN)* connects computers at a given location (that is, within a department, within a building, or within a campus). Local area networks at different locations can be linked to form a *wide area network (WAN)*. For example, a wide area network could connect different plants at different locations of the same company.

Electronic Mail

In electronic mail, or e-mail, messages are composed, transmitted, and usually read on computer screens. Because e-mail conveys a sense of importance and urgency, recipients pay more attention to these messages than they would to letters that arrive by conventional mail.

There are several advantages to using e-mail:

- E-mail can be sent and received on both networked and stand-alone computers that are equipped with modems—devices that transmit electronic signals using telephone lines.
- An e-mail message can be sent simultaneously to several people.
- E-mail has the ability to instantly deliver—day or night—an electronic message to your receiver even if the person is not available. The message is held until the receiver accesses the system and reads the mail.

Employees can use an internal e-mail system to distribute memos, reports, and documents without having to send them through the mailroom. Because the messages are sent directly, the delivery takes less time. Internal e-mail systems are relatively inexpensive, and multiple messages can be sent with just a few keystrokes.

Suppose your supervisor is chairing a meeting this afternoon but needs to confirm the schedule with the presenters. The supervisor sends a draft of the meeting agenda to the participants by e-mail. The participants make corrections to the agenda and send it back to your supervisor by return e-mail. The final agenda is then prepared in time for the meeting. There are two reasons e-mail is the medium of choice: (1) the message reaches the participants quickly, and (2) the reply is short and does not require a hard copy.

In some ways, e-mail is similar to regular mail in that you must have the address of the person to whom you're sending your message.

E-mail addresses have two parts separated by the "at" symbol "@." The part that precedes @ is called the *mailbox* and typically consists of your surname or a series of letters or numbers. The part that follows @ is called the *domain* and represents the system on which you receive e-mail. The domain consists of two or more parts separated by dots. If you are sending a message to someone in your domain, you may omit the domain. The final part in the domain section indicates the kind of system being used. For example:

KEY POINT

Local area networks connect computers at the same site. Wide area networks connect computers at remote sites.

KEY POINT

Electronic mail consists of written messages sent electronically from one computer to another.

Technology

Using e-mail to send messages is convenient provided all parties check their e-mail periodically for incoming messages.

.com (commercial business or organization)
.edu (educational institution)
.gov (government)
.org (nonprofit, nonacademic organization)

Here is a sample e-mail address:

president@whitehouse.gov

The user's name is *president*. In the domain, the location is *whitehouse*, and the system is *gov*. If any part of the address is wrong, the message will be returned to you.

You can send and receive e-mail using one of three basic delivery options:

- Public membership networks such as America Online, CompuServe, or Prodigy.

- Private business networks using specified e-mail software such as *cc: Mail* by Lotus.

- Hybrid service networks like InfoNet, Bitnet, and InterNet and free e-mail services such as Juno and Eudora.

Composing Electronic Messages. E-mail messages are typically short and less formal than a hard-copy document. This doesn't mean the planning and organization of a message are left to chance—you may find yourself doing more planning and organizing of your thoughts before keying an e-mail message. Because the language is less formal, writers sometimes have a tendency to write more emotionally. Keep in mind that the message you send through e-mail is a reflection of you, and your reader may not interpret your emotions in the way you intended. Also remember that privacy is not guaranteed when you use e-mail; others may access your message, and the message could be stored in a computer indefinitely.

Listed in the Memory Hook on page 444 are some guidelines for creating e-mail messages.

E-mail is one communication option available on the Internet.

Internet

Today a new and rapidly expanding global era of communication and commerce exists in the form of the world's largest computer network—the Internet.

The *Internet* is a collection of computers and computer networks located all over the world, all of which share information by agreed-upon Internet protocol. People from all over the world can communicate with one another or locate and retrieve information from anywhere in the world through the Internet. Another term for the Internet is the *information superhighway*.

One of the advantages of the Internet is that everything is done in *real time*, which means the information is transmitted instantaneously. Another advantage is that you have access to thousands of references and resources without ever leaving your computer.

World View

On the Internet, an international address contains a two-digit country code. For example, *uk* for United Kingdom, *de* for Germany, and *fr* for France.

KEY POINT

Some people use a smiley—a group of characters arranged to look like a face—to personalize e-mail messages.

:-(I'm sad.
:-D I'm happy.
:-+ I'm tired.
:-O I'm surprised.

KEY POINT

The Internet is a worldwide computer network that is made up of over 130,000 smaller computer networks.

MEMORY HOOK

Use these guidelines for composing effective e-mail messages:

- **A**void sending angry messages (called *flaming*), and avoid using all-capital letters (called *shouting*).

- **L**imit each e-mail message to only one topic, and identify that topic in the subject line.

- **A**void using wording that you would not want anyone other than the recipient to see.

- **S**tate only the necessary background information in the message.

- **K**eep your e-mail messages short—no more than 25 lines—so that they will fit on one screen.

- **A**lways check e-mail documents to make sure they are free of grammatical, spelling, or typographical errors.

- **U**se short paragraphs, and leave a space between paragraphs.

The Internet was developed in 1969 as a research tool but has since expanded to include commercial, defense, education, and government sites.

There are several ways to access the Internet:

- Use a commercial on-line service, such as America Online, CompuServe, Microsoft Network, or Prodigy. Besides Internet access, these services offer connections to discussion groups and specialized indexes not available through direct Internet access.

- Use an Internet service provider (ISP), a local or national service that provides direct access to the Internet and the use of e-mail.

- Use a local area network that has Internet access, such as a university or a government organization network.

Most commercial on-line services offer Internet access for either a by-the-minute or a monthly fee; most Internet service providers charge a flat monthly fee for unlimited access.

Besides e-mail, several other services are available on the Internet:

- World Wide Web
- Search tools
- On-line databases

- Chat rooms
- Electronic bulletin boards

World Wide Web (WWW).   The *World Wide Web,* or *Web,* is a collection of *home pages*—screens of information that look like magazine pages. These home pages may include colorful logos, graphical icons, pictures with links to other pages, text files, and even video or sound clips.

The Web displays images and eliminates the need to know the Internet address of a particular collection or bit of information. On the Web you can move from site to site by clicking on arrows, buttons, or hypertext links. A *hypertext link* is a word or words that connects material at one site to related information at another site. Hypertext links give the user the ability to click on an image, icon, word, or sentence to get different information. Hypertext links appear as underlined words on Web pages.

The actual location of a home page is reflected in its URL (universal resource locator), which is simply an address your computer and software understand.

You can also view Web pages by using Web browsers and search engines. A *Web browser,* such as Netscape Navigator, is software that helps you view Web pages. When you connect to the Internet, you type the address of a particular Web site in an address box. Note the following examples of Web addresses.

Wall Street Journal	http://www.wsj.com
U. S. Census Bureau	http://www.census.gov
United Nations	http://www.un.org

A *search engine* is software that lets you search for information using a *keyword* or *keywords* that you type in a search window. Some examples of search engines are Alta Vista, Yahoo! and Infoseek. Search engines maintain an index of words that appear on Internet sites. The indexes are narrow in scope: Some are worldwide while others deal with specific industries or topics.

Here's how a search engine works:

1. The user types a keyword or words in a search box.

2. The search engine looks through its index and gives the user a list of sites that contain the keyword or words.

3. The user clicks on the names of sites he or she wants to review.

An important point to remember: No one has authority over the entire World Wide Web. Each resource you tap into is owned and maintained by someone different.

There are many situations for which the World Wide Web can be used in either your professional or your personal life.

- Assume you are working part-time in a law office and one of the partners tells you he needs information on the Claws 'N' Jaws case that was tried in the U.S. Supreme Court in 1993. By using the Web you can familiarize yourself with the formatting of U.S. Supreme

KEY POINT

Hypertext links are similar to cross-references that appear in encyclopedias.

Technology

In a Web address, the letters *http* stand for "hypertext transfer protocol," a communication protocol that moves documents on the Web. The letters *www* stand for "World Wide Web."

Figure 9.6

Court rulings; then you can use the information on that case to summarize the specific details for your employer. What would you do?

- Your employer has asked you to research the topic of harassment in the workplace using sources on the Internet, and then prepare a presentation for the staff on the information you were able to find. What would you do?

- Assume that you will be going on your dream vacation. Use the Web to research travel options, accommodations, and sightseeing attractions. What would you do?

Search Tools. There are some Internet search tools that let you search text files that do not contain graphics.

- Archie is a service that searches for files available by anonymous FTP. *File transfer protocol (FTP)* is a set of formats and rules that allows users to access files among computer systems on the Internet (usually from a computer at a different location from that of their own computer).

- Gopher ("go for" files) is a menu-based search tool allowing access to documents, files, and other services. Gopher permits you to focus on the information you want rather than on the services required to obtain it. An additional searching tool available through Gopher is Veronica. Veronica searches Gopher menus throughout the Internet. Jughead is a tool used to search Gopher menus usually at a specific site.

On-Line Databases. During the late 1980s networked computers were growing at an extraordinary rate and there was a tremendous demand for access to the Internet by the general public. Commercial on-line carriers such as America Online, CompuServe Information Service,

Prodigy, Dow Jones News/Retrieval, Nexis, and others were formed to offer on-line databases to the general public for a fee. This type of on-line database is an external database (compared with the internal database discussed in conjunction with integrated software packages in Section 9.1). Some types of on-line databases include statistical and bibliographic information. The fees for using an on-line database program are based on the amount of time used or on a fixed monthly rate.

Statistical or bibliographic databases can be accessed either on-line or from CD-ROMs. Statistical databases contain numerical data such as employment figures, census reports, and so on; the information is often provided by the United States government. A bibliographic database contains listings of books, magazine articles, and other publications and is used extensively by researchers.

Subscribers must have a modem to access on-line databases. This type of search costs from $20 to $250 an hour, or you may pay a monthly flat fee for unlimited use. CD-ROM databases do not require a modem because once you subscribe to a service you are provided with the disk that contains all the information. Services for updating the CD-ROM are also managed by the on-line provider. Some commercial on-line services have developed their own Web-browsing features.

One business use of statistical or bibliographic on-line services might be to research population growth in a particular region in preparation for developing new products.

Chat Rooms.   A *chat room* is a silent, text-based, real-time conversation among two or more people typing into a window on the computer screen. Other people can see what you are typing as you type, and you can instantly see their responses. The biggest advantage of participating in a chat room is that you get immediate feedback from the other participants. Following an on-line chat can be confusing because there may be many people involved in the on-line discussion, and some may be there for reasons other than discussing the topic. When you leave a chat room and log off the computer, any messages that were created while you were in the chat room disappear. Select chat rooms that deal with a specific area of interest rather that ones of general interest; that way, the conversation will be more focused.

Electronic Bulletin Boards.   *Electronic bulletin boards* (EBBs) are public message centers—electronic versions of a bulletin board. Instead of thumbtacks, you use mouse clicks to post your thoughts, questions, or information. EBBs are also known as *newsgroups*.

The difference between an e-mail message and an electronic bulletin board is the number of people for whom a message is intended. While e-mail is intended for a particular person or persons, everyone who has access to the network has access to messages on a bulletin board. With a modem, appropriate communication software, and a password, you can connect your computer to the network that contains the bulletin board. *Usenet* is a set of world-wide special-interest electronic bulletin boards for sharing public messages and participating in discussion groups.

World View

Some countries have restrictions on Internet use. In China, users are required to register with the police; in Saudi Arabia, only hospitals and universities have Internet access.
—*Human Rights Watch*

Why would you want to use an electronic bulletin board?

- Messages can be read and posted at your leisure.
- Messages are organized by topic and monitored by content.
- Messages can stay up several weeks so you have a backlog of questions and answers.
- On-line services monitor content as well as organize and remove inappropriate messages; these services may even revoke access privileges for people who abuse bulletin boards.

Electronic communication plays a key role in the business world today. Learning about the technology and its applications is essential for success in business communication.

SECTION 9.2   REVIEW

Practical Application

1. List several advantages to using telecommunications in business.
2. Give examples of three situations in which you would use e-mail on the job. Is it appropriate to use e-mail for personal use on the job? Why or why not? Should organizations monitor the use of e-mail at their sites? Why or why not?
3. Research the topic of harassment in the workplace (including sources on the Internet), and prepare a one-page memo for your classmates that presents your findings. You will send your memo by e-mail.
4. Your company is considering installing a voice-mail system, and you have been appointed chairperson of the committee to gather information about voice mail. It is critical that you gather the right type of information and talk to current users of voice-mail systems. You must make a persuasive case to the chief financial officer so he will approve the request to purchase voice mail. In your research, ask voice-mail users to answer these three questions:
   a. What are the benefits your company has derived from using voice mail?
   b. What costs did you incur initially when purchasing the system, and what are your ongoing costs?
   c. Have you experienced any problems with the system you installed? If so, what were they and how were the problems solved?
5. You have sold your current vehicle and have just purchased a new one. You want to be sure that you have insurance coverage on your new vehicle before you leave the car dealer so you call your insurance agent. When you call your agent, you receive his

voice mail. Compose the message that you will leave notifying the agent of your purchase and your need to have insurance.

6. You have just received an e-mail message from an employee in the human resource department indicating that the department is in the process of scheduling an all-staff workshop for training. The employee would like you to tell him what topics would be of interest to you, what day of the week is best for you, and any suggestions you may have on possible presenters.

7. Compose a greeting that will be recorded on your voice mail indicating that you will be away for several days but that callers can either leave a message or contact Tom Rubin at 555-3737 if they need immediate help. Make sure the message is brief but that it contains all necessary information.

Editing Practice

Revise the following telecommunications so that none exceeds 15 words. Aim for brevity, clarity, and completeness.

1. Phillip Goetz expects to arrive in Boston on WeMass Flight 15 on Friday morning at 8 a.m. Please arrange to pick him up at the airport and brief him on the Tracy-Phelps contract en route to the board meeting. (39 words)

2. Our Purchase Order 7683 for four mahogany desks and matching executive chairs has not arrived, and our inventory is depleted. If the order has not yet been shipped, arrange shipment for six of each by the fastest method. (38 words)

3. The computer printout of the March sales forecast was lost and never reached us. Please send two copies by Express Mail immediately. (22 words)

Considerations for Communicating Electronically

SECTION 9.3

OBJECTIVES:
After completing Section 9.3, you should be able to:

1. Discuss the considerations that need to be taken into account when you are transmitting messages.
2. Identify the characteristics of each mode of communication technology.
3. Choose the appropriate mode for transmitting messages in particular situations.

Computers are going to become as necessary to the business world as air.

—Andrew Grove, president of Intel Corporation

Business people deal on a daily basis with different time zones, physical distances, and deadlines. It is important to understand what telecommunication alternatives are available to help you meet these challenges in accomplishing your tasks. Once you identify the communication options you have, you can choose the medium that is most appropriate for the situation.

When deciding which technology-based medium to use for transmitting a message, you must weigh several considerations carefully. The impact of sending a message using a certain technology will vary from receiver to receiver, depending on the receiver's comfort level and understanding of the technology. For example, a message transmitted through the most expedient mode may be seen as more important than one that is sent through other channels and takes a longer time to arrive at the recipient's address. Even methods of special delivery are perceived quite differently, such as the use of e-mail with an "Important" designation versus the use of special delivery mail. In much the same way, the type of message (written or oral) may be perceived very differently by receivers based on their experiences and comfort areas. Usually, a written message gets more attention than an oral message because we tend to think of oral messages as being more informal and, therefore, not as important.

FACTORS TO CONSIDER

The factors that need to be considered when determining what media or technology is most appropriate to a situation include time and speed, quality, confidentiality, cost, volume, personalization, feedback capacity, hard copy availability, and message complexity and intensity.

Time and Speed

Time refers to how fast you can get a message to its intended receiver. The speed with which a message or document reaches its intended receiver is affected by both preparation time and delivery time. The time-speed factor may also be thought of in terms of when (hour or day or week) you are sending the message and when it can be received.

Generally, e-mail is faster than a mailed letter, but with the use of special mail services, the time difference can be insignificant. Faxing also reduces the transmittal time of documents. One big advantage of using e-mail and fax technology is that the message can be delivered even after office hours. Although oral presentations generally take a significant amount of time to prepare and present, if the presentation is videotaped, it can be reused making the initial time and cost worthwhile.

Quality

Quality shows in the ability to deliver a professional-looking message. There are times when the most important factor is not that the message look nicely printed on bond paper. Rather it is more important that

there just be a hard copy of record. With teleconferencing, the quality of the transmission may have an impact on the audience's perception of the quality or value of the presentation.

Quality is especially important when you are sending a message to someone outside the organization. Written messages should be formatted attractively, with appropriate paragraphing and plenty of white space. Both written documents and e-mail messages should be checked for correctness.

Confidentiality

When transmitting any document, you need to determine whether the document contains material that is common knowledge or restricted information. This may determine how the message will be sent. For example, if your company is submitting a bid to provide the new high school with computers for its classrooms, you want to be sure that only the people who need to see the bid have access to it. If unauthorized people see the bid, the result could be disastrous for your business; another organization might underbid you, and your business could face a large loss of income. A written message sent in an envelope marked "Confidential" is usually more confidential than an e-mail or voice-mail message.

Cost

In order to determine the true cost of sending a message, you need to consider not only the actual cost of transmission but also the cost of the equipment and any labor costs associated with sending a message.

Most individuals who use the technology on a daily basis aren't the ones responsible for paying the salaries of the individuals using the technology or the bills for the purchase and maintenance of the equipment. Therefore, they tend to think in terms of the one-time, or "relative," cost of transmitting a message.

E-mail is an inexpensive way to transmit documents, as is the U.S. Postal Service. The cost of a fax is based on the phone charges incurred in sending the fax. If the fax is a local number, the charge is based on local phone rates. If the transmission is long-distance, the charges for the fax are based on long-distance rates and the billing is slightly more than for a local fax. In both instances, fax charges are very reasonable for the quality and speed of service you receive. Special mail services are somewhat more expensive than first-class mail.

You may also want to make souvenirs for your guests to take home as memorandums.

Volume

Volume refers to the number of persons who must receive the same message. There are several media that allow you to send multiple copies of a message with ease.

The most basic of these methods is the form letter that can be personalized with a minimum of effort using word processing software. Often this type of message is not urgent, so it is sent through the U.S. Postal Service as first-class mail. If a form letter is urgent, it may be sent by fax to different destinations.

Multiple copies of the same document may also be sent by e-mail. In this medium the message is exactly the same for all recipients, and the "TO" line lists the names of everyone who will receive the message. An e-mail message sent to multiple receivers is not confidential (everybody gets the same information and everyone can see exactly who is getting the information). It is informal in nature, and it reaches the receiver rather quickly.

If you need to send a brief message to several people at the same location, voice mail may be the most convenient method. Most voice-mail systems have an option for sending the same message to several people. Telephone calls are most convenient when you have just one or two people to contact.

KEY POINT

Messages sent to several people at the same location are easily handled by voice mail or e-mail if the messages are relatively short.

Personalization

You need to know the customers you serve. Some people do not respond well to technology and want the human touch in their dealings with organizations. Assume a caller is trying to reach her counselor at school only to be greeted by this voice-mail message: "This is the Office of Gerald Strong at Union College. I will be in and out of the office today. Please leave a message and I will get back to you as soon as I can." A person who feels comfortable with technology will see voice mail as a normal business practice and will leave a message and wait for the call back. The person who disdains the "cold, impersonal" machine may simply hang up, thinking "If I'm not important enough to have a person take my call, forget it!"

KEY POINT

The sender's level of familiarity with the receiver determines the amount of personalization needed in sending a message.

Feedback Capacity

Written messages elicit no immediate feedback. By the time you get a response to a written message, it may be too late to make adjustments or to consider the feedback for decision making. Oral messages, whether they are by phone, voice mail, videophone, or videoconferencing, provide immediate feedback in the form of questions, comments, tone of voice, hesitation, and nonverbal cues.

Hard Copy Availability

In some cases, it is critical (in fact, it may be a legal requirement) to have a written record of a document or message. Technologies that use a paper-based document such as word processing and fax automatically provide a hard copy of any document that is transmitted. Some legal restrictions may apply to the acceptability of faxes. Check first if you are faxing legal or other sensitive documents.

What about e-mail? E-mail messages can easily be printed from the screen and then filed, but otherwise they do not leave a hard copy. They do, however, remain electronically filed. Be aware that what you say in an e-mail message can be traced back to you!

Message Complexity and Intensity

If a message is complex, you would be wise to send a written document. When a message covers a number of issues or deals with complex issues, most people like to have a hard copy of the message to refer to in subsequent messages or conversations. The hard copy document can be used as a point of clarification, and the receiver and sender do not need to rely on their memory to deal with the situation. If an issue or concern is simple and easy to understand, voice-mail, the telephone, or e-mail may be the most expedient way of conveying the message. Even a simple message needs to be followed up with the information in writing if the consequences could be far-reaching.

A high-intensity message is one that conveys unpleasant information or highly emotional information. For example, persuasive messages are best communicated using a written medium that is capable of carrying complex information in a structured format. Also, emotionally charged messages like performance appraisals are best handled through a hard copy document that is transmitted to the receiver using technology that maintains the confidentiality of the message.

Formality

Some communication technologies are more appropriate for formal communications. For example, annual reports, letters of recommendation, agendas, and so on are more formal: they aren't meant to present the image that issues are negotiable. The concepts are pretty well set, and the transmission of the document to the receiver may be only a courtesy. Informal communications, on the other hand, are written in a conversational tone and encourage input from the receiver: they tend to make the receiver feel like he or she can offer suggestions without fear of repercussions. E-mail and voice mail are both examples of informal communication technology.

Keep in mind that you can also use more than one technology to convey messages. The disadvantage of one medium can be offset by the advantages of another; by using more than one medium, you may stimulate more interest in the message than you would have if only one mode of transmission had been used.

Technology provides us, as communicators, with choices. However, technology does not change our need to carefully analyze each situation on its individual merits, plan and compose our messages with care, and choose our transmission media to derive the maximum return on our efforts. Automatically choosing the latest technology does not necessarily guarantee that you will get the desired response.

SECTION 9.3   REVIEW

Practical Application

1. For each of the following tasks, decide which communication technology would be the most appropriate for the situation. Be prepared to explain the reasoning behind your choice.
   a. A manager needs to warn two employees that their performance is below company standards.
   b. A contractor needs to submit a bid by midnight on Thursday (three days from today) for a large paving project for the county.
   c. The CEO of an international company wants to give a state-of-the-company address to 64,000 employees located at sites in the United States, Canada, England, and Australia.
   d. A national sales manager wants to notify sales representatives (57 of them) that their most popular product will no longer be produced, but a new and improved product will be replacing it.
   e. The chairman of the office technology committee needs to notify committee members of the next meeting and supply them with an agenda for that meeting.
   f. The director of human resource development plans to offer half-day seminars on topics of interest to employees. The plan is to construct a survey and then disseminate it to all staff members to get their input before scheduling any workshops.
2. You work for a consulting company that has been hired by a local medical products company to investigate and make recommendations on how technology can be used to communicate with potential customers. What types of information would be communicated between the business and its customers? Is there a certain type of technology that would work well for each of the types of communication you identified as being used in this organization?
3. At the last minute your supervisor asks you to attend a meeting next week in her place. You want to be sure your own clients are

taken care of while you are gone. A coworker has agreed to help handle your clients if he is available. However, you anticipate that there will be some phone calls requesting service while you are at this conference. Compose the message you will leave on your voice mail while you are gone.

Editing Practice

Spelling Alert! On a separate sheet of paper rewrite the paragraph below, correcting the problems with numbers and any spelling errors.

Too administrative assistants wanted two share the use of a computer workstation equiped with a fax machine an a modem. Both assistants felt this arrangement would work because each assistant types only for hours per ate-hour day. Each assistants works with three executives. The six executives agree two the trade.

CRITICAL THINKING CASE

Selecting the Appropriate Technology. Andrea Dial, an assistant for the human resources manager at Acme Financial Systems, is arranging a one-day conference for employees at the headquarters site. Plans for the conference have been changed to include participants at other company sites. Andrea has been asked to make arrangements for a videoconference set up for the other sites. Andrea needs to provide the participants at the other locations with information on how the videoconference will work at these remote locations. Andrea's supervisor has also given her the responsibility of negotiating the speaking fees with the speakers. These tasks need to be completed rather quickly.

1. What technology or technologies should Andrea use to communicate with the off-site participants?

2. What technology should she use to contact the speakers?

10.1 **Planning Messages**

10.2 **Planning Memos**

10.3 **Memo Parts and Formats**

10.4 **Letter Parts and Formats**

10.5 **Stationery and Envelopes**

Vanessa Sierra had recently been promoted to a supervisory position at Automation Incorporated, a medium-sized engineering company employing about 50 people. She was pleased about the promotion and was eager to do a good job. Vanessa believed that communication was one of her strong points and that additional communication at the company would improve not only company operations but also employee morale.

Vanessa started putting all her observations, suggestions, and ideas in memos and sending them to anyone who could conceivably have any interest in the subjects of her memos. Because she wrote so many memos, she spent very little time planning and organizing them, and they were quite lengthy and wordy. In addition, Vanessa always sent copies to anyone who ranked above her.

To make matters worse, most of the memos contained errors—spelling, grammar, punctuation, and so on. The other employees began to resent receiving a lengthy memo about every little thing when they were accustomed to receiving most of their communication through a brief conversation or phone call. Vanessa's supervisors were tired of the proliferation of memos about details in which they had no interest.

Ken Howie, Vanessa's immediate supervisor, had received several verbal complaints from other employees about Vanessa's memos. Behind Vanessa's back, other employees were referring to Vanessa as the "Memo Queen."

Although Ken realized that Vanessa needed to learn more about the basics of communication—communicating to one's supervisors, as well as to people being supervised—he thought that a good first step might be to point out the spelling, punctuation, and formatting errors in Vanessa's memos. He hoped that Vanessa might write fewer memos if she spent more time on making sure that they were correct. He asked Vanessa to meet with him to discuss her memo writing.

As you read Chapter 10, identify some strategies Vanessa could use to write more effective memos.

Planning Messages

OBJECTIVES:

After completing Section 10.1, you should be able to:

1. Discuss four possible reactions of the reader to your business message and identify which approach would be most appropriate for each reaction.
2. Discuss four or more techniques for achieving a positive, lasting impression with business messages.
3. Describe the use of special formatting and mechanical techniques in business messages.

KEY POINT

Readers will have one of four reactions to a business message: pleased, neutral, displeased, or little or no interest.

Planning is a prerequisite to getting things done.

—Rulon G. Craven, author

In business writing, careful planning and proper formatting are key to producing memos and letters that reflect positively on you and your company or organization.

DETERMINE YOUR READER'S REACTION

The first step in planning a business message is to determine what your reader's reaction will be to your message. Almost all recipients' reactions will fall into one of these four categories: pleased, neutral, displeased, or little or no interest. Depending on what you expect your reader's reaction will be, you will use one of three approaches for planning a message: direct, indirect, or persuasive. See Figure 10.1 below.

Pleased or Neutral Reaction

If your reader will be pleased to get your message (or at least have a neutral reaction), you can get right to the point: the good news or the information. Use the *direct approach,* in which you state the main point of the

Figure 10.1

The reader's reaction to a message depends on the content and the approach the writer used. Which approach might elicit a favorable response?

message in the opening sentence. Follow the opening statement with supporting information. Close with an upbeat ending.

Direct Approach
Good news
↓
Supporting information
↓
Upbeat ending

In a memo, you might close by stating what action to take or by requesting information. In a letter, you should close by reselling your service and/or product and building goodwill.

Displeased Reaction

When you expect the reader to be displeased, unwilling, or even hostile to your message, use the *indirect approach*. With the indirect approach, begin the message with a "buffer" that presents background information.

Indirect Approach
Buffer
↓
Reasons/Explanation
↓
Bad news
↓
Buffer

Never start a message with bad news. This puts the reader in a negative frame of mind. Instead, sandwich the bad news in the middle of the message; start and end with a neutral "buffer" and put the bad news in the middle, after an explanation of why you are saying no.

Little-or-No-Interest Reaction

If your recipient will have little interest in your message, you must sell the recipient on the message you are sending. This type of message calls for the *persuasive approach*. With this approach, you begin by getting the reader's attention in the opening sentence. This "hook" is crucial in encouraging the reader to continue reading. Follow the hook by presenting benefits that generate the reader's interest. Then provide additional information that creates a desire on the reader's part for the plan, product, or service. Close the message by asking for the desired action on the part of the reader.

Persuasive Approach
Attention-getter
↓
Interest
↓
Desire
↓
Action

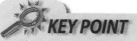
KEY POINT

Use the direct approach when your reader will be pleased or neutral.

KEY POINT

Use the indirect approach when your reader will be displeased.

KEY POINT

Use the persuasive approach when the reader will have little or no interest in the message.

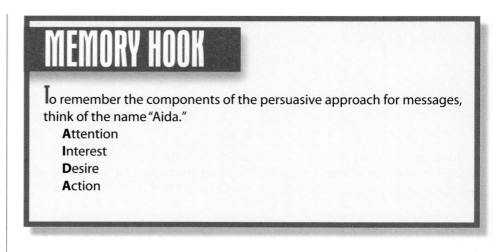

IMPROVING THE MESSAGE CONTENT AND PRESENTATION

Once you determine your reader's reaction and the approach to use in organizing the message, you need to plan the content so that you will make a lasting impression on the reader. Two ways to make such an impression are to use the six Cs of communication and to use special formatting techniques.

Use the Six Cs of Communication

By using the six Cs of communication, you can write messages that are tailored to the reader's needs.

KEY POINT

Using the six Cs of communication ensures that your message is reader-centered.

- **Be clear.** Give specific information, use direct wording, use transitions, and replace any specialized terms or jargon with terms that are familiar to readers.
- **Be complete.** Include all pertinent details so that the reader has all the information needed to make a decision.
- **Be concise.** Get to the point and do it quickly—without being abrupt, curt, or rude. Cut irrelevant words, sentences, or paragraphs. You will save your reader time, and you will improve your letter or memo.
- **Be consistent.** Use the same treatment for similar items, such as listing courtesy titles with names and using two-letter state abbreviations in addresses. Also, use formatting techniques such as indenting, numbering, and single- or double-spacing consistently throughout a document.
- **Be correct.** Verify that the information is accurate. Also, check the document for correct grammar, usage, spelling, and punctuation.
- **Be courteous.** Use the you-attitude, writing your message with the reader's viewpoint in mind.

Use Special Formatting and Mechanical Techniques

Formatting and mechanical techniques can simplify the overall organization of a memo or letter and thereby encourage further reading. Some suggestions for using special formatting techniques follow.

1. Use enumerations to list important items.

   Please complete the following tasks before tomorrow morning:

   1. Make 20 copies of the inventory report and the sales report.
   2. Collate and staple the reports and put a copy in each manager's folder.
   3. Call the managers to remind them of the meeting.

2. Use bullets to emphasize several points when the sequence of the items is not important.

   Here are some topics we will discuss at next week's staff meeting:

   • Orientation program for new employees
   • Stock purchases by employees
   • Employee training programs
   • Education benefit program
   • Severance plan

3. Use bold, underline, italics, solid capitals, or centering to emphasize important details.

   Tomorrow at 9 a.m. Leo Coleman will be here to discuss
   MANAGING CHANGE IN OUR ORGANIZATION

4. Use columns with headings to make reading and understanding easier.

   Below are the inventory figures for March:

Number	Product	Cases
Y-3346	Wallpaper	1300
Z-4384	Cushions	2856
M-8729	Curtains	1438
L-4778	Comforters	1143

5. Use underlining or bold and side headings to show natural breaks in a message.

   Our new vacation policy rewards continued employment.

   Service—6 Months or Less
   Employees who have been with the company 6 months or less will receive one-half day of paid vacation for each month of full-time employment.

   Service—7 to 11 Months
   Employees who have been with the company 7 to 11 months will receive three-fourths of one day of paid vacation for each month of employment.

   Service—One to Two Years
   Employees who have been with the company one to two years will receive fourteen days of paid vacation.

KEY POINT

Use a numbered list (an enumeration) when the sequence of items is important, as is the case for steps in a set of instructions. Use a bulleted list when a series of items follows no particular sequence.

6. Use color coding to attract attention. For example, use yellow paper for all messages from the accounting department. Or use a colored highlighting pen to attract attention. The color used can have a special meaning: For example, blue could be used for general announcements (Our profits are up); red could signify needed information (All expense reports must be turned in by June 6).

Exercise caution in using these special techniques—overuse reduces their effectiveness.

SECTION 10.1   REVIEW

Practical Application

On a separate sheet of paper, answer the following questions.
1. List the four possible reactions by the reader of a business message, and indicate which approach should be used for each reaction.
2. Describe six special formatting and mechanical techniques that can be used with business messages.
3. Why should you be cautious when you use special formatting and mechanical techniques in writing business messages?

Editing Practice

A. On a separate sheet of paper, revise the following expressions to use clearer, more up-to-date wording.
1. In re your letter of the 27th of June, . . .
2. At the present writing we still have not received . . .
3. Please be advised that your dividend will be $6000, not $600.
4. In the event that August 14 is an inconvenient date, kindly let us know when you would like to have the speakers delivered.
5. Due to the fact that property sales are down because of . . .

B. On a separate sheet of paper, revise the following sentences to make them more concise.
1. Prior foresight would have saved us these cost overruns.
2. The same identical error message appeared the last time I used this word processing command.
3. Unless the whole staff cooperates together, we won't finish the manuscript in time for spring publication.

4. Their management styles are both alike.
5. The heating system has been converted over from gas to solar power.

C. On a separate sheet of paper, make the following sentences clearer and more forceful by using simple words.
1. From the expression on Michael's face, we knew that he was engaged in deep ratiocination.
2. The managing partner discommended the proposal.
3. Phyllis was the cynosure of the labor negotiations.
4. His dark blue suit was in every way comme il faut.
5. Her remarks precipitated a veritable brouhaha.

Critical Thinking Skills

Using some special formatting techniques, write the body of a memo using the following information.

In her memo of July 15, your supervisor, Rosa Hernandez, asked you to give her a list of sales by region for April, May, and June. The sales figures are, respectively, Region 1—$23,494, $22,577, $19,482; Region 2—$33,458, $32,332, $25,854; Region 3—$21,589, $21,887, $20,492. Write the body of a memo listing this information in column format.

Planning Memos

SECTION 10.2

OBJECTIVES:

After completing Section 10.2, you should be able to:

1. Name four advantages of using memos.
2. List six purposes of memos.
3. Describe how to tailor the tone of a memo to the recipient.
4. Identify the three elements in the body of a memo.
5. Explain how to write complete, correct, and effective memos.

Memorandums represent more than 50 percent of written communications in businesses today. You send *memos,* as they are often called, to someone within your own organization. Letters, on the other hand, are usually written to people outside your organization. Memos may be sent within a department, among departments, and among company branches at different geographic locations.

IMPORTANCE OF MEMOS

When a matter is important or complicated, employees within an organization should put their thoughts in writing. This is why memos are essential to business communication.

ADVANTAGES OF MEMOS

KEY POINT

Memos are quick, inexpensive, and convenient. Also, they serve as documentation for future reference.

Memos fill the needs for both effective internal communication and written documentation of messages. Organizations are often large and diversified, with branches or divisions of a company located in different states or even countries. Memos are a logical way to coordinate the efforts of many people within an organization.

1. **Memos are quick.** Using technology can reduce the time needed to write and send memos. Many software programs include memo templates that make it easy to compose a memo. By using e-mail and fax machines, a writer can quickly transmit memos to recipients.

2. **Memos are inexpensive.** Compared with telephone calls and meetings, memos are a cost-effective way to transmit messages within an organization because all recipients receive the same information. Using plain paper instead of letterhead or preprinted memo forms also reduces the cost of memos.

3. **Memos are convenient.** Memos offer access to people who are not seen on a regular basis. Memos also minimize interruptions for the receiver. In addition, reading a memo requires less time than a phone call or a personal visit.

4. **Memos are a written record.** Memos serve as a written record for both the reader and the writer. Memos can, for example, clarify instructions or information given orally. In many situations, a well-written memo can help prevent misunderstandings.

Technology

Using e-mail, a writer can send a memo to several people without making separate copies for each recipient. The recipient has the option of printing the e-mail message for future reference.

PURPOSES OF MEMOS

Memos are used for a variety of purposes. The main purposes are to inquire, to inform, to report, to remind, to transmit, and to promote goodwill.

To Request

Use memos to ask for information, action, or reactions. Memos written for this purpose take the direct approach, as in the following examples.

Figure 10.2

Memos offer a quick, convenient way to make inquiries, explain policies, send reminders, and transmit information.

Before the cost estimates for the Bryant project can be completed, we will need revised sales figures from you.

Please make arrangements for a one-day seminar for all trainees.

Will you please review this proposal and give me your opinion of it?

To Inform

Use memos to communicate procedures, company policies, and instructions. If the message contains good news, use the direct approach; if the message contains bad news, use the indirect approach.

> Our safety procedures require a 15-minute break for every 4 hours of work.

> Company policy permits escorted visitors (16 years old and older) to tour our plant.

> Use your key card to enter the Third Avenue gate.

To Report

Use memos to convey organized data such as schedules, sales figures, and names of clients or patients, as in these examples.

> Below is our schedule for the completion of Lincoln Hall.

> Here is a list of the donors who will attend the fundraiser.

A confidential memo giving specifics about a new product was accidentally faxed to a competitor.

To Remind

Use memos as reminders about deadlines, important meetings, and so on. Such reminders should be brief and should use the direct approach.

> Please send me your travel itinerary by May 6.

> Is our appointment with the Southern Telcom representatives on your calendar for Monday, April 3, at 2 p.m. in the main conference room?

To Transmit

Use memos to tell readers about an accompanying message. The memo could describe, explain, or simply identify the attachment or enclosure. The direct approach works best for such memos.

> Attached are the time sheets to be distributed to all hourly employees.

> Enclosed is a printout listing the names and home addresses of all regional managers.

To Promote Goodwill

Use memos to establish, improve, and maintain goodwill. These memos can congratulate, welcome, or convey appreciation.

> Congratulations on your promotion.

> Welcome to Howard Industries.

> Renee, your advertising designs got us the Wright Corporation account. Thanks for a great job!

TONE OF THE MEMO

The tone of a memo depends largely on the position of, and the writer's relation to, the recipient. Relationships are often clear between two people on different levels within an organization. In general, use a more formal tone when addressing top management than when writing to a peer or a subordinate, unless you know that the addressee prefers an informal tone.

Even within clear corporate structures, there will be times when a writer is not certain which tone to use in a memo. The best course in these cases is to choose a balanced tone—neither too formal nor too casual. Avoid using contractions like *you'll* and *here's,* but do not use stilted language either. Stick to business. Note the balanced tone in the following example:

> Here is the report on last month's video camera sales, with the changes you requested yesterday. The figures on Model A26 are now broken down to show the number of these video cameras sold in each sales region. In addi-

KEY POINT

The tone of a memo is determined by (1) the position of the writer in relation to the recipient and (2) the subject matter of the memo.

tion, the appropriate tables now have an added line showing Model A26 sales by region for the same period last year.

Subject matter also determines the choice of tone for a memo. A memo announcing the schedule of the company's bowling team would obviously have a lighter tone than a memo justifying costs that ran over budget. The more serious the topic, the more serious the tone should be.

ORGANIZATION OF THE MEMO

The format and the tone of a memo help the writer convey the message. The memo's organization is another means to the same end. A memo tries to "sell" its reader a particular point of view. This situation is true whether the writer wishes to convince a superior of the need for new office equipment or to convince someone under the writer's supervision of the need to maintain high work standards. A memo is more likely to achieve the writer's goal if it is brief and to the point without seeming abrupt or incomplete.

The organization of the body of a memo should be based on these three elements: (1) a statement of purpose, (2) a message, and (3) a statement of future action, as shown in Figure 10.3 on page 468.

KEY POINT

The body of a memo should contain: (1) a statement of purpose, (2) a message, and (3) a statement of future action.

Statement of Purpose

The subject line of a memo tells the reader what the memo is about but usually does not state the writer's reasons for writing. Often the writer can make the purpose clear simply by referring to an earlier memo or to a previous meeting or telephone conversation. Here are two examples of how a writer can state the purpose of a memo in the first paragraph.

> At the advertising meeting on October 15, you asked me to investigate and report on the comparative costs of print and broadcast advertisements in the Northeast. Here is a summary of my findings.

> Attached is the independent review of our admissions procedures from Dr. O'Hara. We will meet on April 5 from 9 to 11 a.m. in Conference Room A to discuss his recommendations.

Message

After making the statement of purpose, the writer should go directly to the main points of the message. The object is to help the reader grasp the main points as easily as possible, as in these two examples.

> We could admit patients more quickly and efficiently if we gave them a checklist to complete. The checklist would take the place of the long-answer forms now being used.

> A new form has been designed to simplify taking telephone orders. A copy of that form is attached.

Figure 10.3

The body of this memo contains the three organizational elements—purpose, message, and future action.

MEMO TO: Susan C. Rostagno, Advertising and Display ↓2x

FROM: James Roe, Garden Department ↓2x *J.R.*

DATE: July 1, 20— ↓2x

SUBJECT: August Newspaper Advertisements ↓2x

Purpose —— Our semiannual garden clearance sale is planned for August 10 through September 19. We will need to run ads in the local newspapers to announce the sale. ↓2x

Message —— Let's meet on July 5 to discuss copy preparation and photography for the advertisements. ↓2x

Future Action —— Would you let me know when it is convenient for you to meet to plan these ads.

Statement of Future Action

The body of the memo should usually end with a statement of future action to be taken or with a request for further instructions, as illustrated in the following two examples:

> If you would like additional information on the benefits of this proposed checklist, call me at extension 6254. If you wish, I can investigate the amount of time such a checklist would save.

> Please notify me of your decision on this matter by February 16 so that I can either put this procedure into effect or develop a new plan.

SPECIAL TECHNIQUES FOR MEMO EFFECTIVENESS

Memos, like letters, can be effective or ineffective, depending on how they are written. Here are some suggestions for writing effective memos:

1. Cover only one main topic in a memo. When memos cover too many topics, a main thought may go unnoticed or may not receive the attention it deserves.

2. Consistently use a simple, familiar heading that includes the guide words *MEMO TO, FROM, DATE,* and *SUBJECT.* Using the words *MEMO TO* eliminates the need to type the word *MEMORANDUM* at the top of the page. People who receive messages from you regularly will know exactly where to look for specific information. Some companies use printed memo forms or a standardized template (provided with some software programs)

for ease in composing memos. (Detailed information on memo types and parts appears in Section 10.3.)

3. Compose a brief but appropriate subject line. Subject lines should identify the topic, not give all the details. For example:

> SUBJECT: Updated Vacation Policy
>
> SUBJECT: Revised Gorham Contract

4. Present the key idea in the first paragraph. The idea presented at the beginning will usually receive the most attention from the reader.

5. In most instances, use a personal, pleasant, and somewhat informal tone. You will know most of your receivers because they are members of your organization. Special situations, however, such as writing to your superiors or reprimanding an employee, may require a more formal tone.

6. Strive to make memos clear, complete, concise, consistent, correct, and courteous.

In the case study at the beginning of the chapter, Vanessa would have written more effective memos if she had followed the preceding six techniques. Even though you will send most memos you write to people you know, you should not take shortcuts in your memos. An overuse of shortcuts can decrease effectiveness.

SECTION 10.2   REVIEW

Practical Application

On a separate sheet of paper, answer the following questions.

1. In what writing situation would a memo be more appropriate than a letter?
2. In what writing situation would a letter be more appropriate than a memo?
3. Identify and discuss the advantages of sending memos.
4. List and describe the three elements of the body of a memo.
5. Memos have the following purposes:

a. To request	d. To remind
b. To inform	e. To transmit
c. To report	f. To promote goodwill

For each numbered item that follows, write the letter of the purpose that best describes a memo that accomplishes the following:

1. Identifies an attached prospectus
2. Asks about the servicing of company vehicles

3. Announces a new employee dental and vision plan
4. Congratulates someone who has been transferred to another office
5. Lists sales figures for the last three months by division
6. Asks about a production schedule that was due last Friday
7. Explains the company bonus policy
8. Welcomes a new employee
9. Asks for an opinion on a new follow-up system
10. Gives instructions for ordering new computers and printers

Editing Practice

Possessives, Plurals, and Contractions.   On a separate sheet of paper, rewrite each incorrect item by adding, moving, or deleting apostrophes to make the sentences correct. Write *OK* for any sentence that is correct.
1. Lets walk over to Lisas office.
2. Two trainee's are working in the mens Sportswear Department
3. Its almost time for our annual safety inspection.
4. Most manager's agree with the Art Departments new procedures.
5. Until Harry's van is repaired, he is using his son-in-laws car.
6. Luke and Dawn's faces were sunburned after the softball game.
7. One witnesses' statement agreed with Joses.
8. Two employees must check the lock on the bank vaults' door.
9. His sister-in-law's suit was designed by Jones of Dallas.
10. This is Naomi Yonke, our companies computer technician.

Critical Thinking Skills

On a separate sheet of paper, write the body of a memo using information from the following paragraphs. Include a statement of purpose, a message, and a statement of future action. At the end of the memo, identify these three elements.

After six month's full-time employment, employees are eligible for tuition reimbursement for evening and Saturday courses taken at local colleges. Employees must have the course approved by George Earl, human resources manager. Mr. Earl requires each applicant to write a memo to him requesting approval. The memo must list the course title, the credit hours, the dates of the course, the college, the cost, and how successful completion of the course will help the employee perform his or her job.

You want to take Computer Concepts 101 at Cranbury Community College. The course begins on September 7 and meets each succeeding Monday for 12 weeks. The cost is $250 for three credit hours. Taking this computer applications course will help you improve your productivity in processing customer requests. Include your telephone extension and the deadline for enrollment (August 15).

Memo Types and Parts

"Executive overheard talking to a friend: 'My wife tells me I don't display enough passion. Imagine! I have a good mind to send her a memo!'"

—*Reader's Digest*

Even though memos are internal documents, they are a vital link in achieving an organization's objectives. In addition, successful internal communication can be important in achieving your career objectives. Section 10.3 reviews types of memos and memo parts. Selecting the appropriate type of memo for a particular purpose and being familiar with the parts of a memo help you communicate successfully with other members of your organization.

OBJECTIVES

After completing Section 10.3, you should be able to:

1. Describe the standard memo format.
2. Describe three types of printed memo forms and the circumstances in which each should be used.
3. List and describe the parts of a memo.
4. Identify the information that should appear in the heading of a memo.

TYPES OF MEMOS

Memorandums may be printed on plain paper using a standard format or template, or they may be written on preprinted forms.

Standard Memo Format

The standard memo format used on plain paper contains a heading with the guide words *MEMO TO, FROM, DATE,* and *SUBJECT,* which identify the recipient, the writer, the date the memo was written, and the subject of the memo. The guide words can be typed as shown in Figure 10.4 on page 472, or they can be part of a template available on your computer. Guide words may be typed in all-capital letters or with initial-capital letters. Do not, however, mix the all-capital letter format and the initial-capital format within the same memo.

Printed Memo Forms

Using printed forms for specific purposes is a time-saver when one type of information is frequently communicated. Three examples of printed forms are the standard memo, the message memo, and the routing slip.

Standard Memos.   Printed interoffice memo forms make it easy to both write and read memos. A common size of memo forms is 8 1/2 by 11 inches. These forms often list the writer's name and telephone number. The writer simply writes in the appropriate information and forwards the memo.

Figure 10.4

A standard memo format typed on plain paper.

MEMO TO: Rosalie Wheeler, Shipping Department

FROM: Mitch Bentley, Sales Manager ↓2x *MB*

DATE: December 1, 19— ↓2x

SUBJECT: Creative Products Order ↓2x

Please ship the Creative Products Company order (Invoice 3648)
just as soon as you can schedule it. ↓2x

Creative Products had originally requested shipment on December 10
but called this morning asking for immediate shipment. Creative Products
is one of our largest customers, and we want to cooperate. ↓2x

Please send me confirmation when you ship the order.

The heading of a printed memo form, such as the one shown in
Figure 10.5 below, usually contains (1) the name of the company, (2)
the title *Interoffice Memorandum* (or *Interoffice Memo*), and (3) the guide
words *TO, FROM, DATE,* and *SUBJECT*. In some organizations, the preferred sequence is *DATE, TO, FROM,* and *SUBJECT*. In a large organization, the heading may also contain *Department, Location, Telephone
Extension, Fax Number,* and *E-Mail Address.*

Figure 10.5

*This printed memo form
includes the company's name
and the words INTEROFFICE
MEMORANDUM, as well as the
guide words TO, FROM, DATE,
and SUBJECT.*

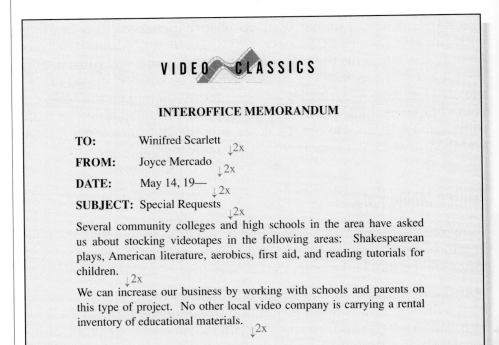

VIDEO CLASSICS

INTEROFFICE MEMORANDUM

TO: Winifred Scarlett ↓2x

FROM: Joyce Mercado ↓2x

DATE: May 14, 19— ↓2x

SUBJECT: Special Requests ↓2x

Several community colleges and high schools in the area have asked
us about stocking videotapes in the following areas: Shakespearean
plays, American literature, aerobics, first aid, and reading tutorials for
children. ↓2x

We can increase our business by working with schools and parents on
this type of project. No other local video company is carrying a rental
inventory of educational materials. ↓2x

Message Memos.   Message memos are used to record phone messages and messages from visitors. These forms consist of lines for the caller's name and telephone number and for a brief message.

Routing Slips.   Routing slips are used to systematically channel messages to specified people. If a routing slip is not used often, the spaces following the guide words for names and office telephone numbers can be left blank. If a routing slip is used often, the names and office telephone numbers should be printed on the form.

MEMO PARTS

A memo has two parts—the heading and the body.

The Heading

The heading of a memo contains the guide words *MEMO TO, FROM, DATE,* and *SUBJECT.*

THE *MEMO TO* or *TO* Line.   The *MEMO TO* or *TO* line contains the first and last name of the person or persons who are to receive the original copy of the memo. Courtesy titles are usually omitted on memos.

> MEMO TO: Carl Martin
> Rodolpho Gonzalez
> Stephanie Grimaldi

The writer should include an addressee's job title in the following situations:

1. When the writer wishes to show deference:

   MEMO TO: Rodolpho Gonzalez, Chief Executive Officer

2. When the addressee has more than one job title and the writer's message concerns the duties that pertain to only one of the titles.

   TO: Stephanie Grimaldi, Chair, Committee on Community Relations
       (Ms. Grimaldi is also the director of personnel.)

3. When the addressee has the same name as another employee, or a very similar name, so that the writer must clarify which person should receive the memo.

   TO: Carl Martin, Assistant Chief Engineer
        (Carol Martin is the production manager.)

In large companies, it helps to include address information in the *MEMO TO* or *TO* line of an interoffice memo. For example:

MEMO TO: Antonio Pappas, Room 3301, Benefits Office

TO: Michelle Gold, Laboratory 3, Research Department

If the memo is being sent to more than a few people, type *See Distribution* or *Distribution Below* on the *TO* line and place the list of

KEY POINT

A distribution list is used when a memo is addressed to more than a few people.

recipients at the end of the memo under the heading *Distribution*. Type *Distribution* on the third line below the reference initials, file notation, or enclosure notation, whichever appears last. Begin typing the list of names on the second line below *Distribution*.

Placing the distribution list at the end gives the memo a more balanced appearance and allows readers to focus on the message and not the list of recipients. List the names of recipients in alphabetical order; this is an objective way to determine the order of names. The memo in Figure 10.6 below shows a distribution list for individuals who are all branch managers.

Figure 10.6

This memo shows how a distribution list is typed. Note that the distribution list is typed in alphabetical order according to last name, since all recipients are of equal rank.

MEMO TO: Branch Managers—Distribution Below
↓2x

FROM: Wilbur Dickson, General Manager
↓2x

DATE: August 28, 19—
↓2x

SUBJECT: Meeting for Branch Managers
↓2x

The Human Resource Department has announced improvements in the employee benefits plan.
↓2x

A meeting to explain our new benefits package will be held on Monday, September 12, at 10 a.m. in Conference Room B adjoining my office.
↓2x

Please read the enclosed booklet about the package before the meeting and let me know if you have any questions about it.
↓2x

dk emp-benf
Enclosure
↓3x

Distribution:

Stella Armes
Michael Diaz
Amy Dillingham
Gilberto Henderson
Tyler Jolley
Judy Myers
Harry Poplin
CamilleWray

The *FROM* Line. The writer may include a job title, department affiliation, room number, and telephone extension in the *FROM* line.

> FROM: Edith L. Fitzpatrick, Researcher, Investment Department,
>   Room 2403, Ext. 988

The *DATE* Line. Write the date in full rather than using abbreviations or all figures.

> Business Style   December 19, 19—
> European Style   19 December 19—

The *SUBJECT* Line. The writer should state the subject of a memo clearly and briefly. To give a memo a more professional appearance, do not abbreviate the word *SUBJECT*. Only in exceptional cases should the subject line require more than a single line. The following examples say all that is necessary; the rest should be left to the body of the memo.

> SUBJECT: Request for Additional Personnel
> SUBJECT: Submitting Time Sheets

World View

The day-month-year style for dates, for example, 5 June 19—, commonly used in military correspondence, is also used in business correspondence in European countries.

The Body

A memo, unlike a business letter, includes no salutation. Instead, it begins with the first paragraph of the message. Leave one blank line between the last line of the heading and the body of the memo. Single-space the body of the memo and use blocked paragraphs with no indenting. The block paragraph style is most often used because it is easy to type; paragraphs may be indented, but they usually are not indented. Many organizations determine these matters according to a style of their own; thus new employees should find out whether there is a "house" style for memos.

Two lines below the body of the memo at the left margin, the typist should type his or her reference initials and any notations (for example, enclosure notations and copy notations) that may be needed. If the writer is the person who typed the memo, no reference initials are needed.

The trend today is to add the document name and location on the same line as or on the line below the reference initials. The notation may include the name of the document file or the location where the document is stored, such as:

> mls\winword\04\proposal   mls
> Enclosure   winword\04\proposal
> c: John W. Palmer

Dana asked Ellen, her new office assistant, to type and send a memo to Terry Israel, director of marketing. Ellen included a courtesy title on the memo and sent it to Mr. Terry Israel. Terry was upset because she did not appreciate being addressed as a man.

The Signature

The writer should sign each memo with a blue or black pen by writing his or her initials after the name on the *FROM* line. Typing or signing your full name at the end of a memo is unnecessary because the full name appears after the guide word *FROM*.

For information about other memo formats, consult a comprehensive reference manual.

SECTION 10.3   REVIEW

Practical Application

On a separate sheet of paper, answer the following questions.

1. What kinds of information are transmitted in message memos?
2. What is the purpose of routing slips?
3. When are distribution lists used in memos?
4. List three reasons why a memo writer would include the addressee's job title on the *MEMO TO* line.
5. What two types of notations might be needed below the typist's initials?
6. Match the lettered words in the second column with the numbered definitions in the first column.

   1. Line listing the topic   a. Distribution
   2. Writer's initials   b. Memo
   3. Written communication within a company   c. Signature
   4. List of persons receiving a memorandum   d. Purpose
   5. Reason for writing   e. Subject

Editing Practice

Missing and Extra Words. On a separate sheet of paper, rewrite the following paragraph, omitting the repeated words and adding missing words.

Aaron Singer of Caralia Draperies will be here tomorrow morning at 10:30 to show us his line window treatments. His best-selling draperies are bow and ribbon swags and eyelet tiebacks. Our our competitors are doing quite with these two styles of, and we have lost some business because do not carry these items.

Punctuation Check. On a separate sheet of paper, correct any punctuation errors in the following sentences. Write *OK* if a sentence has no error.

1. All Bennington Bros. tools have a five-year warranty; in our experience however most tools last for ten or more years.

2. Ms. Pirelli wrote a check for $250.00 for the college's scholarship fund.
3. May we expect your shipment by July 1?
4. We have not yet received payment for last month's order nor have we been paid for goods sent the previous month.
5. If the dates change please let me know immediately.
6. You will be glad to hear, that our new office will be open for business on September 15.

Critical Thinking Skills

You are an assistant to the director of a firm that imports fabrics for the fashion industry. The director has instructed you to report on the fabric choices of 20 prominent designers for the upcoming fall season. After analyzing the collections of major designers, you have learned that of the 20 top designers, all 20 use wool; at least 15 use cashmere and flannel; at least 10 use mohair, corduroy, cotton, and silk (mostly crepe de chine); and 5 use rayon. On a separate sheet of paper, write a memo with column headings that presents this information so that the director can understand it at a glance. Refer to the special formatting techniques discussed in Section 10.1.

Letter Parts and Formats

"A handsome appearance is a silent recommendation."

—*Aristotle*

SECTION 10.4

OBJECTIVES

After completing Section 10.4, you should be able to:

1. Identify both the standard parts and the optional parts of business letters.
2. List the order in which letter parts appear in business correspondence.
3. Explain the use and need for each letter part.
4. Describe four letter formats that are acceptable in business.
5. Describe personal- and social-business letter formats.

Think about the people you have seen within the past 24 hours. Were any two people dressed exactly alike? Did any two people say precisely the same thing?

Chances are that, except for uniformed workers such as police officers, firefighters, and restaurant employees, no two people whom you have seen recently were dressed alike. The *appearance* of each person was different (either slightly or very different) from that of the others. Moreover, the *content* of the conversations you had with various people was probably different.

These two style factors—appearance and content—can also be used to describe a business letter. How does the letter *look,* and what does the letter *say?* The appearance and content of a business letter make up the *style* of a letter, just as a person's manner of dress and the content of his or her conversation contribute to that person's style.

KEY POINT

Appearance contributes to the success of a letter.

The style of a business letter contributes as much to the success of that letter as a person's style contributes to his or her success. If your business letters are to achieve your goals, you must first learn how to control the appearance of a letter, which will be discussed in this section.

THE FIRST IMPRESSION: APPEARANCE

A writer conveys a professional appearance by using standard letter parts and arranging these parts according to accepted letter formats. Using standard letter parts and an accepted letter format ensures that the letter is arranged attractively on the page.

Business Letter Parts

KEY POINT

Letters that do not make a good first impression are not taken seriously by busy professionals.

Business letters often contain many parts. All the standard letter parts, plus some optional ones, are illustrated in Figure 10.7 on page 479.

1. Letterhead. The word *letterhead* refers to either (1) the printed information at the top of business stationery or (2) the actual sheet of paper.

The printed information in a letterhead always includes the company's name, address, telephone number, and/or fax number. The company's slogan, a listing of its divisions, names of key personnel, and/or the company's logo may be included. Companies may also include their Web site and e-mail addresses. See the letters in Figures 10.7, 10.8, and 10.9 on pages 479, 483, and 484 for sample letterheads. A company's letterhead may appear at the top, bottom, or along the side margin of business stationery.

When a letterhead is typed rather than printed, the information should be attractively arranged, starting 1 inch from the top of the page (on line 7). Word processing software simplifies typing a letterhead such as the following:

> Electronic Designs Unlimited
> 575 Harborview Drive
> Chelsea, MA 02150
> 800-555-0123

Technology

*Some word processing programs have a **date code** feature that automatically inserts the current date in a document. However, the date changes each time you subsequently display or print the document. If you want the date to stay the same, do not use a date code.*

2. Date Line. Most companies use a business-style date line with the month spelled in full, the day of the month written in figures and followed by a comma, and all four digits of the year. The European or military style date line starts with the day of the month followed by the month, no comma, and all four digits of the year. Here are examples of each:

Business style: July 10, 19—

European style: 10 July 19—

3. Inside Address. The inside address should match the name and address shown on the envelope, for example:

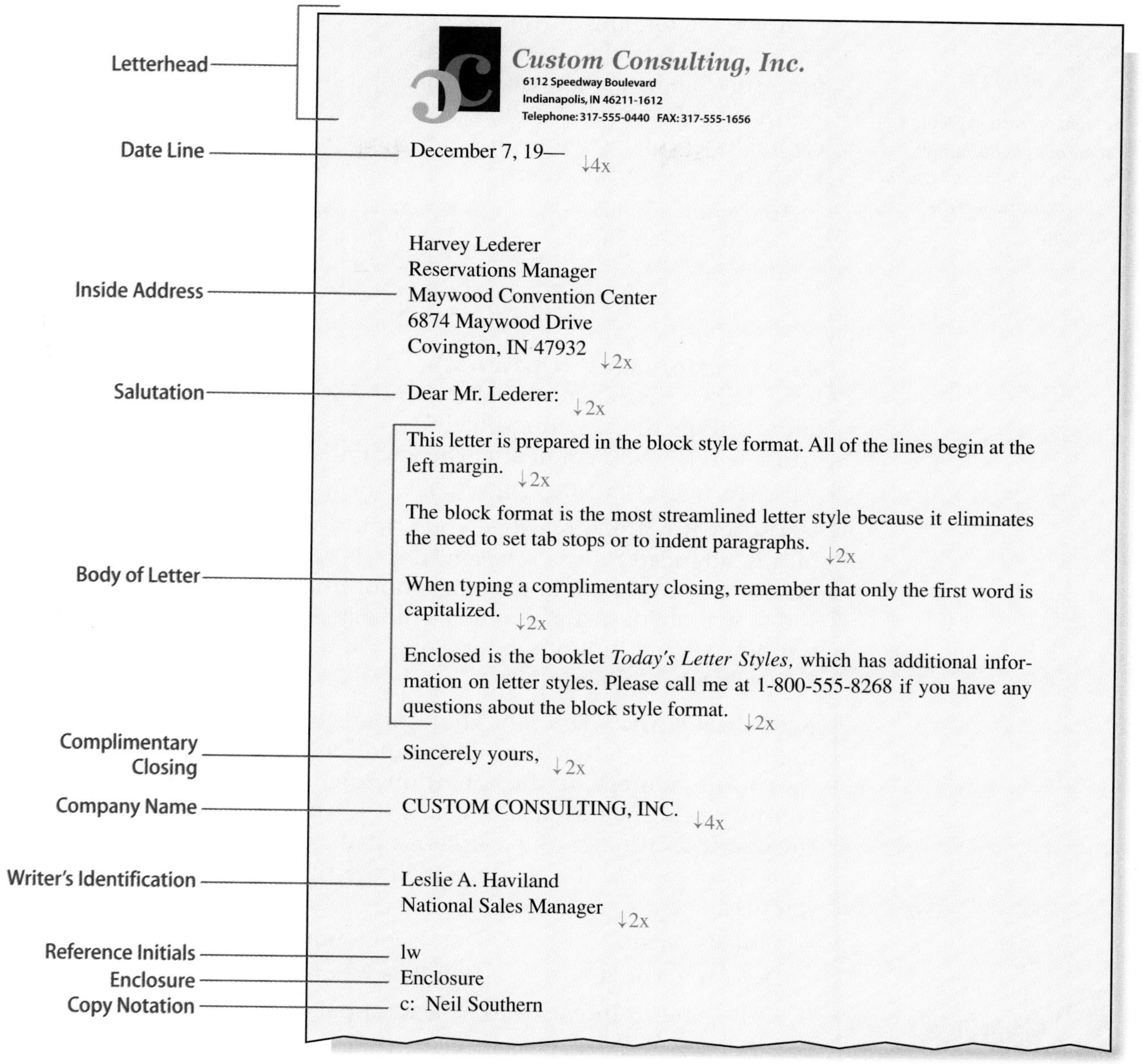

Letterhead

Custom Consulting, Inc.
6112 Speedway Boulevard
Indianapolis, IN 46211-1612
Telephone: 317-555-0440 FAX: 317-555-1656

Date Line — December 7, 19— ↓4x

Inside Address —
Harvey Lederer
Reservations Manager
Maywood Convention Center
6874 Maywood Drive
Covington, IN 47932 ↓2x

Salutation — Dear Mr. Lederer: ↓2x

Body of Letter —
This letter is prepared in the block style format. All of the lines begin at the left margin. ↓2x

The block format is the most streamlined letter style because it eliminates the need to set tab stops or to indent paragraphs. ↓2x

When typing a complimentary closing, remember that only the first word is capitalized. ↓2x

Enclosed is the booklet *Today's Letter Styles*, which has additional information on letter styles. Please call me at 1-800-555-8268 if you have any questions about the block style format. ↓2x

Complimentary Closing — Sincerely yours, ↓2x

Company Name — CUSTOM CONSULTING, INC. ↓4x

Writer's Identification —
Leslie A. Haviland
National Sales Manager ↓2x

Reference Initials — lw
Enclosure — Enclosure
Copy Notation — c: Neil Southern

Ms. Camille R. Barry
Director
Habitat for Humanity
85 East Perth Road
Conway, AR 72032

Mr. Orris Patterson
President
Patterson Consulting
P.O. Box 1473
Golden, CO 80403

Figure 10.7

The block format is very streamlined. Every letter part begins at the left margin, making this format easy to type. This letter shows all the standard parts, as well as some optional ones.

Thus the inside address includes the name of the addressee, the person's title, his or her company's name, street or post office box number, city, state, and ZIP Code.

If the address has a post office box number, type it on the line immediately preceding the city, state, and ZIP Code. The U.S. Postal Service will deliver the mail to the location typed on the line preceding the city, state, and ZIP Code.

If you are sending a letter by a carrier other than the U.S. Postal Service, such as Federal Express, Airborne, or United Parcel Service, you must use a street address; these carriers cannot deliver to a post office box.

For an international address, type the name of the country in all-capital letters on a separate line at the end of the address. Do not abbreviate the name of the country.

Mr. Ferdinand Villa	Ms. Akiko Kagami
Camino de San Rafael	The Togin Building
Málaga 29010	4-1-20 Toranomon
SPAIN	Chuo-Ku, Tokyo, 105
	JAPAN

4. Attention Line (Optional). The attention line is an optional letter part. When used it appears on the second line below the inside address. Type the attention line in all-capital letters or capital and lowercase letters. Use a colon after the word *Attention*.

ATTENTION: TRAINING DIRECTOR   Attention: Office Manager

Use an attention line when you want to stress that the letter is technically intended for the *company,* not the *person.* Also use an attention line when you do not know and cannot find out the name of the person to whom your letter should be directed. In this situation, the attention line should indicate the person's job title such as *Sales Manager* or *Customer Service Representative.*

5. Salutation. The salutation, or greeting, immediately precedes the body of the letter. Type the salutation on the second line below the inside address or the attention line, if one is used. Include a courtesy title such as *Mr.* or *Ms.,* if it is known. If you do not know the courtesy title, use the recipient's first and last name, for example, *Dear Terry Swank.* If you do not know the person's name, use the job title.

Dear Ms. Grant:	Dear Marion Smith:
Dear Mr. Zaborski:	Dear Reservations Manager:

If the letter is intended to be less formal and more friendly, use just the addressee's first name.

Dear Larry: Dear Sally:

A general salutation such as *Ladies and Gentlemen* is used to show that the company is being addressed. When you are writing to an individual whose name and gender you do not know, use a generic salutation such as *Dear Customer, Dear Sales Manager,* and so forth.

Traditionally, the salutation ends with a colon; this is known as *standard punctuation* and is the style most often used by business writers. In *open punctuation,* no punctuation is used after the salutation and complimentary closing. Open punctuation is used by only a small percentage of business writers.

6. Subject Line (Optional). Another optional part is the subject line, which is used to quickly identify the topic of the letter.

Type the subject line in capital and lowercase letters below the salutation, leaving one blank line above and below. See the subject line in Figure 10.8 on page 483.

7. Body.   The body, the main part of the letter, is typed single-spaced with one blank line between paragraphs. A good rule of thumb is to make the first and last paragraphs of the letter a maximum of 4 or 5 lines in length. Other paragraphs should be a maximum of 8 lines in length, depending on the complexity of the message.

8. Complimentary Closing.   The "good-bye" of the letter, the complimentary closing, appears on the second line below the last line in the body of the letter. Some sample complimentary closings are:

Cordially,   Cordially yours,

Sincerely,   Sincerely yours,

Capitalize only the first word in a complimentary closing, and place a comma after the last word if you are using standard punctuation. If you are using open punctuation, do not use a comma.

9. Company Name (Optional).   Some writers (and companies) use a company name; others do not. When used, the company name is typed in all-capital letters below the complimentary closing, with a blank line above and three blank lines below. See Figure 10.7 on page 479 for an example of a company name.

10. Writer's Identification.   The writer's identification consists of the writer's typed name and job title. Type the writer's name on the fourth line below the complimentary closing or the company name, whichever appears last. If the name and title are on the same line, separate them with a comma; if they are typed on two separate lines, no comma is needed.

11. Reference Initials.   Reference initials are the *typist's* initials— the person who typed the letter. Type the reference initials in lowercase letters on the second line below the writer's identification. If the writer's initials are also used, they should appear preceding the typist's

MEMORY HOOK

Remember the difference between standard and open punctuation:

Standard punctuation
Colon after salutation
Comma after
    complimentary closing

Open punctuation
No punctuation after salutation
No punctuation after
    complimentary closing

initials, with a diagonal to separate them. If the writer is also the person who typed the letter, no reference initials are needed.

JHK/prm   RSZ/bar

12. File Name Notation (Optional).   A growing trend with business letters is to include the file name of a document that is created with word processing software. A file name usually consists of one to eight characters, a period, and an extension of one to three characters, as in the following examples:

proposal.131   csmith.let

Type the file name notation on the same line as or on the line below the reference initials.

13. Enclosure Notation (Optional).   When an item or items are sent with the letter, the word *Enclosure* or *Enclosures* is typed on the line below the reference initials or the file name notation, whichever is last.

14. Transmittal Notation (Optional).   A transmittal notation is used to indicate that a letter and enclosure(s) are to be sent by some means other than first-class mail. Type the transmittal notation on the line below the enclosure notation, reference initials, or file name notation, whichever appears last.

By Certified Mail   By Federal Express   By Fax

See Figure 10.10 on page 485 for a sample transmittal notation.

15. Copy Notation (Optional).   When a copy of a letter is to be sent to a person or persons other than the addressee, the writer includes a copy notation such as *c: David Fischer* on the line below the reference initials, the enclosure notation, or transmittal notation, whichever appears last. The abbreviation *c:* or *c* means "copy to."

c: Jerry Habanero   c Melissa Temple|
                     Leroy Vaughn

16. Postscript (Optional).   The postscript is positioned at the *end* of a letter—deliberately or as an afterthought. Because it is part of the body of the letter, it is typed in the same way as the paragraphs in the body of the letter. Type the postscript on the second line below the last notation in the letter. Postscripts may be indicated by typing *PS:* or *PS.* before the message:

PS: Be sure to bring a copy of your report with you.

Business Letter Formats

There are various acceptable formats for letters. Note that the *sequence* of the letter parts (including the optional parts) does not vary from one letter format to another. The differences in formats are primarily concerned with whether a particular part is aligned left, indented, or centered.

Block Format.   In the *block* letter format, all letter parts begin at the left margin except tables and other setoff material. Because there are no

KEY POINT

Acceptable business letter formats are the block, modified-block, modified-block with indented paragraphs, and simplified.

indentions, the block style is easy to set up and, therefore, very popular. See Figure 10.7 on page 479 for an example of a letter in block format.

Modified-Block Format.   Long popular, the *modified-block* format differs somewhat from the basic block style—namely, the date line, the complimentary closing, and the writer's identification begin at the center of the page. (See Figure 10.10 on page 485.)

Modified-Block Format—With Indented Paragraphs.   One variation of the standard modified-block format involves indenting the first line of each paragraph five spaces (1/2 inch) rather than starting them at the left margin. See Figure 10.8 below for an example.

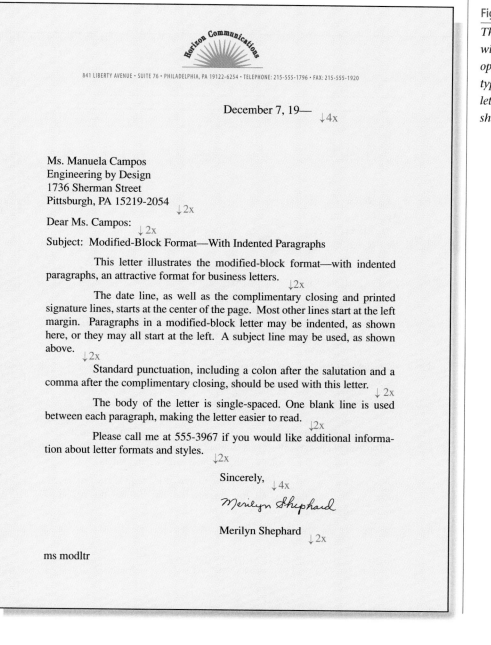

Figure 10.8

The modified-block format— with indented paragraphs. The optional subject line may be typed in capital and lowercase letters below the salutation as shown.

Simplified Format.   In an effort to simplify letter writing, the Administrative Management Society (AMS) developed what it calls the *simplified letter style*. Illustrated in Figure 10.9 below, the simplified letter:

1. Begins each part at the left margin (except unnumbered or unbulleted lists, which are indented five spaces or 1/2 inch). When unnumbered or unbulleted lists are used, leave an extra blank line between entries, particularly if any entry requires more than one line.

2. Omits the salutation and the complimentary closing. A subject line typed in all-capital letters replaces the salutation.

3. Has an all-capital writer's identification line, which consists of both the writer's name and the writer's title all on one line.

Figure 10.9

In the simplified letter format, every letter part begins at the left margin. There is no salutation or complimentary closing; instead, a subject line and a writer's identification line are used.

ORA

O'Donnell Research Associates

546 Harbor Way Circle   Florissant, MO 64056-1546   Telephone: 314-555-7793   FAX: 314-555-7829

October 8, 19—
↓4x

Miss Robin Gossett
Aptos Computer Systems
1102 Eleventh Street
New Haven, CT 06515
↓3x

RESEARCH OF LETTER FORMATS
↓3x

Thank you, Robin, for requesting the results of our research of letter formats used in business. These results indicate that the simplified letter format could save companies time and money by eliminating some parts of the more traditional letter style.
↓2x
The simplified letter has the following features:

- All lines of a simplified letter start at the left margin.
- The salutation is replaced by a subject line in all-capital letters. Two blank lines are placed above and below the subject line to call attention to it.
- The complimentary closing is omitted. Three blank lines precede the writer's name and job title, which are typed in all-capital letters.

Enclosed is a copy of our report on the research of letter styles that includes more detailed information. We encourage you to adopt this letter style for your correspondence; the response will be positive.
↓4x

MARCY GARWOOD, RESEARCH ASSOCIATE
↓2x

Enclosure

Other Letter Formats

In addition to the formats just discussed, you will find the personal-business and the social-business letter formats useful.

Personal-Business Letter Format. *Personal-business* letters generally are not typed on letterhead stationery; instead, plain paper is used. The writer's return address is typed directly beneath the writer's typed signature at the end of the letter. As shown in Figure 10.10 below, begin the writer's name and address on the fourth line below the complimentary closing.

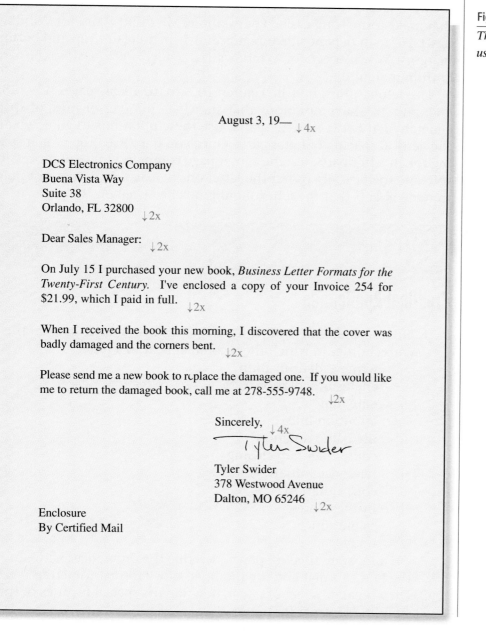

Figure 10.10

This personal-business letter uses a modified-block format.

Social-Business Letter Format. A special format, the *social-business* format (see Section 11.6), is sometimes preferred for letters written to business associates when the subject matter is more social than business.

Formatting Guidelines

Whichever letter style is used, the letter must be typed and formatted properly. The top, bottom, and side margins must be adequate, and the spacing between parts should adhere to certain standards.

Generally, 1-inch top and bottom margins and 1-inch side margins allow you to maximize the amount of copy on a page. Word processing software such as Microsoft Word and WordPerfect have default margins that make formatting easier. For example, Microsoft Word for Windows has 1 1/4 inch default side margins and 1-inch default top and bottom margins. WordPerfect for Windows has 1-inch default side, top, and bottom margins.

The letters illustrated in Figures 10.7 to 10.10 on pages 479, 483, 484, and 485 have notations that show the number of lines of space generally left between letter parts. Use these notations to guide you in the vertical spacing of letter parts. Once you have used the proper spacing for all letter parts, use the center page command in word processing software to vertically center the letter on the page. An important point to remember is that the letter should look balanced on the page.

SECTION 10.4   REVIEW

Practical Application

1. On a separate sheet of paper, write this list of letter parts in the correct order in which they would appear in a letter:
   writer's identification
   enclosure notation
   date line
   attention line
   file name notation
   complimentary closing
   reference initials
   copy notation
   inside address
   salutation
   body
2. On a separate sheet of paper, describe the differences between the block format and the modified-block format for letters.
3. On a separate sheet of paper, describe the special features of the simplified format for letters.

Editing Practice

Updating Vocabulary. On a separate sheet of paper, rewrite these excerpts from business messages, eliminating or replacing all outdated words and expressions.

1. May we meet at your earliest convenience to discuss the Johnson project.
2. Hoping to hear from your soon, I remain, sincerely yours,
3. Kindly advise us of your decision in the very near future.
4. At the present writing, we are revising the production schedule.
5. Due to the fact that manufacturing costs are rising, we must increase prices accordingly.
6. I would very much appreciate some help from you with this matter.
7. We have received your order for a scanner and are shipping it at the present time.
8. Enclosed please find our remittance for Invoice 2032-X.
9. In the event that you have a better suggestion, please advise me of it as soon as possible.
10. Research was not part of the director's purview.

Using Your Word Processor. On a separate sheet of paper, correct the spelling errors in the following paragraph.

Because we specialize in the needs of attornies, our building is uniquely equipped to serve lawyers. Each suite has a large room furnished with shelfs and tables—ideal for a legal liberry. In addition, there are rooms suitible for large and small meetings and, of course, several private offices.

Stationery and Envelopes

"First impressions, you know, often go a long way."

—Charles Dickens

The first impression of a letter will be determined by its physical appearance. That impression will be influenced by the stationery used, the way the letter is folded, and the envelope used.

OBJECTIVES

After completing Section 10.5, you should be able to:

1. Discuss the qualities of stationery that would be appropriate for letterhead.
2. Correctly address an envelope.
3. Fold letters to fit in No. 6 3/4 and No. 10 envelopes.

STATIONERY

Paper

The paper used for letterhead goes a long way toward establishing the impression made by the letter. Paper is available in many different weights and finishes. For letterhead, 16-pound, 20-pound, and 24-pound paper are usually selected. The higher the number, the heavier the paper. The pound designations correspond to the weight of four reams of 8 1/2 by 11-inch paper. A *ream* is 500 sheets of paper. Therefore, if 2000 sheets of paper weigh 20 pounds, the paper is called *20-pound paper*.

The quality of paper is determined by the cotton fiber content, as well as by weight. Letterhead should have at least 25 percent cotton fiber content. The higher the percent of cotton fiber content, the better the quality of the paper. Any document that needs to last ten years or longer should be prepared on paper that is 100 percent cotton fiber content.

Better-quality paper also contains a watermark, which is the "signature" of the paper manufacturer. You can see the watermark by holding the stationery up to the light. If you can read the watermark from left to right, you are looking at the front side of the paper.

Color

Today many colors of paper are used for letterhead. White is the most popular and is always correct. Studies have shown that colors send a message of their own. Most people react to certain colors in a predictable way. Here are some examples:

Colors	What they suggest to the reader
blue	sincere, harmonious
green	cool, restful
buff	dignified, conservative
gray	wise, confident
yellow	cheerful, vigorous
brown	strong, useful

Remember, people read more than the words in your message.

Size

The standard 8 1/2 by 11-inch paper is the size most commonly used for correspondence. Occasionally, a high-ranking employee will send messages of a personal nature—congratulations, thank-yous, condolences—on executive-sized stationery. A sheet of executive stationery measures 7 1/4 by 10 1/2 inches.

Letterhead

Most organizations have a letterhead designed to create the image and impression they wish to convey. All letterheads should include the name of the company, the mailing address, telephone and fax numbers, and possibly an e-mail address. Most letterheads also include a company logo.

The first page of a letter is prepared on letterhead. Continuation pages are prepared on plain paper of the same color, weight, and finish of the letterhead. The continuation page should have a heading that includes the following information: name of recipient, page number, and the same date that appears on the first page of the letter, as shown in the following examples:

Molly Sullivan
Page 2
June 1, 19—

Molly Sullivan   2   June 1, 19—

ENVELOPES

Envelopes should be the same color and quality as the letterhead stationery. The envelope should be large enough to hold the letter and enclosures without excessive folding. Business envelopes come in a variety of sizes, but the two most common are the No. 10 envelope, which measures 9 1/2 by 4 1/8 inches and the No. 6 3/4 envelope, which measures 3 5/8 by 6 1/2 inches. An envelope has three printed or typed parts as follows.

KEY POINT

Envelopes should be the same color and quality as the letterhead stationery.

The Return Address

The return address goes in the upper-left-hand corner of the envelope. Special instructions to be followed after the letter is delivered are indented three or four spaces from the left edge of the envelope and placed two to three lines below the return address. Examples of special instructions are *Reply Requested* and *Personal and Confidential*.

Mailing Notations

Mailing notations go on the upper right side of the envelope three lines below the stamp or postage meter insignia. Mailing notations are instructions for the post office such as *Certified, Air Mail,* and *Registered.*

The Mailing Address

The mailing address should be typed on the envelope so there is a minimum of a 1/2-inch margin on the left and right and a minimum 5/8-inch margin on the bottom. These margins are needed by the U.S. Postal Service so that its scanning equipment will operate properly.

To prepare standard business envelopes (No. 10 envelopes), follow these guidelines:

1. Begin typing the mailing address about 2 1/4 inches from the top of the envelope (on line 14), and about 4 inches from the left edge of the envelope.

2. Use a block-style font; avoid italics and script fonts.

3. Use a block style, starting all lines of the mailing address at the same point.

4. Use single spacing for the address.

5. Type the name and address in capital and lowercase letters or in all-capital letters, with no punctuation. The U.S. Postal Service's optical character readers are programmed to read both styles of address.

6. When using two-letter state abbreviations, capitalize both letters. Do not use a period after a two-letter state abbreviation.

7. Always include the ZIP Code, leaving one space between the state and the ZIP Code.

8. The last line of a United States address should contain the city, state, and ZIP Code. Do not type anything below the city, state, and ZIP Code. The area below the city, state, and ZIP Code is for a bar code that can be scanned by the post office. Many word processing programs can be set to automatically print the bar code below the address. For international addresses, type the name of the country in all-capital letters on the last line of the address.

See Figure 10.11 on page 491 for examples of two properly typed envelopes.

If you need specific formatting instructions for envelopes, refer to a reference manual or business writing handbook.

FOLDING LETTERS FOR ENVELOPES

Letters should be folded so that the thickness of the paper is evenly distributed in the envelope. Figure 10.12 on page 491 shows the proper way to fold a business letter for both a No. 6 3/4 and a No. 10 envelope.

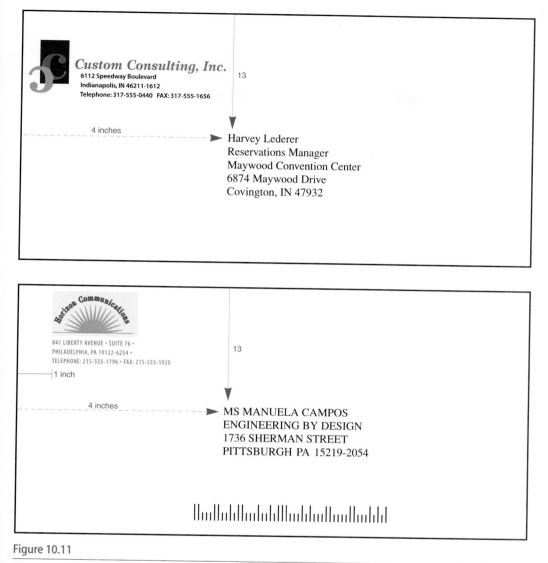

Custom Consulting, Inc.
6112 Speedway Boulevard
Indianapolis, IN 46211-1612
Telephone: 317-555-0440 FAX: 317-555-1656

13

4 inches

Harvey Lederer
Reservations Manager
Maywood Convention Center
6874 Maywood Drive
Covington, IN 47932

Horizon Communications

841 LIBERTY AVENUE • SUITE 76 •
PHILADELPHIA, PA 19122-6254 •
TELEPHONE: 215-555-1796 • FAX: 215-555-1920

1 inch

13

4 inches

MS MANUELA CAMPOS
ENGINEERING BY DESIGN
1736 SHERMAN STREET
PITTSBURGH PA 15219-2054

‖‖‖‖‖‖‖‖‖‖‖‖‖‖‖‖‖

Figure 10.11

The name and address on an envelope should match the inside address of the letter. Note the use of all-capital letters with no punctuation on the envelope addressed to Manuela Campos.

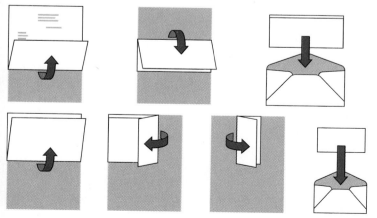

Figure 10.12

To fold a letter for a large envelope:
1. *Place the letter* face up *and fold up the bottom third.*
2. *Fold the top third down to 0.5 inch from the bottom edge.*
3. *Insert the last crease into the envelope first, with the flap facing up.*

To fold a letter for a small envelope:
1. *Place the letter* face up *and fold up the bottom half to 0.5 inch from the top.*
2. *Fold the right third over to the left.*
3. *Fold the left third over to 0.5 inch from the right edge.*
4. *Insert the last crease into the envelope first, with the flap facing up.*

Practical Application

1. An envelope has three parts: return address, mailing notations, and mailing address. On a separate sheet of paper, indicate the section of an envelope to which each of these parts belong:
   sender's name
   Personal and Confidential notation
   recipient's city, state, and ZIP Code
   Registered notation
   sender's mailing address
   recipient's name and job title
   postage stamp
2. Fold an 8 1/2- by 11-inch piece of paper correctly for a No. 10 envelope and another piece of paper for a No. 6 3/4 envelope.

Editing Practice

On a separate sheet of paper, correct the following mailing addresses.
   a. Chicago, Il. 60056
   b. New Orleans, LA
      58678
   c. Margaret English
      3568 Walnut Street
      Rossville, Ill. 60963

      Please Forward

Critical Thinking Skills

Collect four sample letterheads and evaluate them to determine whether all appropriate information is included on them. Write a memo to your instructor giving the results of your evaluation.

Assuring Correspondence Is Correct. Shakell Sa'eed works as an insurance representative for Midwest Assurance. Among his job responsibilities are sending many letters to clients and prospective clients and sending memos to people within the company. All employees are expected to keep a "reading file" containing copies of all correspondence they send. The manager, Elaine Pelligreni, schedules time once a week to read several items of correspondence from each employee's reading file. When Elaine read Shakell's memos and letters, she discovered that he was not very tactful. He frequently used expressions such as *your error, your claim,* and *you failed.* Elaine wondered whether Shakell did not realize that these expressions were negative and could result in the loss of goodwill, or even customer business. The letters and memos also contained spelling, punctuation, and grammatical errors.

Midwest Assurance uses the modified-block style as the company standard for all letters. Shakell used a block style because he thought that it was quicker and because he had learned this style in college. Also, the top margins were small, and the letter parts were not spaced correctly.

Although Elaine was unhappy with Shakell's correspondence, she was hesitant to say anything because Shakell had a nice personality and seemed to get along well with others in the office. He was also eager to learn about the company's products and, most important, he had a natural selling ability.

Today, as Elaine was reviewing Shakell's reading file, she found a letter he wrote several prospective clients guaranteeing a specific rate of return on a mutual fund investment. Elaine was very upset about this, because promising a specific rate of return is a violation of federal law according to the rules of the Securities and Exchange Commission. Such a violation can subject a sales representative and/or a firm to heavy fines and penalties.

1. If you were Elaine, how would you approach the topic of the grammar and formatting errors in Shakell's correspondence?

2. How would you address the serious matter of the violation of federal law?

3. What steps could you and Shakell take to ensure that his future correspondence is acceptable?

SECTIONS

11.1   Informing

11.2   Requesting

11.3   Responding to Requests

11.4   Persuading

11.5   Public Relations Letters

11.6   Social-Business Communications

11.7   Form Paragraphs, Form Letters, and Templates

Chris Ross had worked at Metropolis Medical Center for four years as a medical office assistant. In the *Medical Notes* weekly newsletter, the president of the medical center asked for volunteers to serve on a team to plan some special events and activities to recognize the medical center's 100 years of service to the community. Chris volunteered and was chosen as a member of the Centennial Celebration Team.

The team decided on several events and activities. One was to be a formal gala for approximately 500 people who were contributors to the Medical Center Foundation. The arrangements were made, the guest list was compiled, and the 500 formal invitations were printed and prepared for mailing.

Three weeks before the gala, the invitations were mailed. The next morning the phones did not stop ringing. The first caller said, "I received an invitation to the gala. When is it?" Other callers had the same question. It seems the invitations did not include a date for the gala.

The members of the team were certainly embarrassed. Chris said, "I thought the printer would check that information. I just signed the order form when it came; I assumed the invitation would be correct."

The team members decided to have the invitations reprinted and mailed again. The second invitation would have to be marked as a corrected or revised invitation so people wouldn't think it was a duplicate copy and discard the second one. Unfortunately, marking the second invitation "Corrected" or "Revised" would also draw attention to the error.

The cost of reprinting the invitations and the postage to mail them was an extra expense the team had not planned in their budget. The president of the medical center was not happy about the extra expense.

As you read Chapter 11, identify strategies Chris could have used to ensure that the invitation was complete.

Informing

OBJECTIVES:

After completing Section 11.1 you should be able to:

1. Identify several types of informative messages.
2. Apply the completeness test to all informative messages.

"I only ask for information."

—Charles Dickens, *David Copperfield*

As a business communicator you will often be called upon to write messages to give information to others. Informative messages include giving instructions; giving directions; and making announcements about events, people, meetings, procedures, and so on.

GIVING INSTRUCTIONS

As a business writer, you will have opportunities to provide written instructions on how to complete a task or how to carry out a procedure. Follow these guidelines when writing step-by-step instructions:

1. Number the steps to make them easier to follow, and use phrases rather than complete sentences.
2. Include only necessary information. Avoid giving all the "what ifs" so your instructions won't seem too complex.
3. List the steps in the order they are to be completed.
4. Write the instructions with the user in mind—define unfamiliar terms, and clearly explain complicated items.
5. Avoid unnecessary cross-references to information in another document. Instead, provide all the necessary information in the set of instructions.
6. Use white space, headings, and indentions to make the instructions visually clear. Start each new instruction on a separate line.
7. Test your instructions by having someone try them as written to see if they are clear and complete. The best test is to have someone who does not know the procedure try your instructions.

GIVING DIRECTIONS

When giving directions on getting from one location to another, whether it is to a different location in the building or to a different state, remember that some people learn and comprehend visually and some learn verbally. Keep these guidelines in mind:

- For visual learners, draw a map from the point of departure to the point of destination or, if possible, photocopy a map and use a light-colored highlighter to mark the route.

- For verbal learners, write the directions so that each part of the directions appears on a separate line.
- Differentiate between stop signs and stoplights, indicate turns as right or left, and give specific compass directions as in "Drive north for 2 miles."

MAKING ANNOUNCEMENTS

A great deal of information is communicated through various forms of announcements. Announcements are made through news releases, flyers, and formal cards as well as by memos and letters. As Chris Ross discovered in the case study at the beginning of this chapter, checking announcements for complete details is vital. Every announcement should be checked against the completeness test. Does the announcement include answers to the questions Who? What? Where? When? Why? and How? or How much? Anticipate the questions your receiver may have, and answer them in the announcement.

KEY POINT

Check every announcement for completeness—who, what, where, when, why, and how or how much.

Events

Events such as open houses, anniversary celebrations, special programs, commemorative events, holiday celebrations, ribbon-cutting ceremonies for new buildings or additions to existing buildings, and so on are frequently communicated through announcements.

People

Occasions for announcements about people include when a new employee is hired, when someone is promoted, when a person retires, when someone is elected or appointed to a position, when a person receives an award or another recognition, and so on. An announcement about someone's accomplishments is an excellent way to recognize the person and to let others know about the person's achievements.

Meetings

When meetings are needed, a meeting notice is the most efficient way to get the information to everyone, whether it is sent as a memo, an e-mail message, or a flyer. When meetings are scheduled weeks in advance, a reminder notice close to the date of the actual meeting will probably ensure better attendance.

Procedures

When a new procedure is implemented (for example, a new procedure for ordering supplies), a written, step-by-step guide makes it easier for everyone to follow the new procedure. Many organizations have a procedures book that contains copies of all procedures that have been developed. It is important to date each procedure, including revision dates, so employees can easily identify the most recent version.

Other Occasions

Other examples of occasions for informing include announcing new office hours, a new toll-free telephone number, a new delivery service, a new product, a new address, the opening of a branch office, and so on.

SECTION 11.1   REVIEW

Practical Application

1. Write instructions for someone who has never done a particular task. Some examples include filling a stapler with staples, clearing a paper jam in a printer, making a cake, changing the oil in a car, cooking spaghetti, sending an e-mail message, setting a VCR to record a program, or any other task with which you are familiar.
2. Write directions for a guest speaker to get from a neighboring town to your classroom.
3. Compose an e-mail message to the members of the Employee Benefits Committee about a meeting on Wednesday next week at 2 p.m. in the Bremer Conference Center.

Editing Practice

Plurals and Possessives. On a separate sheet of paper, indicate the correct plural or possessive forms of the words enclosed in parentheses.
1. The managing partner reviews new (attorney) briefs each week.
2. (Marie and Laura) telephone, which they share, is on Marie's desk.
3. All the (attorney) in this company speak Spanish fluently.
4. The two (general manager) reports were in agreement.
5. My (boss) hotel reservation needs to be changed.

Requesting

Many things are lost for want of asking.

—Old English Proverb

Some of the most routine business tasks you will perform involve making requests of some kind—for example, asking for appointments, reserving conference rooms, obtaining price lists and catalogs, asking for copies of reports and studies, seeking technical information about goods and services, and asking favors.

WRITING REQUESTS

Although requests are truly routine, you should not treat them routinely. Moreover, extraordinary requests require extraordinary planning and writing skills! Whether you are simply asking an office supply company for a copy of its catalog or asking a busy, important executive to go out of his or her way to speak at your conference, follow these guidelines when writing requests:

- Be complete.
- Be precise.
- Be reasonable.
- Be courteous.

Be Complete

When writing a request, always ask yourself, "What can I provide the reader to make sure that he or she has *all* the information needed to grant the request?" Also, "Will any more information be helpful for some reason?" Consider the following situations:

You are requesting information from Data-X Company about CD-ROM systems for a report that you are preparing. Tell the reader at Data X the purpose of your request. He or she might have additional materials to share with you or might grant the request solely to get publicity for his or her company.

You are assuming the reader will remember facts from your last letter or your last conversation. Don't assume! Repeat the model or type, the catalog number, the price, the preferred shipping method, and any other facts that will help your reader.

Put yourself in the reader's place so that you can better understand how the reader might feel and what information he or she might need to know. Note how the requests in Figure 11.1 on page 501 and Figure 11.2 on page 502 successfully answer the questions "Who?" "What?" "Where?" "When?" "Why?" and "How?" or "How much?"

OBJECTIVES:

After completing Section 11.2, you should be able to:

1. Write request letters that are complete, precise, reasonable, and courteous.
2. Gather the appropriate facts needed to write a claim letter that is complete and accurate.

KEY POINT

Written requests should be complete, precise, reasonable, and courteous.

In your effort to be complete, however, do not give the reader an excessively detailed description or needless information. For example, decide whether it will help the reader to know that you are planning to write a detailed report about the subject. If it will help, include this fact in your request; if this information is not relevant to the reader, omit it. Likewise, decide whether you must include the model or type, the catalog number, and so on. If all this information is already included in the enclosed purchase order, then there may be no need to repeat it in the letter.

MEMORY HOOK

Apply the five Ws and one H to test the completeness of requests—*"Who?" "What?" "When?" "Where?" "Why?"* and *"How?"* or *"How much?"*

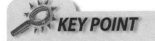
Be Precise

To ensure that your written requests are precise, you should present material in a format that makes it easy to comprehend. Using a table such as the one illustrated below is a precise way to present facts and figures. Proofreading carefully is another way to make your written requests precise. Doing so helps you eliminate errors that may be embarrassing, costly, and time-consuming.

Ristau Computer Supply House
9400 Main Street
Omaha, NE 68114

Attention: Order Department

Please send by UPS the following computer supplies to us. I have enclosed our company check in the amount of $346.20.

Item (Catalog No.)	Quantity (Units)	Unit Price	Total Price
Mouse Pad (42063)	6	$3.75	$ 22.50
Wrist Pad (42068)	6	$5.95	$ 35.70
Copy Stand (42035)	6	$8.50	$ 51.00
Computer Lamp (42092)	6	$39.50	<u>$237.00</u>
		TOTAL	$346.20

We would appreciate receiving the entire order by May 15.

MEMO TO: Sean Dinnocenzo, Office Manager

FROM: Tina Mosher, Copy Room Supervisor *TM*

DATE: December 9, 20—

SUBJECT: Request for Another Duplication Machine

The use of our large duplication machines in the Duplication Room has more than doubled in the past year. The number of copies per day has risen from 12,000 on June 7 to about 26,000 in December. As a result, the length of our turnaround time to duplicate materials has increased from one day to three days. To meet this increase in demand, I propose purchasing a small duplication machine to use for simple, quick duplicating jobs.

This new duplication machine would be used for duplication jobs that take less than ten minutes to complete, thus freeing the Duplication Department to handle larger duplication efforts. The new duplication machine would handle duplexing, collating, and stapling--the most used features. Jobs requiring special features such as special-size paper, enlargement, reduction, and color can be submitted to Duplication Room personnel for copying.

Attached is a comparison of price quotes from two vendors for comparable duplication machines. I would appreciate your feedback on this request by December 14 so that we can take advantage of the vendors' discount offer that is in effect until December 15.

Be Reasonable

Even people who are usually reasonable will sometimes make unreasonable requests when they are faced with job pressures or when they do not fully understand that their request is exceptionally difficult, time-consuming, or complicated.

Consider your request *from the reader's perspective*. Are you requesting too much of someone's time? Are you asking for a character reference from someone who hardly knows you? Can you reasonably expect this person to spend much effort on your request? Consider these factors before making a request.

Figure 11.2   Request Letter.

A request letter should answer the questions "Who?" "What?" "Why?" "When" "Where" and "How?" or "How Much?"

**Sheskey
Insurance
Agency**

617 Crossroad Square Suite 21 Duluth, MN 55346
Telephone: 218-555-9692 FAX: 218-555-9760

September 23, 19--

Ms. Terry P. O'Reilly
Training Director
Quality Insurance Company
130 Nationwide Drive
Columbus, OH 44015

Dear Ms. O'Reilly:

One of your insurance representatives, Irving Chemerinsky, informed me that Quality has produced a research report about the frequency and types of claims filed by policyholders. I would like to obtain this report.

Our company is interested in receiving information for claims relating to both homes and automobiles. We would like to incorporate this information into update sessions for our agents and to disseminate it to agents we may hire in the future.

Irving did not know the answers to these questions: Is the report free, or would there be a charge? What would the charge be? Would I need to buy multiple copies, or could I duplicate portions for our employees?

We want to make applicable portions of the research report immediately available to our personnel. Please give me a call at 501-555-6245 so I can clarify the order, costs, and duplication issues. We are certainly willing to pay duplication costs and costs for mailing the materials by Federal Express two-day delivery service.

Sincerely yours,

Lance Sheskey

Lance Sheskey
President

tr

Be Courteous

KEY POINT

Show courtesy in making requests of others.

Courtesy is a must in business communications. Whether you are requesting something that is legally or morally due to you, something that you have paid (or will pay) for, something that is yours and should be returned, or something that the reader should be delighted to send to you—in every case, you should be courteous in writing your request. Just as you deserve common courtesy, you must show common courtesy.

Although few people intentionally write discourteous requests, in their rush to complete a task, to place an order, to mail a letter, and so on, people *do* sometimes write impolite requests. For example, read this request for a free videotape describing vacation time-shares:

> Send me the free videotape about vacation time-shares at Morning Glory Resorts. I saw it in your ad in *Leisure Days.*

The company *did* advertise free videotapes, obviously in the hope of selling vacation time-shares. Does this mean, however, that the recipient of the request letter does not deserve common courtesy? Of course not! The writer should have shown more thoughtfulness and more respect for the reader by writing the request along these lines:

> Please send me the free videotape advertised in *Leisure Days* magazine that describes vacation time-shares at Morning Glory Resorts. My husband and I enjoy golf and tennis, and your resort sounds like an ideal place to spend our two-week summer vacation each year.
>
> We are also interested in buying a two-week time-share at a ski resort during the month of January. We would also appreciate receiving information about time-shares at winter resorts.
>
> Please mail the video and the other information to us at the address in the letterhead. We look forward to hearing from you.

The writer might have reaped additional benefits from this revised, more courteous request. The recipient will gladly send not only the free videotape advertised in the magazine but also any information about vacation time-shares at winter resorts since the writer took the time to state specific needs and did so *courteously.*

KEY POINT

When communicating a request, write the request that *you* would like to receive if you were the reader.

WRITING CLAIM LETTERS

A *claim letter* is a type of request letter written when there is a problem with a product or service.

The person who writes a claim letter believes, of course, that he or she has been wronged. Indeed, the claim is justified if, for example, the writer:

1. Ordered Model R-75 but received Model R-57.
2. Requested 150 booklets but received only 100.
3. Requested size 10 but received size 14.
4. Enclosed full payment but was billed anyway.
5. Specified brand Q but received brand T.

KEY POINT

A claim letter is written to report a problem with a product or service.

Sometimes, however, the writer *intended* to order brand Q but forgot to specify this particular brand. Or the writer neglected to proofread the order letter or purchase order and did not correct the "100" booklets to "150." Or the writer wrote the check for full payment but did not enclose it. The first step in making a claim, therefore, is to get the facts—before you write your claim.

Get the Facts

Before you make a claim, try to find out what happened and why.

- If part of the order is missing, is there a packing slip that clearly says the rest of the order will be shipped separately? Check your original order to be sure that the "missing" merchandise *was* ordered.

- If merchandise was damaged, should you write your claim to the supplier, or should you write it to the shipping company? You will be embarrassed if you write a strong letter to the supplier and later discover that the shipping company was at fault.

- If the wrong merchandise was delivered, check the original order first. Before you write your claim letter, try to find out if anyone telephoned a change in the order.

When you write a claim letter, you should rely on facts as the basis of your claim. Until you have sufficient facts, do not write the letter. When you do have all the facts, use them to describe the claim completely and accurately.

Describe the Claim Completely and Accurately

It is especially important to be complete and accurate when you are writing a claim letter because, in effect, you are making an accusation. Both to make a convincing argument and to be fair to the reader, you should present all the facts, and you should do so accurately.

Read, for example, the following letter. As you do so, note how the writer cites all the necessary details—size, quantities, times, descriptions, and so on.

> Dear Mr. Barnett:
>
> We have received your invoice for twenty-five 100-pound bags of polypropylene resin for injection-molding concrete. When we placed this order 17 days ago, we stressed the need for speedy delivery of the resin and were promised delivery within 10 days. Your invoice for 25 bags arrived on the tenth day, but we received none of the resin until the fifteenth day, when we received only 5 bags.
>
> We would appreciate your checking your records to make sure that all the resin has been shipped. If so, please notify our shipping company at once. Our customer desperately needs the items to be made from this resin and is understandably upset that we have not delivered them as promised. We are counting on you to help us make up for lost time.
>
> Please telephone me at 614-555-8214 by June 5 to let us know the status of this vital shipment of resin. We will hold your invoice until we receive all 25 bags of resin. Then, of course, we will be happy to send payment.
>
> Sincerely yours,

The writer not only tells the reader *everything* that happened concerning the materials that were ordered but also does so in chronological order. By giving complete information and delivering it accurately, the writer makes an honest, believable claim.

Let's look at another example of a claim letter that is both complete and accurate.

Dear Ms. Draper:

I was distressed to receive your notice of March 1 indicating that you have canceled my homeowner's insurance policy No. AZ1843687 for failure to pay the premium of $350 due on January 15.

On January 4, I mailed Check 186 for $350. On January 17, the check, endorsed by your company and stamped "Paid," was returned to me. I reported this information to you on the back of a notice of cancellation mailed to me January 30. Since I received no further word from you, I assumed that the matter had been resolved.

Enclosed is a photocopy of the front and back of my canceled check. Would you please send me a notice of the reinstatement of my insurance?

Very truly yours,

The letter gives *all* the details—completely and accurately—so that the insurance company can quickly correct its error. Note, however, that even though the above letter presents facts, the writer does not accuse, threaten, or demand.

Avoid Accusations, Threats, and Demands

The goal of the claim letter is to get the missing merchandise, to correct the billing error, to return the damaged goods—in other words, to get results, not to blame, to threaten, or to demand. For example, assume that the preceding letter to the insurance company was not answered in a reasonable time. What would you do? Write a threatening letter? Demand that the company send you a formal apology? These are reactions, not solutions. Writing a letter saying "You know very well that I paid my premium" or "You failed to reply" or "I will sue you" would be a waste of time.

Instead, write a reasonable letter, this time addressed to someone with more authority. For example, a letter to the president of the agency that handles your insurance would probably get results:

Dear Mr. Kovacs:

I am enclosing a photocopy of a letter I wrote to Marie Draper at your main office on March 5. My letter has not yet been acknowledged, and I am concerned about whether my homeowner's insurance is in force.

I would very much appreciate your looking into this matter for me and providing written notification regarding the status of my homeowner's insurance policy.

Very sincerely yours,

KEY POINT

The goal of a claim letter is to get results, not to blame, threaten, or demand.

Without threatening, demanding, or accusing, the letter will get results. After all, if you were the president of the agency, would you overlook this letter? The president would understand that the next step is legal action.

Suggest Reasonable Solutions

KEY POINT

Suggesting a reasonable solution improves your chances of getting a just settlement quickly.

The opposite of accusing, demanding, or threatening is suggesting reasonable solutions. *Remember:* Except in rare circumstances, you are dealing with honest business people who have made a mistake *and realize it.* By suggesting reasonable solutions, you strengthen your chance of getting a just settlement quickly. For example, if you placed an order and received only part of it, one solution might be to indicate that you will accept the missing portion if it arrives by a specific date, as shown by the following statement:

> We will gladly accept the 25 camping tents if they reach us by May 15, the first day of our Great Outdoors Savings Spectacular.

Or suppose that you were overbilled $100 on an order. In this case, you might say:

> We were billed $650 for the merchandise on our Purchase Order 3290, dated July 7. The figure should have been $550. Therefore, please credit our account for $100 and send us a credit memorandum for this amount.

It is usually best to suggest the kind of solution that you consider acceptable. If you received defective merchandise, for example, you might request replacement of the merchandise, cancellation of the order, a credit of the amount to your account, or substitution of a similar item. Suggesting a solution tells the company what kind of action you want taken. When your suggestion is reasonable, there is a good chance that the company will follow it.

SECTION 11.2   REVIEW

Practical Application

1. Write a letter to Alvarez Office Furniture, 1199 Memorial Boulevard, Des Plaines, Illinois 46043, to order a desk. Before writing the letter, answer each of the following questions:
   Why are you writing?
   What kind of desk are you ordering?
   How do you want to pay for and receive the desk?
   When do you want the desk?
   Where do you want the desk delivered?

2. Find in magazines or newspapers two advertisements that invite you to write for additional information about goods and services. Write a letter to each company to ask for a catalog, sample, brochure, or other descriptive information.
3. Write a letter to the Superintendent of Documents, U.S. Government Printing Office, Washington, DC 20402, asking for a list of publications about an occupation that interests you.
4. An advertisement for Rainbow Images Copiers has interested you in a new color copier. Write the company at 999 South Chillicothe Road, Aurora, Ohio 44202, asking for the names and addresses of authorized dealers in your area. Also request appropriate information about the new color copier.

Editing Practice

Using Your Word Processor. On a separate sheet of paper, edit and rewrite the following paragraph, correcting all errors.

Please send me the compleat two-volume set of *Marketing and Distribution.* I understand that for the price of $53.99 I will also receive a one-year subscription to *American Business Today,* along with a callendar for business executives. Please refrane, however, from placing my name on any mailing lists.

Updating Correspondence. On a separate sheet of paper, rewrite these excerpts from letters, replacing any dated expressions.
1. The information in your application has been duly noted.
2. We wish to extend our thanks to you for taking the time to complete the questionnaire.
3. I have before me your letter of October 10.
4. Up to the present writing, we have not received your payment for last month.
5. In the event you will be unable to accept the offer, please advise.
6. I am sending herewith the prospectus for Oakgrove Condominiums, Ltd.

Critical Thinking Skills

Using Courteous Language. How many ways can you express *please* and *thank you* without using the actual words? Consider yourself *good* if you find five ways; *excellent* if you find eight.

Responding to Requests

OBJECTIVES:

After completing Section 11.3, you should be able to:

1. Write answers to requests.
2. Answer requests *promptly* and use a positive approach.
3. Be helpful in answering requests.
4. Apply general sales techniques in responding to requests.
5. Evaluate claim letters received and make appropriate adjustments.
6. Write effective adjustment letters.

You comply with a request more willingly than with an order.

—a Greek philosopher

I f writing requests is a common business task, then answering requests is equally common. In this section you will learn how to effectively answer requests and how to use techniques for both granting and denying requests. You will also learn how to respond to claim letters by sending an adjustment letter granting or denying a claim.

ANSWERING REQUESTS

Common courtesy dictates that a prompt reply be sent to request letters. Whether the response is an easy-to-write positive reply or a more difficult rejection, the reader should not be kept in suspense. Also, the writer should try to *help* the reader as much as possible, even if the request must be refused.

Writing a response—whether the reply is positive or negative—presents an opportunity to promote goodwill and to make a sale. Thus the response should be *sales-minded*. In addition, the response (like the request) should be *specific* and *complete*.

KEY POINT

Common courtesy dictates that a prompt reply be sent in response to a request letter.

Be Prompt

Many companies have policies requiring their employees to respond to letters within 48 hours—some, within 24 hours. Why? These companies realize that being prompt in replying is simply good business.

Even when an inquiry cannot be answered in detail, common business courtesy demands that a reply (at least an acknowledgment of the request) be sent *promptly*.

Dear Mr. Miller:

Your recent request for a price quotation for four 5,000-watt alternators (Bitco No. 4700) is being handled by Beverly Jenrette. Bitco, the manufacturer, now has these alternators on back order. Ms. Jenrette is checking with Bitco to determine how soon these alternators will be available and what the price change (if any) will be.

Ms. Jenrette expects to have this information for you by October 15. In any case, she will write to you before then to give you an update on your request.

Sincerely,

This prompt response (1) acknowledges the request, (2) tells the potential customer specifically who is taking care of the request, and (3) tells when the customer can expect an answer. The writer in this situation would send a copy to Beverly Jenrette and place another copy in a *tickler file*—a reminder file—for October 15.

Because promptness is both a courtesy and a sign of good business, your reader will always be impressed by your quick response. Therefore, take advantage of situations in which promptness will be a plus. Note how one writer capitalized on a quick response:

> When I received your request in this morning's mail, I checked immediately to make sure that we could process the color slides you requested for your March 19 meeting. I am pleased to tell you that we can process and deliver the slides by. . . .

Another shortcut that allows writers to achieve promptness when faced with a large volume of responses is to write a brief message on a preprinted reply card. The card may have blanks that the writer can quickly fill in, or it may simply give a printed message with no blanks. Despite their lack of personalization, preprinted responses allow a company to respond to hundreds or thousands of requests *promptly*. Without printed "Dear Subscriber" responses, such as the one in Figure 11.3, prompt replies would be impossible.

KEY POINT

If a detailed reply is not possible, send an acknowledgment of the request.

Technology

Business writers often use word processing software to help them save time in answering requests promptly—especially when a large volume of replies must be written. Word processing software permits writers to develop individually personalized letters in a short period of time.

Figure 11.3   Printed Form Letter.

A printed form letter helps a company acknowledge all its transactions with customers promptly.

Dear Subscriber:

MANY THANKS . . .

for renewing your subscription to *Political Insights*. Your check for $39—half our usual subscription price—indicates that this publication meets your high standards and expectations because you chose to invest your money in this product.

We believe *Political Insights* presents a variety of issues and perspectives in a different way from any other media. Our magazine attempts to bring the facts to you with many points of view and in an objective, rational way. Our short, easily readable stories allow you to have current information.

By renewing *Political Insights*, you have indicated that we are doing our job in providing the information you need about national and international politics. However, we know it is always possible to improve a product. Therefore, please take a few moments to jot us a note and tell us how we can improve any aspect of your magazine. Simply return your comments in the enclosed, postage-paid envelope.

Sincerely,

Be Helpful

A customer or a potential customer who asks for information expects to receive assistance, whether the customer is asking in person, on the telephone, or in writing.

When responding to a request, try to understand why the person is asking for help, and remember why your company wants you to help.

KEY POINT

In responding to a request, provide additional help or information whenever possible.

Remember, too, that you are the expert. Whether or not you can grant the request, consider if there is something additional you can do to help the person. Do you know of a store where the person can find the product he or she needs? Do you know of a company that makes the product he or she is looking for? Do you know of a book that covers the very topic the person wants to research? Do you know of a service organization that can assist the person?

Note how the writer of the following letter did more than fill the request—the writer anticipated Ms. Harrison's interest in a closely related product. Good sales expertise? Good business? *Both!*

Dear Ms. Harrison:

It's good to know that you are considering the ImageMaker, our telephone facsimile transmitting system. One of our most popular items, the Image-Maker will enable you to send any graphic design 24 by 24 inches or smaller to any office in the world equipped with an ImageMaker and a telephone. The ImageMaker should be particularly valuable to you and your architects in other cities. Now you won't have to wait days to react to one another's latest sketches.

A wonderful complement to ImageMaker is our reducing, high-resolution photocopier, the ImageReducer. With no discernible loss in precision, the ImageReducer will reduce graphic designs as large as 48 by 48 inches to 24 by 24 inches—small enough to be transmitted by the ImageMaker. The combination of the ImageMaker and ImageReducer will save not only the transit time of regular mail or of shipping by an express mail service but also the cost.

We very much appreciate your interest in our products and would be happy to demonstrate them for you soon.

Sincerely,

Although it is rather easy to be helpful when you are granting a request, you can also be helpful many times when you cannot grant the request, as the writer of the following letter proves.

Dear Mrs. Gonzales:

Thank you for your recent order for the 15-millimeter, f/2.8 Caxton underwater lens. Although we generally carry this superb lens, we are currently out of stock, and Caxton will not be shipping more until September or October.

Because you mentioned that you wanted the lens for your upcoming scuba diving trip, I called another supplier to find this lens. Good news: The F Stop, a photography specialty store, has the lens that you want. You may call the F Stop toll-free at 800-555-1800.

Good luck! And please be sure to try us again *next time.*

Sincerely,

This letter writer has certainly won a friend for the writer's company—just by being helpful.

Be Sales-Minded

Whenever you respond to a request letter, you should look for possible ways to make a sale. After all, whether you work in the sales department or not, your company depends on sales to make a profit and to pay your salary.

The hard-sell approach is rarely effective; you will not make much progress by bluntly saying "Buy this product!" Yet you can help sell your company's products or services—by responding promptly to requests and by being helpful. Both responses will make your readers appreciate the quality customer service that your company provides and will convince them to deal with your firm.

In addition to these indirect sales techniques, there are several direct ways to help sell your company's goods and services when you are responding to requests. For example, if you are sending a potential customer a catalog, include *both* an order blank *and* an addressed envelope to make it easy for the customer to place an order. If a customer complains about having had to wait a long time to receive a previous order, take a few minutes to write an apology and an explanation. Better yet, tell the customer to write directly to you next time so that you can personally track the order. Such extras are selling techniques.

Can you uncover the indirect selling methods the writer of this letter used?

KEY POINT

When responding to a request letter, look for ways to sell or resell your products or services.

> Dear Mr. Neumann:
>
> Thank you for asking about the service contract for Gorden's Model-X camcorder. We are pleased to share some information with you.
>
> Mr. Neumann, the enclosed booklet includes a list of all the specific items that are covered by our service contract. In fact, it also lists (in equally large print) the few items that are *not* covered in the contract, so that there will be no surprises if something should happen to the product; you will know exactly what is covered. By doing so, we avoid the unfortunate experience that you described in your letter.
>
> Because service is such an important factor in your buying decision, I recommend that you ask your local Gorden dealers how they rate the service of two or three of the brand names that they sell. (A list of dealers in your area is enclosed.) Further, I invite you to visit Peter Cleary of Cleary & Sons in Woodmere, which I believe is near you. Mr. Cleary has operated an authorized Gorden service center for more than twenty years. Not only will visiting Peter be informative, but also this will give you a chance to meet the person who would service any Gorden product that you own.
>
> Please review the enclosed booklet; then let me know of any way that we can help. You may call me toll-free at 800-555-9250 whenever you have any questions for us. We would be delighted to be of service.
>
> Sincerely,

Throughout the letter the writer stresses what is most important to the reader—*service*.

Be Specific

KEY POINT

Responses to requests should give specific information in terms of amounts of money, dates, and other factual information.

The need to *be specific* is a general rule; it applies to any letter or memorandum, whether the message is a request, a response to someone's request, or any other type of communication.

When acknowledging receipt of money, cite the exact amount:

> We appreciate receiving your Check 3689 for $1,250 in payment of Invoice 17290.

When discussing dates, times, airline flight numbers, or other specific statistics, cite them clearly.

> I am delighted to accept your invitation to discuss my career in textile design with your students. It has been a long time since I visited the Design Institute, and I look forward to our discussion on April 28 at 3 p.m. As you suggested, I will bring samples of my newest designs to share with your students.

> As I mentioned in our conversation earlier today, I will arrive at LaGuardia Airport at 2:30 p.m. on Monday, July 8, on Northeast Airline flight 741. . . .

When you receive something of value, acknowledge its receipt, including any specific information that is appropriate. Remember that your letter will become part of the sender's files—proof that you received the important mailing.

> Your portfolio of industrial photographs arrived this morning. When Carrie Foster, our art director, returns from vacation next week, she will call you to discuss the prints she has selected for the September issue of *Modern Manufacturing*.

When acknowledging receipt of an order, include the date of the order and the purchase number. Although the reader already knows this information, it is repeated because the letter will be filed for future reference. In addition, mention how the materials will be shipped, when the reader can expect to receive the merchandise, and so on.

> We are delighted that you are taking advantage of our annual stock-reduction sale. Your order No. 575, dated June 20, will be shipped by Reliable Parcel Service this afternoon. As you requested, the merchandise will be delivered to your Central Avenue store.

Be Complete

KEY POINT

To give a complete response to a request, outline the specific points mentioned by the person making the request.

Although many writers try to be complete, important information is often omitted due to carelessness.

One way to make sure that your responses are complete is to underline the specific points in the request letter. Another way is to note in the margin each answer to a specific point in the request letter. The underlined points or marginal notes serve as an outline in writing the reply. For example, when Muriel Pisanelli received the letter of inquiry illustrated in Figure 11.4 she made marginal notes to make sure that her response, illustrated in Figure 11.5 on page 514 would be *complete*.

October 27, 19—

Ms. Muriel Pisanelli
Sales Manager
Econ Heating and Cooling
2064 Rendle Avenue
Galveston, TX 77513

Dear Ms. Pisanelli:

I am interested in obtaining information about the addition of your humidifier unit to my gas furnace with heat pump. I have studied your brochure but have some additional questions before deciding whether to invest in this product.

1. Where would the unit be mounted on the furnace? *Back of furnace, halfway btwn. floor & ceiling*

2. What special water hookups would be required? *Usually no*

3. How often would the filter in the unit need to be replaced, and what is the cost? *Once a year; $10*

4. How much installation time would be required by your personnel? *2 hours*

5. How would the presence of a heat pump affect operation of the furnace? *No effect*

6. What would be the total cost of the unit, including installation? *$328*

7. What type of warranty exists for this product? *Full, 10-yr.*

I am thinking about having this product installed before December 25. Please answer these questions in time for me to make my decision.

Very truly yours,

Joe V. Dove

Joe V. Dove
8064 Miles Boulevard
Houston, TX 77034

One technique that fosters completeness is listing major points in a letter item by item. Note how the writer of the follow-up letter in Figure 11.5 on page 514 lists the major points the customer mentioned in his letter, as illustrated in Figure 11.4 above. In the follow-up letter, the writer enumerates each point and discusses them in the same order as in the customer's letter.

ECON
Heating
and Cooling

2064 Rendle Avenue
Galveston, TX 77513
Telephone: 409-555-6218   Fax: 409-555-6359

November 1, 19--

Mr. Joe V. Dove
8064 Miles Boulevard
Houston, TX 77034

Dear Mr. Dove:

Thank you for inquiring about our furnace humidifier. You posed several questions in your October 27 letter that I will answer:

1. The unit would be mounted on the back of the furnace, halfway between floor and ceiling.
2. In many cases, the water hookup is already available but inactive for hook-up of a humidifier unit. We would have to check your situation but could easily tap into a nearby water pipe.
3. The filter costs approximately $10 and should be replaced once a year.
4. Assuming no complicating factors, installation normally takes about two hours.
5. The addition of the humidifier unit would not affect heat pump operation.
6. The total cost of the humidifier unit and installation would be $328.
7. Our humidifier unit carries a full, 10-year warranty.

Enclosed is a brochure that describes the humidifier in which you are interested. I am sure you will find that this unit is an outstanding product for the money.

Please call me at 1-800-555-4216 if you have further questions and to set up a desired installation date.

Sincerely,

Muriel Pisanelli

Ms. Muriel Pisanelli
Sales Manager

lam
Enclosure

Be Positive

The need to *be positive* is especially important when handling problem requests. Saying no to people who have applied for credit, who do not qualify for discounts, whose warranties have expired, who have asked for confidential information, who have requested contributions that must be turned down—these situations require tact and diplomacy from the writer. *Remember:* Whatever the cause of the problem, the writer's goal is to keep the reader's goodwill.

KEY POINT

Written responses that deny a request require tact and diplomacy.

To begin, consider the contrast between the statements listed below. Note how the positive statements say no without greatly hurting the reader's ego.

Negative	Positive
Your product does not meet our specifications.	Our engineers believe that the brand we selected is closest to our specifications.
You do not meet our standards for this particular job.	Although your qualifications are excellent, we feel that we must continue to search for someone who meets all the unique qualifications for this job.
In view of your poor payment record, we are unable to grant you credit.	We shall be glad to evaluate your credit record after you have settled some of your obligations.
We must say no.	Unfortunately, we cannot say yes at this time.
Your prices are too high.	Perhaps, when you have adjusted your prices to make them more competitive, we shall be able to do business with you.

Note how the negative comments stress *you* while the positive comments stress *we*. Always avoid saying "Because of your mistake . . ." or "You failed to. . . ." Placing blame on the reader will accomplish nothing. Remember, preserving goodwill toward your company should be your goal in all business writing.

Although it is important to phrase comments in a positive manner and avoid placing blame, you should not make false statements in refusing a request. If possible, share with the reader some of the genuine reasons why the request is being rejected.

Layoffs this year have reduced our staff, and as a result our remaining employees' workload has increased.

As much as we would like to help you with your research project, gathering the information you requested is beyond our present resources. As you can imagine, Ms. Granger, we simply cannot take that much time away from our usual duties.

Perhaps the most positive aspect of such refusals is to offer the possibility of future cooperation.

Perhaps next year we will be able to . . .

Of course, we will keep your application on file so that . . .

Once again, remember to put yourself in your reader's place. When you consider your reply *from your reader's perspective,* you will seek creative ways to be positive.

FAIRLY EVALUATING CLAIMS AND MAKING ADJUSTMENTS

Whether a business is a multinational corporation or a small family store, it will have customers who claim that they received fewer items than they ordered; damaged goods; the incorrect size, color, or model; unsatisfactory merchandise; and so on. Each customer's claim must be answered, and each situation must be studied. The business must (1) determine whether the claim has any merit and (2) examine how the merchandise was damaged or why the wrong item was shipped so that the same mistake will not happen again.

In many cases an *adjustment* will be made—the customer will receive a full or a partial credit, will be allowed to exchange the merchandise, or will be granted a refund.

Several qualities are required to evaluate a claim, determine a fair adjustment, and approve the adjustment: (1) business experience; (2) company authority; (3) familiarity with company policy, industry standards, and consumer laws; and (4) common sense. You are essentially playing the role of judge; but since you have a vested interest in the case, being impartial is difficult. Yet an equitable adjustment requires you to be reasonable, fair, honest, and impartial in making your decision.

Making the right decision, therefore, is a difficult task. The sources of evidence that you must weigh are the company, the claimant (the person making the claim), the transaction, and, in some cases, the law. Let's look at each source to see how it influences or affects the final decision.

KEY POINT

To evaluate a claim, the employee must consider these sources of evidence:
• The company
• The claimant
• The transaction
• The law

The Company

As an ethical business, your company will want to examine its responsibility in light of a claim. Ask yourself the following questions to determine the extent of your company's responsibility in causing the situation.

• Do you know, without a doubt, that the company is not at fault?

• Could anyone in the company have made a misleading statement?

• Could the advertising be misinterpreted?

• Could your records be at fault?

• Is it possible that someone in the company made a mistake?

If such questioning reveals an element of blame on the part of the company, you, the adjuster, will probably decide to honor the claim, at least in part.

The Claimant

To help you evaluate the claimant's share in causing the claim, ask questions like these:

- Could the claimant be mistaken?
- Is the claim, if true, a reasonable one to make?
- Has the claimant provided all the information you need to check the claim and place responsibility for it?
- Does the claimant have a record of fair dealings with your company?

Even if you find that the claimant is wrong beyond any doubt, good business sense tells you that perhaps the claim should be honored anyway.

The Transaction

The answers to the following questions will help you arrive at an equitable decision about the transaction:

- Did your company carry out all its obligations—both stated and implied—to the customer?
- Has your company made any claims with reference to this product such as, "Double your money back if you are not absolutely satisfied"?
- Were any misleading statements made to the customer by your sales personnel?
- Is there evidence of faulty materials or workmanship in the product?
- Were the instructions for use of the product clear and complete?

If you find a defect either in the product or in the handling of the transaction, you should decide in favor of the claimant. This correction is just one more application of the commonly practiced business rule of trying to please the customer.

Sometimes you will have to seek further information before you can answer the previous questions. You may need to question some of your coworkers or to write the claimant before you have all the facts. The following letter is an example of an inquiry addressed to a claimant.

Dear Mrs. Parker:

Thank you for your October 17 letter about your Healthguard water purifier. We are sorry that you are having problems with the purifier, a product that is usually quite reliable.

We cannot locate a copy of your warranty agreement, which should be on file here. The period of the warranty is normally one year. If you could send us the transaction number from the top right corner of your receipt, we could confirm the purchase. If you do not have the receipt, then please give us the name of the dealer from whom you made the purchase and the approximate date of purchase.

As soon as we receive the information, we will be happy to make an adjustment.

Sincerely yours,

When you receive the necessary information, you will be able to make an equitable decision on the claim.

The Law

In some cases, there may be laws that will affect your decision regarding a claim. Laws intended to protect consumers, for example, allow a consumer to cancel certain contracts within three days "without penalty or obligation." State or local laws may apply in special situations in your industry.

In any case, you should realize that there are potential legal problems in some situations. Although you have learned that you should not threaten when making a claim, many writers will threaten you with legal action in their first claim letters just because they believe that making such threats will get results. Does your company have a policy that requires all employees to notify the legal department any time there is a possibility of a lawsuit? Whether it has such a policy or not, you *should* notify someone in authority (perhaps your supervisor *and* the legal department) whenever legal action is even remotely possible.

WRITING ADJUSTMENT LETTERS

After probing all the sources of evidence and reviewing all the facts in a claim, you may determine that (1) the claim is indeed allowable, (2) the claim is only partially allowable, or (3) the claim is not allowable. Now comes the task of using your writing skill to respond to a claim letter with an adjustment letter.

An Allowable Claim

Mistakes occur in every business. What separates a well-run business from a poorly run business is not *whether* the company makes mistakes but *how it handles* its mistakes.

Question: What do you do when the error is yours? *Answer:* Grant the adjustment and admit that it was your fault, without arguing or trying to avoid responsibility. Note the following letter.

> Dear Dr. Hargrove:
>
> A new barometer has been shipped to you by airfreight.
>
> From your description in your December 9 letter, we believe that your aneroid barometer was mistakenly calibrated for use as an altimeter. We manufacture altimeters and aneroid barometers using the same mechanism—only the calibrations are different. Somehow the wrong model number and nameplate were placed on the barometer you received. Please accept our sincere apology. We are reviewing our procedures in an effort to prevent this kind of mix-up from happening again.
>
> If we can be of further assistance to you, Dr. Hargrove, please write or call.
>
> Sincerely yours,

The writer admits the error without hedging and strives to keep the customer's goodwill. In an effort to maintain goodwill, indeed, some companies will even grant doubtful claims if the costs are not excessive. In this way they develop an excellent reputation among their customers and gain new business.

A Partially Allowable Claim

Allowing a claim is rather easy. Slightly more difficult is reaching a compromise with a claimant. For instance, if the transaction involves a heavy piece of equipment worth $10,000, the manufacturer will probably be reluctant to exchange the equipment and pay for double shipping charges besides. Yet that may be what the claimant asks for.

Suppose, for example, that a recent purchaser of a commercial automatic film processor wants to exchange the processor. The customer states that the processor is unsatisfactory because the developed film comes out wet instead of dry. You feel certain that the problem is caused by failure of the small fan under the drying hood. Replacement of the fan will take one of your technicians ten minutes and cost you only $25. Exchanging the entire processor, which weighs 200 pounds and is valued at $9,000, will be expensive because of shipping costs. Moreover, the customer will have to wait at least three weeks for a new processor. You decide to seek a compromise adjustment.

How much of an adjustment a company makes in a case like this depends on company policy. You believe that the customer will be satisfied with the processor after the fan is replaced. You are also willing to offer the customer a $100 discount toward the purchase price as compensation for the inconvenience caused by the failure of the fan. Your letter describing this proposed adjustment might read as follows:

Dear Ms. Sanders:

Thank you for your letter about your new SuperSpool Rapid Film Processor. Replacing the fan under the drying hood is the solution. Although we thoroughly test each processor before it leaves our plant, the machines are sometimes damaged by rough handling in transit.

Exchanging your processor for a new one would require subjecting another unit to the hazards of shipping. In addition, you would be without a processor for at least three weeks. We seriously question the wisdom of exchanging the entire unit when only one small component is the cause of all the trouble.

Ms. Sanders, we want you to be satisfied with our products and service. We realize that the fan's failure has inconvenienced you. We can send a service technician to your plant with a new drying fan. Replacement of the defective fan should take only ten minutes, and you can test the processor immediately to make sure that everything is working properly. In addition, we have enclosed a $100 discount certificate.

Please call our service center at 555-2243 to make an appointment for our service technician to visit your plant.

We are also confident that your SuperSpool Rapid Film Processor will provide good service for years to come.

Sincerely yours,

The writer is trying to reach a fair settlement with the customer. Nonetheless, Ms. Sanders may reply by asking to be compensated for all the film wasted as a result of the fan's failure.

A Nonallowable Claim

Although a business may strive to satisfy its customers and may have the most lenient claim policy in its industry, it will encounter situations in which claims simply cannot be allowed. One customer, for example, may try to return a perfectly good lamp that he ordered simply because he no longer wants that style. Another customer may wrongly insist that she ordered merchandise before a price increase. If the business granted such claims once, it would set a questionable precedent. Besides, granting such a claim would be poor business. Whatever the reason, the company is faced with the uncomfortable but necessary task of saying no to a customer.

Assume, for example, that you are employed by Essex Distribution Company, a computer products wholesaler. Last month you featured a special offer on the complete Epic Model KL computer system. In your mailer to dealers, you specifically stated that you are discounting your current inventory of the KL model by 30 percent "to make room for new inventory." Many dealers took advantage of the superb discount offer. You specifically stated in the mailer that this sale was a "clearance sale" and that no returns would be permitted.

Patrice Clemente, manager of the Metropolitan Computer Center, purchased 50 of the discounted Epic KL systems, sold 20, and then asked permission to return the remaining 30 systems. Because Metropolitan is a good customer, in the past you have "bent the rules" to allow Ms. Clemente special return privileges for unsold merchandise. However, you simply cannot accept the 30 Model KL systems. You must write to Ms. Clemente to tell her this, but you must also try to retain her goodwill—and her future business. To do so, perhaps you would send the following letter.

Dear Ms. Clemente:

Thank you for complimenting us on our special offers on the top brand names in computers. We at Essex pride ourselves on being the number-one computer distributor in the state, and we sincerely appreciate having the opportunity to do business with the number-one computer store in the state, Metropolitan Computer Center.

As you know, Ms. Clemente, no other distributor has offered such a drastic discount on Epic computers as our recent 30 percent discount. We did so, frankly, because we were forced to make room for new inventory. We simply had to clear our stock at the time of the special sale. That's why we specifically stated that the sale was on a no-return basis. I'm sure that you, too, have been faced with similar situations.

As much as we would like to help you, we really cannot accept a return of 30 Epic KL systems. For one reason, we now have on order more than 500 of the new Epic XP systems. As you can imagine, these 500 systems will take up much warehouse space as well as inventory dollars. We are also increasing our inventory of other major brands so that we can continue to deliver to dealers like Metropolitan all computer merchandise in the minimum amount of time. By serving you better, of course, we help you to serve *your* customers better.

May I make a suggestion? A few days ago Bill Kline of Computer World (in the Warren Mall) was eager to get more Epic Model KL systems. Perhaps you can arrange to sell your stock to Mr. Kline. Of course, if I should hear of any other dealers who are looking for Epic KLs, I will be sure to call you.

By the way, let me give you some "advance notice" of a special sale we are planning for next month. We will be offering the popular Speedex disk drive for only $125 and the Lark 2400 modem for only $195!

Sincerely yours,

Although the reply is clearly no, the letter has a positive tone and maintains the customer's goodwill.

Practical Application

A. On a separate sheet of paper, write a letter answering each of the following requests.
  1. Steven Crowell, 23 Saltway Drive, Saltway, Florida 33596, requested from your company, Allword Publishing Inc., a copy of your new magazine, *Video Visions*. Demand has exceeded expectations, and the first issue has sold out. Write an appropriate response to Mr. Crowell's October 1 letter.
  2. Gladys Simon, sales manager for Bermuda Beauty Lawn Products, 1132 South Market Avenue, Claremore, Minnesota 54335, has received an order from the Howard House and Garden Shop, 853 Wallace Street, Dearfield, Illinois 62705. The order, dated March 1, is large and is the first received from the Howard House and Garden Shop. John Rosetti, the manager of Howard, wants to know the terms of payment and how and when the merchandise is to be shipped. Write Ms. Simon's reply to Mr. Rosetti.
  3. Alice O'Toole, director of public relations for Advantage Office Systems and Networks, 332 Phillips Avenue, Manchester, New Hampshire 03110, has telephoned Craig Curtis, chief advertising consultant for New England Best Business Consulting, 212 Crofts Street, Peterborough, New Hampshire 03484, and asked him to make a presentation entitled "Advertising in the Electronic Age" at the convention of the New England Advertising League. The presentation is to take place on June 24 at the Merrick Hotel in Cambridge, Massachusetts 02138, starting at 4:30 p.m. Mr. Curtis is to make a 40-minute presentation and then participate in a 20-minute discussion period. The meeting will be held in the Peerless Ballroom and will be followed by dinner at 5:30. Mr. Curtis is invited to the dinner as a guest of the Advertising League. Write the letter that Ms. O'Toole should send to Mr. Curtis to confirm all the details of his participation in the convention.

B. On a separate sheet of paper, write a letter expressing each of the following claim or adjustment messages.
  1. Write a letter for William Roland, the manager of Le Crépuscule, a French restaurant located at 665 Darien Street, Omaha, Nebraska 68108. Today Mr. Roland has received a new, heavy-duty commercial food processor, but his chef shows him that it does not slice foods as precisely as advertised. Write the manufacturer, Whirling Wonder Kitchen Co., One Bluegrass Way, Lexington, Kentucky 40506, requesting replacement of the food processor.

2. You work in the claims and adjustments department of Whirling Wonder Kitchen Co. You receive a letter from the manager of Le Crépuscule (see 1 immediately above) requesting replacement of a food processor that is not slicing evenly. You know from experience that uneven slices usually result from a damaged slicing disk. Write Mr. Roland, the manager of Le Crépuscule. First, ask whether the food processor performs correctly with other attachments, such as the two-bladed knife and the shredding disk. Explain that if the machine does correctly dice, chop, grate, grind, and shred, the problem is definitely the damaged slicing disk. Offer to replace the slicing disk at no cost if this is the problem.

3. Review the letter of adjustment addressed to Ms. Sanders (page 520) concerning the problem film processor. Assume that Ms. Sanders is not satisfied with your offer to replace the fan and to give her a $100 discount. Instead, Ms. Sanders agrees to accept replacement of the fan, but she also wants full compensation for all film wasted as a result of the defective fan. You decide to write Ms. Sanders offering to send a claims adjuster to her photography business to examine the wasted film and determine its value. But you also decide not to commit yourself at this point to pay for all film wasted. Write the letter.

Editing Practice

Applied Psychology. On a separate sheet of paper, rewrite the following sentences so that each promotes goodwill.

1. There is no chance that we can deliver your order on time because many smarter consumers placed their orders before you.
2. Because you were careless and forgot to write your taxpayer's identification number on the form, we are returning it to you.
3. You must be too lazy to open your mail, because we have already written you once about this matter.
4. Your October 3 letter fails to explain satisfactorily your delay in paying.
5. Your inability to operate computer equipment means that we will have to send a technician to your office.
6. We will repair the cabinet that you claim was damaged in transit.
7. You are the only person who ever found our sunscreen product unsatisfactory.
8. You neglected to send us the sales receipt for your stolen watch when you filed your claim.
9. You complained that Order 977 did not arrive on time.
10. You made a mistake of $27 on our March 15 invoice.

Persuading

Would you persuade, speak of interest, not of reason.

—Ben Franklin, *Poor Richard's Almanac*

Next to the face-to-face visit of a sales representative, sales and other persuasive letters represent the most effective, direct contact a business can have with the customer. You should know the guidelines for writing sales letters because most business letters are really sales letters written to promote the sales of goods or services.

WRITING SALES LETTERS

Businesses spend millions of dollars on sales letters every year because letters have two major advantages over radio and television advertisements. First, letters give recipients something they can put their hands on and see or read more than once. Second, letters sent to a carefully selected audience can be more direct and personal than commercials, which are produced for a mass audience.

Targeting Audiences

Think about the sales letters you receive. They range from offers to sell magazines or insurance to invitations to collect a free prize when you visit a time-share condo in your area. Do you think that everyone on your street or in your town gets the same sales letters that you do? You might be surprised to learn that marketing specialists make a living by choosing very select target audiences for different products and services. A *target audience* is a group of potential customers chosen on the basis of certain characteristics such as age, geographic location, income, or lifestyle.

If the new product, for example, is exercise equipment, the target audience will be fitness trainers or athletes who might be able to use such equipment. If the product is a new line of children's clothing, the target audience will be families with young children. Of course, finding the target audience is not always as easy as in the two preceding examples. Companies that want to sell a new product for businesses, such as a digital camera (or color laser printer), may have to do extensive research to determine the best target audience.

When the target audience for a product is the general public, the challenge facing writers of sales letters is to determine which of the following buying motives are most likely to appeal to the readers.

Understanding Buying Motives

Identifying buyers' needs and wants and then satisfying those needs and wants is the key to understanding buying motives.

Identifying Needs and Wants.   In general, people buy products and services to satisfy specific needs and wants. People's needs are, of course, vital but relatively few: food, shelter, clothing, and perhaps transportation. People's wants, by contrast, are endless. People want not just any food, but delicious food; not just any shelter, but a comfortable apartment or house; not just any clothes, but the latest fashions. As you learned in Chapter 1, most people also want security, status, the approval of others, health, personal attractiveness, conveniences (such as microwave ovens and garage door openers), and various forms of recreation and entertainment.

While people are usually aware of their wants in a general way, they may not know how a new product or service would fulfill any of those wants. The job of a sales letter writer, therefore, is to convince people that a specific product or service will satisfy one or more of their wants.

Satisfying Needs and Wants.   To make readers interested in a product or service, a sales letter writer must show how purchasing the item will provide the reader with prestige, good health, fun, beauty, savings, romance, freedom from drudgery, and so on. For example, the following list indicates the kinds of personal wants and needs that can be satisfied by the products and services shown.

Product or Service	Want or Need
Central air conditioning	Comfort
Microwave oven	Convenience
Toothpaste	Health and attractiveness
Home swimming pool	Recreation, status or prestige
Outdoor lighting	Security
Charitable contribution	Self-esteem

OBJECTIVES OF SALES LETTERS

After identifying the target audience's motives for buying a particular product or service, the writer proceeds to write the sales letter. Keep in mind, however, that there is no standard formula for all sales letters. They can vary in length, organization, and content. However, an effective sales letter generally accomplishes the following five objectives.

1. Attract the reader's attention.
2. Establish a close relationship with the reader.
3. Appeal to one or more specific buying motives.
4. Persuade the reader to act.
5. Provide the reader an opportunity to act.

KEY POINT

Sales letters are written to appeal to a target audience.

Attracting Attention

A sales letter must immediately attract favorable attention. The appearance of a sales letter often makes the difference between whether the letter is read or tossed into the wastebasket. Because appearance starts with the envelope, sales letters often come in envelopes that promise big prizes, valuable certificates, and great savings inside. Creative advertisement writers take advantage of computers to add personalized attention-getting questions to envelopes. "Where would you take your next FREE vacation, Mrs. Martin?" Many readers would react by opening the envelope to see what they have to do to get a free vacation.

Once a reader opens the envelope, other factors come into play. For example, heavy-stock stationery and an engraved letterhead give an appearance of importance, or the facsimile of a telegram gives the appearance of urgency. An enclosed free sample is another good way to get a reader's attention.

Establishing Familiarity

To keep the sales prospect reading, the writer needs to establish a familiar tone with the reader. One way to achieve this goal is to refer to the reader as *you* as often as possible. Another good device for establishing a mood of familiarity is to start the letter with a rhetorical question. If you combine these two techniques, you might develop an opening sentence such as the following.

Isn't it time you took a really good photograph?

Would you like to lose 5 pounds in a week?

You can also establish a familiar tone with the reader in the first paragraph by (1) using imperative sentences; (2) using informal punctuation such as dashes, exclamation points, underscores, ellipses, and parentheses; (3) using contractions; (4) using short, informal sentences; (5) repeating the reader's name in the letter; and (6) complimenting the reader. The sentences that follow are additional opening lines that illustrate these techniques.

Opening	Product or Service
Protect your family with Burglar Beware.	Security system
Now! Do it . . . don't wait a minute longer. Health—happiness—fitness: they're all yours at Exercise World!	Fitness Club
Mr. and Mrs. Engles, don't you want your child to get better than average grades?	Encyclopedias

Appealing to Buying Motives

Now the writer uses market research and other knowledge about the target audience of the sales letter to make a connection between the features of the product or service and the presumed buying motives of the reader. The goal is to induce the reader to buy. Incentives to buy are called *sales appeals,* and they are the main act of the sales letter. Keep in mind, therefore, that the envelope, the stationery, and the opening line only set the stage. Notice how the following excerpts use sales appeals to stimulate the reader's buying motives.

Sales Appeal	Buying Motive
Your family will ask for more each time you serve Rosa's Best macaroni and cheese.	Family approval
You can get twice the work done in half the time if your employees use Famous Maker computers.	Convenience and economy
You can relive all your happy moments time and time again if you record them with a Video-Play camcorder.	Enjoyment
Don't drive just any car. Drive a car that people will notice. Drive an elegant Mercedes!	Personal status

The sales appeal brings the reader to the point of wanting to buy a product. The writer must then nudge the reader just a little further by persuading that person to act on his or her desire to buy.

Persuading Someone to Act

To increase the pressure on the reader to say "Yes, I want to buy this!" the writer often uses techniques that help develop a close relationship between writer and reader. The most effective of these techniques is the rhetorical question. Although a sales letter may contain several rhetorical questions at various points, a question can be used most effectively after the sales appeal. For example, after the virtues of the product have been described and the sales appeal has been made, imagine how effective questions such as the following could be.

Do pressures, deadlines, and difficult people leave you feeling frazzled?

Are your fuel bills too high?

Would you like to be free from back pain?

After answering yes to rhetorical questions like these, readers are as ready to act as they will ever be. The writer's job, however, is still not over.

KEY POINT

The goal of a sales letter is to persuade the reader to buy a specific product or service.

KEY POINT

The rhetorical question is the most effective technique to develop a close relationship between the writer and the reader.

Providing the Opportunity to Act

What happens if the reader has no opportunity to act on an urge to buy? Writers of sales letters include at least one of the following opportunities for immediate reaction.

1. A postage-paid reply card
2. An order form
3. Coupons
4. A toll-free, 24-hour telephone number

The sample letter in Figure 11.6 gives the reader simple instructions:

Figure 11.6 Sales Letter With a Return Card.

The sales letter makes the reader's response to the offer very easy. All the reader needs to do is write a reply on the postage-paid return card.

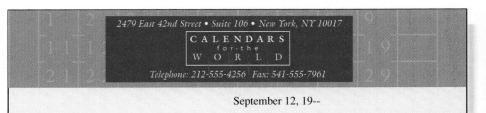

2479 East 42nd Street • Suite 106 • New York, NY 10017

CALENDARS
for the
W O R L D

Telephone: 212-555-4256 | Fax: 541-555-7961

September 12, 19--

Mr. Elwin Hemsley
1295 Amber Way
Memphis, TN 38119

Dear Mr. Hemsley:

Studies show that . . .

. . . the successful people in business control time and do not let time control them.
. . . remembering important events strengthens friendships and relationships.
. . . being organized and getting things done result in advancement opportunities.

We know these statements describe you, Mr. Hemsley, because you purchased one of our convenient Day Planners last year for just $102. You and the many other individuals who use our day planning products are better organized and get more accomplished than those who do not use them.

Now we offer you a special, three-year subscription to calendar refills for 1998, 1999, and 2000 for an incredible $72.86. The price includes shipping and handling for all three years. Your l998 calendar will ship immediately.

To reserve your Day Planner fillers and have them shipped at the appropriate times, just check the "Yes" option on our enclosed return card, and mail it to us. We will bill you later.

Your time is valuable, Mr. Hemsley. Let our Day Planner continue to help you make the most of it by acting now on this special offer.

Sincerely,

Mason Hicks

Mason Hicks
President

Enclosure

WRITING CREDIT AND COLLECTION LETTERS

Another type of persuasive letter is the *collection letter,* a letter in which a company reminds certain customers that they have not paid their bills. Collecting an overdue account is not an easy task because no one likes to ask for money. Yet businesses must ask—or lose money. The goal, therefore, is to get customers to pay without losing their goodwill.

Making Sure Customers Understand Credit Terms

The terms of credit should always be explained to the customer at the time credit is granted. In fact, the law requires such explanation. In commercial credit (between a wholesaler and a retailer), it is also advisable to review credit terms pleasantly, but firmly, when acknowledging a customer's first order. If the terms are 30 days net, expect your money in 30 days and do not hedge with weak statements like "We hope you will send your check in 30 days." Instead, say, "Our terms are 2 percent discount if you pay within 10 days; the net amount is due in 30 days."

Assuming Customers Will Pay

When a customer first fails to pay a bill on time, it is wise to assume that this failure is an oversight. Therefore, if the usual monthly statement does not produce results, companies often send the customer a second statement a week or ten days later. Sometimes this second statement is stamped "First Reminder" or "Please Remit." Some credit departments use printed reminder forms such as the one shown in Figure 11.7.

Most customers will respond to gentle hints that their accounts are overdue. Remember, therefore, that the first reminder should never be an attack. Rather, it should be a highly impersonal nudge.

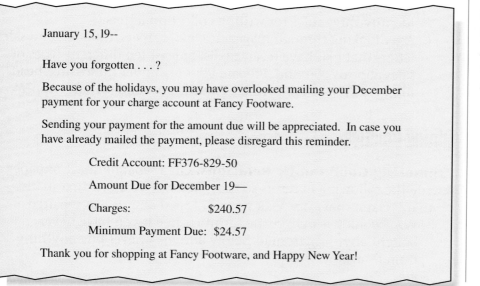

January 15, 19--

Have you forgotten . . . ?

Because of the holidays, you may have overlooked mailing your December payment for your charge account at Fancy Footware.

Sending your payment for the amount due will be appreciated. In case you have already mailed the payment, please disregard this reminder.

Credit Account: FF376-829-50

Amount Due for December 19—

Charges: $240.57

Minimum Payment Due: $24.57

Thank you for shopping at Fancy Footware, and Happy New Year!

Figure 11.7   Overdue Reminder Form.

An impersonal printed form provides a gentle reminder that an account is overdue.

Sending Additional Reminders and Follow-Up Letters

If there is no payment after a second statement and a reminder, most companies will send a series of three to five follow-up letters before turning the account over to a lawyer or a collection agency.

In a five-letter follow-up series, the first follow-up letter, though clear and firm, should still give the customer the benefit of the doubt. The second letter, which should be mailed no later than 15 days after the first letter, should remain friendly and courteous but should be firmer and more insistent than the first. The third letter should be even more insistent and forceful, and the fourth letter should demand payment. The fifth letter, then, should state what legal action will be taken if the delinquent customer fails to take advantage of this last opportunity to pay. The goal of this last letter is to urge the reader to pay the bill in order to avoid legal action.

SECTION 11.4   REVIEW

Practical Application

On a separate sheet of paper, answer the following questions.

1. What two advantages do sales letters have over radio or television commercials?
2. Define the term *target audience*.
3. List the five objectives of a sales letter.
4. Name some ways that prospective buyers can act immediately after they finish reading a sales letter.
5. Identify three rules for writing collection letters.
6. After looking through magazines, newspapers, catalogs, and sales letters that you have received, list at least ten different types of sales appeals you find. Prepare your list under these three headings: (1) Type of Product, (2) Trade Name, and (3) Sales Appeal.

Editing Practice

Promoting Good Public Relations. On a separate sheet of paper, rewrite the following excerpts so that they will be more diplomatic.

1. You claim that your VCR was not tested after it was repaired.
2. Why would we deliver the furniture free if you have never bought anything from us before and may never buy anything from us again?

3. Because you didn't include your warranty number, we won't repair your CD player.
4. Don't expect a discount if you don't remember to include your coupons.
5. If you don't pay your bill immediately, you'll be sorry.

Critical Thinking

Write a sales letter—including an attention-getting envelope—that asks young married couples to buy a mobile home. Be sure to attract the readers' attention, set up a close relationship, appeal to a specific buying motive, persuade the readers to act, and give them an opportunity to act.

Public Relations Letters

Modern businesses and persons and organizations that seek publicity must recognize their obligations to the public and to the press.

—Henry F. Woods, Jr.

OBJECTIVES:
After completing Section 11.5, you should be able to:

1. Write a letter effectively promoting a new business.
2. Write a letter encouraging charge account use.
3. Apply general public relations techniques to the writing of routine business letters.

*P*ublic relations is the business of influencing the public's feeling or attitude toward a company or an organization. Business and industry spend many millions of dollars a year on magazine and newspaper advertisements, radio and television commercials, billboard signs, cards, posters, and letters intended not only to sell a specific product but also to promote good public relations. Favorable public relations with a business means that the public has a positive opinion of the company or organization; unfavorable public relations, a negative opinion.

Major corporations have public relations departments that specialize in creating favorable images of their firms and minimizing the negative impact when their firms get unfavorable news coverage in the media. Although you may not work in the public relations department, as an employee you will certainly affect your company's public image.

Whenever you communicate with the public as a representative of your company—when you talk with or write to anyone outside the company—you have an opportunity to affect the public's attitude toward your firm. Your communication skills, therefore, can contribute to your firm's favorable public image.

KEY POINT

Public relations is the business of positively influencing the public's feeling or attitude toward a company or an organization.

KEY POINT

Every employee affects his or her company's public image.

SPECIAL PUBLIC RELATIONS OPPORTUNITIES

You have seen signs that say, for example, "Working Hard to Keep You and Your Family Safe . . . SAFE-TEE SMOKE DETECTORS." This sign is not designed specifically to sell Safe-Tee's Model 121-E smoke detector or to sell Safe-Tee's line of products but instead to promote the Safe-Tee Company in general. The ad is designed to convince you that the Safe-Tee Company has your safety in mind. Why? So that when you *do* shop for smoke detectors, you will (unconsciously or otherwise) select Safe-Tee—a name you can trust.

The public relations specialist looks for opportunities to show the company in the best possible light. When an employee receives a commendation from his or her community for civic work, the company might send a news release to various newspapers to share this good news with the public. The good civic work of one of its employees helps to enhance the firm's image. On the other hand, the public relations specialist tries to minimize anything the public could interpret in a negative way.

Unfavorable public opinion can ruin a firm. For example, if a newspaper report states or implies that the All-Natural Breads Company uses chemical preservatives and artificial coloring despite claims that its breads contain only natural ingredients, public opinion of that company will certainly drop—even if the report is later proved false. Consumers who remember the negative report may start buying another brand if they doubt the integrity of the company.

Knowing the benefits of good public relations, all businesses strive to create—and to keep—a favorable image of their organizations in the eyes of the public. An oil company may televise a short film showing the public that the company works to protect the environment wherever it drills for oil. A well-known, reputable person may narrate the film to lend it additional credibility. At no time does the narrator say "Buy your oil and gas from Enviro-Go." Instead, the narrator points out all the benefits the company offers the public.

The public relations specialist tries to win friends and customers when faced with the opportunity to:

- Promote a new business.
- Announce a special privilege or service to preferred customers.
- Offer special incentives to encourage charge customers to use their credit cards.
- Welcome new residents (new *potential customers*) to the community.
- Congratulate someone for a special achievement.
- Invite someone to a lecture, art show, demonstration, or film.
- Thank someone for his or her business.

Let's take a closer look at some of these special public-relations opportunities.

Promoting a New Business

To promote a new business, the first step toward establishing good public opinion is to announce the grand opening—for example, in a letter such as this one:

> May we introduce you to—Constance Devane, chef and managing partner of Maple Grove's newest and most exciting restaurant:
>
> A SPLENDID AFFAIR
>
> Chef Devane, a graduate of the American Culinary Arts Institute and the author of two best-selling cookbooks, has practiced her culinary magic in several fine restaurants in New York City and Boston. *Good Food Magazine* has hailed Constance Devane as "one of America's most creative young chefs."
>
> Dining at A Splendid Affair is the ultimate dining experience. Surrounded by understated elegance, you and your guests will be attended by a well-trained staff who will describe in detail the tempting appetizers, entrées, and desserts that Chef Devane and her staff will prepare for you.
>
> Reservations are necessary, and all major credit cards are accepted. As a courtesy to all guests and for your personal dining pleasure, separate dining rooms are reserved and designated as smoking and nonsmoking.
>
> Join us at A Splendid Affair for a relaxed evening of fine dining.
>
> Cordially,

This letter alone, however, is only one step in a public relations campaign. To effectively promote this grand opening requires newspaper ads, spot announcements on local radio stations, circulars, and news releases, all focused on the general theme and tone of this letter. Together, these messages make up a public-relations campaign that will surely reach the potential diners who live or work in the Maple Grove area.

Through these public-relations communications, A Splendid Affair seizes every opportunity to put its name before potential customers in a favorable light.

Handling Other Special Opportunities

The sharp businessperson has an eye for opportunities to improve public relations—and takes every advantage of those opportunities. For examples of how to *create* letters for special occasions, see the letters illustrated in Figure 11.8 and Figure 11.9 on pages 534 and 535.

KEY POINT

Astute business people look for opportunities to improve public relations.

EVERYDAY PUBLIC RELATIONS OPPORTUNITIES

Unless your job is in the public relations department, you may not have all the special public relations opportunities that have been discussed so far. But the techniques will be useful because you *will* have everyday opportunities to improve public relations for your company.

In Figure 11.8 below, note how the writer of the letter uses a rhetorical question to catch the reader's interest. The writer continues the letter by stating how the company can assist the reader.

Figure 11.8   Sales Letter With a Special Offer.

Many companies use sales letters to attract interest in a product or service through special promotions.

DESTINATIONS UNLIMITED
344 East Canyon Place
Tucson, AZ 85704
Telephone: 520-555-8728
Fax: 520-555-8728
E-mail: destunl@cactusnet.com

April 14, 20--

Ms. Victoria Masters
28 Frances Avenue
Phoenix, AZ 85022

Dear Ms. Masters:

Do you need a vacation? Like many people, you probably enjoyed your last few days away from the office during the holidays. That seems so long ago as you wade through the endless piles of paper on your desk, as you sort through endless requests, and as you hurry from one meeting to another.

We invite you to visit our summer getaway representative at the Travel Center. We can offer you many alternatives for the weekend, week, or month vacation that you deserve. We can offer suggestions that fit your preferences. We have the networking capability to make all arrangements so you don't have to worry about any details. All you have to do is think about a glorious vacation that lies ahead for you beyond that stack of papers on your desk!

Right now, you can take advantage of many airline and tour discounts. Give yourself something to look forward to. Come in and talk to one of our representatives today.

Sincerely yours,

Gloria Bean

Gloria Bean
Travel Manager

Figure 11.9 Public Relations Letter.

Coastal Electronics

335 North Beach Avenue
Alhambra, CA
Telephone: 818-555-8835

July 24, 20—

Mrs. Jean Craig
15620 Vernon Park Avenue
Pasadena, CA 91116

Dear Mrs. Craig:

Congratulations! You now own your big screen television you purchased one year ago. Our enclosed canceled note is your record that all payments have been made on this product.

We are sorry to lose you as a customer because you have always made all your payments on time. We hope you will consider us again to finance your purchase of additional major household items.

Please file our enclosed certificate that will entitle you to our lowest possible finance rates when you seek loans from us for indoor and outdoor household items as well as new vehicles. Present the certificate to a representative at any one of our conveniently located offices for service on your loan requests. We will be most pleased to work with you again.

Cordially yours,

Cynthia A. Lopez

Cynthia A. Lopez
Vice President

Figure 11.9 Public Relations Letter.

The writer makes an opportunity to contact a former customer. While thanking her for her patronage, the writer also reminds the customer that she has credit privileges with the company the next time she considers making a purchase.

Note in the following letter that the writer *sells the company.* In other words, the writer employs good public relations techniques in replying to a routine request for information.

Dear Mr. Gould:

All of us here appreciate your thinking of the Little Creek Inn as *the* place to hold your annual sales conventions. Thank you for the compliment!

For several years now, you have used our facilities to host your special dinners, to demonstrate products to customers, to train your new representatives, and to lodge your employees and guests whenever they are in our area. We do, indeed, make a special effort to make all your meetings successful because your appreciation of our efforts always shows.

Mr. Gould, we sincerely enjoy serving you, your employees, and your customers. Thank you for doing business with us.

Cordially yours,

As you see, then, public relations is part of every letter you write for your company. When you write your letters, even *routine* letters, look for ways to incorporate good public relations techniques.

Practical Application

1. Suppose that you are a college graduate with five years of business experience as (a) an administrative assistant in an attorney's office, (b) a travel agent in a large agency, or (c) a tax accountant in a public accounting firm.

    You decide to set up your own (a) legal secretarial service, (b) travel agency, or (c) tax accounting business.

    You choose to begin promoting your new business by writing a letter and sending it to 100 businesses in the community. You wish to emphasize both your business experience and your excellent college education. Write a letter that includes all the details that will improve your chances of attracting clients.

2. You work for Newlook Decorators, an interior decorating firm that is introducing a new line of furniture and decorations this spring. A special preview showing of the new line is planned for charge customers, including family and friends, at the Newlook Showroom, 657 Woodside Avenue, March 21, from 6 p.m. until 9 p.m. You are assigned to write a letter of invitation. Admission will be by ticket only, and you are enclosing a ticket with each invitation. The general public will not see the new line until March 28. Write a letter that makes the most of this occasion.

3. You are manager of Lindemann's Hardware Store, an established business on the outskirts of a large city. Traditionally, your customers have come from the city. New towns and neighborhoods are springing up beyond city limits, however, and you are looking for a way to develop business with the residents of these new areas. You decide to write a letter, enclosing a discount coupon worth $5, that invites each resident of the new areas to visit your store. Write an appealing invitation addressed to new residents.

Editing Practice

Editing to Improve Writing Techniques. On a separate sheet of paper, edit the following sentences to improve any poor writing techniques.

1. Arriving to pick up the package, I asked the messenger to wait while the cover letter was signed by Ms. Drake.
2. Employees must now submit their health insurance claim to Robert Bergman in the personnel office.
3. Ellen borrowed the dictionary which was on my desk.
4. Judy said she couldn't find any stamps for the letters after looking in the desk drawers.
5. You can use either of these four spreadsheets as a model for your training course.

Social-Business Communications

Persuade him with kindly gifts and gentle words.

—Homer, *The Illiad*

OBJECTIVES:
After completing Section 11.6, you should be able to:

1. Use the correct social-business letter format both on plain stationery and on printed stationery.
2. Write effective congratulatory letters, thank-you letters, and condolence letters.
3. Correctly write—and reply to—formal invitations.

When you buy a new car or a new home, start a new business, get a promotion, or get married, you expect your lifelong friends and your closest relatives to congratulate you—to show somehow that they share the joy of the occasion. On the other hand, if you suffer the loss of a loved one, you expect those same friends and all your other close relatives to show their sympathy for you. Common courtesy and tradition require people to communicate their congratulations or their sorrow in these instances.

In business, likewise, common courtesy and tradition demand that business workers send *social-business communications* to congratulate someone on a special occasion, express condolence when a business associate suffers the loss of a loved one, reply properly to a formal invitation, thank someone for a special favor or a gift, and so on. Just as you would appreciate hearing from your coworkers and business associates in these situations, you should let them hear from you whenever appropriate.

SOCIAL-BUSINESS LETTER FORMAT

As you learned in Section 10.4, the *format* of a letter refers to the arrangement of letter parts on the page.

On Company Letterhead

For a social-business letter typed on company letterhead, use the social-business letter format illustrated in Figure 11.10. As you see, in this social-business letter format, the letter parts are in the usual position *except* the inside address is placed last, positioned at the bottom of the page. In addition, there is a change in the usual punctuation pattern for business letters: The salutation ends with a comma rather than with a colon. Reference initials, copy notations, and so on, are not included.

World View

Traditions for congratulating someone may differ from culture to culture.

KEY POINT

The inside address is placed at the end of the letter in the social-business letter format.

Figure 11.10 Congratulatory Letter on Standard Letterhead.

Prepared in modified-block style, this letter illustrates the two unique features of social-business letters: (1) the inside address is positioned at the bottom of the letter and (2) the salutation ends with a comma, not a colon.

Lakeside Community College
DEPARTMENT OF COMPUTER SCIENCE

2525 ERIE AVENUE
PAINESVILLE, OH 44077
TELEPHONE: 216-555-3576
FAX: 216-555-7413
E-MAIL: LUNGREN@LCC.EDU

November 24, 19–

Dear Ms. Gomez,

Congratulations on your recent promotion to Executive Editor. As an author who has worked with you for six years, I know the promotion is well deserved.

You have played an important part in developing the concept for my computer applications text. You have also secured approved funding, completed and implemented input from reviewers, and kept me on track in terms of meeting manuscript and production deadlines.

As a result of your efforts, my text is now being used in high schools around the country. Not only do you have superb editorial skills but also you have the people skills to pull everyone together as a team to complete this project.

I hope your promotion will not affect our working relationship when the text revision begins. I look forward to working with you again. I do wish you continued success in your new position and with all projects for which you have increased responsibility.

Sincerely,

Henry A. Lungren

Henry A. Lungren
Associate Professor

Ms. Carolyn Gomez
Harbor Publishers
50 Excelsior Avenue
Columbus, OH 43230

KEY POINT

Executives frequently use executive sized letterhead for social-business correspondence.

Some companies provide *executive* letterhead for social-business and other letters. Executive stationery measures 7 1/4 by 10 1/2 inches (monarch) or 5 1/2 by 8 1/2 inches (baronial). Standard stationery, on the other hand, measures 8 1/2 by 11 inches. Many people consider these sizes especially fitting for executive correspondence.

Whether you are using monarch or baronial letterhead or standard-sized stationery, follow the same format described.

On Plain Stationery

When a social-business letter is typed on stationery with no printed letterhead, include the return address as you would for personal-business letters. See the letter illustrated in Figure 11.11 on page 539.

754 Old Mill Road
Terre Haute, IN 47802
September 4, 19–

Dear Ms. Chan,

Please allow me to offer my best wishes to you upon your election as national president of the National Reading Literary Council. You have shown your dedication to the goals of this organization at both the local and state levels.

With your experience, you will continue to work hard and be influential in helping everyone learn to read. By doing so, you will improve the quality of life of many people nationwide.

I know you will have a productive and successful term in this very important leadership position.

Cordially yours,

James E. Vandenberg

Ms. Helen Chan
17 Layson Drive
Fayette, IA 52142

Figure 11.11   Congratulatory Letter on Plain Stationery.

This social-business letter, prepared on plain, 8 1/2- by 11-inch stationery, follows the modified-block style with indented paragraphs.

CONGRATULATIONS LETTERS

Special honors and special events provide ideal public-relations opportunities. They present you with an appropriate occasion to say "Congratulations!" Your reader will appreciate your thoughtfulness, and you will certainly win favor both for yourself and for your company. *Remember:* Everyone wants to be respected and admired, and a congratulatory message shows your respect and admiration for someone's accomplishment or recognition.

For Promotions

The degree of friendliness or informality of your congratulatory note will depend on the specific relationship you have with the reader. For two examples of similar congratulatory notes (one more formal and the other more casual), see the letters in Figure 11.10 and Figure 11.11 respectively.

Congratulatory letters often are written to employees of the same company. In fact, it is virtually *mandatory* for executives to acknowledge promotions of employees in their company. The following letter is written to a valued employee:

Dear Preston,

Congratulations to you on your promotion to District Manager. You certainly are "the right person for the right job."

KEY POINT

Congratulatory letters can be an effective public relations tool.

Catherine Terranova has been talking about promoting you to this position since she became Marketing Manager six months ago. All of us in management are equally convinced that you will be able to continue to turn in the high sales volume for which the Southern District is well known.

In any case, Preston, I certainly am happy to welcome you to the sales management team for our Consumer Division, and I wish you success in your new position.

Sincerely,

For Anniversaries

A coworker's anniversary also calls for written congratulations. Note the friendliness and informality—and the sincerity—of this letter:

Dear Gene,

Congratulations on your tenth year with Vector Products Inc. I remember your first day with the company, when Len Denaro introduced you to me and my staff. When Len retired one year later, I *knew* that you were the right person to replace him—and you've continued to prove that for the last nine years.

Gene, I think you know just how pleased I've been to have the opportunity to work with you during your time here. Thanks to your manufacturing expertise and management leadership, our Production Department is the best in the industry. My staff and I appreciate your fine work. You certainly help make things easier for the rest of us!

Cordially yours,

For Retirements

The retirement of a coworker or of a business associate also deserves recognition. Retirement letters deserve extra care; if you are not sure that the person welcomes retiring, be especially sensitive to the retiree's feelings in writing the note.

Dear Veronica,

What will Clarion Advertising be like without you? Our clients, our suppliers, and of course all our coworkers have come to depend on that smiling face, that cheerful voice, and that friendly attitude whenever we approach the Graphic Arts Department. It seemed as if you were always there to help a lost visitor, to reroute a messenger, and to answer the phone when no one else was around. I know that you were always there to help me.

Thank you, Veronica, for all you have done to help me since the first day I joined the company. All my best wishes to you in your retirement. I hope that you will enjoy many years of health and happiness with your family and your good friends. I hope, too, that you will visit us from time to time.

Sincerely,

For Individual Honors

When a business friend or associate has been named, appointed, or elected to a special position, show your congratulations with a message such as the one illustrated in Figure 11.11 on page 539.

THANK-YOU LETTERS

During our daily interaction with people, we always have many opportunities to say "Thank you." A special occasion, however, requires a *written* thank-you—for example, when we receive a gift, hospitality, or special courtesy from a business associate.

For Gifts

Business executives may receive gifts from suppliers and vendors. When they do, courtesy demands that they write a thank-you note to the giver.

KEY POINT

In many cases a written thank you is expected. A timely thank-you letter demonstrates to employers that you are a thoughtful person who knows business etiquette.

> Dear Matthew,
>
> Thank you for your thoughtfulness in sending me such a beautifully bound edition of *Modern Art in America*. You certainly selected a book of very special interest to me, as you very well know. Since I received your package late Friday afternoon, I have done little else but read, read, read. Admittedly, I spent lots of time on the photographs too!
>
> Matthew, please accept my sincere appreciation to you for your kindness. You may be sure that I will enjoy this book again and again.
>
> Cordially yours,

Some companies have policies prohibiting employees from accepting such gifts under any circumstances. If your firm has such a policy, you will of course adhere to it. Your thank-you letter, then, will require a different approach.

> Dear Matthew,
>
> Thank you for your thoughtfulness in sending me such a beautifully bound edition of *Modern Art in America*. You certainly selected a book of very special interest to me, as you very well know.
>
> I wish, Matthew, that company policy permitted me to keep this thoughtful gift, but we have a specific policy that prohibits my doing so. Therefore, when I have completed reading the book, I will give it to the company library with this inscription: "Donated to the Owens-Mandel Library by Ridgefield Printers, Inc."
>
> Matthew, please accept my sincere appreciation to you for your kindness. You may be sure that I will borrow this book from the library often; when I do, I will remember your thoughtfulness.
>
> Cordially yours,

For Hospitality

A business associate's hospitality is not to be taken for granted. Even if the person is also an employee of your company, he or she still deserves a thank-you letter for special hospitality.

Dear Mrs. Allen,

Thank you for the many courtesies extended to me on my recent visit to Evanston. My stay was certainly much more pleasant because of your thoughtfulness in arranging for my comfort.

The high spot of the entire visit was the evening spent in your beautiful home. You and Mr. Allen are most gracious hosts. The food was excellent; the conversation, stimulating; the people, delightful. The time passed so quickly that I was embarrassed to find that I had stayed so long—so engrossed and comfortable was I in being part of such good company.

Enclosed is a small token of my appreciation for the many kindnesses shown me. I shall not soon forget my visit to Evanston.

Sincerely yours,

For Recommendations

Many businesses flourish almost solely on the basis of the recommendations of clients, friends, suppliers, and other business associates. When someone recommends you or your firm, he or she is doing you a special favor—a favor that deserves a thank-you letter.

Dear Ms. Boyle:

This morning we visited Bruce Stargell of Stargell's Sports Center, Inc. Mr. Stargell mentioned your recommendation when he placed an order for display and storage equipment for the chain of new stores that he will open this fall.

We thank you, Ms. Boyle, for recommending us to Mr. Stargell. We appreciate the order immensely, but not one bit more than we appreciate your confidence in us. Please accept our thanks for this favor. I hope we will be able to repay your kindness at the earliest opportunity.

Cordially yours,

KEY POINT

Thank-you letters build business relationships with coworkers and colleagues at other companies.

CONDOLENCE LETTERS

When business associates and friends suffer tragedies or misfortunes, common courtesy requires you to communicate your sympathy with a condolence letter. Depending on your specific relationship, you may send a printed sympathy card.

Condolence letters are difficult to write simply because it is difficult to console and comfort someone who has recently suffered a tragic loss. For the same reason, however, condolence letters are always very much appreciated. The important element is to let your business associate or friend know that you are thinking of him or her. You may type a condolence letter, but if you really wish to give your letter a personal touch, write a legible handwritten note.

> Dear Sandy,
>
> The news of your brother's untimely death yesterday has stunned and saddened me. I know that you have suffered a great loss. Please accept my sincere sympathy.
>
> When my mother died last year, a friend sent me a copy of Dylan Thomas's poem "And Death Shall Have No Dominion." I found the poem, a copy of which is enclosed, a source of consolation again and again. I hope the poem will serve you as well as it did me. My heart goes out to you and your family in your time of grief.
>
> Sincerely yours,

KEY POINT

Common courtesy requires you to send a condolence message when business associates and friends suffer tragedies or misfortunes.

FORMAL INVITATIONS AND REPLIES

From time to time, business people receive formal invitations to such events as an open house, a special reception to honor a distinguished person, a special anniversary, or a formal social gathering. Such invitations are usually engraved or printed and are written in the third person.

The illustration in Figure 11.12 shows a formal printed invitation. An acceptance or a refusal is usually handwritten. Handwritten invitations and replies are written on personal stationery or special note-sized stationery. Plain white notepaper may also be used.

The Plaza Health Spa

requests the pleasure of your company
at its presentation of expanded health facilities
Friday, the sixth of February
at six o'clock
1244 North Hamilton Road in Middleport.

Our health bar will be serving refreshments.

R.S.V.P.

Figure 11.12 Printed Invitation.

A printed formal invitation is usually written in the third person.

Practical Application

1. Annette Rossi was a classmate of yours in college. You read in the newspaper that Annette, after only three years at Harvest Investing, has been chosen Outstanding Financial Analyst. Annette's reward is twofold: a promotion to Assistant Director of Financial Analysis and an expense-paid tour of the Far East. Write a letter of congratulation to Annette on her achievements.

2. You have just returned from a business trip to Louisville, Kentucky. During your three-day stay in Louisville, you were the house guest of Barbara and Peter Brandon, longtime friends of your family. Barbara even met you at the airport and insisted on personally driving you to your business appointments, rather than having you experience the difficulty of getting around a strange city in a rented car. Write a note of thanks to the Brandons, who live at 87 Mark Twain Drive, Louisville, Kentucky 40204. Today you ordered a gift to be sent to them as a small token of your appreciation.

3. You have just learned of the illness and death of Helga Olson, the wife of one of your company's suppliers who had become a friend of yours. In addition to her husband, Mrs. Olson leaves a married daughter (Anne) and three grandchildren. Write a letter of condolence to Frederick Olson, Director of Marketing for Ludlow Manufacturing, 668 West Ludlow, St. Louis, Missouri 63399.

Editing Practice

Electronic Mail. You received the following wordy e-mail message on your computer. On a separate sheet of paper, rewrite it in 60 words or less.

One of the nation's outstanding experts on stress is Dr. Alice Burns of New York City. We are fortunate to be able to have Dr. Burns as a speaker for two presentations that she will give here in our company auditorium next month.

The title of her talk is "Stress on the Job." The first presentation will be at 10 a.m. on April 18; the second presentation will be at the same time on the next day, April 19. Each speech will be one hour long, and each will be followed by a session during which Dr. Burns will answer questions from the audience.

If you are interested in hearing this noted author and lecturer, you are welcome to attend either one of the scheduled sessions. Because seats are limited, of course, we ask you to notify the Training Department if you are interested in hearing Dr. Burns.

Form Paragraphs, Form Letters, and Templates

I for one appreciate a good form letter, having worked on Capitol Hill and learned several dozen cordial ways to say nothing.

—Carrie Johnson

OBJECTIVES:

After completing Section 11.7, you should be able to:

1. Explain the advantages and disadvantages of using form letters.
2. Name and describe the three categories of form letters.
3. Create and use a form letter with variables.
4. Create form paragraphs and use them to develop form letters.
5. Create a form letter.

You have learned that writing quality business communications takes much time and effort. Because time and effort cost money, many companies look for acceptable ways to reduce the amount spent. One very good way to reduce writing costs is to use form letters. *Form letters* are letters in which the same message is sent to many addressees. Sometimes details of the message, called *variables,* change from letter to letter. Sometimes form letters are composed by combining various pre-written paragraphs, called *boilerplate,* into a particular communication.

ADVANTAGES OF USING FORM LETTERS

Here are the major advantages of using form letters.

1. Using form letters saves time in planning, dictating, and transcribing.
2. Company representatives can respond more quickly to routine writing situations, and thus the receiver gets an answer sooner.
3. The content quality will be better. Much time and thought can go into writing form letters.
4. Fewer errors will result because the spelling, punctuation, and grammar have to be approved only once.
5. Form letters and paragraphs do not have to be retyped. They are simply selected and printed.

DISADVANTAGES OF USING FORM LETTERS

As with most good ideas, there are some disadvantages of using form letters. Here are three:

1. Some of the "personal touch" can be lost in mass-producing letters. Attempts should be made to make letters more personal. You could, for example, include the person's name within a sentence. "I look forward to seeing you, Ms. Tate, on Friday at 2 p.m."

2. If readers find out that they have received a form letter, they may feel somewhat disappointed. A manager, for example, wrote you a congratulatory message when your son finished college. You felt good about the letter until your coworker showed you one exactly like it when his daughter finished college. The purpose of the letter was goodwill, and the goodwill was lost. For this reason form letters should be revised and updated at least once a year. Do not knowingly send personal form letters to people who would have the opportunity to compare content.

3. The use of form letters and boilerplate can be abused. Some business writers use them when they are inappropriate or when they do not quite fit the situation.

TYPES OF FORM LETTERS

Executives often find that they are repeatedly writing the same content in response to frequently occurring—almost identical—writing situations. When this happens, they should invest some time and effort in developing general responses that can be used and reused. These general responses fall into three main categories.

- Form letters
- Form letters with variables
- Letters with form paragraphs

Form Letters

KEY POINT

Form letters are used to respond to identical situations.

Form letters are used to respond to identical situations. The letter shown in Figure 11.13 would be used to respond to any general inquiries about Alaska cruises. The entire body of the letter remains the same; the date, inside address, salutation, and reference initials are the only changes. These letter parts are highlighted in the example. Figure 11.14 shows the form letter with the highlighted information filled in.

Form Letters With Variables

Form letters with variables are used when similar, but not identical, responses are needed. In addition to the date, inside address, and salutation, other details are changed throughout the body of the letter. These changes are called variables. Figure 11.15 on page 549 shows a form letter with the variables highlighted. The letter in Figure 11.16 on page 549 is in finished form, with specific information added for the variables.

Current Date

Name
Address
City, State ZIP Code

Salutation:

Thank you for inquiring
For the past several years
area of our country have

I am enclosing a brochur
cruise packages. You ca
determine the one that be

When you are ready, plea
it to me at your earliest p
lar, they tend to fill up qu

If you have other questio
me help you make the de

??
Enclosure

DESTINATIONS UNLIMITED
344 East Canyon Place
Tucson, AZ 85704
Telephone: 520-555-8728
Fax: 520-555-8728
E-mail: destunl@cactusnet.com

February 10, 20--

Ms. Marie Cola
117 Orchard Avenue
Raleigh, NC 26701

Dear Ms. Cola:

Thank you for inquiring about our great cruises to our 49th state, Alaska. For the past several years, our six cruise packages to this great beautiful area of our country have continued to become increasingly popular.

I am enclosing a brochure that summarizes the dates and costs of the many cruise packages. You can readily see the differences among the packages and determine the one that best fits your preferences.

When you are ready, please complete our enclosed reservation form and return it to me at your earliest possible convenience. Since these cruises are so popular, they tend to fill up quickly.

If you have other questions, please call me at my number shown above. Let me help you make the details for your memorable vacation.

Sincerely,

DESTINATIONS UNLIMITED

Renee Weaver

Renee Weaver
Manager

dp
Enclosure

Letters With Form Paragraphs

For similar writing situations that occur frequently but vary in content, experienced business communicators use form, or boilerplate, paragraphs. Paragraphs dealing with most common situations are written. Each paragraph has a number. Instead of dictating or keying each letter, the originator gives the office assistant the date, inside address, salutation, and a list of paragraphs by number. A letter that uses form paragraphs and sample boilerplate for those paragraphs is shown in Figure 11.17 on page 550.

Using the word processing program on a computer makes writing letters with form paragraphs even easier. Boilerplate paragraphs and complete letters can be stored on disk and retrieved and altered as necessary. Only the variables need to be typed. As a result, routine letters can be prepared quickly and efficiently.

MERGED LETTERS

Merged letters save time when you need to send the same letter to a group of people. Merging requires two files—a *data file,* which contains the names and addresses of people on your mailing list, and a *form file,* which contains the form letter and the codes to merge the information with the data file. The two files are merged, and your letters are printed so that each letter appears to be individually typed and addressed.

An advantage to merged letters is that the next time you wish to send a letter to this group of people, you need only to change the body of the letter.

TEMPLATES

Many word processing programs today come with templates of letters. A *template* contains the format for a letter and can include the letterhead in addition to the skeleton of a letter. To use a template, you insert the template into your blank document or open a copy of the template, add the text in the places indicated, and print. This saves time and helps the user who is unsure of the correct letter format. Unfortunately, not all templates in all software are set up according to the correct formats you learned about in Chapter 10.

Current Date

Name
Address
City, State ZIP Code

Salutation:

Your reservations for eight tickets to see "A Funny Thing Happened on the Way to the Forum" have been made, and your tickets are enclosed. You should be pleased with the seats you have been assigned. Four individuals will sit in Row 3, center; four individuals will sit in Row 3, center.

A total amount of $640, including taxes and service fees has been charged to your These tickets cannot be exchanged, and no refunds can be given.

We thank you for ordering tickets from us, and we know you will enjoy this fabulous and funny Broadway musical. Seeing this

DESTINATIONS UNLIMITED
344 East Canyon Place
Tucson, AZ 85704
Telephone: 520-555-8728
Fax: 520-555-8728
E-mail: destunl@cactusnet.com

August 15, 19–

Mr. Tom Finney
1223 Hummingbird Place
Fort Pierce, FL 32548

Dear Mr. Finney:

Your reservations for two tickets to see "A Funny Thing Happened on the Way to the Forum" have been made, and your tickets are enclosed. You should be pleased with the seats you have been assigned. Two individuals will sit in Row 4, center.

A total amount of $160, including taxes and service fees has been charged to your MasterCard credit card. These tickets cannot be exchanged, and no refunds can be given.

We thank you for ordering tickets from us, and we know you will enjoy this fabulous and funny Broadway musical. Seeing this show will certainly enhance your trip to New York City.

Sincerely,

Jacqueline McNeill

Jacqueline McNeill
Ticket Agent

AMBROSE LEGAL SERVICES

2203 Seahorse Place
Orlando, FL 32822

Telephone: 407-555-4159
Fax: 407-555-4367

April 5, 19—

Ms. Patty Linowski
5822 Cleveland Avenue
Tampa, FL 33612

Dear Ms. Linowski:

1   Thank you for expressing an interest in employment with our firm. We feel complimented that you want to discuss your career plans with us.

4   Before we consider you for any position, your application file must be complete. Please send us the name, company name (if appropriate), address, and phone number of three references.

5   As soon as we receive the information requested, we will call you to arrange an interview with our human resources manager.

6   Thank you for your interest in Ambrose Legal Services. We look forward to hearing from you.

Sincerely,

Michael Ambrose

Michael Ambrose
Senior Partner

SECTION 11.7   REVIEW

Practical Application

1. List and describe the three main categories of form letters.
2. Using the form letter in Figure 11.6, page 549, write a letter to Denis Prior, Post Office Box 2849, Birmingham, AZ 85643. You made reservations for Mr. Prior for four tickets in Row 8, center, to see "Bells Are Ringing." A total amount of $400 was charged to Mr. Prior's Visa credit card.

Editing Practice

Missing Words. A word has been left out of each of the following sentences. Select a word that will correctly complete each sentence, and write it on a separate sheet of paper.

1. A helpful highway gave us directions to your plant.
2. We were late for the ceremony, because we trouble with our car.
3. Most of the employees have decided participate in the dental insurance program.
4. Our sales representative in your area Carla White.
5. Newspaper advertisements radio advertisements aroused our interest.

CRITICAL THINKING CASE

A Public Relations Problem. The Pine County Medical Center periodically prepares and mails a newsletter, *Your Health,* to patients and prospective patients. The current issue contained an article informing the recipients of an upcoming seminar on the medical center's state-of-the-art Bone Densitometer. A simple test with this machine can determine the patient's risk of developing osteoporosis.

The article said the seminar would begin at 7 p.m. However, the doctor presenting the seminar had asked to have the seminar scheduled at 7:30 p.m. because of a prior obligation.

The newsletter mailing list included the name of a woman who had recently died at the medical center. The woman's husband, very upset about receiving the newsletter addressed to his deceased wife, called the director of the medical center to complain.

A day or two after the newsletter was mailed, the doctor presenting the seminar called the medical center director; the doctor was annoyed that the seminar was to start earlier than he had requested. After all, he was donating his time to present the seminar.

1. What would be the best way to handle the error in the time of the seminar?
2. What should the medical director do about the newsletter's being mailed to the deceased woman?

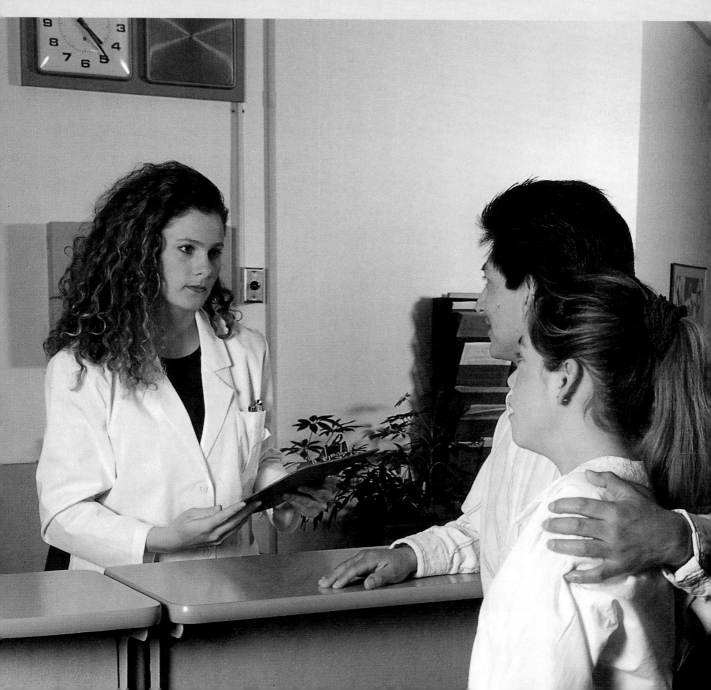

12.1   **The Importance of Good Customer Service**

12.2   **Maintaining Good Customer Service**

12.3   **Improving Contact With Customers**

12.4   **Responding to Customer Service Needs**

John and Sarah rushed to the emergency room of a large metropolitan medical center after being awakened at 11:30 p.m. by a telephone call delivering the alarming news that Sarah's father apparently had had a heart attack. John and Sarah entered a bustling reception room and hurried to the receptionist's desk.

John and Sarah heard one side of the receptionist's phone conversation. "I'll be late getting off from work tonight. We have several critical patients who have just arrived. Can you pick up something for dinner?

John waited patiently and then interrupted the receptionist, "Please, can you help me?"

"Sir," the receptionist responded, her expression showing her annoyance at being interrupted, "I'll be with you just as soon as I finish this call."

Sarah interjected, "Please, we just received a telephone call that my father was brought here and ..."

"Ma'am," the receptionist impatiently interrupted, "I said that I will be with you just as soon as I finish this call. What's his name?" Then the receptionist continued with her telephone conversation.

"Now, what is it you want?" the receptionist scowled.

Sarah, who was very upset, asked the receptionist about her father. After getting Sarah's father's name, the receptionist gave Sarah a clipboard with a questionnaire. "Fill this out. We need his insurance information."

Sarah completed the insurance questionnaire and returned it to the receptionist, who was talking on the telephone again. The receptionist took the clipboard from Sarah and motioned for her to take a seat. The receptionist continued to chat on the phone.

Fifteen minutes later, John and Sarah again approached the receptionist's desk. The night shift receptionist was now on duty. Sarah emphatically said, "I want to know how my father is."

The night shift receptionist asked for the patient's name and immediately telephoned to find out his status. A moment later the receptionist reported that the emergency room physician was transferring Sarah's father to a room for overnight observation. "If you and your husband will go to Room 385, Dr. Feldman will talk with you. He has been waiting for you for a half hour. He has some good news. Your father did not have a heart attack."

John and Sarah thanked the receptionist and hurried to see Sarah's father. Several days later, they began to think about the treatment they had received from the first receptionist.

As you read Chapter 12, identify some strategies the first receptionist could have used to promote positive customer relations.

The Importance of Good Customer Service

OBJECTIVES:

After completing Section 12.1, you should be able to:

1. Explain the concept of customer service.
2. Understand the importance of customer service.
3. Define *external* and *internal* customers.

It is not the employer who pays the wages. Employers only handle the money. It is the customer who pays the wages.

—Henry Ford

In the emergency room situation described in the case study at the beginning of this chapter, the receptionist was obviously annoyed when John and Sarah interrupted her telephone conversation. She should have been attentive to Sarah and John, welcomed their questions, requested the needed insurance information, and directed them to someone who would be able to provide information about Sarah's father. John and Sarah were surely experiencing stress and were probably bewildered by their unfamiliar surroundings.

In situations like this, you should be seen as a friendly, knowledgeable, and helpful representative of your company. If you represent a company in any capacity, the customer will believe that you can help him or her with a need or concern. Provide help, even if it simply involves directing a customer to the appropriate office or staff member.

In situations like the one in the case study, the hospital's administrative staff is required to obtain insurance and other information about a patient through contact with the patient's family. But, it is not necessary to explain hospital procedures to a family member in order to satisfy the internal needs of the hospital. Family members do not need to have this procedural information. There is a way to obtain the needed information from the patient and the patient's family while maintaining a courteous approach. An appropriate response to John and Sarah by the first receptionist could have been, "The emergency room physician is evaluating your father. He will speak to you just as soon as he has completed his examination. Will you please complete this admission form while you are waiting?" In this—and every—situation, treat the customer exactly the way you would want to be treated if your roles were reversed.

CUSTOMER SERVICE DEFINED

Customer service is a function that should exist and be practiced throughout every business organization. Very simply defined, *customer service* is the performance of activities or services for the purpose of ensuring customer satisfaction. Customer satisfaction occurs when the customer's needs are met and when the customer feels valued by the company. One way to accomplish this goal is to provide goods and ser-

KEY POINT

Customer service is the performance of activities or services for the purpose of ensuring customer satisfaction.

vices to the customer when and where they are needed and at a competitive price. Making customers feel valued instills the feeling that their business is appreciated, that they will be treated with respect, and that their business will receive conscientious attention.

The requirement that customer service procedures be implemented throughout an organization must come from top management. Without top management's support and specific directives to key employees, customer service will not receive the attention it deserves.

THE NEED FOR CUSTOMER SERVICE

Why should your company implement customer service procedures? Outstanding customer service helps you retain your current customers and attract new ones. Outstanding customer service also helps develop a reputation that encourages customers and prospective customers alike to do business with you. Satisfied customers become loyal customers, who continue to use your product or service; this results in repeat business. Most chief executive officers report that it is much easier to keep a customer than to attract a new one. In addition, many businesses derive much of their new business through recommendations, called *referrals,* from satisfied customers.

EXTERNAL AND INTERNAL CUSTOMERS

Many times, we think of customers as being exclusively from outside the organization. Recently, however, companies have come to realize that there are two categories of customers: external and internal. *External customers* are persons outside your organization who purchase your goods or services, thereby generating the money and profits that let you continue in business. Your company may deal with external customers face-to-face or by telephone, fax, e-mail, or some other method of communication.

An *internal customer* is a coworker or supervisor—someone within your own organization—who depends on products, supplies, or services that you deliver to him or her. Suppose, for example, you work in the Marketing Department. Before the Marketing Department determines the selling price for a certain item, someone from Marketing requests the cost figures for the item from the Cost Department. The Marketing Department is the internal customer of the Cost Department. If the Marketing Department asks the Accounting Department for the credit rating of a prospective customer, the Marketing Department is an internal customer of the Accounting Department. Nowadays, much emphasis is being placed on maintaining positive relationships between internal customers. Improving these relationships can help a business run more smoothly.

KEY POINT

Outstanding service helps a business retain current customers and attract new ones.

KEY POINT

External customers are people outside your organization who purchase your goods or services.

KEY POINT

An *internal customer* is someone within your own organization who depends on products, supplies, or services that you provide.

Practical Application

A. Review the case study on page 553. On a separate sheet of paper, write one to four paragraphs describing things the first receptionist should have done to establish good customer service.

B. Interview a customer service representative at a local business, such as a retail store or at a government agency. Does the organization have a written customer service policy and guidelines for employees to follow? Are staff members given training in how to handle customer inquiries? On a separate sheet of paper, write a memo to your instructor describing the customer service policy and practices of the organization.

C. Role-play a customer service situation involving a face-to-face conversation or a telephone call from a customer (internal or external). You may choose to show both the "wrong" way and the "right" way to handle a particular situation.

SECTION 12.2

OBJECTIVES:
After completing Section 12.2, you should be able to:

1. Understand the importance of positive customer contact.
2. Discuss customer service guidelines for limited contact situations.
3. Explain how companies can be accessible to their customers.
4. Understand the importance of knowledgeable responses to customers.
5. Explain the role of continuous contact with customers.

Maintaining Good Customer Service

A satisfied customer tells 5 people; a dissatisfied customer tells 25 people.

—Author unknown

Customer service is a complex function that has many facets. Let's look at some of them.

CUSTOMER SERVICE AS AN ONGOING FUNCTION

Some people view customer service as a problem-solving function that comes into play only when there has been a complaint. In fact, customer service should be an ongoing function that is proactive in anticipating problems and managing problems that surface.

CUSTOMER CONTACT

Any employee who comes in contact with a customer directly or indirectly can influence that customer's perception of your company and its products and services. Contact through any of the usual communications media—advertisements, telephone, fax, e-mail, letters, and conversations—can increase or diminish the likelihood that a customer or potential customer will do business with your firm.

As with many communication situations, first impressions are important in establishing a good rapport between customers and company representatives. Company representatives should exhibit positive attitudes and perform their jobs in such a way that they cultivate trust.

Business environments such as restaurants, retail shops, and government agencies offer opportunities to cultivate a positive customer service image. Use the following guidelines when working in a business environment in which only limited contact with external customers takes place.

Customer Service Guidelines for Limited Contact Situations

1. Greet the customer with a smile and an appropriate greeting.
2. Address the customer by name.
3. Be attentive to the customer.
4. Assist the customer in conducting his or her business.
5. Thank the customer.
6. Say good-bye with a smile.

When a customer speaks, you should listen. If you are a sales representative, for example, you should get to know your customers and what is important to them. However, avoid being intrusive. You should make notes each time you visit a customer or talk with a customer on the telephone. As soon as the contact is completed, enter important information about that call into a file on your computer. If a computer is unavailable, you can use the traditional method of writing your notes on index cards. Include information pertinent to the contact and also include information about the customer's personal interests. You might write: "Rachel's son will graduate from college in May. Send him a card." Another entry might be: "Mark and his wife are expecting a child in July." Or, "Emile will be competing in the local marathon in February." Keep the information current and read your file on each customer before making a call or visit. Your customers will be impressed by your "memory," but you are really just being organized and "doing your homework." This tactic demonstrates that you respect and value the customer and that you value the business the customer conducts with you.

KEY POINT

Any employee who comes in contact with a customer directly or indirectly can influence that customer's perception of the company and its products and services.

World View

Establishing good eye contact is a practice that may not be seen as positive by individuals from countries outside the United States. For example, in some Latin American countries, direct eye contact is considered to be rude, and averting the eyes is a sign of respect.

KEY POINT

When a customer speaks, listen attentively.

Accessibility

Your company is accessible if it offers services for its customers that make it convenient to conduct business. Many companies implement policies that make it easy to purchase a product or service or obtain information. For example, many banks offer automated teller machines (ATMs) and 24-hour banking via computers. Many retail stores remain open at convenient hours and offer trouble-free return policies.

Some companies may establish a toll-free telephone number or an e-mail address to answer customer questions. The numbers or addresses are frequently found in advertisements and on literature that accompanies a product or service. By calling the toll-free number, for example, a customer might be inclined to order additional products and services. Customer-service representatives, such as the ones shown in Figure 12.1, are often a customer's first contact with a company.

Often, appliance retailers maintain a hotline that enables them to respond to customer concerns in a timely manner. When there is a problem, often the customer wants an immediate solution. For example, a customer called a hotline asking for recommendations on how to remove offensive odors from a refrigerator. Her problem was not due to a defective refrigerator but was the result of food spoilage caused by a power outage. The customer service associate recommended placing charcoal (the kind used in fish tanks) in the refrigerator. The suggestion worked; and the pleased customer perceived the appliance company as being helpful.

Figure 12.1

Accessibility is essential in maintaining satisfied customers and clients. What options for obtaining information might companies make available to customers?

Knowledgeable Responses

People who come into direct contact with customers should be knowledgeable about the product or service, as well as company policies. By being familiar with the company's products and services, you will be more likely to positively influence your customers. When customers ask questions, they should get answers in a timely fashion. If you don't know the answer to a question, don't make one up. Simply tell the customer that you will find out the information from someone else. Don't let that promise be "lip service." If you say that you will get information for a customer, be sure that you do it as soon as it is feasible to do so. To give knowledgeable responses to customers and clients, do the following:

1. Familiarize yourself with the products and services your company offers.

2. Know the functions of key departments and personnel. You need to know to whom you can refer a customer or client.

3. Have copies of pertinent company information, such as brochures, flyers, catalogs, and so on, available for your reference.

4. Provide the customer or client with specific information, such as dates, costs, and product or service specifications.

KEY POINT

People who come into contact with customers should be knowledgeable about the product or service, as well as company policies.

Continuous Contact

After you have sold a product or provided a service, keep the customer informed. Let the customer know if merchandise will be delayed or if there is a shipping problem. If there are changes in the service that your company has provided, such as a change in a policy or a warranty, notify the customer in writing or with a telephone call. Let the customer know what to expect.

Even after the sale has been made and the customer has paid for the merchandise, you should follow through and reinforce the relationship between the company and the customer. For example, a communications provider called a customer to ask how a new telephone system was performing: "How is your caller-identification system working?" A dermatologist called a surgery patient several days after the procedure to find out whether she was experiencing any difficulties. A computer sales representative called clients who had recently bought computers and software to ask whether he could provide additional technical assistance: "Are you adapting to your new system easily?"

In any situation in which employees are in direct contact with the public, that contact becomes the basis for the customer's judgment about the services or products provided by the company. If the contact situation is pleasant and rewarding, the customer will likely view the company positively; any unpleasantness will create negative impressions and discourage the customer from doing business with the company.

KEY POINT

Maintain continuous contact with customers to reinforce the relationship between your company and the customer.

Practical Application

A. On a separate sheet of paper, answer the following questions.
  1. Explain the importance of viewing customer service as an ongoing function.
  2. Describe the guidelines for limited contact situations with customers.
  3. Identify some examples of technologies that companies use to be accessible to customers.
  4. Explain the importance of making knowledgeable responses and maintaining continuous contact in customer service situations.
B. Observe customer service techniques at three local businesses such as restaurants, supermarkets, and video stores. In a two-page written report, compare the positive and negative actions that you observed. Close your report with a summary of your findings.

Editing Practice

Editing for Redundancies. Eliminate all unnecessary repetitions in the sentences below.
  1. We are planning to revert back to personal contact as our main sales strategy.
  2. These forms confuse me because they are both alike.
  3. With every new subscription, a utilities disk is sent free, gratis.
  4. By the time I arrived, the presentation was over with.
  5. Please repeat the instructions again so that everyone understands them.
  6. Do you know what files are stored inside of this cabinet?
  7. Past experience shows that Michael is reliable.

Critical Thinking Skills

Select a local company that has a customer service department. Schedule an appointment with the head of this department. Make up a list of questions to ask this person. Interview the department head about the company's customer service policies. If you have his or her permission, tape-record the interview. Write a report on the interview in the form of a dialogue. The report should consist of three parts: an introductory paragraph, the dialogue, and a closing paragraph. Use the following format for the dialogue:

Your Name: Good morning, Mr. Ortega.
Mr. Ortega: Good morning. Welcome to Jarvis Manufacturing.

Improving Contact With Customers

Goodwill is the one and only asset that competition cannot under-sell nor destroy.

—Marshall Field

OBJECTIVES:

After completing Section 12.3, you should be able to:

1. Describe the importance of initial and continuing customer contacts.
2. Discuss procedures for receiving the public.
3. List guidelines for effective telephone communication with customers.
4. Identify the expectations of customers when they call a company.

oth initial contacts and continuing contacts a customer has with your firm can be important in either establishing or maintaining good customer relations. Every employee has an opportunity to influence a customer's image of your firm. The assistant who greets visitors and answers telephone calls can have a significant impact on a customer's perception of your firm. A sales representative who has product knowledge instills confidence in the company. A friendly and helpful assistant who directs a visitor or caller to the person who can best offer assistance creates customer goodwill. Good customer service skills are critical, not only for the sales representative and the assistant but also for everyone in the organization. How a company welcomes its guests is important. Information on how a company should receive the public follows.

RECEIVING THE PUBLIC

Although in many companies a designated employee greets visitors to the office or business, other employees have contact with the public. In legal offices, dentists' offices, travel agencies, and most retail establishments, this situation applies to every employee. You should, therefore, be familiar with the basic procedures for meeting the public.

Give Prompt Attention to Visitors

Recognize a visitor's presence immediately. Even if you are busy, interrupt your work for a moment to smile and say to the new arrival, "I'll be with you in a moment. Would you like to sit down?"

Greet Visitors Pleasantly

Greet visitors with a pleasant smile and tone of voice, and show friendliness by using their names in your greeting whenever possible. Add a personal touch to your greeting, such as "Good morning, Mr. Brackett.

KEY POINT

Both initial and continuing contacts a customer has with your firm are important in either establishing or maintaining good customer relations.

Ignoring a customer who is waiting in person for assistance while you are on the phone can cause the customer to react to you and your firm in a negative way.

It's a pleasure to see you again." Such friendly greetings make callers feel that they are getting special treatment and put them in a positive frame of mind to do business with your company.

Be Courteous to All Visitors

KEY POINT

Every visitor should receive friendly and courteous treatment.

Every visitor should receive friendly and courteous treatment, regardless of the purpose of the visit. Even if the visitor is obviously upset about something and acts accordingly, you must overlook any discourtesy and show that you are understanding. It may be that your visitor is annoyed about what he or she believes is "unfair treatment" from your company. There may be some justification for this belief so you now have an opportunity to mend a business problem. Even if you can do nothing about the situation, you can listen in an understanding way to the complaint. Treating an annoyed customer discourteously will only tend to make the situation worse. Usually people respond well to pleasant treatment. Therefore, your courteous attitude is likely to help calm the visitor and give your company a chance to make amends.

Apologize for Delays

World View

In England, instead of complaining, customers are more likely to get assistance by putting themselves at the mercy of the company. For example, a customer might say, "I've reviewed the statement of my account and I really need your help in trying to sort it out."

If an appointment cannot be kept promptly by the person who is to receive the visitor, you should explain the delay ("I'm sorry, Mr. Crouch, Ms. Wong has been delayed at a meeting"), and you should tell the visitor about how long the wait will be ("Ms. Wong should be back in about 20 minutes"). Make the visitor comfortable (a selection of current magazines and today's newspaper should be available, or offer a cup of coffee if it is convenient to do so).

The undistinguished appearance of some visitors may lead you to believe that they could not possibly have business of interest to anyone in the company. Don't be too sure! A person who is indifferent to personal appearance may be a VIP—perhaps even the most important stockholder in the company. Everyone is entitled to your most courteous treatment.

Find Out the Purpose of the Visit

Almost every caller will have an appointment with a member of the company. For example, a visitor may say to you, "I am Mary O'Neill; I have an appointment with Paul Morgan." You will escort Mrs. O'Neill to the appropriate office or telephone Mr. Morgan to inform him that his visitor has arrived. If you do not know whether the visitor has an appointment, you must ask, "May I help you?" or "Whom do you wish to see?" If the visitor has no appointment, take his or her name, the name of the company he or she represents (if any), and the purpose of

Figure 12.2

When meeting with customers, be prompt, courteous, and tactful in your comments. How should you respond to a visitor's inquiries about sensitive topics such as company business or personnel?

the call. Relay this information to the person whom you think can be of most help to the caller. After getting permission to show the visitor in, invite him or her to follow you to the appropriate office. Then present the visitor like this: "Mr. Morgan (host), this is Mary O'Neill (visitor)."

Be Discreet and Tactful

Protect both your employer's and the company's interests by being discreet in your comments to visitors. For example, if your employer is late arriving at the office in the morning or returning from lunch, it is not appropriate to supply these details to the visitor. Instead of saying, "Mrs. Stein is late getting in this morning," say, "I expect Mrs. Stein about 9:15." If she is late returning from lunch, you might say, "Mrs. Stein had an important luncheon meeting and should return shortly." Avoid making conversation about company business or personnel. If the subject comes up, be noncommittal and change the topic of conversation as quickly as you can. Never engage in negative statements such as "Business has really been slow lately" or "We just can't keep good sales representatives longer than six months."

Be discreet in giving any opinions solicited by the visitor. The person the visitor has come to see may have a different opinion from your own. For example, the visitor may want to show you certain products and ask whether you think your company might be interested in buying them. Unless you are responsible for company purchases, however, you should not give an opinion about the company's possible interest in buying the products. Of course, you should not be rude even if you are pressured for comment. Simply say pleasantly, "My responsibilities do not include purchasing our company's supplies. Thus, I'm unfamiliar with the qualities the company requires for such products."

COMMUNICATING BY TELEPHONE

Many transactions are handled by telephone. All telephone relationships—regardless of the initial contact system your company uses—require special consideration. In almost all cases, the customer expects speed, knowledge, courtesy, and action. If you answer the telephone with these expectations in mind, you will represent your company positively.

Speed

Since the customer has called rather than visited, he or she is interested in saving time. Although the customer's expectation of a speedy response is frequently unrealistic (even unreasonable), how you handle the call contributes to the customer's attitude during the call and afterward.

Knowledge

If you have answered the call, you are expected to know anything and everything the customer asks. It is important to ascertain quickly what is being requested. Do not assume that the first statement or request is the customer's primary motive for calling; getting to that may take a while. Respond in those areas in which you are qualified and quickly redirect the customer to other staff members if necessary. If possible, after making the transfer, check to find out whether the transfer occurred. There is nothing more frustrating to a customer who has called long distance to be transferred to another extension and get a busy signal or to be accidentally disconnected. Sometimes you must resist transferring the call altogether. Do not transfer a customer to someone else just because it is inconvenient for you to handle the situation. Do not transfer a customer to someone else unless you are fairly sure that person can help the customer more quickly than you can.

Courtesy

Always use a respectful tone when answering calls from customers. Maintaining a courteous tone will often be difficult, especially when the day grows long or the customer becomes hostile. However impatient and frustrated you become, remember that each call is a new situation to the caller. Therefore, you have an opportunity to make a friend each time the telephone rings. No matter how far up or down the chain of

Sending a fax addressed "To Whom It May Concern" will certainly reduce the likelihood of a positive response—or of any response.

command you are, a customer remembers discourtesy—and often the name attached to it.

Action

When you make a commitment to a customer, make sure that you keep that commitment. If you promised to send a technician to repair a telephone system, send the technician at the specified time. If you promised to replace a defective product, do so as soon as possible. Broken commitments foster distrust.

SECTION 12.3   REVIEW

Practical Application

A. For a one-week period, keep a personal log in which you note the companies you visit alone or with family or friends. Record the favorable verbal and nonverbal messages conveyed by company personnel.
B. Identify a product or service that you or your family would like to have more information about. Make a list of the questions you will ask by phone to obtain the desired information.
C. With several classmates, develop and role-play telephone situations in which:
  • You must put the other person on hold
  • You must transfer someone to another party
  • You cut off the other person and that person calls back
  • You answer someone else's telephone and must handle the call
  • You clearly know that the company is at fault for nonperformace of a product
  • You do not know who is at fault for the nonperformance of a product
  • A customer is calling for information about your company, services, or products
  • A customer is calling about a matter indirectly related to your company's services or products

OBJECTIVES:

After completing Section 12.4, you should be able to:

1. Discuss suggestions for responding to customer service needs.
2. Explain why telephone technology can be a detriment to customer satisfaction.
3. Identify the advantages and disadvantages of customer service policies or procedures.

Responding to Customer Service Needs

The customer may not always be right, but you always want him to be a customer.

—Author unknown

The obvious solution to customer complaints is preventive action. A visitor to the Scottsdale Princess hotel in Arizona was impressed with the exceptional service she was experiencing from all levels of the hotel staff. After the visitor commented on the exceptional service to the manager, a spokesperson from the Human Resources Department related that customer service was part of the training each associate received. The spokesperson said that associates are encouraged to help make memories for the guests and to cater to the "internal guest" by becoming a "team player" when working with fellow associates. The spokeswoman showed the guest a card that is given to all associates to remind them of the level of service that guests should receive. The following two quotes are from that card.

> We provide our guests a unique and luxurious resort experience through attentive and professional service.
>
> By anticipating needs and exceeding expectations, we provide our guests with sincere, personalized service, ensuring a memorable stay.

Top management must set the standard for good customer service attitudes. The need for good customer service must be communicated throughout the organization. No matter how hard an organization tries, however, there will be some dissatisfied customers. The goal, then, is to minimize customer dissatisfaction and to take corrective action when it does occur.

KEY POINT

The goal of customer service procedures is to minimize customer dissatisfaction and to take corrective action when problems occur.

KEY POINT

Sometimes technology that is intended to simplify customer service increases customer frustration.

TECHNOLOGY AND CUSTOMER SATISFACTION

Sometimes technology that is intended to simplify customer service increases customer frustration. Imagine how you would feel if you called a company with regard to a defective product and were connected to the following message:

"Hi! Blue Ridge Satellite Communications. If you want to subscribe to our services, press 1 now. If you want information about your bill, press 2 now. If you want Customer Service, press . . ."

If your company chooses to use such technology or, because of its size, is forced to use such technology, your "live" voice or presence becomes especially important. When your personal contact with a customer occurs, his or her stress level is probably already high, a result of normal customer concern compounded by the impersonal and complex answering system that finally led to you. Again, your recognition of the customer's state of mind is crucial. Greet the customer by making a positive statement: "Hi. I'm Delores in Customer Service. May I help you?"

When formal greetings are required, express genuine interest in helping the caller. "Hello. This is Zach Milligan at J & J Electronics. Thanks for calling. How may I help you?" Control your speed of delivery and tone of voice to avoid the impression that you have answered that same way 30 times already, just this morning. It helps to vary your responses to avoid the impression of a worn-out greeting. Communicating boredom or impatience in the delivery of a "warm" greeting is worse than bland impersonality.

Maintaining your air of helpfulness decreases a customer's resistance and establishes a basis for success. Never respond to a customer's demand for speed with frustration. Simply tell the customer when you can do something. If the complexity of the request clearly requires a face-to-face exchange, suggest that a visit would be more productive and arrange for the customer to meet with you or someone who can provide the needed assistance.

Here are some suggestions for dealing with customers who have a complaint or need to exchange an item.

1. Answer the telephone call or the letter promptly. Take careful notes of all important details.

2. If a customer becomes hostile, maintain self-control. You must remember that you represent your company and that little or nothing is to be gained by allowing yourself to become angry.

3. Express interest in and an understanding of the caller's problem. "Yes, I can see why you were concerned about your telephone bill, Mr. Hathaway, but I am sure we can correct it quickly."

4. Don't blame someone else for the problem.

5. Tell the caller what action you will take. If the customer has experienced problems, make repairs and exchanges cheerfully. Provide whatever relief is available through warranties and company policy.

6. If you cannot make the adjustment yourself, refer the caller to someone who can. Don't make the caller repeat the entire story to someone else; each time the message must be repeated to another person, the caller becomes angrier.

7. Take the action that you promised the customer as soon as possible.

8. Follow up within three to five days to make sure that the customer is now satisfied.

World View

Greeting a customer in his or her native tongue demonstrates an effort to be friendly. Here are some frequently used English words and their French and Spanish equivalents.

English	French	Spanish
Hello	Bonjour	Hola
Good-bye	Au revoir	Adios
Thank you	Merci	Gracias

KEY POINT

Be sure to follow your company's customer service policies or procedures.

CUSTOMER SERVICE POLICIES AND PROCEDURES

Most companies have customer service policies or procedures. Be sure that you follow them. Policies and procedures set up by a company determine the boundaries of your behavior as an employee. Do not assume, however, that the company's recommended procedures anticipate every situation. Also, do not assume that company procedures are infallible. Of course, you cannot make policy by yourself or make arbitrary changes that do not conform to the spirit of company policy. You should be especially careful of personal interpretation in situations when such policy protects the company and you from legal repercussions.

Policies have their limits. They are merely a set of guidelines that cannot apply to all individual circumstances or to the personalities of your customers. Every contact situation requires your alertness, sensitivity, and judgment in handling customers in the best interest of a positive relationship.

SECTION 12.4 REVIEW

Practical Application

A. On a separate sheet of paper, write a description of a recent exchange in which you or a friend were angered or frustrated by an employee at a company or business. Identify the factors that produced the frustration and explain how, in the role of the employee, you would have handled the situation better. Do not mention the name of the company or the real names of the employees involved.

B. With a classmate, ad-lib in front of the class a telephone exchange between a customer and a company representative. Sit several feet away from your classmate and at an angle so that you can hear each other but not see each other. The customer cannot understand why her electric bill for August was 50 percent higher than the July bill. The customer is frustrated and a bit pushy, with the attitude "you people have done something wrong, and I want it fixed, now!" The customer service representative for the power company has to respond to the customer in a appropriate manner to resolve the problem. After five or six minutes of this exchange, ask the class for an evaluation of the two sides.

C. Assume that you work in a bank. On a separate sheet of paper, write a customer service policy for the employees in your branch office.

Customer Dissatisfaction. Wendy Lopez needed to purchase an upgrade package for her word processing software. After consulting the Yellow Pages, she decided to visit a store whose name she recognized and that had recently advertised a sale on television.

Upon entering the store, Wendy received a blank stare from three employees who stood to the side of the entrance, and they continued their conversation. She moved to the back of the store and searched the shelves in the "Computer Software" section. Wendy didn't see what she wanted. A salesperson walked by, and Wendy asked for assistance. "I don't work in this section," was the response as the salesperson kept walking. Wendy walked to the back of the store where the Service Department was located. Four customers stood in line with no salespersons visible. When a salesperson finally appeared from behind a closed door behind the counter, Wendy asked where the software upgrade packages were kept. "You'll have to ask in Customer Service" the salesperson replied. "Which is where?" Wendy asked in an irritated voice. "Up front" the salesperson answered.

Frustrated, Wendy went to Customer Service where she was told to locate someone in the software section who could help her. Upset with the lack of service, Wendy calmly asked to see the store manager. She knew that she would probably not be shopping at this store again. However, Wendy wanted management to know why. She felt if management knew how customers were being treated by store personnel that steps might be taken to correct the situation. The store manager thanked Wendy for her comments and apologized for her frustration and inconvenience. He then led Wendy to the software section and located her upgrade package from a top shelf. He also gave Wendy a ten percent discount coupon. Wendy bought the package but had mixed feelings about doing any future business with this store.

1. What would have been appropriate behavior on the part of the employees who stood at the entrance of the store? The employee who walked by Wendy in the software section? The person in the Service Department? The person in the Customer Service Department?

2. Was Wendy justified in speaking with the store manager about the service? Why or why not?

3. Should Wendy have bought the merchandise? Why or why not? Should she return to do business at this store? Why or why not?

CHAPTER

13 Writing Reports and Special Communications

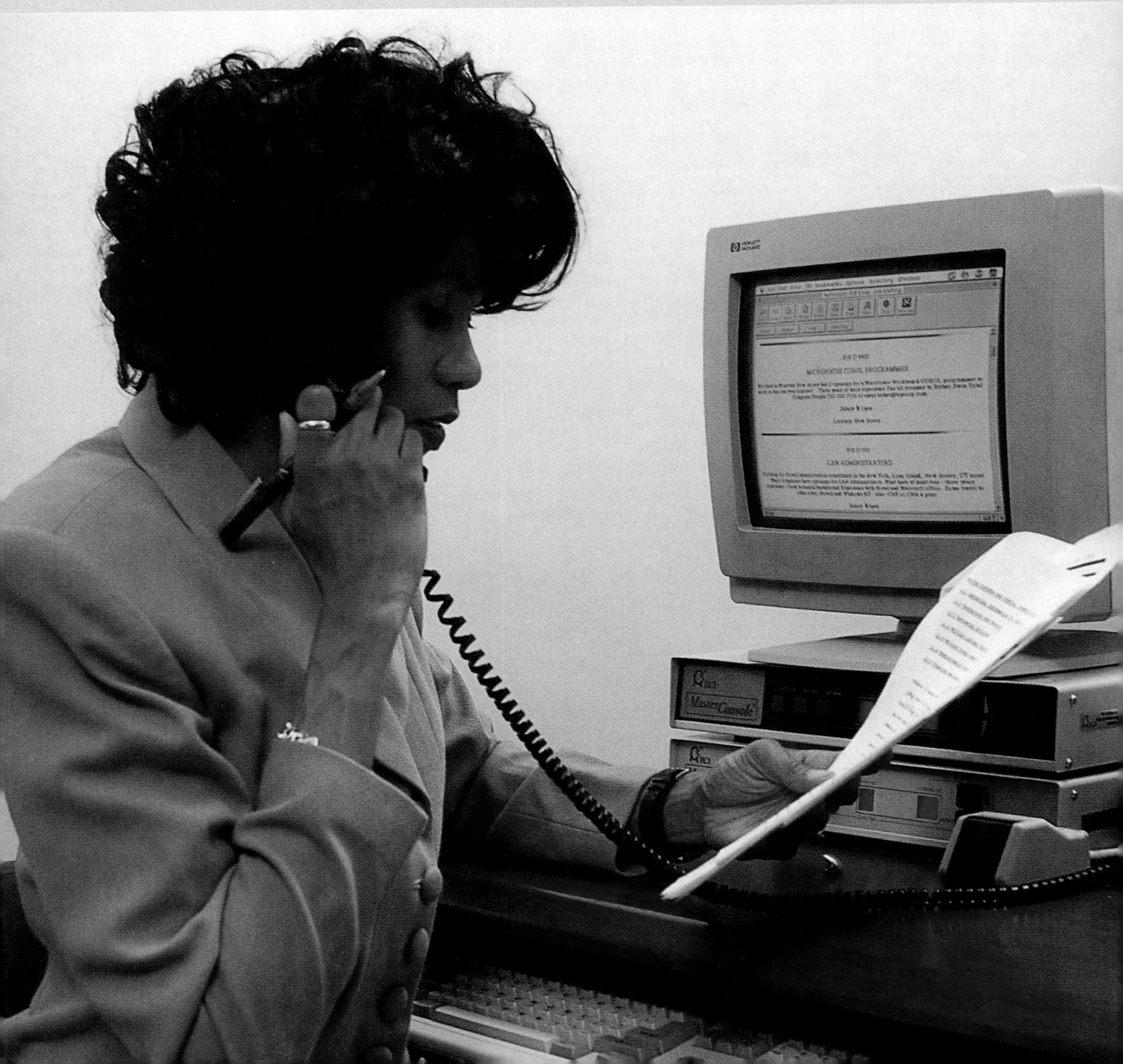

13.1 Gathering Information for Reports

13.2 Technology and Reports

13.3 Reviewing Articles and Documenting Sources

13.4 Writing Informal Reports

13.5 Writing Formal Reports

13.6 Keeping Meeting Records

13.7 Preparing News Releases

Tonya Sands was the administrative assistant in the Richardsville Chamber of Commerce office. She received a phone call from Dr. Dave Ehman, the career dean at the local Richardsville Community College, requesting information on the current skills needed for entry-level office employees. The community college faculty wanted to start the process of revising and updating curriculums to better prepare its students for employment, and the faculty wanted to base the changes on the current needs of employers. Dr. Ehman needed the survey information in order to prepare a report for the college board on revising and updating curriculums.

Ms. Shirleen Hackman, executive director of the chamber, said that Tonya would work with her to conduct a survey of local and regional employers. The survey would focus on gathering information regarding skills and training that entry-level employees would need for target employers.

Tonya met with Ms. Hackman to discuss who would write the survey, what questions would be asked, and to whom the survey would be sent. Ms. Hackman recommended that Tonya contact the human resources departments at target employers in the area to find out the names of company officials who would receive the survey.

The first step in preparing for the survey would be to target important employers in the area, both local and regional. Tonya decided to use the chamber of commerce's Web site to contact these businesses. She knew that Richardsville's Web site was linked to the Web sites for other cities in the state and with other states. Once she has gathered the information, Tonya will compile the results of the survey for Ms. Hackman and Dr. Ehman.

With feedback from her inquiry on the chamber of commerce's Web site, Tonya identified 300 employers to receive the survey. She typed the survey, duplicated the copies, ordered the mailing labels from a small local mailing service, and mailed the surveys.

By the due date, Tonya had received responses from over 70 percent of the recipients. Now that she had the information, she was ready to compile the report.

As you read Chapter 13, identify some tasks that Tonya needs to complete in order to compile the report.

Gathering Information for Reports

OBJECTIVES:

After completing Section 13.1, you should be able to:

1. Identify the two basic types of reports and give some examples of each.
2. Identify primary and secondary sources of information and give some examples of each.

Knowledge is of two kinds. We know a subject ourselves, or we know where we can find information upon it.

—Samuel Johnson

TYPES AND PURPOSES OF REPORTS

Before writing a report, you need to determine the purpose of your report and analyze your audience. The purpose of your report will determine the type of report you prepare.

Informative Report

An *informative report* gives facts and other information on some aspect of an organization's operations. Examples of informative reports include reports on company policies and procedures; sales reports of company's products or services; and reports on patient admissions, clients served, cases processed, bids submitted, customer service requests, and so on. An informative report usually identifies a problem or gives background information but does not make recommendations or persuade.

Periodic Reports.   Many informative reports are prepared at regular intervals so they are also considered periodic reports.

Progress Reports.   A progress report gives the current status of a project, tells what has been completed since the last progress report, and says when the project will be completed.

Analytical Report

An *analytical report* examines a situation or problem, draws conclusions, and makes recommendations in addition to providing information and data. This type of report may explore the feasibility of taking possible actions by looking at several alternatives, systematically analyzing each alternative, and then making recommendations.

Examples of analytical reports are justification reports, feasibility studies, and proposals. These three types of reports are very similar.

KEY POINT

The purpose of your report determines the type of report you prepare.

KEY POINT

An *informative report* gives facts and other information.

Justification Reports. A *justification report* is usually prepared for someone at a higher level of management; it gives the rationale for a recommendation or a decision. Sample subjects would include making a major expenditure for new equipment, expanding facilities, hiring additional personnel, and so on.

Feasibility Studies. A *feasibility study* describes the pros and cons of proceeding with a project in addition to giving the costs and a time frame for the project. This type of report would include recommendations on whether or not to go ahead with the project.

Proposals. A *proposal* is a report that may be prepared for someone inside or outside your company. A proposal is designed to persuade the reader to purchase your products or services, to adopt your idea or plan, or to provide or donate money or services for a worthwhile project. The proposed may offer a solution to a problem; the proposal report usually gives the cost of the plan.

KEY POINT

An *analytical report* examines a situation or problem, draws conclusions, and makes recommendations.

GATHERING INFORMATION

The value of any report depends on the quality of the material going into it. A term used by computer specialists—*GIGO* (pronounced "guy-go"), standing for "*g*arbage-*in*, *g*arbage-*out*"—expresses this idea vividly. With reliable facts behind it, a reliable report can be written; with questionable data, only a questionable report can result.

Information for reports can be obtained through two types of sources—*primary sources* of data and *secondary sources* of data. Your first step should be to see what secondary data already exist to save yourself the time and trouble of gathering data that may already be available. Also, you want to include in your report the information that is common knowledge.

KEY POINT

Obtain information for reports by consulting primary and secondary sources of data.

Secondary Sources of Information

A *secondary source* is a document or other material that contains information gathered by someone else. This information is usually published in books and periodicals, or it may be found in company records and reports. Today secondary information is also widely available through electronic sources. In gathering secondary information, you should be familiar with the authoritative references in your field. There are, in addition, many general references that are invaluable helps to every writer, some of which are listed here.

Indexes. An index includes a list of the titles of articles appearing in a variety of periodicals. *Periodicals* are journals, magazines, pamphlets, newsletters, and so on that are published on a regular basis. Such indexes include the *Readers' Guide to Periodical Literature,* the *Business Periodicals Index,* and *The New York Times Index.*

KEY POINT

A *secondary source* is a document or other material that contains information gathered by someone else.

Almanacs and Yearbooks. These sources contain concise information on important events that occurred during a given year. Examples include *The World Almanac and Book of Facts, Information Please Almanac,* and *Facts on File.*

Databases. A *database* is an electronic version of a print index. See the discussion of on-line services on the Internet in Section 13.2 for more on databases.

Periodicals. Periodicals that are of general interest to report writers include magazines such as *Time, U.S. News & World Report,* and *Business Week.* Newspapers such as *The Wall Street Journal, The Washington Post,* and *The New York Times* are reliable secondary sources of information. Many professional journals are published in every field, and the applicable ones should also be reviewed frequently by report writers.

Naturally, anyone doing research must first learn how to find and use books, periodicals, card catalogs, databases, and various indexes as well as the many sources available through the Internet.

After you know the topic of your report, make a list of keywords and key phrases that might give you information on your topic. Also make a list of the sources (books, periodicals, magazines, and so on) that you plan to search for additional information on your topic.

A word of caution about secondary data—always check the date of publication and the source. You don't want to use outdated information, and you want it to be from a credible (reputable and unbiased) source. For example an article on the benefits of certain medication for hyperactive children published by a drug company that manufactures and sells the medicine may present a slanted view. Remember, just because information appears in print doesn't necessarily make it true.

Use the following checklist to help you determine the reliability of a secondary source of information:

- Does the source provide current information on the topic?
- Is the source reliable?
- Is the information pertinent to your topic?
- Is the author an authority on the subject?
- Does the author identify his or her opinions?

When the information you need is not available from secondary sources, you have to gather the information and collect the data for your report from primary sources.

Primary Sources of Information

A *primary source* is a source from which information or data are obtained firsthand for your particular need. Primary source data may be obtained through surveys (such as questionnaires), personal interviews, or telephone interviews as well as through observation or experimenta-

---

KEY POINT

Remember, just because information appears in print doesn't necessarily make it true.

KEY POINT

A *primary source* is a source from which information or data are obtained firsthand.

tion. Eyewitness accounts, given by someone who experienced the event firsthand, are also considered primary sources.

One problem with many primary sources is the accuracy of the information you receive. For example, many people will not bother to complete and return a questionnaire so you may not get a representative sampling. Other people may not answer the questions truthfully so your results are not accurate.

Surveys are done to identify customer likes and dislikes, to identify customer wants and needs, to poll patients on the care they received, to learn the level of customer or client satisfaction, to determine public opinion on a controversial topic or project, and so on. Surveys can be conducted by several methods.

Telephone Surveys.   To conduct an effective telephone survey, identify yourself and your organization, and state the purpose of the survey at the beginning of the telephone interview; ask questions that provide data that can be compared or measured; and keep the number of questions manageable.

Questionnaires.   Determine what types of questions will yield the most helpful answers to get the data you are seeking. The most effective types of questions to yield measurable data include yes-or-no questions, multiple choice questions, ranking according to preference, and rating in order of importance. For example, a questionnaire on a new product line to be sent to current and potential customers might ask the respondent to rank the new products in the order in which they might be purchased.

Interviews.   To gather information by interviewing, you should first familiarize yourself with the topic and terminology of your subject and create a list of relevant questions to ask. Next, you should identify an expert on the subject and schedule an appointment for the interview. Begin the interview by explaining the purpose of the interview and giving an estimate of how much time you need. Continue the interview by asking your questions in an objective manner, and thank the person for his or her time at the conclusion of the interview. Always ask at the end of the interview if the interviewee has anything he or she would like to add; there may be relevant information that you did not ask about in your interview.

For example, to gather information about starting a recycling program at your workplace, you might interview a representative from a recycling company. Your questions could cover costs, pickup, and types of materials accepted for recycling.

Observations.   Objectively observing a practice or procedure can help you determine if the procedure and policy could be improved. Use facts and statistics, not opinions, to present your observations. For example, you might record the number of telephone calls received in a doctor's office during the lunch hour. Your observations may be used to change the policy of closing the office between noon and 1 p.m. for lunch. Staggered lunch hours may better serve the patients.

Practical Application

1. Identify the two major types of reports and give an example of each type.
2. Explain the difference between secondary and primary sources.
3. List four examples of secondary sources.
4. Identify and describe four methods for gathering primary data.
5. Identify the primary and secondary sources you would use to gather information on the following topics:
   a. Electronic banking
   b. Business ethics
   c. Cross-cultural communication
   d. Electronic résumés

Editing Practice

Proofreading. Can you find any errors in the following paragraph? Write the corrected words on a separate sheet of paper.

The first 20 seconds in a job intervew our the most important. The first impression at a job intervew is a mayor factor in weather or not your will be hired. You should make I contact, smile, and give a firm hanshake as soon as you met the interviewer's.

SECTION 13.2 Technology and Reports

OBJECTIVES:

After completing Section 13.2, you should be able to:

1. Identify three electronic media sources for research.
2. Explain briefly how the Internet can be used for research, and identify some types of information you can access on the Internet.

Information networks straddle the world. Nothing remains concealed. But the sheer volume of information dissolves the information. We are unable to take it all in.

—Günther Grass, German author

Technology has opened a whole new world of electronic resources to help the researcher and report writer. These sources are available in public and university libraries. Also, some large organizations as well as some medical facilities have libraries of their own. Individuals can access these sources from their offices or homes through the Internet.

COMPUTERIZED LIBRARY LISTINGS

Today most libraries have automated card catalogs that tell you not only what books are in this library but also what books are in other library systems.

Searching Library Listings

Computerized card catalogs can be searched in the same manner as the hard copy card catalog files: by author, by title, and by subject. You can also search for keywords and get a listing of all the books that may have information about the keywords. When you are learning to use the computerized card catalog, ask the librarian for help, or use the help menu on the screen. Reference librarians are specially trained to help you locate information on just about any topic.

KEY POINT

Computerized card catalogs can be searched by author, by title, and by subject.

Using CD-ROMs

Much of the information that is available in traditional hard copy format is now available on CD-ROM (*CD-ROM* is an acronym for *c*ompact *d*isc—*r*ead-*o*nly *m*emory). A CD-ROM holds up to 250,000 pages of text; telephone directories, encyclopedias, genealogy records, and so on are available on CD-ROM. CD-ROMs are also used for some full-text articles from periodicals and references, and for abstracts of articles.

Search a CD-ROM using keywords for the subject you are interested in to get the most references. Print the list of references, choose the relevant ones, and then review those sources. Use the help feature on the CD-ROM, or ask the librarian for help.

THE INTERNET

The Internet is the fastest-growing electronic source of information. Literally, people from all over the world and in all professions, including governments and educational institutions, can exchange and retrieve information through the Internet. Internet tools that can be used to find information include the World Wide Web, on-line services, and browsers.

KEY POINT

The Internet is the fastest-growing electronic source of information.

World Wide Web

The World Wide Web (WWW) is a segment of the Internet that contains electronic documents. Information on the Web is in the form of Web pages that contain text, graphics, and highlighted words, called *hypertext,* to link pages. Hypertext appears as highlighted words on a Web page. Clicking with your mouse on a highlighted word leads you to another Web page that contains related information. Many companies, government organizations, and schools have their own Web pages.

On-Line Services

On-line services are self-contained fee-based services that provide extensive resources to their members. Typical resources are discussion groups, e-mail, on-line banking, news, software, and so on. Popular on-line services include America Online, CompuServe, Prodigy, and Microsoft Network. Business-oriented on-line services include Nexis and Lexis. These database services are highly reliable; businesses pay fees to access them.

Internet service providers, also called Internet access providers, only offer access to the Internet and the World Wide Web—not any other services.

Browsers

A *browser,* also known as a *search engine,* allows you to quickly access specific information on the Internet about a subject of interest to you.

Popular browsers include Netscape Navigator, Yahoo, and Mosaic. Browsers are in a constant state of change as they alter their appearance and as new ones spring up. Browsers fall into different categories; some are broader than others. For example, you can execute general subject searches using browsers such as Yahoo and Galaxy. You can access Web databases with browsers such as Alta Vista, Excite, or Infoseek.

SEARCHING THE INTERNET FOR INFORMATION FOR A REPORT

You must give some thought to how you will approach your search on the Internet. Develop a plan to make the best use of the browsers. Such a plan might include the steps in the following chart:

Tips for an Internet Search
1. Identify the topic you want to research.
2. Determine keywords to use for your search. For example, if you are searching for job listings, you might use keywords such as *job listings, employment opportunities*, and *job postings*.
3. Choose a browser or browsers to assist in your search. If necessary, do some research on the browser and how it works to identify the appropriate Web pages for your search.

4. Develop a plan for using the keywords and the browsers to search for the information you need.

5. Begin searching using your first keyword and first choice for a browser.

6. Examine the information you receive initially and adjust your plan, perhaps using a different browser as necessary to obtain the information you seek.

7. Repeat the procedure in step 6 for each keyword that you have identified.

The sample screens shown in Figure 13.1 and Figure 13.2 illustrate some steps in a keyword search on the Internet.

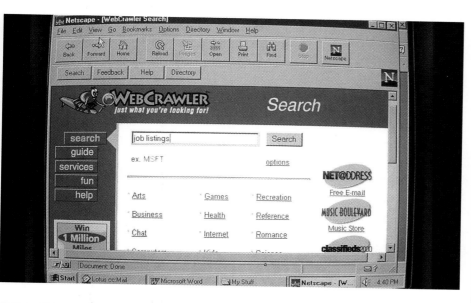

Figure 13.1   Internet Browser.

A browser such as Netscape Navigator allows you to explore the Internet. Use a search engine to look for information that matches your keyword(s).

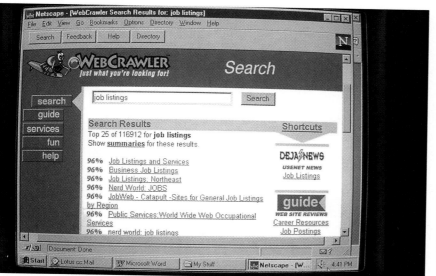

Figure 13.2   Internet Search Engine.

The window on a search engine displays the results of a keyword search of the World Wide Web.

Practical Application

1. Identify some electronic sources to use in gathering information.
2. List three or four keywords you might use to conduct an Internet search on purchasing a new car.

Editing Practice

Missing Words. One or two words have been left out of each of the following sentences. On a separate sheet of paper, write a word (or words) that will correctly complete each sentence.

1. I hope you were pleased with angel calendar we sent to you.
2. A donation card and pre-addressed envelope enclosed for your convenience.
3. Yes, I want give a special gift to help the flood victims in South America.
4. The hope of rebuilding a life will become a reality through the generous contributions people like you.
5. Your donation will play important role in helping victims of the flood.

SECTION 13.3

OBJECTIVES:

After completing Section 13.3, you should be able to:

1. Make a source card or bibliography card for a working bibliography.
2. Identify three methods of documenting sources.
3. Document information taken from electronic sources such as the Internet.

Reviewing Articles and Documenting Sources

Basic research is what I am doing when I don't know what I am doing.

—Wernher von Braun, American engineer

Once you have identified the sources of information for your report, you need to read and review the articles and take notes.

WORKING BIBLIOGRAPHY

As you consult the various reference works pertinent to the topic of your report, you should make a list of the books, periodicals, reports, and other sources to be used as references in the report. This preliminary list of sources is called the *working bibliography.* If you make each entry of the working bibliography on a separate card (3 by 5 or 4 by 6 inches), the final bibliography of sources actually used will be easier to assemble because you can simply arrange the cards in the appropriate order. You will also find the bibliography cards useful when footnoting material in the report.

A bibliography or source card for a book or reference should contain all the information shown in Figure 13.3.

In addition, it is helpful to include for your own use the library's call number for the reference.

When consulting a magazine, newspaper, or other periodical, prepare a bibliography card like the one illustrated in Figure 13.4.

KEY POINT

A working bibliography is a preliminary list of sources.

Cormier, Robin A.

Error-Free Writing: A Lifetime Guide to Flawless Business Writing, Prentice-Hall, Inc., Englewood Cliffs, NJ, 1996

Lancaster, Hal

"Solving Conflicts in the Workplace Without Making Losers"

The Wall Street Journal,
May 27, 1997, p B1
Vol. IC, No. 102

Figure 13.3 Bibliography Card for a Book.

This bibliography card for a book lists the author's full name (last name first); complete title (underlined) and edition, if applicable; publisher's name and location; and publication date (latest copyright date).

Figure 13.4 Bibliography Card for an Article.

A bibliography card for an article should include full name of the author (last name first); title of the article (in quotation marks); name of the publication (underlined) and location, if it is a newspaper; date, volume, and number of the publication; and page number on which the article appears.

Highlighting

Many times you will have a photocopy of the article or a printout from the computer. Start by reading the article. As you read, underline or highlight the information you might need. This practice will make note taking easier.

Note Taking

Taking notes from your sources helps you pick out the information you can use, organize the information, and retain the information. You should use note cards for taking notes because they are sturdy and can be sorted and re-sorted easily.

Taking detailed notes as you read makes it easier for you to organize and write a report. This practice gives you a great deal of information, which you can use as the basis for your report.

When you take notes from your reading, follow these tips:

KEY POINT

Identify each source carefully on a separate card when you take notes from your reading.

- Identify each source, including the name of the writer, the title of the work, the name of the publisher, and the date published.
- Use a new card for each new source or topic. Normally, summary statements or phrases with page references are sufficient for note cards.
- Copy quotations word for word, exactly as they appear in the source. Enclose each quotation in quotation marks, and list the number of the page from which the quotation was taken.

As you organize your research, include a brief subject reference at the top of each note card; for example, if you are tracing the development of a product, you might identify each card by subject references like "year," "developer," or "site of development."

Plagiarism and Paraphrasing

KEY POINT

Plagiarism is using someone else's exact written words without giving credit.

KEY POINT

Paraphrasing is taking someone else's idea and stating it in your own words.

Careful note taking will help you to keep from plagiarizing material. *Plagiarism* is using someone else's words, exact or paraphrased, or ideas and using them as your own; that is, without giving credit to the original author. *Paraphrasing* is taking someone else's idea and stating it in your own words. When you paraphrase, give credit to the original author.

Credit for exact written words (quotes) and paraphrases can be given to the originator by doing the following:

- Mentioning the source in your text.
- Using quotation marks for direct quotes.
- Documenting the source in a footnote or endnote.

Avoid plagiarism by following a simple rule: When taking notes from published sources, use quotation marks around any material that you copy word for word. When writing your report, either quote and acknowledge the source or summarize the material in your own words and acknowledge the source.

DOCUMENTATION FORMATS

Several methods of documenting sources are used in the business world today. Some organizations have even adopted their own format for documentation. Some of the more widely used formats appear in *The Chicago Manual of Style, The Publication Manual of the American Psychological Association,* and *The MLA Style Manual.*

KEY POINT

Several methods of documenting sources are used in the business world today.

Chicago Style

The documentation format preferred in the humanities, *The Chicago Manual of Style,* is well established and has been used for years. This style uses consecutive raised (superscript) numbers to identify quoted or paraphrased ideas throughout the report. Complete information on the source for each number is either given as a footnote at the bottom of the page or on an endnote page, usually titled "Notes," at the end of the report. Note the example:

. . . cost of technology.[1]

Bibliography. In addition to your "Notes" page, you will also need, after the body of the report, a *bibliography*—that is, an alphabetical listing by author's last name of all the sources used in your report. If a source has no author, it is alphabetized by the first important word in the title of the work. A hanging indention style (first line of each entry located at the left margin with the second and succeeding lines indented one-half inch) with a blank line between each entry facilitates quickly locating a particular reference.

For detailed information on this documentation format, see Chapter 15 in *The Chicago Manual of Style,* 14th edition, published by The University of Chicago Press (1993).

APA Style

The American Psychological Association (APA) style gives reference information immediately following the quote or paraphrased material in the body of your report. APA style is heavily used in the social science and education fields. APA style emphasizes the date of publication because in these fields it is important that information be current. The author's name, the year of publication, and the page numbers are separated by commas and given in parentheses in the text. If the author's name is given as part of the quote or paraphrased material, it does not need to be included again in the parentheses.

... cost of technology (Pearman, 1995, p. 36).

References. A "References" section is the same as the bibliography in *The Chicago Manual of Style.* The entries are arranged in alphabetical order by author's last name, and a hanging indention style is used for ease of locating information quickly.

For additional information on APA style see the *Publication Manual of the American Psychological Association,* 4th edition, published by the American Psychological Association (1994).

MLA Style

The MLA style was developed by the Modern Language Association and is heavily used in the humanities area. MLA style emphasizes the page number to facilitate locating the exact information. It is similar to APA style in many ways. The author's last name and the page number appear in parentheses immediately following the quoted or paraphrased material. One difference is that no comma is used to separate the author's name and the page number.

... cost of technology (Pearman 36).

Works Cited. The complete list of sources used in an MLA paper is given at the end of the paper. This list is titled "Works Cited" and is similar to the bibliography used in *The Chicago Manual of Style.* The entries are double-spaced and arranged in alphabetical order by the author's last name. A hanging indention style makes it easy to locate a specific source quickly.

For detailed information on MLA style, see Joseph Gibaldi's *MLA Handbook for Writers of Research Papers,* 4th edition, published by The Modern Language Association of America (1995).

Documenting Electronic Sources

When you cite material taken from an electronic source, such as an on-line database or a Web page on the Internet, you need to provide enough information so that someone reading your report can access the source. With electronic sources, this means identifying information such as that described in the following chart.

Source	Citation Information
e-mail	Author's name; e-mail address; subject line; date the message was posted
Gopher	Author's name; title of the document; the Gopher address; date the material was accessed
mailing list	Author's name; e-mail address; subject line; date the message was posted; mailing list address; date the material was accessed
Web site	Author's name; title of the document; last date updated or revised; the address of the Web site; date you accessed the site

For detailed information on citing electronic sources, consult *The Chicago Manual of Style;* the *Publication Manual of the American Psychological Association;* or the *MLA Handbook for Writers of Research Papers.*

SECTION 13.3   REVIEW

Practical Application

1. Look up one or two articles on a topic of interest, photocopy the articles, and make source cards for each article.
2. Photocopy a short article, take notes on what you read, and paraphrase information you might use in a report.

Editing Practice

Editors' Alert. Find the incorrect word or error in each sentence. Write the correct substitution on a separate sheet of paper.

1. Marcy told the members that she wood not except any additional orders after the deadline.
2. Please let me no weather their is a carrying case four the projection devise .
3. The presentor asked the staff for they're vacation request forms buy too o'clock tomorrow.
4. Since there payment is now for months passed due, a penalty will be imposed.
5. The fifth addition of the book will be published early next year.

Writing Informal Reports

OBJECTIVES:

After completing Section 13.4, you should be able to:

1. Write an informal report in correct memorandum form.
2. Use a variety of forms of presentation for an informal report.
3. Prepare and present an unsolicited report.

Information is the oxygen of the modern age. It seeps through the walls topped by barbed wire, it wafts across the electrified borders.

—Ronald Reagan, 40th President of the United States

In the business world, the report is probably the primary method for providing information. The information in a report is intended to help executives, supervisors, managers, department heads, and others to understand their roles and perform their duties more effectively. Many of these people also write reports to supply others with essential information. Therefore, anyone who wishes to succeed in today's business world must be able to gather information and prepare reports.

A report may be given orally, but usually it is written. Important information in an oral report may be quickly forgotten, especially statistical data. Even a forceful oral report will grow weaker with each passing day, whereas a written report can be referred to again and again. Each reading of the report reinforces the message conveyed in the report. Moreover, a precise and permanent record exists in the report itself.

One way to classify reports is according to the length of the report—*informal* reports are usually shorter, and *formal* reports are usually longer. Because formal reports usually require extensive research, documentation, investigation, and analysis, the style of the presentation is usually different from the style used for a short report.

KEY POINT

One way to classify reports is by length. *Informal reports* are usually shorter, and *formal* reports are longer.

STYLE OF INFORMAL REPORTS

In Chapter 10 you learned how to use a memorandum as a means of corresponding with other employees within an organization. The same memorandum form is used for writing informal reports, hence the name *memorandum report*.

The memorandum report begins with the same information contained in the memorandum form you learned to use for interoffice correspondence.

MEMO TO:

FROM:

DATE:

SUBJECT:

Whether you use this format exactly as it is or adapt it will depend upon the report style preferred by the company where you work. *How* you use this format will depend on a number of variables.

KEY POINT

The memorandum form is used for writing informal reports. Usually the standard memo heading (*MEMO TO, FROM, DATE,* and *SUBJECT*) is used. However, this heading can be adjusted to fit individual or company preferences.

The *TO* Line

The way you address the person to whom the report is going depends primarily upon the degree of formality or informality of your office atmosphere. For instance, if everybody is on a first-name basis and if the report is of a personal nature, use the person's name.

MEMO TO: Sam Whitman

If the report will be read by other people besides the supervisor or if the report will be filed for future reference, use the person's name and job title.

MEMO TO: Samuel Whitman, Marketing Manager

The *FROM* Line

The *FROM* line should match the degree of formality of the *TO* line. For an informal memorandum report written only for your supervisor's information, list only your name.

MEMO TO: Sam Whitman

FROM: Kim Mason

For a report that is not for the exclusive information of the supervisor or that is to be filed for future reference, include your name and job title.

MEMO TO: Samuel Whitman, Marketing Manager

FROM: Kimberly Mason, Administrative Assistant

The *SUBJECT* Line

The *SUBJECT* line should be a comprehensive, yet clear and precise, statement that will prepare a reader for rapid assimilation of the information given in the report. Composing a good *SUBJECT* line, therefore, requires a high degree of skill.

Let's look at some illustrations. In the following examples, note how the specific subject lines immediately orient the reader to the information in the report.

General	Specific
SUBJECT: Sales Projections	SUBJECT: Third-Quarter Sales Projections, By Product
SUBJECT: Employee Absenteeism	SUBJECT: Causes of Employee Absenteeism

The *DATE* Line

Because reports may be updated or business conditions may change, every report should show the date on which it was written. In addition, dating a report makes it easier to locate a copy of the report.

Wherever dates are given in the body of a report, those dates must be specific. Instead of writing, "Last Friday, we sent , . . ," write, "On Friday, May 10, 19—, we sent. . . ."

File Copies

Whenever you write an informal report, even if you think it is not important, be sure to make a copy for your own files. At least keep a copy of your informal report on a computer disk from which the report could be printed if it is needed again. Anything important enough to be put in writing is important enough to be retained. You may never need to refer to your file copy, but someone else in the company may need some of the information contained in the report sometime in the future.

PLANNING AND WRITING INFORMAL REPORTS

Many people think that writing involves merely sitting down and dashing off a few words. Partly as a result of this widespread but false notion, good business writers are scarce and, therefore, very much in demand.

Indeed, first-class writing of any kind involves hard work and results from much thought, careful planning, and excellent training. Before you can write informal reports of the highest quality, you need to study, think about, and apply the following principles.

Be Clear, Complete, Correct, and Concise

As you know, *concise* writing should also be complete writing. To be concise, you must say everything that needs to be said, but you must say it in the fewest possible words.

You are also well aware that your writing must be clear and complete. You would not write a fuzzy sentence like this:

> Tom Bennett told Mr. Delgado about the construction delays about the industrial park, and he said he would have the report to Mr. Delgado by Friday.

Instead, you would write a clear, complete message, such as this one:

> Tom Bennett told Mr. Delgado that he would have the report on the construction delays at the industrial park on Mr. Delgado's desk on Wednesday, October 20, 20—.

All reports must be correct in every detail. Perhaps we should use the stronger term *accurate,* because any information important enough to be reported must be more than substantially correct; it must be *completely* accurate. For example, if you are asked to report the number of free-sample requests that come in on a given day, you'd better be sure that you give an exact, not an approximate, count.

Wording

The wording of reports differs from that of letters. A letter is designed to do more than convey a message, for its accompanying purpose is to win new customers or clients for the company and to retain old ones. Therefore, the tone of a letter is warm and friendly. A report, on the other hand, is a straightforward, factual presentation—and it should be worded as such.

As an illustration, read the following opening paragraph of a letter answering a request for information about your company's free tuition program for employees.

> In response to your April 10 request, we are pleased to tell you that we do provide free tuition for employees taking work-related courses in local schools under the following circumstances: [At this point, you would itemize and explain the circumstances under which your company pays the tuition for its employees.]

Now, note how the wording changes when the same information is given in a report.

> Employees taking work-related courses in local schools will be reimbursed for tuition when the following requirements have been met:
>
> 1. The course has been approved in advance by the employee's supervisor.
> 2. The employee earns a grade of B or better.
> 3. The employee has been with the company for one year or more.

KEY POINT

A report is a straightforward, factual presentation of information.

FORMS OF PRESENTATION

How brief or how detailed should your informal report be? Should you give the requested information in a single paragraph? Should you present the information in outline form? Should you tabulate the information? Should you show the information in a graph?

Because *you* are preparing the report, *you* are the one who must answer these questions. Only you are close enough to the situation to know why the report was requested, to project the probable uses of the information, and so on. In order to make a wise decision about the form your report should take, though, you must be familiar with the different types of presentations and their uses.

KEY POINT

Three basic forms of presentation are used in reports: paragraph form, outline form, and table form.

Technology

Computer-generated spreadsheets are often part of formal and informal reports. Spreadsheets are useful for presenting statistical information.

Paragraph Form

The paragraph form is often used for the presentation of simple facts. For example, if your supervisor has requested that you report how many hours of overtime were paid the previous month—and you are certain that the only statistic of interest is the total number of hours—you might write the following in a memo-style report:

> In the month of March 19—, the total number of hours of overtime in the Accounting Department was 15 hours.

Or, if you want to give a little extra information, you might add the following to the above statement:

> There are 35 employees in the department, and 7 employees (20 percent) accounted for the 15 hours of overtime.

Outline (List) Form

If, however, you know that your supervisor has a personal interest in the staff, you might correctly believe that you should list the names of the people who worked overtime. You could present all the information necessary in outline (or list) form.

> Information regarding overtime in the Accounting Department during March 19—is as follows:
>
> 1. Total employees in department   35
> 2. Total hours of overtime   15
> 3. Employees working overtime   7 (20 percent)
>
>   Mark Petrone, 2 hours
>   Cynthia Rogers, 2 hours
>   Ruth Stein, 2 hours
>   Kenneth Ulrich, 1 hour
>   Alicia Velez, 3 hours
>   Robert Williams, 4 hours
>   Steven Wimmer, 1 hour

Note how the outline form is used to highlight the suggestions in the unsolicited memo report shown on Figure 13.5 on page 591.

Table Form

Statistics such as dates and amounts of money are easier to comprehend and compare when presented in table form.

KEY POINT

In some cases, a table is the most effective way to present information. The advantage of a tabulated presentation is that the reader can more easily see the total situation at a glance without wading through a great many words. The decision to tabulate should be influenced by the amount and the kind of information to be included as well as by the uses to which the information is likely to be put. In table form, the example overtime report would look like this:

ACCOUNTING DEPARTMENT OVERTIME

Month of March 19—

Employee	Hours	Reason
Petrone, Mark	2	To complete January billing
Rogers, Cynthia	2	To prepare for business trip
Stein, Ruth	2	To prepare expense statement
Ulrich, Kenneth	1	To complete checking cost estimates
Velez, Alicia	3	To prepare cost analysis
Williams, Robert	4	To analyze travel expenses
Wimmer, Steven	1	To complete January billing

Total employees: 35
Overtime hours: 15
Total employees working overtime: 7
Percentage of employees working overtime: 20

UNSOLICITED REPORTS

An unsolicited report is, quite simply, one that you make on your own initiative rather than one you are asked to prepare. In business, any idea for increasing efficiency, saving money, increasing productivity, or increasing

Figure 13.5   Unsolicited Memo Report

Ideas for increasing efficiency, productivity, or profitability are often welcomed. Note how the SUBJECT line in this unsolicited report appeals to the reader's interest.

MEMO TO: Elizabeth Wang

FROM: Peter White

DATE: May 5, 20—

SUBJECT: Increasing Credit Card Use

Our firm has issued 2,320 credit cards to customers during the past 12 months. However, a survey made recently by our credit department indicates that only 40 percent of these credit card holders have made purchases exceeding $50 during this period. The average charge is $35.

A national study recently made by the American Credit Association revealed that the average single purchase by credit card holders is $75. This figure would seem to indicate that we are not getting the maximum benefits from the credit cards we issue and that we should be able to increase our volume of credit business by encouraging greater use of credit cards by our customers.

I am, therefore, recommending that we undertake a campaign to encourage customers who hold our credit cards to make greater use of them. The initial steps of this campaign should include the following:

1. Preparing folders encouraging new customers to apply for credit cards. An application form should be a part of this folder, which would be available not only in the credit office but also at numerous locations within our stores.

2. Placing full-page advertisements in all regional newspapers, explaining how customers can use their credit cards more extensively without getting into economic difficulties.

3. Buying television time for spot announcements with a theme similar to that of the newspaper advertisements.

I would suggest that representatives from both the credit and the marketing departments form a committee to plan the strategies of this program no later than the end of this month.

I will be happy to discuss any aspects of these suggestions with you at your convenience.

as

profits will usually be welcome. It's advisable to put your idea in writing so that you can present it in the most complete, logical, and generally effective manner. See the unsolicited report shown in Figure 13.5.

How do you go about preparing and submitting an unsolicited report? Before you begin to write, consider these details.

The *TO* Line

You will want to direct your suggestion or idea to the person who has the authority to put it into effect. Usually this person will be your supervisor; but even if it happens to be someone else, courtesy and protocol demand that the suggestion be routed *through* your supervisor to that other person. For example:

MEMO TO: Antonia Dawson [the "authority" person]
            Dan Spivack [your supervisor]

KEY POINT

The *Subject* line should identify the subject of the report for the reader.

The *SUBJECT* Line

In any report, the *Subject* line should tell the reader what the report is about. In an unsolicited report, though, you should write the *Subject* line so that it will appeal to the reader's particular interest. For example, if you know that your supervisor is particularly interested in increasing new subscriptions, you might use the following *Subject* line.

SUBJECT: Suggestions for Increasing New Subscriptions

SECTION 13.4   REVIEW

Practical Application

1. Your supervisor, Ms. Marion Hoskins, wants to purchase a personal computer so that she can work at home during the evenings and weekends. She asks you to check the prices of computers. Since Ms. Hoskins has specified what she needs, you investigate only models that meet her specifications. You obtain the following information:

   (1) ACI,—monochrome display, $1,200; color display, $1,495; Tecniq,—monochrome display, $1,400; color display, $1,680; Saporo,—monochrome display, $999; color display, $1,300; and CompPute,—monochrome display, $2,200; color display, $2,600.

All carry 1-year warranties, and service contracts are available after the expiration of the warranty. Both the ACI and the Tecniq are available at Super Computer and each comes with a carrying case. The Saporo is available at Red Barn Computer Sales, and the company will extend its warranty for 6 additional months if the system has not required service during the first year. The CompPute is available at CompPute, Inc., which provides a free spreadsheet program with each purchase.

Organize this information into a concise, easy-to-read memorandum to Ms. Hoskins.

2. Select two stocks or bonds that are listed in your local newspaper's stock market report. From the information that is provided in the newspaper, write an informal report about the status of these two securities during the past five days. Address the report to your instructor.

3. Prepare a tabulation report, similar to the one shown on page 590 in Section 13.4, for the information given below.

Sources of Employees Hired During the Year 19—: The state employment service referred 36 candidates; 16 were hired. Local college placement offices referred 27 candidates; 19 were hired. Private placement services referred 41 candidates; 17 were hired. Newspaper advertising resulted in 53 candidates; 10 were hired. Unsolicited applicants included 6 candidates; 1 was hired. Notices in employee service magazines resulted in 12 candidates; 7 were hired.

4. From *one* of the following areas—accounting, word processing services, marketing, personnel, or communications—indicate three *SUBJECT* Lines that would be likely for short reports. For example, a possible *SUBJECT* Line for a short report in the marketing area might be "Sources of New Clients."

Editing Practice

Using Your Word Processor and Proofreading. Can you find any spelling or homonym errors in the following excerpt from a magazine's circulation department report? Write the correct word or words on a separate sheet of paper.

Newsstand sales plus subscription sales of the magazine acceded 1.5 million copies in the month of December. Clearly, the principle reason for this sharp increase in sales is that our radio and television advertising in November and December was well planned. Indeed, we expect sales of our Febuary addition to reach 1.6 million copies; sales should than level off in the months of March and April and (as usual) decrease over the summer months.

Writing Formal Reports

OBJECTIVES:

After completing Section 13.5, you should be able to:

1. List and describe the main sections of a formal report.
2. Explain how to plan and write a formal report.
3. Explain how to write progress reports.
4. Describe the mechanics of report writing.

Knowledge is the most democratic source of power.

—Alvin Toffler

How do formal reports differ from the memorandum reports that you learned to write in the previous section? Formal business reports, in addition to being longer than the informal memorandum report, are usually concerned with more complex problems or questions necessitating investigation, analysis, research, and documentation. Some typical formal report subjects might be an analysis of the methods of marketing a company's products; a study to determine how to modernize a particular aspect of a business, such as a study to determine which type of computer accounting and billing system to install; or an experiment to determine how to improve the quality control of a product.

The writing of a formal business report may require weeks or even months of extensive research and reading related to the topic of the report. The completed report could contain anywhere from several pages to more than a hundred pages. Regardless of its length, however, a formal report must be accurately documented and well written, because often the report is the basis upon which a company decides whether or not to spend many thousands of dollars.

Not everyone is capable of writing an effective formal report. Even though an executive, an engineer or a technician may conduct the research that is the basis for the report, often an administrative assistant will be closely involved in the report preparation.

 **KEY POINT**

Formal reports often cover more complex problems and questions that frequently require extensive study or investigation.

PREPARING TO WRITE FORMAL REPORTS

Not all reports look alike. There are some variations in the style and form used in formal reports. These variations are usually determined by the nature of the subject being investigated. For example, a technical report that specifies the requirements for manufacturing computer components may be organized in outline form with very little text. Similarly, the reports of chemists, engineers, and other scientists are likely to include many tables, charts, and graphs, with a relatively small amount of narrative interpretation. On the other hand, many business reports are mainly narrative, possibly with some tabular material. Despite this variation in the style and form, most formal reports include these main sections:

Introduction

Summary

Body of the report

Conclusions and recommendations

Supplementary material

Before beginning to write a formal report, the writer-investigator must first determine the purpose and the scope of the report. To make this determination, the investigator must gather reliable facts, assemble and analyze those facts, draw conclusions from the factual analysis, and, finally, make recommendations that are reasonable in view of company needs.

Defining Purpose and Scope

Why is the report being written? The answer to this question should appear in the introduction of the report. For example, in a study to determine whether a company should disband its word processing center and let each department handle its own communication needs, the purpose of the report might be stated as follows:

1. To determine current methods of preparing communications.
2. To determine the efficiency of these methods.
3. To determine the feasibility of returning responsibility for correspondence and report writing activities to individual departments.

A report writer must avoid selecting a topic that is too large in scope to be handled effectively. The experienced report writer, therefore, clearly defines the scope of the problem and sets boundaries that keep the research within reason. For example, think how difficult it would be to do research for a report entitled "Telephone Techniques of Office Workers." This topic is much too broad in scope to be treated in one report, if it could be treated at all. The topic needs to be limited to a more specific group. A revised title that would be more practical might read "Telephone Techniques of Customer Service Representatives of the Arco Electronics Company."

ORGANIZING THE REPORT

After all the material related to the topic has been collected and studied, the writer can begin to organize the report. At this time, the note cards should be revised, sorted by topic, and tentatively organized into a logical sequence for the report.

Outline

Using organized note cards as a guide, the writer creates an outline to serve as the structure, or framework, of the report. The outline should be kept as simple as possible. While determining the outline, the writer should keep in mind the kinds of topic headings the report requires. If outline entries are carefully thought out, many of them can be used as topic headings in the final report.

Headings

Most books, articles, and business reports use headings to indicate the organization of the material. Headings of equivalent weight should be formatted alike. For example, the main divisions of an article, a report, or a chapter in a book may be centered, and the subdivisions of each main heading may be typed as paragraph headings. When there are more than two divisions, however, the following arrangement of headings (excluding the report title) should be used:

CENTERED FIRST-ORDER HEADING

Side Second-Order Heading

Run-In Third-Order Heading. Text follows on the same line. . . .

If the report writer is consistent in the use of headings, the reader will better understand the report's organization and content. Consistency should be observed in the wording as well as in the style of the headings. In general, a topic form is preferred to a sentence form. For example, "How to Write Reports" is preferable to "This Is How to Write Reports."

WRITING THE REPORT

There are considerable differences between the informal writing style of business letters and memorandums and the writing style commonly found in formal reports. These differences are examined in the following discussion.

Writing Style

Long business reports are important documents upon which management bases many of its high-level decisions. Consequently, such reports tend to be written in a serious, formal style, usually in the third person. The impersonal style helps the writer avoid interjecting a personal tone that might weaken a report by making it seem merely a statement of one person's opinions and beliefs. The more the writer can de-emphasize the *I* and cite facts to back the evaluation, the more objective and more persuasive the report will be.

In the following example the writer carefully avoids any expressions that may imply that the evaluations are based on personal opinions instead of sound reasons and facts.

The evidence revealed by this survey indicates that the modified-block style of letter takes 15 percent more typing time than the simplified style.

Use of the simplified letter style would be appropriate for New Visions Entertainment, Inc., because the style has the modern look of simplicity and is also faster and easier to type.

Three of the five departments studied use mixed punctuation; however, adoption of open punctuation would have the following advantages: [Explanation of these advantages would follow.]

The same impersonal writing style illustrated above should characterize every section of the report. *Remember*: Making it possible for the reader to reason from the facts presented is an important factor in the success of any business report.

Title Page

The title page usually includes the complete title of the report, the name and title of the author, the name and title of the person for whom the report is prepared, and the date the report is submitted. These items should be attractively arranged on the page. A typical title page is shown in Figure 13.6.

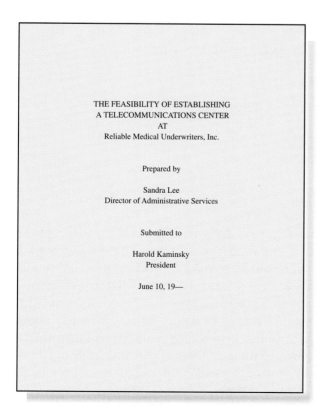

THE FEASIBILITY OF ESTABLISHING
A TELECOMMUNICATIONS CENTER
AT
Reliable Medical Underwriters, Inc.

Prepared by

Sandra Lee
Director of Administrative Services

Submitted to

Harold Kaminsky
President

June 10, 19—

Figure 13.6   Title page for a report

This title page shows the complete title of the report, the name and title of the author, the name and title of the person for whom the report is prepared, and the date the report is submitted.

Table of Contents

This section is prepared after the report has been completed. It should start at the top of a new page and list in sequence each separate part of the report. The main part of the report, the body, should list the side headings used and possible paragraph headings. The paragraph headings would be indented to indicate they are a lower level. Use dot leaders to align the elements of the report with the page number they start on as illustrated here:

CONTENTS

INTRODUCTION 1

    Statement of Purpose 1

    Scope or Limitations 2

    Procedures 3

SUMMARY 5

BODY OF REPORT (list actual title) 6

    List Side heading 6

    List Side heading 7

        List Paragraph heading 7

        List Paragraph heading 8

    List Side heading 9

CONCLUSIONS AND RECOMMENDATIONS 10

APPENDIX 12

BIBLIOGRAPHY 14

Introduction

The introduction section tells the reader why the report was written, what the scope of the report is, and how the data were gathered.

Suppose that Harold Kaminsky, president of Reliable Medical Underwriters, Inc., has assigned Sandra Lee, the director of administrative services, the job of investigating the feasibility of establishing a central telecommunications center as a way to improve the company's correspondence function and also to cut costs. In the introduction to such a report, Ms. Lee would include the *purpose* and *scope* of the report, as well as a description of the *procedures* followed to collect and analyze the data presented in the report.

Statement of Purpose. First, the writer should state the problem that the report addresses—the need to improve the handling of correspondence as well as to cut costs. Next, the writer should list the objectives of the report as in the following example:

> This report was prepared at the request of Mr. Kaminsky, president of Reliable Medical Underwriters, Inc. The report addresses the need to improve the processing of correspondence and the need to cut the costs of processing correspondence. The purposes of the report are:
>
> 1. To determine current practices used in preparing communications.
> 2. To identify the equipment used to prepare communications.
> 3. To determine the costs involved in preparing communications.
> 4. To determine whether a telecommunications center would improve the quality and decrease the cost of communications.

Scope or Limitations. A brief statement of the scope of the investigation may be included in the introduction.

> This investigation is limited to the communication practices in the home office of Reliable Medical Underwriters, Inc., in Lexington, Massachusetts.

Procedures. The introductory section of the report should describe the methods that were used to collect and analyze the data. Here is an example:

> Information for this report was collected through interviews with all department supervisors and all technical writers. The questionnaire in Appendix C of this report was completed by each supervisor and each technical writer.
>
> Major manufacturers of computer equipment were contacted, and each demonstrated its equipment. In addition, current periodicals were consulted to identify recommended practices for handling communications.

Summary

The summary is placed early in the report (following the introduction). The summary may range from one paragraph to several pages, depending on the amount of material covered. The following example is the opening paragraph of the summary of the feasibility study to determine whether a telecommunications center should be established at Reliable Medical Underwriters, Inc.

> This study recommends that a telecommunications center be established at the home office of Reliable Medical Underwriters, Inc., and shows that such a center would improve correspondence practices and decrease correspondence costs. The specific data gathered during this investigation resulted in the following conclusions that led to the above recommendation:
>
> 1. Dictation and transcription processes takes more time than necessary.
> 2. There is a great variation in letter styles used throughout the company.
> 3. Responding to correspondence often takes two to three days.
> 4. Many letters that are individually written could well be form letters.

KEY POINT

A summary contains the most significant information in capsule form, which helps the reader who cannot take time to read the entire report.

Body of the Report

The body is the actual report. In this section the writer tells what research was done, how it was done, and what the writer found. For example, in the report on the telecommunications center at Reliable Medical Underwriters, Inc., the body of the report would include the following:

- An analysis of responses to the questionnaire
- The results of the interviews with supervisors and technical writers
- A comparison of telecommunications equipment from major manufacturers
- A comparison of survey results with recommended practices for handling communications in other companies.

Writing the body of the report should present few difficulties if the writer follows a carefully prepared outline and has detailed notes. The writer should stick to accurate, verifiable facts and present them in a clear, concise manner. The suggestions given in Chapter 7 for forceful, clear writing apply also to writing reports.

Conclusions and Recommendations

This section can easily be the most important one in any report, for it is here that the real results of the report appear. The writer's conclusions tell the busy executive, on the basis of the most reliable data available, "Here is what the report tells us."

Personal observations should be kept to a minimum—conclusions should be drawn only from the facts. In light of the conclusions and from experience with the company, the writer can make recommendations. As a guide to making worthwhile recommendations, the writer should refer to the listed purposes of the report. As a rule, there should be at least one recommendation for each stated purpose.

By referring to the purposes stated in the introduction of the report on the feasibility of establishing a telecommunications center at Reliable Medical Underwriters, Inc., the writer might include the following conclusions and recommendations.

From an analysis of the data gathered in this study, the following conclusions are drawn:

1. Current dictation and transcription practices waste time.
2. Almost half the letters that are individually written could be form letters or could make use of form paragraphs.
3. Little use is made of available dictation equipment.

4. Most of those who dictate do not know how to dictate properly.

5. Administrative assistants are rarely permitted to compose letters.

6. Only half of the administrative assistants have word processing equipment.

7. A variety of letter styles is used, depending upon each writer's preference.

With these conclusions in mind, the following actions are recommended:

1. Purchase personal computers for all administrative assistants.

2. Make dictation equipment available to each executive.

3. Provide each executive with instruction on how to dictate properly and how to use dictation equipment properly.

4. Adopt the simplified letter as the standard letter style to be used throughout the company.

5. Record comparative communication costs as a basis for determining whether personal computers should be purchased for administrative assistants in the branch offices of the company.

Supplementary Material

Supplementary material, which is given after the conclusions and recommendations, provides substantiating data for the report. One or all of the features discussed below may be included.

Illustrations. A formal report can often be enhanced by the use of graphics or illustrations. When should graphic displays be used to supplement the material in your report? Consider using graphics when any or all of the following situations occur:

1. The information—ideas, facts, or figures—being presented is complex, and illustrations will help simplify it.

2. Visuals can reinforce the logic of your conclusions and recommendations.

3. You are comparing or contrasting two sets of data, or you are analyzing trends.

4. Statements need to be documented, and tables and other displays will provide the necessary information.

What kinds of graphic or visual displays should be included? The kind depends on the information you are presenting and your purpose in presenting this information. The possibilities include:

Tables. To provide a visible comparison of two or more sets of data and ready access to information.

Bar Graphs. To depict relationships between fixed groups of data or to compare or contrast two sets of data.

Line Graphs. To illustrate trends or show how sets of data have changed over a period of time.

Pie Charts. To show the relationships between parts and a whole.

Diagrams, Flowcharts, Organizational Charts. To simplify complex relationships or operations.

Photographs. To document information or statements.

Refer to Figure 13.7 and Figure 13.8 below for some examples of illustrations used to present data in a report.

How graphic displays are prepared varies from company to company. Unless you are a business writer with artistic ability, you may wish to have visuals prepared by your corporate art department or by an independent artist or agency. Another alternative is to use a graphics software program to prepare visuals. Several excellent programs that produce sophisticated, professional-looking graphic displays are available, and they are easy to learn.

Appendix. The appendix consists mainly of supporting information to back up the material in the body of the report. Long tables, charts, photographs, questionnaires, letters, and drawings are usually placed in this section. By including such material at the end of the report, you keep the body of the report free of the kind of detail that makes reading difficult.

Bibliography. This section is an alphabetic listing of all the references used in the report. Bibliographic entries are listed in alphabetic order by author. Forms for book and periodical entries are shown in the following examples.

Books

Braun, Harold F., *Communication Procedures,* Westly Book Company, New York, 19—.

Schrag, A. F., *How to Dictate,* McGraw-Hill Book Company, New York, 19—.

Periodicals

Greene, Arnold, "Word Processing Centers," *The Office Worker,* Vol. XV, No. 6, 19—, pp. 89—100.

Zane, Anthony, "Cutting Communication Cost," *The Executive,* Vol. IV, No. 3, 19—, pp. 34—38.

Figure 13.7 Bar Graph

Bar graphs may show relationships between fixed groups of data.

Figure 13.8 Pie Chart

Pie charts show the relationship between parts and a whole.

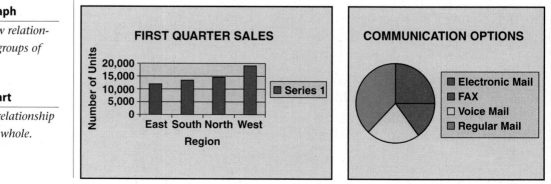

LETTER OR MEMO OF TRANSMITTAL

A short letter or memo of transmittal, composed after the report has been completed, accompanies the report. If the report is to be sent to someone outside the organization, compose a transmittal *letter*. If the report is to be sent to someone within the organization, use a transmittal *memo*. The letter or memo of transmittal usually contains such information as:

- A reference to the person who authorized the report.
- A brief statement of the general purpose of the report.
- Appropriate statements of appreciation or acknowledgment.

PROGRESS REPORTS

To complete an investigation and prepare the written report may take months. When such is the case, it is a good idea to keep the person who requested the investigation informed about the progress being made. How many progress reports will be called for depends upon how much time elapses following the original request.

A progress report generally is made in memorandum form. Suppose that you were requested on April 30 to make an investigation of the feasibility of establishing a telecommunications center at the home office of Reliable Medical Underwriters, Inc. On May 15, you might prepare the following memorandum:

> On April 30 you asked me to investigate the feasibility of purchasing personal computers for administrative assistants in our building. I have now completed the preliminary investigation and am ready to analyze the data I have gathered. I am also in the process of investigating computer equipment available from the leading manufacturers. I expect to complete my investigation and analysis by May 30 and to submit the completed report to you on or before June 10.

MECHANICS OF REPORT WRITING

An immaculate physical appearance, expert placement, and careful attention to the mechanics of English, spelling, and punctuation emphasize the importance of the finished report. For this reason, mechanics, as well as organization and writing style, are important in preparing the report.

All the mechanics of English, spelling, and punctuation discussed in earlier chapters apply to report writing. Some suggestions for setting up a report are also necessary, and they are presented in the following paragraphs.

Paragraphing

Use common sense and show variety in paragraphing; try to avoid too many long and too many short paragraphs. Keep in mind that the topic sentence, which tells what the paragraph is about, frequently comes first. Also, the closing sentence is often used to summarize the meaning of the paragraph.

Headings

Be generous in using headings. Take care to leave plenty of white space around major headings, tables, and other display elements. Be sure that all headings of the same value within a section are parallel in wording. For example:

Nonparallel	**Parallel**
The Introduction	Writing the Introduction
The Body	Writing the Body
How to Write the Closing	Writing the Closing

Notes

KEY POINT

Ideas taken from someone else or from another source should be footnoted even if you are not quoting the material word for word. Taking credit for an idea presented by someone else is a form of plagiarism, in the same way that using the words of someone else without enclosing those words in quotation marks is plagiarism.

Use footnotes or endnotes to give credit when citing the ideas of others, either verbatim or modified. A footnote is placed at the bottom of the page carrying the footnoted item; endnotes are grouped together and listed at the end of the report. Number notes consecutively, whether they appear at the bottom of the footnoted page or are grouped at the end of the report. Since note styles vary, it is advisable to consult the company's reference manual or a standard reference manual.

Graphics

Select carefully any tables, charts, diagrams, photographs, drawings, and other illustrated materials used to supplement the writing. To promote better understanding of the contents, choose the items that contribute most to the report. Eliminate any items that are not pertinent.

Typing Format

Observe these rules of good manuscript form:

1. Keyboard and print all reports on standard 8 1/2- by 11-inch paper. Legal-sized paper will not fit standard office files.

2. Use double spacing except for long quotations (usually three or more lines), for which single spacing is preferred. Print on only one side of each sheet.

3. Leave ample margins. Commonly accepted margins are:

   Left margin: 1 1/2 inches to provide for side binding.

   Other margins: Allow 1 inch.

   First page only: When the page contains the title, allow a 2-inch top margin.

4. Always prepare at least one file copy.

5. Traditionally, the first page does not show a page number when the page contains the title. All other pages, beginning with 2, should be numbered in the upper-right corner.

6. Follow this pattern for any material presented in outline form:

   I.
      A.
         1.
            a.
               (1)
                  (a)

Binding

Bind the report attractively. Many types of binding, from the single staple to an elaborate sewn binding, can be used. Reports that are subject to frequent, rigorous use should be placed inside a special hardback report folder for protection. Do not rely on a paper clip to bind the report; the chances of losing part of the report are very high.

SECTION 13.5   REVIEW

Practical Application

1. In memorandum report form, write a report for your instructor that describes the function of each of the following parts of a report:

   a. Title page
   b. Table of contents
   c. Introduction
   d. Summary
   e. Body of the report
   f. Conclusions and recommendations
   g. Supplementary material

2. Write a progress report for your employer, Fidelma Cassidy, using the following information:
    a. Nature of the study: dictation habits of executives at ABC Company.
    b. Assigned March 31; due May 1; progress report April 16.
    c. Completed so far: interviews with 20 executives, the total number of executives in the company; visits and interviews with three distributors of dictating equipment.
    d. Remaining research: library research, analysis of data gathered, determination of conclusions and recommendations. Add any additional items you think should be included.
3. You were asked on May 2 by your department manager, Michael Patel, to write a report on employee turnover. You gather the following data from the human resource department as well as by surveying the employees, interviewing a representative group of employees, and holding some informal small group meetings. Here are your notes.
    a. Annual turnover rate: manufacturing employees, 20 percent; office employees, 15 percent.
    b. Reasons given for leaving the company (in order of frequency): Manufacturing—working conditions undesirable, higher salary in another company, friction with supervisors, little opportunity for advancement. Office—better salary, little opportunity for further advancement, poor working conditions, friction with managers, difficult commuting, inadequate employee benefits.
    c. Recommended actions: Encourage frequent departmental meetings to give employees an opportunity to express their opinions; institute training programs for supervisors; initiate a salary survey of similar businesses and similar jobs; study promotion policies; hire a management consultant to make recommendations concerning employee benefits; consider the possibility of designating a personnel relations counselor to handle grievances.
    d. Department managers are to consider the turnover problem with reference to their experiences with employees under their supervision, are to be prepared to discuss the problem further, and are to make recommendations at a special meeting to be held on August 18. Prior to this meeting, by August 3, managers should submit a memorandum on morale in their departments.
    e. In the interviews and informal meetings you learn that there seems to be an atmosphere of unrest and that morale is generally low. The commuting problem may be eased shortly, when the proposed new bus route (direct from the Riverside area) goes into operation.

Editing Practice

Editing for Writing Power. On a separate sheet of paper, edit or rewrite these sentences for the purpose of improving writing power.

1. Ms. Andrews is the new administrative assistant, and she is very proficient in computer operations.
2. Her major is economics, but marketing also interests her.
3. Spend an afternoon at the job fair, and there you can learn about job opportunities for recent college graduates.
4. Desiring to avert a strike, a discussion of fringe benefits was held.
5. Not having been able to obtain any information about loans, and as he did not know the procedures for making such loans, the new manager decided we must deal on a cash basis.
6. The manager refunded my money, when I returned the floppy disks.
7. I liked the graphics in your report. They were readable. They contained accurate and complete information.
8. Although wanting information for his report, but he felt he had invested enough time, Ed began the writing without it.
9. The report to the executives about the new billing system that was started for the Toledo branch, was long and complicated so then the credit manager had to call a special meeting to explain it.
10. The report on sight possibilities here in Davenport was given by the reality agents.

Keeping Meeting Records

OBJECTIVES:

After completing Section 13.6, you should be able to:

1. Record and prepare for distribution a set of minutes for a meeting.
2. Explain the role of group recorder at meetings conducted by the interaction method.

Many ideas grow better when transplanted into another mind than in the one where they sprang up.

—Oliver Wendell Holmes, Jr.

Every organization, business or social, has meetings and must keep a record of what happens at these meetings. These records of the proceedings of meetings, called *minutes,* are another type of report used in business. The minutes serve as a permanent record of the decisions reached and the actions that are to be taken. The minutes can also be used to inform those who were not at the meeting of what took place. At one time or another, most business employees serve as recorder in a group or committee and are responsible for keeping an accurate set of minutes.

RECORDING THE MINUTES

The accurate recording of the proceedings of all meetings is an important function, for the minutes usually serve as the only historical record of a meeting.

There is probably no one best way to record what happens at a meeting. If an agenda of the meeting has been prepared beforehand, the assistant or recorder should receive a copy. As you learned in Chapter 8, an agenda is a brief chronological list of the business to be transacted at the meeting and acts as a guide to the person presiding at the meeting. The agenda also helps the assistant check that all scheduled items are accounted for in the minutes. Much of the success of good note taking revolves around the personal efficiency of the assistant. However, any assistant preparing to record the proceedings of a meeting should find the following general guidelines helpful:

1. List the name of the group, committee, or team and whether the meeting is a regular or special one.

2. Record the day, date, time, and place of the meeting.

3. List the persons attending and those absent. In a small group, list actual names; in a large group, however, either state the number of people present, as in "Forty-five members were present," or list the names of the absentees only.

4. In the opening section of the minutes, mention that the minutes for the previous meeting were read and approved, amended, or not approved.

5. Record the important points in the discussion of each item on the agenda. Presenting supporting facts helps those who were present recall the discussion and informs those who were not present. Reports or papers read during the meeting are often attached to the final minutes because it is usually not possible for the assistant to record verbatim all such information.

6. Record verbatim all resolutions and motions, as well as the names of the persons who introduced and seconded the motions. If the assistant was unable to record the resolution or motion verbatim, the assistant should request that the motion be repeated or even put in writing so that the exact motion is recorded.

7. Keyboard, edit, and prepare the minutes in final form. Sometimes, the assistant may want to get another person's approval before issuing the minutes in final form. The assistant signs the minutes, thus certifying their accuracy according to his or her notes. Sometimes the presiding officer countersigns them.

8. File one copy of the minutes in the folder, notebook, or binder used for this purpose. Usually minutes are duplicated and sent to each member of the group and to designated officers who would be interested in the business of the meeting.

KEY POINT

Minutes are the written record of a meeting.

FORMAT OF MINUTES

Various formats are used for meeting minutes. Regardless of the format used, all essential information should appear in a neat, well-arranged form. Some organizations prefer to emphasize the main points on the agenda by using a standardized format.

The minutes shown in Figure 13.9 illustrate an acceptable format. Notice the standard pattern and the topical headings that are used for all meetings of this group and the way in which the motions and the discussion are summarized.

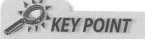

KEY POINT

Companies or organizations may specify a particular format for minutes. New employees or new members of an organization who are asked to take minutes should ask to see copies of the most recent minutes.

Figure 13.9   Minutes of a Meeting in Two-Column Format

This two-column format for minutes uses topical headings.

ASSOCIATION OF BEST COMPANY EMPLOYEES
MINUTES OF MEETING OF APRIL 19, 19—

TIME, PLACE, ATTENDANCE	The monthly meeting of the Association of Best Company Employees was held in the Blue Room at 5:30 p.m. The president, Jan Dixon, presided. All members and officers were present.
MINUTES	The minutes of the last meeting on March 15, 19—, were read and approved.
OFFICERS' REPORTS	Treasurer: The treasurer reported receipts of $650, disbursements of $150, and a balance of $967 as of April 1, 19—. Tony Valenti moved the acceptance of the report. Anne Terry seconded the motion. Motion carried.
COMMITTEE REPORTS	Chairperson William Ferris presented the report of the nominating committee. The nominees are:

President:	Meg Andrews
Vice President:	James Brown
Secretary:	Antonio Valdez
Treasurer:	Garth Kimberly

Rosa Sanchez moved that nominations be closed and that a unanimous ballot be cast for the slate of officers presented by the committee. The motion was seconded by Yamen Abdulah. Motion carried.

UNFINISHED BUSINESS	Plans for the Annual Retirement Dinner to be held June 30 were discussed. Tory's Inn and Edwin's were suggested for this event. The president will report to the group at the next meeting about these restaurants.
NEW BUSINESS	The president reported that the Board of Directors is considering a policy change regarding tuition reimbursement for college courses taken. The change would involve getting approval for each course in advance. The feeling of the group was to recommend to the board that the words "unless prior approval is not feasible" be added to this change in policy.
ADJOURNMENT	The meeting adjourned at 6:15 p.m.

Respectfully submitted,

Ivy Lewis

Ivy Lewis

Practical Application

1. Assume that you are the assistant of the Millstone Employees' Association, charged with the responsibility for taking minutes at all meetings and distributing copies to each member. From the following information, prepare in a concise format the minutes of the latest meeting:

   a. The regular meeting, held in Room 5A, Tyler Building, was called to order by President Karl Swensen at 5:30 p.m., March 15, 19—.

   b. A correction in the minutes of the preceding meeting (February 15) was approved: Ina Singer, not Rita Singer, was appointed chairperson of the Welfare Committee.

   c. Karen Bjorn reviewed employee suggestions for January. Awards of $100 each for two accepted suggestions were approved. Ms. Bjorn was to make arrangements for presenting the awards at the spring banquet.

   d. Revised written procedures for handling employee suggestions were presented by Jack Stuhlman. They were accepted with editorial revision to be made by a committee appointed by the president.

   e. The meeting was adjourned at 6:15 p.m., with the understanding that the next meeting would be a dinner meeting at Jackson's Restaurant, April 21, to begin at 6:30 p.m.

   f. The following members were absent: Holden, Yates, Witmer.

2. Do research about how meetings are conducted using the interaction method. Try to interview people who have attended such meetings. Then write a report that explains how the method works and that states whether you think meetings conducted this way are more productive.

Editing Practice

Spelling Check. On a separate sheet of paper, correct any spelling errors in the following paragraph.

   Harrison, who dislikes meetings, thought the comittee meeting was a waist of time. Everyone else, of corse, disagreed. Alice Croft chaired the meeting and encouraged the members to participat fully. Clark recorded the minuets—a task that he enjoys and takes seriusly. We were all accomodating, and we listened to one another's ideas. Accept for Harrison, we all left the meeting convinced that a productive meeting had been adjorned.

Preparing News Releases

SECTION 13.7

Communication is something so simple and difficult that we can never put it in simple words.

—T. S. Mathews

OBJECTIVES:

After completing Section 13.7, you should be able to:

1. Explain the purpose of a news release.
2. Write a news release, using the correct form.

Public relations specialists use a particular type of report called a *news release* to inform the media of newsworthy events. They hope that the media will prepare a story for publication or broadcast based on the news release. Knowing how to prepare news releases is another way of making yourself valuable to your employer.

THE FUNCTION OF THE NEWS RELEASE

An important means of getting the planned publicity of business into the hands of the public is the news release. Whenever a business plans an announcement or an event that it considers newsworthy or capable of enhancing its public image, its public relations personnel prepare and submit a news release to various news outlets for publication or broadcasting. Such a news announcement may publicize the introduction of a new line or new product, or it may concern the awarding of some honor to a member of the organization. Any item that will interest the public and create goodwill for the organization is an appropriate subject for a news release.

Any news story sent by a company must be approved for release. In large companies, the director of public relations would have this responsibility. In small companies, individual department heads might handle their own news and distribute it in keeping with company policy, or releases might be issued from the office of the president or of one particular executive.

To be printed or broadcast and thereby serve its purpose, the release must be newsworthy; that is, the contents of the release must be of sufficient interest to the public. Naturally, the writing style of the news release, as well as the form in which it appears, will have a strong effect on the news editor who decides whether or not the story is worth printing or broadcasting.

KEY POINT

A news release does not have a single prescribed format. However, following certain rules in preparing a news release will provide greater assurance that the story will be published.

THE FORM OF THE NEWS RELEASE

With hundreds of releases coming to their desks each week, news editors will select for publication or broadcast the items that require the least amount of rewriting, everything else being equal. Therefore, the news release must give complete, accurate information in a news style of writing that presents the facts in a clear and interesting way.

Many organizations use a special form for issuing news releases. These forms are arranged so that editors can get to the heart of the story without wasting time. Like a letterhead, a news release form usually contains the name and address of the company or organization and the name, address, and telephone number of the person responsible for issuing the release to the public as shown in Figure 13.10.

Figure 13.10   News release

A news release must give complete, accurate information in the news style of writing. Note that this company uses a special preprinted form for its news releases.

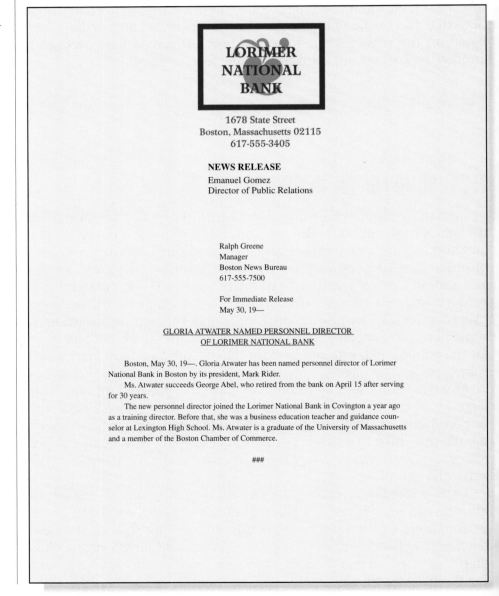

1. Double-space the news release and leave room in the margins for editing by the news editor.

2. Include a tentative headline in all-capital letters to identify the story. An editor may change this title to fit the space requirements and style of the publication or broadcast.

3. Indicate the time when a story may be published. In the example in Figure 13.10, note the prominence of the phrase *For Immediate Release*. A release may be sent to the media before an event occurs so that news will reach the public at almost the same time the event takes place. For example, if a company plans to announce a million-dollar gift to a local hospital at a banquet on Saturday, June 25, the release might read *For release after 6 p.m., Saturday, June 25.*

4. In a long release, insert subheads between parts of the release to guide the editor who wants to scan the story.

5. If there is more than one page to the release, type the word *MORE* in parentheses at the end of each page but the last one. At the end of the last page, type the symbols -XXX-, ###, oOo, or type END to indicate the end of the release.

Technology

Many word processing software packages contain templates for news releases. The placement of the date, title, city and state of origin, and company name and address will vary depending on the template used.

WRITING THE NEWS RELEASE

However good the form of a written communication, the subject and the words determine whether the release will be read and used. In writing a news release—just as in writing letters, memorandums, and reports—certain guides will help the writer develop an effective writing style and will improve the chances of getting the release printed. Especially important is the arrangement of paragraphs in the news release.

The opening paragraph of a news release should summarize the entire story and present the most newsworthy information first. In this opening section, the writer should give the *who, what, where, when, why,* and *how* of the news story in such a form that this paragraph can stand by itself, as in the following example.

Ms. Pamela Browning has been named international marketing director of New Millennium Electronics, Inc., by its president, Hayden Bartholomew.

Each succeeding paragraph should supply background facts in the order of decreasing importance. In this way, editors who need to shorten the release because of space or time limitations can easily shorten the story from the bottom up. For example, notice that the first two paragraphs in the news release in Figure 13.10 make a complete news story by themselves. The remainder of the copy provides additional details. A common practice is to include quotations from an official or another important person commenting on the news in the release.

KEY POINT

The opening paragraphs of a news release should summarize the story and present the most newsworthy information first, including *who, what, where, when, why,* and *how.*

KEY POINT

The first one or two paragraphs should provide a complete story. The rest of the news release provides additional details.

Practical Application

1. The AEP (Association for Environmental Protection) held its first organizational meeting in your community last evening. Margot Hayden was elected president, and you were elected assistant treasurer. The technical adviser is Professor Sidney Allen, chairperson of the Science Department of Mercer County College. The group plans to meet monthly on the first Wednesday of each month. Its aims are to publicize instances of local pollution and toxic-waste dumping, to investigate possible conservation measures in the community, and to recommend publicity to make the community more conservation-oriented.

   Write a news release about the organization—its officers, aims, plans—for your local newspaper. Supply any additional facts that you feel are needed.

2. Your boss, George Theopolus, vice president of Northwest Paper Company of Portland, Oregon, requests that you write a news release for the news outlets in the Portland area announcing the retirement of the company president, Philip Suarez, at the end of this year. Mr. Suarez has been with the company for 25 years, serving as president for the last ten years. He started his career with the company as a shop supervisor and then became factory manager within two years. Mr. Suarez became a vice president shortly thereafter and remained in that position until ten years ago, when the board of directors elected him president. Following his retirement, Mr. Suarez will serve as chairman of the board of directors. Mr. Suarez lives in Seacrest with his wife, Anita. Mr. Suarez has served on the Portland Chamber of Commerce for five years and is a member of the Portland Rotary Club.

   Using an acceptable format, write a news release. Supply any information that should be included.

Editing Practice

Supply the Missing Words. On a separate sheet of paper, fill in the word or words that you think are needed in each sentence.

1. If this booklet does not give you the ———— you desire, please write us again.
2. Thank you for being so ———— in filling our order for eight laser printers.
3. We are happy to tell you that your ———— has been established at the Crawford Hotel.

Doing Your Homework. The Danstown Carnegie Library had been in existence for almost 100 years in a town with a population of about 40,000 people. Many of the library patrons were very proud of the building and did not want to see it altered or abandoned even though the library had run out of space and needed expensive repairs.

The library director, Nancy Holler, and the five department heads had talked informally for several months about building a new library that would include adequate room for the collection, a community meeting room, and facilities for today's electronic library sources.

After much discussion at a regular staff executive committee meeting, the committee unanimously agreed to ask the Library Board for approval and funding for construction of a new library building.

The committee members compiled a list of reasons they felt the town needed a new library and presented the list to the Library Board at its next regular meeting.

Several board members agreed that they personally would like to have a new library. Questions were raised that the staff executive committee could not answer: What will happen to the old building? What will the building cost? What additional costs (insurance, utilities, water, maintenance, and so on) are anticipated? Where will the money come from? After a lengthy discussion, the president of the Library Board told the group that no action could be taken at this time because the group had not "done their homework." The staff executive committee were disappointed; they assumed that because they saw a need for the new building, the board would approve their request.

Analyze the situation in the case, and answer these questions:

1. What do you think was meant by the comment that the staff had not "done their homework"?

2. What kind of primary data should have been gathered? What kind of secondary data might have helped convince the board to build a new library?

3. What might have been more convincing to the Library Board than a list of the reasons why the staff executive committee felt a new library should be built?

CHAPTER 14

Finding, Accepting, and Leaving Employment

SECTIONS

14.1 Communicating in the Job Search

14.2 The Effective Employment Interview

14.3 Communicating and Your Career

Harold is one of ten graduates at Centerville Community College to be interviewed for two positions that would begin June 1 at HiTech Solutions, Inc., a local computer company. Lonnell Russell, HiTech's interviewer, will meet with all ten as a group at the college to tell them about the company and the two available positions. All had similar academic programs, each had at least a 3.5 grade point average, and all had work experience.

Harold arrived late for the group meeting and took a seat near the door. Mr. Russell was telling the group about HiTech and the two available positions. Harold felt uncomfortable as he glanced around the room. Everyone else wore a business suit. He had on jeans, a school sweatshirt, and a baseball cap.

After Mr. Russell finished the information session, he asked those students who were interested to sign up for an appointment at his office the next day. Harold signed up for the 1:30 slot.

Harold was determined to dress appropriately and to arrive early for the interview—two tasks that he hadn't accomplished at the group meeting. On the day of the interview, Harold was running late. To save time, he ate on the way. Harold noticed that his gas gauge was on empty. He stopped at a self-service gas station and filled up his gas tank. In his haste, Harold spilled some gas on his shoes. He used the napkins that came with his meal to wipe his shoes. Soon after, he arrived at the interview site.

In the reception area, Harold sat down beside his classmate Max Wilson and started a conversation. The receptionist asked, "Sir, may I help you?"

From his seat, Harold identified himself and told the receptionist he had an appointment with Mr. Russell.

Max asked Harold, "What's that spot on your shirt?"

"Must be catsup from the french fries. Got a Kleenex?"

"And, what's that smell?" Max queried.

"Must be the gas that sloshed on my shoes. Sorry," Harold said apologetically.

Mr. Russell's administrative assistant walked over to Max and Harold. Max stood up, while Harold sat and rubbed the stain on his shirt. Ms. Moreno took Max to Mr. Russell's office for his interview. Harold finally gave up on the stain.

What would have been your first impression of Harold? As you read Chapter 14, consider how Harold could have better prepared for his interview.

Communicating in the Job Search

OBJECTIVES:

After completing Section 14.1, you should be able to:

1. Analyze yourself and your qualifications.
2. List methods for assessing the job market.
3. Write a résumé and an application letter that market your qualifications to prospective employers.
4. Identify strategies for preparing a résumé that can be scanned or faxed.
5. Explain how to use a portfolio in the job search process.

Choose a job you like and you'll never have to work a day in your life.

— Confucius

Finding the position you want is similar to taking a comprehensive final exam. You must review everything you have learned and apply it to a specific situation. The information and related assignments in this chapter will prepare you for your job search. The process will be easier if you approach it systematically in separate steps. You need to:

1. Analyze yourself and your qualifications.
2. Assess the job market.
3. Market yourself.

ANALYZING YOURSELF AND YOUR QUALIFICATIONS

The first step in the job search process is to analyze yourself and your qualifications. You need to consider what kind of work interests you and what qualifications you have that would help you perform the work.

KEY POINT

Begin the job search by analyzing yourself and your qualifications.

Career Goals

To determine your career goals, ask yourself these questions: What position do I have now? What position do I want when I graduate? What position do I want two years from now? What position do I want five years from now?

Education

Think about how education affects your career goals: What courses, degrees, or training have prepared me for my career goals? Can I achieve my career goals with the education I now have? Do I need additional courses to qualify for the position I want? Will I need additional education and training for the position I want in the future?

Experience

Analyze your work experience by asking yourself these questions: What work experience do I have that is related to the position I want? How is this experience related to my career goals? If I do not have related experience, how can I acquire such experience before graduation? Do I have additional—though unrelated—experience that will demonstrate a successful work history?

Personal Characteristics

Define your personal characteristics by asking yourself these questions: What are my major strengths and weaknesses? Do I enjoy working with data, computers, or people, or a combination of these? Do I like variety? Do I want responsibility? Do I like challenges and problem solving? Would I accept a position that offers advancement but frequently requires overtime?

KEY POINT

Look for connections between your personal characteristics and work experience to identify the type of work you enjoy doing.

Your Ideal Job

Now, you should become very specific. Begin by describing your ideal potential employer and the position you would want with that firm. It is okay to dream a little when writing this description—your goal is to determine the type of position you want. Here are some questions to consider when writing the description of your ideal job:

- What products or services am I interested in providing?
- What position do I want?
- Am I looking for a career opportunity that offers promotions, transfers, additional education, and training?
- Do I want to work in a small community or a large city, in the United States or internationally?
- Would I like to work for a small, medium, or large company?
- What salary range would I be looking for?
- How important are benefits such as a flexible schedule, vacation policy, health insurance, and retirement options?
- Am I prepared to travel for my job?

Compare your description of your ideal company and position, with your analyses of your goals, education, experience, and personal characteristics to see how the two sets of information fit. If almost everything is in agreement, proceed to the next step. If your personal assessment and the description of your ideal position and company do not agree, work through both sets of information again to decide where you should make changes.

For example, you may find that the type of job you want as a computer programmer exists but that the available positions are in Southern California, and you were hoping to work in Texas. Should you stick to your original plan or rethink your choices? You must consider your choices and establish your priorities. This leads to the second step in the job search: assessing the job market.

ASSESSING THE JOB MARKET

KEY POINT

Assess the job market to find positions that meet your specifications.

After you have analyzed yourself and your qualifications and identified the type of employment you want, begin looking for positions that meet your specifications. There are many convenient sources of information on job opportunities. Depending on the size and geographic region of your desired location, some sources may be more accessible than others.

Your Personal Contact Network

Your personal contact network of friends, relatives, and college instructors can be an effective source of employment opportunities, particularly in a small community. Instructors frequently are contacted by alumni or local businesses requesting recommendations for job vacancies. Employees of a company often know when positions will become available because of transfers, promotions, resignations, retirements, and the creation of new positions. Inform people in your personal contact network about the kind of job you are seeking and the date when you will be available to accept a position. Even if your personal contacts do not know of an available position, they may know others who do.

Your Professional Contact Network

KEY POINT

Personal and professional contacts often provide leads for job opportunities that are not advertised.

You should establish your own professional contact network of friends and acquaintances in the business world using the following tips.

Join the College Affiliate of Civic and Professional Organizations. The Rotary Club sponsors Rotoract—its collegiate organization—on many campuses, and International Management Accountants (IMA) encourages student participation in its organization.

Use Every Opportunity to Mingle With Professionals in Your Chosen Field. When you hear a guest speaker at a conference, be sure to talk with the speaker after the presentation. Introduce yourself, express your appreciation for the speaker's time and expertise, and comment on some specific point that was made during the presentation.

Arrange to Meet Professionals Who Are Affiliated in Some Way With Your College. Find out if the department in your major has a board of advisors or a similar group. You might suggest holding a reception that gives students the opportunity to interact with members of this group.

Acquire Work Experience Through Internships, Summer Jobs, and Part-Time Employment. In addition to the work experience such positions provide, you develop relationships with professionals who can serve as mentors and sources of recommendations. You also develop links to other employers who might have available positions that match your qualifications. Internships and temporary employment situations also give you a chance to see if a career in a particular field is right for you.

Build Cordial Relationships With the Business Professionals With Whom You Work. Through your job performance, impress upon the employer your willingness to accept new assignments and to work as a team member. Many employers use internships and temporary employment situations to determine the potential that temporary employees possess for permanent employment. Employers particularly look for traits that are complex to measure, such as the ability to work in teams, a positive attitude, and creativity in coming up with new ideas or suggestions for solving problems.

College Placement Centers

Most educational institutions have placement offices whose career counselors are eager to assist you in finding a position. Visit your school's placement center to see what services are available. Besides listing employment requests from area businesses, career counselors also arrange job fairs that bring potential employers to the campus to interview students. Many career placement centers offer software programs that help you make career decisions, as well as books, pamphlets, and magazines related to current employment trends.

A comprehensive center would offer workshops on résumé preparation and interviewing techniques. Comprehensive placement centers also serve as the disbursement center for employment-related credentials that each student selects to be sent to prospective employers. These credentials would include a résumé, a list of references, and an unofficial transcript.

Often, career counselors can help you get a part-time job while you are in school. Many college placement centers offer to help students even after they graduate. If you want to change positions several years after you graduate, contact your college's career placement center and ask if you can still use its services.

KEY POINT

College placement centers offer assistance in writing résumés, researching employers, and preparing for interviews.

Newspaper Advertisements

The classified advertisement section of newspapers carries announcements of job openings in many types of business positions. Generally, the Sunday edition of a newspaper has the most extensive listings. If you want to apply for a position in a distant city, you should start checking the classified advertisements several months in advance for available positions in that location. Your college library, local library, or bookstore may subscribe to a newspaper for the city you have chosen. If not, you may need to take out a short-term subscription to the newspaper.

Specialized Journals

Another place to look for employment opportunities is in specialized journals, such as those for accountants, medical personnel, office personnel, teachers, and other professionals. The *College Placement Annual,* which offers information on a variety of employment opportunities, is available through college placement centers. This publication lists employers alphabetically and geographically. It also gives general background information about companies and lists anticipated position openings.

On-Line Searching for Employment

There are many employment-related sites on the Internet and the World Wide Web that make it possible to conduct an on-line employment search. Many companies have home pages on the World Wide Web that provide information about the company and employment opportunities. Also, many on-line services provide job postings, employer profiles, and résumés for review by employers. Many of these sites allow you to post your résumé electronically, for free or for a fee. Later in this section you will learn how to write an electronic résumé.

Some on-line employment services and their Internet addresses at the time this text was printed appear below.

America's Job Bank	http://www.ajb.dni.us
CareerMosaic	http://www.careermosaic.com
CareerPath	http://www.careerpath.com
Help Wanted USA	http://iccweb.com
The Monster Board	http://www.monster.com
NationJob Network	http://www.nationjob.com
Online Career Center	http://www.occ.com

Technology

Some on-line job search services allow only companies who have paid a fee to access the résumés posted by the service. Other services make their résumé postings available to anyone who has Internet access.

Placement Agencies and Employment Contractors

Private employment agencies exist in most metropolitan areas. Some of these agencies fill job openings in a wide range of occupations, while others focus on one area of employment such as management, construction, or office personnel. These agencies charge a fee, which is usually a percentage of the annual salary for the position. The fee is paid by the company seeking to fill a vacancy or by the person getting the job.

Employment contractors, also known as temporary agencies, employ personnel in response to specific industry requests. These agencies "lease" employees to a company on a temporary basis. Temporary workers gain valuable workplace experience, establish a positive relationship with a company, and possibly attain permanent employment.

MARKETING YOURSELF

After deciding what position you want and are qualified for, you begin the application process. You can answer advertisements, or you can apply directly to companies in which you are interested. Your résumé, application letter, list of references, and portfolio are the items you use to market yourself to prospective employers. These four items present your qualifications and assets to a prospective employer.

KEY POINT

Use a résumé, an application letter, a list of references, and a portfolio to market yourself to potential employers.

Résumé Content

The *résumé* is an outline or summary of your background and qualifications for the job you want. As you prepare your résumé, remember that the care with which it is prepared and the information that it supplies often determine whether you will be invited for an interview. Proofread and edit your résumé carefully to make sure that the spelling, grammar, and facts are correct and that the wording is clear. Ask several people to proofread your résumé as well. Creating a résumé that is error-free will make the all-important first impression a favorable one.

Always be honest when listing your qualifications in a résumé. Fabricating academic credentials or job titles and responsibilities is not worth the risk involved. Falsifying your credentials or application documents is grounds for immediate termination in many companies.

Federal law prohibits employers from asking the age, sex, marital status, religion, or race of applicants. Therefore, supplying such information is optional. If you consider any of this data an asset, you can include it on your résumé. The preference, however, is to omit such information.

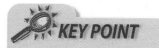

KEY POINT

A *résumé* is a summary of your educational background, work experience, and special skills and qualifications.

KEY POINT

Be honest when listing your qualifications in a résumé.

Résumé Parts

Résumés have standard parts, which make it easy for prospective employers to review a job candidate's credentials. You can individualize the information in these standard parts to present your qualifications in the best light. Include the following major sections in your résumé.

Identification. Begin with your name, address, and telephone number. If applicable, include a fax number or e-mail address. If you have a temporary address while you are in college, be sure to include your temporary as well as your permanent address information. You may want to have the following heading above your temporary address: Address Until May 10, 1999.

Career Objective. Your career objective should express your employment goal. If you are preparing your résumé for an advertised position, you may want to be very specific, such as *A position as a paralegal in the area of probate, trusts, and estates.* If you are preparing a résumé to send to many companies, your career objective should be somewhat general, such as *A position as a nursing assistant in a clinic setting.* You also have the option of not including a career objective.

Education. If you have attended several colleges, list your most recent education first. Include your degree, college, and major; also list your grade point average if it is 3.2 on the 4.0 scale or higher. If you have not yet received a degree, list the date the degree will be awarded: *Associate of Arts in Accounting to be awarded May 1999.* As a prospective college graduate, your education can be your strongest selling point.

Special Skills. Use this optional category to list distinctive competencies such as proficiency in another language, ability to interpret for the hearing-impaired, and experience with specific software programs.

Experience. You have several options in listing work experience. You may choose to list all experience, even though it may be unrelated to the position for which you are applying. A steady work history demonstrates that you are industrious, have initiative, and are dependable. List your current or most recent work experience first and continue backward. Give the months and years of employment, such as *May 1997-June 1999,* along with the company name, city, state, and ZIP Code. Include brief, specific descriptions of your job responsibilities using active verbs:

Reduced mailing costs by 10 percent.

Developed training program for new salespeople.

Increased the sales of electronics equipment by 25 percent.

Implemented voice-mail system to handle customer inquiries.

If you have had many jobs, you may use the heading "Selected Experience" or "Related Experience" to focus on the jobs most related to the position you seek. Use one of these headings to let potential employers know that your résumé does not include your entire employment history.

KEY POINT

Listing an objective on your résumé shows you have a career goal and makes it easier for a recruiter to identify the type of position for which you qualify.

KEY POINT

Expand the education section by listing courses in your major, particularly if you have little work experience. List the topic of the course (*Managerial Accounting*) rather than the specific course title (*Accounting 320*).

MEMORY HOOK

Use action verbs in your résumé to describe your work responsibilities:

achieved	developed	initiated	reduced
arranged	evaluated	managed	researched
completed	expanded	minimized	simplified
coordinated	implemented	organized	solved
created	improved	presented	supervised
designed	increased	programmed	trained

KEY POINT

If you have ample work experience in your field of interest, emphasize this fact. If you have had military service or are active in campus organizations highlight these activities.

Activities. List your participation in school and community organizations, sports, and volunteer activities. Specify any offices you held in organizations, such as president, secretary, or treasurer. This section demonstrates your leadership and community involvement, qualities that many employers look for in job candidates. You can expand the section on activities to include special recognitions such as dean's list, academic scholarships, honor fraternities, and so on. If you expand this list, use a heading such as "Honors and Activities."

KEY POINT

Remind students to use the same stationery and typeface for their list of references as they did for their résumés.

References. Use the statement *References supplied on request* to indicate that you will provide references when a prospective employer requests them. As part of the résumé preparation process, you should prepare a references list.

You should carefully select three references who know you well and who will communicate with prospective employers on your behalf. You could choose an instructor in your major field, a former employer or supervisor, and someone who knows you personally but is not a relative. Give the name, job title (if applicable), complete address, and telephone number of each reference.

As a courtesy, you should ask each person before you give his or her name as a reference. Although you may request permission by telephone or in person, you may also request this information in writing, as in the following example.

> Would you be willing to serve as a reference for me in my job search? As you are aware, I will graduate in May 1998 from Central Piedmont Community College with an Associate Degree in Computer Science. Enclosed is a copy of my résumé for your reference.
>
> Please indicate your answer in the space provided and return this letter to me in the enclosed envelope by March 15.

KEY POINT

Always ask for permission before listing someone as a reference.

World View

Take the opportunity to travel internationally if you get the chance. International travel can be a plus when you are applying for positions that require extensive traveling.

Résumé Types

Résumé formats are usually chronological, functional, or a combination of these two types.

- **Chronological Résumés.** These résumés stress time by listing education and experience in reverse chronological order, with the most recent work experience listed first, as shown in Figure 14.1. Chronological résumés are appropriate when you have a steady work history and work experience in your field of interest.

Figure 14.1   Chronological Résumé.

Joan Knight chose to use a chronological format for her résumé to emphasize her work experience. Note the use of bulleted lists to highlight job responsibilities.

JOAN R. KNIGHT
206 Median Avenue
Stillwater, Oklahoma 74075
405-555-2841

OBJECTIVE   Position as sales representative with an opportunity for advancement to sales management

EXPERIENCE   **Sales Representative**
Colonial Insurance Company, Stillwater, Oklahoma
May 1996 to Present

- Increased sales volume by 12 percent
- Developed home page for Colonial Internet site
- Established computerized record keeping system
- Recruited two additional sales representatives

Customer-Service Representative
Americo Credit Services, Oklahoma City, Oklahoma
January 1994 to April 1996

- Handled billing inquiries from customers
- Inputted data for credit reports

Sales Associate
Dustin Department Store, Oklahoma City, Oklahoma
January 1992 to December 1993

- Simplified inventory procedure for housewares department
- Designed sales displays
- Supervised three part-time employees

EDUCATION   **Associate of Arts Degree** to be awarded May 9, 1998
Tri-County Community College, Stillwater, Oklahoma

- Emphasis in Marketing
- Minor in Psychology
- 3.8 overall GPA/4.0 Scale

SPECIAL SKILLS   Bilingual in English and Spanish
Proficient in Microsoft Word, PowerPoint, and Excel
Experienced in budgeting and allocating resources

HONORS AND   Dean's List all semesters
ACTIVITIES   Top Sales Award, Colonial Insurance, 1996
Colonial Chairman's Round Table, 1994 and 1995

REFERENCES   Provided on request

KEY POINT

As a courtesy, you should supply your references with a copy of your résumé so that they will be prepared to answer questions about you. You should also notify your references when you accept a position.

- **Functional Résumés.** These résumés emphasize skills and related accomplishments and de-emphasize work experience, unlike chronological résumés. A functional résumé, as shown in Figure 14.2, is appropriate for recent graduates who wish to emphasize their education and training over their work experience.

- **Combination Résumés.** These résumés combine the best features of chronological and functional résumés to present a prospective employee's qualifications. As shown in Figure 14.3 on page 628, a combination résumé emphasizes skills while also mentioning work experience.

OOPS!

Be sure not to mispell words on a résumé.

Figure 14.2 Functional Résumé.

Michael Valencia chose the functional format for his résumé to stress his coursework and skills and to make up for his limited work experience.

MICHAEL TODD VALENCIA, III
938 Oakbrook Lane
St. Louis, Missouri 63132-4461
314-555-3814
E-mail:tvalencia@louis.net

Objective	Position as a computer software technician
Education	Associate of Arts Degree in Computer Technology, expected December 1999 Mid-State Community College, St. Louis, Missouri • Emphasis in Microcomputer Systems Management • 3.4 Grade Point Average/4.0 Scale • Internship with leading telecommunications firm
Selected Coursework	AC/DC Electronics Industrial Electronics Logic and Program Design RF Communications
Computer Skills and Expertise	Troubleshooting telecommunications equipment Installing software on networked computers COBOL, RPG, C Lotus and Dbase IV Microsoft Office 97 Corel WordPerfect Suite 7
Leadership Roles	President, Mid-State Computer Club Treasurer, Office Education Association Senator, Student Government Association Vice-President, Fellowship of Christian Athletes
Experience	World Wide Tours, Inc., St. Louis, Missouri, 1997-1999 • Developed computerized tracking system to track tour registration and monitor payment schedules • Implemented computerized catalog of tours Metropolitan Realty, Inc., St. Louis, Missouri 1996-1997 • Designed World Wide Web page with real estate listings • Computerized sales contract procedures, saving two hours per home closing
Interests	Chess Swimming Web page design
References	Supplied on request

World View

One way to prepare for today's global marketplace is to study a foreign language.

While writing a résumé is not a difficult task, it's definitely worth your while to devote some time and effort to doing it well. A sloppy, poorly written, or incomplete résumé is likely to be tossed aside by a potential employer—and with it your chance for a job. If you are just beginning your academic career, you should start building your résumé by acquiring work experience, doing volunteer work, and participating in appropriate campus organizations. Establishing a solid work history can assist you in the job search by providing sources for excellent recommendations on your job performance. Having a sufficient work background in your field of interest and being involved in a variety of activities certainly makes writing your résumé much easier.

Figure 14.3   Combination Résumé.

Wendy Zhao chose the combination format to emphasize her blend of experience, skills, and training.

WENDY ZHAO

543 West Woodlawn Avenue
Meadowlark Subdivision
Shelby, North Carolina 28150

Telephone: 704-555-3284
Fax: 704-555-3429
E-Mail: Zhao@Shelby.net

OBJECTIVE   Position as an administrative assistant in a human resource department.

PROFILE
- Excellent oral and written communication skills
- Proficient in using word processing and desktop publishing applications in Microsoft Office 97 and Corel WordPerfect Suite 7
- Typing speed of 75 words per minute
- Adept at integrating spreadsheets and graphic elements into reports

CERTIFICATIONS
- Professional Secretary Certification, 1996
- Notary Public, 1995

EXPERIENCE   **Executive Secretary**, J & J Manufacturing, Charlotte, North Carolina
June 1995 to present
- Conduct software training classes for management
- Arrange domestic and international travel for company executives
- Write company newsletter
- Coordinate quarterly board meetings
- Supervise two administrative assistants

Secretary, Bingham, Bingham, and Schmidt, Attorneys at Law, Charlotte, North Carolina, April 1990 to May 1995
- Scheduled appointments and court dates
- Assisted attorneys in preparing and filing briefs
- Handled correspondence for three attorneys

EDUCATION   **Associate of Arts in Secretarial Science**
Holly Hills Community College, Shelby, North Carolina, May 1997
Selected coursework in addition to major: human resources management, decision making, psychology

**HONORS
AND
ACTIVITIES**
Outstanding Student Award, 1997
Software Applications Award, 1996
Dean's List, six semesters
Vice President, Phi Beta Lambda
Secretary, Holly Hills Honor Society
Member, Students Against Drunk Driving (SADD)

**VOLUNTEER
EFFORTS**
Habitat for Humanity
Community Shelter

REFERENCES   References furnished upon request

Formatting a Résumé

Once you have identified the information to include in your résumé, you need to arrange and format the information for the most attractive, professional, and eye-catching appearance. Use the following guidelines.

Guidelines for Formatting a Résumé

- Limit your résumé to one page, unless you have extensive work experience. While your résumé should contain all pertinent information, it should not be crowded.

- Place your résumé attractively on the page. Include an eye-appealing combination of printed information and white space to make the résumé easy to read.

- Use 1-inch side and bottom margins and a 1 1/2-inch top margin.

- Use headings with bold or capital letters to identify your sections of work experience, education, activities, and skills.

- Select a readable font in 11- or 12-point type for your text and a somewhat larger font, such as 14-point type, for headings. The smallest acceptable font is a 10-point size, and it should be used sparingly and reserved for less important details.

- Select a good-quality paper with matching envelopes. Ideally, your matching envelopes should be large enough to accommodate your résumé and application letter unfolded. Use the same type and color stationery for your résumé, application letter, and list of references. White stationery is used most often, but light colors such as cream, buff, or gray are acceptable.

- Avoid stapling the application letter and résumé because the receiver often must separate them for photocopying or scanning.

Preparing a Technologically Friendly Résumé

To take advantage of all the employment opportunities available today, job applicants must consider how to prepare a résumé to be viewed electronically. Résumés may be scanned by a computer, entered in a database, posted on the Internet, sent via e-mail, or faxed.

Increasingly, companies review résumés using databases and computer scanners to reduce the cost and time involved in assessing job applicants. Computers are programmed to scan résumés for specific keywords or nouns associated with a particular industry and specific positions within that industry. If a résumé contains enough keywords or nouns to match an advertised job, the applicant is selected for further consideration.

Technology

Many word processing programs have résumé templates. These templates can be helpful if you have never prepared a résumé. However, because other applicants may use the same template, you should develop a customized résumé.

KEY POINT

Consider having a résumé service help you complete the content as well as format your résumé.

OOPS!

Lagging behind in technological skills poses a treat to job security.

MEMORY HOOK

To prepare an electronically friendly résumé, use keywords such as the following to describe your accomplishments and responsibilities.

ability to implement	leadership
accurate	multitasking
analytical ability	problem solving
communication skills	public speaking
customer-oriented	relocation
detail-minded	self-starter
flexibility	team player

Besides the traditional method of submitting résumés by mail, job applicants now have the opportunity to post résumés on the Internet. These postings can be viewed 24 hours a day, 365 days of the year and are available to Internet users in the United States and in over 100 other countries. Many on-line services offer tips for writing a résumé that can be scanned or searched for keywords.

Here are some guidelines to help you correctly prepare your résumé in a way that will be compatible with computers, fax machines, photocopiers, and scanners.

- Use keywords and nouns, not action verbs, to describe your responsibilities and accomplishments. Refer to the Memory Hook on this page for some sample keywords.
- Place keywords within the text of your résumé, or group them in a separate paragraph at the end.
- Align text at the left margin.
- Avoid using centered or right justification.
- Do not use tabs or indenting.
- Single-space the text.
- Remove hard returns to allow the text to wrap.
- Do not condense the spacing between letters.
- Use asterisks instead of bullets.
- Do not use italic, script, or underlined text.
- Use a font size of 11 to 14 points.
- Use a readable typeface such as Helvetica, Times, Palatino, or Courier.

KEY POINT

Job seekers may need to prepare two different résumés—a traditional résumé that uses action verbs, and a technologically friendly résumé that emphasizes key words.

Technology

When you prepare your own résumé, you can save and easily update it on disk. You can also easily tailor your résumé to specific employment interview situations.

- Avoid using horizontal or vertical lines, which are difficult for computers to read.
- Do not use two-column text.
- Put your name at the top of the page, followed by your career objective on the second line.
- Send an original of your résumé, not a copy.
- Use 8 1/2- by 11-inch paper in a light color such as white, eggshell, beige, or light gray.
- Print your résumé on a laser printer for the best quality.
- Do not staple or fold your résumé.
- Use the high-resolution or detailed mode when faxing your résumé to make it easier to read.

It is a good idea to follow-up an electronically sent résumé with a printed résumé, application letter, and list of references for any job that you feel is a possible match for you. You should, however, exercise caution in sending personal information and your list of references over the Internet to employers that you do not know by reputation.

The Application Letter

After you have prepared your résumé and targeted prospective employers, you are ready to organize your application letter, often called a cover letter. The application letter is a companion document to your résumé and list of references; to show this connection, use the same stationery and typeface for all three documents.

Remember that the application letter is intended to highlight your most important qualifications and to persuade the employer to grant you a personal interview. Your résumé will help the employer determine whether you have the education and skills required for the job. A sample application letter appears in Figure 14.4 on page 632.

In writing an application letter, always address the letter to a specific recipient. Use the person's name, if you know it. If you cannot find out the person's name, use a job title, such as *Dear Human Resources Manager* or *Dear Personnel Director*.

Get to the Point Immediately. In the first paragraph of your application letter, you should:

- State your intent to apply for a position with the company.
- Describe the position for which you are applying.
- Indicate how you learned about the position. If you are submitting a résumé to a company that has no advertised openings in your field of interest, identify the type of position that interests you.

There is no one best opening for an application letter. The following opening sentences are suggestions that have been used successfully. Adapt them to suit your needs.

KEY POINT

The purpose of the résumé and application letter is for you to get an interview. The purpose of the interview is for you to get the job.

KEY POINT

In an application letter: (1) Get to the point immediately. (2) Tell why you should be considered. (3) Show a willingness to work and learn. (4) Make it easy for the employer to ask for an interview.

For newspaper ads:

Please consider me an applicant for the position of management trainee, as advertised in the August 25 issue of the *Orlando Times.*

The position of paralegal, which you advertised in the April 1 issue of the *Gazette,* matches my qualifications and experience. Please consider me an applicant for this position.

For referrals:

A mutual friend, Linsey Howie, suggested that I contact you concerning a position as administrative assistant with your company.

Figure 14.4
Application Letter

Notice how the job seeker (1) identifies the position being applied for; (2) gives reasons why the job seeker should be considered; (3) shows a willingness to work and learn; and (4) makes it easy to set up an interview.

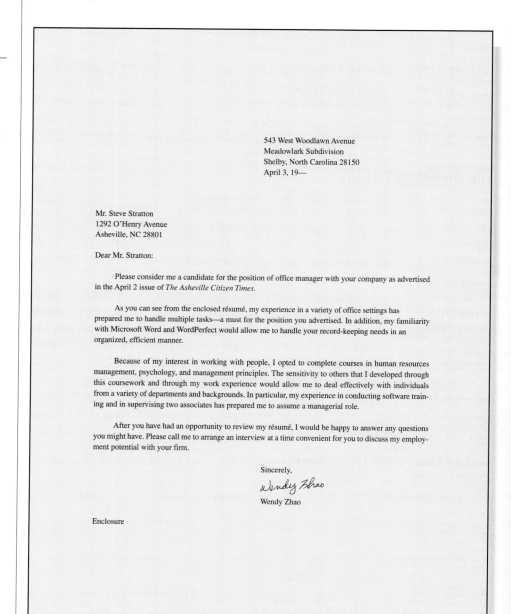

543 West Woodlawn Avenue
Meadowlark Subdivision
Shelby, North Carolina 28150
April 3, 19—

Mr. Steve Stratton
1292 O'Henry Avenue
Asheville, NC 28801

Dear Mr. Stratton:

Please consider me a candidate for the position of office manager with your company as advertised in the April 2 issue of *The Asheville Citizen Times.*

As you can see from the enclosed résumé, my experience in a variety of office settings has prepared me to handle multiple tasks—a must for the position you advertised. In addition, my familiarity with Microsoft Word and WordPerfect would allow me to handle your record-keeping needs in an organized, efficient manner.

Because of my interest in working with people, I opted to complete courses in human resources management, psychology, and management principles. The sensitivity to others that I developed through this coursework and through my work experience would allow me to deal effectively with individuals from a variety of departments and backgrounds. In particular, my experience in conducting software training and in supervising two associates has prepared me to assume a managerial role.

After you have had an opportunity to review my résumé, I would be happy to answer any questions you might have. Please call me to arrange an interview at a time convenient for you to discuss my employment potential with your firm.

Sincerely,

Wendy Zhao

Wendy Zhao

Enclosure

Your company has been recommended to me by Mrs. Nancy Berga, the placement director of Midlands Community College, as one with exceptional opportunities for accountants. Might you have a position for a self-starter who has two years of experience with accounts payable?

For applications made directly to a company, whether or not a position is open:

I believe my qualifications for a position as insurance sales representative will interest you.

I am interested in working for a progressive real estate firm such as yours. My enclosed résumé lists my qualifications for the position.

Here are five reasons why you should consider me for a sales position with Kramer and Cola.

Tell Why You Should Be Considered.   In the second paragraph of your application letter, state how your skills and accomplishments make you a desirable candidate for the position referred to in the first paragraph. Your goal is to convince the employer that you are the best person for the job. Don't be afraid to write about your accomplishments. For example:

As you can see from my enclosed résumé, coursework in accounting, human resource management, and economics has prepared me to assess a variety of financial and personnel needs. In all my courses, I consistently ranked in the top 5 percent of my class.

Of course, the nature of the second paragraph will depend on what you have to sell. If your work experience is limited and unlikely to impress the employer, you should emphasize your education and training. In such a case, you might follow the above paragraph with a statement such as this:

Of particular interest to me in the accounting courses I completed were the applications of accounting theory to computerized procedures and equipment. Working for a large organization such as Johnson Associates would allow me to implement my training with spreadsheets and databases on a wide scale.

The writer of the following paragraph lacks business experience but compensates for this lack by demonstrating interest and enthusiasm.

I am very interested in working as a paralegal for Dunn and Kellerman. As a result of conversations with Yukio Tanaka, a paralegal with your firm, I feel that the varied duties and opportunities for advancement fit well with my legal research background. With my willingness to learn and attention to detail, I can be an asset to Dunn and Kellerman within a short period of time.

If you have had work experience that is related to the position for which you are applying, make the most of it, as in the following example.

As an intern with Evans-Henshaw & Company last summer, I participated on the total quality management team that drafted information processing procedures. This opportunity gave me valuable experience in team problem solving that I could put to use for your company.

KEY POINT

Use the you-attitude in an application letter, focusing on skills and qualifications you offer the employer.

Show a Willingness to Work and Learn. The employer who hires you is taking a risk that you may not be suitable for the position. One of the best ways to convince the employer of your suitability is to demonstrate a willingness to learn and to express genuine interest in the job. The following are examples of ways you can convey your enthusiasm:

As a self-starter who absorbs new information quickly, you will find me willing to learn and eager to improve.

I am not afraid of hard work; in fact, I enjoy it.

You will find I am a quick learner and am adept at problem solving.

Make It Easy for the Employer to Ask for an Interview. Write the last paragraph of your application letter with the aim of asking the prospective employer for an interview. Make it easy for the employer to contact you by including your telephone number and the best time to reach you.

I look forward to meeting with you to discuss the paralegal position available with your firm. You may contact me at 314-555-7613 or at the address at the top of the letter. I am available to meet with you between 11 a.m. and 3 p.m. Monday through Thursday.

Some job seekers prefer to follow up on the letter rather than wait for the employer to contact them. For example:

If it is convenient for you, I am available for an interview between 9 a.m. and 5 p.m. on Tuesdays and Thursdays until April 1. After you have had a chance to review my qualifications, I will contact you to request an appointment.

The Application Form

Most companies require prospective employees to fill out an application form for their files. In some cases, you will be asked to complete the form at the company office; in others, you will take the form home to complete. In either case, you must provide accurate information regarding your education, work experience, and references.

Be sure to take a copy of your résumé and list of references whenever you go to a company to apply for a job. Most of the information needed for the application form will be on your résumé. If you haven't memorized your social security number, it is a good idea to take your social security card with you. If you complete the application form at home, photocopy the form and complete the photocopy as a rough draft. Then copy your responses on the original application form.

As part of the application process, many companies may also ask you to take tests that evaluate your skills and aptitudes. These might include tests of your typing and computer skills, spelling and grammar, or basic math. If you apply for a government job, you will need to take a civil service test.

Portfolios

Portfolios are gaining in popularity and acceptance in the job search arena. *Portfolios* are folders or notebooks containing evidence and examples of your achievements and skills. For many years, artists, models, and advertising associates have used portfolios to display examples of their work while on interviews. Now, prospective employees in other fields have noted the value of this method.

A résumé and a list of references form the basis of the portfolio, but your creativity and your prospective employment position determine the contents of your portfolio. For example, prospective teachers may include lesson plans and pictures of their bulletin board displays in their portfolios. Potential sales representatives might include pictures and scripts or videos of mock sales presentations they have developed. Administrative assistants may include examples of correspondence or spreadsheets. Medical personnel would have copies of their license and certificates for completing specialized training.

Every item in your portfolio should be of high quality. Start with an attractive binder that has pockets for odd-shaped items such as a video. You may choose to laminate some items, but documents such as your résumé, transcripts, and certificates should be placed in sheet protectors, not laminated.

Portfolios become a conversation piece during an interview. Thus, you should include items that you want to talk about because they accentuate your strengths. Professional portfolios are built over time. As you complete a course or master a new skill, select and accumulate class- or work-related projects that could be used in your portfolio.

KEY POINT

A portfolio is a collection of evidence and examples that highlight your achievements and skills.

SECTION 14.1   REVIEW

Practical Application

1. List four sources you might consult for information about job openings in your chosen career.
2. Make a list of your personal characteristics and your work experience. Use this list to write a description of your ideal job.
3. Identify two people who could serve as personal contacts and two people who could serve as professional contacts for you.
4. Based on your education, work experience, and skills, determine which résumé style is best for you. Explain your choice.
5. Write your résumé using the style you selected in 4 above. Use one of the sample résumés in Figures 14.1, 14.2, and 14.3 as a guide.

6. From the "Help Wanted" advertisements in your local newspaper, select a position that appeals to you and for which you are qualified (or will be upon graduation). Write an application letter answering the advertisement, and enclose a résumé that is targeted specifically for this job.
7. Identify someone whom you would like to list as a reference. Write a letter to this person asking permission to use his or her name as a reference.
8. Make a list of the items that would be appropriate for a portfolio in your chosen career. Explain why each item would be useful in presenting your qualifications.

Editing Practice

Editors' Alert. On a separate sheet of paper, rewrite the following sentences for clarity and correctness.
1. Having arranged for a seminar, the conference room was reserved by Carol.
2. Each of the 3 applicants are qualified.
3. Who's computer did you use, his or mine?
4. Its company policy to provide insurance for each employees dependants.
5. After we identified how to develope a new proceedure, the meeting was scheduled by us for Febuary 1.
6. The report is up-to-date and will be distributed tommorow.

Sound-Alikes. On a separate sheet of paper, choose the sound-alike word that correctly completes each of the following sentences.
1. Mr. Whitaker told the sales representative that we would not (except, accept) defective merchandise.
2. We use the new software program to (excess, access) the database.
3. Because the account is now 30 days (past, passed) due, we must impose an interest charge.
4. The manager asked the members of her staff for (they're, their, there) views on the new procedure.
5. We gave two (complementary, complimentary) tickets for the game to the top five sales representatives.
6. Severe (weather, whether) is expected by midnight tonight.

Critical Thinking Skills

Analyze. Why is it important to analyze yourself and your qualifications before you begin your job search?

The Effective Employment Interview

Luck is what happens when preparation meets opportunity.

—Anonymous

Your job interview may be the critical factor in determining whether or not you are hired. For that reason, it is essential that you be well prepared for the interview. No matter how impressive your background, your résumé, and your application letter, you may fail to be hired if you cannot "sell" yourself when you meet a prospective employer face to face. In Section 14.1, you learned that a résumé and application letters are the first phase in marketing yourself to potential employers. The interview is the second phase of the marketing process.

In an interview, you have an opportunity to sell yourself every time you speak. Your responses to questions, your descriptions of experiences and activities, your explanations of procedures and methods—all contribute to the interviewer's impression of you. Therefore, you must prepare thoroughly for the interview.

MENTAL PREPARATION FOR THE INTERVIEW

Although you were not conscious of it at the time, you began preparing for a job interview some time ago. You chose the type of work you wanted to do; then you acquired the education and training necessary for your chosen career. You then targeted prospective employers, compiled a résumé and a list of references, wrote an application letter, and obtained the interview. Now you must prepare for the job interview itself.

Remember the Goal of the Interview

Remember that your goal is twofold: to sell yourself and to find out if the job fits your qualifications and career plans.

Research the Prospective Employer

Conduct some research on your prospective employer. Find out about the company's products, services, and history. Knowing something about the organization will help you decide whether it is a place you

OBJECTIVES:
After completing Section 14.2, you should be able to:

1. Name two goals of an employment interview.
2. Prepare questions to ask the interviewer.
3. Anticipate questions you will be asked at the interview.
4. List the steps you can take to follow up an interview.

KEY POINT

To prepare mentally for an interview:
1. Remember the goal of the interview.
2. Research the prospective employer.
3. Prepare questions to ask the interviewer.
4. Know your strengths and weaknesses.
5. Anticipate questions.
6. Become knowledgeable about industry trends and current events.

KEY POINT

Researching information about a prospective employer makes you knowledgeable about the company and helps you determine if you would like to work there.

would like to work. Also, you should have a strong answer to the often-asked interview question, "Why are you interested in employment with our company?" To be effective, your answer should demonstrate that you know something about the company. "I have always been interested in investments, and I know that your company is one of the leading investment firms in this area."

Follow these guidelines in researching a company:

- Speak with the person who referred you to the organization or to an employee of the organization to find out the information you need.
- Explore the Internet for information about the company or organization. Many companies have home pages on the World Wide Web that provide background information about the company, including the type of business and a description of its products and services.
- Search print or computerized databases in the library for information about local, national, or international companies.
- Obtain a copy of the company's annual report.
- Contact the chamber of commerce for information on companies in the area—the type of business, years of operation, and number of employees.

Prepare Questions to Ask the Interviewer

KEY POINT

Prepare questions about the company and the position based on information in the job posting and on your research of the company.

Researching a company will help you prepare to ask the interviewer intelligent questions. Here are some examples:

- I read that your company exports products to South America. What percentage of your product is shipped abroad?
- I know that your company has eight branch offices. Which office is experiencing the most growth?

After you are comfortably into the interview, you should also plan to ask some questions related to the prospective job. Questions you might ask the interviewer include:

- What are the opportunities for advancement?
- Would travel be required for this position?
- Are internal candidates being considered for this position?
- How soon will the decision for this position be made?
- What is the starting date for the position?
- Does the company provide training and additional education for employees who want to develop their skills?
- What benefits do you provide for employees?

Sometimes, a job applicant knows the salary offered for a position—at least the general range—before the interview. However, if you do not know the salary, and the interviewer has not mentioned it, you should ask about the salary near the end of the interview.

Know Your Strengths and Weaknesses

As a job applicant, you are a sales representative, and the product you are selling is yourself. Preparing a résumé gives you an excellent opportunity to put on paper what you have to sell—to emphasize your strengths and to present your education, experience, and special interests and skills in a way that makes you a strong candidate for the job. You should know your qualifications so well that you can communicate them orally without hesitation.

> **KEY POINT**
>
> Highlight strengths you have that fit the position for which you are interviewing.

Anticipate Questions

Anticipate questions that the interviewer may ask about your education, work experience, and personal qualities. Here are examples of possible interview questions:

- Why did you select this particular course of study?
- Which of these courses did you like best? Why? Which course did you like the least? Why?
- Tell me something about your course in communications (or some other subject).
- I see by your application that you worked as an intern at Austin Accounting for one semester. Describe the work you did. What did you like most about your job? What did you like least?
- What hobbies or activities do you enjoy in your spare time?
- Were you active in school organizations? Which ones?
- Do you like to write? How would you rate your English skills?
- Tell me about yourself. (This request will give you a chance to emphasize your most salable features, such as what do you do best?)
- Summarize your college courses and your work experience. (Emphasize the college courses or your work experience that will best support your qualifications for this job.)
- What are your strongest points? your weakest points?
- Tell me why you think you should be hired for this position.
- Why do you want to work for this company?

- Why did you leave your last position?
- What job would you like to have five years from now?
- Would you be willing to work overtime if necessary?
- Would you be willing to travel?
- Would you be willing to relocate?

Answers to such questions will help the interviewer assess your qualifications for the position, determine how quickly you would adjust to the job, and gauge your potential for growth.

Become Knowledgeable About Industry Trends and Current Events

Acquire a working knowledge of trends and issues in the industry (for example, insurance, banking, medical, legal, travel) in which the company does business. Also, keep up to date about local and national current events. Read a local newspaper to learn about issues, as well as cultural and civic events. Such knowledge demonstrates interest in the business and thoroughness in preparing for the interview.

PHYSICAL PREPARATION FOR THE INTERVIEW

Make sure you have the information and materials you need to keep your appointment and do well.

Confirm Your Appointment

About one week before the interview, write a letter or make a telephone call to confirm the appointment time, date, and place.

> Thank you for the opportunity to interview for the paralegal position with Grant and Jennings, Inc. I look forward to meeting with you on Tuesday, April 19, at 10:30 a.m., in your Locust Street offices.

Get Directions to the Interview Site

Ask the interviewer or that person's assistant for directions to the interview site. If you are taking public transportation, double-check the departure times and the travel time. If your interview is in a city or town with which you are unfamiliar, get a map of that city and study it. If possible, drive to the interview site the day before the interview to determine the travel time, route, and exact location of the interview. Make sure you have enough gas—or transportation money—for the trip.

KEY POINT

To prepare physically for an interview:
1. Confirm your appointment.
2. Get directions to the interview site.
3. Identify items to take.
4. Get a good night's sleep.

Identify Items to Take

To be prepared, take the following items to an interview:

- Two black ballpoint pens and a legal pad for taking notes.
- Three or four copies of your résumé and list of references, placed in a professional-looking folder with the legal pad mentioned above. Often you will interview with more than one person, and each interviewer may or may not have a copy of your résumé. Also, you can use an extra copy of your résumé as a reference in completing a job application form.
- A portfolio, if appropriate, that contains documents or projects that demonstrate your knowledge and qualifications for the position.
- A list of questions to ask the interviewer. Keep this list in the folder with your résumé. You should not read the list to the interviewer, but have it available to refresh your memory. You might review the list while waiting for your appointment.

Get a Good Night's Sleep

Part of your preparation should include eight to ten hours of sleep the night before the interview. Being sharp for the interview will boost your energy level and help you in answering questions.

THE INTERVIEW

When you arrive at the interview site, state your name and the purpose of your visit. While you wait, review your résumé, check your completed application form, skim any literature about the company that may be available in the reception area, or otherwise occupy yourself. Always convey a professional image.

Interviewing—From the Interviewer's Perspective

Most interviewers have three standard goals for an interview:

1. To give the applicant general information about the company and specific information on the position. Sometimes the interviewer will give the applicant printed information about the company and a printed job description.

2. To establish a positive rapport that makes the interview comfortable for the applicant. A skilled interviewer will try to put the applicant at ease to facilitate the interview process.

3. To get enough information from the candidate to make a decision about the person's suitability for employment with the company.

Making a Positive First Impression

Your punctuality and appearance contribute to the impression you make. Follow these suggestions to create a positive first impression.

Arrive Early for Your Appointment.　Allow an extra 30 minutes to arrive at the interview site. Traffic problems, weather, or simply getting lost could cause you to be late. Last-minute traffic delays can cause you to feel frustrated and apprehensive and cause you to feel stressed.

Dress in a Businesslike Way.　It is most important to look your best at an employment interview. Therefore, it's a good idea for men to take an extra shirt and tie and for women to take an extra blouse and hosiery for obvious reasons.

- Make sure your hair, nails, and shoes are neat and clean.
- Avoid bright colors; stick to neutral or conservative colors such as blue, green, gray, and brown.
- Men should wear a suit and tie. A suit is preferred over slacks and a sport coat.
- Women should wear a skirted suit. You want the interviewer to perceive you as a professional and the skirted suit contributes to that image. Avoid carrying a purse. Put your car keys and any other essentials in a pocket or a briefcase that contains your résumé.
- Be conservative about accessories. Avoid dangling and gaudy jewelry. Steer clear of anything that would be controversial. Men should not wear earrings, and women should limit their rings to one finger per hand.

Check Your Appearance While You Are Waiting to Be Called for the Interview.　Visit the restroom and make sure your hair and clothes are neat.

Demonstrate Your Self-Confidence by Using Good Posture. The impression you make when you first walk into the room will very likely influence the interviewer's attitude toward you throughout the entire interview. Preparing yourself, as outlined in this chapter, is the key to building self-confidence.

Beginning the Interview

When you are ushered into the interviewer's office, try to be relaxed (though not casual or arrogant) and to look pleasant. Follow these guidelines to get the interview off to a good start.

- Greet your interviewer with a firm handshake, a smile, and good eye contact. Introduce yourself and express your interest in employment with the company. Seat yourself only when you are invited to do so.

- Keep with you the materials you have brought. Don't place anything on the interviewer's desk unless you are invited to do so. When asked about your education and work experience, give the interviewer your résumé if you haven't already done so. Say something like: "Here is my résumé, which summarizes that information. I also have completed the application form." Then hand both to the interviewer.

- Follow the interviewer's lead. You will know at once—whether the interviewer is going to ask most of the questions or prefers that you take the initiative.

During the Interview

During the interview, you should conduct yourself in a professional manner when answering questions. Follow these suggestions:

Be Attentive and Speak Clearly. Face and speak directly to the interviewer. Don't stare at the floor or out the window while either of you is talking. Shift your gaze from the interviewer's eyes occasionally, but leave no doubt that you are talking and listening to him or her.

Speak slowly and enunciate carefully. Give your answers and statements in a straightforward manner; show that you have thought them through and that you can speak with precision. Give short answers that sufficiently answer the questions. For example, if you are asked this question, "I see you have had one course in accounting. Did you like it?" it is not enough simply to say yes. You might add, "I enjoyed the course very much, and I plan to take more accounting in evening school."

Be specific and honest about your qualifications. "My accounting courses consisted of principles, cost, and tax. In the cost course we were introduced to computerized accounting, and I especially enjoyed that." Or "One of the most challenging tasks in my internship was handling customers' reservations. It wasn't always easy to meet their requests since we had so many clients, but I was successful and learned much from the experience." When asked about your achievements or experiences, show the interviewer appropriate items from your portfolio.

KEY POINT

Usually, the interviewer will direct the proceedings.

KEY POINT

Be relaxed and follow the interviewer's lead.

Don't try to take so many notes in the interview that you are writing more than listening.

Figure 14.5

During an interview you should be attentive, speak clearly, and express confidence.

Be noncommittal about controversial matters. Try to respond positively to questions that ask you to critique yourself or someone else. If you are asked your opinion about your previous supervisor or place of work and your opinion isn't especially favorable, say something like this: "My work there gave me some valuable experience, and I enjoyed much of it" or "Ms. Adams was often helpful; I believe I profited from working with her."

Be objective in explaining why you left other positions. If you make negative comments about the people or the company policies of former employers, you may give the impression that you are a complainer. Say something like this: "I found it difficult to adjust to some of the procedures and to the unusual hours at Haggerty's." The interviewer will appreciate your frankness as well as your discretion.

Avoid bragging when you are asked about your strengths. Respond by identifying your strongest point, as in the following example: "I am very task oriented and work diligently until the project is completed."

When asked about your biggest weakness, answer the question truthfully and positively. "I'm a perfectionist and always want my work to be the best that I can do. However, I am working on this concern and find that I am now able to complete a project sooner that doesn't require perfection."

Express Confidence. If asked about leisure activities, mention activities that involve either physical energy or mental capabilities. Good answers would include jogging, playing tennis, reading, and working on your computer. Avoid giving poor answers such as watching television, shopping, and sleeping that might create a negative impression. Develop constructive leisure activities if you don't have any, because many interviewers ask this question to find out if you have initiative.

Relax and smile occasionally. Remember that the interviewer needs someone to fill an open position and is just as eager to make a decision in your favor as you are to get the job. Most interviewers are pleasant, friendly, and understanding.

Avoid nervous habits such as brushing lint off clothing, straightening and restraightening your tie, fussing with hair, toying with an object such as a purse or a paper clip, and putting hands to your face. Give your full attention to the interviewer.

Avoid the temptation to read materials on the interviewer's desk. This action could provide a negative impression about you.

If your interview involves dining, the best advice is to follow the lead of your interviewer. Ask for suggestions on menu items, but don't order the most expensive meal listed. Avoid foods such as spaghetti that are messy to eat. Let your interviewer begin eating first. Enjoy your meal, but remember that you are still under scrutiny. Use your best manners, and be sure to thank the interviewer for your meal.

Ending the Interview. The interviewer generally will let you know when the interview is over. The usual sign is to rise. As soon as the interviewer rises, you should also do so. The exchange that takes place might be something like the following conversation.

Interviewer (rising): I enjoyed meeting and talking with you.

Applicant (rising): Thank you, Ms. Alyman. I enjoyed meeting you and appreciate your letting me interview with your company.

Interviewer: We have your telephone number, and we will call you just as soon as we have reached a decision.

Applicant: Thank you. I'll look forward to hearing from you.

Interviewer: Good-bye.

Applicant: Good-bye.

Leave quickly and thank the receptionist as you depart.

Following Up the Interview

As soon as feasible after the interview, make notes of the names and titles of the people with whom you talked. Later the same day, write a summary from notes and memory of the facts you learned in the interview and the opinions you formed about the company and the job for which you were interviewed. If you are interviewing for jobs in several different companies, this written summary will prove an excellent way to refresh your memory about an interview when you are trying later to make your final job choice.

OOPS!

"What do you make here?" Asking this question during a job interview can prevent you from being considered for the position because it makes you look unprepared.

KEY POINT

As soon after the interview as feasible, make notes of the names and titles of the people with whom you spoke.

Interview Follow-Up Letters. After you have been interviewed, it is a good strategy to write the interviewer. Getting the follow-up letter on the interviewer's desk a day or two after the interview will make an extremely good impression on the interviewer. The follow-up letter puts your name before the interviewer again, and it gives you a second opportunity to sell yourself by mentioning pertinent qualifications. A basic follow-up letter might read as follows:

> Dear Ms. Tyson:
>
> Thank you for meeting with me on April 15 to discuss the medical assistant position at Rose Valley Clinic.
>
> Your description of the position gave me a clear picture of the responsibilities that a medical assistant has at your facility. The duties you discussed fit well with my training and my internship experience at Belmont Manor.
>
> After visiting your facility, I am convinced I could make a positive contribution to your patient-care team. I look forward to hearing from you soon.

If you have not heard from the company in one to two weeks after the interview, you may want to write a follow-up letter. Send a follow-up letter to each person with whom you interviewed. In the letter, express your continued interest in the position and ask that your application remain on file. In another month, if you are still looking for a position, write another letter reiterating your interest in a position with the company.

> On April 2 I interviewed with you for the position of computer operator. At the interview, you indicated that you would make a decision within two to three weeks.
>
> I am still very interested in the position and would like you to keep my application current. Please contact me at 216-555-4253 if you need additional information about my qualifications.

Handling Rejections. Be positive, but be realistic. You may get the job for which you interview, but you may not. Whether you are turned down once or many times, don't take the rejection personally. Depending on the job market at the time you are applying, you may need to go on many interviews to get the job that you really want. You must view each interview as a learning experience. Use again the strategies that worked well, and eliminate or improve the ones that were ineffective.

SECTION 14.2   REVIEW

Practical Application

1. Prepare written answers to each of the following questions and statements likely to come up in an employment interview.
   a. Why do you want to work for our company?
   b. What kind of work do you enjoy doing most?
   c. What kind of work do you enjoy doing least?
   d. What are your job goals for the next five-year period?
   e. Tell me about yourself.
   f. Why did you leave your last position?
   g. How do you spend your spare time?
2. List eight dos and eight don'ts in preparing for an interview.
3. List ten dos and ten don'ts to be observed during the interview.
4. Assume you are being interviewed for a position at York Travel Services. Your interviewer says, "I notice that Fred Gustafson was your supervisor at Metro Travel. I've heard that he is a tough person to get along with. Did you like working with him?" Compose the answer you would give your interviewer.

Communicating and Your Career

The quality of a person's life is in direct proportion to their commitment to excellence, regardless of their chosen field of endeavor.

—Vincent Lombardi, former coach of the Green Bay Packers

As you have learned in this text, written, oral, and nonverbal communication skills play a critical role in the job application and interview process. Once you have been offered a position, you must communicate your acceptance or refusal. Once you are on the job, you will have the opportunity to polish your skills. In other words, the written and oral communication skills you learn in school form the base for the skills you will use throughout your career.

SECTION 14.3

OBJECTIVES:
After completing Section 14.3, you should be able to:

1. Write letters accepting or declining a position.
2. List guidelines for resigning a position.
3. Explain why communication is essential to successful employment.

ACCEPTING OR DECLINING A POSITION

Suppose that you receive a letter offering you a position in a company to which you applied. You decide to take the job. If you are to start work almost immediately or if a reply has been requested by a certain date, you should probably telephone to inform the employer of your decision. Writing a letter is appropriate if your reporting date is two or more weeks away or if the representative is out of town. You might use the style illustrated in the following letter.

> I am pleased to accept the position as editorial assistant with the catalog department of Gilreath Exports. I know that I shall enjoy working with you in designing and producing your promotional and sales materials.
>
> As you requested, I shall report to work on Monday, September 18. Thank you for the confidence you have expressed in me by giving me this opportunity.

Some companies send a letter outlining the job offer and requesting that the applicant sign and date the letter and return it by a specified date to accept the offer.

You may, however, decide not to take the position. Declining a job offer should be done tactfully because you may be interested in working for that firm later in your career. Here is a sample letter.

> Thank you for offering me the position of office manager for your medical practice. Since we last talked, I have been offered and have accepted a position as office manager in a real estate office. Working in a real estate office will help me achieve my long-term goal of becoming a commercial real estate sales representative. My new employer is already encouraging me to begin studying for the licensing exam.
>
> Thank you, Ms. Reynolds, for your time and courtesy in interviewing me. I appreciate your considering me for the position in your office.

Occasionally, it may be necessary to inform an employer that you will not be taking a job that you have already accepted. You should avoid this situation if at all possible. If, however, you find yourself in this awkward position, you need to give the firm offering the first job some solid reasons justifying your change of heart. Here is a sample.

> This morning, I received an offer from another firm that closely matches my qualifications and career plans. The person who will be my supervisor in this firm considered my experience and education sufficient to place me well above entry-level status. In addition, he has arranged for me to take several advanced training courses in my field of interest.
>
> I feel that I must accept this opportunity, which means declining the position you offered me. I apologize for any inconvenience my decision may cause you.

After you have accepted a job, you should personally thank each person who helped you get the job. You should write a brief note or letter to the people who provided job leads, introductions to potential employers, or personal references.

You will be pleased to learn that I have accepted a position as medical technologist with Harris Regional Laboratories, Inc., in Chicago. The staff of Harris Regional performs diagnostic tests for eight large hospitals. I start work next week, and I am eager to begin my new position. The job fits well with my qualifications.

Thank you very much for letting me use your name as a reference. I am sure that your recommendation was instrumental in my being hired.

LEAVING A POSITION

Most people change jobs several times in the course of their careers. You may leave a position for another job or for personal reasons. Resigning from a job requires almost as much tact, diplomacy, and care as applying for a job. You should leave on good terms with your employer. You may want to work for this company again someday, or you may need to use your supervisors as references. Follow these guidelines when you resign from a job:

1. Make an appointment with your immediate supervisor, and hand your letter of resignation to him or her.

2. In your letter and in the comments you make during the appointment, indicate that you enjoyed working for the organization and with the other employees. You might mention that the experience gained with the company has helped you develop in your career.

3. Give a two-week advance notice that you are leaving, unless your company handbook or employment agreement specifies a longer time period.

4. If you are leaving under unpleasant circumstances, express your reasons in a positive way: "I feel that Guffy Accounting will offer me some new challenges and a greater opportunity for advancement."

5. Make certain that all your work is up to date and that your papers and files are clearly marked and well organized.

6. Leave a list of instructions or suggestions that may be helpful for your successor.

Here is a sample letter of resignation.

Last week, I received a job offer from Savannah Computer Solutions in Georgia. They have offered me a position as senior systems analyst, which represents a major career advancement for me. I have accepted the position.

Please accept my resignation effective November 8. I would be happy to help you find and train a replacement for my position.

Working with you, Alicia, has been a pleasure. You hired me directly after my college graduation, and you helped me grow and develop my skills in computer programming. I have learned a great deal about programming and troubleshooting in working with you and the other programmers in our department. I appreciate DataTrac's investment in my career development.

SECTION 14.3   REVIEW

Practical Application

1. Assume that you have accepted a position as office assistant with Worldwide Travel Agency, 1400 Springfield Avenue, Lansing, Michigan 48901. Write a letter of acceptance to Patricia C. Smith, the director of the agency. In addition, write a letter to William Mazur, your communications teacher at Salem Community College, who served as a reference for you.
2. Although you accepted the position with Worldwide Travel and are scheduled to start work on June 1, on May 22 you were offered a better position with Worldwide's main competitor. This position has greater potential for advancement, a higher starting salary, and better fringe benefits. You have decided to accept the better offer. Write another letter to Patricia C. Smith at Worldwide, explaining why you have changed your mind and must decline the position.

Editing Practice

The Supervising Editor. The following sentences lack writing polish. Edit and rewrite them on a separate sheet of paper.
1. Nothing should be done to change the procedure. You must see to it that it doesn't.
2. The ruling which takes affect today is the one concerning tardiness.
3. The reason Mel was late is because he had to pick up a report from another branch.
4. I have difficulty in distinguishing one to the other.
5. Under the last line in the return address on the envelope is to be printed his name and title.

Critical Thinking Skills

Explain. On a separate sheet of paper, write a memo to new employees explaining why communication is the key to successful employment in your company.

Making a Mess of Marketing Yourself. Tracy Stires was ready to graduate from her local community college with a degree in computer science. For three months, she had been sending her résumé and application letter to firms in her area and nationwide. She knew the job market was competitive, but her six-page résumé and two-page letter of application looked impressive and summarized in great detail her jobs and education. However, with all her efforts, Tracy had not received one request for an interview.

One day while reading her college's newspaper, Tracy discovered an article about the services offered by the college's Career Services and Placement Office (CSPO). Counselors would review and help revise students' letters of application and résumés to yield the best possible results. The CSPO would match students with prospective employers and even set up the interviews. Students could also view tapes of practice interviews.

Tracy called the CSPO and made an appointment with Linda Donley, a counselor. Linda asked Tracy to bring copies of her latest résumé and letter of application.

At the meeting, Linda read Tracy's documents and discovered that the length was excessive and that they contained many format and typographical errors. "Tracy, I see you have not included an objective, references, and nonacademic activities," Linda asked.

"I didn't know I was supposed to," Tracy replied.

"I also notice that during the last three summers you were neither working nor going to school." Tracy thought it best not to tell Ms. Donley she had spent this time in California surfing with her friends.

"Do you send this résumé and letter to every company?"

"Of course," Tracy said proudly. "Do you have any ideas where I can send my résumé? I can't wait for an interview."

1. What guidelines could you give Tracy for the length and content of her résumé? application letter?

2. In what ways can Tracy tailor her employment documents for various firms to which she is applying?

3. What format guidelines could you give Tracy for producing documents that employers will read and that will stand out?

4. How should Tracy have responded to the question about what she was doing during the last three summers?

Answers to Checkups

Chapter 3
Expanding Language Skills

Section 3.1

Checkup 1, page 65

1. we (P), ticket (N), play (N), New York City (N)
2. I (P), Yvette Wilson (N), our (P), reservations (N), we (P), her (P)
3. They (P), software (N), Denver (N), month (N)
4. You (P), I (P), Tuesday (N), expansion (N)
5. She (P), Nashville (N), Memphis (N), sights (N)
6. David (N), Tamara (N), me (P), Midwest (N), their (P), part (N), country (N)

Checkup 2, page 66

1. seems
2. was planning
3. hired, promoted
4. has been

Possible verbs for sentences 5 through 8:

5. received, completed, finished, met (action); started, began (action)
6. is (being)
7. passed (action)
8. plans (action)

Checkup 3, page 68

1. adjective
2. adjective, adverb, adjective
3. adverb, adjective
4. adjective, adverb
5. adjective, adverb, adjective
6. adjective, adverb

Checkup 4, page 69

1. P (With), P (on), C (or)
2. P (to), P (for)
3. P (of), C (nor), P (through), P (during)
4. C (and), P (to), P (in), P (with)
5. P (on), C (but), P (on)

Checkup 5, page 71

1. person spoken about
2. person spoken about
3. person speaking

4. things spoken about
5. persons spoken about

Checkup 6, page 72

1. employees (simple)
2. participant (simple)
3. Harrison or Margaret (compound)
4. folders (simple)
5. salons and store (compound)

Checkup 7, page 73

1. are the newest members of our department.
2. has enrolled in the computer applications course.
3. should have at least three year's experience.
4. is scheduled for March 15.
5. have responded favorably to the new ad campaign.

Checkup 8, page 74

1. INT
2. IMP
3. D
4. E
5. D

Checkup 9, page 75

Clauses for 2, 4, and 5 will vary. Examples are in parentheses.

1. sentence
2. dependent (, he will announce the personnel changes.)
3. sentence
4. dependent (, there will be an in-service training session.)
5. dependent (, she will ask for volunteers to work overtime to cover the vacancy.)

Checkup 10, page 77

1. VP, PP, PP
2. IP, VP, IP, PP
3. IP, PP, PP
4. IP, PP, VP, PP
5. VP, PP

Checkup 11, page 79

Answers will vary. Possible rewrites are in parentheses.

1. fragment (, we must get signatures from both Jan and Bill.)
2. fragment (, we can complete the transaction today.)
3. sentence
4. sentence
5. fragment (, it has now expired and must be renewed.)

Section 3.2

Checkup 1, page 83

1. lenses, lenses
2. countries
3. attorneys
4. OK
5. Averys
6. OK
7. editors in chief
8. daughters-in-law
9. Barrys
10. supplies

Checkup 2, page 85

1. Misses Brown (or Miss Browns)
2. 20s
3. I's
4. OK
5. Jordans
6. OK
7. men
8. Messrs. Crantz and Fenner, Mses. Hillsdale and Kramer

Checkup 3, page 87

1. solos, videos
2. beliefs, loaves
3. portfolios, dittos
4. leaves, thieves
5. tomatoes, mosquitoes
6. watches, brushes
7. radios, concertos
8. bailiffs, handkerchiefs
9. trios, volcanoes
10. knives, gulfs

Checkup 4, page 88

1. analyses
2. pants
3. bacteria
4. OK
5. OK
6. thousand
7. dozen shrimp
8. OK

Section 3.3

Checkup 1, page 92

1. employees'
2. representatives'
3. employee's, company's

4. executives'
5. Riley's
6. OK
7. father's
8. men's

Checkup 2, page 94

1. Carmine and Rosa's wedding
2. his helping
3. your sending
4. Donna's
5. OK
6. someone else's (*Rob's* is possessive because the word *suggestion* is understood after *Rob's.*)
7. supervisors'
8. our working together

Checkup 3, page 97

1. change *there's* to *theirs*
2. change *whose* to *who's* (or *who is*)
3. change *they're* to *there*
4. change *Whose* to *Who's* (or *Who is*)
5. change *theirs* to *there's* (or *there is*)
6. change *its* to *it's* (or *it is*)
7. OK
8. change *its* to *it's* (or *it is*)

Section 3.4

Checkup 1, page 100

1. OK
2. change *her* to *she*
3. change *I* to *me* (Exception to rule: *to be* has the pronoun *him* before it.)
4. OK
5. I

Checkup 2, page 103

1. whom
2. Whoever
3. who
4. whom
5. who
6. whoever
7. OK
8. OK
9. change *whomever* to *whoever*
10. OK

Checkup 3, page 106

1. change *him* to *he*

2. OK
3. change *we* to *us*
4. change *we* to *us*
5. change *I* to *me*
6. change *he* to *him*
7. change *her* to *she*
8. change *her* to *she*
9. OK
10. change *me* to *I*
11. change *we* to *us*
12. OK

Checkup 4, page 107

1. that he himself wants to
2. they themselves decided to cancel
3. OK
4. OK
5. Judith and I
6. As Scott and he
7. Bill and I

Section 3.5

Checkup 1, page 110

1. has accepted
2. seemed
3. was; was announced
4. invited
5. want
6. are

Checkup 2, page 112

1. paint, painted, painted, painting
2. carry, carried, carried, carrying
3. type, typed, typed, typing
4. answer, answered, answered, answering
5. bake, baked, baked, baking
6. mark, marked, marked, marking
7. marry, married, married, marrying
8. trust, trusted, trusted, trusting
9. use, used, used, using
10. walk, walked, walking, walking

Checkup 3, page 113

Main verbs are underlined.

1. want
2. have already received
3. have been waiting
4. need
5. will be inspecting
6. can complete

7. will enter
8. will introduce
9. has been drafting
10. has been promoted

Checkup 4, page 117

Answers will vary. Sample sentences are given.

1. The detectives have questioned the suspects.
2. She wished for a break in the weather.
3. Dave has refused to adjust the schedule.
4. He evaluates all employees fairly.
5. George had remembered my birthday.
6. They are speaking at the luncheon.
7. The authors will have corrected all the errors.
8. My sister will be graduating in May.

Checkup 5, page 119

1. change *spoken* to *has spoken* (or *spoke*)
2. change *had began* to *had begun*
3. change *has went* to *has gone* (or *went*)
4. OK
5. change *seen* to *has seen* (or *saw*)
6. change *knowed* to *knew*
7. OK

Checkup 6, page 121

1. is (B)
2. is (B)
3. has been deliberating
4. was employed
5. have been (B) (*been* is the main verb; *have* is a helper)
6. have been sympathizing

Checkup 7, page 122

1. change *were* to *was*
2. OK
3. change *is* to *were*
4. change *was* to *were*
5. change *was* to *were*

Checkup 8, page 124

1. has told (T)
2. have left (I)
3. has been (B)
4. had been appointed (T)
5. will be (B)
6. will be televised (T)
7. apology (DO); him (IO)
8. report (DO); pilot (IO)
9. books, magazines (DO)
10. awards (DO); Fred, Marta (IO)

Checkup 9, page 125

1. set
2. lay
3. laid
4. rise
5. raise
6. sits
7. raised
8. set

Section 3.6

Checkup 1, page 129

1. wants; his
2. has; its; its
3. is; its
4. does; its
5. are; their; them
6. is; her; she

Checkup 2, page 131

1. change *there's* to *there are*
2. change *are* to *is*
3. change *are* to *is*
4. change *there's* to *there are*
5. change *there is* to *there are*
6. change *There is* to *There are*

Checkup 3, page 132

Simple subjects are given in parentheses.

1. OK (Anyone)
2. he or she must . . . present his or her (executive) You may use plurals to make the sentence more readable: Executives permitted to use the exercise facilities must present their identification at the desk when entering.
3. has submitted (Nobody)
4. wants; his or her (Each)
5. his or her (manager)
6. has (Neither)

Checkup 4, page 134

1. change *are* to *is*
2. change *is* to *are*
3. change *are printed* to *is printed*
4. change *was discussing* to *were discussing*
5. change *are leaving* to *is leaving*
6. change *were told* to *was told*
7. change *is used* to *are used*
8. change *have been criticized* to *has been criticized*

Checkup 5, page 136

1. change *have risen* to *has risen*
2. change *was damaged* to *were damaged*
3. OK
4. change *is concerned* to *are concerned*
5. OK
6. change *has already begun* to *have already begun*

Checkup 6, page 137

1. change *have* to *has*
2. change *are* to *is*
3. change *is* to *are*
4. change *are* to *is*
5. change *are* to *is* . . . *their* to *his or her*
6. change *is* to *are*

Checkup 7, page 138

1. are; their
2. is
3. likes; her
4. have
5. have; their

Checkup 8, page 139

1. OK
2. change *has* to *have* . . . *it* to *them*
3. OK
4. change *collects* to *collect* . . . *his* to *their*
5. change *has* to *have*
6. change *is* to *are*

Section 3.7

Checkup 1, page 144

1. Jack's (P, PR); two (L); well-known (C, D); spring (D)
2. three (L); his (P); younger (D); this (DM); Kansas City (PR)
3. Bill's (P, PR); six-month (C, L); beautiful (D)
4. Carla's (P, PR); crucial (D); new (D); West Coast (C, PR); insurance (D)
5. These (DM); tax-free (C); their (P); new (D)
6. third (L); T-shirt (C, D); substantial (D); our (P); struggling (D)
7. special (D); new (D); these (DM); important (D)
8. Dallas (PR); that (DM); our (P); their (P); Goldberg's (P, PR)

Checkup 2, page 146

1. change *fuller* to *more nearly full*
2. change *more better* to *better* . . . *more quiet* to *quieter* . . . *more big* to *bigger*

3. OK
4. omit *very*
5. change *the most* to *more*
6. omit *more*
7. change *largest* to *larger*
8. omit *very*

Checkup 3, page 148

1. change *court appointed* to *court-appointed*
2. OK
3. change *any one* to *either*
4. change *one another* to *each other*
5. change *any* to *any other*
6. change *anyone* to *any other*
7. change *five time* to *five-time*
8. change *any* to *any other*
9. change *15 minute* to *15-minute* . . . *two hour* to *two-hour*
10. change *word of mouth* to *word-of-mouth*

Checkup 4, page 150

1. PA
2. PN
3. PA; PA
4. PN
5. PN

Section 3.8

Checkup 1, page 155

1. SC; SA
2. SC
3. CA
4. SC
5. SA; SA; CA
6. SA; SC
7. SC; SA; SA
8. SA; CA; SA

Checkup 2, page 158

1. change *angrily* to *angry*
2. OK
3. change *real* to *really*
4. change *some* to *somewhat*
5. change *real* to *really*
6. OK
7. OK
8. change *sure* to *surely*
9. change *badly* to *bad*
10. change *good* to *well*

Section 3.9

Checkup 1, page 162

Prepositions are underlined.

1. of the reimbursement requests, on my desk, to the Accounts Payable Department
2. of the partners, with the billing procedures
3. into the conference room, with her assistant
4. on the site, of the midtown helicopter landing pad, by the planning board
5. in a hurry, to the airport
6. in my desk drawer
7. Between you and me, in that stock
8. for the delay, on the telephone

Checkup 2, page 165

1. change *in regards* to *in regard*
2. OK
3. change *different than* to *different from*
4. change *angry at* to *angry with*
5. change *plans on opening* to *plans to open*
6. OK
7. change *discrepancy in* to *discrepancy between*
8. change *retroactive from* to *retroactive to*
9. change *identical to* to *identical with*
10. OK

Checkup 3, page 168

1. change *between* to *among*
2. change *in* to *into*
3. change *besides* to *beside*
4. omit *of* from *all of*; omit *at*
5. omit *from*
6. omit *to*
7. omit *of* from *all of these*
8. omit *of* from *Both of the*
9. omit *for* from *like for*
10. OK
11. change *in* to *into*
12. change *inside of* to *within*

Section 3.10

Checkup 1, page 173

1. as soon as (S)
2. While (S)
3. both . . . and (CR)
4. and (CO)
5. If (S)
6. Unless (S)
7. whether . . . or (CR)

8. that (S)
9. either . . . or (CR)
10. or (CO)

Checkup 2, page 175

1. OK
2. change *like* to *as if* (or *as though*)
3. change *except* to *unless*
4. change *like* to *as if* (or *as though*)
5. change *without* to *unless*
6. change *like* to *as if* (or *as though*)
7. change *without* to *unless*
8. change *and* to *but*
9. change *because* to *that*
10. change *which* to *who* (or *that*)

Checkup 3, page 176

Sample sentences:

1. OK
2. You may send us your travel plans by telephone, by fax, or by e-mail.
3. Cathy enjoys reading, exercising, and traveling.
4. Fred, the cafeteria manager, said that the squash could be eaten steamed, fried, or raw.
5. Our response should be courteous, quick, and accurate.
6. The dietician told the patient that avoiding certain foods is necessary, but exercising is also essential to his overall health program.

Checkup 4, page 177

Sample sentences:

1. Among the activities I like best are both reading mystery novels and "surfing" the Internet.
2. In an effort to save fuel, we are trying either to form car pools or to use public transportation.
3. Coupons are usually mailed either to our best customers or to our prospective customers.
4. Our public relations brochure is both well written and colorfully illustrated.
5. For 50 years the antique shop has been owned by either Mr. Roselli or his father.
6. Selma went neither to the hospital nor to the clinic.

Chapter 4
Applying the Mechanics of Style

Section 4.1

Checkup 1, page 185

1. Q
2. P
3. P
4. Q
5. P
6. Q
7. P
8. P

Checkup 2, page 186

1. OK
2. change *$114.00* to *$114*
3. OK
4. change *$500.* to *$500*
5. change *Inc..* to *Inc.*
6. change *III.,* to *III,*

Checkup 3, page 187

Commas may be used for the periods in sentences 2, 3, and 8.

1. change to *ago, Andrea*
2. change to *Friday. She* or *Friday; she*
3. change to *deposit. He* or *deposit; he*
4. change to *hour, she*
5. OK
6. change to *hours when*
7. change to *meeting, we*
8. change to *morning. We*

Checkup 4, page 189

1. change to *rain?*
2. change to *presentation.*
3. OK
4. change to *airport.*
5. OK
6. change to *he?*
7. change to *car.*
8. change to *they?*

Section 4.2

Checkup 1, page 194

1. omit comma after *a.m.*
2. OK

3. omit comma after *drove*
4. add semicolon after *William*
5. add comma after *New York*
6. omit comma after *December*
7. add comma after *July*
8. OK

Checkup 2, page 196

1. add comma after *train*
2. OK
3. omit *and*
4. omit comma before *&*
5. add comma after *etc.*
6. add comma after *reservations*
7. replace comma after *airplane* with a semicolon
8. add comma after *Mark*

Checkup 3, page 199

1. add comma after *recommendation*
2. add comma after *airplane*
3. add comma after *October 1*
4. omit comma after *representative*
5. add commas after *approved* and after *moreover*
6. add comma after *manager*
7. add comma after *vacation*
8. omit comma after *software*
9. OK
10. add comma after *therefore*

Checkup 4, page 201

1. omit commas after *staff* and *CPA*
2. omit comma after *stationery*
3. add commas after *alternative* and *think*
4. OK
5. omit commas after *technician* and *lab*
6. add commas after *Steven* and *office*
7. add commas after *solution* and *yesterday*
8. OK
9. omit comma after *attorney*
10. add commas after *received* and *owned*

Checkup 5, page 204

1. add comma after *2002*
2. add commas after *divisions* and *Pharmaceuticals*
3. add comma after *Tennessee*
4. add comma after *Inc.*
5. OK
6. add comma after *Leonard*
7. add commas after *Madison* and *Wisconsin*
8. add comma after *Jr.*
9. OK
10. add comma after *Billings*

Checkup 6, page 205

1. add commas after *statement* and *checks*
2. omit comma after *shift*
3. OK
4. add commas after *outlet* and *South*
5. omit comma after *products*
6. omit commas after *gear* and *catalog*

Checkup 7, page 206

1. OK
2. *solid, high-yielding*
3. OK
4. *creative, talented*
5. *brilliant, ambitious, resourceful*
6. OK

Checkup 8, page 207

1. add commas after *Charlotte plant* and *Nashville plant*
2. add comma between *risky* and *risky*
3. add comma after *Ms. Adams*
4. add comma between *many* and *many*
5. add commas after *Industries* and *Communications*
6. add comma after *truth*

Section 4.3

Checkup 1, page 213

1. change *student,* to *student;*
2. change *view,* to *view;*
3. change *$1000,* to *$1000;*
4. change *period,* to *period;*
5. change *intriguing,* to *intriguing;*
6. OK
7. change *January,* to *January;*
8. change *machines,* to *machines;*

Checkup 2, page 215

1. change *service: My* to *service: my*
2. change *action. Go* to *action: Go*
3. change *areas;* to *areas:*
4. change *procedures,* to *procedures:*
5. change *arrived;* to *arrived:*
6. OK

Checkup 3, page 217

1. change *cruise fax* to *cruise–fax*
2. change *complete but* to *complete–but*
3. OK
4. change *pools, these* to *pools–these*
5. change *Shop, Shutter* to *Shop—Shutter*

Checkup 4, page 218

1. change *fruit—.* to *fruit.*
2. OK
3. change *them—?* to *them?—who*
4. change *work,—these* to *work—these*
5. OK
6. Change *available—? by* to *available?—by*

Section 4.4

Checkup 1, page 222

1. change *proposal"* to *proposal,"*
2. change to *catalog," said Pete, "will*
3. change to *so-called photo opportunity*
4. change *Fragile,* to *"Fragile,"*
5. change to *'Handle With Care.'"*
6. change to *"Stella Abernathy,"*
7. change to *session," announced . . . Mr. Norton, "because*
8. change to *announced, "Maria . . . Montreal."*

Checkup 2, page 225

1. change to *personnel" :*
2. change to *taxi!"*
3. OK
4. Change to *overstated" ;*
5. Change to *appliances" ?*
6. Change to *Taken."*
7. Change to *"Waste not, want not*
8. Use underscore or italics for *Interviews That Impress*

Checkup 3, page 227

1. OK
2. Change to *(we think . . . so),*
3. change to *marked),*
4. OK
5. Change to *page 34),*
6. Change to *Travel (formerly . . . Services"), is*
7. Change to *March 15.)*
8. Change to *move)?*

Section 4.5

Checkup 1, page 232

1. change to *One . . . One . . . Three*
2. change to *No,*
3. change to *"Tips for Business and Pleasure Traveling"* and *International Business and Marketing*
4. change to *"Continue*
5. change to *following: An*

6. change to *"Sincerely"*
7. change to *Significantly*
8. change to *Remember: When*
9. change to *"Labor-Management Problems and How to Avoid Them"*
10. OK

Checkup 2, page 235

1. change to *Computers in Schools Association . . . Hancock Building*
2. change to *Fourth of July . . . Von Hoffman*
3. change to *Chinese*
4. change to *Monday . . . August . . . autumn*
5. change to *Mexican*
6. change to *Sioux City*
7. change to *Von Aspern . . . Inn . . . Lake Lure*
8. change to *"Creativity in Business: A Guide . . .*

Checkup 3, page 237

1. change to *manager . . . Rotary Club . . . private dining room . . . hospital*
2. OK
3. Change to *president . . . Nashville*
4. Change to *cookies*
5. Change to *advertising agency*
6. Change to *Shipping and Receiving Department . . . Kennedy Memorial Hospital*
7. Change to *west*
8. Change to *president*
9. Change to *vans*
10. Change to *Federal*

Section 4.6

Checkup 1, page 241

1. OK
2. Change to *Mr. Gordon responded*
3. Change to *Senator*
4. Change to *Dr. Jacquelyn R. Benton will* or *Jacquelyn R. Benton, Ph.D., will*
5. Change to *Dr. Evelyn S. Stanley has* or *Evelyn S. Stanley, Ph.D., has*
6. Change to *Mr.*

Checkup 2, page 246

1. change *N.C.,* to *North Carolina,*
2. change *lb* to *pounds*
3. change *R.A.M. and R.O.M.* to *RAM and ROM*
4. change *10:30 AM* to *10:30 a.m.*
5. change *Wed., Dec. 9* to *Wednesday, December 9,*
6. change *CM* to *centimeters*
7. change *IND.,* to *Indiana,*

8. change *Tex. . . . Calif. . . . Ore.* to *Texas . . . California . . . Oregon*

Section 4.7

Checkup 1, page 251

1. change *12* to *Twelve*
2. change *1,000* to *thousand*
3. OK
4. Change *18th-century* to *eighteenth-century*
5. Change *9* to *nine*
6. Change *1970's* to *1970s*
7. Change *1/10* to *one-tenth*
8. Change *22* to *Twenty-two*
9. OK
10. Change *ten and a half* to *10.5 (or 10-1/2)*

Checkup 2, page 253

1. change *9 months to 1 year* to *nine months to one year*
2. change *two hundred seventy* to *270*
3. change *$360.00* to *$360*
4. change *50¢* to *$.50*
5. change *$.75* to *75 cents*
6. change *five . . . seven* to *5 . . . 7*
7. change *twelve* to *12*
8. change *13* to *13th*
9. OK
10. Change *$7* to *$7 million*

Checkup 3, page 255

1. change *three and a half parts . . . two parts* to *3-1/2 parts . . . 2 parts*
2. OK
3. OK (or *3rd of July*)
4. OK
5. Change *twelve feet . . . twenty feet* to *12 feet . . . 20 feet*
6. Change *May 2nd, 1996* to *May 2, 1996*
7. Change *three o'clock* to *3 o'clock*
8. Change *Jul 30 87 employees* to *July 30, 87 employees*

Chapter 5
Reading Effectively

Section 5.1

Checkup 1, page 263

1. speed; comprehension
2. reading for pleasure; specific data; retention or analysis; checking and copying

3. Less time: reading for pleasure and for specific data; More time: reading for retention and analysis and checking and copying

Section 5.2

Checkup 1, page 270

Answers will vary. Possible answers:

1. favorable opportunity or circumstance
2. property, character, attribute
3. in-cor-po-rat-ed
4. accomplishable, accomplisher

Chapter 6
Improving Listening Skills

Section 6.1

Checkup 1, page 288

1. False
2. False
3. True
4. False
5. True
6. False

Checkup 2, page 294

1. False
2. True
3. False
4. True
5. True

Chapter 7
Sharpening Writing Skills

Section 7.2

Checkup 1, page 324

1. taping
2. transmitted
3. wedding
4. OK
5. territories
6. scarring
7. believe
8. miscellaneous

9. necessarily
10. OK

Checkup 2, page 325

1. reversible
2. defendant
3. deductible
4. remittance
5. OK
6. Illegible

Checkup 3, page 326

1. complexion
2. ambitious
3. anxious
4. conscientious
5. beneficial

Checkup 4, page 327

1. particles
2. stationery; inventory
3. calendars
4. statistical; technical
5. exceeded

Section 7.4

Checkup 1, page 340

1. The samples you requested in your April 5 letter are enclosed.
2. Material on the Thornton account is in three large files.
3. Please include your payment with the completed order form.
4. Please give me your response by Friday.
5. To be successful, you should try harder.

Checkup 2, page 342

1. Although some additional options were presented, the manager decided to go with Susan's proposal.
2. Because the report is due March 4, Jeff has been working long hours on the calculations.
3. Despite the costs involved, we are committed to expanding our markets overseas.
4. Because our accounting department is understaffed, we propose hring three additional accountants.
5. Save the files in a new directory on the computer, and print a copy of each file.

References

To keep up to date on the subject of business communication, you should consult professional journals both in business and in communication. In addition, some of the following books may be of interest:

Axtell, Roger E., *Do's and Taboos of Using English Around the World*, John Wiley & Sons, Inc., New York.

Cormier, Robin A., *Error-Free Writing: A Lifetime Guide to Flawless Business Writing*, Prentice-Hall, New Jersey.

Flower, Linda, *Problem-Solving Strategies for Writing*, Harcourt Brace Jovanovich.

Tebeaux, Elizabeth, *Design of Business Communication: The Process and the Product*, Macmillan, New York.

Consult reference sources such as the following when in doubt about facts, spelling, or usage:

The American Heritage Dictionary of the English Language, Houghton Mifflin, Boston.

Bartlett, John, *Bartlett's Familiar Quotations*, Little, Brown, Boston.

Bernstein, Theodore, *The Careful Writer: A Modern Guide to English Usage*, Atheneum, New York.

Camp, Sue C., *Developing Editing Skill*, Glencoe/McGraw-Hill, Columbus, Ohio.

Camp, Sue C., *Developing Proofreading Skill*, Glencoe/McGraw-Hill, Columbus, Ohio.

The Chicago Manual of Style, University of Chicago Press, Chicago.

Fowler, H.W., *The New Fowler's Modern English Usage*, Oxford University Press, New York.

Gibaldi, Joseph, *MLA Handbook for Writers of Research Papers*, Modern Language Association of America, New York.

Hosler, Mary Margaret, and Charles E. Zoubek, *20,000+ Words*, Glencoe/McGraw-Hill, Columbus, Ohio.

Lee, Jo Ann, and Marilyn L. Satterwhite, *The Irwin Office Reference Manual*, Irwin Mirror Press, Richard D. Irwin, Inc., Burr Ridge.

Publication Manual of the American Psychological Association, American Psychological Association, Washington D.C.

Robert's Rules of Order, Berkley Publications, New York.

Roget's International Thesaurus, HarperCollins Publishers, New York.

Sabin, William A., *The Gregg Reference Manual*, Glencoe/McGraw-Hill, Columbus, Ohio.

Strunk, William, Jr., and E. B. White, *The Elements of Style*, Macmillan, New York.

Webster's Collegiate Dictionary, Merriam-Webster, Springfield, Massachusetts.

Note: Since these books are revised frequently, the edition numbers and dates of publication have not been given. Ask for the latest edition.

Note: Italicized page numbers indicate material in figures.

Abbreviations, 240–245
    address, 243–244, 480, 490
    all-capital, 44–45, 85, 242–243
    business, 243–244
    in companies and organizations, 203, 242–243
    days and months, 245
    degrees or titles, 203, 240–241
    initials, 241, 475, 481–482
    language differences and, 44–45
    miscellaneous, 245
    No., 245
    in personal names, 240–241
    sentences ending in, 185
    time expressions, 244
    units of measure, 244
Absolute adjectives, comparing, 146
Abstract words, 310
Academic degrees
    abbreviations of, 240–241
    commas with, 203
Accessibility, in customer service, 558
Accuracy, 504–505, 588
Accusations, 505–506
Acknowledgment
    of invitations, 54, 543
    of receipt of order, 512
    of requests, 508–509, 512
Acronyms, 44–45, 243
Action verbs, 66, 110, 157
Active listening, 285–286, 289–294
Active voice, 343, 364
Actual message, 11
Address(es)
    abbreviations in, 243–244, 480, 490
    electronic mail, 442–443
    inside, 478–480, 537, *538*
    mailing, 490
    in memo headers, 473
    numbers in, 253
    return, 489
Adjectival phrase, 161
Adjectives, 67, 142–149
    adverbs confused with, 156–158

articles, 67, 142
    commas with modifying, 206
    comparison of, 144–146
    compound, 143, 148
    demonstrative, 143–144
    descriptive, 142
    infinitive phrases as, 76
    limiting, 143
    overused, 316–317
    possessive, 142
    predicate, 149
    prepositional phrase as, 76
    proper, 143, 234
Adjustment letters, 516, 518–521
Administrative Management Society (AMS), 484
Adverbial clauses, 154
Adverbs, 67–68, 152–158
    adjective-adverb confusions, 156–158
    comparison of, 153–154
    conjunctive, 154
    defined, 152
    identifying, 152–153
    infinitive phrases as, 76
    pitfalls with, 155–156
    position of, 155
    prepositional phrase as, 76
Advertisements, newspaper, 622, 632
Afterthoughts, dashes with, 216
Age bias, 57
Agenda of meeting, 400–401, *401*, 442, 608
Ages, spelling out, 250–251
Agreement, predicate. See Predicate agreement
agree with, agree to, 163–164
all, both, 166
Allowable claim, 519
Almanacs, 574
almost, most, 158
a.m., p.m., 244, 254
American Psychological Association (APA) documentation format, 583–584

America Online, 186, 443, 446–447, 578
among, between, 166
Ampersand (&), 196
Analytical reports, 572–573
and, 69, 136–137, 172, 174, 193
and so, 342
Anecdotes, 422
angry with, angry at, 164
Anniversaries
    congratulations letters for, 540
    spelling out, 250–251
Announcements, written, 497–498
Antecedents, 107, 128–139, 138, 335–336. *See also* Predicate agreement
Antonyms, 318–319
any, anyone, anybody, 132, 147
anything, 132
Apostrophes
    in contractions, 95–96, 227–228
    plural form of nouns with, 85
    possessive form of nouns and, 91–94
Appeals, sales, 527
Appearance, 8, 27
    bias based on, 57
    of letters, 477–486
    oral communication and, 387–388, 416–419
Appendix, 602
Application form, 634
Application letter, 631–634, *632*
Appointments
    confirming, 640
    delays in, 562
    receiving visitors for, 561–564
Appositives, 94, 105, 202
Archie, 446
are, our, 96
Articles (*a, an, the*), 67, 142
as, as if, as though, 104–105, 175
as regards, 164–165
at, to, 167
Atmosphere, 383, 402

Attention, attracting, 526
Attention line, 480
Attitude, positive, 15, 288, 407, 421,
     514–515
Audience
     awareness of, transmitting, 418
     eye contact with, 389–390, 422, 643
     of sales letters, targeting, 524
     of speech, 411
     words suited to, using, 314, 361–362
Audiovisual materials, 414–416
Auxiliary (helping) verbs, 77, 112–113
Awareness of audience, transmitting,
     418

bad, badly, 156, 157
Balancing techniques (parallel
     structure), 176–177, 344–347
Bar graphs, 601, *602*
Baronial letterhead, 538
Barriers, to effective communication,
     9–10
because, 174
behind, 167
being that, 174
"Being" verbs, 100, 101, 110, 120–121,
     149, 157
beside, besides, 166
between, among, 166
Bias, 56–59, 287–288
Bias-free language, 56–59
Bibliography
     in American Psychological
          Association (APA) format, 584
     in *Chicago Manual of Style* format,
          583
     in formal report, 602
     in Modern Language Association
          (MLA) format, 584
     working, 581, *581*
Binding, report, 605
Biographical names, 309
Block letter format, *479*, 482–483
     modified, 483, *485*
          with indented paragraphs, 483, *483*
     salutation in, 480
Body language, 5, 7, 45, 297–298, 388,
     419
Body movement, 390
Boilerplate paragraphs, 545, *550*
Bold type, 461
both, all, 166
Brand names, 45, 237
British English, 308
Browsers, 445, 446, 578
Bullets, 461
Business abbreviations, 243–244
Business cards, 42
Business communication, 24–29
     components of, 26–27

cross-cultural communication in,
     41–49
ethics in, 50–53
importance of good, 24–25
skills, developing, 27–29,
     460
Business letters. *See* Letter(s)
but, 69, 172, 174, 193
Buying motives, 525

Calendar dates. *See* Dates
Caller ID, 434
Camera-ready copy, 37
Capitalization, 230–237
     all-capital abbreviations, 44–45, 85,
          242–243
     after colons, 215, 231
     of commercial products, 237
     dictionary information on, 306–308
     first words, 231
     main words, 232
     names of persons, places, and things,
          233–234
     of personal and official titles, 236
     pitfalls with, 235–236
     proofreaders' marks for, *359*
     of proper adjectives, 234
     of short forms, 235–236
Career goals, 618, 624
Case forms of pronouns. *See* Pronoun(s)
Casual conversations, listening in,
     296–298
CD-ROMs, 447, 577
Cellular phones, 35, 36, 380, 438–439
Centuries, spelling out, 251
Chairperson of meeting, 402–406, 442
Charts, 602
Chat rooms, 447
Chicago Manual of Style documentation
     format, 583
Chronological résumés, 626, *626*
Citations, documenting, 580–585
City names, abbreviating, 243
Claim(s)
     allowable, 519
     evaluating, 504, 516–518
     nonallowable, 520–521
     partially allowable, 519–520
Claim letters, 503–506
Clarity, 28, 365
     of informal report, 588
     of speech, 412
     of writing, 460
Clause(s), 74–75
     adverbial, 154
     agreement problems with intervening,
          130–131
     balancing, 347
     dependent, 75
          comma, rules for, 198–200

relative pronoun (*who, that, which*),
     138, 174, 204, 332–333
subordinating conjunctions,
     introducing, 154
independent, 75
     comma splice, 187
     conjunctive adverbs joining, 154
     punctuation between, 194,
          195–196, 211–213
introductory, punctuating, 198–199
proper subordination of ideas in,
     341–342
in thought units, 332
who, whom (or *whoever, whomever*)
     used in, 102–103
Clichés, 44, 317–318
Clip art, 432
Closing remarks after speech, 423
Clothing styles, 45
Code of ethics, 53, *53*
Collection letters, *529*, 529–530
Collective-noun simple subject,
     predicate agreement with, 133
College Placement Annual, The, 622
College placement centers, 621
Colon, 213–215
     capitalizing first word after, 215, 231
     dashes vs., 215
     at end of quotation, 224
     in letter salutation, 480
Color, of stationery, 488
Color coding, 462
Columns, 461
Combination résumés, 627, *628*
Comma(s), 192–209
     before abbreviations after personal
          names, 241
     with appositives, 202
     avoiding use of, 196
     with calendar dates, 203
     in compound sentence, 193–194
     between consecutive numbers, 255
     with degrees, titles, and other
          explanatory terms, 203
     in direct address, 207
     at end of quotation, 223, 224
     with explanatory elements, 201
     following introductory words,
          phrases, and clauses, 197–199,
          212
     with interrupting elements, 200
     with modifying adjectives, 206
     in numbers and between unrelated
          numbers, 208, 255
     for omissions, 207
     with parenthetic elements, 200–201
     pitfalls with, 205, 208–209
     with repeated expressions, 207
     separating subject from predicate, 205
     separating verb from object, 205
     in series, 195–196, 206

Commas *(cont.)*
  with state names, 204
  with subordinate clause following
    main clause, 199–200
  in weights, capacities, and
    measurements, 209
  in *which* and *that* clauses, 204
Comma-for-period fault, 187
Comma splice, 187
Common-gender nouns, 131–132
Common nouns, 64–65, 82
Communication
  avoiding discrimination in, 56–59
  business, 24–29
  components of, 6–7, *6*
  defined, 4
  to develop goodwill, 11–12, 466,
    514–515
  factors influencing, 7–11
  to inform. *See* Informing
  to inquire. *See* Requests
  interpersonal skills, developing,
    11–15
  means of, 7
  nonverbal, 3, 5, 7, 17, 45, 388, 419
  to persuade. *See* Persuading
  purposes of, 5–6
  six Cs of, 27–29, 365–367, 460
  types of, 4–5
Communication breakdowns, avoiding,
  9–10
Communication networks, 37, 441–448
  electronic mail (e-mail), 442–443. *See
    also* Electronic mail (e-mail)
  Internet, 443–448. *See also* Internet
  local area networks, 442
  wide area networks, 442
Communication skills, 17–23
  business, 27–29, 460
  combining, for effectiveness, 18–22
  roles of, 18–22
  of sender and receiver, 8, 11–15
  value of, 22–23
Company letterhead, 478, *479*, 488–489,
  537–538
Company names, 196, 203, 242–243,
  481
Company recognition, congratulations
  letter for, 541
Company research, for employment
  interview, 637–638
Comparative degree, 144, 145, 153–154
Comparison(s)
  of adjectives, 144–146
  of adverbs, 153–154
  balancing, 344–345
  double, 146
Complaints, handling telephone,
  564–565
Completeness
  of communication, 28, 365–366

of requests, 499–500, 504–505
of responses to requests, 512–514
of writing, 460
Complete predicate, 72
Complexity, and electronic
  communication, 453
Complimentary closing, 231, 481
Compliments, 383
Compound adjectives, 143, 148
Compound nouns, 82–83, 93
Compound objects, pronouns in, 103
Compound sentence, punctuating,
  193–194, 211–213
Compound subject, 72
  predicate agreement with, 136–138
  pronouns in, 104
Comprehension
  listening, 289–294
  reading, 272–275, 276–278, 300
CompuServe, 186, 443, 446–447, 578
Computer(s), 37, 430
  electronic office, communicating in,
    34–39
  proofreading on, 369–370
  See also Software, computer; Word
    processing software
Computer-assisted data search, 446–447
Computer-friendly résumés, 629–631
Computer workstation, 37
Conciseness, 28, 366, 383, 408, 460,
  588
Conclusion
  to formal report, 600–601
  of meeting, 405
  of speech, 423
Condensed expressions, punctuating,
  187
Condolence letters, 542–543
Conference calls. *See* Teleconferencing;
  Videoconferencing
Conferences. *See* Meeting(s)
Confidence
  in giving speeches, 418
  and job interview, 642, 644–645
Confidentiality, 15, 52–53, 429, 437,
  451
Congratulations letters, 539–541
Conjunctions, 69, 171–177
  balancing, 346–347
  coordinating, 172, 176
  correlative, 172, 177
  misplaced, 177
  omission of, semicolon to indicate,
    212
  parallel structure and, 176
  pitfalls with, 174–175
  repeated, in series, 196
  so and *and so* faults, 342
  subordinating, 154, 172–173
Conjunctive adverbs, 154
Connotation, 314–315

Consecutive numbers, 255
Consistency, 28, 366, 460
Consonants, doubling final, 323–324
Continuation pages, 489
Contractions, 95–96, 227–228
Conversation. *See* Oral communication
Conversational atmosphere, 383
Coordinating conjunctions, 172, 176
Coordination vs. subordination, 341
Copy notations, 482
Correctness, of communication, 29, 367,
  460
Correlative conjunctions, 172, 177
Coupons, 528
Courtesy, 15, 29
  acknowledging invitations, 54
  acknowledging requests, 508–509
  of condolence letters, 542–543
  editing for, 367
  making introductions, 54, 422, 423
  in meetings, 407–408, 422, 423
  in requests and responses, 502–503
  smoking policies and, 54
  in telephone communication, 384,
    564–565
  of thank-you letters, 54, 541–542
  to visitors, 562
  of writing, 460
Courtesy titles, 84–85, 240–241, 473,
  480
CPU (central processing unit), 37
Credit letters, *529*, 529–530
Cross-cultural communication, 41–49
  domestic, 41–43
  greetings in, 46, 435, 480, 567
  international, 43–49
Cues, verbal and nonverbal, 292–293
Cultural diversity, 10, 20, 41–49
Culture
  defined, 41
  in domestic communication, 41–43
  in international communication,
    43–49
Currency, differences in, 48
Customer service, 553–569
  customer contact and, 557–565
    accessibility and, 558
    continuous contact, 559
    knowledgeable responses in, 559,
      564
    receiving the public, 561–564
    telephone communication,
      564–565
  defined, 554–555
  external and internal customers,
    555
  need for, 555
  as ongoing function, 556
  policies and procedures, 568
  responding to requests, 508–521
Customs, 20

Dangler, 335
Dashes, 215–218
Databases, 574
Database software, 37, 428–429, *429*, 431–432
Data files, 548
Date code, 478
Dates
    abbreviations in, 245
    commas with, 203
    figures in, 255
    in informal reports, 587–588
    in letters, 478
    in memos, 475
    and secondary source information, 574
Days
    abbreviations for, 245
    capitalization of, 234
Decades, spelling out, 251
Decimal numbers, 254
Declarative sentences, 74, 184, 189
Dedicated word processors, 430. *See also* Word processing software
Definitions
    dictionary, 270, 306
    multiple, awareness of, 44
    quotation marks around, 222
Degrees, academic. *See* Academic degrees
Delays, in appointments, 562
Demands, 505–506
Demonstrative adjectives, 143–144
Denotation, 314–315
Dependent clause, 75
    comma rules for, 198–200
    relative pronoun (*who, that, which*), 138, 174, 204, 332–333
    subordinating conjunctions introducing, 154
Derivatives, 269–270, 308
Descriptive adjectives, 142
Descriptive words, 319
Desktop publishing software, 35, 37, 432
Diagrams, 602
Dialect, 43
Dictation, 380
Dictionary, 268–270, *269*, 306–309, *307*
    electronic, 311, 430
    plurals requiring, 86–88
    spelling pitfalls requiring, 324–327
    of synonyms, 311
different from, 165
Diplomacy, 514–515, 649–650
Direct address, commas in, 207
Direct approach, in writing, 458–459
Directions
    giving, 496–497
    for job interview site, 640
    parentheses for enclosing, 226

Direct object, 122–123
Direct questions, 188
Direct quotation, 221, 231
Disability bias, 57, 59
discrepancy in, discrepancy between, discrepancy among, 164
Discretion with visitors, 563–564
Discrimination, 56–59
Distance learning, 441
Distractions, 9, 18
Distribution lists, 473–474, *474*
Diversity, 10, 20, 41–49
Division, word, 269, 308
Documentation of sources, 580–585
    formats for, 583–585
    highlighting in, 582
    note taking in, 582
    paraphrasing in, 582–583
    plagiarism in, 582–583, 604
    working bibliography in, 581, *581*
Document name, 475, 482
Dollar amounts, 186
Domain, electronic mail, 442–443
Double comparisons, 146
Double negatives, 155–156
Dow Jones News/Retrieval, 447
Downward communication, 25
Dress, 45, 390, 417, 642

each, 132
each other, 147
Editing, *361*, 365–367
Education
    assessing, 618
    communication skills used in, 19–22
    on résumé, 624
Educational teleconferencing, 441
either, neither, 132, 147
Electronic bulletin boards (EBBs), 447–448
Electronic communication, 34–39, 427–455
    desktop publishing and, 35, 37, 432
    factors to consider, 449–454
    information processing, 428–429
    integrated software in, 431–432
    optical character recognition (OCR), 432
    teleconferencing, 4, 299, 405, 439–441
    videoconferencing, 4, 299, 440–441
    See also Telecommunications; Word processing software
Electronic mail (e-mail), 35, 36, 38, 442–444
    advantages of, 450, 451, 452, 464
    composing, 443
    documenting, 584–585
Electronic meetings. *See* Teleconferencing

Electronic reference tools, 311
Electronic sources
    documenting, 584–585
    using, 574, 576–579, 622
Elliptical expressions, 70
else, "more than" comparisons using, 147
Emotional distractions, 9, 18
Empathy, 14
Emphasis
    colons for, 214
    highlighting for, 300, 582
    underscoring (italics) for, 461
Employment
    accepting or declining position, 648–649
    career goals, 618, 624
    leaving a position, 649–650
    See also Job search
Employment contractors, 623
Employment interview, 634, 637–646
    behavior during, 641–645
    following up, 645–646
    planning for, 637–641
    See also Job search
Enclosure reminder, 482
Endnotes, 583, 604
English as a second language (ESL), 13, 44
    figures of speech and, 10
    translations, 27, 45, 153
Enumerations, 461
    as informal report form, 590
    in response to requests, 513, *513*, *514*
    semicolon before, 212–213
    See also List(s)
Enunciation, 393–397, 643
Envelopes, 244, 489–491, *491*, 526
Environment, office, 18, 36
Errors, proofreading for, 358–360
Esteem needs, 13
etc., 195
Ethics, 50–53
    code of ethics and, 53, *53*
    confidentiality and, 52–53
    defined, 50
    ethical communication and, 52
    facts vs. opinions in, 51
Ethnic bias, 57–58
Etiquette, 45, 54. *See also* Courtesy
Etymology, 269–270
Evaluation
    of claims, 504, 516–518
    listening and, 292–293
    of oral presentation, 421
Events, announcing, 497
everyone, everybody, 132
Exclamation points, 70, 189–190, 224
Exclamatory sentences, 74
Executive-sized stationery, 488, 538

Experience
    and job search, 619, 621, 624
    in receiving communication, 8
Explanatory elements, punctuating, 201,
    212–213
Expressions
    interrupting, 342
    overused, 316–318
    transitional, 154, 351–353, 362
External communication, 27
External customers, 555
External database, 429
Eye contact, 46, 297, 389–390, 418,
    422, 643

f, fe, plural or nouns ending in, 87
Face-to-face conversation, 379,
    382–383, 440–441
Facial expressions, 389
Facilitator of meeting, 402–406, 442
Facilities, meeting, 401–402
Facsimile (fax) machines, 37, 437,
    450
Facts
    for claim letters, 504
    consistency in, 28
    opinions vs., 51, 407
Familiar tone of sales letter, 526, *528*
Feasibility studies, 573
Feedback, 7
    electronic communication and, 452
    questions and, 12–13
Figures, numbers expressed in, 252–255
Figures of speech, 44
File copies of informal report, 588
File name notation, 475, 482
File transfer protocol (FTP), 446
Flaming, 444
Flowcharts, 602
Flow of communication, 25
Follow-up
    on employment interview, 645–646
    letters in, 530, 646
Footnotes, 583, 604
Force (volume) of voice, 391
Foreign nouns, 87–88, 134
Formal invitations and replies, 54, 543,
    543
Formal meetings, 405
Formal reports, 594–605
    letter of transmittal, 603
    mechanics of, 603–605
    organizing, 595–596
    preparing to write, 594–595
    progress reports, 572, 603
    purpose and scope of, 595, 598–599
    style, 596–597
    supplementary material, 601–602
    writing, 596–605
    See also Reports

Format
    business letter, 482–486, 537–538
    documentation, 583–585
    memo, 471–476
    minutes of meeting, *609*
    news release, *612*, 612–613
    paragraph, 353–354
    report, 583–585, 604–605
    résumé, *626–628*, 629–631
    special techniques for, 461–462
Form files, 548
Form letters, 545–550, *547, 549, 550*
Form paragraphs, 545, 548, *549*
Fractions, 250
Fragments, 78
French, 54
Friendliness, 384, 418
from, off, 167
From line
    in informal report, 587
    in memos, 475
Functional résumés, 627, *627*
Future perfect tense, 115, 117
Future progressive tense, 116, 117
Future tense, 115, 116

Gender bias, 56–57
Geographical names. *See* Place names
Gerund, 93–94
Gerund phrases, 198
Gestures, 388, 419
Gifts, thank-you letters for, 54, 541
GIGO (garbage-in, garbage-out), 573
Global changes, 369–370
good, well, 158
Goodwill, 11–12
    memos and, 466
    positive attitude and, 514–515
Gopher, 446, 584–585
Grammar checkers, 364–365, 430
Graphic displays, 45, 414–416, 432,
    601–602, 604
Greetings, cultural differences in, 46,
    435, 480, 567
Grooming, 390, 417, 642
Group communication. *See* Meeting(s)

Handbook of style in dictionary, 309
Handouts, 416
Hands, placement of, while speaking,
    388
Handwritten messages, 54
Hard copy, 452–453
he, 335
Headings, 461
    capitalization in, 232
    in formal reports, 596, 604
    in memos, 468–469, *472,* 473–475
    punctuating, 185

    résumé, 629
    side, 461
Hearing, 284
help, 167
Helping verb, 77, 112–113
Highlighting information, 300, 582
Holidays
    capitalization of, 234
    domestic, 43
    international, 48
    religious, 42, 48
Home pages, 445
Homonyms, 95–96, 311–313
Honesty, 50–51
Honors, congratulations letters for, 541
Horizontal communication, 25
Hospitality, thank-you letters for, 54,
    542
Human interest stories, 422
Humor, 42, 413
Hypertext links, 445, 577–578
Hyphenation
    in compound adjectives, 148
    dictionary information in, 269, 308
    in titles, 232

I-attitude, 15, 339–340
Ideal job, 619–620
identical with, 165
Idiomatic usage, 34, 162–165, 317
Illiteracies, 311
Illustrations
    in dictionary, 270
    in formal reports, 601–602, 604
Imperative sentences, 70, 74
Imperative sentences, periods after, 184
in, into, 167
in back of, 167
Inc., 242
Incomplete sentences, 187
Indefinite numbers, 250
Indefinite-word subject, predicate
    agreement with, 132
Independent clauses, 75
    comma splice, 187
    conjunctive adverbs joining, 154
    punctuation between, 194, 195–196,
        211–213
Indexes, 573
Indirect approach, in writing, 459
Indirect object, 122–123
Indirect question, 185, 189
Indirect quotations, 221
Indirect sales techniques, 508, 511, *535*
Infinitive phrases, 76, 197–198
Infinitives, 100, 101, 114, 124
Inflectional forms, 270, 308
Informal reports, 586–592
    formal reports vs., 594
    forms of presentation, 589–591

Informal reports *(cont.)*
   planning and writing, 588–589
   style of, 586–587
   unsolicited, *591*, 591–593
   See also Reports
Information processing, 428–429
Information superhighway. *See* Internet
Informative reports, 572
Informing, 5, 379, 496–498
   giving directions, 496–497
   giving instructions, 496
   making announcements, 497–498
   memos for, 465
   reports for, 572
in front of, in back of, 167
Initials, 241
   reference, 475, 481–482
Inquiries, 5. *See also* Requests
in regard to, 164–165
inside, outside, 166
Inside address, 478–480, 537, *538*
Instruction, 379, 380
Instructions, giving, 496
Intended message, 11
Intensive use of pronouns ending in *self*,
   106–107
Interaction method, 405–406
Interest, 8
Interjections, 70
Internal communication, 26–27. *See
   also* Electronic mail (e-mail);
   Meeting(s); Memos
   (memorandums)
Internal customers, 555
Internal database, 428–429
International settings, 21
   cross-cultural communication and,
     43–49
   greetings and, 46, 435, 480, 567
Internet, 38, 186, 443–448, 622
   accessing, 444
   chat rooms, 447
   documenting sources on, 584–585
   electronic bulletin boards, 447–448
   on-line databases, 446–447, 574,
     577–579
   search tools, 445, 446, 578
   World Wide Web (WWW), 38,
     445–446, 577–579, 584–585,
     622
Interpersonal skills, 11–15, 380–381
Interpretation
   listening, 284
   message, 7, 11
Interrogative sentences, 74. *See also*
   Questions
Interrupting elements, 342
   comma with, 200
   with *who* and *whom* in clauses, 103
Interviews, 379
   employment, 634, 637–646

as primary sources, 575
Intonation, 391
Intransitive verbs, 123, 125
Intrapersonal skills, 11
Introduction
   of formal report, 598–599
   of persons, 54
   of speaker, 422, 423
   of speech, 422, 423
Introductory words, phrases, and
   clauses
   commas following, 197–199
   semicolons following, 212
Inverted sentence, agreement problems
   in, 74, 130
Invitations, formal, 54, 543, *543*
irregardless, 311
Irregular verbs, 117–125
   principal parts of, 118–119
   transitive vs. intransitive, 122–123
it, indefinite, 335
Italics (underscoring)
   for emphasis, 461
   for titles of works, 223
its, it's, 95

Japanese, 54, 480
Jargon, 10, 44
Jaws, developing flexible, 395
Job, resigning from, 649–650
Job offer, accepting or declining,
   648–649
Job search, 617–635
   analysis of self and qualifications,
     618–620
   application form, 634
   application letter, 631–634, *632*
   job market, assessment of, 620–623
   marketing of self in, 623–635
   portfolios in, 635, 641
   résumé and, 623–631, *626–628*, *632*,
     639
   See also Employment interview
Joint ownership, possessive of, 93
Journals, professional, 574, 622
Jr., 203, 241
Justification reports, 573

Keywords, 445, 574, 578–579, 630
Knowledge, 8
   in customer service, 559, 564

Language differences, 9–10, 20
   abbreviations and, 44–45
   punctuation and, 188
   translations and, 27, 45, 153, 222
Language structure, 64–81
   clauses and phrases, 74–77

parts of speech, 64–70
   sentences, 70–75
Laptop computers, 38, 39, 415
Laser printers, 35, 38
Lateral communication, 25
Latin words, plurals of, 87
lay, lie, 124–125
Leader of meeting, role of, 402–406,
   442
Legal issues, evaluating claims and, 518
Letter(s), 477–491
   to accept or decline job offer,
     648–649
   adjustment, 516, 518–521
   appearance of, 477–486
   application, 631–634, *632*
   claim, 503–506
   content of, 460, 477
   credit and collection, *529*, 529–530
   envelopes, 244, 489–491, *491*, 526
   folding for envelopes, 490–491
   follow-up, 530, 646
   form, 545–550, *547*, *549*, *550*
   formats, 482–486, *483–485*, 537–538
   message control in, 350
   parts of, 478–482
   persuasive, 459, 524–530
   planning, 458–462
   public relations, 531–535, *534–535*
   reader's reaction, 458–460
   of resignation, 649–650
   sales, 524–528, 631–634
   special techniques for, 461–462
   stationery for, 488–489, 537–538
   of transmittal, 603
   See also Requests; Social-business
     communications
Letterhead, 478, *479*, 488–489,
   537–538
Lexis, 578
Library research, 573–574, 577–579
lie, lay, 124–125
like, 168
   as, as if, or *as though* vs., 175
   for *that*, 175
like for, 168
Limiting adjectives, 143
Line graphs, 601
Linking (no-action) verbs, 66, 157
Lips, developing mobile, 395–396
List(s)
   capitalization in, 231
   distribution, 473–474, *474*
   See also Enumerations
Listed items, colons before, 213–214.
   See also Enumerations
Listening skills, 15, 18–19, 283–303
   active, 285–286, 289–294
   in casual conversations, 296–298
   in conference situations, 298–301
   customer service and, 557

Listening skills *(cont.)*
   improving, 289–294
   in meetings, 298–301, 403–404
   model for, 284
   as neglected skill, 284–285
   overcoming barriers, 286–288
   passive listening and, 285
   talking vs., 287, 382–383, 404
Local area network (LAN), 442
Ltd., 242
ly, words ending in, 67–68, 152–153.
      See also Adverbs

Mail, guidelines for addressing,
      243–244
Mailbox, electronic mail, 442
Mailing address, 490
Mailing lists, electronic, 584–585
Mailing notations, 489
Main verb, 77, 112–113
Manager/chairperson of meeting,
      402–406, 442
Meaning, shades of, 314–315
Measurement(s)
   abbreviating, 244
   commas in, 209
   figures for, 254
   international differences in, 48
Meeting(s), 399–408
   agenda of, 400–401, *401*, 442, 608
   announcing, 497
   facilities for, 401–402
   formal, 405
   interaction method for, 405–406
   listening in, 298–301, 403–404
   managing, 402–406, 442
   participating in, 379, 403–404,
      406–408
   planning, 400–402
   preparation for, 406
   records of, 405, 607–609, *609*
   teleconferencing and, 4, 299, 405,
      439–441
   tone of, 402
   videoconferencing and, 4, 299,
      440–441
Memorandum report, 586–592
Memorized speech, avoidance of,
      418
Memos (memorandums), 463–476
   advantages of, 464
   formal reports vs., 594
   headings on, 468–469, *472*, 473–475
   importance of, 464
   as letter of transmittal, 603
   message control in, 350
   organization of, 467–468, *468*
   parts of, 473–476
   planning, 463–469
   purposes of, 464–466

special techniques for, 461–462,
      468–469
   style, 473–476
   tone of, 466–467
   types of, 471–473
Merged letters, 548
*Merriam-Webster's Collegiate
      Dictionary, Tenth Edition,*
      268–269, *269*, *307*, 318
Message, 6, 11
   assessing, 294
   complete, 365–366
   composing electronic, 38
   consistency in, 366
   in memos, 467
   of paragraphs, 350, 362
   social-business. *See* Social-business
      communications
   of speaker, 287
Message control, 350
Message interpretation, 7, 11
Message memos, 473
Message transmission, 7, 11
Microcomputers, 37, 430. *See also*
      Computer(s)
Minutes of meeting, 405, 607–609,
      609
Miscommunication, 11
Modems, 38
Modern Language Association (MLA)
      documentation format, 584
Modified-block format, 483, *485*
   with indented paragraphs, 483, *483*
Modifiers
   balancing, 345
   commas with, 206
   repeated, 147
   See also Adjectives; Adverbs
Monarch letterhead, 538
Money, figures to express sums of,
      252–253
Months
   abbreviating, 245
   capitalization of, 234
"More than" comparisons, 147
most, almost, 158
Motivation, 8
Multiculturalism, 20
   cross-cultural communication and,
      41–49, 435, 480, 567
   language differences and, 9–10, 20,
      44–45
Multitasking, 437

Name(s)
   biographical, 309
   capitalization of, 233–234
   company, 196, 203, 242–243, 481
   personal, 64, 65, 233, 240–241

place, 64, 65, 204, 233–234,
      243–244, 309
   plural forms of, 82
   plurals of titles with, 84–85
   product, 45, 237
   of speaker, ending introduction with,
      423
   state, 204, 243–244
   use of person's, in one-to-one
      communication, 382
Needs, human, 13–15, 525
Negatives, double, 155–156
Negative words, 315–316, 339–340
neither, either, 132, 147
Nervousness, 390
Netscape, 579
Networks
   communication. *See* Communication
      networks
   personal contact, 620
   professional contact, 620–621
never vs. *not*, 156
Newsgroups, 447–448
Newspaper advertisements, 622, 632
News releases, 611–613, *612*
Nexis, 447, 578
no., 245
Noise, 287
Nominative pronouns, 95, 103, 104,
      149
Nonallowable claim, 520–521
Nondiscriminatory language, 56–59
Nonverbal communication, 3, 5, 7, 17,
      45, 388, 419
Nonverbal cues, 292–293
no one, nobody, 132, 147
nor, or, 69, 137–138, 172, 193
not any, none, 132, 147
Notations
   mailing, 489
   memo, 475
Note cards, 278–279
   bibliography, 581, *581*
   for speeches, 418
Notes
   customer contact, 557
   delivery of speech from, 418–419
Note taking
   for formal reports, 582
   listening and, 293, 294, 300–301
   for meetings, 300–301, 408
   note cards in, 278–279, 581, *581*
   in preparing for speech, 413–414
   for reading comprehension, 274,
      276–278
   for research, 278–279, 581, *581*
Nouns, 64–65
   collective, 133
   common, 64, 82
   compound, 82–83, 93
   foreign-origin, 87–88, 134

Nouns *(cont.)*
   infinitive phrases as, 76
   plural forms of, 81–88
      with apostrophes, 85
      of common nouns, 82
      of compound nouns, 82–83
      ending in *f* or *fe*, 87
      ending in *o*, 86
      ending in *y*, 83, 322
      foreign nouns, 87–88
      irregular, 85
      possessive form for, 91
      of proper nouns, 82
      with special changes, 85
      of titles with names, 84–85
      troublesome forms, 88
   possessive forms of, 91–94
   prepositional phrase as, 76
   pronoun agreement with common-gender, 131–132
   proper, 64–65, 82, 143
   See also Pronoun(s)
number
   abbreviation for (*no.*), 245
   as singular or plural, 135
Number, subject-predicate agreement in, 129
Number(s), 249–255
   commas in and between unrelated, 208
   figures to express, 252–255
   indefinite, 250
   in parentheses, 185–186
   words to express, 249–251

o, nouns ending in, plural of, 86
Object(s)
   commas separating verbs from, 205
   compound, pronouns in, 104
   direct, 122–123
   indirect, 122–123
   of prepositions, 161
Objective pronouns, 99, 101, 102, 104
Objectives, listening, 299
Observations, 575
o'clock, 254–255
off, from, 167
Office, traditional vs. electronic, 36
Omissions
   apostrophes for, 227–228
   commas for, 207
   of conjunction, 212
   of preposition, 346
one another, 147
One-to-one communication, 382–385
   guidelines for, 382–385
   receiving the public, 561–564
   on telephone, 380, 383–385, 434–435, 564–565

On-line databases, 446–447, 574, 577–579
On-line employment services, 622
On-line services, 578
Open punctuation, 480, 481
Opinions, facts vs., 51, 407
opposite, 168
Optical character recognition (OCR), 432
or, nor, 69, 137–138, 172, 193
Oral communication, 4–5, 7, 10, 13, 17, 18, 20–21, 377–425
   appearance and, 387–388, 416–418, 418–419
   effective, 387–397
   effective business relationships through, 380–381
   enunciation and pronunciation, 269, 308, 393–397, 643–644
   forms of, 379–380, 382
   importance of, 378
   improving skills at, 381
   listening skills and, 283–303, 382–383, 403–404
   in meetings, 379, 399–408
   one-to-one. *See* One-to-one communication
   role of, in business, 378–379
   speech qualities, 390–393
   by telephone, 380, 383–385, 434–435, 564–565
   See also Speeches
Oral reports, 586
Order forms, 528
Organizational charts, 602
other, "more than" comparisons using, 147
our, are, 96
Outline(s)
   capitalization in, 231
   of formal report, 596
   as informal report form, 590
   for reading comprehension, 274–275
   for speech, 418
Out-of-date words, 316
outside, inside, 166
Overhead transparencies, 414–416, 432
Overused words and expressions, 316–318, 363

Pagers, 4, 36, 438
Paper, quality of, 488, 629
Paragraphs, 350–356
   boilerplate, 545, 548, *550*
   form, letters with, 545, 548, *549*
   format, 353–354
   as informal report form, 589–590
   length of, 351, 353
   message of, 350, 362
   sentence length and structure, 354–356, 363–364

   transitional devices for, 154, 351–353, 362
   unity of, 351
   variety in, 604
Parallel structure, 176–177, 344–347
Paraphrasing, 582–583
Parentheses, 185–186, 225–227
Parenthetic elements, comma with, 200–201
Parliamentary procedure, 405
part from, part with, 164
Partially allowable claim, 519–520
Participation, in meetings, 379, 403–404, 406–408
Participial phrases, 198
Parts of speech, 64–70
Passive listening, 285
Passive voice, 343, 364
Past participle, 112, 118–119, 124
Past perfect tense, 115, 117
Past progressive tense, 116, 117
Past tense, 112, 114, 116
   of *to be*, 120
   of irregular verbs, 118–119, 124
Percentages, figures for, 254
Period fault, 187
Periodicals, 574, 622
Periodic reports, 572
Periods, 184–187, 223, 224
Person, subject-predicate agreement in, 129
Personal-business letter format, 485, *485*
Personal characteristics, assessing, 619
Personal computers (PC), 37, 430. *See also* Computer(s); Software, computer
Personal contact network, 620
Personality, 8
Personalization, electronic communication and, 452
Personal names, 64, 65, 309
   abbreviations in, 240–241
   capitalizing, 233
Persuading, 6
   in letters, 459, 524–530
Photographs, 602, 604
Phrase(s), 74, 75, 76–77
   adjectival, 161
   agreement problems with intervening, 130–131
   gerund, 198
   infinitive, 76, 197–198
   introductory, punctuating, 197–199
   participial, 198
   prepositional, 68–69, 76, 161–162, 198
   pronoun, 104
   in thought units, 331–332
   transitional, 154, 351–353, 362
   verb, 77, 112–113, 120–121
Physical appearance. *See* Appearance

Physical distractions, 9, 18
Physical needs, 13
Pie charts, 602, *602*
Pitch of voice, 391–392, 419
Placement agencies, 623
Place names, 64, 65
    abbreviating, 243–244
    capitalizing, 233–234
    states, 204, 243–244
Plagiarism, 582–583, 604
Planned repetition of words, 340
Planning business messages
    employment interview, 637–641
    formal reports, 594–595
    informal reports, 588–589
    letters, 458–462
    meetings, 400–402
    memos, 463–469
plan to, 165
Plural forms of nouns. *See under* Nouns
p.m., a.m., 244, 254
Poise, 420–421
Policies
    customer service, 568
    smoking, 54
Portfolios, in job search, 635, 641
Positive attitude, 15, 288, 407, 421,
    514–515
Positive degree, 144, 145
Positive words, 339–340
Possessive adjectives, 142
Possessive forms of nouns, 91–94
Possessive pronouns, 95–96
Postage-paid reply cards, 528
Post office box numbers, abbreviating,
    243
Postscript, 482
Posture, 388, 642
PowerPoint, 415–416
Preciseness, 500
Predicate(s)
    commas separating subjects from,
        205
    inverted order of, 74, 130
    normal order of, 73–74
    in sentence, 72–74
Predicate agreement, 128–139
    with compound subjects, 136–138
        joined by *and*, 136–137
        joined by *or* or *nor*, 137–138
    in relative-pronoun clauses, 138
    with simple subjects, 128–132
    with special subjects, 133–135
        collective-noun simple subject, 133
        foreign-noun subject, 134
        a number, the number, 135
        part, portion, or amount subject,
            134–135
Predicate nominatives, 149
Prefixes
    in antonyms, 318–319

capitalizing, 233, 236
    in names of persons, 233
    spelling pitfalls involving, 324–325
Prejudice, 58–59
Prepositional phrase, 68–69, 76,
    161–162, 198
Prepositions, 68–69, 161–168
    balancing, 346
    conjunctions vs., 176
    identifying, 161–162
    idiomatic use of, 162–165
    objective pronouns of, 101
    object of, 161
    pitfalls with, 166–168
Presentation graphics software,
    415–416, 432
Presentations, oral. *See* Speeches
Present participle, 112, 118–119, 124
Present perfect tense, 115, 116
Present progressive tense, 115–116, 117
Present tense, 112, 114, 116
    of *to be*, 120
    of irregular verbs, 118–119, 124
pretend that, 174–175
Previewing, 273, 277
Primary sources, 573, 574–575
Printed forms, 471–472, *472*
Printers, laser, 35, 38
Privacy, 52–53
Procedures
    announcing, 498
    customer service, 568
    in formal reports, 599
    parliamentary, 405
Prodigy, 443, 446–447, 578
Productivity, office, 35–36
Product names, 45, 237
Professional contact network, 620–621
Professional courtesy. *See* Courtesy
Professional life, communication skills
    used in, 19–22
Progressive tenses, 115–116, 117
Progress reports, 572, 603
Promotion
    congratulations letter for, 539–540
    of new business, letter for, 533
Promptness
    punctuality and, 402, 642
    in responding to requests, 508–509
Pronoun(s), 65
    as adjectives, 143
    agreement with common-gender
        nouns, 131–132
    agreement with subject, 129
    in appositives, 105
    case forms of, 99–107
        nominative, 95, 103, 104, 149
        objective, 99, 101, 102, 104
        possessive, 95–96
        special, 101–105
    in compound subjects or objects, 104

ending in *self*, 106–107
references, indefinite and confusing,
    335–336
relative, 138, 174, 204, 332–333
    with *than* or *as*, 104–105
    which clauses, 138, 204, 332–333
See also Nouns
Pronoun phrases, 104
Pronunciation, 269, 308, 393–397,
    643–644
Proofreading, 263, 358–360, 367–371
    checklists for, 370, 371
    importance of, 370
    marks for, 358–360, *359–360, 361*
    for quality, 368
    for self and others, 368
    steps in, 370–371
    technology and, 369–370
Proper adjectives, 143, 234
Proper nouns, 64–65, 82, 143
Proposals, 573
Pseudohomonyms, 312, 313
Public, receiving the, 561–564
Public relations
    letters, 531–535, *534–535*
    news releases, 611–613, *612*
    oral communication and effective,
        380–381
Public speaking. *See* Speeches
Punctuality, 402, 642
Punctuation
    apostrophes, 85, 91–96, 227–228
    colons, 213–215, 224, 231, 480
    comma. *See* Comma(s)
    dashes, 215–218
    exclamation points, 70, 189–190, 224
    omitting, 10
    open vs. standard, 480, 481
    parentheses, 185–186, 225–227
    periods, 184–187, 223, 224
    question marks, 188–189, 224
    quotation marks, 220–224
    semicolons, 194, 195–196, 211–213,
        214, 224
    terminal, 184–190
Purchasing, oral communications in,
    379

Quality
    and electronic communication, 35,
        450–451
    of paper, 488, 629
    proofreading for, 368
Question marks, 188–189, 224
Questionnaires, 575
Questions
    direct, 188
    in employment interview, 638–640,
        641
    in getting feedback, 12–13

Questions *(cont.)*
  indirect, 185, 189
  listening and, 294, 300
  for news releases, 613
  punctuating, 188–189
  requests phrased as, 184
  after speeches, 418, 419–420
  verb phrase in, 113
  who, whom in, 102
Quotation(s)
  direct, 221, 231
  indirect, 221
  punctuation at end of, 223–224
  within quotations, 221
Quotation marks, 220–224

Racial bias, 57–58
raise, rise, 124–125
Readability, 354, 430
Reading of speech, avoiding, 418
Reading skill, 21, 261–282
  adjustment to material and purpose,
    263
  assessing, 262
  comprehension, 272–275, 276–278,
    300
  improving, 262–265
  speed, 263–265
  vocabulary and, 267–270
real, really, 157
Reasonableness, 501, 506
reason is that, 174–175
Receiver, 7, 8, 10, 11, 14–15, 287. *See
    also* Audience
Receiving the public, 561–564
Recommendations
  on formal reports, 600–601
  thank-you letters for, 54, 542
Recorder of meeting, 405, 607–609,
    609
Records, meeting, 607–609
Reference initials, 481–482
Reference materials, 306–310, 318
  dictionary. *See* Dictionary
  electronic reference tools, 311
  thesaurus, 309–310, 311, 318
  for writing reports, 573–574
References (directions), parentheses for
    enclosing, 226
References with résumé, 625, 626
Referrals, application letter
    following up on, 632–633
Reflexive use of pronouns ending in
    self, 107
regard, regards, 164–165
Regional differences, 43
Rejection, handling, 646
Relative-pronoun clauses, 138, 174,
    204, 332–333
Religions, 42, 48

Religious bias, 57
Reminders
  follow-up letters as, 530
  memos as, 466
Repetition(s)
  of conjunctions, 196
  of modifier, 147
  planned, 340
  punctuating, 207, 216
Reply cards, postage-paid, 528
Reports, 572–609
  documenting sources for, 580–585
  electronic sources for, 574, 576–579,
    584–585
  formal, 594–605
  format of, 583–585, 604–605
  gathering information for, 573–579
  informal, 586–592
  memos as, 465
  minutes of meeting, 405, 607–609,
    609
  oral, 586. *See also* Speeches
  preparing to write, 573–579
  purpose and scope of, 572–573,
    598–599
  technical, 594
  types and purposes of, 572–573
Requests, 499–521
  answering, 508–521, *509, 513, 514,
    535*, 589
  claim letters, 503–506
  memos for, 464–465
  phrased as questions, 184
  writing, 499–503, *501, 502*
  See also Letter(s)
Rereading, for reading comprehension,
    275, 300
Research
  computerized library listings and,
    577–579
  library, 573–574, 577–579
  on-line databases and, 446–447,
    577–579
Resigning from job, 649–650
Responses
  in customer service, 559, 566–568
  to requests, 508–521, *509, 513, 514*
  to sales letters, 527–528
Résumé, 623–631, *626–628, 632*, 639
  computer-friendly, 629–631
  format of, *626–628*, 629–631
  parts of, 624–625
  in portfolios, 635, 641
  of speaker, 422
  types of, 626–628
Retirement, congratulation letters for,
    540
retroactive to, 165
Return address, 489
Reviewing, for reading comprehension,
    275

Revising, 360–365
  checklists for, 363, 364
  editing, 365–367
  in word processing, 430
rise, raise, 124–125
Robert's Rules of Order, 405
Roget's International Thesaurus, 309
Roman numerals, punctuating, 185
Routing slips, 473–474, *474*
RSVP notation, 54

Sales
  responding to requests and, 508, 511
  role of oral communication in, 378
  See also Customer service
Sales appeals, 527
Sales letters, 524–528, 631–634
Sales techniques, indirect, 508, 511, *535*
Salutation, 231, 480
Scanners, 35, 36, 37, 432
Scanning, 273
Search-and-replace feature, 430
Search engines, 445, 446, 578
Secondary sources, 573–574
Security needs, 13
self, pronouns ending in, 106–107
Self-actualization needs, 13
Semicolons, 211–213
  colons vs., 214
  in compound sentence, 194
  dashes vs., 215–216
  at end of quotation, 224
  in series, 195–196
Sender, 6, 8, 10, 11, 287
Sense verbs, 157
Sentence fragments, 78
Sentences, 338–347
  abbreviations at end of, 185
  active vs. passive voice in, 343
  balancing techniques in, 176–177,
    344–347
  compound, 193–194, 211–213
  declarative, 74, 184, 189
  defined, 70
  exclamatory, 74
  imperative, 74, 184
  incomplete, 187
  interrogative, 74. *See also*
    Questions
  inverted, agreement problems in, 74,
    130
  inverted order of, 74, 130
  length, variety in, 354–355
  normal order of, 73–74
  numbers at beginning of, 249–250
  parentheses within, 226–227
  proper subordination of ideas in,
    341–342
  punctuation. *See* Punctuation
  simple, 193

Sentences *(cont.)*
    structure, 70–75, 354–356, 363–364
    word usage in, 339–340
Separate ownership, possessive of, 93
Sequence, consistency of, 28
Series
    commas in, 195–196, 206
    of questions, punctuating, 188
    semicolons in, 195–196
set, sit, 124–125
Shades of meaning, 314–315
she, 335
Short forms, capitalizing, 235–236
Shouting, in electronic mail, 444
Side headings, 461
Signature, on memo, 475–476
Signs and symbols in dictionary, 309
Simple predicate, 72
Simple sentence, punctuating, 193
Simple subject, 71–72, 128–132
Simplified letter style, 484, *484*
since, 174
sit, set, 124–125
Slang, 10, 44, 222, 314, 317
Smoking policies, 54
so, 342
Social-business communications, 379,
    537–543
    condolence letters, 542–543
    congratulations letters, 539–541
    formal invitations and replies, 54,
        543, *543*
    letter format, 486, *538, 539*
    thank-you letters, 54, 541–542
Social life, communications skills used
    in, 19–22
Social needs, 13
Software, computer, 37, 428–432
    communications, 431–432
    database, 37, 428–429, *429*, 431–432
    desktop publishing, 35, 37, 432
    presentation graphics, 415–416, 432
    spreadsheet, 37, 428, *429*, 431
    suites, 431–432
    Web browser, 445, 446, 578
    word processing. *See* Word
        processing software
some, somewhat, 158
someone, somebody, 132
Speaking rate (tempo), 392–393
Speaking skills, 20–21
Specificity, in responding to requests,
    512
Specific words, 44, 310, 363
Speech, parts of, 64–70
Speeches, 379, 380, 410–423
    audience of, 411
    closing remarks after, 423
    conclusion of, 423
    delivering, 418–419
    developing, 411–413

    evaluating, 421
    gathering and organizing data,
        413–414
    introducing speaker, 422
    outlining and organizing, 418
    practicing, 414–416
    previewing speaking assignment, 411
    purpose of, 411
    questions after, 418, 419–420
    time allowed for, 411, 418, 419
Speech qualities, 390–393
Spelling, 250–251, 313–314, 321–328
    analyzing and learning, 327
    dictionary information on, 306,
        324–327
    doubling final consonant, 323–324
    ei and *ie* words, 322
    final *y*, 322
    ful, ous, lly endings, 322–323
    guides to correct, 322–324
    pitfalls in, 324–327
    spelling checkers, 311, 369, 430
Spelling checkers, 311, 369, 430
Spreadsheet software, 37, 428, *429*, 431
Sr., 203, 241
Stage fright and stage presence,
    420–421
Standard memo format, 471–472
Standard punctuation, 480, 481
Statement of future action, in memos,
    468
State names, 204, 243–244
Stationery, 488–489
    letterhead, 478, *479*, 488–489,
        537–538
    for social-business communications,
        537–538
Stereotypes, 10, 58–59, 287–288
Stories, use of, 422
Street names, abbreviating, 243
Subject(s)
    commas separating predicate from,
        205
    compound, 72, 136–137
        predicate agreement, 136–138
        pronouns in, 104
    inverted order of, 74, 130
    normal order of, 73–74
    predicate agreement with. *See*
        Predicate agreement
    pronoun agreement with, 129
    pronoun as, 99
    in sentence, 70–72
    simple, 71–72, 128–132
Subject line
    in informal report, 587
    in letter, 480–481
    in memos, 467, 468–469, 475
    in unsolicited report, 592
Subordinating conjunctions, 154,
    172–173

Subordination
    coordination vs., 341
    of ideas in sentence, proper, 341
Suffixes, 236, 325–327
Suites, software, 431–432
Summarizing, 216, 293, 404–405, 423,
    599
Superlative degree, 145, 153–154
Supplementary material, in report,
    601–602
sure, surely, 157
Surveys, telephone, 575
Syllables, dictionary information on,
    269, 308
Synonyms
    in dictionary, 270, 308, 318
    dictionary of, 311
    in thesaurus, 309–310, 311, 318

Table of contents, 598, *598*
Tables
    in formal reports, 601, 604
    as informal report form, 590–591
Tact, using, 407, 563–564, 649–650
Talking, vs. listening, 287, 382–383,
    404
Target audience, 524
Technical reports, 594
Technical writers, 594
Technology
    and applications, 36–39
    and customer satisfaction, 566–567
    impact of, 34
    productivity and, 35–36
    proofreading and, 369–370
    See also Electronic communication;
        Word processing software;
        specific types
Telecommunications, 434–448
    cellular phones, 35, 36, 380,
        438–439
    communication networks and,
        441–448
    fax machines, 37, 437, 450
    modem and, 38
    pagers, 4, 36, 438
    teleconferencing, 4, 299, 405,
        439–441
    telephone, 434–437
    videophones, 438
Telecommunications devices for the
    deaf (TDD), 434
Teleconferencing, 405, 439–441
    audio, 439–440
    distance learning, 441
    videoconferencing, 4, 299, 438,
        440–441
Telephone
    audio teleconferencing, 439–440
    cellular, 35, 36, 380, 438–439

Telephone *(cont.)*
  communication by, 380, 383–385,
    434–435, 564–565
  originating calls, 384–385
  receiving calls, 385
  toll-free numbers, 528, 558
Telephone surveys, 575
Templates, 548, 629
Tempo (speaking rate), 392–393
Temporary ("temp") agencies, 623
Tense of verbs, 111–112, 114–117, 120,
  123, 124
Terminal punctuation, 184–190
Thank-you letters, 54, 541–542
than, pronouns with, 104–105
that, 138, 204
  because or *like* for, 174–175
  as demonstrative adjective, 143
  where for, 156
  who or *which* vs., 174
their, there, they're, 96
theirs, there's, 96
Thesaurus, 309–310, 311, 318
these, those, 143–144
"They say," 335–336
this, 143, 336
Thought unit
  clauses in, 332
  defined, 330
  phrases in, 331–332
  reading in, 264
  who-did-what violation of, 333–334
  words in, 330, 331
Threats, 505–506
thus, ambiguity of, 334
Time expressions, abbreviating, 244
Time limits, for speeches, 411, 418, 419
Time zones
  domestic, 43
  international, 47, 450
  voice mail and, 435
Timing
  punctuality and, 402, 642
  technology and, 35
Title page of formal report, 597, *597*
Titles, personal
  abbreviating, 240–241
  capitalizing, 236
  commas with, 203
  courtesy, 84–85, 240–241, 473, 480
  plural of names with, 84–85
Titles of publications
  capitalizing, 232
  hyphenated, 232
  punctuating, 185, 223
to, at, 167
to be, 100, 101, 120–121, 157
To line
  in informal report, 587
  in memos, 473–474
  in unsolicited report, 592

Toll-free telephone numbers, 528, 558
Tone
  audience and appropriateness of,
    361–362
  of business communication, 26–27
  familiar, 526, *528*
  of meeting, 402
  of memos, 466–467
  of sales letter, 526
  of voice, 392
Tongue, developing lively, 396–397
Transitional devices, 154, 351–353, 362
Transitive verbs, 122–123, 125
Translations, 27
  problems with, 45, 153
  quotation marks for, 222
Transmittal
  letter of, 603
  memos for, 466
Transmittal notation, 482
Transportation errors, 640
Treatment, consistency of, 28
Typographical errors, proofreading for,
    358–360

Underscore (italics)
  for emphasis, 461
  for titles of works, 223
Unethical communication, 52–53
Unity in writing, paragraph, 351
unless, 175
Unnecessary words, 316, 363
Unsolicited reports, *591,* 591–593
Upward communication, 25
Usenet newsgroups, 447

Variables, 545, *549, 550*
Variety in writing, 354–355, 604
Verb(s), 66, 109–125
  action, 66, 110, 157
  agreement of subject and, 129.
      See also Predicate agreement
  balancing, 345–346
  "being," 100, 101, 110, 120–121, 149,
    157
  commas separating object from, 205
  defined, 109
  helping (auxiliary), 77, 112–113
  identifying, 109–110
  infinitives, 100, 101, 114, 124
  irregular, 117–125
    principal parts of, 118–119
    transitive vs. intransitive, 122–123
  linking (no-action), 66, 157
  main, 77, 112–113
  objective pronouns of, 101
  regular, 111–117
    conjugation of, 116–117

  principal parts of, 111–112,
    114–117
  of sense, 157
  tense of, 111–112, 114–117, 120,123,
    124
Verbal communication, 4–5, 7, 10, 17,
    18, 20–21
Verbal cues, 292–293
Verb phrases, 77, 112–113, 120–121
Videoconferencing, 4, 299, 438,
    440–441
Videophones, 438
Visitors, receiving, 561–564
Visual aids, 45, 414–416, 432
Vocabulary, 264, 267–270, 291, 327.
    See also Word(s)
Voice
  active, 343, 364
  force (volume), 391
  passive, 343, 364
  pitch (voice level), 391–392, 419
  tone of, 392
Voice mail, 4, 35, 36, 380, 385,
    435–437, 438, 452
Volume
  of electronic communication,
    451–452
  of voice, 391

Wants and needs, identifying and
    satisfying, 525
was, vs. *were,* 121
Web browsers, 445, 446, 578
Webster's Collegiate Thesaurus,
    309–310
Weights, commas in, 209
well, good, 158
were, vs. *was,* 121
where, 167
  for *that,* avoidance of, 156
which clause, 138, 204, 332–333
who, which, that, 138, 174
who, whom, 101–103
Who-did-*what* principle, 333–334
whoever, whomever, 101–103
whose, who's, 96
Wide area network (WAN), 442
with regard to, 164–165
Word(s)
  abstract, 310
  antonyms, 318–319
  audience and using suitable, 314
  to avoid, 315–318
  capitalizing, 231
  colorful, vivid, and specific, using,
    44, 310, 363
  correct usage of, 311–314, 339–340,
    367
  descriptive, 319
  developing creativity in, 318–319

Words *(cont.)*
  explanatory or enumerating,
    semicolon before, 212–213
  to express numbers, 249–251
  homonyms and pseudohomonyms,
    95–96, 311–313
  improving choice of, 311
  introductory, punctuating, 197–199,
    212
  negative, 315–316, 339–340
  new, using, 268
  numbers expressed in, 249–251
  out-of-date, 316
  overused, 316–318, 363
  in parentheses, punctuation with,
    226–227
  planned repetition of, 340
  positive, 339–340
  reviewing choice of, 362–364
  setting of, by dashes, 217–218
  shades of meaning, 314–315
  sound of, 340
  specific, 44, 310, 363
  spelling. *See* Spelling
  synonyms, 270, 308, 309–310, 311,
    318
  in thought units, 330, 331

transitional, 154, 351–353, 362
  unnecessary, 316, 363
Word-conscious, becoming, 268
Word information in dictionary,
  306–308
Wording of informal report, 589
Word origin, 269–270
Word processing software, 35, 311, 430,
  431, 452, 509
  form letters and paragraphs, 406,
    545–550
  grammar checkers, 364–365, 430
  special techniques for memos and,
    461–462
  spelling checkers, 311, 369, 430
  templates, 548, 629
  thesaurus feature, 310, 311
Word tools. *See* Reference materials
Working bibliography, 581, *581*
World Wide Web (WWW), 38,
  445–446, 577–579, 584–585,
  622
worst way, 156
Writer's identification, 481
Writing, 13, 17, 18, 21–22, 305–375,
  457–551
  effective paragraphs, 350–356

effective sentences, 338–347
formatting techniques for, 461–462.
  See also Format
to inform, 496–498
  announcements in, 497–498
  directions in, 496–497
  instructions in, 496
planning for effective, 458–462
proofreading, 358–360
to request, 499–506
responding to requests, 508–521
revising, 360–365, 365–367
structuring phrases and clauses,
  330–336
  See also Letter(s); Memos
  (memorandums); Reports
Written communication, 5, 10–11
Written messages, 7
Written records, 452–453

y, plural form of nouns ending in, 83,
  322
Yearbooks, 574
You-attitude, 14–15, 339–340
your, you're, 96

ZIP Codes, 243, 432, 479, 490